2ND EDITION

D1239989

Early American
Pattern Glass

COLLECTOR'S IDENTIFICATION & PRICE GUIDE

Darryl Reilly • Bill Jenks

© 2002 by

Krause Publications

Published by

krause publications

700 E. State Street • Iola, WI 54990-0001
Telephone: 715/445-2214
Web: www.krause.com

Please call or write for our free catalog of publications.
Our toll-free number to place an order or obtain a free catalog is 800-258-0929
or please use our regular business telephone 715-445-2214.

Library of Congress Catalog Number: 2002105097
ISBN: 0-87349-438-5

Printed in the United States of America

TABLE OF CONTENTS

ACKNOWLEDGMENTS

Ushering *Early American Pattern Glass* into the 21st Century was no easy undertaking. As enthusiasts of pressed glass will readily agree, to date all listings of patterned glass fall short of recording true values. In fact, for the past 10 or more years, prices have been associated with the moderate to low-end of the price structure. Unrealistic and outmoded, such estimates devaluate the true nature of investment-quality glassware and inhibit the collector in his or her ambition of creating a collection of lasting worth.

In attempting to present a realistic price structure, we have been privileged to enlist the special talents and expertise of several well-known individuals. Foremost in their endeavor to contribute the most up-to-date materials on prices were Jeff and Beverly Evans of Green Valley Auctions, located in picturesque Mt. Crawford, VA. Recognized nationally as the premier auction house in the field of specialized Early American pattern glass catalogued auctions, Jeff and Beverly unselfishly provided their complete collection of catalogues and auction results of each catalogued auction conducted at the Green Valley gallery. Through their busiest moments of biweekly and specialized antiques auctions, Jeff somehow always created the time to review the multitude of flint glass prices we uncannily e-mailed him at the oddest hours. His passion for pattern glass and knowledge of rarities became an endless source of information, especially when dealing with the older flint patterns. The field of Early American pattern glass will be forever indebte to Jeff and Beverly and the learned staff at Green Valley Auction and their dedication to the research and preservation of pressed glassware.

Our sincere thanks to Stephan H. Chapman and Walter A. Hulkkonen , Shadyside, MD. Avid collectors of exceptional examples of pattern glass, both Steve and Wally graciously opened their home and their extensive collection of pattern glass rarities to our camera. Their willingness to share their knowledge of collecting and glassware is reflected in their personal collection as well as the multitude of prices they reviewed and pondered. Many of the color and black and white photographs included in this book reflects a very small sampling of their exemplary collection and Steve's acute knowledge of photographing glassware.

Harold and Gail Essmaker of Sault Ste. Marie, MI also graciously opened their home to our cameras. Known throughout pattern glass circles as a collector's collector, the Essmaker collection houses numerous rarities rarely encountered on today's market. For the time and hospitality they've shown in the preparation of this book, we note our sincerest thanks. Many photographs from the Essmaker collection are included in this work including the blue Log Cabin covered sugar bowl that graces our cover.

A sincere "Thank You" is likewise extended to Larry W. Dosier of Rhoadsville, VA. When learning of our proposed book project, Larry took time away from his own pursuits to photograph his collection of pattern glass.

Our sincerest "Thanks" to Rick and Ricki Thompson from Missouri who proved invaluable in their ability to add pertinent historical and pricing information for the new patterns we have added. Experienced dealers in Early American pattern glass, their familiarity with and knowledge of patterns and designs often illuminated what seemed to be the darkest moment.

We are equally grateful and indebted to a special group of individuals for the time and effort they have invested in this undertaking. The time and energy each has taken from his or her own special interests and projects will always be appreciated. For want of a better approach of displaying fairness (and all are exceptional), we list them in alphabetical order: Richard Adams and Frank Renner (RFD Antiques, Fleetwood, PA), Lee Briggeman (Frosted Dolphin Antiques, Fertile, Iowa), Jon Clark (J. Clark Antiques, London, Ontario, Canada), Doug & Coila Hales (Coila's Antiques, FL), Kay Converse (Birch Run, MI), Eva Cromer (Dillsburg, PA), Dr. Henry Erlich, (Allentown, PA), Mr. & Mrs. Stauffer (CT), Helen Goldberg (Helen Goldberg Antiques, Pittsboro, NC), Al and Grace Guido (FL), Peg Gross (Doylestown, PA), Elaine and Bill Henderson (EAPG, Inc., Albuquerque, NM), Joyce and Clay Holland (Park City, FL), Charlie and Nellie

Huttunen (Northport, NY), Bill and the late Carolyn Jessup (West Chester, PA), Joyce and Seth Johnston (Johnston Antiques, Monroe, OH), Ed and Willi Kleppinger (New Orleans, LA), Alan and Andrea Kopple (Iris Cottage Antiques, Canaan, NY), Cat Krivda (Chesterville Antiques, Mt. Vernon, OH), Jim Ludescher (Jim's Antiques, Dubuque, IA), Jim Masterson (Royal Oak, MI), Walter and Joan Mendes (Westward Ho Antiques, Madison, AL), Phyllis Petcoff (Wickliffe, KY), Mark Coxe Prime (Atglen, PA), Arlene Rabin (Allentown, PA), Chris and Rena Reynolds (C&R Antiques, Brandford, CN), Rick Saffol and Stephen Sekac (Southern Gents Antiques, New Oxford, PA), Jane Stahl (FL), Miriam and Dale Stock (Stock's Antiques, Dillsburg, PA), Gary & Kimberly Stack (Wyoming, PA), Ray Stutsman (Elkhart, IN), Miriam & Anthony Randazzo (Tillie's Antiques & Trinkets, Edwardsville, PA), Ronald Warman and Gary Weber (Over the Hill Antiques, Plains, PA), and Jerry Wood (The Wood Post, Quincy, LA). Last but certainly not least we extend a sincere "Thank you" to Jim and Patty Chambers, managers of the Eastern National Antiques Show and Sale at the Farm Show Complex in Harrisburg, PA. Through the efforts of the Chambers family, Early American pattern glass was given a lasting home in which to be admired and collected. As the adage insists, "It's easy to look good when you surround yourself with the best...."

As in past efforts, we acknowledge the fact that we will be forever indebted to the late Harry Robinson of Shippensburg, PA. Through his friendship and love of patterned glass, we were delighted to have worked with Harry in photographing his goblet collection now permanently on display in the Shippensburg Historical Society, Shippensburgh, PA. Many of the goblet examples used within this book are a result of the many hours spent with Harry.

— *Darryl Reilly and Bill Jenks*

INTRODUCTION

The most often asked question outside of the collecting field is "Why is it called 'Early American'?" The words *early American* echo picturesque recollections of the bygone pioneer days: pine furnishings lapped in multicolored quilts and coverlets accentuated by a diverse assembly of stone and graniteware. A more meaningful manner of defining "Early American" as it pertains to the pressed glassware of the 19th Century would be to characterize it as *early* American. As subtle a nuance as it may appear, *early* may properly be assigned to its time of manufacture, American referring to its country of origin and "pattern glass" to its genus or form. Through years of literary bandying, the less formal but more familiar EAPG (**E**arly **A**merican **P**attern **G**lass) anagram has likewise emerged both phrase and anagram successfully delineating the pressed glass tableware produced in America throughout the 19th Century.

As devotees of the glassware known as Early American pattern glass are aware, American pressed glass chronologically falls into three well-defined periods. (A) The Lacy Period, (B) the Flint Period, and (C) the Non-flint Period, each a product of the creative power of imagination and discovery. Characterized by high-profiled designs consisting of finely placed stippling, output of the Lacy Period spanned the earliest years of pressed glass production, roughly from 1830 to the 1840s. Ushering in an entirely new design concept, the Flint Period (developing through the 1840s and lasting until the Civil War) dramatically changed the appearance of pressed tableware. By eliminating the use of the stipple as the dominant element of decoration and replacing it with more simple geometric designs, a new breed of decoration was created. The addition of lead to the glass formula at this time also produced a glass that was heavy, brilliant, and resonant in nature. It was, however, the non-Flint Period that inevitably changed the production and direction of the American pressed glass industry. Dependent upon the use of lead for the war effort, it was the exchange of lime for lead in the standard glass formula by William Leighton, Jr., in 1862, that heralded the emergence of Non-flint glass. Lighter, less brilliant and without resonant quality, the new glass of the non-flint period proved to be less expensive yet ideal for the glassware from 1860 onward. Coupled with the new advances in pressing and the power of the industrial revolution, designs became more complicated in detail and craftsmanship.

Such a compressed overview of American pressed glass must be considered simplistic at the very least. Nurtured by invention, mechanical development and advancement in technology each acting as a common catalyst, it was the glass pioneer's brute desire to create and willingness to learn that conceived and nourished the pressed glass industry of the 19th Century. From this fundamental desire to create emerged the multitude of glassware designs we term Early American.

Shell and Jewel green water pitcher.

PRESSED GLASS V.S. PATTERNED GLASS

Although sharing the same elemental makeup, all pressed glass is not pattern glass although pattern glass is pressed. At first glance, such a statement may sound contradictory. On further reflection, however, it is easily understood. When the proper amount of molten glass is compressed into a full-size mold, the resulting glass object is pressed. Tableware produced in this fashion is pressed glassware. To differentiate pattern glass from pressed glass there must exist at least one common denominator. For the sake of argument, let us designate this denominator as the design or pattern. And while literally thousands of pressed glass designs were issued, let us further narrow the criteria to include only those designs produced in forms large enough to constitute a basic 4-piece table setting as pattern glass. Unlike pressed glass, which may or may not be pattern ornamented, collectible pattern glass (beginning with the basic butter dish, creamer, spoon holder and sugar bowl) will include a barrage of complementary articles such as bowls, compotes, dishes, salt- and peppershakers, syrup jugs and so forth.

Literally thousands of designs have been employed during the heyday of Early American pattern glass (1850-1910). Because of this extensive number, the patterns included in this book reflect those that have traditionally enjoyed sustained favor within the collecting community. Because of interest and disinterest, a number of collectors may exhibit displeasure in discovering certain favored patterns absent from the listings while a number of new designs have been added. Hopefully within subsequent editions, the circle will turn and a number of new and exciting design additions will be added.

Fine Cut and Block covered sugar bowl.

BUYING EARLY AMERICAN PATTERN GLASS

Newcomers to the field of collecting pattern glass are occasionally confronted with the thought of "Where do I begin to acquire items for my collection?" The answer is basic and simple: the pattern glass dealer. For more than half a century, dealers in pattern glass have served the enthusiast. Armed with the knowledge and understanding of their profession, many offer specialized services including (a) matching and (b) seek-and-find services. A majority of dealers maintain want lists and quickly respond to collectors when special items of interest become available.

Assembling a collection of glassware can be enjoyable and challenging. For lasting value, examples in mint or perfect condition are most desirable. Defects including chips, scratches, discoloration and the cloudiness caused

by the deposit of calcium all detract from the item and its true value. Missing pieces such as lids and original stoppers likewise affect value and usually cause a reduction of its overall worth. Such items when purchased fill a void in a collection until finer examples can be acquired.

Today, the advancement and interest in Early American pattern glass have become so widespread that it has caused the creation of numerous clubs to arise on a national level. One of the most exciting of these clubs is the Early American Pattern Glass Society. Founded but a few years ago by Columbus, Ohio-based Jo and Bill Reidenbach, today the club boasts a sprawling membership. Each year at the Spring edition of the Eastern National Antiques Show & Sale held at the Farm Show Complex in Harrisburg, PA, the Society holds its annual convention, drawing collectors and members from across the country. A complete membership directory is issued on a yearly basis while a well-written newsletter offers members yet another avenue in which to come together and share in their collective knowledge.

As widespread a collectible as pattern glass has become, its presence often arises in numerous areas: auctions, antique co-ops, shows, and individually owned shops to name but a few. As mentioned above, it is always advisable to know your dealer and his or her reputation. Reliable, honest, and dedicated to their first love, dealers in pattern glass are well acquainted with their glassware and will happily stand behind each sale.

Thousand Eye high-standard true open compote.

SURFING THE INTERNET

As a baby boomer of the 1950s Northeast, one of the better slices of growing up was the fact that life was less complicated. The radio and Saturday movie matinees were important facets of growing up. But the overall tempo of living differed. Things were simple. Most of the time people would walk. On special occasions, public transportation was the only way to go and, more often than not, that too was limited.

In today's world of computer chips and portable Internet connections, for many of us childhood seems all too surreal. Gone are the boundaries, whether real or imaginary, that confined our wanderings and interests to a regional level. With a click of the mouse the only confines we might now encounter are incorrect Internet addresses and the limits imposed upon our credit cards. With the beginning of the new millennium the Internet has emerged as the single-most factor of influence in the fields of antiquities. In a single "click" we can access the Web sites and Internet-galleries across air and water...many never before available to the general public. Furnished with shopping carts and the ability to instantly estimate the final shipping charge and cash out, the Internet has inadvertently replaced the Sunday drive.

Whether we like it or not, the Internet is here...and it's here to stay. However, as boundless and imaginative as it appears, it has radically altered the nature of the business of antiques. By removing the adventure of discovery, it has stripped the profession of that one element that makes collectors and dealers what they are: fun. The personal, one-on-one repartee between the buyer and the seller has been replaced by instant messaging and lists of e-mail. The anticipation of discovering the new and the exciting is gone. The touching and the feeling of the object are lost. Indeed, the advent of the Internet has been the demise of so many of the co-ops, the group shops, and the individual shops that once dotted the highways and byways of our need to discover. And when things tend to become tedious and colorless, we too often choose to discard them and turn to other pursuits.

One of the most popular novelties of the Internet is the so-called E-auction. Laden with offerings ranging from trash to treasure, E- auctions afford buyers the opportunity to bid on items of interest. Bidding is incremental and the high or final bid purchases the item in question. Simple and ideal but the differences between the gallery or real-world auction and the online or E-auction are numerous and important: galleries or real-time auctions offer the buyer the opportunity to handle the merchandise. Each item can be examined prior to sale and condition and authenticity can be noted and considered. Better auction houses offer very few items at reserve (the least amount at which the seller is willing to sell). And at an absolute auction there are no reserves whatsoever. One of the most important elements of the gallery auction is the ability to become aware of the underbidder or the other person who is bidding. Alas, when the bidding is over and the jaunt to the check-out counter is complete, we depart with our purchases to have and to hold.

Unlike the galley or real-time auction house, bidding on the Internet can be quite a different experience. Condition and authenticity are findings often, but not always, stated by the seller. Often these findings (authenticity and condition) are open to debate as the seller's opinion many dramatically differ from that of the buyer's. Because the Internet has yet to be disciplined by federal law, these terms and conditions vary as diversely as the number of e-sellers. The same differences apply to return privileges, shipping costs, and the newly-introduced and overly-used insistence of the "restocking charge." Unlike the auction gallery, where legitimate grievances might be discussed, return privileges lay solely on the seller's whim. Shipping charges often range from the actual cost of shipping to an exaggerated sum including the cost of the box and its paper stuffing. And when a disgruntled buyer encounters an unsatisfactory item and arranges its return, he or she may also experience the surprise of being charged an additional sum (including return shipping) for the seller to place the item back into their inventory.

Like any auction, E-auctions can be an enjoyable and profitable experience. But whether it is online or in the gallery, common sense should dominate our bidding. Knowing the reputation and reliability of the seller is always important and there are a multitude of fine dealers on the Internet and in the gallery. Also, there are bargains to be had through both mediums and each offers the buyer a different and unique set of circumstances. As someone once said, "When in doubt...don't."

REPRODUCTIONS AND LOOK-ALIKES

In retrospect, the same pioneering ambition that created the foundation for the identification and collection of Early American pattern glass also created its own ghosts. Labeled "reproductions" and "look-alikes," these specters of Early American pattern glass have haunted collectors and dealers from their earliest appearance in 1924. Fueled by suspicion and distrust, by the early 1930s forgers presumably inundated the market with reproductions and look-alikes. Often thought to have been skillfully seeded throughout specified areas, what we now know as the "reproduction craze" rooted and quickly bloomed into a state of near-panic. For more than half a decade, these fears of reproductions and fakes have possessed well-meaning collectors as suspicions curtailed the popularity of many patterns.

Considering the volume of authentic glassware produced, it is safe to declare that very bothersome reproductions of Early American pattern glass have actually been produced. Besides the earliest attempts by L.G. Wright and other entrepreneurs to copy items from original molds, museums have commissioned a large majority of imitations on the market today. It is with regret, however, that most of those patterns chosen to become the victims of misuse by copy and imitation are those of the most importance to the collector.

Unlike early reproductions (made from original molds), today's copies are produced from new molds. Despite the advancement of technology and the wizardry of modern electronics, new items possess a number of telltale signs. As a general rule of thumb, reproductions lack in both the quality and craftsmanship of genuine pattern glass. Often the pattern or design on reproductions is ill-executed and its details are often missing or differ considerably from the original concept. Reproductions tend to be heavier in weight than their antique counterpart and their dimensions do not always conform to original sizing. Unlike the crystal-clear quality of most antique examples, a majority of pattern glass copies tend to be drab in appearance. Because of low-grade ingredients, new glass appears less than clear and often tinged in amethyst, blue, green or yellow highlights.

When a suspect item is encountered, it is advantageous to compare that item to a known original. When comparison is impossible, noting the detail, quality and workmanship is perhaps the best test for authenticity. Is the item in question of the quality you would expect of the pattern and does it reflect the quality of its maker? Does the pattern detailing reflect the work of fine workmanship and is the detail crisp and sharp? Is the glass of normal clarity and is the weight of the object in proportion to is size and shape?

Regrettably, the nuances of each pattern's individual reproductions cannot be listed in a general guide to pattern glass. A complete study of reproductions can be found in our book *Identifying Pattern Glass Reproductions* (Wallace-Homestead Book Company, 1993). Although difficult to locate, the book is certainly worth the hunt. The following guide is a quick checklist to consider when encountering a suspect item:

(A) Are the edges of the glass blunt to the touch? Original examples feel dull because of years of handling.

(B) Does the item feel exceptionally heavy or weighty? Because of the method in which they are made, reproductions frequently are heavier than their antique counterpart.

(C) Does the surface of the item feel slick to the touch? Unlike antique glassware, modern glass contains an abundant amount of sodium, which acts like a magnet in attracting dust and moisture producing a greasy feeling.

(D) Does the color appear to be of the same color as an original? Although colors will vary to a degree on old glass, modern colors simply appear too modern.

(E) Do the design and details appear sharply chiseled and well molded? Reproductions inevitably lack in detail and craftsmanship and upon comparison to an original will readily reveal these deficiencies.

Whenever encountering a suspect item, it is wiser to pass on its purchase than to forever doubt its authenticity. Of course, the advice of a pattern glass dealer is invaluable.

HOW TO USE THIS GUIDE

Every guide begins with a special intent. Our ambition in writing *Early American Pattern Glass* was to present the collector and dealer with a new attitude toward value. Without doubt, many will suffer from sticker shock as prices are transported from the funky 1990s to the spunky 2000s. Happily, fine pattern glass escalates in value like an investment portfolio and today well-planned collections bring high-end returns on the auction block.

Like previous endeavors, we have arranged patterns in alphabetical order and by popular name. When a pattern name is original (that is, the name given it by its manufacturer) it is designated as **OMN**. Additional names by which a design has been historically known are listed as "AKA" (also known as). Dates of production are designated as "**c.**" or **circa** indicating the year in which a particular design may have first appeared. Reproductions and Look-alikes refer to reissues (new examples produced from original molds) or new items (examples produced from newly created molds) that have been noted.

Although we attempted to do away with abbreviations, the following proved essential:

AKA: also known as
ER: Exceptionally rare
EX: Extremely rare
Gal: Gallons
Pt(s): Pint, pints
Qt(s): Quart(s)
R: Rare
S: Scarce
VR: Very rare

Popularity, availability, condition, and age all combine to create worth. Values herein were procured from many venues: auction results, dealers, collectors, and alas Web sites. Suggested prices should be considered the retail or selling price for examples of glassware in mint or perfect condition. For examples in less than mint condition, value becomes the buyer's prerogative. Damage, missing parts, calcium deposits and other defects greatly decrease the value of collectible glassware and should be seriously considered

No book of value should be considered complete or definitive. Collecting and dealing in Early American pattern glass is somewhat like a kaleidoscope: the more often we look into the nature of the glassware the more we become aware of new colors, dimensions and forms.

Heart with Thumbprint emerald green stand oil lamp.

FACTORY "CODE LETTERS"

Because the United States Glass Company and its associated firms produced so much of the glassware contained within *Early American Pattern Glass*, using factory "code letters" whenever possible seemed logical. The following list makes up those glass factories comprising the United States Glass Company from its inception in 1891.

U.S. GLASS FACTORY MEMBERS

A	Adams & Company, Pittsburgh, PA
B	Bryce Brothers, Pittsburgh, PA
C	Challinor, Taylor & Company, Tarentum, PA
D	George Duncan & Sons, Pittsburgh, PA
E	Richards & Hartley, Tarentum, PA

F	Ripley & Company, Pittsburgh, PA
G	Gillinder & Sons, Pittsburgh, PA
H	Hobbs Glass Company, Wheeling, WV
J	Columbia Glass Company, Findlay, OH
K	King Glass Company, Pittsburgh, PA
L	O'Hara Glass Company, Pittsburgh, PA
M	Bellaire Glass Company, Findlay, OH
N	Nickel Plate Glass Company, Fostoria, OH
0	Central Glass Company, Wheeling, WV
P	Doyle & Company, Pittsburgh, PA
R	A.J. Beatty & Sons, Tiffin, OH
S	A.J. Beatty & Sons, Steubenville, OH
T	Novelty Glass Company, Fostoria, OH
U	U.S. Glass Company, Gas City, IN
GP	U.S. Glass Company, Glassport, PA

The names and locations of all other glass houses represented by glassware in this work are as follows:

AMERICAN GLASS HOUSES:

Atterbury & Company, Pittsburgh, PA
Bakewell, Pears & Company, Pittsburgh
Beatty, A.J. & Sons, Steubenville, OH
Beatty-Brady Glass Company, Dunkirk, IN
Bellaire Goblet Company, Bellaire and later Findlay, OH
Boston Silver Glass Company, East Cambridge, MA
Brilliant Glass Works, Brilliant, OH
Bryce, Higbee & Company, Pittsburgh, PA
Bryce, McKee & Company, Pittsburgh, PA
Bryce, Richards & Company, Pittsburgh, PA
Bryce, Walker & Company, Pittsburgh, PA
Cambridge Glass Company, Cambridge, OH
Campbell, Jones & Company, Pittsburgh, PA
Canton Glass Company, Canton, OH
Cape Cod Glass Company, Sandwich, MA
Central Glass Company, Wheeling, WV
Challinor, Taylor & Company, Pittsburgh, PA
Columbia Glass Company, Findlay, OH
Co-Operative Flint Glass Company, Beaver Falls, PA
Crystal Glass Company, Bridgeport, OH
Curling, Robertson & Company, Pittsburgh, PA
Dalzell, Gilmore & Leighton, Findlay, OH
Dugan Glass Company, Indiana, PA
Duncan & Miller Glass Company
Federal Glass Company, Columbus, OH
Findlay Flint Glass Company, Findlay, OH
Fort Pitt Glass Works, Pittsburgh, PA
Fostoria Glass Company, Fostoria, OH;
   also Moundsville, OH

George A. Duncan & Sons, Pittsburgh, PA
George Duncan & Sons, Pittsburgh, PA
George Duncan=s Sons & Company, Washington, PA
Gillinder & Sons, Philadelphia, PA
Greensburg Glass Company, Greensburg, PA
Grierson & Company, Pittsburgh, PA
Heisey, A.J. Company, In c., Newark, OH
Higbee, J.B. Glass Company, Bridgeville, PA
Hobbs, Brockunier & Company, Wheeling, WV
Ihmsen & Company, Pittsburgh, PA
Indiana Glass Company, Dunkirk, IN
Indiana Tumbler & Goblet Company, Greentown, IN
King Glass Company, Pittsburgh, PA
King, Son & Company, Pittsburgh, PA
Kokomo Glass Manufacturing Company, Kokomo, IN
LaBelle Glass Company, Bridgeport, OH
Lyon, James B. & Company, Pittsburgh, PA
McKee & Brothers, Pittsburgh, PA
McKee Brothers, Jeannette, PA
McKee Glass Company, Jeannette, PA
McKee-Jeanette Glass Company, Jeanette, PA
Model Flint Glass Works, Albany, IN.; also Findlay, OH
National Glass Company, Dunkirk, IN. Also Pittsburgh, PA
New England Company, East Cambridge, MA
New Martinsville Glass Manufacturing Company, New
   Martinsville, WV
Nickel Plate Glass Company, Fostoria, OH
Northwood, H. Company, Wheeling, WV
Ohio Glass Company, Somerville, OH
Ohio Flint Glass Company, Lancaster, OH
Pioneer Glass Works, Pittsburgh, PA
Portland Glass Company, Portland, ME
Richards & Hartley Glass Company, Tarentum, PA
Riverside Glass Works, Wellsburg, WV
Sandwich Glass Company, Sandwich, MA
Specialty Glass Company, East Liverpool, OH
Steimer Glass Company, Buckhannon, WV
Tarentum Glass Company, Tarentum, PA
Thompson Glass Company, Uniontown, PA
Union Glass Company, Somerville, MA
Union Stopper Company, Morgantown, WV
Westmoreland Specialty Glass Company, Grapeville, PA
Windsor Glass Company, Pittsburgh, PA

CANADIAN GLASS HOUSES:

Diamond Glass Company, Ltd., Montreal, Quebec, Canada
Jefferson Glass Company, Toronto, Ontario, Canada

STATE OF THE MARKET

by Jeffrey S. Evans
Green Valley Auctions, Inc., Mt. Crawford, VA

Readers of price guides should always keep this caveat in mind: Evaluation in any field of collecting has never been—and never will be—an exact science. While this price guide is the first publication on early American pattern glass to attempt to take into account the new factors in the market outlined below, one must still remember that price guides are just what their titles state, mere guides to assist in ascertaining the value of a particular article.

Bearing this in mind, the authors, by revising their original 1990 guide, clearly demonstrate that early American pattern glass has enjoyed a grand resurgence of popularity over the last decade. Several key factors, which have greatly magnified the visibility of our field, continue to be the driving forces behind its rebirth. One of the key factors has been public auctions. Arguably, the true value of any given item is the price achieved through competition between two knowledgeable bidders. While this venue is a dependable gauge most of the time, it still harbors an occasional aberration brought on by "auction fever." To be totally accurate, one needs to scrutinize the results from several years worth of records in order to determine an appropriate value.

To use an example close to home, as one of the nation's leaders in high-profile cataloged auctions of EAPG, Green Valley Auctions' Early American Glass department holds and continues to achieve new world record prices for rare pieces in this field. Our professional and authoritative illustrated catalogs have been among the major forces in elevating pattern glass back to the importance that it held in the 1930s and 1960s. Dealers (including the authors of this guide), collectors and museums often use our past catalogs and prices realized sheets as important evaluation tools for today's market. Detailed catalogs are also enticing seasoned collectors and investors from other fields to cross over into our own as many are recognizing the tremendous values currently available in EAPG, especially when compared to similar material in their own fields. This, coupled with the already high demand and short supply of rarities, should keep the upper end EAPG market strong far into the future.

Another key to the resurgence of EAPG collecting has been the development of a totally new market with the emergence of Internet auctions, especially on the popular eBay site. While EAPG makes up only a small fraction of the overall Internet antiques and collectibles world, this new venue has exposed pattern glass to a much broader audience than had been previously possible. A large portion of this audience is comprised of relatively new collectors along with many others who are located in areas of the country that contain little or no pattern glass. This group is the main reason that the middle and lower level markets have shown an increase in price and demand over the past several years. Provided that this interest in Internet auctions continues to be strong and the quantity of pattern glass does not overwhelm the demand, glass in this range should continue to prosper nicely.

Yet another factor that has added to the resurgence of EAPG is the demand from the sector of the market that is not only collecting, but actually using their collection for entertaining and decorating. Martha Stewart and various home decor magazines have been the driving force behind this trend. For example, cake stands, which until recent years had been one of the white elephants of the field, are now in great demand because of the practical usability and elegance they provide when stacked as pyramids. So-called "buttermilk" goblets, which as we all know are pedestal-footed sugar bowls missing their lids, continue to be in high demand for use as mixed drink containers. Other forms that are regaining popularity on today's dinner table are spooners, celery vases, butter dishes, water pitchers and a variety of drinking vessels.

Despite the increased demand for these forms, the goblet continues to be far and away the most collected article in all of pattern glass. From the publication of Millard's two volume reference in 1938, to Metz's follow-up in 1958, and another two volumes authored by the Unitts in 1971, the goblet has been the form of choice by those wishing to assemble a collection featuring an example of every pattern ever produced. This is not a task for those easily discouraged since there are over 2,000 different examples to search for when one takes into account varying colors and decorations. Our firm has sold several collections of goblets, each numbering over 1,200 different patterns, and all have yielded previously uncataloged patterns and variants.

The majority of EAPG collectors, however, collect by pattern and not by form. After all, this is the way that pressed pattern glass production evolved in the 1850s. Mass production of many different forms in the same pattern allowed the middle class to attain "matching" tableware, an accomplishment previously available only to the upper classes. Many of the most popular patterns of the period have remained at the top of the field, while others have fallen out of favor. For instance, Bellflower, the earliest pattern produced in a wide variety of forms, continues to be the most widely collected pattern from the flint period of EAPG production. Patterns close behind in desirability are Horn of Plenty, New England Pineapple and Early Thumbprint, all of which are available in a broad range of forms, greatly enhancing their appeal to collectors. Other early flint patterns that are every bit as desirable, but not as widely collected, because of their scarcity are Cable, Bulls Eye and Diamond Point, Washington, Diamond Thumbprint, and Magnet and Grape with Frosted Leaf.

From the non-flint era, animal and historical patterns continue to top the list of collectible patterns. Jumbo and Monkey both remain in extremely high demand despite the limited number of forms made in each pattern. Demand for Westward Ho, Three Face, U.S. Coin and Frosted Lion is also exceptionally strong, with many of the rarities in these patterns selling in the four-figure range. The naturalistic patterns of the 1870s continue to attract more and more collectors because of their clean, attractive design and classic forms. Leading patterns in this group include Holly, Lily-of-the-Valley and Bleeding Heart, with all becoming scarcer in today's market.

Demand for the later Victorian patterns, most of which are available in a wide variety of colors, has been up and down over the past ten years. Greentown patterns have stayed fairly steady, with the very rare pieces appreciating in value nicely. The market for other patterns of this period seems to be more closely tied to color rather than pattern. Vaseline and blue are presently the most hotly collected colors, with green and amber being the most difficult to sell. Keep in mind, however, that, as with all tastes, this ranking is subject to change without notice. Collectors of decorated pattern glass have been growing by leaps and bounds in recent years also. Far out in front in this category are ruby stained wares. With the simple addition of copper sulfate, an unremarkable clear piece was transformed into a very rare and desirable article worth up to a hundred times more. Other decorations like amber and blush-staining have gained in popularity also, but not nearly to the extent of ruby.

As with all fields of antiques and collectibles, the availability of published scholarly works and research material always promotes demand and desirability. Because of the recent emergence of several different original company catalogs, collecting by manufacturer has become a new area of interest for many. Companies whose wares have become hotly collected because of these publications are Riverside Glass Works and Central Glass, both of West Virginia. This list is destined to grow as more research and factory catalogs come to light.

Collector organizations have also played an important factor in our field regaining the prestigious status it once held. The Early American Pattern Glass Society, which was officially chartered in 1994 and currently has over 700 members, has put forth a tremendous effort towards this comeback. By holding their national convention in conjunction with the Eastern National Antiques Show in Harrisburg, PA, each spring, they have provided an ideal setting for collectors from across the country to assemble and promote pattern glass. More information on this group can be found at its Web site, *www.eapgs.org*. Similarly, museums are another great resource for pattern glass collectors. The Corning Museum of Glass, the world's leading glass repository, is currently expanding its holdings of EAPG. Through the generosity of the John and Elizabeth Welker Memorial Fund (administered by the EAPGS), and other private donations, great strides have been made in this endeavor.

The single biggest deterrent to promoting and expanding EAPG collecting has been, and continues to be, the threat of reproductions. This threat is in no way relegated only to pattern glass, but is a problem in all fields of collecting. Some patterns over the years, like Daisy and Button, have become almost un-sellable because of this problem. Luckily, widespread reproductions in a single pattern are rather limited. Once a collector becomes familiar with his/her pattern of choice it becomes easy to determine the forms that need to be scrutinized and/or avoided.

New research is currently being undertaken by several authorities to alleviate the problem of reproductions. Our gallery, for instance, published the definitive comparison of the original Westward Ho goblet and the 1930s and 1960s reproductions, which was included in our 2000 auction catalog of the Bette and Chub Wicker collection. Another comparison, which finally makes it simple to differentiate between the original and reproduction Morning Glory goblets, is available on our Web site at *www.greenvalleyauctions.com*. Research of this type is extremely important in cultivating and maintaining confidence in all areas of antiques.

Over the past 10 years, Early American pattern glass has matured from a "collectible" into an "antique." With this maturity, it has gained a well-deserved aura of respect from the antiques world in general. It has been a great pleasure and honor to observe and contribute to its resurgence over the last decade and I look forward to its continued strong growth.

ACTRESS

OMN: Opera. **AKA:** Annie, Jenny Lind, Pinafore, Theatrical.

Non-flint. Adams & Co., Pittsburgh, PA, c. 1880.

Original color production: Clear, clear with acid finish. **Notes:** Items in the pattern exhibit views of early stage actresses. Pieces in clear or clear with frosting are priced the same.

Reproductions and Look-a-Likes: 9-1/8" l. relish dish, embossed *"Love's Request is Pickles"* (honey amber, Midwest rue, Siegel green, Wistar purple). Imperial Glass Corporation, Bellaire, OH. Often impressed with Imperial's "IG" logo. Additional unmarked reproductions are known in amethyst, blue, vaseline, and in the opalescent colors of green, purple, and vaseline. Saltshaker with excess glass in base in amber, clear, and blue.

Actress clear frosted champagne book.

Actress covered cheese dish.

Known Items:	Clear
Bowl, footed	
Covered	
6" d.	$100.00
7" d.	110.00
8" d. *"Miss Neilson"*	125.00
9-1/2" d.	150.00
Open with smooth rim	
6" d.	35.00
7" d.	45.00
8" d. *"Miss Neilson"*	55.00
9-1/2" d.	75.00
Butter dish, covered *"Fanny Davenport and Miss Neilson"*	150.00
Cake stand, high standard *"Annie Pixley and Maud Granger"*	
9-1/2" d.	250.00
10" d.	275.00

Known items:	Clear
Celery vase, footed *"HMS Pinafore"*	225.00
Champagne, 5" h.	750.00
Cheese dish flat with cover *"The Lone Fisherman, Two Dromios"* base	350.00

Compote

Covered, high standard

8" d.	175.00
9-1/2" d.	200.00
10" d.	225.00

Open, high standard

10" d.	95.00
12" d.	325.00

Creamer, *"Fanny Davenport and Miss Neilson"*	75.00
Goblet, *"Kate Claxton and Lotta Crabtree"*	150.00
Marmalade jar with cover	125.00
Mug, *"HMS Pinafore"*	95.00
Pickle dish, flat, oblong, *"Love's Request is Pickles"*	45.00

Pitcher

Milk, 1-qt., 6-1/2" h. *"HMS Pinafore Fancy Davenport"*	450.00
Water, 1/2-gal., 9" h. *"Romeo and Juliet Balcony Scene"*	575.00

Platter, bread

"HMS Pinafore," 7-1/2" x 12"	110.00
"Miss Neilson" and motto, 9" x 13"	95.00

Relish dish, flat, oblong

4-1/2" x 7"	50.00
5" x 8"	55.00
5-1/2" x 9"	65.00

Saltshaker	125.00

Sauce dish, round

Flat

4-1/2" d.	15.00
5" d.	20.00

Footed

4-1/2" d.	15.00
5" d.	20.00

Spoon holder, *"Mary Anderson and Maud Granger"*	65.00
Sugar bowl, covered, *"Kate Glaxton and Lotta Crabtree"*	150.00

ADONIS

OMN: AKA: Pleat and Tuck, Washboard.

Non-flint. McKee & Brothers, Pittsburgh, PA, c. 1897.

Original color production: Blue, canary yellow, clear.

Reproductions and Look-a-Likes: None known.

Adonis syrup, water pitcher, and celery vase.

Known items:	Blue	Canary	Clear
Bowl			
Oval, open, flat	$35.00	$25.00	$15.00
Round, open, flat with beaded rim			
5" d.	35.00	35.00	15.00
8" d.	65.00	75.00	20.00
Butter dish with cover	125.00	125.00	45.00
Cake stand on high standard			
10-1/2" d.	325.00	300.00	95.00
Celery vase, collared base with			
scalloped rim	85.00	75.00	35.00
Compote			
Covered on high standard			
8" d.	125.00	110.00	55.00
Open on high standard			
4-1/2" d. (jelly)	45.00	45.00	15.00
Creamer	55.00	50.00	30.00
Pitcher			
Milk, 1-qt.	85.00	75.00	45.00
Water, 1/2-gal.	125.00	125.00	55.00

Known items:	Blue	Canary	Clear
Plate, round			
8" d.	35.00	35.00	18.50
10" d.	65.00	55.00	25.00
Relish tray, flat	25.00	25.00	12.50
Saltshaker	75.00	55.00	35.00
Sauce dish, round, flat with beaded rim			
4" d.	12.50	12.50	5.00
4-1/2" d.	15.00	15.00	8.50
Spoon holder	65.00	55.00	30.00
Sugar bowl with cover	85.00	75.00	35.00
Syrup	325.00	275.00	95.00
Tray, water, 11"	65.00	55.00	30.00
Tumbler, water, flat	45.00	45.00	20.00

Alabama castor set.

Adonis water tray.

ALABAMA

OMN: U.S. Glass No. 15062-Alabama.
AKA: Beaded Bull's Eye and Drape.

Non-flint. United States Glass Co., Pittsburgh, PA, c. 1899.

Original color production: Clear. Occasional items may be found in clear with ruby stain and emerald green.

Reproductions and Look-a-Likes: None known.

Known items:	Clear
Bowl, open, flat	
Rectangular	$35.00
Round, master berry, 8" d.	95.00
Butter dish with cover, flat	125.00
Cake stand on high standard	225.00
Caster set, 4-bottles in original silver plate stand	200.00
Celery	
Tray	30.00
Vase	85.00
Compote on high standard	
Covered	110.00
Open, 5" d. (Jelly)	45.00
Creamer	
Individual	65.00
Table size	55.00
Cruet with original patterned stopper	125.00
Dish, open, flat, single-handled (jelly)	25.00
Honey dish, covered, square (R)	375.00
Mustard pot with original notched covered lid	125.00
Pickle dish	15.00
Pitcher, water with pressed handle, 1/2-gal.	110.00
Saltshaker	75.00
Sauce dish, round, 4" d.	
Flat	10.00
Footed	15.00
Spoon holder	65.00

Alabama creamer.

Known items:	Clear
Sugar bowl with cover	85.00
Syrup	225.00
Toothpick holder	75.00
Tray, water, round, 10-1/2" d.	110.00
Tumbler, water, flat	65.00

Alabama cruet.

ALMOND THUMBPRINT

AKA: Almond, Finger Print, Pointed Thumbprint.

Flint, non-flint. Bakewell, Pears & Co., Pittsburgh, PA, c. 1860s. Non-flint examples reissued by the United States Glass Co., Pittsburgh, PA. after 1891.

Original color production: Clear. Blue, milk white, or any other color would be considered rare.

Reproductions and Look-a-Likes: None known.

Almond Thumbprint punchbowl.

Known items:	Flint	Non-flint
Bottle, cologne, footed, o.s.	$125.00	$85.00
Butter dish with cover	65.00	35.00
Celery vase	75.00	35.00
Champagne		
Barrel	65.00	35.00
Straight-side	45.00	25.00
Compote with covered		
High standard		
4-3/4" d. (Jelly)	85.00	45.00
7" d.	110.00	55.00
10" d.	175.00	75.00

Almond Thumbprint covered sweetmeat.

Known items:

	Flint	Non-flint
Low standard		
4-3/4" d. (Jelly)	45.00	25.00
7" d.	55.00	30.00
Creamer	85.00	35.00
Cruet, footed (2 styles) with original stopper	95.00	45.00
Decanter with original stopper	110.00	55.00
Eggcup, single, footed with cover	35.00	20.00
Goblet		
Barrel	45.00	25.00
Straight sided	35.00	15.00
Pitcher, water, 2-gal.	225.00	85.00
Punch bowl	450.00	125.00
Salt		
Dip	10.00	5.00
Master		
Covered	95.00	45.00
Open	35.00	15.00
Spoon holder	45.00	25.00
Sugar bowl with cover	85.00	35.00

Known items:

	Flint	Non-flint
Tumbler		
Flat	75.00	35.00
Footed	55.00	35.00
Wine, 4" h.		
Barrel	45.00	15.00
Straight sided	35.00	12.50

AMAZON

OMN: AKA: Sawtooth, Sawtooth Band.

Non-flint. Bryce Brothers, Pittsburgh, PA, c. 1890-1891. United States Glass Co., Pittsburgh, PA. at Factory "B," c. 1891-1904.

Original color production: Clear (plain, engraved). Amber, amethyst, blue, canary yellow, clear with ruby stain, or any other color would be considered rare.

Reproductions and Look-a-Likes: None known.

Amazon four-piece table set.

Known items:

	Clear
Banana stand on high standard	$75.00
Bowl, flat	
Oval with cover, 6-1/2"	65.00
Round	
Covered	
5" d.	35.00
6" d.	40.00
7" d.	45.00
8" d.	55.00
9" d.	85.00

Amazon cake stand.

Amazon celery vase.

Known items:	Clear
Open, round	
Flared, plain rim	
5" d.	15.00
6" d.	15.00
8" d.	35.00
Scalloped rim	
5" d.	15.00
6" d.	15.00
7" d.	25.00
8" d.	35.00
Butter dish, footed with cover	65.00
Cake stand on high standard	
8" d.	95.00
9" d.	110.00
10" d.	125.00
Celery vase	
Flat	30.00
Footed	35.00
Champagne, 5" h.	45.00
Claret 4-1/2" h.	45.00
Compote	
High standard	
Covered	
4-1/2" d. (Jelly)	35.00
5" d.	35.00
6" d.	45.00

Known items:	Clear
7" d.	55.00
8" d.	85.00
Open	
Flared, deep bowl	
4-1/2" d.	15.00
5" d.	20.00
6" d.	25.00
7" d.	30.00
8" d.	35.00
Round, flared bowl	
5" d.	20.00
6" d.	25.00
7" d.	30.00
8" d.	35.00
9-1/2" d.	55.00
Saucer-shaped bowl	
8" d.	45.00
9" d.	55.00
10" d.	65.00
Low standard, open, 4" d.	15.00
Cordial	35.00
Creamer, table size	35.00
Cruet with original "fist" or *Maltese cross* stopper	55.00
Dish	
Oval, covered, flat with lion handles	
6" l.	65.00
7" l.	75.00
8" l.	85.00

Amazon goblet.

Amazon syrup pitcher.

Known items:	Clear
Round, open, shallow with lion handles	
4-1/2" d.	25.00
6" d.	35.00
Eggcup, open, single	25.00
Goblet	
6" h.	35.00
Miniatures	
Butter dish, flat with cover	110.00
Creamer, footed	50.00
Spoon holder	50.00
Sugar bowl, footed with cover	85.00
Pitcher, water, 1/2-gal.	75.00
Relish tray	15.00
Salt	
Dip	
Individual, 1-1/2" h.	5.00
Master	25.00
Shaker	35.00
Sauce dish, round	
Flat	
Flared scalloped rim	
4" d.	5.00
4-1/2" d.	5.00

Known items:	Clear
Footed	
4" d.	8.00
4-1/2" d.	8.00
Spoon holder	30.00
Sugar bowl with cover	55.00
Syrup	75.00
Tumbler, water, flat, 1/2-pt.	25.00
Vase, flower, on high standard with ruffled rim	
Double-bud	65.00
Single-bud	45.00
Wine	25.00

APOLLO (Adam's)

Apollo four-piece table set.

OMN: AKA: Canadian Horseshoe, Frosted Festal Ball, Shield Band, Thumbprint and Prisms.

Non-flint. Adams & Co., Pittsburgh, PA, c. 1875. United States Glass Co., Pittsburgh, PA, at Factory "A," Pittsburgh, c. 1891 to 1899.

Original color production: Clear, clear with frosted finish (plain, copper wheel engraved). Clear with ruby stain, clear with blue, pale yellow, dark green, or any other color is considered rare.

Reproductions and Look-a-Likes: None known.

Apollo water pitcher.

Apollo syrup pitcher, seven-piece berry set.

Known items:	Clear	Clear/Frosted
Bowl		
Desert, open, oblong	$20.00	$35.00
Open flat		
Flared bowl		
5" d.	15.00	25.00
6" d.	20.00	30.00
7" d.	25.00	35.00
8" d.	35.00	45.00
Round bowl		
5" d.	15.00	25.00
6" d.	20.00	30.00
7" d.	25.00	35.00
8" d.	35.00	45.00
Salad, round	65.00	95.00
Butter dish with cover		
Flanged rim	85.00	110.00
Plain rim 6" d.	45.00	55.00

Known items:	Clear	Clear/Frosted
Cake stand on high standard		
8" d.	65.00	85.00
9" d.	75.00	95.00
10" d.	85.00	110.00
12" d.	135.00	175.00
Celery		
Tray	20.00	25.00
Vase	30.00	40.00
Compote		
Covered on high standard, 6" d.	85.00	135.00
Open		
High standard, smooth rim		
5" d.	15.00	25.00
6" d.	25.00	35.00
7" d.	35.00	45.00
8" d.	45.00	55.00
Low standard		
5" d.	15.00	25.00
6" d.	20.00	30.00
7" d.	25.00	35.00
8" d.	35.00	45.00
Creamer	35.00	45.00
Cruet with original stopper	55.00	110.00

Apollo flared bowl, cruet, water pitcher, and deep bowl.

Known items:	Clear	Clear/Frosted
Dish, pickle 15.00		20.00
Eggcup, open, single 25.00		45.00
Goblet 35.00		45.00
Lamp, kerosene, 10" h. 85.00		125.00
Pickle tray .15.00		20.00

Pitcher

    Bulbous

	Clear	Clear/Frosted
Milk, 1-qt. 55.00		110.00

    Water

	Clear	Clear/Frosted
1/2-gal. 65.00		95.00
1-gal. 85.00		150.00
Tankard. 1-gal. 75.00		135.00
Plate, square, 9-1/2" 25.00		35.00

Salt

	Clear	Clear/Frosted
Master, flat 25.00		35.00
Shaker 35.00		45.00

Sauce

    Flat with smooth rim

      Flared bowl

	Clear	Clear/Frosted
3-1/2" d. 5.00		8.00
4" d. 5.00		8.00

      Round bowl

	Clear	Clear/Frosted
3-1/2" d. 5.00		8.00
4" d. 5.00		8.00

    Footed, round with smooth rim

	Clear	Clear/Frosted
3-1/2" d. 5.00		8.00
4" d. 7.50		15.00
5" d. 10.00		20.00
Spoon holder 35.00		45.00
Sugar bowl, footed with cover. 55.00		75.00
Sugar shaker 75.00		125.00
Syrup 110.00		175.00
Tray, water, round 65.00		95.00
Tumbler, water, 3-1/2" h. 30.00		40.00
Wine 25.00		30.00

ARCHED GRAPE

Flint, non-flint. Boston & Sandwich Glass Co., Sandwich, MA, c. 1870s.

Original color production: Clear.

Reproductions and Look-a-Likes: None known.

Arched Grape spooner.

Known items:	Non-flint
Butter dish with cover $65.00
Celery vase. 55.00
Champagne 85.00
Compote, with cover high standard 125.00
Creamer 45.00
Goblet 45.00
Pitcher, water with applied handle, 1/2-gal. 350.00
Sauce dish, round, 4" d.
Flat 5.00
Footed. 8.00
Spoon holder 35.00
Sugar bowl with cover 55.00
Wine 35.00

ARGUS

OMN: Concave Ashburton. **AKA:** Argus-Creased, Argus-Faceted Stem, Argus (5-Row), Barrel Argus, Hotel Argus, Master Argus, Tall Argus, Thumb-print.

Original color production: Clear. Any item in color would be considered a rarity.

Flint. Adams & Co., Pittsburgh, PA, c. 1872 (only the 2-pt. tumbler). Bakewell, Pears & Company, Pittsburgh, PA, c. 1870. King, Son & Co., Pittsburgh, PA, c. 1875. McKee & Brothers, Pittsburgh, PA, c. 1865.

Reproductions and Look-a-Likes: Butter dish by the Imperial Glass Co. (amber, heather and verde). Covered low-footed compote, creamer with pressed handle, goblet, plate, flat round sauce dish, sherbet, covered sugar bowl, tumblers: iced tea, highball, old-fashioned, juice or cocktail and the wine (amber, blue, clear, cobalt blue, green, gray, olive green, ruby) by the Fostoria Glass Co. (each embossed with the "*H.F.M.*" monogram).

Argus goblet, champagne, and wine.

Known items:	Clear
Ale glass, footed, 5-1/2" h.	$110.00
Beer glass, flat	95.00
Bottle, bitters	75.00
Bowl	
Covered with collared base, 6" d.	110.00
Open, flat, 5-1/2" d.	45.00

Known items:	Clear
Butter dish with cover, 6-1/2" d.	85.00
Celery vase, footed	
Cut ovals	135.00
Pressed ovals	110.00
Champagne with cut or pressed ovals, 5-1/4" h.	
Barrel-shaped bowl	85.00
Flared bowl	85.00
Compote	
Covered	
High standard	
6" d.	85.00
8" d., patterned base	175.00
9" d.	225.00
Low standard	
6" d.	45.00
9" d.	75.00
Open, 10-3/8" d.	225.00
Cordial	75.00
Creamer with applied handle	150.00
Decanter	
1-pt.	95.00
1-qt.	95.00
Eggcup, single, open, footed	
Handled	85.00
No handle	20.00
Goblet	
Cut ovals	110.00
Pressed ovals	65.00
Honey dish, round, flat	15.00
Jelly glass	55.00
Lamp, oil	
Collared base, 4" d.	150.00
Footed	225.00
Mug with applied handle	95.00
Paperweight	325.00
Pickle jar	225.00
Pitcher, water with applied handle, 1/2-gal.	850.00
Punch bowl, pedestaled with scalloped rim	
11-1/2" d.	650.00
14-1/8" d.	1250.00
Salt	
Individual, round, flat	15.00
Master, open, footed	35.00
Sauce dish, round, flat, 4-1/4" d.	8.00

Argus goblet.

Known items:	Clear
Spoon holder	45.00
Sugar bowl with cover	85.00
Tumbler	
Flat	
1/2-pt.	75.00
Bar	75.00
Ship	85.00
Whiskey with applied handle	110.00
Footed	
4" h.	65.00
5" h.	85.00
Wine, 4" h.	45.00

ART

OMN: AKA: Jacob's Tears, Job's Tears, Teardrop and Diamond Block.

Non-flint. Adams & Company, Pittsburgh, PA. Introduced c. 1889 with production continued by the United States Glass Company at Factory "A," c. 1891.

Original color production: Clear, clear with ruby stain. Ruby-stained items were produced after Adams' merger into the United States Glass Company.

Reproductions and Look-a-Likes: Covered compote on high standard (clear, clear with cranberry stain, and milk white).

Known items:	Clear	Clear w/Ruby
Banana stand		
High standard, 10" l.	$150.00	$450.00
Low standard, 10" l.	95.00	175.00
Biscuit jar with cover	325.00	850.00
Bowl, round		
Covered, collared base		
Belled bowl		
6" d.	65.00	—
7" d.	85.00	—
8" d.	100.00	—
Flared bowl		
6" d.	65.00	—
7" d.	85.00	—
8" d.	100.00	—
Open		
Collared base with flared bowl		
6" d.	25.00	—
7" d.	35.00	—
8" d.	45.00	—
9" d.	65.00	—
10" d.	85.00	—

Art covered sugar bowl.

Art cruet, goblet, water pitcher, and biscuit jar.

Art sugar bowl, butter dish, and creamer.

Known items:	Clear	Clear w/Ruby
Flat		
Flared		
7" d.	25.00	—
8" d.	35.00	—
8-1/2" d.	45.00	—
9" d.	65.00	—
10" d.	85.00	—
With pointed end, 8"	95.00	150.00
Butter dish with cover.	75.00	175.00
Cake stand on high standard		
7-3/4" d.	75.00	—
9" d.	95.00	—
10" d.	110.00	—
10-1/2" d.	125.00	—
Celery vase	30.00	85.00
Compote on high standard		
Covered		
6" d.	85.00	125.00
7" d.	110.00	175.00
8" d.	135.00	225.00
Open		
Belled bowl		
6" d.	40.00	—
7" d.	50.00	—
8" d.	65.00	—
Round bowl		
6" d.	35.00	—
7" d.	45.00	—
8" d.	55.00	—

Known items:	Clear	Clear w/Ruby
9" d.	65.00	—
10" d.	85.00	—
Scalloped rim with shallow bowl		
8" d.	65.00	—
9" d.	85.00	—
10" d.	95.00	—
Creamer, flat with applied handle		
Hotel, round, squatty	110.00	—
Table size	75.00	135.00
Tankard, 1/2-pt.	65.00	125.00
Cruet with applied handle and original stopper (blown, not pressed)	125.00	375.00
Dish, preserve, oblong, 8" l.	35.00	75.00
Goblet	65.00	225.00
Mug	85.00	175.00
Pickle dish, rectangular	25.00	65.00
Pitcher with applied handle		
Milk, 1-qt.	125.00	225.00
Water		
Bulbous, 1/2-gal.	225.00	450.00
Squat, square		
3-pts.	175.00	275.00
2-1/2-qts.	200.00	325.00
Plate, round, 10" d.	65.00	—
Relish tray	20.00	55.00
Sauce dish		
Flat		
Round		
4" d.	15.00	—
4-1/2" d.	15.00	—

Known items:	Clear	Clear w/Ruby
Pear-shaped, pointed at one end		
4" d.	25.00	55.00
4-1/2" d.	30.00	—
Square, 4-1/4"	25.00	—
Footed, round		
4" d.	20.00	—
4-1/2" d.	25.00	—
Spoon holder, flat	35.00	85.00
Sugar bowl with cover		
Hotel	65.00	125.00
Table	65.00	125.00
Tumbler, water, flat	75.00	110.00

ARTICHOKE

OMN: Fostoria No. 205-Valencia. **AKA:** Frosted Artichoke

Non-flint. Fostoria Glass Co., Moundsville, WV, c. 1891.

Original color production: Clear, clear and frosted. Limited production in clear (prices for all clear are the same as clear with frosting).

Reproductions and Look-a-Likes: Goblet (clear with frosting). L.G. Wright Glass Co., New Martinsville, WV. Unmarked. Note: A goblet was not originally produced in the *"Artichoke"* pattern.

Known items:	Clear w/Frosting
Bobeche	$35.00
Bowl, open, round, flat	
7" d.	150.00
8" d.	175.00
9" d.	250.00
10" d.	275.00
Butter dish with cover	225.00
Cake stand on high standard	325.00

Artichoke ice-cream set.

Known items:	Clear w/Frosting
Compote	
High standard	
Covered	
6-1/2" d.	325.00
7" d.	375.00
8" d.	450.00
Open, 10" d.	350.00
Low standard, open with shallow bowl, 8" d.	225.00
Creamer	150.00
Cruet with original stopper	325.00
Finger bowl with matching underplate, 4" d.	150.00
Goblet (reproduction by Wright not made originally)	25.00
Lamp, oil	
Finger with grip	
Flat	275.00
Footed	450.00
Miniature with matching shade	425.00
Stand (all glass)	
7-1/2"	450.00
8-1/2"	500.00
9-1/2"	525.00
Nappy, triangular, handled	175.00
Pitcher, water, 1/2-gal.	
Bulbous	450.00
Tankard	350.00
Rose bowl	150.00
Saltshaker (VR)	225.00
Sauce dish, round	
Flat	65.00
Footed	75.00
Spoon holder, double handled	150.00
Sugar bowl, covered	175.00

Known items:	Clear w/Frosting
Syrup pitcher	325.00
Tray, water, round	200.00
Tumbler, water, flat	125.00
Vase	
6" h.	110.00
9-1/2" h.	175.00

ASHBURTON

OMN: Ashburton, Double Flute. **AKA:** Barrel Ashburton, Choked Ashburton, Dillaway, Double Flute, Double Knob Stem Ashburton, Flaring Top Ashburton, Giant Straight Stemmed Ashburton, Large Thumbprint, Near Slim Ashburton, Proxy Ashburton, Semi-Squared Ashburton, Short Ashburton, Slim Ashburton, and Tailsman Ashburton.

Flint, non-flint. Predominant production by the New England Glass Company, East Cambridge, MA, c. 1869. Also produced by Bakewell, Pears & Co., Pittsburgh, PA, c. 1875. Bellaire Goblet Co. via the United States Glass Co., Pittsburgh, PA, after 1891. Bryce, Richards & Co., c. 1854. Bryce, McKee & Co., Pittsburgh, PA, c. 1854. Boston & Sandwich Glass Co., Sandwich, MA.

Original color production: Clear (plain, enameled, engraved). Examples in amber, amethyst, blue-green, canary yellow, emerald green, milk white, opal, opaque white, or any other color would be considered rare.

Reproductions and Look-a-Likes: Ashtray, low flat bowl; goblet (10-oz., 12-oz.); saltshaker; sherbet; tumblers (82-oz., 10-oz., 12-oz.); wine by Libbey Glass Co. (clear, amber); ashtray; low-footed cake stand; candlestick; claret; 7-1/2" h. covered compote; high-standard open compote with flared rim; open high-standard compote with lipped rim; creamer; goblet; water pitcher with pressed handle; sherbet; covered sugar bowl; tumblers (iced tea, old-fashioned), wine by the Westmoreland Glass Company (amber, Bermuda Blue, brown, clear, flame, milk white, milk white decorated, olive green, pink).

Ashburton celery.

Known items:	Clear
Ale glass	
6-1/2" h.	$125.00
Long Tom (R)	225.00
Bottle	
Bitters	75.00
Water or tumble-up with matching tumbler	325.00
Bowl, open, round, flat, 6-1/2" d.	110.00
Butter dish with cover (2 styles)	125.00
Celery vase	
Scalloped rim, 10-1/4" h.	165.00
Smooth rim, 9-1/4" h.	150.00
Champagne	
Flared bowl	85.00
Straight-sided bowl	75.00
Claret, 5-1/4" h.	95.00
Compote, open on low standard, 7-1/2" d.	125.00
Cordial, 4-1/4" h.	
Flared bowl	135.00
Round bowl	110.00
Creamer with applied handle	225.00
Decanter	
With bar lip or heavy collar	
1-pt.	65.00
3-pts.	75.00
1-qt.	85.00

Ashburton whiskey.

Known items:	Clear
With stopper	
1/2-pt.	110.00
1-pt.	125.00
3-pts.	150.00
1-qt.	175.00
Eggcup, open, footed	
Double	125.00
Single	20.00
Flip	
Handled	225.00
Non-handled	175.00
Goblet	
Flared bowl	55.00
Straight-sided bowl	45.00
Honey dish, round, flat, 3-5/8" d.	10.00
Lamp	325.00
Mug	
Beer with pressed handle	125.00
Pony	110.00
Pitcher, water with applied handle, 6-5/8" h.	950.00
Plate, 6-5/8" d.	125.00
Sauce dish, round, flat, 4-1/4" d.	8.00
Spoon holder (2 sizes)	65.00

Known items:	Clear
Sugar bowl with cover	
Large	150.00
Small	125.00
Toddy jar, with cover, handled and matching under plate, 1-qt.	650.00
Tumbler	
Bar, 3-3/8" h.	95.00
Footed	65.00
Handled, 2-pt.	125.00
Sarsaparilla	75.00
Ship	
1/3-pt.	85.00
1/2-pt.	95.00
Soda	110.00
Tap	
1/3-pt.	65.00
1-pt.	75.00
Water, flat, 3-3/4" h.	85.00
Whiskey, flat	65.00
Whiskey, flat with applied handle	125.00
Wine	
Flared bowl	45.00
Round bowl	35.00

ATLANTA (Fostoria)

OMN: Fostoria No. 500-Atlanta. **AKA:** Clear Lion Head, Frosted Atlanta, Late Lion, Square Lion, Square Lion Heads.

Non-flint. Fostoria Glass Co., Moundsville, WV, c. 1895 through 1900.

Original color production: Clear, clear with satin finish (plain, engraved). Items in clear with ruby stain, clear with amber stain, and camphor glass are considered rare. Notes: Items are generally square in shape and adorned with well-sculpted faces of lions.

Reproductions and Look-a-Likes: Goblet (clear), unmarked.

Atlanta covered sugar bowl.

Atlanta creamer.

Known items:	Clear	Clear/Frosted
Banana stand with folded		
sides on high foot	$325.00	$450.00
Bowl, open, scalloped rim, square		
Flat		
6" sq.	55.00	65.00
7" sq.	65.00	75.00
8" sq.	85.00	100.00
Butter dish with cover.	125.00	150.00
Cake stand on high standard		
9-1/4" sq..	150.00	225.00
10" sq.	225.00	275.00
Celery vase	85.00	110.00
Compote		
High standard		
Covered		
5" sq.	110.00	135.00
6" sq.	135.00	150.00
7" sq.	150.00	175.00

Atlanta creamer, butter dish, sugar bowl, and spoon holder.

Known items:	Clear	Clear/Frosted
Open, scalloped rim		
4-3/4" sq.	75.00	95.00
5" sq.	65.00	75.00
6" sq.	75.00	85.00
7" sq.	95.00	100.00
Low footed, open with		
scalloped rim, 8" sq.	125.00	150.00
Creamer	85.00	100.00
Cruet with original stopper (R).	375.00	550.00
Dish, preserve, rectangular		
6" l.	45.00	55.00
7" l.	55.00	65.00
8" l.	65.00	75.00
Eggcup, open, single	85.00	110.00
Goblet	125.00	175.00
Marmalade jar with cover	175.00	275.00
Mustard jar with cover.	150.00	250.00
Pitcher, water, 1/2-gal..	450.00	550.00
Relish dish	55.00	65.00
Salt		
Dip, individual	65.00	100.00
Master, open, flat	125.00	135.00
Shaker	85.00	110.00
Sauce dish, flat, 4" sq..	35.00	45.00
Spoon holder	65.00	85.00
Sugar bowl with cover	110.00	135.00
Syrup pitcher (VR)	550.00	850.00

Known items:	Clear	Clear/Frosted
Toothpick holder	45.00	55.00
Tumbler, water	100.00	135.00

Atlanta goblet.

ATLAS

OMN. AKA: Bullet, Cannon Ball, Crystal Ball, Knobby Bottom.

Non-flint. Designed and patented by Henry J. Smith (pattern No. 19,427, registered November 12, 1889). Bryce Brothers, Pittsburgh, PA, c. 1889. Production continued by the United States Glass Co., Pittsburgh, PA, at Factory "A" and Factory "B," c. 1891 to at least 1904.

Original color production: Clear, clear with ruby stain (plain, engraved).

Reproductions and Look-a-Likes: None known. Some pieces confused with the Candlewick pattern by Imperial.

Atlas celery vase, covered compote, and syrup.

Known items:	Clear	Clear w/Ruby
Bowl, flat		
Covered		
5" d.	$35.00	$65.00
6" d.	45.00	75.00
7" d.	55.00	85.00
8" d.	75.00	125.00
Open		
5" d.	15.00	35.00
6" d.	20.00	40.00
7" d.	25.00	45.00
8" d.	45.00	65.00
Butter dish with cover		
Hotel size	55.00	95.00
Table size	55.00	95.00
Cake stand on high standard		
8" d.	75.00	175.00
8-1/2" d.	85.00	185.00
9" d.	110.00	225.00
10" d.	135.00	275.00
Celery vase, flat.....................	35.00	85.00
Champagne, 5-1/2" h.	45.00	85.00
Compote		
Covered on high standard		
5" d.	85.00	150.00
7" d.	95.00	165.00
8" d.	125.00	225.00

Atlas champagne.

Atlas high-standard cake stand.

Known items:	Clear	Clear w/Ruby
Open		
High standard, flared rim,		
5" d.	35.00	75.00
Low standard		
5" d.	25.00	45.00
7" d.	35.00	55.00
8" d.	45.00	65.00
Cordial	55.00	95.00
Creamer with cover		
Hotel size	45.00	85.00
Table size	45.00	85.00
Finger or waste, bowl	45.00	65.00
Goblet	35.00	65.00
Marmalade jar with cover	125.00	275.00
Mug	25.00	55.00
Pitcher, tankard		
Milk, 1-qt.	65.00	125.00
Water, 1/2-gal.	85.00	175.00
Salt		
Dip, individual	8.00	—
Master, round, flat	15.00	—
Shaker	35.00	—

Known items:	Clear	Clear w/Ruby
Sauce dish, round		
Flat, 4" d.	8.00	25.00
Footed		
4" d.	10.00	30.00
4-1/2" d.	12.50	35.00
Spoon holder		
Hotel size	45.00	75.00
Table size	35.00	65.00
Sugar bowl with cover		
Hotel size	55.00	85.00
Table size	55.00	95.00

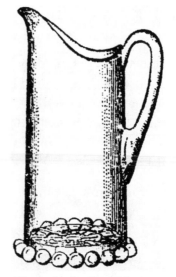

Atlas tankard water pitcher.

Atlas toothpick holder, saltshaker, wine, and cordial.

Known items:	Clear	Clear w/Ruby
Syrup pitcher		
Toothpick holder	20.00	35.00
Tray, water, round	95.00	225.00
Tumbler		
Water, 1/2-pt.	35.00	75.00
Whiskey, 1-gill	25.00	45.00
Wine	35.00	65.00

AURORA (Brilliant)

OMN: AKA: Diamond Horseshoe, Diamond Horse Shoe.

Non-flint. Brilliant Glass Works, Brilliant, OH, c. 1888-1902. Greensburg Glass Co., Greensburg, PA, c. 1890. McKee Brothers, Pittsburgh, PA, c. 1902 (items in chocolate only).

Original color production: Clear (plain, engraved). Items in clear with ruby stain were decorated by the Pioneer Glass Co., Pittsburgh, PA. Odd items are also known in chocolate.

Reproductions and Look-a-Likes: None known.

Known items:	Clear	Clear w/Ruby
Bowl, round, flat		
5" d.	$15.00	$35.00
6" d.	20.00	45.00
8" d.	30.00	65.00
Butter dish with cover	45.00	150.00
Cake stand on high standard	75.00	275.00
Celery vase	35.00	85.00
Compote on high standard		
Covered		
6" d.	55.00	125.00
7" d.	75.00	150.00
8" d.	110.00	225.00

Aurora high-standard covered compote.

Aurora water set with ice bowl, tumblers, pitcher, and under tray.

Aurora water tray.

Aurora wine.

Known items:	Clear	Clear w/Ruby
Open		
6" d.	35.00	95.00
7" d.	45.00	110.00
8" d.	50.00	135.00
Creamer	35.00	85.00
Decanter, 11-3/4" h. with		
original stopper	55.00	135.00
Goblet	45.00	95.00
Mug with pressed handle	35.00	75.00
Olive dish, oblong	20.00	45.00
Pickle dish, fish shaped	15.00	30.00
Pitcher		
Milk, 1-qt.	45.00	150.00
Water, 1/2-gal.	75.00	225.00
Plate, bread, 10" d.		
Plain center	25.00	65.00
Star center	30.00	75.00
Relish tray, oval with handle	15.00	35.00
Saltshaker	30.00	65.00
Sauce dish, 4"		
Flat	5.00	20.00
Footed	8.00	25.00
Spoon holder	35.00	85.00
Sugar bowl with cover	40.00	125.00
Tray, round		
Water	45.00	85.00
Wine	35.00	65.00

Known items:	Clear	Clear w/Ruby
Tumbler		
Handled	30.00	75.00
Scalloped base	25.00	65.00
Waste bowl	35.00	75.00
Wine	20.00	65.00

AUSTRIAN

OMN: Indiana Tumbler & Goblet Co. No. 200, Federal No. 110. **AKA:** Fine Cut Medallion, Paneled Oval Fine Cut, Western.

Non-flint. Indiana Tumbler & Goblet Co., Greentown, IN. Introduced in August 1897. Federal Glass Co., Columbus, OH, c. 1914. Indiana Glass Co., Dunkirk, IN, c. 1907.

Original color production: Amber, canary yellow, clear (plain, gilded), green. All items were not made in all colors. Also, the experimental colors of cobalt blue, Nile green, opaque colors, chocolate.

Reproductions and Look-a-Likes: None known.

Austrian seven-piece water set with tumblers, pitcher, and under tray.

Austrian sugar bowl, butter dish, spoon holder, and creamer.

Known items:	Amber	Canary	Clear	Green
Banana stand	$450.00	—	$225.00	—
Bowl, open				
Rectangular				
5" x 7-1/4"	—	—	85.00	—
5-1/4" x 8-1/4"	—	195.00	75.00	—
Round				
Deep, 8" d.	—	275.00	75.00	—
Shallow	—	—	65.00	—
Butter dish with cover	—	475.00	250.00	—
Compote, open				
High standard				
4-1/4" d.	—	225.00	75.00	—
8" d.	—	325.00	85.00	—
Low standard	—	250.00	110.00	—
Cordial	275.00	165.00	75.00	300.00
Creamer, open or covered				
4-1/4" h.	—	150.00	35.00	225.00
Large, rimless	—	225.00	85.00	—
Small, pedestaled base	—	200.00	65.00	—
Goblet	—	250.00	75.00	—
Miniatures				
Butter dish with cover	—	550.00	275.00	—
Creamer, 4" h.	225.00	150.00	75.00	—
Mug	—	—	75.00	—
Spoon holder	—	150.00	85.00	—
Sugar bowl with cover	—	225.00	175.00	—

Austrian rose bowl.

Austrian wine.

Known items:	Amber	Canary	Clear	Green
Nappy, flat with cover and double handles	275.00	85.00	—	
Pitcher, water	—	550.00	250.00	—
Plate, square	—	—	95.00	—
Punch cup	225.00	135.00	25.00	—
Rose bowl				
Small	—	225.00	85.00	—
Medium	—	—	110.00	—
Large	—	250.00	125.00	—
Saltshaker	—	150.00	65.00	—
Sauce dish, flat				
Round				
4-1/4" d.	—	—	10.00	—
4-1/2" d.	—	55.00	12.50	—
Square	—	75.00	15.00	—
Spoon holder	—	150.00	65.00	—
Sugar bowl with cover				
2-1/2" d.	—	135.00	45.00	—
4" d.	—	325.00	75.00	—
Small with pedestaled base	—	250.00	95.00	—
Tumbler	325.00	150.00	45.00	—
Vase				
6" h.	—	200.00	50.00	—
8" h.	—	250.00	75.00	—
10" h.	—	375.00	85.00	—
Wine	375.00	225.00	35.00	275.00

AZTEC

OMN. AKA: New Mexico.

Non-flint. McKee Glass Co., Jeannette, PA, c. 1894 through 1915.

Original color production: Clear, milk white.

Reproductions and Look-a-Likes: Butter dish with cover (clear, colors), one-piece and two-piece 10-qt. punch bowls (clear and colors without the "Pres-Cut" trademark), 5-ounce punch cup (clear), toothpick holder marked with the Fenton Art Glass Company logo.

Aztec punch set.

Known items:	Clear
Bonbon dish, footed, 7" d.	
Round	$20.00
Triangular	20.00
Bottle, water	55.00
Bowl, open	
Round	
Deep bowl	
Flared rim, scalloped	
9" d.	45.00
10-1/2" d., lemonade or eggnog	65.00

Known items:	Clear
Regular with scalloped rim	
7" d.	30.00
8" d.	40.00
Shallow with scalloped rim	
7" d.	25.00
8" d.	35.00
10-1/2" d.	55.00
Triangular with deep scalloped bowl	
7"	35.00
8"	45.00
Finger bowl with matching underplate	65.00
Butter dish with cover	
Round	65.00
Square	75.00
Cake plate, tri-cornered	45.00
Candlestick	85.00
Celery	
Tray, 11" l.	30.00
Vase, flat	45.00
Champagne, 5-oz.	45.00
Claret, 4-oz.	35.00
Cologne bottle	
Globular	35.00
Tall	40.00
Compote, open on high standard	55.00
Condensed milk jar with notched lid	75.00
Cordial	
3/4-oz.	35.00
1-oz.	35.00
Cracker jar with cover	110.00
Creamer	
Individual or "berry"	15.00
Table size	35.00
Tankard	20.00
Cruet, 6-oz. with original stopper	45.00
Cup, custard	8.50
Decanter, wine	75.00
Dish, flat, handled, 5"	
Round	15.00
Square	20.00
Triangular	18.50
Goblet, 9-oz.	45.00

Aztec wine.

Known items: **Clear**

Jar, covered

    Crushed fruit, with spoon

        Squat **125.00**

        Tall **175.00**

    Puff, 3-1/4" d. **35.00**

Lamp with matching globe, 18-1/4" h. **225.00**

Marmalade or pickle jar, same as condensed milk jar

    but without notch in lid **85.00**

Pitcher

    Lemonade **75.00**

    Tankard with pressed handle **85.00**

    Water with applied handle **110.00**

Plate

    Cake, flat with scalloped rim

        5-1/2" d. **15.00**

        9-1/2" d. **25.00**

    Dinner, 10" d. **45.00**

Punch bowl, 8-qt.

    Flat **65.00**

Known items: **Clear**

    Footed

        One piece **95.00**

        Two piece **85.00**

Punch bowl under plate (also known as the "torte plate"),

    21-1/2" d. **45.00**

Relish tray **15.00**

Rose bowl **35.00**

Saltshaker

    Bulbous **35.00**

    Tall **30.00**

Sauce dish, flat

    Heart shaped **35.00**

    Round, scalloped

        4" d. **8.00**

        4-1/2" d. **8.50**

    Triangular, 4-1/2" **10.00**

Sherbet, footed **12.50**

Spoon holder **35.00**

Straw holder with cover, 12-1/4" h. **275.00**

Sugar bowl

    Covered

        Scalloped rim **45.00**

        Smooth rim **55.00**

    Open, flat, handled (also known as the

        "berry sugar") **20.00**

Syrup **85.00**

Toothpick holder **30.00**

Tray, flat

    Olive **15.00**

    Pickle **15.00**

Tumbler

    Iced tea **35.00**

    Water **30.00**

    Whiskey **25.00**

Vase with scalloped rim, 10" h. **30.00**

Whiskey jug with handle and original stopper **125.00**

Wine

    2-oz. **25.00**

    3-oz. **25.00**

BABY FACE

OMN: Cupid

Non-flint. McKee & Brothers, Pittsburgh, PA, c. 1880.

Original color production: Clear with acid finish (plain, copper wheel engraved). **Note:** The most prominent features of this pattern are the well-formed faces of babies that adorn both the stem and finial of most items. All clear pieces are very rare and priced the same as clear with frosting. Etched items are worth 10-20% more.

Reproductions and Look-a-Likes: Although reproductions have been listed in the early literature of pattern glass, known examples have yet to surface.

Baby Face table creamer.

Baby Face high-standard covered compote.

Known items:	Clear w/Frosting
Butter dish with cover	$325.00
Celery vase	225.00
Champagne	750.00
Compote	
Covered on high standard with belled bowl	
7" d.	350.00
8" d.	550.00
Open	
High standard with belled bowl	
7" d.	325.00
8" d.	375.00
Low standard, 8" d.	325.00
Creamer	225.00
Goblet	550.00
Knife rest (Not part of original production)	135.00
Pitcher, water, pedestaled, 1/2-gal.	3,500.00

Baby Face close-up of pattern on water pitcher.

Known items:	Clear w/Frosting
Spoon holder	175.00
Sugar bowl with cover	275.00
Wine	225.00

Baby Face water pitcher.

BALL AND SWIRL

OMN: Ray. **AKA:** Swirl and Ball.

Non-flint. McKee & Brothers, Pittsburgh, PA, c. 1894.

Original color production: Clear, clear with acid finish, clear with ruby stain (plain, copper wheel engraved).

Reproductions and Look-a-Likes: Ashtray; banana stand on high standard; basket with handle (5-1/2" d., 7" d.); bowls (6-1/2" d., 10" d.); cake stand on high standard (6" d., 10" d.); two-light candelabra; 4" h. candlestick; covered candy dish; covered 7" d. compote; open 7" d. compote with flared rim; open 7-1/2" d. compote with turned edge; footed creamer; 2-oz. oil cruet; wine decanter; 8-oz. goblet; footed mayonnaise; 5" l. heart-shaped nappy with handle; 5-1/2" d. flared nappy with handle; 5-1/2" d. plain nappy with handle; 6-1/2" d. water pitcher; 8" d. plate; 10" d. plate; plate with turned up edges; 12" d. dinner plate; 18" d. torte plate; 3-part, 9" d. round relish; 5" d. rose bowl, high standard sherbet, low standard sherbet, double handled sugar bowl, iced tea (10-oz., 12-oz.), 8-oz. water tumbler, fan-shaped footed vase; 9" h. footed vase with flared rim; 2-oz. wine (Amber, amethyst, blue, clear, cerise, crimson mother-of-pearl, green marble slag, milk white, purple carnival, purple marble slag). Westmoreland Glass Company, Grapeville, PA. Often embossed "WG" or marked with a paper label.

Known items:	Clear
Banana stand, high standard, 10" l.	$55.00
Bowl, finger	20.00
Butter dish with cover	45.00
Cake stand on high standard, 10" d.	75.00
Candlestick	45.00
Compote	
Covered on high standard, 9" d.	85.00

Ball and Swirl creamer.

Ball and Swirl cake stand.

Known items:	Clear
Open on high standard	
Jelly	15.00
9" d., with smooth rim	35.00
Creamer	25.00
Decanter, wine	55.00
Dish, jelly, flat with handle	10.00
Goblet	25.00
Mug	
Large	30.00
Medium	20.00
Small	15.00
Pickle tray	15.00
Pitcher	
Milk, 1-qt., tankard	35.00
Water, 1/2-gal.	
Bulbous	55.00
Tankard	45.00
Plate, cake, flat	25.00
Salt/pepper shakers with original glass holder	35.00
Sauce dish, round, footed	5.00
Spoon holder	25.00
Sugar bowl with cover	35.00
Syrup	55.00
Tray, cordial	30.00
Tumbler	
Water	15.00
Handled	20.00
Wine	15.00

BALTIMORE PEAR

OMN: Gypsy. **AKA:** Double Pear, Fig, Maryland Pear, Twin Pear.

Non-flint. Adams & Co., Pittsburgh, PA, c. 1874. The United States Glass Co., Pittsburgh, PA, at Factory "A," c. 1891.

Original color production: Clear. A very rare version of the creamer and water pitcher are known with a shell motif under the spout.

Reproductions and Look-a-Likes: Bowl 8" d. ; butter dish; creamer; goblet; 9" d. plate; 10" d. plate; 4-3/4" d. round flat sauce dish; covered sugar bowl; double-handled tray (clear, milk white, pink opaque [Shell Pink]). Jeanette Glass Co., Jeanette, PA; L.G. Wright Glass Company, New Martinsville, WV; others. Unmarked.

Known items:	Clear
Bowl	
Collared base	
Covered	
5" d.	$95.00
6" d.	110.00

Baltimore Pear water pitcher and goblets.

Baltimore Pear celery vase.

Known items: **Clear**

    7" d. **125.00**

    8" d. **175.00**

    9" d. **275.00**

Open

    5" d. **45.00**

    6" d. **55.00**

    7" d. **65.00**

    8" d. **85.00**

    9" d. **110.00**

Flat base

   6" d. (AKA: "butter nappy")

    Flared rim **85.00**

    Plain rim **75.00**

   8" d., master berry **125.00**

Baltimore Pear covered butter.

Known items: **Clear**

Bread plate, round, 12-1/2" d. 110.00

Butter dish

    Covered, flat, 6-1/2" d. 150.00

Cake stand on high standard

    9-1/4" d. 325.00

    10" d. 375.00

Celery vase 110.00

Compote, covered

   High standard

    5" d. 110.00

    6" d. 150.00

    7" d. 175.00

    8" d. 225.00

    8-1/2" d. 275.00

   Low standard

    5" d. 95.00

    6" d. 110.00

    7" d. 125.00

    8" d. 175.00

Creamer 55.00

Goblet 110.00

Honey dish, 3-1/2" d.

    Octagonal, flat 25.00

   Round

    Flat 25.00

    Footed 35.00

Pickle tray, oblong. 85.00

Baltimore Pear creamer, butter dish, sugar bowl, and spoon holder.

Known items:	Clear
Pitcher	
Milk, 1-qt.	225.00
Water, 1/2-gal.	150.00
Plate, round	
8-1/2" d.	65.00
9" d.	85.00
10" d.	95.00
Relish tray	95.00
Sauce	
Collared base, round	
4" d.	25.00
4-1/2" d.	30.00
Flat, octagonal	
4" d.	20.00
4-1/2" d.	25.00
Spoon holder	55.00
Sugar bowl with cover	95.00

Baltimore Pear covered sugar.

BAMBOO

OMN: LaBelle No.365. **AKA:** Bamboo Edge.

Non-flint. LaBelle Glass Co., Bridgeport, OH, c. 1883.

Original color production: Clear (plain, copper wheel engraved). Add 20-30% for engraved items.

Reproductions and Look-a-Likes: None known.

Bamboo celery vase.

Known items:	Clear
Butter dish with cover	$150.00
Celery vase	110.00
Compote on high standard	
Covered	
7" d.	150.00
8" d.	225.00
9" d.	325.00
Open, oval	95.00

Bamboo covered butter.

Bamboo high-standard covered compote.

Bamboo creamer.

Known items:	Clear
Creamer	85.00
Pitcher, water, 1/2-gal.	350.00
Relish tray	
7" l.	55.00
8" l.	75.00
9" l.	85.00

Known items:	Clear
Saltshaker (R)	225.00
Sauce dish, 4" d.	
Flat	15.00
Footed	25.00
Spoon holder	75.00
Sugar bowl with cover	125.00
Tumbler	95.00

BANDED BUCKLE

OMN: Union.

Non-flint. King, Son and Co., Pittsburgh, PA, c. 1875.

Original color production: Clear. Blue or any other color would be considered rare.

Reproductions and Look-A-Likes: None known.

Banded Buckle eggcup.

BARBERRY

OMN: Berry. **AKA:** Olive, Pepper Berry.

Non-flint. McKee & Brothers, Pittsburgh, PA, c. 1880. The Boston & Sandwich Glass Co., Sandwich, MA, c. 1850s-1860s.

Original color production: Clear. Amber, blue or any other color would be considered rare.

Reproductions and Look-a-Likes: None known.

Barberry spooner.

Known items:	Clear
Bowl, open, flat with smooth rim, 8" d.	$55.00
Butter dish with cover	95.00
Compote on high standard, round, 6" d.	
Covered	125.00
Open	45.00
Creamer, footed with applied handle	85.00
Eggcup, open, single	25.00
Goblet	35.00
Jam jar with cover	95.00
Pickle dish, oval	15.00
Pitcher, water, 1/2-gal.	350.00
Salt, master, open	
Flat, oval, 3-1/3" l.	45.00
Footed	35.00
Spoon holder	35.00
Sugar bowl with cover	95.00
Syrup pitcher (R)	275.00
Tumbler, water, flat	65.00
Wine	30.00

Known items:	Clear
Bowl, flat	
Covered	
6" d.	$65.00
8" d.	110.00
Open	
Oval	
6" l.	25.00
7" l.	30.00
8" l.	35.00
9" l.	45.00

Known items: Clear

Round, shallow with smooth rim

5" d. 20.00

7" d. 25.00

8" d. 35.00

9" d. 45.00

Butter dish with cover, 6" d.

Design on rim 150.00

Plain rim 75.00

Cake stand on high standard 225.00

Compote

High standard

Covered

6" d. 85.00

7" d. 110.00

8" d. 150.00

Open

7" d. 55.00

8" d. 75.00

Low standard

Covered

6" d. 65.00

7" d. 85.00

8" d. 110.00

Open

7" d. 35.00

8" d. 45.00

Creamer 75.00

Cup plate, 3" d. 35.00

Eggcup, single, open 45.00

Goblet 45.00

Honey dish, round, flat 10.00

Pickle tray, oval with taper at one end, 7" l. 18.50

Pitcher, water, bulbous with applied handle,

1/2-gal. 325.00

Plate, round, 6" d. 35.00

Salt, master, open, footed 45.00

Sauce dish, round, 4" d.

Flat 8.00

Footed 15.00

Spoon holder, footed 35.00

Sugar bowl with cover 75.00

Syrup pitcher with applied handle 225.00

Tumbler, water, footed 85.00

Wine 45.00

BARLEY

AKA: Sprig.

Non-flint. Maker unknown. Attributed to Campbell, Jones & Co., Pittsburgh, PA. Researchers traditionally base this attribution on the design patented as No. 12,647 by James Dalzell on January 3, 1882 for a wheelbarrow master salt bearing the "Barley" pattern. To date, no proof has emerged indicating that the design covered by the Dalzell patent covered the complete Barley line.

Original color production: Clear. Amber or any other color would be considered rare.

Reproductions and Look-a-Likes: None known.

Barley set.

Known items: Clear

Bowl, open, flat

Oval, 10" l. $35.00

Round, 8" d., master berry 45.00

Butter dish with cover 55.00

Cake stand on high standard

8" d. 55.00

9" d. 65.00

9-1/2" d. 75.00

10" d. 125.00

Celery vase 45.00

Compote

Covered

High standard

6" d. 75.00

8-1/2" d. 95.00

Known items: **Clear**

Low standard

     6" d. 55.00

     8-1/2" d. 75.00

Open on high standard, 8-1/2" d. 45.00

Creamer..................................... 30.00

Dish, oval, open, flat (vegetable)

     5-1/4" x 7-1/2" l. 25.00

     6-1/2" x 9-1/2" l. 30.00

Goblet 45.00

Honey dish, flat, 3-1/2" d. 15.00

Marmalade jar with cover 85.00

Pickle

     Castor in silver plate frame 150.00

     Dish.................................... 15.00

Pitcher, water

     Bulbous, applied handle................ 225.00

     Pressed handle......................... 55.00

Plate, round, 6" d. 35.00

Platter, oval, 13" l x 8" 45.00

Relish, 7" x 8" 30.00

Sauce dish, round

     Flat, sunburst center, 4-1/2" d. 8.00

     Footed

         4" d. 10.00

         5" d. 12.50

Spoon holder 25.00

Sugar bowl with cover 45.00

Tray, bread................................. 35.00

Wine....................................... 30.00

BARRED OVAL(S)

Barred Oval carafe and tumbler.

OMN: United States Glass No. 15004. **AKA:** Banded Portland, Banded Portland-Frosted, Buckle, Frosted Banded Portland, Purple Block, Oval and Crossbar.

Non-flint. George Duncan & Sons, Pittsburgh, PA, c. 1892. The United States Glass Co., Pittsburgh, PA, at Factory "D."

Original color production: Clear, clear w/frosting, Clear with ruby stain (plain, copper wheel engraved).

Reproductions and Look-a-Likes: Basket with applied handle; bell; round open 6-1/2" d. bowl; round open 8-1/2" d. bowl; 6" h. candlestick; light, covered sugar bowl; 8-1/2" h. swung vase (carnival, clear, Periwinkle blue, ruby). Fenton Art Glass Company, Williamstown, WV. Often embossed with the Fenton logo.

Known items:	**Clear**	**Clear w/Ruby**
Bottle, water	$65.00	$325.00
Bowl, open, flat		
Round		
7" d.	25.00	75.00
8" d.	35.00	85.00
9" d.	55.00	125.00
Square		
7"	45.00	95.00
8"	75.00	125.00
Butter dish with cover	65.00	150.00
Cake stand on high standard, 10" d.	125.00	650.00
Celery		
Tray....................	35.00	75.00
Vase, 6-1/2" h...........	45.00	95.00

Barred Oval cruet.

Barred Oval spoon holder, sugar bowl, creamer, and butter dish.

Known items:	Clear	Clear w/Ruby
Compote on high standard		
Covered		
7" d.	95.00	375.00
8" d.	110.00	450.00
Open		
7" d.	45.00	110.00
8" d.	50.00	125.00
Creamer	45.00	95.00
Cruet with original stopper	95.00	375.00
Dish, open, oblong, flat		
7" l.	15.00	55.00
8" l.	20.00	60.00
9" l.	25.00	65.00
Goblet	150.00	350.00
Lamp, oil		
High standard		
7-1/2" h.	150.00	—
9" h.	175.00	—
Parlor with matching		
half shade	1,500.00	—
Pickle dish, rectangular, 6" l.	15.00	45.00
Pitcher		
Milk, 1-qt.	95.00	275.00
Water, 1/2-gal.	110.00	350.00
Plate, cheese		
6" d.	25.00	65.00
7" d.	30.00	75.00
Sauce dish, flat		
Round		
4" d.	5.00	20.00
4-1/2" d.	5.00	20.00

Barred Oval saltshaker.

Known items:	Clear	Clear w/Ruby
Square		
4" d.	8.00	20.00
4-1/2" d.	8.00	20.00
Saltshaker	55.00	95.00
Spoon holder	35.00	85.00
Sugar bowl with cover	55.00	125.00
Tumbler, water, flat	40.00	75.00

BASKETWEAVE

Non-flint. Maker unknown, c. mid-1880s. Attributions have been placed on the Boston & Sandwich Glass Co., Sandwich, MA, based on the discovery of shards at the factory site.

Original color production: Amber, apple green, blue, clear, vaseline. Odd items in milk glass may occasionally be found.

Reproductions and Look-a-Likes: Goblet, tumbler, water pitcher, water tray (amber, blue, clear, green, yellow).

Basketweave goblet.

Basketweave pitcher.

Known items:	Amber	Apple Green	Blue	Clear	Vaseline
Bowl, round, flat					
Covered with handles	$35.00	$75.00	$65.00	$30.00	$95.00
Open					
Berry, master.............	35.00	65.00	55.00	25.00	85.00
Finger or waste..........	25.00	45.00	35.00	20.00	50.00
Butter dish with cover	55.00	110.00	75.00	45.00	125.00
Compote					
Covered, 7" d.					
High standard..........	65.00	110.00	95.00	55.00	125.00
Low standard	45.00	85.00	75.00	40.00	95.00
Open					
High standard	30.00	45.00	50.00	25.00	55.00
Low standard..........	25.00	40.00	45.00	20.00	50.00
Creamer	35.00	65.00	50.00	30.00	85.00
Cup and saucer	40.00	75.00	60.00	30.00	95.00
Dish, open, oval, flat	25.00	45.00	35.00	20.00	55.00
Eggcup					
Double	35.00	75.00	65.00	30.00	95.00
Single	25.00	55.00	45.00	20.00	65.00
Goblet	30.00	65.00	40.00	15.00	55.00
Mug	25.00	45.00	40.00	20.00	55.00
Pickle dish.................	15.00	35.00	25.00	15.00	40.00

Known items:	Amber	Apple Green	Blue	Clear	Vaseline
Pitcher					
Milk, 1-qt.	95.00	135.00	125.00	45.00	175.00
Water, 2-gal.	35.00	75.00	65.00	30.00	95.00
Plate, cake, handled, 11" d.	20.00	35.00	30.00	15.00	40.00
Salt, master, open					
Flat, oblong	25.00	45.00	40.00	25.00	55.00
Footed	25.00	50.00	45.00	20.00	65.00
Sauce dish, round, flat.	5.00	10.00	8.00	5.00	12.50
Spoon holder	30.00	75.00	65.00	25.00	85.00
Sugar bowl with cover	45.00	95.00	85.00	35.00	110.00
Syrup pitcher	110.00	225.00	150.00	85.00	275.00
Tray, water with "rural" scene in center	35.00	55.00	45.00	25.00	65.00
Tumbler, water, flat	20.00	65.00	50.00	20.00	75.00
Wine	20.00	45.00	40.00	15.00	55.00

BEADED ACORN MEDALLION

AKA: Beaded Acorn.

Non-flint. Boston Silver Glass Co., East Cambridge, MA, c. 1869. Also attributed to the Boston & Sandwich Glass Co., Sandwich, MA, based on shards found at the factory site.

Original color production: Clear.

Reproductions and Look-a-Likes: None known.

Beaded Acorn Medallion goblet.

Known items:	Clear
Bowl, fruit, open	$65.00
Butter dish with cover	110.00
Champagne	95.00
Compote with cover	
High standard, 8" d.	175.00
Low standard, 9" d.	150.00
Creamer, 5-3/4" h.	75.00
Eggcup, open, single	45.00
Goblet	55.00
Honey dish, flat, 3-1/2" d.	15.00
Lamp, marble base with brass standard	175.00
Pitcher, water, bulbous with applied handle, 1/2-gal.	375.00
Plate, round, 6" d.	45.00
Relish, oval, flat, deep	
Large	35.00
Small	30.00
Salt, master, open, footed with smooth rim	35.00
Sauce dish, round, flat with smooth rim, 4" d.	5.00
Spoon holder	35.00
Sugar bowl with cover	75.00
Wine	35.00

BEADEDBAND

Non-flint. Maker unknown, c. 1884.

Original color production: Clear. Amber, blue or any other color would be considered rare.

Reproductions and Look-a-Likes: None known.

Beaded Band compote.

Known items	Clear
Butter dish with cover	$45.00
Cake stand on high standard	
7-1/2" d.	55.00
9" d.	65.00
10" d.	85.00
Compote	
Covered	
High standard	
7" d.	85.00
8" d.	95.00
Low standard, 8" d.	65.00
Open, high standard	
9-1/2" d.	35.00
10" d.	45.00

Known items	Clear
Creamer	30.00
Goblet	35.00
Pickle jar with cover	110.00
Pitcher, water, 1/2-gal.	95.00
Relish tray	
Double, flat	15.00
Single	20.00
Sauce dish, round	
Flat	5.00
Footed	5.00
Spoon holder	30.00
Sugar bowl with cover	40.00
Syrup pitcher, lid dated "June 29, 84"	125.00
Wine	15.00

BEADED GRAPE MEDALLION

Flint, non-flint. The Boston Silver Glass Co., East Cambridge, MA, c. 1869. Attributed to the Boston & Sandwich Glass Co., Sandwich, MA, based on shards found at the factory site. When "banded," the design is referred to as Beaded Grape Medallion-Banded.

Original color production: Clear. Designed by Alonzo C. Young and patented May 11, 1869 under the mechanical patent No.90,040.

Reproductions and Look-a-Likes: Goblet (clear, clear with stain, colors) marked with "R" in shield on base.

Known items:	Clear
Bowl, open, flat	$55.00
Butter dish with cover, 6" d.	95.00
Cake stand on high standard, 11" d.	550.00
Castor set with original stoppers in original period holder	
4-bottles	225.00
5-bottles	275.00
Celery vase	135.00
Champagne	95.00

Beaded Grape Medallion celery.

Known items: **Clear**

Compote

    Covered

        High standard. 175.00

        Low standard 125.00

    Open, high standard

        7-1/4" d. 100.00

        8" d. 125.00

Creamer with applied handle 65.00

Dish with cover

    Oval

        Collared base, 7" x 10" 175.00

        Flat, 9-1/4" x 9-1/2" 150.00

Eggcup. 40.00

Goblet

    Stippled base 30.00

    Stippled base, 3 clear beaded ovals and clusters of

        grapes. 65.00

    Stippled base, 3 small clear beaded ovals . . . 50.00

Honey dish, flat, 3-1/2" d. 15.00

Pickle dish, flat. 35.00

Pitcher, water, bulbous with applied handle,

    1/2-gal. 275.00

Plate, round, 6" d. 55.00

Relish dish, marked with "Mould Pat'd May 11, 1869"

    Covered 175.00

    Open. 55.00

Salt

    Dip, individual 15.00

    Master, open

        Flat, oval 45.00

        Footed, smooth rim. 35.00

Sauce dish, round, flat, 4" d. 5.00

Spoon holder 35.00

Sugar bowl with cover 85.00

Tumbler, footed 65.00

Wine 75.00

BEADED MIRROR

AKA: Beaded Medallion.

Flint, non-flint. The Boston Silver Glass Co., East Cambridge, MA, c. 1869. Attributed to the Boston & Sandwich Glass Co., Sandwich, MA, based on shards found at the factory site.

Original color production: Clear.

Reproductions and Look-a-Likes: None known.

Known items: **Clear**

Bottle, castor

    Mustard $30.00

    Oil, original stopper. 35.00

    Shaker. 25.00

Butter dish with cover 95.00

Castor set, 5-bottles in original pewter frame. 325.00

Celery vase. 85.00

Compote with cover on high standard 150.00

Creamer 65.00

Eggcup, open, single 30.00

Goblet. 45.00

Beaded Mirror spooner.

Beaded Mirror sugar bowl.

Known items:	Clear
Salt master, open, footed	35.00
Sauce dish, round	
Flat	5.00
Footed	8.00
Spoon holder	35.00
Sugar bowl with cover	75.00

BEADED SWIRL

Beaded Swirl seven-piece water set.

OMN: George Duncan No. 335. **AKA:** Swirled Column.

Non-flint. George Duncan & Sons, Pittsburgh, PA, c. 1890. The United States Glass Co., Pittsburgh, PA, after 1891.

Original color production: Clear, emerald green (plain, gilded). Electric blue, clear with amber stain, clear with ruby stain, milk white or any other color would be considered rare. Issued in both a flat and a 3-legged form.

Reproductions and Look-a-Likes: None known.

Known items:	Clear
Pitcher	
Milk, 1-qt.	350.00
Water, 1/2-gal.	275.00
Plate, round, 6" d.	35.00
Relish tray	25.00

Beaded Swirl butter dish, creamer, spoon holder, and cruet.

Beaded Swirl sugar shaker.

Beaded Swirl syrup pitcher.

Known items:	Clear	Emerald Green
Bowl		
Covered, round with 3-legs		
7" d.	$35.00	$45.00
8" d.	45.00	55.00
9" d.	55.00	65.00
Open		
Oval, flat		
7" l.	12.50	15.00
8" l.	15.00	20.00
9" l.	20.00	25.00
Round with scalloped rim		
Flat		
7" d.	12.50	15.00
8" d.	15.00	20.00
9" d.	25.00	30.00
3-legged		
7" d.	15.00	20.00
8" d.	20.00	25.00
9" d.	30.00	40.00
Butter dish with cover		
Flat	35.00	65.00
Footed	55.00	75.00
Cake stand on high standard	85.00	125.00

Known items:	Clear	Emerald Green
Celery		
Tray		
Cupped, flat	15.00	20.00
Straight	15.00	20.00
Vase, flat	25.00	35.00
Creamer		
Flat		
Table size	25.00	35.00
Tankard	30.00	45.00
Footed, table size	35.00	55.00
Cruet with cut or pressed stopper	45.00	85.00
Cup		
Custard with handled	5.00	8.00
Sherbet without handle	8.00	10.00
Eggcup	15.00	20.00
Finger or waste bowl	20.00	30.00
Goblet	35.00	55.00
Pitcher, water, bulbous, 1/2-gal.	55.00	75.00
Plate for sherbet	10.00	15.00
Relish tray	12.50	15.00
Saltshaker		
Squat	20.00	35.00
Tall	20.00	35.00
Sauce dish, round		
Flat		
4" d.	5.00	8.00
4-1/2" d.	5.00	8.00
3-legs		
4" d.	8.00	10.00
4-1/2" d.	8.00	10.00

Known items:	Clear	Emerald Green
Spoon holder		
Flat	20.00	35.00
Footed	30.00	40.00
Sugar bowl with cover		
Flat	30.00	40.00
Footed	35.00	45.00
Sugar shaker (VR in color)	35.00	110.00
Syrup (VR in color)	55.00	125.00
Tumbler	20.00	25.00
Wine	10.00	15.00

BEADED TULIP

OMN: Andes. **AKA:** Tulip.

Non-flint. McKee & Brothers, Pittsburgh, PA, c. 1895.

Original color production: Clear. Blue, emerald green, or any other color would be considered rare.

Reproductions: None known.

Beaded Tulip pitcher.

Known items	Clear
Bowl, open, oval, flat, 9-1/2" l.	35.00
Butter dish, flat with cover	125.00

Known items	Clear
Cake stand on high standard	150.00
Champagne	110.00
Compote, 8" d.	
Covered	85.00
Open	35.00
Creamer	45.00
Dish, ice cream, oblong	40.00
Goblet	45.00
Marmalade jar with cover	95.00
Pickle dish, oval, flat	15.00
Pitcher	
Milk, 1-qt.	55.00
Water, 1/2-gal.	75.00
Plate	
Bread	35.00
Sandwich, 6" d.	45.00
Relish dish	15.00
Sauce dish, round, leaf-shaped edges, 4"	
Flat	8.00
Footed	8.00
Spoon holder	95.00
Sugar bowl with cover	100.00
Tray, round	
Water	55.00
Wine	45.00
Wine	25.00

Beaded Tulip spooner.

BEAUTIFUL LADY

Non-flint. Bryce, Higbee & Co., Pittsburgh, PA, c. 1905.

Original color production: Clear.

Reproductions and Look-a-Likes: None known.

Beautiful Lady banana stand.

Known items:	Clear
Banana stand on high standard	$55.00
Bowl, open, 9" d.	
Collared base	25.00
Flat	20.00
Butter dish with cover	75.00
Cake stand on high standard	
6-1/4" d. (child's)	45.00
9-1/2" d.	65.00
Celery vase	45.00
Compote on high standard	
Covered	85.00
Open	35.00
Creamer, 5" h.	45.00
Cruet with original stopper	55.00
Goblet	45.00
Pitcher	
Milk	35.00
Water, 1/2-gal.	65.00

Known items:	Clear
Plate	
Round	
Bread	30.00
Dinner	
8" d.	25.00
9" d.	30.00
11" d.	35.00
Square, 7"	30.00
Saltshaker	35.00
Spoon holder	45.00
Sugar bowl with cover	65.00
Tumbler, water, flat	30.00
Vase, 6-1/2" h.	20.00
Wine	15.00

BELLFLOWER

OMN: R.L. Pattern. **AKA:** Ribbed Bellflower, Ribbed Leaf.

Flint, non-flint. Attributed to the Boston & Sandwich Glass Co., Sandwich, MA, based on shards found at the factory site. Later produced by Bryce, McKee & Co., Pittsburgh, PA.

Original color production: Clear. Amber, cobalt blue, fiery opalescent, green, milk white, opaque blue, sapphire blue or any other color is considered very rare. Produced with either a single or a double vine of bellflowers and berries. An uncommon adaptation of the design incorporates cut bellflowers, rather than pressed.

Reproductions and Look-a-Likes: Creamer with applied handle; 8-oz. goblet; 1-qt. milk pitcher; covered sugar bowl; 8-oz. tumbler (clear, canary, emerald green, sapphire blue, peacock blue). Imperial Glass Corporation, Bellaire, OH. Embossed "MMA."

Bellflower assortment.

Bellflower celery vase.

Known items: **Clear**

SINGLE VINE-FINE RIB

Bowl,

    Open, flat

        Oval

           9-1/4" l........................ **$425.00**

        Round

           Plain rim with rayed base

               6" d. (R)....................... **125.00**

               8" d. (R)....................... **200.00**

           Scalloped rim

               7-3/4" d. with scallop and point rim

                   (VR) **650.00**

               8" d. with six large scallops **250.00**

           Covered, round, footed, 8" d......... **675.00**

Butter dish with cover and hexagonal-acorn finial

    Beaded base **175.00**

    Flanged base......................... **325.00**

    Plain base **150.00**

    40 ray base **225.00**

Cake stand (produced from a footed compote)

    6" d., with plain scalloped edge and sunburst

        center (VR)........................ **4,000.00**

    8-1/2" d., 3" h. with rayed-scalloped rim and

        patterned base (VR) **5,500.00**

    8-1/2" d., curiosity with the design against a fine

        diamond point background (VR)...... **9,500.00**

Castor with patterned bottom

    Bottles

        Mustard.......................... **75.00**

        Oil with original stopper............ **135.00**

        Shaker **65.00**

Known items: **Clear**

    Stands

        Pewter, period

            Signed by maker................. **325.00**

            Unmarked **150.00**

        Silverplate or Britannia............... **65.00**

Celery vase

    Banded unpatterned rim, 8" h............. **500.00**

    Patterned rim

        8-1/8" h. **325.00**

        7-3/4" h. **275.00**

Champagne

    Barrel-shaped bowl with knob-stem

        Plain base, 5-1/4" h. **165.00**

        Rayed base, 5-1/4" h. **175.00**

    Straight-sided bowl with plain, 3" clear marginal

        band around bowl.................... **135.00**

Compote

    Covered with hexagonal acorn-finial

        High standard

            6" d. **450.00**

            8" d. **650.00**

Bellflower decanter and stopper.

Bellflower double vine decanter.

Known items:	Clear
Low standard	
7" d.	325.00
8" d.	375.00
Open	
High standard	
Domed patterned base	
Patterned to edge	
9" d.	325.00
9-7/8" d. (sometimes called punch bowl)	425.00
Unpatterned edge, 9" d.	450.00
Clear scalloped rim	300.00
Plain base with scalloped rim	225.00
Low standard	
Domed patterned base	
Clear scalloped rim	
7" d.	150.00
8" d.	175.00
Rayed with scalloped rim	175.00
Plain base with scalloped rim	125.00
Creamer	
Pattern to end of lip, 6" h.	450.00
Plain lip	325.00

Known items:	Clear
Decanter (R)	
Heavy bar lip	
1-pt., 8-1/4" h.	275.00
1-qt., 9-1/2" h.	225.00
Matching patterned stopper	
1-pt., 11-1/2" h.	1,000.00
1-qt., 12-1/2" h.	1,250.00
Plain rim, not ground for stopper	325.00
Eggcup, open	
Flared	35.00
Straight-sided	30.00
Goblet	
Knob stem, SV-FR	
Barrel shape	
Plain base 5-3/4" h.	45.00
Rayed base 5-3/4" h.	55.00
Loops under goblet bowl, 5-5/8" h.	300.00
Plain stem, SV-FR	
Rayed base to edge, 6-1/8" h.	40.00
Rayed base with straight-sided bowl and 2" clear marginal band around top of bowl.	65.00
Straight stem with design to top of bowl	45.00

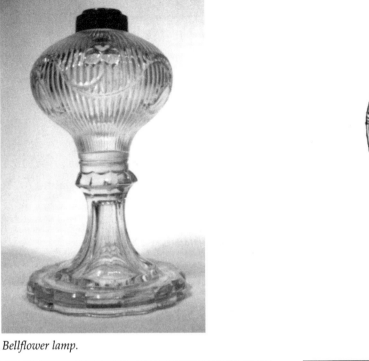

Bellflower lamp.

Bellflower rare covered compote.

Known items:	Clear
Hat, fashioned from a tumbler (ER)	**4,500.00**
Honey dish, round, flat	
3" d., scalloped rim	
Rayed base	**110.00**
Star base (R)	**225.00**
3-1/4" d., plain rim, rayed base.	**85.00**
3-1/2" d.	**35.00**
Lamp	
Interior patterned font, brass stem,	
marble base	**475.00**
Outside patterned font	
All glass, with scalloped base (coal	
or whale oil), 7-1/4" h.	**225.00**
Bracket, pattern on top, plain ribbing	
below, 10-point star base	**1,800.00**
Glass font with brass stem and	
marble base	**325.00**
Mug with applied handle, 2-7/8" h. (VR)	**1,250.00**
Pickle dish.	**65.00**
Pitcher, helmet-shaped with applied handle	
Milk, 1-qt. (ribbed to the end of lip), 7" h. . . .	**1,850.00**
Water, 1/2-gal.	**450.00**
Plate, 16 scallops, 47 ever rays, 6-1/4" d.	**125.00**
Relish dish, open, flat with rayed base.	**75.00**

Known items:	Clear
Salt, master, footed	
Beaded rim, open	**95.00**
Scalloped edge, open	
Clear scallop.	**65.00**
Rayed base with 15 scallops	**55.00**
Scallop and point between, 2-3/4" h.	**75.00**
Sauce dish, round, flat, various types	**10.00**

Bellflower single vine footed true open bowl.

Bellflower single vine oil lamp.

Known items: **Clear**

Spoon holder, footed

    40 rayed base with ribs to edge, 5-1/2" h. .. **65.00**

    45 ray base with unpatterned scallops,

    5-1/2" h. **95.00**

    Rayed to top of scalloped rim **40.00**

Sugar bowl with cover

    Octagonal shaped on low foot with high domed

    lid with rayed base and mushroom finial

    (VR). **2,200.00**

    Pedestaled with acorn finial **175.00**

Syrup with applied hollow handle

    Round

        6" h. **650.00**

        7" h. **450.00**

    Ten-sided with flared foot and 10-pointed rosette

    base (VR)

        5-1/2" h. to neck **3,500.00**

        6-3/4" h. to neck **2,250.00**

Tumbler

    Water, flat

        Design to rim, vine flows left

        Typical design, 3-1/2" h. **200.00**

        Untypical, 2 veined leaves, 2, 3-petalled

        clovers, & 2 bellflowers rotating together,

        3-1/2" h. **85.00**

Known items: **Clear**

    Unpatterned rim, with 3/8" clear marginal

    band, vine flows right **85.00**

    Whiskey, flat, 2-7/8" h., vine flows left **375.00**

Wine

    Barrel-shaped bowl with rayed base

    3-7/8" h. **150.00**

    Straight-sided bowl with plain stem and rayed

    base 4-1/8" h. **135.00**

    Straight-sided bowl with plain, 1/4" clear

    marginal band around bowl 4" h. **150.00**

DOUBLE VINE-FINE RIB:

Compote, open

    High standard, 8" d. **$375.00**

    Low standard with scalloped rim, 7" d. **225.00**

Creamer with rayed foot and applied handle **325.00**

Decanter (R)

    Bar lip, 1-qt. **275.00**

    With matching patterned stopper

        1-1/2-pts. **550.00**

        1-qt. **750.00**

Goblet with bellflowers (VR). **275.00**

Pitcher, helmet-shaped with applied handle

    Milk, 1-1/2-pts. (ribbed to end of lip),

    7-5/8" h. (R) **2,250.00**

Bellflower single vine syrup.

Bellflower spoon holder.

Bellflower water pitcher.

Known items:	Clear
Water, 1-1/2 qts.	
8-1/4" h.	550.00
8-3/4" h.	650.00
Salt, master, open, footed	75.00
Spoon holder, footed	
Clear with scalloped rim and short stem,	
5" h.	150.00
Rayed to top of rim	125.00
Sugar bowl with cover and acorn finial on low foot . . .	225.00
Tumbler, footed, 4-7/8" h.	750.00

SINGLE VINE-COARSE RIB:

Bowl, unpatterned foot	
7-1/4" d. with 12 scallops.	$275.00
8-3/8" d. with 14 scallops.	300.00
Butter dish, round, flat with cover	
Mushroom finial	225.00
Rose bud finial.	375.00
Champagne, barrel-shaped bowl with plain stem,	
5-1/4" h.	135.00
Compote	
High standard with scalloped rim	
Patterned base with clear marginal bands	
around top and bottom	375.00
Domed foot, 8" d.	
Clear scallops	175.00
Rayed scallops.	200.00
Low standard, 9" d.	150.00

Known items:	Clear
Eggcup, open, single	
Flared bowl	40.00
Straight-sided bowl	35.00
Goblet	
Plain stem, rayed base, 5-7/8" h.	40.00
Ribbed-paneled bowl with small	
bellflowers (R)	125.00
Stippled bellflower (VR)	275.00
Variation, 12 fluted panels around lower	
portion of bowl with hexagonal stem	
and plain foot (VR)	325.00
Lamp, bracket (VR).	1,800.00
Pitcher, with applied handle, 1-qt., ribbed to top	
of lip	850.00
Syrup, with applied handle and 10-panels	750.00
Sugar bowl with cover	
Mushroom finial.	150.00
Octagonal finial.	175.00
Tumbler	
Water	
Clear marginal band around top	110.00
Straight-sided with plain base (vine flows	
right), 3-1/2" h.	125.00
Whiskey with applied handle (R)	425.00
Wine, rayed base 4-1/4" h.	225.00

CUT BELLFLOWERS:

Known items:	Clear
Celery vase with pedestal and scalloped rim, dv.	1,400.00
Champagne, dv. 5" h.	1,500.00
Compote, high standard, plain stem and base, 8-1/4" d.	1,750.00
Decanter, 1-pt., dv. with original stopper	2,250.00
Goblet, dv., 6-1/4" h.	1,250.00
Tumbler, water, 3-1/2" h.	850.00
Wine, dv., 4" h.	1,000.00

MISCELLANEOUS:

Cologne bottle either marked "cologne" or suited with a plain space for a paper label	650.00
Goblet (fine ribbing) with Bellflower border (ER)	1,250.00
Plate, fine diamond background, 6" d.	1,000.00
Sugar bowl, covered with additional leaves on vine, lid rest on narrow rim within bowl, 8" h.	475.00

Bethlehem Star goblet.

BETHLEHEM STAR

AKA: Bright Star, Six Point Star, Star Burst.

Non-flint. Indiana Glass Co., Dunkirk, IN, c. 1912. Jefferson Glass Co., Toronto and Montreal, Canada.

Original color production: Clear.

Reproductions and Look-a-Likes: None known.

Known items:	Clear
Bowl, master berry, flat, 8-1/2" d.	$45.00
Butter dish with cover	85.00
Celery	
Tray, flat	25.00
Vase, handled (S)	75.00
Compote with cover on high standard	
4-1/2" d. (Jelly)	50.00
5" d.	65.00
8" d.	95.00
Creamer, 5" h.	35.00
Cruet with original stopper	55.00
Goblet	50.00

Known items:	Clear
Pitcher	
Milk, 1-qt.	65.00
Water, 1/2-gal.	95.00
Relish dish, flat	15.00
Sauce dish, round, flat, 4-3/4" d.	10.00
Spoon holder	35.00
Syrup	110.00
Sugar bowl with cover	65.00
Toothpick holder	50.00
Tumbler, water	35.00
Wine	75.00

BEVELED DIAMOND AND STAR

OMN: Tarentum's Albany. **AKA:** Diamond Prism, Diamond Prisms, Princeton.

Non-flint. Tarentum Glass Co., Tarentum, PA, c. 1894.

Original color production: Clear, clear with ruby stain.

Reproductions and Look-a-Likes: None known.

Known items:	Clear	Clear w/Ruby
Bowl, open, flat		
7" d.	$15.00	$45.00
8" d.	20.00	55.00
Butter dish flat with cover	45.00	125.00
Cake stand on high standard		
9" d.	65.00	225.00
10" d.	85.00	275.00
Celery vase	30.00	110.00
Cheese dish flat with cover	75.00	250.00
Compote on high standard		
Covered		
5" d.	55.00	225.00
7" d.	75.00	275.00
Open with serrated rim		
5" d.	35.00	150.00
7" d.	45.00	175.00
8" d.	55.00	225.00
Cracker jar with cover	85.00	275.00
Creamer, tankard, 5-1/2" h.	35.00	95.00
Cruet with original patterned stopper	45.00	225.00
Decanter with original patterned stopper, 10-3/4" h.	65.00	175.00

Known items:	Clear	Clear w/Ruby
Goblet (S)	85.00	325.00
Pickle dish, flat	15.00	35.00
Pitcher		
Milk, 1-qt.	55.00	200.00
Water, 1/2-gal., applied handle		
Bulbous	65.00	325.00
Tankard	55.00	225.00
Plate, round	15.00	35.00
Sauce dish, round		
Flat	5.00	20.00
Footed	7.00	25.00
Spoon holder	30.00	75.00
Sugar bowl with cover	45.00	110.00
Sugar shaker	55.00	185.00
Syrup pitcher, 7" h.	75.00	275.00
Toothpick holder	20.00	95.00
Tray, round		
Bread, 7" d.	30.00	65.00
Water	40.00	85.00
Tumbler, water, flat	20.00	55.00
Wine, 4" h.	25.00	45.00

Beveled Diamond and Star goblet.

BIGLER

Flint. Attributed to the Boston & Sandwich Glass Co., Sandwich, MA, based on shards found at the factory site, c. 1850s. Other factories.

Original color production: Clear. Amethyst, greenish-yellow or any other color would be considered rare.

Reproductions and Look-a-Likes: Goblet (clear).

Known items:	Clear
Ale	$125.00
Bowl, open, round, flat	
Flared rim, 6-5/8" d.	45.00
Straight-sided, 10" d.	65.00
Butter dish with cover	150.00
Celery vase	125.00
Champagne	95.00

Bigler champagne.

Known items:	Clear
Compote, open on high standard, 7" d.	75.00
Creamer	150.00
Cup plate	25.00
Decanter, bar lip	
1-pt.	75.00
1-qt.	95.00
Eggcup, open, double footed	75.00
Goblet	
Short stem	55.00
Tall stem	65.00
Lamp on glass standard, whale oil	275.00
Mug with applied handle	150.00
Plate, toddy, round, 6" d.	45.00

Bigler whiskey.

Known items:	Clear
Spoon holder	45.00
Sugar bowl with cover	125.00
Salt, master, open, footed	30.00
Tumbler, flat	
Water	65.00
Whiskey	95.00
Wine	35.00

BIRD AND STRAWBERRY

OMN: Indiana Glass No. 157. **AKA:** Blue Bird, Flying Bird and Strawberry, Strawberry and Bird.

Non-flint. Indiana Glass Co., Dunkirk, IN, c. 1914.

Original color production: Clear, clear with blue-green-red stain.

Reproductions and Look-a-Likes: 8-3/8" l., oval relish tray (clear, blue); 6-1/2" d. covered high standard compote (clear, pale green).

Bird and Strawberry pattern close-up.

Known items:	Clear	Clear w/Stain
Bowl, open		
Flat, round		
5" d.	$35.00	$75.00
9-1/2" d.	125.00	225.00

Bird and Strawberry compote.

Bird and Strawberry heart relish.

Known items:	Clear	Clear w/Stain
10" d. 135.00		250.00
10-1/2" d., flared 135.00		325.00
Footed		
Oval, 4-legged,		
master berry.......75.00		225.00
Round, 3-legged, 5" d. 55.00		175.00
Butter dish flat with cover on		
flanged rim.................150.00		325.00
Cake stand on high standard,		
9-1/4" d.....................75.00		—

Known items:	Clear	Clear w/Stain
Celery		
Tray, flat 110.00		225.00
Vase...................150.00		300.00
Compote		
Covered on high standard		
4-1/2" d., jelly (R) ...250.00		550.00
5-3/8" d. (VR).......275.00		750.00
6-1/2" d. 175.00		450.00

Bird and Strawberry decorated spoon holder.

Bird and Strawberry water pitcher.

Bird and Strawberry water set.

Known items:	Clear	Clear w/stain
Open on high standard		
4-1/2" d., jelly (R)	225.00	650.00
7-3/4" d.	135.00	—
Creamer	85.00	175.00
Cup, punch	35.00	65.00
Goblet		
Barrel-shaped bowl	550.00	1,500.00
Flared bowl (R)	850.00	2,500.00
Hat, made from a tumbler (VR)	1,850.00	—
Pitcher, water with pressed handle	325.00	650.00
Plate		
Chop, round		
11" d.	175.00	275.00
12" d.	200.00	325.00
Sandwich, 6-1/4" d. (R)	225.00	300.00
Relish dish, heart shaped	95.00	350.00
Sauce dish, round		
Flat	20.00	65.00
Footed, 3 feet, 4" d.	35.00	85.00
Spoon holder	95.00	225.00
Sugar bowl with cover and double handled	135.00	275.00
Tumbler		
Lemonade, 4-3/8" h.	75.00	175.00
Water, 4" h.	65.00	150.00
Wine	65.00	375.00

Bird and Strawberry creamer.

BLACKBERRY

AKA: Messereau Blackberry.

Non-flint. Hobbs, Brockunier & Co., Wheeling, WV, c. 1870.

Original color production: Clear, milk white. Designed by John H. Hobbs and patented under patent No. 3,829; February 1, 1870.

Reproductions: Goblet; creamer; spoon holder; covered sugar bowl (milk white, color).

Known items:	Clear	Milk White
Butter dish with cover		
Insert for ice (R)	$150.00	$175.00
Plain	45.00	65.00
Celery vase		
High standard, 8-1/4" h.	95.00	110.00
Low standard, 6-1/2" h.	65.00	85.00
Compote with cover		
5-1/2" d.	125.00	150.00
7" d.	150.00	175.00
Creamer	45.00	35.00

Blackberry rare water pitcher.

Blackberry milk white goblet.

Known items:	Clear	Milk White
Dish, open, oval, flat		
8-1/4" l.	30.00	45.00
9-1/4" l.	35.00	55.00
Eggcup, open		
Double	35.00	45.00
Single	30.00	35.00
Goblet		
No date	45.00	95.00
Patent dated *"Pat. Feb. 1870"*		
(R)	150.00	175.00
Honey dish, round, flat, 3-1/4" d.	8.00	10.00
Lamp, oil, brass stem, and marble base		
8-1/2" h.	150.00	—
9-1/2" h.	175.00	—
11-3/4" h.	225.00	—
Pitcher, water, bulbous with applied handle,		
1/2-gal. (ER)	850.00	2,200.00
Relish, flat	15.00	15.00
Salt, master, open, footed	45.00	40.00
Sauce dish, round, flat, 4-1/2" d.	8.00	5.00
Spoon holder	35.00	30.00
Sugar bowl with cover	65.00	85.00
Syrup pitcher (R)	325.00	650.00
Tumbler, water, flat	85.00	225.00

BLAZE

OMN:

Flint. New England Glass Co., East Cambridge, MA, c. 1869.

Original color production: Clear. Canary or any other color would be considered rare.

Reproductions and Look-a-Likes: None known.

Known items:	Clear
Bowl, round, flat	
Covered	
5-1/2" d.	$85.00
6" d.	95.00
7" d.	110.00
8" d.	150.00
Open	
5" d.	30.00
5-1/2" d.	35.00
6" d.	40.00
7" d.	50.00

Known items:	Clear
Butter dish, flat with cover	95.00
Celery vase	125.00
Champagne	135.00
Cologne bottle with original stopper	150.00
Compote	
Covered	
High standard	
Deep bowl	
6" d.	125.00
7" d.	150.00
8" d.	225.00
Shallow bowl	
6" d.	110.00
7" d.	135.00
8" d.	175.00
Low standard	
Deep bowl	
6" d.	100.00
7" d.	125.00
8" d.	150.00
Shallow bowl	
6" d.	95.00
7" d.	110.00
8" d.	135.00

Blaze champagne.

Known items:	Clear
Open	
High standard	
Deep bowl	
6" d.	40.00
7" d.	45.00
8" d.	55.00
Shallow bowl	
6" d.	40.00
7" d.	45.00
8" d.	55.00
9" d.	65.00
10" d.	85.00
Low standard	
Deep bowl	
6" d.	35.00
7" d.	40.00
8" d.	45.00
9" d.	55.00
10" d.	65.00
Shallow	
6" d.	35.00
7" d.	40.00
8" d.	50.00
Creamer	150.00
Cup, custard with handle	20.00
Dish, open, oval, flat	
7" l.	35.00
8" l.	40.00
9" l.	45.00
10" l.	55.00
Eggcup, open with applied handle	125.00
Goblet	75.00
Honey dish, 3-1/2" d.	10.00
Plate, cheese, round, 7" d.	55.00
Sauce dish, round, flat, 4" d.	5.00
Spoon holder	35.00
Sugar bowl with cover	110.00
Tumbler	
Flat	
Water, 2-pt.	95.00
Whiskey	110.00
Footed	65.00
Wine	75.00

Bleeding Heart water pitcher and four, footed tumblers.

BLEEDING HEART

Bleeding Heart creamer butter, sugar, spoon holder, sugar bowl.

OMN: King's Floral Ware, U.S. Glass No. 85-New Floral.

Non-flint. King, Son & Co., Pittsburgh, PA, c. 1875. The United States Glass Co., Pittsburgh, PA, at Factory "C." Attributed to the Boston & Sandwich Glass Co., Sandwich, MA, based on shards found at the factory site. The Specialty Glass Co., East Liverpool, OH (goblet and mug only). Covered items with a cable cord edge where covers join and possessing a row of dots on the outer underside of the rim have traditionally been attributed to the Boston & Sandwich Glass Co.

Original color production: Clear. Milk white or any other color would be considered rare.

Reproductions: None known.

Bleeding Heart high and low-footed covered compotes.

Known items:	Clear
Bowl, flat	
Covered, round	
6" d.	$125.00
9-1/4" d.	225.00
Open	
Oval	
5" l.	15.00
7" l.	25.00
7-1/4" l.	30.00
8" l.	40.00
9" l.	50.00
9-1/4" l.	55.00
Round	
5" d.	20.00
7" d.	35.00
8" d.	65.00
Butter dish flat with cover	125.00
Cake stand on high standard	
9" d.	110.00
10" d.	150.00
11" d.	225.00
Compote	
High standard	
Covered	
6" d.	175.00
7" d.	225.00
8" d.	275.00
Open, 5" d.	65.00
Low standard	
Oval	250.00

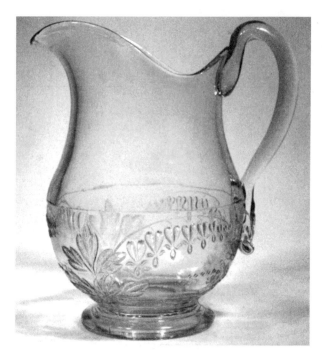

Bleeding Heart water pitcher.

Known items:	Clear
Round, covered	
7" d.	150.00
7-1/4" d.	175.00
8" d.	200.00
Open, 8-1/4" d.	85.00
Creamer	
Flat with pressed handle	55.00
Footed with applied handle, 5-3/4" h.	95.00
Eggcup, open, footed (2 styles)	45.00
Egg server, footed with cover (VR)	2,250.00
Goblet	
Barrel-shaped bowl with heavy design and knob stem	75.00
Jelly container with flimsy design and plain stem	30.00
Straight-sided bowl with knob stem	55.00
Straight-sided bowl with thin design and knob stem	35.00
Honey dish, round, flat, 3-1/2" d.	15.00
Mug, pressed handle, 3-1/4" h.	45.00
Pickle tray, oval, pear-shaped, 8-3/4" l.	25.00
Pitcher, bulbous with applied handle	
Milk, 1-qt.	275.00
Water, 1/2-gal.	325.00

Known items:	Clear
Plate, round (S)	110.00
Platter, oval	150.00
Relish tray	
4 divisions	225.00
Oval, 5-1/2" l.	15.00
Salt, master	
Flat, oval, open, smooth rim	175.00
Footed, round with cover	275.00
Sauce dish, flat	
Oval	
4" l.	15.00
5" l.	20.00
Round	
4" d.	8.00
5" d.	10.00
Spoon holder, pedestaled	45.00
Sugar bowl with cover (2 styles)	125.00
Tumbler	
Flat, 2-pt.	175.00
Footed	125.00
Waste bowl	110.00
Wine	175.00

BLOCK AND FAN

OMN: Richards & Hartley No. 544. **AKA:** Block with Fan, Block with Fan Border, Red Block and Fan, Romeo.

Non-flint. Richards & Hartley Glass Co., Tarentum, PA, c. 1885. The United States Glass Co., Pittsburgh, PA, at Factory "F" after 1891.

Original color production: Clear, clear with ruby stain.

Reproductions and Look-a-Likes: None known.

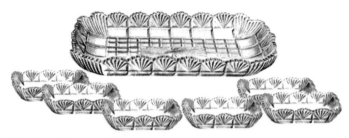

Block and Fan seven-piece ice cream set.

Block and Fan saltshaker.

Known items:	Clear	Clear w/Ruby
Biscuit jar with cover............$85.00		$225.00
Bowl, open		
Rectangular, 6" x 10"......30.00		65.00
Round		
Collared base		
7" d. 35.00		75.00
8" d. 45.00		95.00
10" d. 55.00		125.00
Flat base		
6" d. 25.00		50.00
7" d. 30.00		65.00
8" d. 35.00		75.00
9-1/2" d. 55.00		110.00
10" d. 65.00		135.00
Butter dish with cover...........75.00		175.00
Cake stand on high standard		
9" d. 95.00		325.00
10" d. 110.00		375.00
Carafe, 8-1/2" h 55.00		125.00
Castor set tray 25.00		45.00

Block and Fan high-standard compote.

Known items:	Clear	Clear w/Ruby
Celery		
Tray.................30.00		65.00
Vase.................45.00		110.00
Compote, round on high standard		
Covered		
7" d. 110.00		275.00
8" d. 125.00		325.00
Open with scalloped rim		
7" d. 45.00		100.00
8" d. 55.00		110.00
Creamer with pressed handle		
Individual 25.00		45.00
Table size 45.00		110.00
Cruet, 4-oz. with original stopper . 50.00		250.00
Decanter with handles 85.00		275.00
Dish, open, flat		
Oblong, ice cream........30.00		65.00
Rectangular 30.00		55.00
Goblet, 6" h. 65.00		225.00
Ice bucket 75.00		175.00
Lamp, oil 150.00		—
Pickle dish, oblong 20.00		35.00

Block and Fan syrup, condiment set, and sugar shaker.

Known items:	Clear	Clear w/Ruby
Pitcher		
Milk, 1-qt.	55.00	175.00
Water, 1/2-gal.	65.00	225.00
Plate, round		
6" d.	25.00	45.00
10" d.	30.00	65.00
Relish tray, oval	25.00	55.00
Rose bowl, 7" d.	55.00	110.00
Saltshaker, tall	25.00	75.00
Sauce dish, round		
Flat		
4" d.	5.00	20.00
5" d.	8.00	20.00
Footed		
3-3/4" d.	5.00	25.00
4" d.	8.00	25.00
5" d.	10.00	25.00
Spoon holder	35.00	75.00
Sugar bowl with cover	65.00	110.00
Sugar shaker	85.00	225.00
Syrup pitcher	175.00	325.00
Tumbler, water, flat	45.00	75.00
Waste bowl	40.00	95.00
Wine, 3-3/4" h.	85.00	175.00

BOW TIE

OMN: Thompson No. 18. **AKA:** American Bow Tie.
Non-flint. Thompson Glass Co., Uniontown, PA, c.
1889.

Original color production: Clear.

Reproductions and Look-a-Likes: None known.

Bowtie goblet.

Known items:	Clear
Bowl, open	
Flat	
Rectangular with scalloped rim	
4-1/4" x 7"	$45.00
5-1/4" x 8"	55.00
5-5/8" x 9"	65.00
Round	
Flared rim, 8" d.	65.00
Scalloped rim, 10-1/4" d.	85.00
Smooth rim	
6" d.	35.00
7" d.	45.00
8" d.	55.00
10-1/4" d.	65.00
10-5/8" d.	85.00
Footed with plain rim, 10" d. (fruit)	110.00
Butter dish flat with cover	150.00
Butter pat, flat, 2-3/4" d.	45.00
Cake stand on high stand, 9-1/4" d.	275.00
Celery vase	125.00
Compote, open	
High standard	
Flared with scalloped rim	
7" d.	135.00
9" d.	150.00

Bowtie orange bowl.

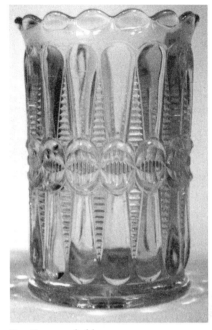

Bowtie spoon holder.

Known items:	Clear
Smooth rim	
5-1/2" d.	65.00
8-1/4" d.	100.00
9-1/4" d.	150.00
10-3/8" d.	225.00
Low standard	
Scalloped rim	
6-1/2" d.	55.00
8" d.	75.00
Smooth rim	
6-1/2" d.	55.00
8" d.	75.00
Creamer, 5" h.	55.00
Goblet	125.00
Jam jar with cover, 4-1/2" h.	110.00
Pitcher	
Milk	
5-1/2" h.	150.00
6-1/2" h.	175.00
Water	
7" h.	200.00
8" h.	225.00
9" h.	275.00
Punch bowl, flat, one-piece with scalloped rim	225.00
Relish dish, rectangular	35.00
Salt	
Individual, 1-1/2" d.	45.00
Master, open, round with smooth rim, 3-1/8" d.	85.00
Shaker	95.00

Known items:	Clear
Sauce dish, round, 4" d.	
Scalloped rim	
Flat	20.00
Footed	25.00
Smooth rim	
Flat	20.00
Footed	25.00
Spoon holder, flat	75.00
Sugar bowl with cover	135.00
Tumbler, water, flat, 4" h. (R)	100.00

BRILLIANT (Riverside)

Brilliant seven-piece water set.

OMN: Riverside No. 436-Brilliant. **AKA:** Petaled Medallion, Miami.

Non-flint. Riverside Glass Works, Wellsburg, WV, c. 1895.

Original color production: Clear, clear with ruby stain (plain, engraved, sometimes souvenired). Odd items may be found in clear glass with amber stain.

Reproductions and Look-a-Likes: None known.

Brilliant sugar bowl, creamer, spoon holder, butter dish.

Known items:	Clear	Clear w/Ruby
Bowl, open, flat, master berry	$55.00	$125.00
Butter dish with cover	75.00	175.00
Celery vase	95.00	150.00
Compote on high standard		
Covered		
5" d.	85.00	225.00
6" d.	100.00	250.00
7" d.	135.00	325.00
Open		
5" d.	65.00	135.00
7" d., plain rim	125.00	250.00
7" d., fluted rim	135.00	275.00
Creamer		
Individual	25.00	55.00
Table size	45.00	95.00
Cruet with original stopper	85.00	175.00
Goblet	65.00	135.00
Pitcher, water, 1/2-gal.	110.00	225.00

Brilliant rare condiment set.

Known items:	Clear	Clear w/Ruby
Saltshaker	40.00	75.00
Sauce dish, round, flat	10.00	45.00
Spoon holder	35.00	85.00
Sugar bowl		
Individual, true open	35.00	65.00
Table size with cover	65.00	125.00
Syrup pitcher	125.00	325.00
Tray, spoon or condiment	75.00	150.00
Toothpick holder	40.00	125.00
Tumbler, water, flat	30.00	75.00
Wine	40.00	85.00

BRITANNIC

OMN: AKA: Brittanic.

Non-flint. McKee & Brothers Glass Works (under the National Glass Co.), Pittsburgh, PA, c. 1894 until sometime after 1903.

Original color production: Clear, clear with ruby stain, clear with amber stain (plain, engraved). Emerald green or any other color would be considered rare.

Reproductions: None known.

Known items:	Clear	Clear w/Ruby
Basket, fruit	$65.00	$225.00
Banana stand	135.00	375.00
Bottle		
Cologne with original stopper	45.00	125.00
Water	65.00	150.00

Britannic tumbler.

Known items:	Clear	Clear w/Ruby
Bowl, open		
Oblong		
Crimped rim	30.00	45.00
Smooth rim	30.00	45.00
Oval, shallow bowl with serrated rim		
7" l.	30.00	45.00
8" l.	35.00	55.00
9" l.	40.00	65.00
Round, 8" d.		
Crimped rim	45.00	55.00
Smooth rim	45.00	65.00
Square		
Cupped rim	30.00	45.00
Smooth rim	35.00	55.00
Butter dish with cover	75.00	150.00
Cake stand		
9" d.	95.00	325.00
10" d.	125.00	375.00
Castor set, 4 bottles in glass holder	225.00	550.00
Celery		
Tray	30.00	65.00
Vase	45.00	110.00

Known items:	Clear	Clear w/Ruby
Compote on high standard, round, open		
Flared with scalloped rim		
7-1/2" d.	35.00	85.00
8-1/2" d.	45.00	95.00
10" d.	65.00	125.00
Smooth rim		
5" d.	15.00	35.00
6" d.	35.00	85.00
7" d.	45.00	95.00
8" d.	55.00	110.00
Creamer with applied handle		
Bulbous	45.00	95.00
Tankard	40.00	125.00
Cruet with original stopper	55.00	225.00
Cup, custard	15.00	35.00
Dish		
Olive, handled, flat		
Crimped rim	20.00	35.00
Smooth rim	20.00	35.00
Pickle, flat		
Crimped rim	20.00	40.00
Smooth rim	35.00	45.00
Goblet	35.00	95.00
Honey dish, square with cover	275.00	450.00
Jar, cracker with cover	95.00	275.00
Lamp		
Low foot with handle (2 styles)	95.00	—
Stand (all glass)		
7-1/2" h.	135.00	—
8-1/2" h.	150.00	—
Mug, 3-3/4" h.	25.00	45.00
Pitcher, water with applied handle, 1/2-gal.		
Bulbous	75.00	175.00
Tankard	85.00	200.00
Rose bowl	35.00	75.00
Saltshaker, squat	25.00	65.00
Sauce dish		
Round		
Flat	5.00	30.00
Footed	5.00	30.00
Square	8.00	35.00
Spoon holder	35.00	85.00

Known items:	Clear	Clear w/Ruby
Sugar bowl with cover	55.00	150.00
Syrup pitcher	95.00	325.00
Toothpick holder	20.00	85.00
Tray, ice cream	45.00	100.00
Tumbler, water, flat	35.00	55.00
Vase	30.00	75.00
Wine	20.00	45.00

BROKEN COLUMN

OMN: U.S. Glass No. 15,021-Bamboo. **AKA:** Broken Column with Red Dots, Irish Column, Notched Rib, Rattan, Broken Irish Column, Ribbed Fingerprint.

Non-flint. Columbia Glass Co., Findlay, OH, c. 1888. The United States Glass Co., Pittsburgh, PA, after c.1893 at Factory "E" and Factory "J."

Original color production: Clear, clear with ruby stain. Ruby stained items were likely produced after Columbia Glass joined the United States glass combine in 1891. A limited number of odd items may be found in cobalt blue.

Reproductions and Look-a-Likes: flat open 8" d. bowl; flat open 8-1/2" d. open bowl; 10-oz. creamer with pressed handle, goblet, 40-oz. water pitcher; 8" d. round plate; round, 4-1/2" d. flat sauce dish; 4-5/8" d. flat sauce dish; spoon holder; covered sugar bowl; flat water tumbler (clear). Items are often impressed with either "S.I." (Signifying the Smithsonian Institution) or "MMA." (Signifying the Metropolitan Museum of Art). Other reproductions produced by the L.G. Wright Glass Company, New Martinsville, WV, are not marked.

Known items:	Clear	Clear w/Ruby
Banana stand		
Flat	$85.00	—
High standard	375.00	1,250.00
Basket with applied handle, 12" h.. .	125.00	—
Biscuit jar with cover.	200.00	2,750.00
Bottle, water	275.00	1,000.00

Broken Column covered sugar.

Known items:	Clear	Clear w/Ruby
Bowl, flat		
Covered, deep		
5" d.	85.00	350.00
6" d.	110.00	500.00
7" d.	125.00	600.00
8" d.	150.00	750.00
Open		
Deep		
5" d.	35.00	125.00
6" d.	45.00	150.00
7" d.	55.00	175.00
8" d.	85.00	225.00
Shallow		
5" d.	30.00	110.00
6" d.	40.00	125.00
7" d.	50.00	150.00
8" d.	75.00	175.00
9" d.	110.00	325.00
Butter dish with cover	150.00	600.00
Cake stand on high standard		
9" d.	150.00	800.00
10" d.	225.00	900.00
Celery		
Tray, oval, 7" l.	45.00	150.00
Vase, 6" h.	110.00	300.00

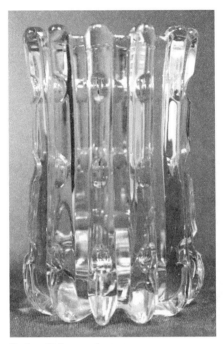

Broken Column celery vase.

Broken Column covered compote.

Known items:	Clear	Clear w/Ruby
Champagne.	275.00	850.00
Claret	150.00	700.00
Compote		
Covered on high standard		
5" d.	110.00	400.00
6" d.	125.00	550.00
7" d.	175.00	800.00
8" d.	225.00	1,000.00
Open		
High standard		
Belled bowl		
5" d.	55.00	225.00
6" d.	65.00	250.00
7" d.	85.00	275.00
8" d.	110.00	325.00
Flared bowl		
5" d.	55.00	225.00
6" d.	65.00	250.00
7" d.	85.00	275.00
8" d.	110.00	325.00
Round bowl		
5" d.	45.00	200.00
6" d.	55.00	225.00

Known items:	Clear	Clear w/Ruby
7" d.	75.00	250.00
8" d.	100.00	325.00
Low standard, 5" d. . .	45.00	175.00
Creamer	65.00	275.00

Broken Column cracker jar.

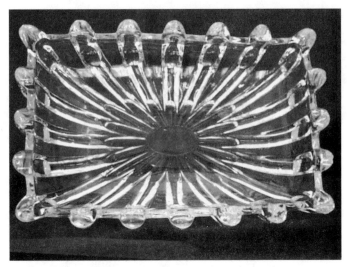

Broken Column relish.

Known items:	Clear	Clear w/Ruby
Cruet with original stopper, 6-oz.	175.00	750.00
Cup, custard	25.00	175.00
Decanter, wine with lapidary stopper	150.00	1,100.00
Dish, open, flat		
Rectangular		
5-1/2" l. (Olive)	55.00	125.00
7" l.	65.00	150.00
8" l.	75.00	175.00
9" l.	85.00	225.00

Broken Column syrup.

Broken Column wine.

Known items:	Clear	Clear w/Ruby
Finger bowl	55.00	150.00
Goblet	110.00	550.00
Honey dish, round, flat	20.00	55.00
Humidor with original silver plated lid (VR)	650.00	—
Pickle		
Castor in silverplate frame	175.00	850.00
Jar with original glass cover	350.00	1,000.00
Pitcher, water with pressed handle, 1/2-gal.	150.00	650.00
Plate, round		
4" d.	35.00	75.00
5" d.	40.00	85.00
6" d.	45.00	95.00
7" d.	55.00	110.00
7-1/2" d.	65.00	135.00
8" d.	85.00	175.00
Relish, oval, flat		
4" x 7-1/2"	55.00	125.00
5" x 11"	85.00	175.00
Saltshaker	95.00	275.00
Sauce dish, round, flat, 4" d.	25.00	75.00
Spoon holder	75.00	150.00

Broken Column sugar shaker.

Known items:	Clear	Clear w/Ruby
Sugar bowl with cover	125.00	500.00
Sugar shaker...................	175.00	450.00
Syrup pitcher	275.00	850.00
Tumbler, water, 9-oz., 4" h........	75.00	150.00
Wine, 4" h.....................	175.00	525.00

BUCKLE, EARLY

OMN: Gillinder No. 15. **AKA:** Buckle.

Flint, non-flint. Maker unknown. Often attributed to Gillinder & Sons, Pittsburgh, PA, c. late 1870s. Also, the Boston & Sandwich Glass Co., Sandwich, MA, and the Union Glass Co., Somerville, MA, based on shards found at each factory site.

Original color production: Clear. Sapphire blue, opaque white or any other color would be considered rare.

Reproductions and Look-a-Likes: None known.

Known items:	Flint	Non-Flint
Bowl, open, flat		
8-1/4" d. with original wire basket frame...	$125.00	$85.00
9" d.	150.00	110.00
10" d.	225.00	150.00

Buckle rare opaque white goblet.

Known items:	Flint	Non-Flint
Butter dish with cover	95.00	55.00
Cake stand on high standard, 9-3/4" d.	350.00	175.00
Celery vase	125.00	65.00
Champagne	85.00	45.00

Buckle wine.

Buckle spoon holder.

Known items:	Flint	Non-Flint
Compote, 6" d.		
Covered		
High standard	125.00	85.00
Low standard	110.00	65.00
Open, 8-1/2" d.		
High standard	65.00	45.00
Low standard	55.00	35.00
Creamer with applied handle	150.00	95.00
Eggcup, open, single	35.00	20.00
Goblet	45.00	30.00
Pickle dish, flat	30.00	15.00
Pitcher, water, bulbous with applied		
handle, 1/2-gal. (rare)	1,500.00	350.00
Relish tray, oval	25.00	15.00
Salt, master, open		
Flat, oval	45.00	30.00
Footed		
Plain rim	35.00	20.00
Scalloped rim	35.00	20.00
Sauce dish, round, flat, 4" d.		
Cable edge rim	12.50	8.00
Plain rim	12.50	8.00
Spoon holder, footed, 5-1/2" h.	55.00	35.00
Sugar bowl with cover	125.00	65.00
Tumbler, water, flat	85.00	45.00
Wine	75.00	30.00

BUCKLE WITH STAR

OMN: Orient. **AKA:** Buckle and Star, Late Buckle and Star.

Non-flint. Bryce, Walker & Co., Pittsburgh, PA, c. 1880. The United States Glass Co., Pittsburgh, PA, at Factory "B."

Original color production: Clear. Amber or any other color would be considered rare.

Known items:	Clear
Bowl, oval, flat	
Covered, 6" l.	$65.00
Open with plain rim	
6" l.	20.00
7" l.	25.00
8" l.	30.00
9" l.	35.00
10" l.	45.00
Butter dish flat with cover	55.00
Cake stand on high standard	75.00
Celery vase	45.00
Cologne bottle, bulbous with pedestaled base and original stopper	65.00

Buckle with Star celery vase.

Buckle with Star bulbous water pitcher.

Buckle with Star syrup.

Known items:	Clear
Compote on high standard	
Covered, 7" d.	95.00
Open, 9-1/2" d.	55.00
Creamer with pressed handle, 6" h.	35.00
Goblet	35.00
Honey dish, round, 3-1/2" d.	
Flat	5.00
Footed	8.00
Mug	55.00
Mustard, oval with cover	65.00
Pickle dish, round, flat, handled	15.00
Pitcher, water, bulbous with applied handle, 1/2-gal.	225.00
Relish tray	15.00
Salt, master, open, footed	25.00
Sauce dish, round with star in center	
Flat	
4" d.	5.00
4-1/2" d.	5.00
Footed	
4" d.	5.00
4-1/2" d.	5.00
Spoon holder	30.00
Sugar bowl with cover	55.00
Syrup with applied handle	175.00

Known items:	Clear
Tumbler, water	
Handled	95.00
No handle	55.00
Wine	20.00

BUDDED IVY

Non-flint. Maker unknown, c. 1870.

Original color production: Clear.

Reproductions and Look-a-Likes: None known.

Known items:	Clear:
Butter dish, flat with cover	$65.00
Compote with cover	
High standard	85.00
Low standard	35.00
Creamer with pressed handle	35.00
Eggcup, open, footed	35.00
Goblet	45.00
Pitcher, water with applied handle, 1/2-gal.	175.00
Relish tray	15.00

Budded Ivy pattern illustration.

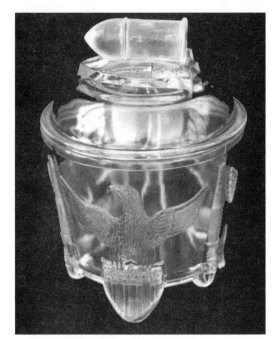

Bullet Emblem covered sugar.

Known items:	Clear:
Sauce dish, round, 4" d.	
Flat	5.00
Footed	8.00
Spoon holder	35.00
Sugar bowl with cover	55.00
Syrup pitcher	175.00
Wine	30.00

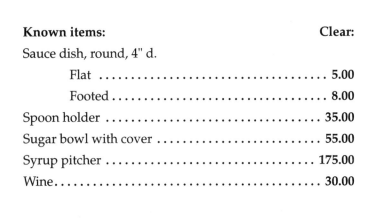

Bullet Emblem creamer, covered sugar.

BULLET EMBLEM

AKA: Bullet, Eagle and Shield, Eagle and Arms, Emblem, Shield.

Non-flint. U.S. Glass Company, Pittsburgh, PA, c. 1898.

Original color production: Clear. Clear with red, white & blue and silver bullet.

Reproductions and Look-a-Likes: None known.

Known items:	Clear	Clear w/Paint
Butter dish with cover	$400.00	$650.00
Creamer	200.00	350.00
Spoon holder	175.00	325.00
Sugar bowl with cover	325.00	550.00

BULL'S EYE

OMN: New England Glass Co.'s Lawrence.

Flint, non-flint. Boston & Sandwich Glass Co., Sandwich, MA, c. 1860s. New England Glass Co., East Cambridge, MA, c. 1869.

Original color production: Clear. Fiery opalescent, milk white or any other color in flint glass would be considered rare.

Reproductions and Look-a-Likes: None known.

Bull's Eye goblet.

Known items:	Clear
Bottle	
Bitters	125.00
Castor	
Mustard	45.00
Oil with original stopper	55.00
Shaker	35.00
Cologne with original stopper	175.00
Water or tumble-up with tumbler	450.00
Butter dish with cover	225.00
Celery vase	125.00
Champagne	135.00
Compote, open	
High standard	125.00
Low standard	95.00
Creamer with applied handle	175.00
Cruet with original stopper	150.00
Decanter	
With bar lip	
1-pt.	150.00
1-qt.	200.00
With original patterned stopper	
1-pt.	325.00
1-qt.	450.00
Eggcup, footed	
Covered	550.00
Open	55.00

Known items:	Clear
Goblet	
Knob stem	95.00
Plain stem	75.00
Jar, with cover and plain stopper, 5" h.	135.00
Jelly glass (claret)	175.00
Lamp, oil	
All glass	325.00
Marble base with brass stem	225.00
Mug with applied handle, 3-1/2" h.	250.00
Pickle dish, oval	35.00
Pitcher, water with applied handle, 1/2-gal.	750.00
Pomade jar with cover	125.00
Relish tray, oval	35.00
Salt	
Oblong, flat	65.00
Round	
Individual	30.00
Master footed with cover	275.00
Spoon holder	65.00
Sugar bowl with cover	175.00
Tumbler	
Water	125.00
Whiskey	150.00
Wine	45.00

Bull's Eye tumbler.

BULL'S EYE AND DAISIES

Bull's Eye and Daisy seven-piece berry set.

OMN: U.S. Glass No. 15,117-Newport. **AKA:** Bull's Eye and Daisy, Knobby Bull's Eye.

Non-flint. The United States Glass Co., Pittsburgh, PA, at Factory "F" and Factory "P," c. 1909.

Original color production: Clear, clear with amethyst, blue, green and pink stain, emerald green, clear with ruby stain (plain, gilded). Clear with ruby stain add 100% to all clear prices.

Reproductions and Look-a-Likes: 9-oz. goblet, swung footed vase (amber, blue, canary yellow, milk white, sapphire blue).

Bull's Eye and Daisy spoon holder.

Known items:	Clear	Clear w/Stain	Green
Bowl, open, flat,			
master berry 30.00		65.00	55.00
Butter dish with cover. 55.00		110.00	85.00
Celery vase 35.00		75.00	65.00
Creamer. 30.00		45.00	45.00

Bull's Eye and Daisy tumbler.

Known items:	Clear	Clear w/Stain	Green
Cruet with original stopper.	55.00	125.00	95.00
Decanter	85.00	110.00	125.00
Dish, round			
Jelly, 3-handled	15.00	25.00	25.00
Olive, handled.	15.00	25.00	25.00

Bull's Eye and Daisy wine.

Bull's Eye and Daisy water pitcher.

Known items:	Clear	Clear w/Stain	Green
Goblet	25.00	45.00	40.00
Pickle dish, boat shaped	15.00	25.00	25.00
Pitcher, water, 1/2-gal.	65.00	95.00	85.00

Known items:	Clear	Clear w/Stain	Green
Saltshaker	30.00	45.00	45.00
Sauce dish, round, flat	5.00	10.00	10.00
Spoon holder with double handles	30.00	40.00	40.00
Sugar bowl with cover	45.00	55.00	55.00
Syrup pitcher	95.00	150.00	175.00
Tumbler, water, flat	25.00	30.00	35.00
Wine	15.00	35.00	40.00

BULL'S EYE AND FAN

OMN: U.S. Glass No. 15,160. **AKA:** Daisies in Oval Panels.

Non-flint. The United States Glass Co., Pittsburgh, PA, c. 1904.

Original color production: Clear, clear with amethyst or pink stain; solid emerald green; sapphire blue (plain, gilded).

Reproductions and Look-a-Likes: None known.

Bull's Eye and Fan creamer, sugar bowl, butter dish, and spoon holder.

Known items:	Blue	Clear	Green	Pink or Amethyst Stain
Biscuit jar with cover	$375.00	$135.00	$225.00	$200.00
Bowl, open, flat 5" d., pinched ends	35.00	15.00	30.00	20.00

Known items:	Blue	Clear	Green	Pink or Amethyst Stain
8" d., master berry, round-crimped sides........ 85.00		30.00	65.00	40.00
Butter dish, with cover				
Quarter pound.............. 110.00		45.00	85.00	55.00
Table size 135.00		65.00	110.00	75.00
Cake stand on high stand				
8" d. 125.00		65.00	95.00	75.00
9" d. 150.00		85.00	110.00	95.00
Celery				
Tray 7 x 12 .... 50.00		25.00	40.00	30.00
Vase....................... 65.00		35.00	55.00	40.00
Champagne, 6-oz. 85.00		45.00	65.00	50.00
Compote, open on high standard with saucer bowl				
5-1/2" d. jelly............... 85.00		35.00	50.00	40.00
8-1/2" d. 100.00		35.00	55.00	45.00
Creamer				
Individual, tankard 45.00		20.00	40.00	30.00
Table size, 5-1/2" h. 85.00		35.00	65.00	45.00
Cruet with original stopper, 5-oz.... 225.00		85.00	135.00	110.00
Cup, custard 35.00		15.00	25.00	20.00
Goblet 85.00		25.00	50.00	35.00
Mug, lemonade, 5" h. 95.00		35.00	65.00	45.00
Pitcher				
Lemonade, footed.............. 125.00		45.00	85.00	55.00
Milk, 8" h. straight-sided 135.00		55.00	95.00	65.00
Water, tankard, 2-gal. 150.00		65.00	100.00	75.00
Plate				
7" sq....................... 75.00		35.00	55.00	45.00
11" d. 75.00		40.00	65.00	50.00
Relish tray....................... 35.00		15.00	30.00	20.00
Sauce dish, round, flat, 4" d......... 20.00		8.00	15.00	10.00
Sherbet, footed with flared top 95.00		45.00	75.00	55.00
Spoon holder 65.00		30.00	45.00	35.00
Sugar bowl with cover 95.00		45.00	75.00	55.00
Syrup pitcher 450.00		125.00	225.00	150.00
Toothpick holder 55.00		20.00	35.00	25.00
Tumbler, water, flat 65.00		20.00	50.00	25.00
Vase, swung 75.00		45.00	65.00	50.00
Wine.......................... 45.00		15.00	35.00	20.00

BULL'S EYE AND FLEUR-DE-LIS

AKA: Bull's Eye and Princess Feather, Bull's Eye with Fleur-de-lis, Bull's Eye with Princes' Feather, Prince's Feather, Princess Feather.

Flint. Traditionally attributed to the Union Glass Co., Somerville, MA, c. 1850s. Shards are also known to have been uncovered at the site of the Boston & Sandwich Glass Co., Sandwich, MA.

Original color production: Clear. Amber or any other color would be considered rare.

Reproductions and Look-a-Likes: None known.

Bull's Eye and Fleur-de-lis decanter.

Known items:	Clear
Ale glass, footed (R)	$850.00
Bottle, cologne	275.00
Bowl, fruit, open, round, flat, 8" d.	135.00
Butter dish with cover	275.00
Carafe	250.00
Celery vase	425.00
Champagne (R)	1,500.00

Known items:	Clear
Compote, open	
High standard	225.00
Low standard	110.00
Creamer, 6-1/2" h.	375.00
Decanter with bar lip	
1-pt.	225.00
1-qt.	250.00
Eggcup, open, footed	95.00
Goblet	175.00
Honey dish, round, flat	15.00
Lamp	
Finger, small	225.00
Stand, all glass font with brass stem and marble base	250.00
Whale oil, 10" h., all glass	375.00
Mug with applied handle	850.00
Pitcher, water with applied handle, 1/2-gal.	1,500.00
Salt, master, open, footed	125.00
Sauce dish, round, flat	20.00
Spoon holder	110.00
Sugar bowl with cover	225.00
Tumbler	
Water	175.00
Whiskey, 3-1/4" h.	325.00
Wine (2 styles)	275.00

Bull's Eye and Fleur-de-leis goblet.

BULL'S EYE WITH DIAMOND POINT

OMN: New England Glass Co.'s Union. **AKA:** Bull's Eye Diamond, Owl.

Flint. New England Glass Co., East Cambridge, MA, c. 1869.

Original color production: Clear. Fiery opalescent, milk white or any other color would be considered rare.

Reproductions and Look-a-Likes: None known.

Bull's Eye with Diamond Point goblet.

Known items:	Clear
Bottle, water with original tumbler	$1,250.00
Bowl, open, flat	
5" d.	55.00
6" d.	65.00
7" d.	75.00
8" d.	95.00
Butter dish, covered	375.00
Celery vase, footed	275.00
Champagne	650.00

Known items:	Clear
Claret (jelly glass)	850.00
Cologne bottle with original stopper	325.00
Compote, open	
High standard	
6" d.	85.00
7" d.	110.00
8" d.	125.00
9" d.	150.00
10" d.	225.00
Low standard	
6" d.	65.00
7" d.	75.00
8" d.	85.00
9" d.	110.00
10" d.	125.00
Creamer	425.00
Decanter	
Bar lip	
Pt.	275.00
Qt.	325.00
With original stopper	
Pt.	550.00
Qt.	650.00
Eggcup	150.00
Goblet	250.00
Honey dish, 3-1/2" d.	25.00
Lamp, oil	
Finger with applied handle	225.00
Stand, all glass	325.00
Mug with applied handle	1,250.00
Pitcher, water with applied handle	2,500.00
Salt master, footed	85.00
Sauce dish, flat, round, 4" h.	30.00
Spoon holder	175.00
Sugar bowl with cover	275.00
Syrup with applied handle, original top	375.00
Tumbler	
Water	225.00
Whiskey	450.00
Wine	325.00

BUTTON ARCHES

Button Arches goblet.

Button Arches cruet, celery vase, and syrup.

OMN: Duncan No. 39. **AKA:** Scalloped Diamond, Scalloped Diamond-Red Top, Scalloped Daisy-Red Top.

Non-flint. George Duncan Sons & Co., Washington, PA, c. 1897. Duncan & Miller Glass Co. c. 1900.

Original color production: Clear, clear with ruby stain and frosted band, clambroth, opaque white (plain, engraved, later souvenired). Ruby-stained items were decorated by the Oriental Glass Co., Pittsburgh, PA.

Reproductions and Look-a-Likes: Covered butter dish, cordial, individual creamer, table size creamer, goblet, spoon holder, covered sugar bowl, toothpick holder (clear, clear with light ruby stain). Westlake Ruby Glass Works, Columbus, OH. Permanently unmarked, but originally identified by a paper label.

Known items:	Clear	Clear w/Ruby
Bowl, master berry, open, flat, 8" d.	$35.00	$95.00
Butter dish, flat with cover on flanged base	65.00	150.00
Cake stand on high standard with turned down rim, 9" d.	95.00	275.00
Celery vase	35.00	85.00
Compote, open on high standard		
Jelly	25.00	45.00
Large with deep flared round bowl	55.00	110.00
Creamer		
Individual, 2-3/4" h.	20.00	35.00
Table size	40.00	75.00
Cruet with original stopper	65.00	225.00
Cup, custard	15.00	25.00
Goblet	25.00	55.00
Mug with handle, 4-oz.	25.00	45.00
Mustard with original notched cover and underplate	75.00	150.00
Plate, 7" d.	25.00	45.00
Pitcher, tankard		
Milk, 1-qt.	55.00	110.00
Water, 1/2-gal.	95.00	150.00
Saltshaker		
Short	25.00	45.00
Tall	30.00	50.00
Sauce dish, round, flat, 4" d.	5.00	15.00
Spoon holder	25.00	40.00
Sugar bowl with cover	45.00	65.00
Syrup pitcher with glass lid, 12-oz.	65.00	225.00
Toothpick holder	20.00	25.00
Tumbler, water, flat, 4" h.		
Handled	20.00	35.00
Handleless	30.00	45.00
Wine, 4-1/8" h	15.00	30.00

Button Arches punch cup, tumbler, and saltshaker.

Button band creamer, sugar bowl, butter dish, and spoon holder.

BUTTON BAND

OMN: Wyandotte. **AKA:** Umbilicated Hobnail.

Non-flint. Ripley & Co., Pittsburgh, PA, c. 1886. The United States Glass Co., Pittsburgh, PA, at Factory "F" after 1891.

Original color production: Clear (plain, copper wheel engraved).

Reproductions and Look-a-Likes: None

Button Band rare five-bottle castor set.

Known items:	Clear
Bowl, open, round, flat, 10" d.	$35.00
Butter dish with cover	95.00
Cake stand on high standard, 10" d.	135.00

Known items:	Clear
Cake basket with pewter bail handle	125.00
Castor set, 5 bottles in original silver plate or glass holder	225.00
Celery vase	55.00
Compote, round	
High standard	
Covered	
6-1/2" d.	110.00
9" d.	135.00
Open, jelly	35.00
Low standard, open, 9" d.	65.00
Creamer	
Legged, 5-1/2" h.	65.00
Tankard	85.00
Cruet with original stopper	95.00
Goblet	75.00
Pitcher	
Milk, 1-qt.	110.00
Water, 1/2-gal.	135.00
Plate, round	45.00
Saltshaker (S)	75.00
Sauce dish, round, flat	12.50
Spoon holder	45.00
Sugar bowl with cover	75.00
Tray, water	85.00
Tumbler, water, flat	40.00
Wine	45.00

CABBAGE LEAF

AKA: Frosted Cabbage Leaf.

Non-flint. Original manufacturer unknown, c. 1883.

Original color production: Clear, clear with acid finish, amber, blue.

Reproductions and Look-a-Likes: Goblet, plate with "rabbit" center, wine (amber, amber frosted, blue, blue frosted, clear, clear frosted). L.G. Wright Glass Company, New Martinsville, WV, unmarked.

Cabbage Leaf creamer.

Known items:	Clear	Clear w/Frosting
Bowl, master berry, open, round	$225.00	$375.00
Butter dish with cover	425.00	650.00
Celery vase	150.00	225.00
Cheese dish with cover	1,500.00	2,250.00

Known items:	Clear	Clear w/Frosting
Compote, covered on high standard (several sizes)		
Large	850.00	1,000.00
Medium	700.00	850.00
Small	625.00	700.00
Creamer	150.00	175.00
Goblet (reproduction only)	15.00	20.00
Pickle dish, flat, leaf-shaped	125.00	225.00
Pitcher, water, 1/2-gal.	1,000.00	2,500.00
Plate with *Rabbit Head* center	225.00	350.00
Sauce dish, round, flat with *Rabbit Head* center	75.00	100.00
Spoon holder	125.00	150.00
Sugar bowl with cover	325.00	450.00
Tumbler	225.00	350.00
Wine (reproduction only)	10.00	15.00

CABBAGE ROSE

OMN: Central No. 140-Rose.

Non-flint. Central Glass Co., Wheeling, WV, c. 1870.

Originally named *"Rose,"* the pattern was conceived and patented by John Oesterling, July 26, 1870.

Original color production: Clear.

Known items:	Clear
Bottle, bitters, 6-1/4" h.	$150.00
Bowl, flat	
Oval, open, 6" l.	35.00
Round	
Covered	
6" d.	55.00
7" d.	65.00
7-1/2" d.	75.00

Cabbage Rose celery vase.

Cabbage Rose covered compote.

Known items:	Clear
Open	
5" d..	25.00
6" d..	30.00
7" d..	35.00
7-1/2" d..	35.00
Butter dish with cover.	95.00
Cake stand on high standard	
9" d.	75.00
9-1/2" d.	85.00
10" d.	95.00
11" d.	110.00
12" d.	135.00
12-1/2" d.	150.00
Celery vase	125.00
Champagne.	85.00
Compote	
Covered on high standard	
Deep bowl	
6" d.	65.00
6-1/2" d.	75.00
7" d.	85.00
7-1/2" d.	85.00
8" d.	95.00
8-1/2" d.	100.00
9" d.	125.00

Known items:	Clear
Regular bowl	
8" d.	100.00
9" d.	125.00
10" d.	150.00
Shallow bowl	
6" d.	55.00
7" d.	65.00
8" d.	85.00
Low standard	
Deep bowl	
7" d.	65.00
8" d.	75.00
9" d.	95.00
Regular bowl	
8" d.	75.00
9" d.	85.00
10" d.	100.00
Shallow bowl	
6" d.	45.00
7" d.	55.00
8" d.	65.00
Open on high standard	
6-1/2" d.	35.00
7-1/2" d.	45.00
8-1/2" d.	55.00
9-1/2" d.	75.00

Known items: **Clear**

Creamer with applied handle, 5-1/2" h. 85.00

Eggcup, single, open

       Handled 225.00

       Handleless 65.00

Goblet (2 styles) 65.00

Mug 85.00

Pickle dish. 20.00

Pitcher

       Milk, 1-qt. 225.00

       Water

              1/2-gal. 275.00

              3-pt. 300.00

Relish dish, tapered at one end, 8-1/2" l., with

       "rose filled horn of plenty" center 25.00

Salt, master, open, footed, beaded rim 45.00

Sauce dish, round, flat, 4" d.. . . . . 8.00

Spoon holder 45.00

Sugar bowl with cover 150.00

Tumbler, water, flat 65.00

Wine. 75.00

CABLE

> **AKA:** Atlantic Cable, Cable Cord.
>
> Flint. The Boston & Sandwich Glass Co., Sandwich, MA, c. 1850.
>
> **Original color production:** Clear. Clear with amber stain, jade green, opalescent, opaque green, blue, white, translucent turquoise-blue or any other color would be considered rare.
>
> **Reproductions:** Goblet, champagne (clear flint, non-flint, colored non-flint). L.G. Wright Glass Company, New Martinsville, WV, unmarked. Other producers.

Known items: **Clear**

Bowl, open

       Flat, 9" d.. . . . . $125.00

       Footed, 8" d. 85.00

Butter dish with cover. 225.00

Cake stand on high standard, 9" d. (produced from a

       footed compote) (ER) .4,500.00

Castor bottle

       Mustard. 55.00

       Oil with original stopper 85.00

       Shaker 45.00

Cable four-bottle castor.

Known items: **Clear**

Celery vase. 110.00

Champagne, 5" h. 375.00

Compote, open

       High standard

              5-1/2" d., jelly. 95.00

              10" d. 550.00

       Low standard

              7" d. 75.00

              9" d. 110.00

              11" d. 175.00

Creamer with applied handle 325.00

Decanter

       Bar lip

              1-pt. 175.00

              1-qt. 225.00

       Original stopper

              1-pt. 550.00

              1-qt. 650.00

Eggcup 65.00

Goblet

       Gentleman's, 6-1/4" h. 125.00

       Ladies', 5-1/2" h.. . . . . 275.00

Honey dish, round, flat 25.00

Cable creamer.

Cable syrup.

Cable goblet.

Known items:	Clear
Lamp, whale oil	
Finger, applied handle	225.00
All glass	275.00
Brass standard with marble base	175.00
Mug with applied handle	750.00

Known items:	Clear
Pitcher with applied handle	
Milk, 1-qt. (VR)	1,850.00
Water 1/ 2-gal. (R)	1,500.00
Plate, round, 6" d.	110.00
Pomade jar with cover	850.00
Salt	
Individual, flat	35.00
Pedestaled	75.00
Sauce dish, round, flat	15.00
Spoon holder	55.00
Sugar bowl with cover	175.00
Syrup pitcher with applied handle	800.00
Tumbler	
Water	
Flat	150.00
Footed	375.00
Whiskey, flat	250.00
Wine	275.00

CALIFORNIA

OMN: U.S. Glass No. 15,059-Beaded Grape. **AKA:** Beaded Grape and Vine, Grape and Vine.

Non-flint. United States Glass Co., Pittsburgh, PA, c. 1899.

Original color production: Clear, emerald green (plain, gilded).

Reproductions and Look-a-Likes: Ashtray, square, 5"; bowl, covered, flat, 4" sq., 7" sq.; bowl covered, footed, 5" sq., 7" sq.; bowl, open, flat, 7" sq., 9" sq.; bowl, open, footed, 5" sq., 7" sq., 9" sq; box, chocolate, flat, rectangular; cake stand on high standard, 11" sq.; candlestick, 4"; compote on high standard, square, covered, 5" h., 7" h., 9" h.; compote on high standard, open, flared bowl, 7" h., 9" h., 12" sq.; creamer, table size, individual; cup and saucer set; decanter with matching stopper; fruit cocktail; 8-oz. goblet; 5" sq. covered honey dish; footed mayonnaise; footed parfait; plate, round, 6" d. (bread and butter), 7" d. (salad), 8-1/2" d. (luncheon), 10-1/2" d. (dinner), 11" d. (sandwich), 12-1/2" d. (serving), 15" d. (torte); plate, square, 6" (bread and butter), 7" (salad), 8-1/2" (luncheon), square, 10-1/2" (dinner), 11" (sandwich), 12-1/2" (serving), 15" (torte); saltshaker; 4" sq. flat sauce dish; sherbet; open table size sugar bowl; open individual sugar bowl, covered table sugar bowl; flat, 5-oz tumbler (juice), flat, 8-oz. tumbler (water), 10-oz. tumbler (Iced tea); crimped footed, 6" h. vase; footed, bell-shaped 9" h. vase; footed crimped, 9" h. vase; wine (amber, amethyst, blue, Brandywine blue, clear, green, golden sunset, honey, ice blue, laurel green, milk white, milk white decorated, milk white with gold). Westmoreland Glass Company, Grapeville, PA. Unmarked, embossed with the Westmoreland "WG" logo or identified with a paper label.

California bread plate.

California goblet.

Known items:	Clear	Emerald Green
Bowl, flat, square		
Covered		
7"......................	$65.00	$85.00
8"......................	75.00	95.00
9"......................	95.00	110.00

Known items:	Clear	Emerald Green
Open		
5-1/2".............	10.00	15.00
6".................	15.00	20.00
7".................	20.00	25.00
7-1/2"..............	25.00	30.00
8".................	30.00	40.00
9".................	55.00	75.00
Butter dish, covered	95.00	100.00
Cake stand on high standard, 9" sq........................	225.00	275.00
Celery		
Tray, oblong.............	30.00	40.00
Vase	35.00	65.00

California square plate.

Known items:	Clear	Emerald Green
Compote, square on high standard		
Covered		
4"	55.00	65.00
7"	85.00	95.00
8"	95.00	110.00
9"	110.00	125.00
Open		
4"	25.00	30.00
5"	30.00	35.00
6"	35.00	45.00
7"	45.00	50.00
8"	65.00	75.00
9"	85.00	95.00
Cordial	125.00	175.00
Creamer	35.00	45.00
Cruet with original stopper	95.00	125.00
Goblet	75.00	125.00
Olive dish, square, flat with		
single tab handle	20.00	30.00
Pickle dish, rectangular	20.00	30.00
Pitcher		
Round, tankard, water,		
1/2-gal.	110.00	125.00
Square		
Milk, 1-qt.	85.00	110.00
Water, 1/2-gal.	100.00	125.00
Plate, dinner, square		
8-1/4"	40.00	45.00
8-1/2"	40.00	45.00
Preserve dish, oblong, flat	30.00	35.00

Known items:	Clear	Emerald Green
Saltshaker	35.00	45.00
Sauce dish, flat, square		
No handle		
3-1/2"	5.00	8.00
4"	8.00	10.00
4-1/2"	10.00	10.00
Tab-handled		
3-1/2"	15.00	15.00
4"	20.00	20.00
4-1/2"	22.50	25.00
Spooner	35.00	45.00
Sugar bowl, covered		
Flat base	65.00	65.00
Low footed, 4" (also known as the *"Austrian"* sugar)	85.00	95.00
Toothpick holder	45.00	65.00
Tray, bread, rectangular (R)	85.00	125.00
Tumbler, water, round, flat	35.00	45.00
Vase, pin-up (R)		
6" h.	65.00	85.00
9" h.	85.00	110.00
12" h.	110.00	125.00
Wine	45.00	65.00

CANADIAN

Non-flint. Manufacturer unknown, c. 1870s.

Original color production: Clear.

Reproductions and Look-a-Likes: 6-3/4" h. lamp base (white camphor).

Known items:	Clear
Bowl	
Covered, flat, tab-handled, 6" d.	$225.00
Open, footed, no handles, 7" d.	85.00
Butter dish with cover	225.00
Celery vase	125.00
Compote	
Covered	
High standard	
6" d.	125.00
7" d.	150.00
8" d.	175.00

Canadian three-piece table set.

Known items:	Clear
Low standard	
6" d.	125.00
7" d.	150.00
8" d.	175.00
Open	
High standard	
6" d.	55.00
7" d.	65.00
8" d.	75.00
Low standard	
6" d.	50.00
7" d.	55.00
8" d.	65.00
Creamer, 6" h.	75.00
Goblet	65.00
Jam jar with cover, 6-1/2" h. (R)	375.00
Mug, small	65.00
Pitcher	
Milk, 1-qt.	175.00
Water, 1/2-gal.	150.00

Known items:	Clear
Plate with tab handles	
6" d.	45.00
8" d.	55.00
9-1/2" d.	75.00
10" d.	95.00
12" d.	110.00
Sauce dish, round, 4" d.	
Flat	25.00
Footed	30.00
Spoon holder, 5-3/4" h.	65.00
Sugar bowl with cover	175.00
Wine, 4-1/8" h.	45.00

Canadian covered butter dish.

CANE

OMN: McKee's Hobnail. **AKA:** Cane Insert, Cane Seat, Hobnailed Diamond and Star.

Non-flint. McKee Brothers, Pittsburgh, PA, c. 1885.

Original color production: Amber, apple green, blue, clear, vaseline.

Reproductions and Look-a-Likes: None known.

Cane goblet.

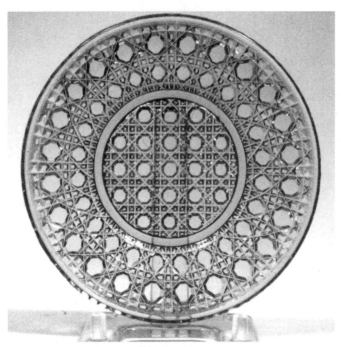

Cane plate.

Known items:	Amber	Blue	Clear	Green	Vaseline
Bowl, open					
Oval, 9-1/2" l.	$15.00	$20.00	$15.00	$25.00	$25.00
Round					
Berry, master	35.00	40.00	30.00	45.00	50.00
Finger or waste	30.00	35.00	25.00	40.00	40.00
Butter dish, flat with cover	55.00	65.00	45.00	75.00	85.00
Celery vase	35.00	50.00	35.00	55.00	65.00
Compote, open on low standard, 5-3/4" d.	25.00	30.00	20.00	35.00	35.00
Creamer	35.00	45.00	30.00	50.00	55.00
Goblet	35.00	45.00	25.00	45.00	45.00
Match holder, kettle-shaped	20.00	25.00	15.00	25.00	30.00
Pickle dish, flat	20.00	25.00	15.00	25.00	30.00
Pitcher					
Milk, 1-qt.	55.00	55.00	45.00	65.00	75.00
Water, 1/2-gal.	65.00	65.00	55.00	75.00	85.00
Plate, toddy, 4-1/2" d.	10.00	15.00	5.00	15.00	15.00
Relish tray	20.00	25.00	15.00	25.00	25.00
Saltshaker	30.00	40.00	25.00	45.00	50.00
Sauce dish, round, 4-1/2" d.					
Flat	5.00	8.00	5.00	8.00	8.00
Footed	8.00	10.00	8.00	10.00	10.00
Slipper	45.00	55.00	35.00	75.00	65.00
Spoon holder	25.00	35.00	20.00	40.00	45.00
Sugar bowl with cover	40.00	50.00	35.00	55.00	65.00
Tray, water	35.00	55.00	35.00	65.00	65.00
Wine	15.00	25.00	15.00	30.00	30.00

CARDINAL

AKA: Blue Jay, Cardinal Bird.

Non-flint. Traditionally attributed to the Ohio Flint Glass Company, Lancaster, OH, c. 1875.

Original color production: Clear.

Reproductions and Look-a-Likes: Creamer, goblet (Blue, clear, green). Both the L.G. Wright Glass Company, New Martinsville, WV and the Summit Art Glass Company, Mogadore/Rootstown, OH. Unmarked.

Cardinal covered sugar.

Known items:	Clear
Bowl, open, flat, master berry	$175.00
Butter dish with cover	
Regular	125.00
With *"Redbird, Pewitt, Titmouse"* center	225.00
Cake stand on high standard (R)	1,500.00
Creamer, 5-3/4" h.	45.00
Goblet	55.00
Honey dish, round, flat, 3-1/2" d.	10.00
Pitcher, water, 1/2-gal. (R)	2,500.00

Sauce dish, round
    Flat
        4" d. 5.00
        4-1/2" d. 8.00
        5" d. 10.00
    Footed
        4" d. 8.00
        4-1/2" d. 10.00
        5" d. 15.00
Spoon holder 45.00
Sugar bowl with cover 100.00

CATHEDRAL

OMN: Orion. **AKA:** Waffle and Fine Cut.

Non-flint. Bryce Brothers, Pittsburgh, PA, c. 1885. The United States Glass Co., Pittsburgh, PA, after 1891.

Original color production: Amber, amethyst, blue, clear, clear with ruby, vaseline. Clear items with ruby stain were produced after Bryce Brothers merged with the United States Glass Company.

Reproductions: None known.

Cathedral covered butter dish.

Known items:	Amber	Amethyst	Blue	Clear	Vaseline
Bowl, open, found, flat					
Crimped rim					
6" d.	$25.00	$35.00	$25.00	$20.00	$30.00
7" d.	30.00	45.00	35.00	25.00	35.00
8-1/2" d.	40.00	55.00	45.00	35.00	45.00

Cathedral sugar bowl, creamer, spoon holder, and butter dish.

Known items:	Amber	Amethyst	Blue	Clear	Vaseline
Smooth rim					
6" d.	25.00	35.00	25.00	20.00	30.00
7" d.	30.00	45.00	35.00	25.00	35.00
8-1/2" d.	40.00	55.00	45.00	35.00	45.00
Butter dish, covered.	65.00	125.00	85.00	55.00	95.00
Cake stand, high standard, 10" d.	85.00	175.00	110.00	75.00	135.00
Celery, boat shaped, 10" l.	50.00	75.00	55.00	45.00	65.00
Compote on high standard					
Covered, 7-1/4" d.	110.00	275.00	150.00	95.00	175.00
Open with ruffled rim					
8-1/2"d	40.00	65.00	45.00	35.00	50.00
9-1/2" d.	50.00	75.00	65.00	45.00	75.00
10-1/2" d.	65.00	85.00	75.00	55.00	85.00
Creamer					
Flat (S)	65.00	—	—	45.00	85.00
Footed, 6-1/2" h.	40.00	85.00	50.00	35.00	65.00
Cruet with original stopper	125.00	—	—	85.00	175.00
Goblet	35.00	85.00	45.00	30.00	55.00
Pitcher, water, bulbous, applied handle	175.00	—	—	135.00	275.00
Relish tray, fish-shaped					
Oval, 8-1/2"	30.00	55.00	40.00	25.00	50.00
Round, 5-3/4"	45.00	—	55.00	35.00	—
Salt, boat-shaped	15.00	25.00	20.00	15.00	20.00
Sauce dish, round, smooth or ruffled rim					
Flat, 4" d.	5.00	20.00	10.00	5.00	10.00
Footed, 4" d.	8.00	20.00	15.00	8.00	15.00
Spoon holder	40.00	65.00	45.00	35.00	55.00
Sugar bowl, covered	65.00	110.00	75.00	55.00	85.00
Tumbler, water, flat, 3-3/4" h.	35.00	75.00	45.00	30.00	55.00
Wine, 4-3/8" h.	35.00	65.00	45.00	20.00	50.00

Cathedral covered compote.

Center Medallion covered sugar.

CENTER MEDALLION

OMN: Lilyware. **AKA:** Jersey Lily Ware. Lily Langtree. Non-flint. Riverside Glass Works, Wellsburg, WV, c. 1883. **Original color production:** Clear (plain, engraved). **Reproductions and Look-a-Likes:** None known.

Center Medallion creamer.

Center Medallion covered butter.

Known items:	Clear
Butter dish with cover	
Flat	$175.00
Footed	225.00
Celery vase	125.00
Compote, covered	
High standard	
7"	225.00
8"	275.00

Center Medallion spoon holder.

Center Medallion table set.

Known items:	Clear
Low standard or flat	
7"	150.00
8"	200.00
Creamer	125.00
Lamp, oil on high standard	
7-1/2" h.	175.00
8-1/2" h.	225.00
9-1/2" h.	250.00
Nappy	45.00
Pitcher, water	375.00
Saltshaker	65.00
Sauce dish	
Flat, round with 4 peg feet	65.00
Footed	20.00

Known items:	Clear
Spoon holder	95.00
Sugar bowl with cover	150.00
Syrup	425.00
Tray, bread	
7"	125.00
8"	150.00

CHAIN

Non-flint. Maker unknown, c. 1870s.

Original color production: Clear.

Reproductions and Look-a-Likes: None known.

Chain covered sugar bowl.

Known items:	Clear
Butter dish with cover	$55.00
Celery vase	35.00
Compote, covered on high standard	85.00
Creamer	30.00
Goblet	35.00
Pickle dish	15.00
Pitcher	
Milk, 1-qt.	65.00
Water, 1/2-gal.	85.00

Chain goblet.

Chain with Star creamer.

Known items:	Clear
Plate, round	
7" d.	15.00
11" d.	25.00
Relish tray, oval	15.00
Sauce dish, round	
Flat	5.00
Footed	5.00
Spoon holder	30.00
Sugar bowl with cover	45.00
Wine	20.00

CHAIN WITH STAR

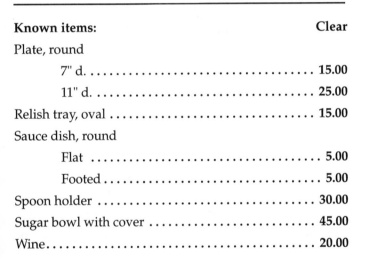

OMN: Bryce No.79. **AKA:** Chain, Frosted Chain.

Non-flint. Bryce Brothers, Pittsburgh, PA, c. 1882. The United States Glass Co., Pittsburgh, PA, c. 1891.

Original color production: Clear.

Reproductions and Look-a-Likes: None known.

Known items:	Clear
Bowl, open	
Flat, shallow, 7-1/2" d.	$25.00
Low footed, scalloped, 9-1/2" d.	35.00

Known items:	Clear
Butter dish on low foot with cover	55.00
Cake stand on high standard	
8-1/4" d.	55.00
9-1/2" d.	65.00
10-1/2" d.	75.00
Compote	
Covered	
High standard	
7" d.	85.00
9" d.	110.00
Low standard, 9" d.	65.00
Open	
High standard with scalloped rim	55.00
Low standard, 7" d.	35.00
Creamer, 5-1/2" h.	35.00
Goblet	35.00
Pickle dish, oval	15.00
Pitcher, water with applied handle and circular foot, 9-1/4" h.	150.00
Plate	
Bread, round with tab-handles, 11" d.	35.00
Dinner, round	
7" d.	25.00
10" d.	35.00

Chain with Star open compote.

Chain with Star spooner.

Known items:	Clear
Saltshaker	45.00
Sauce dish, round, 4" d.	
Flat	5.00
Footed	5.00
Spoon holder	35.00
Sugar bowl with cover	55.00
Syrup pitcher	175.00
Wine	20.00

CHANDELIER

OMN: O'Hara No.82-Crown Jewels.

Non-flint. O'Hara Glass Co., Pittsburgh, PA, c. 1888. The United States Glass Co., Pittsburgh, PA, at Factory "L" after the 1891 merger.

Original color production: Clear (plain, engraved).

Reproductions and Look-a-Likes: None known.

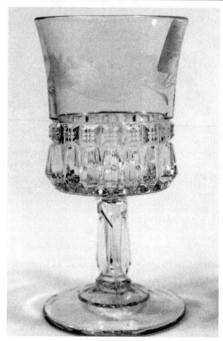

Chandelier goblet.

Known items:	Etched	Plain
Banana stand		
High standard	$225.00	$150.00
Low standard	175.00	135.00
Bowl, open, flat with flared rim		
6" d.	45.00	35.00
7" d.	55.00	45.00
8" d.	65.00	55.00
Butter dish with cover	150.00	110.00
Cake stand, high standard, 10" d.	225.00	135.00
Celery vase	55.00	45.00
Compote on high standard		
Covered, round		
6" d.	135.00	95.00
7" d.	175.00	110.00
8" d.	225.00	135.00

Chandelier water set.

Known items:	Etched	Plain
Open		
Round		
9-1/2" d.	95.00	75.00
10" d. (Fruit)	110.00	85.00
Square, 9"	135.00	110.00
Creamer, 5" h.	65.00	45.00
Finger bowl	45.00	35.00
Goblet	125.00	95.00
Inkwell, marked *"Davis Automatic Inkstand, patented May 8, 1889"*	—	125.00
Pitcher, water, tankard with applied reeded handle		
1/2-pt.	100.00	65.00
1-pt.	110.00	85.00
1-qt.	135.00	110.00
1/2-gal.	200.00	150.00
Salt		
Master, open, flat, 2" h., 2-3/4" d.	—	55.00
Shaker, tall	75.00	50.00
Sponge dish	—	45.00
Spoon holder	55.00	40.00
Sugar bowl with cover	110.00	85.00
Sugar shaker	150.00	110.00
Tray, water, round, handled	110.00	85.00
Tumbler, water, flat	65.00	45.00
Violet bowl	—	35.00

CHERRY

Non-flint. Bakewell, Pears & Co., Pittsburgh, PA, c. 1870. The pattern was designed by William M. Kirchner and patented as patent No. 3,954 April 5, 1870.

Original color production: Clear, milk white.

Reproductions and Look-a-Likes: Champagne, goblet (clear, contemporary colors, milk white). Unmarked.

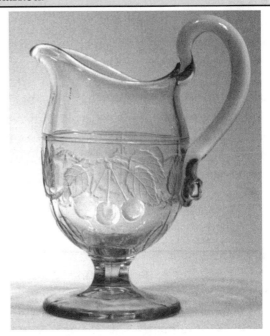

Cherry creamer.

Known items:	Clear	Milk White
Butter dish flat with cover	$150.00	$200.00
Celery vase.	275.00	—
Champagne	175.00	—
Compote		
Covered on high standard, 8" d.	225.00	—
Open, 8" d.		
High standard	110.00	275.00
Low standard.	85.00	200.00
Creamer with applied handle	125.00	225.00
Goblet	65.00	125.00
Pitcher, water (ER)	2,500.00	—
Plate, 7-1/2" d.	95.00	—
Sauce dish, round, flat	10.00	15.00
Spoon holder with pedestaled base . .	65.00	110.00
Sugar bowl with cover	135.00	200.00
Wine	110.00	—

CHERRY THUMBPRINT

AKA: Cherry & Cable, Cherry with Thumbprints, and Paneled Cherry.

Non-flint. H. Northwood Company, Wheeling, WV, c. 1904. Westmoreland Glass Company, Grapeville, PA 1907.

Original color production: Clear, clear with color stain. Also can be found in iridescent colors.

Reproductions and Look-a-Likes: Butter dish with cover (miniature, table size); celery vase with handle (miniature, table size); cookie jar with cover and double handles (miniature, table size); creamer with pressed handle (miniature, table size); pitcher with pressed handle (miniature, table size); punch bowl (miniature); punch cup (miniature); spoon holder with handles (miniature, table size); sugar bowl with cover (miniature, table size); water tumbler. Mosser Glass, Inc., Cambridge, OH (amethyst Carnival, clear decorated). Often embossed **"M,???"** within a circle.

Compote with cover on low standard; cookie jar with cover and double handles; individual creamer; covered square honey dish; individual double-handled sugar bowl. (Mint green, milk white, milk white decorated with "roses & bows," decorated vaseline). Often embossed "WG" or found with a paper label. Westmoreland Glass Company, Grapeville, PA.

Known items:	Clear w/color stain
Bowl, open, flat, master berry	$75.00
Butter dish with cover	110.00
Celery vase with handles	85.00
Cracker jar, handled with cover	150.00
Creamer	55.00
Cup, punch	20.00
Pitcher, water with pressed handle, 1/2-gal.	85.00
Punch bowl with stand	375.00
Sauce dish, round	25.00
Spoon holder	55.00
Sugar bowl with cover	40.00
Tumbler, water, flat	35.00

CLASSIC

Non-flint. Gillinder & Sons, Philadelphia, PA, c. 1875.

Original color production: Clear with frosting. Items were originally produced with either collared or footed bases, footed bases being either stippled or frosted. Initial production began with open-legged bases that were shortly substituted with thick collared bases less vulnerable to breakage. Plates often contain the name *"Jacobus"* inconspicuously embossed within the design.

Reproductions and Look-a-Likes: None known.

Cherry Thumbprint butter.

Classic covered butter dish.

Classic assortment of plates.

Known items: **Clear w/Frosting**

Butter dish with cover, 6-1/2" d.
> Collared base $250.00
> Log feet 325.00

Celery vase
> Collared base 110.00
> Log base 175.00

Compote with cover
> Collared base
>> 7-1/2" d............................ 275.00
>> 8-1/2" d............................ 300.00
> Log feet
>> 7-1/2" d............................ 350.00
>> 8-1/2" d............................ 375.00

Creamer
> Collared base 95.00
> Log feet 125.00

Goblet 350.00

Marmalade jar with cover
> Collared base 275.00
> Log feet 425.00

Pitcher
> Milk, 1-qt.
>> Collared base 375.00
>> Log feet 850.00
> Water, 1/2-gal.
>> Collared base 275.00
>> Log feet 550.00

Plate, dinner, round, 10-1/2" d.
> "Blaine" 425.00
> "Cleveland" 425.00
> "Hendricks" 375.00
> "Logan" 375.00
> "Warrior" 150.00

Classic covered sugar bowl.

Known items: **Clear w/Frosting**

Sauce dish, round, 4-1/4"
> Collared base........................... 25.00
> Log feet................................ 45.00

Spoon holder
> Collared base........................... 85.00
> Log feet............................... 110.00

Sugar bowl with cover
> Collared base.......................... 150.00
> Log feet.............................. 250.00

CLASSIC MEDALLION

AKA: Cameo.

Non-flint. Richards & Hartley Glass Co., Tarentum, PA, c. 1870s.

Original color production: Clear. Finials are either conventional or tiny lion.

Reproductions and Look-a-Likes: None known.

Known items: **Clear**

Bowl, open, round
> Flat, straight-sided, 7-1/2" d. $45.00
> Footed, 6-1/4" d........................ 40.00

Butter dish with cover 110.00

Celery vase................................. 85.00

Classic Medallion covered sugar.

Known items:	Clear
Compote, round	
Covered,	
High standard	225.00
Low standard, 7-1/2" d.	
Conventional finial	125.00
Tiny Lion finial (ER)	1,500.00
Open, low standard, 7" d.	65.00
Creamer, 5-1/2" h.	35.00
Pitcher, water, 1/2-gal.	325.00
Sauce dish, round, footed	12.50
Spoon holder	35.00
Sugar bowl with cover	85.00

CLEAR DIAGONAL BAND

AKA: California State.

Non-flint. Maker unknown, c. 1880s.

Original color production: Clear. Any item in color would be considered rare.

Reproductions and Look-a-Likes: None known.

Known items:	Clear
Bowl, footed with cover	$55.00
Butter dish with cover	45.00
Cake stand on high standard	85.00
Celery vase	35.00
Compote with cover on high standard	65.00
Creamer, with pressed handle, 6" h.	30.00
Dish, oval, open, flat	15.00

Clear Diagonal Band covered marmalade.

Clear Diagonal Band compote.

Known items:	Clear
Goblet	25.00
Marmalade jar with cover	95.00
Pitcher, water, 1/2-gal.	55.00
Plate, dinner, round, 7-1/4" d.	25.00
Platter with "*Eureka*" imprinted in the center	55.00
Relish tray, oval	15.00
Saltshaker	25.00
Sauce dish, round	
Flat	5.00
Footed	5.00

Known items:	Clear
Spoon holder	25.00
Sugar bowl with cover	35.00
Wine	15.00

CLEMATIS

AKA: Fuchsia (Unitt).

Non-flint. Maker unknown, c. 1875-1885.

Original color production: Clear.

Reproductions and Look-a-Likes: None known.

Clematis covered butter dish.

Known items:	Clear
Bowl, open, oval, flat	$30.00
Butter dish with cover	95.00
Creamer, 5-1/2" h.	75.00
Goblet	55.00
Pickle tray	15.00
Pitcher, water, 1/2-gal.	275.00
Sauce dish, round, flat, 4" d.	8.00
Spoon holder	45.00
Sugar bowl with cover	85.00

COLORADO

OMN: U.S. Glass No. 15,057-Colorado. **AKA:** Jewel, Lacy Medallion.

Non-flint. The United States Glass Co., Pittsburgh, PA, c. 1899 to about 1920.

Original color production: Blue (initially called *"Dewey Blue"*), clear, green (engraved, gilded, plain, souvenired). Items in black, clear with ruby stain, vaseline or any other color would be considered rare.

Reproductions and Look-a-Likes: Flat toothpick holder (blue, clear, green).

Known items:	Blue	Clear	Green
Banana dish, low footed with 2 folded beaded sides	$55.00	$25.00	$45.00
Bowl, open			
Round, footed			
Beaded rim			
5" d.	25.00	15.00	20.00
6" d.	30.00	15.00	25.00
7" d.	45.00	20.00	35.00
8" d.	85.00	35.00	55.00
Crimped rim			
5" d.	25.00	15.00	20.00
6" d.	30.00	15.00	25.00
7" d.	45.00	20.00	35.00
8" d.	65.00	30.00	45.00
Flared rim			
5" d.	35.00	20.00	25.00
6" d.	45.00	20.00	30.00
7" d.	55.00	30.00	40.00
8" d.	75.00	35.00	50.00
Smooth rim			
5" d.	35.00	20.00	25.00
6" d.	45.00	20.00	30.00
7" d.	55.00	30.00	40.00
8" d.	75.00	35.00	50.00
Triangular, low footed			
With finger grip			
4"	45.00	25.00	35.00
5"	55.00	30.00	45.00

Colorado covered butter dish.

Known items:	Blue	Clear	Green
Without finger grip			
4"	30.00	15.00	20.00
5"	40.00	20.00	25.00
6"	50.00	20.00	45.00
Violet, footed	50.00	20.00	45.00
Butter dish, covered, footed	275.00	65.00	125.00
Cake stand, on high standard (R)			
9" d.	200.00	95.00	125.00
10-1/2" d.	275.00	110.00	200.00
Celery vase	125.00	55.00	75.00
Cheese dish, open, round on low foot with beaded rim	65.00	30.00	35.00
Cologne bottle, 4-oz.	225.00	65.00	125.00
Compote, open on high standard			
Crimped rim			
5" d.	45.00	20.00	35.00
6" d.	55.00	25.00	45.00
7" d.	65.00	30.00	45.00
8" d.	85.00	45.00	65.00
9" d.	125.00	55.00	85.00
Flared rim			
5" d.	45.00	25.00	30.00
6" d.	55.00	25.00	45.00
7" d.	65.00	30.00	55.00
8" d.	85.00	45.00	65.00
9" d.	125.00	55.00	85.00
Creamer, bulbous with applied handle			
Breakfast	45.00	25.00	30.00
Individual	35.00	15.00	20.00
Table sized	95.00	45.00	85.00

Known items:	Blue	Clear	Green
Cup, custard with applied handle			
Large (round)	35.00	20.00	25.00
Small (tapered base with flared rim)	35.00	20.00	25.00
Dish			
Crimped rim, 8" d.	50.00	25.00	40.00
Flared edge, 8" d.	50.00	25.00	40.00
Scalloped rim, handled			
4" d.	35.00	20.00	30.00
5" d.	35.00	20.00	30.00
Jar, cracker with cover	450.00	125.00	275.00
Olive dish	40.00	20.00	30.00
Pickle dish	40.00	20.00	30.00
Pitcher, bulbous with applied handle			
Milk, 1-qt.	275.00	95.00	150.00
Water, 1/2-gal.	550.00	125.00	250.00
Plate, round, footed			
6" d.	50.00	15.00	45.00
8" d.	65.00	20.00	50.00
Saltshaker, bulbous, footed	225.00	85.00	150.00
Sauce dish, round, footed, 4" d.			
Crimped rim	35.00	10.00	20.00
Flared rim	35.00	10.00	20.00
Ruffled rim	35.00	10.00	20.00
Sherbet cup (tapered base with beaded rim)			
Large	30.00	20.00	25.00
Small	30.00	15.00	20.00
Spittoon (lady's)	85.00	35.00	45.00
Spoon holder, footed	95.00	45.00	55.00
Sugar bowl			
Individual, true open (known as the "café sugar")			
Handled	45.00	20.00	35.00
Handleless	45.00	20.00	35.00
Table sized, covered	125.00	65.00	75.00
Toothpick holder, footed	85.00	35.00	45.00
Tray			
Calling card	45.00	25.00	35.00
Jewel	45.00	25.00	35.00
Tumbler			
Lemonade, handled	110.00	45.00	65.00
Water	65.00	30.00	45.00
Vase, footed			
12" h.	125.00	35.00	65.00
16" h.	175.00	55.00	85.00

COLUMBIAN COIN

OMN: United States Glass No. 15,005 1/2. **AKA:** Columbus Coin, Spanish Coin.

Non-flint. The United States Glass Company, Pittsburgh, PA, at Factory "O," c.1893.

Original color production: Clear (plain, frosted or stained with gold); lamps in milk white opaque. Clear with amber stain, clear with ruby stain or any other color would be considered very rare.

Reproductions and Look-a-Likes: None.

Columbian Coin goblet.

Columbian Coin ale.

Known items:	Clear	Clear w/Frosting or Gold
Ale goblet, 7" h.	$125.00	$175.00
Bowl, round, flat		
Covered, plain rim		
6" d.	275.00	350.00
7" d.	300.00	400.00
8" d.	350.00	450.00
Open, plain rim		
6" d.	175.00	225.00
7" d.	200.00	250.00
8" d.	250.00	350.00

Known items:	Clear	Clear w/Frosting or Gold
Open, scalloped rim		
6" d.	250.00	350.00
7" d.	300.00	400.00
8" d.	350.00	600.00
Butter dish with cover	200.00	250.00
Cake stand, high standard, 10" d.		
(R)	350.00	450.00
Celery vase...................	225.00	275.00
Champagne, 5-1/2" h.	225.00	350.00
Claret, 4-3/4" h................	150.00	175.00
Compote, round		
Covered, straight sided		
High standard		
6" d. 275.00		300.00
7" d.............300.00		325.00
8" d.............325.00		350.00
Low standard, 6" d....200.00		250.00
Open		
Flared, high standard		
7" d.............200.00		275.00
8-1/2" d.........225.00		300.00
9-3/4" d.........250.00		325.00
10-1/2" d........350.00		450.00

Columbian Coin milk-white lamp.

Columbian Coin syrup.

Known items:	Clear	Clear w/Frosting or Gold
Plain rim, belled bowl, high standard		
7-1/4" d. 225.00		275.00
8-1/2" d. 250.00		300.00
9-3/4" d. 275.00		325.00
10-1/2" d. 350.00		350.00
Scalloped, high standard,		
7-1/4" d. 250.00		350.00
Scalloped, low standard		
6" d. 250.00		300.00
7" d. 350.00		400.00
Creamer. 125.00		175.00
Cruet with original stopper 300.00		400.00
Epergne with single lily 750.00		950.00
Goblet, 6-1/2" h. 175.00		225.00
Lamp, oil		
High Standard		
Flared or tapered font		
8-1/2" h. 300.00		350.00
9" h. 325.00		375.00
9-1/2" h. 375.00		425.00
10" h. 400.00		475.00

Known items:	Clear	Clear w/Frosting or Gold
Round font, paneled		
8" h. 250.00		300.00
8-1/2" h. 275.00		325.00
9" h. 300.00		350.00
9-1/2" h. 325.00		375.00
10" h. 350.00		400.00
10-1/2" h. 375.00		425.00
11" h. 400.00		450.00
11-1/2" h. 450.00		475.00
Square font (has coins)		
8" 250.00		275.00
8-1/2" h. 275.00		300.00
9" h. 300.00		325.00
9-1/2" h. 325.00		350.00
10" h. 350.00		375.00
10-1/2" h. 400.00		450.00
11" h. 425.00		475.00
11-1/2" h. 450.00		500.00
Footed, plain or round font		
4-7/8" h. 300.00		350.00
5-1/4" h. 325.00		350.00

Known items:	Clear	Clear w/Frosting or Gold
Mug, beer with pressed handle	225.00	325.00
Pickle dish, oblong	100.00	125.00
Pitcher with pressed handle		
Milk, 1-qt.	350.00	450.00
Water, 1/2-gal.	325.00	400.00
Preserve, 8"x 5"	100.00	125.00
Saltshaker (tall), 3" h.	95.00	110.00
Sauce dish, round		
Plain		
Flat		
3-3/4" d.	35.00	45.00
4-1/4" d.	45.00	55.00
Footed, 3-3/4" d.	45.00	55.00
Spoon holder	100.00	275.00
Sugar bowl with cover	175.00	225.00
Syrup pitcher with original dated pewter lid	600.00	750.00
Toothpick holder	100.00	125.00
Tray, water, 10" d.	250.00	275.00
Waste bowl	125.00	175.00
Tumbler, water, flat	110.00	150.00
Wine	150.00	200.00

COMET

Flint. Boston & Sandwich Glass Co., Sandwich, MA, c. late 1840s, early 1860s.

Original color production: Clear. Sapphire blue, canary yellow or any other color would be considered rare. Documentation of table pieces would be appreciated.

Reproductions and Look-a-Likes: None known.

Known items:	Clear
Butter dish with cover	—
Compote, open on low standard	—
Creamer with applied handle	—
Goblet, 6" h.	$175.00
Mug with applied handle	1,250.00
Pitcher, water with applied handle, 1/2-gal.	7,500.00
Spoon holder	—

Comet goblet.

Known items:	Clear
Sugar bowl with cover	—
Tumbler, flat	
Water	150.00
Whiskey	225.00

CORD AND TASSEL

Non-flint. LaBelle Glass Co., Bridgeport, OH, c. 1872. Central Glass Co., Wheeling, WV, c. 1879.

Original color production: Clear. Designed by Andrew H. Baggs, assignor to LaBelle Glass Co. and patented under patent No. 6,002 July 23, 1872. The design was reissued by the Central Glass Co., Wheeling, WV, after the patent expiration period of 32 years.

Reproductions and Look-a-Likes: None known.

Known items:	Clear
Bottle	
Barber with ceramic pourer	$135.00
Castor	
Mustard	40.00
Oil with original stopper	45.00
Shaker	35.00

Cord and Tassel bowl.

Known items: **Clear**

Bowl, open, oval, flat. 65.00

Butter dish with cover. 175.00

Cake stand on high standard, 9-1/2" d. 275.00

Castor set, 5 bottles, silverplate or Britannia frame . . . 375.00

Celery vase 110.00

Compote, covered on high standard 225.00

Cordial. 125.00

Creamer

       Applied handle 150.00

       Pressed handle. 55.00

Eggcup, open, single 45.00

Goblet 95.00

Lamp, footed with applied finger grip. 110.00

Mug with applied handle. 225.00

Mustard jar with cover 125.00

Pickle dish, oval. 35.00

Pitcher, water with applied handle, 1/2-gal. 650.00

Saltshaker, bulbous 85.00

Known items: **Clear**

Sauce dish, round, flat 15.00

Spoon holder 45.00

Sugar bowl with cover 125.00

Syrup pitcher 225.00

Tumbler, water. 110.00

Wine 35.00

Cord and Tassel goblet.

CORD DRAPERY

AKA: Indiana Tumbler No. 350-Indiana.

Non-flint. National Glass Company Combine, c. 1901. Indiana Tumbler & Goblet Company, Greentown, IN, c. 1898. Indiana Glass Company, Dunkirk, IN, after 1907.

Original color production: Amber, blue, clear, emerald green. Examples in canary yellow, chocolate, opaque white or any other color would be considered rare.

Reproductions and Look-a-Likes: None known

Cord Drapery covered bowl.

Cord Drapery covered bowl, syrup, cruet, and footed bowl.

Known items:	Clear	Amber	Cobalt	Emerald Green
Bowl				
Open				
Flat				
Oval	$35.00	$165.00	$165.00	$165.00
Rectangular	95.00	225.00	250.00	225.00
Round				
6-1/4" d. with fluted rim	55.00	150.00	175.00	165.00
7" d.	35.00	—	—	—
8" d.				
Plain rim	40.00	145.00	160.00	175.00
Ruffled rim	85.00	—	—	—
Footed				
Covered				
6-1/4" d.	95.00	225.00	—	—
8-1/4" d.	150.00	325.00	—	—
Open				
6-1/4" d.				
Plain rim	65.00	150.00	185.00	175.00
Ruffled rim	110.00	225.00	250.00	225.00
8-1/4" d.				
Plain rim	85.00	175.00	225.00	200.00
Ruffled rim	110.00	225.00	250.00	235.00
Butter dish with cover				
4-3/4" d.	150.00	325.00	375.00	275.00
5-1/8" d.	95.00	275.00	300.00	275.00
Cake plate	55.00	195.00	235.00	200.00
Cake stand	150.00	375.00	450.00	—
Celery vase	135.00	—	—	—
Compote, round on high standard				
Covered				
4-1/4" d.	75.00	300.00	325.00	275.00
6-1/2" d.	95.00	—	—	—
9" d.	135.00	—	—	—

Cord Drapery covered butter.

Cord Drapery water pitcher.

Cord Drapery wine.

Known items:	Clear	Amber	Cobalt	Emerald Green
Open				
Plain rim				
5-1/2" d. 85.00		—	—	225.00
7-1/2" d. ....—		—	—	275.00
8-1/2" d. 110.00		—	300.00	—
Ruffled, 10" d. 165.00		—	425.00	—
Creamer				
4-1/4" h. 65.00		150.00	200.00	195.00
4-3/4" h. 65.00		150.00	200.00	195.00
Cruet with original stopper 150.00		575.00	750.00	650.00
Cup, punch. 20.00		135.00	175.00	—
Goblet 135.00		275.00	350.00	325.00
Mug, footed 75.00		185.00	225.00	200.00
Pickle dish, 9-1/4" l. 35.00		150.00	175.00	165.00
Pitcher, water, 1/2-gal. 95.00		275.00	325.00	300.00
Saltshaker 75.00		175.00	225.00	200.00
Sauce dish, round				
Flat with hand-fluted rim. ... 65.00		100.00	135.00	110.00
Footed				
3-7/8" d. 20.00		75.00	110.00	100.00
4-1/8" d. 20.00		75.00	125.00	110.00
Spoon holder 55.00		135.00	185.00	175.00
Sugar bowl with cover 85.00		175.00	225.00	250.00
Syrup pitcher 175.00		425.00	475.00	450.00
Toothpick holder 125.00		375.00	475.00	—
Tray, water. 125.00		275.00	325.00	300.00
Tumbler, water 75.00		175.00	225.00	200.00
Wine. 85.00		250.00	325.00	300.00

CORDOVA

OMN:

Non-flint. O'Hara Glass Co., Pittsburgh, PA, c. 1891.
The United States Glass Co., Pittsburgh, PA, c. 1891.
Designed by John G. Lyon and patented December
16, 1890.

Original color production: Clear. Individual items
in clear with ruby stain and solid emerald green
may be discovered.

Reproductions and Look-a-Likes: None known.

Cordova vase.

Known items:	Clear
Bowl, flat	
Covered	
6" d.	$35.00
7" d.	45.00
8" d.	55.00
9" d.	75.00
Open	
Flared bowl	
6" d.	15.00
7" d.	20.00
8" d.	25.00
9" d.	35.00

Known items:	Clear
Straight bowl	
6" d.	15.00
7" d.	20.00
8" d.	25.00
9" d.	35.00
Butter dish with cover, handled	55.00
Cake stand on high standard, 10" d.	85.00
Casserole, flat	
Flared rim	
6" d.	35.00
8" d.	45.00
Plain rim	
6" d.	35.00
7" d.	40.00
8" d.	45.00
Catsup with cover, handled	65.00
Celery vase	35.00
Cologne bottle, 4-oz. with original cover	35.00
Compote	
Covered	
High standard	
Flared bowl	
7" d.	75.00
8" d.	85.00
9" d.	95.00
Straight-sided	
6" d.	65.00
7" d.	75.00
8" d.	85.00
Low standard	
Round (berry bowl)	45.00
Square (fruit bowl)	35.00
Cracker jar with cover	95.00
Creamer	
Individual, 3-1/4" h.	15.00
Table size	35.00
Cruet with original stopper	55.00
Cup, custard or punch	15.00
Dish	
Almond, round, handled, 5" d.	20.00
Jelly, round, handled, 5"	15.00
Cheese	25.00
Olive, triangular shape	15.00

Known items:	Clear
Finger bowl	25.00
Hatpin holder, 6" h.	45.00
Inkwell with original metal top	125.00
Mug with handle	30.00
Mustard jar with cover	45.00
Nappy, flat with handle, 6" d.	15.00
Pickle jar with cover	85.00
Pitcher, tankard	
Milk	
2-pt.	45.00
1-pt.	55.00
1-qt.	65.00
Water, 1/2-gal.	75.00
Punch bowl	125.00
Salt	
Individual, round, flat	5.00
Shaker	20.00
Sauce dish, round, flat	
4" d.	5.00
4-1/2" d.	5.00
Spoon holder	20.00
Sugar bowl with cover	
Individual	15.00
Table size	35.00
Syrup pitcher	75.00
Toothpick holder	15.00
Tray	
Lemonade	45.00
Water	55.00
Tumbler, water, flat	15.00
Vase, bud	
Flared top	
7" h.	15.00
8" h.	20.00
9" h.	25.00
Straight top	
7" h.	15.00
8" h.	20.00
9" h.	25.00

COTTAGE

OMN: Cottage (Adams', Bellaire No.456 [only goblet]). **AKA:** Dinner Bell, Fine Cut Band.

Non-flint. Adams & Co., Pittsburgh, PA, c. 1874. The United States Glass Co., Pittsburgh, PA, at Factory "A" after 1891. Bellaire Goblet Co, c. 1891 (only goblet).

Original color production: Clear. Items in amber, blue, clear with ruby stain, and emerald green are considered scarce.

Reproductions and Look-a-Likes: 5-3/8" h. goblet, wine (amber, blue, clear). Unmarked.

Cottage compotes, saltshaker, syrup, and cruet.

Known items:	Clear
Banana stand on high standard	$325.00
Bowl, open, flat	
Oval	
Deep	
7-1/2" l.	35.00
9-1/2" l.	45.00
Shallow	
7-1/2" l.	25.00
9-1/2" l.	35.00
Round	
Deep	
Berry, master, 10" d.	65.00
Finger or waste	50.00
Fruit	45.00

Cottage high-standard cake stand.

Cottage water set.

Known items:	Clear
Shallow with cover, 8" d..............	**75.00**
Butter dish	
Flat	
Dinner bell lid (S)..................	**325.00**
Flanged with flared bowl and cover....	**55.00**
Footed with cover	**75.00**
Cake stand on high standard	
9" d.	**65.00**
10" d.	**95.00**
Celery vase, pedestaled	**45.00**
Champagne............................	**85.00**
Claret	**75.00**
Compote	
Covered	
High standard	
6" d............................	**95.00**
7" d............................	**110.00**
8" d............................	**135.00**

Known items:	Clear
Low standard	
6" d............................	75.00
7" d............................	85.00
8" d............................	110.00
Open	
High standard	
4-1/2" d. (Jelly)	15.00
5" d............................	25.00
6" d............................	35.00
7" d............................	45.00
8" d............................	55.00
9" d............................	75.00
10" d............................	95.00
Low standard	
6" d............................	30.00
7" d............................	35.00
8" d............................	45.00
Creamer, 5-1/4" h....................	30.00
Cruet, with applied handle and original stopper ...	150.00
Cup, custard with handle	20.00
Goblet	35.00
Mug....................................	30.00
Pickle dish, leaf-shaped	20.00
Pitcher	
Milk	
1-pt.	55.00
1-qt.	65.00
Water, 1/2-gal....................	85.00

Known items: **Clear**

Plate, round

    6" d. 20.00

    7" d. 25.00

    8" d. 35.00

    9" d. 55.00

    10" d. 85.00

Relish tray 25.00

Salt

    Master, flat, square 75.00

    Shaker, bulbous 55.00

Sauce dish, round

    Flat, flared rim

        4" d. 8.00

        4-1/2" d. 8.00

    Footed

        4" d. 10.00

        4-1/2" d. 10.00

Saucer (for custard cup) 25.00

Spoon holder, pedestaled 30.00

Sugar bowl with cover 55.00

Syrup pitcher

    Applied handle 150.00

    Metal handle with screw top lid 95.00

Tray, water, round 55.00

Tumbler, water, flat 75.00

Wine 25.00

CROESUS

OMN: Riverside No.484.

Non-flint. Riverside Glass Works, Wellsburg, WV, c. 1897. McKee & Brothers, Pittsburgh, PA, c. 1901.

Original color production: Amethyst, green (McKee Glass Co.), clear (Riverside Glass Works), plain, gilded.

Reproductions and Look-a-Likes: Creamer, butter dish, spoon holder, sugar bowl, toothpick holder, water tumbler (amethyst, clear, green with or without gilding) by the Guernsey Glass Company, Cambridge, OH, Smith Glass, Corning, Arkansas and the Summit Art Glass Company, Akron, OH.

Croesus compote.

Known items:	Amethyst	Clear	Green
Bowl			
Covered, footed, 7" d.	$525.00	$275.00	$325.00
Open, footed with scalloped rim			
7" d.	225.00	110.00	125.00
8" d.	300.00	150.00	175.00
9-1/4" d., shallow	325.00	135.00	185.00
Butter dish with cover	300.00	150.00	175.00
Cake stand on high standard,			
10" d.	650.00	350.00	385.00
Celery vase	475.00	275.00	325.00
Compote on high standard			
Covered			
5" d.	475.00	125.00	250.00
6" d.	650.00	175.00	350.00
7" d.	825.00	200.00	450.00
Open, scalloped rim			
4" d.	425.00	200.00	250.00
5" d.	425.00	175.00	250.00
6" d.	600.00	200.00	350.00
7" d.	775.00	250.00	450.00

Croesus covered bowl.

Croesus water pitcher.

Known items:	Amethyst	Clear	Green
Saltshaker			
Bulbous	125.00	55.00	75.00
Cylinder	125.00	55.00	75.00
Sauce dish, round, 4" d.	85.00	40.00	45.00
Spoon holder	135.00	75.00	95.00
Sugar bowl with cover			
Breakfast	500.00	250.00	275.00
Table size	225.00	125.00	150.00
Toothpick holder	195.00	75.00	95.00
Tray, condiment	150.00	65.00	85.00
Tumbler, water, flat	125.00	55.00	75.00

CRYSTAL WEDDING (Adams)

OMN. AKA: Collins, Crystal Anniversary.
Non-flint. Adams & Co., Pittsburgh, PA, c. 1890.
The United States Glass Co., Pittsburgh, PA, c. 1891.
Designed by James B. Lyon and patented under
patent No. 8,464, July 6, 1875.

Original color production: Clear, clear with frosting, clear with ruby stain (plain, banded, engraved).
Etchings include *"Fern & Berry," "Bird in Bower,"*
"Rose Sprig," and *"Bird and Cattails."* Any item in
clear with amber stain, cobalt blue, and vaseline are
considered rare.

Reproductions and Look-a-Likes: Candlestick; 6-
1/2", 8" h., 10" h., 12-1/4" h. high standard covered
compotes; 6" low standard candy dish (clear, clear
with light ruby stain, plain, enamel decorated); goblet (clear, clear with light cranberry stain); banquet
lamp (clear).

Croesus cruet with original stop.

Known items:	Amethyst	Clear	Green
Creamer			
Breakfast	275.00	150.00	185.00
Individual or *"berry"*	300.00	135.00	175.00
Table size	200.00	125.00	150.00
Cruet with original stopper			
Large	525.00	225.00	275.00
Small	525.00	225.00	275.00
Pickle dish	130.00	65.00	75.00
Pitcher, water with applied handle, 1/2-gal.	525.00	285.00	325.00
Plate, footed			
8-1/2" d.	185.00	100.00	110.00
10" d. (Cake)	325.00	175.00	185.00

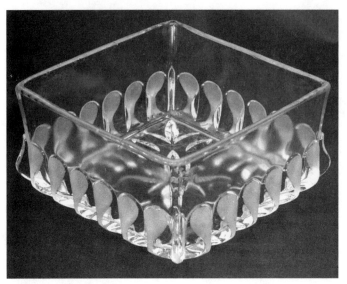

Crystal Wedding bowl.

Crystal Wedding etched covered bowl.

Crystal Wedding covered sugar.

Crystal Wedding etched tankard.

Known items:	Clear	Clear w/Frosting	Clear w/Ruby
Banana dish on high standard (AKA: *"fruit basket"*)	$150.00	$225.00	$550.00
Bowl, square, flat			
Covered			
6" sq.	85.00	110.00	175.00
7" sq.	95.00	135.00	250.00
8" sq.	110.00	175.00	275.00

Known items:	Clear	Clear w/Frosting	Clear w/Ruby
Open			
Design on lower half of scalloped bowl, beaded rim			
6" sq. 55.00		85.00	135.00
7" sq. 65.00		95.00	150.00
8" sq. 85.00		110.00	175.00

Crystal Wedding high-standard banana stand.

Crystal Wedding square water pitcher.

Crystal Wedding rare etched syrup.

Crystal Wedding tumbler, master salt, and saltshaker.

Known items:	Clear	Clear w/Frosting	Clear w/Ruby
Design covering entire scalloped bowl, 8" sq.	150.00	225.00	325.00
Butter dish with cover.	125.00	175.00	275.00
Cake stand on high standard, 10" sq.	225.00	325.00	475.00
Celery vase, flat	85.00	110.00	175.00
Claret	225.00	375.00	475.00
Compote			
Covered			
High standard			
6" sq.	100.00	135.00	225.00
7" sq.	125.00	175.00	275.00
8" sq.	150.00	225.00	325.00

Known items:	Clear	Clear w/Frosting	Clear w/Ruby
Open with scalloped rim			
High standard			
6" sq	65.00	95.00	135.00
7" sq.	85.00	110.00	150.00
8" sq.	125.00	150.00	175.00
Low standard			
5" sq.	50.00	85.00	110.00
6" sq.	75.00	95.00	135.00
7" sq.	95.00	110.00	150.00
8" sq.	125.00	150.00	175.00
Creamer, square, flat with applied handle	85.00	110.00	150.00
Cruet with original stopper (R)	275.00	450.00	950.00
Goblet, 5-3/4" h.	95.00	135.00	175.00
Lamp, oil, tall			
Banquet with non-matching font	325.00	—	—
Table			
7-1/2" h.	275.00	475.00	—
8-1/2" h.	325.00	525.00	—
9-1/2" h.	425.00	575.00	—

Crystal Wedding covered bowl.

Known items:	Clear	Clear w/Frosting	Clear w/Ruby
Nappy, flat with handle, 4-3/4" sq.	35.00	55.00	65.00
Pickle dish, rectangular	25.00	45.00	55.00
Pitcher, tankard with applied handle.			
Round			
Milk			
1-pt.	175.00	225.00	425.00
1-qt.	225.00	275.00	475.00
Water, 1/2-gal.	325.00	375.00	550.00
Square			
Milk, 1-qt.	275.00	375.00	425.00
Water, 1/2-gal.	375.00	475.00	575.00
Plate, cake, 10" sq.	135.00	175.00	275.00
Relish tray	35.00	45.00	65.00
Salt			
Master, square			
Design on entire item	85.00	110.00	150.00
Design half way up from base	65.00	85.00	110.00
Shaker, pyramid-shaped	110.00	150.00	225.00
Sauce dish, square			
Flat, design covers entire item			
4" sq.	25.00	30.00	45.00
4-1/2" sq.	30.00	35.00	45.00
Footed	35.00	35.00	50.00

Known items:	Clear	Clear w/Frosting	Clear w/Ruby
Spoon holder	65.00	75.00	110.00
Sugar bowl with cover	110.00	135.00	175.00
Syrup pitcher (R)	450.00	650.00	1,250.00
Tumbler, water, flat	75.00	85.00	125.00
Vase, bouquet			
Footed, twisted stem	325.00	—	—
Swung style	275.00	—	—
Wine	175.00	225.00	325.00

CUPID AND VENUS

OMN: Richards & Hartley No. 500. **AKA:** Guardian Angel, Minerva.

Non-flint. Richards & Hartley Glass Co., Pittsburgh, PA, c. 1875. The United States Glass Co., Pittsburgh, PA, c. 1891.

Original color production: Clear. Scant production in amber, blue, and vaseline.

Reproductions and Look-a-Likes: None known.

Cupid and Venus closeup.

Cupid and Venus handled bread plate.

Cupid and Venus wine.

Cupid and Venus milk pitcher.

Known items:	Clear
Bowl, flat, open, oval	
6" l.	$110.00
7" l.	125.00
8" l.	135.00
Butter dish with cover	225.00
Celery vase, pedestaled	55.00
Champagne	125.00
Compote	
Covered	
High standard	
6" d.	150.00
7" d.	175.00
8" d.	225.00

Known items:	Clear
Low standard	
6" d.	95.00
7" d.	110.00
8" d.	135.00
Creamer, 6" h.	45.00
Cruet, with applied handle and *"Maltese Cross"* stopper (R)	1,500.00
Goblet	95.00
Marmalade jar with cover	110.00
Mug	
Large, 3-1/2" h.	65.00
Medium, 2-1/2" h.	55.00
Small, 2" h.	45.00
Pickle castor, complete in silver plate frame	225.00
Pitcher	
Milk, 1-qt.	75.00
Water, 1/2-gal.	95.00
Plate, bread, handled, 10-1/2" d.	45.00
Sauce dish, round	
Flat	
4" d.	25.00
4-1/2" d.	30.00
Footed	
4" d.	10.00
4-1/2" d.	12.50
5" d.	15.00
Spoon holder	35.00
Sugar bowl with cover	150.00
Wine, 3-3/4" h.	85.00

CURRANT

OMN: Currant Ware. **AKA:** Currant Double Row.

Non-flint. Campbell, Jones & Co., Pittsburgh, PA, c. 1871. Attributed to the Boston & Sandwich Glass Co., Sandwich, MA, based on shards found at the site of the factory. Designed by Mary B. Campbell and patented under patent No. 4,774 April 11, 1871.

Original color production: Clear.

Reproductions and Look-a-Likes: None known.

Currant celery vase.

Known items:	Clear
Bowl, open, oval, flat	
5" x 7"	$35.00
6" x 9"	45.00
Butter dish with cover	110.00
Cake stand on high standard	
9-1/2" d., plain standard	125.00
10-1/2" d., hexagonal standard	150.00
11" d.	175.00
Celery vase, pedestaled	110.00
Compote, round	
Covered	
High standard	
8" d.	135.00
9" d.	150.00
12" d.	450.00

Known items:	Clear
Low standard, 8" d.	110.00
Open	
High standard with scalloped rim, 6" d.	55.00
Low standard, 6" d.	45.00
Creamer, footed with applied handle	75.00
Eggcup, single, open, footed	45.00
Goblet	45.00
Honey dish, 3-1/2" d., with or without cable edge	20.00
Jam jar, covered	125.00
Pitcher with applied handle	
Milk, 1-qt.	225.00
Water, 1/2-gal.	275.00
Plate	
5" x 7"	35.00
6" x 9"	45.00
Relish dish, oval	20.00
Sauce dish, flat	
With cable edge	
Flat	
4" d.	10.00
4-3/4" d.	15.00
Footed	
4" d.	15.00
4-3/4" d.	20.00
Without cable edge	
Flat	
4" d.	5.00
4-3/4" d.	8.00
Footed	
4" d.	10.00
4-3/4" d.	12.50
Spoon holder	45.00
Sugar bowl with cover	110.00
Tumbler, water, footed	65.00
Wine (S)	55.00

CURRIER AND IVES

OMN: Eulalia.

Non-flint. Co-Operative Flint Glass Co., Beaver Falls, PA, c. 1898.

Original color production: Clear. Any Item in amber, blue, clear with ruby stain, cobalt blue, milk white and vaseline would be considered rare.

Reproductions and Look-a-Likes: Pencil tray (clear, marked *"Avon"*).

Currier and Ives cup.

Currier and Ives creamer.

Known items:	Clear
Bowl, open, oval, flat, canoe-shaped, 10" l.	$45.00
Butter dish, rectangular with cover	125.00
Celery vase	55.00
Cake stand, high standard	135.00
Compote on high standard, round, 7-1/2" d.	
Covered	175.00
Open, scalloped rim	65.00
Creamer, 6-1/4" h.	65.00
Cup/saucer	55.00
Decanter with original stopper, 12" h.	55.00
Goblet	
Knob stem	35.00
Plain stem	25.00

Currier and Ives footed tumbler.

Known items:	Clear
Lamp, oil	
Finger with applied handle	95.00
High standard	
7-1/2" h.	150.00
8-1/2" h.	110.00
9-1/2" h.	125.00
Mug	15.00

Currier and Ives tray.

Known items:	Clear
Pickle dish	20.00
Pitcher	
Milk, 1-qt.	75.00
Water, 1/2-gal.	45.00
Plate	
Bread with handles	30.00
Dinner	
7" d.	20.00
10" d.	30.00
Relish dish	
Boat-shaped, 6" l.	25.00
Oval	20.00
Salt	
Master, open	65.00
Shaker, tall	55.00
Sauce dish	
Flat, round	15.00
Oval	20.00
Spoon holder	55.00
Sugar bowl with cover	85.00
Syrup pitcher	125.00
Tumbler, water	
Flat	55.00
Footed	75.00
Tray, water, round with *"Balky Mule"* center	
9-1/2" d.	45.00
12-1/4" d.	50.00
Wine, 3-1/4" h.	15.00

CURTAIN TIE BACK

Non-flint. Maker unknown, c. 1860s.

Original color production: Clear.

Reproductions and Look-a-Likes: None known.

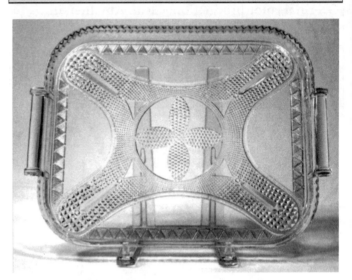

Curtain Tie Back Water Tray.

Known items:	Clear
Bowl, open, square, flat	
7" sq.	$25.00
7-1/2" sq.	30.00
Butter dish with cover	65.00
Celery	
Tray	25.00
Vase	45.00
Compote with cover on high standard	95.00
Creamer	35.00
Goblet	
Designed on base	40.00
Plain base	35.00
Pickle dish	15.00
Pitcher, water, 1/2-gal.	65.00
Plate, bread	15.00
Relish tray	15.00
Saltshaker, tall	35.00
Sauce dish, round	
Flat	5.00
Footed	5.00
Spoon holder	30.00

Known items: Clear

Sugar bowl with cover 45.00

Tray, water, rectangular, handled 95.00

Tumbler, water, flat 35.00

Wine... 20.00

CURTAIN

OMN: Sultan.

Non-flint. Bryce Brothers, Pittsburgh, PA, c. late 1870s.

Original color production: Clear.

Reproductions and Look-a-Likes: None known.

Curtain compote.

Known items: Clear

Bowl

   Round

      Collared base

      Covered

         5" d. $45.00

         6" d. 55.00

         7" d. 65.00

         8" d. 85.00

      Open

         5" d. 25.00

         6" d. 30.00

         7" d. 35.00

         8" d. 45.00

Curtain water pitcher.

Known items: Clear

   Flat, open

      7-1/2" d.......................... 35.00

      8" d............................. 45.00

Butter dish with cover 55.00

Cake stand on high standard

      8" d................................. 65.00

      9" d................................. 85.00

      9-1/2" d............................. 95.00

      10" d................................ 125.00

Caster set, 5 bottles, silver plate frame 225.00

Celery

      Boat.................................. 25.00

      Tray.................................. 20.00

      Vase

         Plain rim 30.00

         Scalloped rim 40.00

Compote on high standard

      Covered

         6" d. 65.00

         7" d. 75.00

         8" d. 95.00

         10" d. 125.00

      Open

         6" d. 35.00

         7" d. 40.00

         8" d. 45.00

         10" d. 75.00

Known items:	Clear
Creamer	45.00
Cruet with original stopper	65.00
Goblet	35.00
Mug, large	25.00
Mustard pot	35.00
Pickle dish	15.00
Pitcher	
Milk, 1-qt.	100.00
Water, 1/2-gal.	135.00
Plate, square	
Bread	30.00
Dinner	
7" sq.	35.00
8" sq.	45.00
Saltshaker	35.00
Sauce dish, round	
Collared base	
4-1/2" d.	8.00
4-3/4" d.	8.00
Flat	
4-1/2" d.	5.00
4-3/4" d.	5.00
Spoon holder	30.00
Sugar bowl with cover	55.00
Tray, water, round	65.00
Tumbler, water, flat	30.00

Cut Log Juice or Champagne Tumbler

CUT LOG

OMN: Ethol. **AKA:** Cat's Eye and Block.

Non-flint. Bryce, Higbee & Co., Pittsburgh, PA, c. 1889. Westmoreland Specialty Glass Co., Grapeville, PA, c. 1896.

Original color production: Clear. Camphor or any other color would be considered rare.

Reproductions and Look-a-Likes: None known.

Known items:	Clear
Banana stand (R)	$650.00
Bowl, flat	
Oblong	
Relish, 8" l.	35.00
Vegetable, 9-1/4" l.	55.00

Cut Log creamer.

Known items:	Clear
Round	
7" d.	55.00
8" d.	75.00
Butter dish with cover	135.00
Cake stand on high standard	
9-1/4" d.	175.00
10-1/2" d.	225.00
Celery	
Tray	35.00
Vase	65.00

Cut Log goblet.

Cut Log individual creamer.

Cut Log high-standard cake stand.

Cut Log individual sugar bowl, creamer, and covered horseradish.

Known items:	Clear
Compote	
Covered on high standard	
5" d. (Jelly)	45.00
6-1/4" d.	125.00
7-1/2" d.	150.00
8" d.	175.00
Open	
High standard	
Flared rim	
5-1/4" d.	55.00
6" d.	45.00

Known items:	Clear
7-1/2" d.	55.00
8" d.	75.00
8-1/2" d.	95.00
Scalloped rim	
6-1/8" d.	45.00
10-3/4" d.	110.00
Low standard	
Flared	
Scalloped rim	
9-3/4" d.	75.00
10" d.	95.00

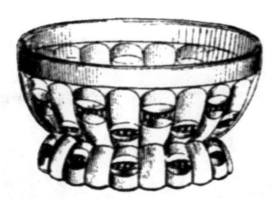

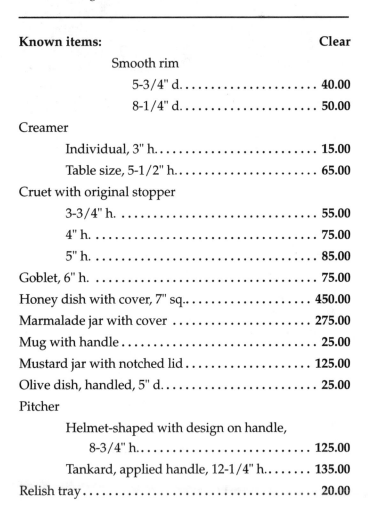

Cut Log rare master salt.

Cut Log tankard water pitcher and champagnes.

Known items:	Clear
Smooth rim	
5-3/4" d.	40.00
8-1/4" d.	50.00
Creamer	
Individual, 3" h.	15.00
Table size, 5-1/2" h.	65.00
Cruet with original stopper	
3-3/4" h.	55.00
4" h.	75.00
5" h.	85.00
Goblet, 6" h.	75.00
Honey dish with cover, 7" sq.	450.00
Marmalade jar with cover	275.00
Mug with handle	25.00
Mustard jar with notched lid	125.00
Olive dish, handled, 5" d.	25.00
Pitcher	
Helmet-shaped with design on handle, 8-3/4" h.	125.00
Tankard, applied handle, 12-1/4" h.	135.00
Relish tray	20.00

Known items:	Clear
Salt	
Master, flat, round, 3" d. (R)	135.00
Shaker, 2-1/4" h.	85.00
Sauce dish, round	
Flat	35.00
Footed	
Plain rim, 4-1/4" d.	40.00
Scalloped rim, 4-1/2" d.	45.00
Spoon holder	55.00
Sugar bowl with cover	
Individual, 3-1/4" h.	75.00
Table size, 5-1/8" h.	110.00
Tumbler, flat	
Water, 3-1/4" h.	85.00
Juice, 3-1/2" h.	65.00
Vase, flat (various sizes)	125.00
Wine, 4" h.	20.00

DAHLIA

AKA: Stippled Dahlia.

Non-flint. Portland Glass Co., Portland, ME, c. 1865. Canton Glass Co., Canton, OH, c. 1880.

Original color production: Amber, apple green, blue, clear, vaseline.

Reproductions and Look-a-Likes: None known.

Dahlia pattern close up.

Known items:	Amber	Blue	Clear	Green	Vaseline
Bowl, oval, open, flat, 8-3/4" l.	$30.00	$35.00	$25.00	$45.00	$50.00
Butter dish with cover.	65.00	85.00	55.00	95.00	110.00
Cake stand on high standard					
9-1/2" d.	85.00	110.00	75.00	125.00	135.00
10" d.	110.00	125.00	95.00	150.00	175.00
Champagne, 5" h.	85.00	100.00	75.00	110.00	125.00
Compote on high standard, round					
Covered					
7" d.	125.00	150.00	125.00	175.00	200.00
8" d.	150.00	175.00	150.00	200.00	225.00
Open, 8" d.	55.00	65.00	55.00	75.00	75.00
Creamer.	35.00	40.00	30.00	40.00	40.00
Eggcup, open					
Double.	125.00	135.00	110.00	135.00	150.00
Single.	40.00	45.00	35.00	45.00	50.00
Goblet, 5-3/4" h.	60.00	85.00	55.00	100.00	110.00
Mug with handle					
Large	55.00	65.00	55.00	65.00	75.00
Small.	45.00	50.00	45.00	50.00	55.00
Pickle dish.	25.00	30.00	20.00	30.00	35.00
Pitcher					
Milk, 1-qt.	65.00	75.00	55.00	95.00	85.00

Dahlia eggcup.

Dahlia mug.

Known items:	Amber	Blue	Clear	Green	Vaseline
Water, 1/2-gal.					
Applied handle	135.00	150.00	125.00	175.00	225.00
Pressed handle	75.00	85.00	65.00	110.00	125.00
Plate, round					
Bread, 7" d.	25.00	30.00	20.00	40.00	45.00
Dinner, handled, 9" d.	20.00	25.00	15.00	45.00	50.00
Platter, oval, 11" l.					
With fan handles	35.00	40.00	30.00	40.00	45.00
With grape handles	45.00	50.00	40.00	55.00	50.00
Relish					
Dish, 9-1/2" l.	20.00	20.00	15.00	25.00	25.00
Jar, small handled mug with original notched handle with "pickle" finial (R)	250.00	275.00	225.00	300.00	325.00
Salt, individual, footed	35.00	35.00	30.00	35.00	45.00
Sauce dish, round with scalloped rim, 4" d.					
Flat	5.00	8.00	5.00	10.00	10.00
Footed	8.00	10.00	8.00	15.00	15.00
Spoon holder	35.00	40.00	35.00	45.00	50.00
Sugar bowl with cover	55.00	75.00	55.00	95.00	110.00
Wine	55.00	75.00	55.00	85.00	100.00

DAISY AND BUTTON

OMN: Doyle's No. 300, Bryce's *Daisy & Button*, *Fashion*, Hobbs' No. 101, Duncan's *Octagon Rosette*.

Non-flint. Bryce Brothers, Pittsburgh, PA. Doyle & Company, Pittsburgh, PA, c. 1880s. Hobbs, Brockunier & Company, Wheeling, WV, c. 1885.

Original color production: Amberina, amber, blue, clear, apple green, vaseline.

Reproductions and Look-a-Likes: Vastly reproduced in both original and contemporary colors and forms.

Daisy and Button four-lobe water tray.

Known items:	Amber	Blue	Clear	Green	Vaseline
Ale glass with stem					
4-oz.	$25.00	$65.00	$30.00	$75.00	$85.00
4-1/2-oz.	30.00	75.00	35.00	85.00	100.00
5-oz.	35.00	95.00	55.00	110.00	125.00
Basket with applied handle	35.00	85.00	45.00	110.00	150.00
Bottle					
Bar with original faceted stopper	85.00	175.00	95.00	200.00	225.00
Caster					
Mustard	30.00	35.00	25.00	45.00	55.00
Pepper	30.00	35.00	25.00	45.00	55.00
Vinegar with original stopper	40.00	45.00	35.00	55.00	75.00
Cologne with original faceted stopper	35.00	65.00	35.00	85.00	95.00
Bowl					
Covered, round, flat with tab handles and faceted finial, 8" d.	135.00	250.00	125.00	275.00	325.00
Open					
Collared, oval with scalloped rim	85.00	125.00	75.00	150.00	175.00
Flat					
Octagonal with scalloped rim, 10"	175.00	275.00	150.00	300.00	350.00
Round					
Deep					
Finger with smooth rim	30.00	45.00	20.00	50.00	55.00
Flared scalloped rim, 6" d.	30.00	45.00	20.00	50.00	55.00
Ice bowl with smooth rim and drainer	—	—	95.00	—	225.00

Daisy and Button bulbous water pitcher

Daisy and Button canoe-shaped relish.

Known items:	Amber	Blue	Clear	Green	Vaseline
Pointed and scalloped rim,					
8" d.	35.00	65.00	35.00	75.00	85.00
Scalloped rim					
9" d.	45.00	75.00	45.00	85.00	110.00
9-1/2" d.	55.00	95.00	55.00	100.00	125.00
10" d.	65.00	110.00	65.00	125.00	150.00
Shallow bowl					
5-1/2" d.	20.00	45.00	20.00	50.00	55.00
7" d.	20.00	45.00	20.00	50.00	75.00
9" d. (AKA: "Crown Bowl")					
with 4 tab-handles	45.00	95.00	45.00	110.00	125.00
Square with scalloped rim					
Flared sides, 5".	15.00	35.00	15.00	40.00	45.00
Straight-sided					
5".	15.00	35.00	15.00	40.00	45.00
6"	15.00	40.00	15.00	45.00	55.00
8-1/2"	35.00	65.00	35.00	75.00	85.00
Triangular with scalloped rim	30.00	55.00	25.00	65.00	85.00
Butter dish, flat with cover					
Quarter pound	65.00	95.00	55.00	125.00	150.00
Table size					
Round	65.00	100.00	55.00	125.00	150.00
Square	75.00	125.00	65.00	150.00	175.00
Butter pat					
Clover-leaf shape.	5.00	10.00	5.00	15.00	20.00
Round with smooth rim	5.00	10.00	5.00	15.00	20.00
Square	5.00	10.00	5.00	15.00	20.00
Canoe					
4"	15.00	25.00	15.00	30.00	35.00
8-1/2"	25.00	35.00	25.00	45.00	55.00
12"	65.00	85.00	65.00	110.00	125.00
14"	85.00	100.00	85.00	150.00	175.00

Daisy and Button deep master berry.

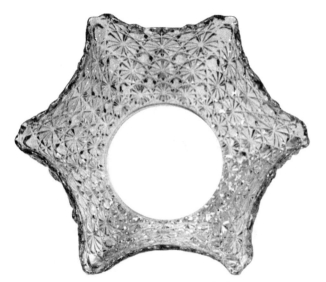

Daisy and Button lampshade.

Known items:	Amber	Blue	Clear	Green	Vaseline
Castor set					
4 bottles with original glass holder..	225.00	225.00	195.00	250.00	300.00
5 bottles in original metal holder ...	275.00	275.00	225.00	300.00	375.00
Celery					
Yachet shaped	45.00	65.00	35.00	85.00	110.00
Vase					
Hat-shaped	65.00	95.00	55.00	125.00	150.00
Tall, square with tab handled rim .	55.00	65.00	45.00	75.00	95.00
Cheese dish with matching underplate					
and cover	135.00	175.00	125.00	200.00	225.00
Compote on high standard					
With cover, 6" d...................	75.00	95.00	55.00	125.00	150.00
Without cover, 8" d................	35.00	45.00	30.00	55.00	85.00
Creamer					
Individual					
Barrel-shaped with hand tooled					
rim and applied handle..........	25.00	30.00	15.00	35.00	40.00
Round with pinched spout and					
applied handle	25.00	30.00	15.00	35.00	40.00
Table size, bulbous on collared base,					
6" h.	35.00	50.00	25.00	55.00	65.00
Tankard, flat with applied handle	35.00	55.00	25.00	65.00	75.00
Cruet with applied handle and original faceted stopper					
Bulbous	85.00	150.00	55.00	225.00	275.00
Tall, straight-sided	75.00	125.00	45.00	150.00	175.00
Cup, punch with applied ring handle	15.00	25.00	10.00	30.00	35.00

Daisy and Button milk pitcher.

Daisy and Button rare catsup bottle.

Known items:	Amber	Blue	Clear	Green	Vaseline
Dish, open					
Oval, 10" l.	45.00	65.00	35.00	75.00	85.00
Rectangular, shallow	35.00	55.00	25.00	65.00	75.00
Eggcup, open, single	35.00	50.00	30.00	85.00	95.00
Goblet					
Barrel shaped bowl	35.00	65.00	35.00	75.00	85.00
Straight-sided bowl	30.00	50.00	30.00	65.00	75.00
Ink well, chair-shaped with cat lid (VR)	300.00	475.00	375.00	550.00	650.00
Lamp, oil on high standard, all glass with patterned font	110.00	200.00	125.00	225.00	350.00
Match safe, flat with two compartments	45.00	65.00	35.00	85.00	110.00
Mug, lemonade with applied handle, 3-1/4" h.	65.00	110.00	65.00	125.00	135.00
Pickle					
Castor, complete in silver plate holder	135.00	250.00	125.00	300.00	350.00
Dish					
Fish-shaped	25.00	35.00	20.00	45.00	55.00
Yachet-shaped	20.00	30.00	15.00	40.00	50.00
Jar with original matching lid	95.00	150.00	85.00	175.00	200.00
Whisk broom tray					
Large	35.00	45.00	30.00	55.00	65.00
Small	30.00	40.00	25.00	45.00	55.00

Daisy and Button sauce dish.

Daisy and Button scalloped berry.

Known items:	Amber	Blue	Clear	Green	Vaseline
Pitcher					
Bulbous					
Milk, 1-qt. with applied air-twist					
handle, 8" h.	75.00	150.00	125.00	200.00	275.00
Water with applied reeded handle,					
1/2-gal.	150.00	350.00	275.00	375.00	425.00
Tankard with applied handle					
Milk, 1-qt.	45.00	110.00	50.00	135.00	150.00
Water, 1/2-gal.	55.00	125.00	65.00	150.00	225.00
Plate					
Leaf-shaped, 5"	10.00	25.00	15.00	30.00	35.00
Round					
With scalloped rim					
6" d. (Sugar underplate)	10.00	25.00	10.00	30.00	40.00
7" d. (Butter underplate)	15.00	30.00	15.00	35.00	45.00
7-1/2" d. (Cheese underplate)	20.00	35.00	20.00	40.00	50.00
10" d. (Dinner plate)	25.00	45.00	25.00	55.00	65.00
Square, 7"	15.00	35.00	35.00	45.00	65.00
Platter					
Oval, double-handled, 13" l.	30.00	40.00	25.00	45.00	65.00
Rectangular with four applied feet	35.00	45.00	35.00	55.00	75.00
Punch bowl, on standard	150.00	250.00	175.00	275.00	250.00
Salt					
Individual					
Band master's hat, 2" h.	55.00	75.00	45.00	125.00	95.00
Hat with brim	25.00	35.00	15.00	110.00	55.00
Rectangular, flat	5.00	10.00	5.00	15.00	15.00
Triangular	10.00	15.00	5.00	15.00	15.00
Tub with tab handle					
1-3/4" d.	10.00	15.00	8.00	25.00	25.00
2" d.	15.00	20.00	10.00	30.00	30.00

Daisy and Button yachet.

Known items:	Amber	Blue	Clear	Green	Vaseline
Master					
Canoe, 5" l.	20.00	25.00	15.00	35.00	40.00
Hat with brim	25.00	35.00	15.00	95.00	65.00
Shoe with low heel, 4-1/2" l.	35.00	45.00	30.00	175.00	65.00
Yachet	20.00	25.00	15.00	35.00	40.00
Shaker					
Flat					
Bulbous	30.00	35.00	20.00	45.00	50.00
Slender	25.00	30.00	15.00	40.00	45.00
Tapered	20.00	30.00	15.00	35.00	40.00
Footed, tall	30.00	45.00	25.00	65.00	55.00
Sauce dish, flat					
Octagonal	10.00	15.00	10.00	20.00	25.00
Round					
Flared rim	5.00	10.00	5.00	15.00	18.00
Four folded edges	5.00	10.00	5.00	15.00	20.00
Pointed and scalloped rim	5.00	10.00	5.00	15.00	20.00
Smooth scalloped rim	5.00	10.00	5.00	15.00	20.00
Square					
4 pointed scallops on rim	8.00	15.00	8.00	20.00	25.00
Point and scallop rim					
4" d.	5.00	10.00	5.00	15.00	20.00
4-1/2" d.	5.00	10.00	5.00	15.00	20.00
Triangular	5.00	15.00	5.00	22.50	25.00
Shade, glass with 4" fitter opening					
Crimped	125.00	150.00	110.00	175.00	225.00
Round	95.00	110.00	85.00	125.00	150.00
Shoe					
Baby bootie shape marked					
"PATd Oct 16, 86"	35.00	55.00	25.00	95.00	85.00
Boot shaped	30.00	50.00	20.00	85.00	55.00
Sietz bath tub (R)	110.00	150.00	85.00	175.00	225.00
Slipper					
Flat, 11-1/2" l.	150.00	200.00	125.00	325.00	225.00

Known items:	Amber	Blue	Clear	Green	Vaseline
High heel					
With clear toe (Duncan version, marked "*PATD OCT 19/86*")					
4-1/8" l.	30.00	35.00	25.00	110.00	45.00
5" l.	35.00	40.00	30.00	125.00	50.00
Low heel with patterned toe (Bryce version, marked "*PATD OCT 19 1886*")	35.00	40.00	30.00	125.00	45.00
Spoon holder					
Hat-shaped	75.00	95.00	55.00	150.00	110.00
Point and scallop rim.	30.00	45.00	35.00	65.00	75.00
Sugar bowl					
Table-sized with cover					
Round					
Small.	40.00	50.00	35.00	65.00	75.00
Tall with faceted knob finial and tab handles	75.00	95.00	65.00	110.00	125.00
Square, footed	40.00	55.00	40.00	75.00	95.00
Syrup with pressed handle					
Table sized.	135.00	225.00	125.00	325.00	275.00
10-oz.	125.00	200.00	110.00	275.00	250.00
Toothpick holder					
Barrel-shaped with metal band around rim.	30.00	40.00	25.00	50.00	45.00
Bulbous with scalloped rim	25.00	35.00	20.00	45.00	50.00
Cat on a pillow	75.00	95.00	65.00	125.00	110.00
Coat scuttle	45.00	55.00	35.00	85.00	65.00
Hat					
With flared brim	25.00	35.00	20.00	85.00	75.00
With plain rim	30.00	40.00	25.00	110.00	85.00
Kettle	25.00	35.00	20.00	45.00	40.00
Match box with four feet.	35.00	45.00	30.00	55.00	65.00
Round					
With collared base.	30.00	40.00	25.00	50.00	55.00
Flat.	25.00	35.00	20.00	45.00	50.00
With pedestal, smooth rim and patterned base.	40.00	50.00	35.00	65.00	75.00
Three legged.	30.00	35.00	25.00	45.00	50.00
Tray					
Dust pan	35.00	55.00	35.00	75.00	85.00
Ice cream	75.00	125.00	65.00	225.00	200.00
Water					
Clover leaf-shaped	110.00	175.00	95.00	225.00	250.00
Oblong with cut corners.	135.00	225.00	125.00	275.00	300.00
Round	175.00	225.00	150.00	325.00	300.00
Triangular-shaped and tab-handled.	150.00	200.00	175.00	225.00	250.00

Known items:	Amber	Blue	Clear	Green	Vaseline
Tumbler, flat					
Champagne......................... 35.00		45.00	35.00	75.00	85.00
Water					
Pattern only on base 20.00		25.00	10.00	35.00	40.00
Pattern on lower half 30.00		35.00	20.00	45.00	65.00
Pattern on lower three quarters 35.00		45.00	25.00	55.00	75.00
Patterned to rim.................. 40.00		55.00	30.00	65.00	75.00
Whiskey with pattern on lower half 20.00		35.00	25.00	55.00	65.00
Umbrella with original handle					
Footed 125.00		125.00	125.00	325.00	300.00
Plain............................ 110.00		150.00	95.00	275.00	250.00
Wall pocket					
Canoe-shaped...................... 75.00		95.00	55.00	125.00	135.00
Vase 55.00		85.00	45.00	110.00	125.00
Whisk broom holder, canoe shaped ... 175.00		275.00	150.00	325.00	350.00
Wine.................................. 25.00		35.00	20.00	55.00	45.00

DAISY AND BUTTON WITH CROSSBARS

OMN: Richards & Hartley No. 99, Mikado. **AKA:** Daisy and Thumbprint Crossbar, Daisy and Button with Crossbar and Thumbprint, Daisy with Crossbar.

Non-flint. Richards & Hartley Glass Co., Tarentum, PA, c. 1885. United States Glass Co., Pittsburgh, PA, after 1891.

Original color production: Amber (dark), amber (light), blue, canary yellow, clear. (Plain, less often engraved).

Reproductions and Look-a-Likes: None known.

Daisy and Button with Crossbars water set.

Known items:	Amber	Blue	Canary Yellow	Clear
Bottle, ketchup with original stopper........	$75.00	$125.00	$150.00	$65.00
Bowl				
Oval, open, flat				
6" l................................. 25.00		30.00	30.00	20.00
8" l................................. 30.00		35.00	35.00	25.00
9" l................................. 35.00		40.00	40.00	30.00
Butter dish covered with flanged base				
Flat.................................. 55.00		75.00	85.00	55.00
Footed 65.00		85.00	95.00	65.00

Daisy and Button with Crossbars table set showing flat & footes butter dishes.

Known items:	Amber	Blue	Canary Yellow	Clear
Celery vase	45.00	55.00	65.00	40.00
Compote, round				
Covered				
High standard				
7" d.	85.00	100.00	110.00	85.00
8" d.	95.00	110.00	125.00	95.00
Low standard				
7" d.	65.00	85.00	95.00	65.00
8" d.	75.00	95.00	110.00	75.00
Open				
High standard				
7" d.	35.00	55.00	65.00	35.00
8" d.	45.00	65.00	75.00	45.00
Low, collared base				
7" d.	25.00	45.00	55.00	25.00
8" d.	35.00	55.00	65.00	35.00
Creamer				
Individual	25.00	30.00	35.00	25.00
Table size	30.00	40.00	45.00	30.00
Cruet with original stopper	65.00	125.00	135.00	55.00
Dish, preserve, open				
7" d.	25.00	30.00	30.00	25.00
8" d.	30.00	35.00	35.00	30.00
9" d.	35.00	40.00	40.00	35.00
Finger or waste bowl	35.00	45.00	45.00	30.00
Goblet	30.00	50.00	55.00	30.00
Jar, pickle with cover	110.00	135.00	150.00	95.00
Lamp, oil				
7-1/2" h.	150.00	175.00	175.00	125.00
8-3/4" h.	175.00	200.00	200.00	135.00
9-1/2" h.	200.00	225.00	225.00	150.00
10-1/4" h.	225.00	250.00	250.00	175.00

Daisy and Button with Crossbars lamp.

Known items:	Amber	Blue	Canary Yellow	Clear
Mug with pressed handle				
Large, 3" h.	30.00	35.00	35.00	30.00
Small	20.00	25.00	25.00	20.00
Pickle dish, oblong	15.00	20.00	20.00	15.00
Pitcher				
Milk, 1-qt.	40.00	65.00	75.00	35.00
Water, 1/2-gal.	50.00	75.00	85.00	45.00
Plate, bread, round	25.00	45.00	45.00	25.00
Saltshaker	30.00	35.00	40.00	25.00
Sauce dish, round, 4" d.				
Flat	5.00	8.00	8.00	5.00
Footed	8.00	10.00	10.00	8.00
Spoon holder, footed	25.00	35.00	35.00	25.00
Sugar bowl with cover				
Individual	20.00	35.00	35.00	20.00
Table size	45.00	55.00	55.00	45.00
Syrup pitcher	125.00	175.00	175.00	110.00
Toothpick holder	20.00	25.00	30.00	20.00
Tumbler, water, flat	25.00	35.00	40.00	25.00
Tray, water, round	50.00	55.00	55.00	45.00
Wine	20.00	30.00	35.00	20.00

DAISY AND BUTTON WITH NARCISSUS

OMN: Indiana Glass No. 124. **AKA:** Daisy and Button with Clear Lily.

Non-flint. Indiana Glass Co., Dunkirk, IN, c. 1910.

Original color production: Clear, clear with cranberry stain.

Reproductions and Look-a-Likes: Flat oval bowls, vases and the wine (amber, dark blue, clear, green, yellow).

Daisy and Button with Narcissus tray.

Known items:	Clear
Bowl, open	
Oval, footed, 6" x 9-1/4" l.	$45.00
Round, flat	
7-1/4" d.	30.00
8-1/4" d.	45.00
Butter dish with cover	65.00
Celery	
Tray, oval	25.00
Vase	30.00

Known items:	Clear
Compote, open	
High standard	
Jelly, 5" d.	25.00
Fruit, large	65.00
Low standard	35.00
Creamer	35.00
Cup, punch or custard	15.00
Decanter with original stopper, 1-qt.	85.00
Goblet	45.00
Pickle tray, oblong, 9" l.	25.00
Pitcher	
Milk, 1-qt.	75.00
Water, 1/2-gal.	95.00
Relish dish, oval	15.00
Saltshaker	35.00
Sauce dish, round, deep	
Flat	
4-1/4" d.	5.00
4-3/4" d.	5.00
Footed	
4-1/4" d.	8.00
4-3/4" d.	8.00
Spoon holder	35.00
Sugar bowl with cover	50.00
Tray, 10" d.	
Water, plain edge	35.00
Wine, serrated rim	30.00
Tumbler, water, flat (2 sizes)	25.00
Wine	15.00

DAISY AND BUTTON WITH THUMBPRINT PANEL

Daisy and Button with Thumbprint seven-piece water set.

OMN: Adams' No. 86. **AKA:** Daisy and Button with Amber Stripe, Daisy and Button with Thumbprint, Daisy and Button Thumbprint.

Non-flint. Adams & Company, Pittsburgh, PA, c. 1886. The United States Glass Company, Pittsburgh, PA, c. 1891.

Original color production: Clear, clear with amber, blue and pink stain. The solid colors of amber, blue and vaseline. Clear with ruby stain, solid green or any other color would be considered rare.

Reproductions: 8-oz. goblet, water pitcher, 4-3/4" h. wine (amber, amethyst, amberina, amber satin, blue, clear, clear with painted panels, green, milk white, pink, ruby, vaseline). L.G. Wright Glass Company, New Martinsville, WV. Unmarked.

Daisy and Button with Thumbprint assortment.

Known items:	Clear	Clear w/Stain	Solid Amber	Solid Blue	Solid Vaseline
Bowl					
Heart-shaped, 7"..............	$25.00	$55.00	$30.00	$35.00	$40.00
Oval, 9" l......................	30.00	65.00	35.00	40.00	45.00
Square					
Covered					
6" d......................	65.00	125.00	75.00	85.00	95.00
7" d......................	75.00	150.00	85.00	95.00	110.00
8" d......................	85.00	175.00	95.00	110.00	125.00
Open					
6" d......................	25.00	55.00	30.00	35.00	45.00
7" d......................	35.00	65.00	40.00	45.00	55.00
8" d......................	45.00	75.00	50.00	55.00	65.00
Waste or finger	30.00	55.00	30.00	35.00	40.00
Butter dish with cover...............	55.00	125.00	55.00	65.00	75.00
Butter pat, square...................	15.00	35.00	15.00	20.00	20.00
Cake stand on high standard..........	85.00	225.00	95.00	110.00	135.00
Celery vase	35.00	85.00	35.00	45.00	55.00
Champagne..........................	75.00	125.00	75.00	85.00	85.00
Claret	65.00	110.00	65.00	75.00	75.00
Compote, square, covered on high standard					
6" d........................	85.00	150.00	95.00	110.00	125.00
7" d........................	95.00	175.00	110.00	125.00	150.00
8" d........................	110.00	225.00	125.00	150.00	175.00
Creamer with applied handle, 5-1/4" h. ..	35.00	65.00	35.00	40.00	45.00
Cruet with original stopper	65.00	225.00	75.00	95.00	110.00

Known items:	Clear	Clear w/Stain	Solid Amber	Solid Blue	Solid Vaseline
Goblet	35.00	75.00	35.00	45.00	50.00
Lamp, oil, finger with applied handle	125.00	325.00	150.00	175.00	200.00
Mug	25.00	55.00	30.00	35.00	35.00
Pickle dish	15.00	45.00	15.00	20.00	20.00
Pitcher, water with applied handle, 1/2-gal.	95.00	275.00	100.00	125.00	135.00
Plate, bread, oval	30.00	55.00	30.00	35.00	40.00
Salt					
Master, open, flat	15.00	55.00	15.00	20.00	25.00
Shaker	25.00	85.00	30.00	35.00	40.00
Sauce dish, round or square, 4-1/2"					
Flat	5.00	15.00	5.00	8.00	8.00
Footed	8.00	20.00	8.00	10.00	10.00
Spoon holder	30.00	65.00	30.00	35.00	40.00
Sugar bowl with cover	35.00	85.00	35.00	45.00	50.00
Syrup pitcher	95.00	375.00	110.00	150.00	175.00
Tray, water, oblong with double handles	45.00	85.00	45.00	50.00	55.00
Tumbler, water, flat	25.00	65.00	25.00	35.00	40.00
Wine	15.00	55.00	15.00	25.00	30.00

DAISY AND BUTTON WITH V ORNAMENT

OMN: Beatty No. 555, 558-Vandyke. **AKA:** Daisy with V Ornament.

Non-flint. A.J. Beatty & Co., Steubenville, OH, c. 1886-1887. The United States Glass Co., Pittsburgh, PA, c. 1892. Federal Glass Co., Columbus, OH, c. 1914.

Original color production: Amber, blue, clear, vaseline (plain, less often engraved).

Reproductions and Look-a-Likes: None known.

Daisy and Button with "V" ornament spooner.

Known items:	Amber	Blue	Clear	Vaseline
Bowl, octagonal				
Berry, deep with flared rim				
5-1/2" d.	$25.00	$30.00	$20.00	$40.00
8-1/2" d.	45.00	65.00	35.00	85.00
10" d.	55.00	75.00	45.00	95.00
Finger, bulbous, flat				
Belled with smooth rim (originally cataloged as "Style A")	25.00	35.00	25.00	45.00
Smooth rimed (originally cataloged as "Style B")	25.00	30.00	25.00	40.00
4-scalloped rim (originally cataloged as "Style C")	35.00	40.00	30.00	50.00
6-scalloped rim (originally cataloged as "Style AD")	30.00	45.00	30.00	55.00
Butter dish with cover	65.00	80.00	65.00	110.00
Celery vase				
Crimped, 4-scallop rim	40.00	55.00	35.00	65.00
Flared rim	35.00	50.00	30.00	55.00
Straight-sided	30.00	45.00	30.00	50.00
Creamer	30.00	40.00	30.00	45.00
Dish, open, oblong, deep	25.00	30.00	25.00	35.00
Match holder	35.00	40.00	35.00	40.00
Mug				
No. 2 (largest)	30.00	40.00	30.00	45.00
No. 3	30.00	35.00	30.00	40.00
No. 4	30.00	30.00	30.00	35.00
No. 5 (smallest)	25.00	30.00	25.00	30.00
Pickle jar with cover	95.00	125.00	85.00	150.00
Pitcher with applied handle				
Milk, 1-qt.	50.00	75.00	45.00	95.00
Water, 1/2-gal.	75.00	110.00	65.00	135.00
Plate ("V" Ornament omitted in design), round				
With scalloped rim				
6" d.	25.00	30.00	25.00	35.00
7" d.	30.00	35.00	30.00	45.00
With scalloped edge and deep rim				
6" d.	15.00	25.00	15.00	30.00
7" d.	20.00	30.00	20.00	35.00
8" d.	25.00	35.00	25.00	40.00
9" d.	35.00	45.00	35.00	50.00
Sauce dish, flat				
Octagonal with scalloped rim, 4" d.	5.00	10.00	5.00	15.00
Round, shallow bowl, 4" d.	5.00	10.00	5.00	15.00
Straight-sided, 5" d.	5.00	10.00	5.00	15.00

Known items:	Amber	Blue	Clear	Vaseline
Shade, gas w/4" d. fitter opening	65.00	85.00	55.00	125.00
Sherbet cup, handled.	20.00	25.00	20.00	30.00
Spoon holder, flat.	30.00	35.00	30.00	45.00
Sugar bowl with cover	45.00	55.00	45.00	65.00
Toothpick holder	20.00	25.00	20.00	30.00
Tray water.	65.00	85.00	55.00	135.00
Tumbler, water				
7-1/2-oz..	25.00	35.00	25.00	45.00
9-oz.	30.00	45.00	30.00	55.00

DAKOTA

OMN: AKA: Baby Thumbprint, Thumbprint Band, Thumbprint Band-Clear, Thumbprint Band-Red Top.

Non-flint. Ripley & Co., Pittsburgh, PA, c. 1885. The United States Glass Co., Pittsburgh, PA, c. 1898.

Original color production: Clear, clear with ruby stain (plain, engraved, souvenired.) Cobalt blue or any other color would be considered rare. Issued in two conspicuous forms: (a) a "hotel set" distinguished by ruffled edges and flat bases, and (b) a "household set" distinguished by plain edges and pedestaled, circular bases. Popular engravings include No. 76 (*Fern & Berry*), No. 79 (*Fish*), No. 80 (*Fern, Butterfly & Bird*), and No. 157 (*Oak Leaf*). Further documented engravings include *"Bird & Flowers," "Bird & Insect," "Buzzard," "Crane Catching Fish," "Fern without Berry," "Ivy & Berry," "Peacock," "Spider and Insect in Web," "Stag," "Swan,"* and *"Vintage Grape."*

Reproductions and Look-a-Likes: 11" h. tankard water pitcher with pressed handle (clear, clear with light cranberry stain). Marked with an embossed "R" within a shield.

Dakota covered sugar bowl.

Known items:	Clear	Clear w/Etching	Clear w/Ruby
Basket, cake with metal bail, 10" d.			
Flat. $250.00		$400.00	—
Footed with 4 clear			
applied ball feet .275.00		450.00	—

Known items:	Clear	Clear w/Etching	Clear w/Ruby
Bottle with original stopper			
Cologne (R) 85.00		175.00	350.00
Pepper sauce with original			
top (VR). 110.00		225.00	—
Bowl, open, round, flat			
Master berry with			
flared rim 110.00		175.00	350.00
Waste with smooth rim . . .45.00		95.00	125.00
Butter dish, covered			
Hotel. 45.00		95.00	175.00
Table size 35.00		65.00	150.00
Cake cover (high domed) (VR)			
8" d. 550.00		850.00	—
9" d. 750.00		1,000.00	—
10" d. 950.00		1,250.00	—

Dakota rare castor set.

Dakota tankard pitcher.

Known items:	Clear	Clear w/Etching	Clear w/Ruby
Cake stand, high standard			
8" d.	85.00	110.00	325.00
9" d.	95.00	125.00	—
9-1/2" d.	110.00	150.00	—
10" d.	125.00	175.00	375.00
10-1/2" d.	150.00	200.00	—
Celery vase			
Hotel	25.00	45.00	95.00
Table	30.00	45.00	—
Compote on high standard			
Covered			
5" d. (S)	75.00	135.00	225.00
6" d.	55.00	85.00	—
7" d.	65.00	95.00	—
8" d.	75.00	125.00	325.00
9" d.	95.00	225.00	—
Open			
5" d.	35.00	55.00	—
6" d.	25.00	35.00	—
7" d.	30.00	40.00	—
8" d.	35.00	45.00	125.00
9" d.	40.00	50.00	—

Known items:	Clear	Clear w/Etching	Clear w/Ruby
Creamer with applied handle			
Hotel	85.00	150.00	250.00
Table sized	35.00	55.00	125.00
Cruet with original stopper	150.00	275.00	350.00
Cruet under tray (VR)	150.00	350.00	—
Goblet	15.00	35.00	65.00
Honey dish, round, 3-1/2" d.			
Flat	15.00	30.00	45.00
Footed	12.00	25.00	35.00
Mug with applied handle (R)	225.00	450.00	—
Pitcher with applied handle, flat			
Cider, straight-sided, 9-1/4" h.	65.00	125.00	150.00
Tankard			
Milk			
1-pt.	125.00	250.00	350.00
1-qt.	85.00	175.00	185.00
Water, 1/2-gal.	75.00	150.00	175.00
Saltshaker			
Hotel	95.00	225.00	—
Table	35.00	85.00	125.00

Dakota water set.

DEER AND DOG

AKA: Frosted Dog.

Non-flint. Gillinder & Sons, Philadelphia, PA, c. 1870s.

Original color production: Clear, clear with frosted finials (plain, engraved). Note: Finials are in the shape of fine sculpted frosted dogs.

Reproductions and Look-a-Likes: None known.

Deer and Dog covered butter.

Known items:	Clear	Clear w/Etching	Clear w/Ruby
Sauce dish, round			
Flat			
4" d............12.00		30.00	45.00
5" d............15.00		35.00	50.00
Footed			
4" d............10.00		25.00	35.00
5" d............10.00		25.00	35.00
Spoon holder			
Hotel 75.00		110.00	150.00
Table sized 25.00		40.00	85.00
Sugar bowl with cover			
Hotel 75.00		110.00	150.00
Table sized 30.00		65.00	110.00
Tray, water, round, piecrust rim			
Hotel 250.00		450.00	—
Table size, 13" d.....150.00		275.00	—
Wine, 10-1/2" d.....110.00		225.00	—
Tumbler, water, flat 25.00		45.00	55.00
Wine.................15.00		45.00	45.00

Known items:	Clear w/Etching
Butter dish with cover $225.00	
Celery vase, pedestaled	
Signed Gillinder 175.00	
Unsigned 110.00	
Champagne, 5-1/2" h. 250.00	
Compote	
Covered	
High standard, round	
7" d...........................275.00	
8-1/4"d........................350.00	
Low standard, oval	
7-3/4" l. 425.00	
9-1/4" l. 450.00	

Deer and Dog spoon holder.

Deer and Dog covered oval bowl.

Deer and Dog covered compote.

Deer and Dog covered sugar.

Known items:	Clear w/Etching
Cordial	275.00
Creamer	110.00
Goblet	
Bulbous bowl	95.00
"U"-shaped bowl	125.00
Marmalade jar with cover	550.00
Pitcher, water, tankard with applied handle, 10" h.	325.00
Plate, Barry center, 10-1/4" d.	95.00

Known items:	Clear w/Etching
Relish, Barry center	65.00
Sauce dish, round	
Flat	25.00
Footed	45.00
Spoon holder	95.00
Sugar bowl with cover	175.00
Wine	150.00

DEER AND PINE TREE

OMN: McKee's Band Diamond. **AKA:** Deer and Doe.

Non-flint. McKee & Brothers, Pittsburgh, PA, c. 1886.

Original color production: Amber, apple green, blue, canary yellow, clear (plain, less often gilded). Not all items were produced in all colors.

Reproductions and Look-a-Likes: Goblet (clear). L.G. Wright Glass Company, New Martinsville, WV. Unmarked.

Deer and Pine Tree pattern close up.

Deer and Pine Tree footed sauce.

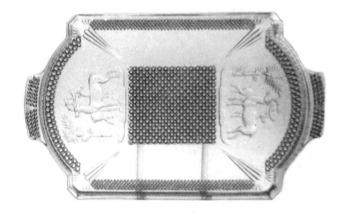

Deer and Pine Tree water tray.

Known items:	Amber	Blue	Clear	Green
Bowl, waste, open, footed.	—	—	$125.00	—
Butter dish with cover.	—	—	275.00	—
Cake stand on high standard.	—	—	225.00	—
Celery vase.	—	—	175.00	—
Compote, on high standard, covered				
7" l.	—	—	225.00	—
8" l.	—	—	275.00	—
9" l.	—	—	325.00	—
Creamer, 5-1/2" h.	—	—	95.00	—
Dish, open, oblong, flat				
5-1/2" x 7-1/4".	—	—	65.00	—
5-1/2" x 8".	—	—	75.00	—
5-3/4" x 9".	—	—	95.00	—

Deer and Pine Tree milk pitcher.

Known items:	Amber	Blue	Clear	Green
Goblet ....—	—	110.00	—
Jar, marmalade with cover ....—	—	325.00	—
Mug				
Large..................................... 85.00	95.00	65.00	110.00
Small..................................... 65.00	75.00	45.00	85.00
Pickle dish, oblong.............................—	—	45.00	—
Pitcher				
Milk, 1-qt.....................................—	—	225.00	—
Water, 1/2-gal................................—	—	175.00	—
Plate, bread, oblong........................ 125.00	135.00	45.00	150.00
Sauce dish, oblong				
Flat				
4" l. ....—	—	22.50	—
4-1/2" l. ....—	—	30.00	—
Footed				
4" l. ....—	—	35.00	—
4-1/2" l. ....—	—	40.00	—
Spoon holder ....—	—	85.00	—
Sugar bowl with cover ....—	—	175.00	—
Tray, water, 11" x 15" ....—	—	350.00	—

DELAWARE

OMN: Diamond's No. 206-New Century, U.S. Glass No. 15,065-Delaware. **AKA:** American Beauty, Four Petal Flower.

Non-flint. The United States Glass Co., Pittsburgh, PA. Introduced in 1899.

Original color production: Clear, clear with rose stain, emerald green (plain, gilded). Amethyst (VR), clear with ruby stain (VR), milk white with blue stain (S), opaque white (R), opaque ivory (R).

Reproductions and Look-a-Likes: Four Piece Table Set.

Known items:	Clear	Green w/Gold	Rose w/Gold
Banana bowl, open, flat, 11" l.. . . .	$35.00	$45.00	$85.00

Delaware cruet with faceted stopper.

Delaware scarce tall lampshade.

Delaware scarce flared lampshade.

Delaware tankard water pitcher.

Known items:	Clear	Green w/Gold	Rose w/Gold
Basket, bride's in silver plate holder			
Oval, 11" l.	85.00	125.00	175.00
Round, 8" d.	65.00	85.00	125.00
Bowl, round, smooth rim			
Berry, master, 8" d.	30.00	55.00	75.00
Finger	20.00	35.00	45.00
Butter dish, covered	55.00	85.00	125.00
Celery vase, 8" h.	35.00	75.00	95.00
Claret jug	45.00	110.00	175.00
Creamer			
Individual	15.00	30.00	40.00
Table size	35.00	55.00	75.00
Cruet with original stopper	95.00	250.00	375.00
Cup, custard	15.00	35.00	45.00
Pin tray	35.00	55.00	85.00
Pitcher, water	55.00	150.00	225.00

Known items:	Clear	Green w/Gold	Rose w/Gold
Pomade box with original jeweled cover	175.00	275.00	450.00
Puff box with original jeweled cover	175.00	275.00	450.00
Saltshaker, tall (VR)	150.00	275.00	375.00
Sauce dish, flat			
Boat shaped, 5" l.	5.00	15.00	35.00
Round, 4" d.	5.00	15.00	35.00
Shade (R)			
Electric	15.00	45.00	65.00
Gas, bulbous	15.00	45.00	65.00
Spoon holder	30.00	55.00	75.00
Sugar bowl, covered			
Individual	35.00	45.00	55.00
Table size	45.00	85.00	110.00
Toothpick holder	35.00	85.00	150.00
Tumbler, water, flat	25.00	45.00	55.00

Known items:	Clear	Green w/Gold	Rose w/Gold
Vase			
6" h. (Smooth rim)	25.00	45.00	65.00
9-1/2" h. (Ruffled rim)	35.00	75.00	95.00

DEWDROP AND RAINDROP

OMN: Kokomo No. 50, Federal No. 50. **AKA:** Dew with Raindrop, Dewdrop and Rain.

Non-flint. Kokomo Glass Co., Kokomo, IN, c. 1901. Federal Glass Co., Columbus, OH, c. 1913-14. Indiana Glass Co., Dunkirk, IN, c. 1902.

Original color production: Clear. Cordial (amber, blue, clear with light ruby), sherbet cup (clear), goblet (clear), wine (clear).

Reproductions and Look-a-Likes: Wine (clear).

Dew and Raindrop punch cup.

Known items:	Clear
Bowl, open, master berry, flat, 8" d.	$45.00
Butter dish with cover	85.00
Cordial	20.00
Creamer	40.00
Goblet with dewdrop stem	55.00
Mug	35.00
Pitcher, water, 1/2-gal.	110.00
Saltshaker	35.00

Known items:	Clear
Sauce dish, round, flat	
4" d.	8.00
4-1/2" d.	10.00
Sherbet cup	20.00
Spoon holder	35.00
Sugar bowl with cover	55.00
Tumbler, water, flat	45.00
Wine with plain stem	15.00

DEWDROP IN POINTS

OMN: Greensburg Glass No. 67.

Non-flint. Brilliant Glass Works, Brilliant OH, c. 1888. Greensburg Glass Co., Greensburg PA, c. 1889.

Original color production: Clear

Reproductions and Look-a-Likes: None Known.

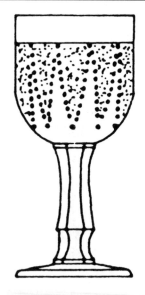

Dew Drop in Points pattern illustration.

Known items:	Clear
Butter dish with cover	$55.00
Cake stand on high standard, 10-1/2" d.	85.00
Compote	
Covered on high standard	75.00

Known items: **Clear**

    Open

        High standard

            7" d. 30.00

            8" d. 35.00

        Low standard 30.00

Creamer. 35.00

Goblet 35.00

Pickle dish. 15.00

Pitcher, water with pressed handle, 1/2-gal. 135.00

Plate, round

        Bread 25.00

        Dinner, handled, 12" d. 15.00

Platter, bread, handled with vine border, 11-3/4" l. 25.00

Sauce dish, round, 4-1/2" d.

        Flat 5.00

        Footed 5.00

Spoon holder 30.00

Sugar bowl with cover 45.00

Wine. 20.00

DEWDROP WITH STAR

Dewdrop with Star compote.

AKA: Dewdrop and Star, Dewdrop with Small Star, Star and Dewdrop.

Non-flint. Campbell, Jones & Co., Pittsburgh, PA, c. 1877. Designed by Jenkins Jones and patented under the design patent Nos. 10,096 and 10,297, July 17, 1877.

Original color production: Clear.

Reproductions and Look-a-Likes: Goblet (not original to the pattern); 7-1/4" d., 7-1/4"d. round plates; footed open master salt; footed sauce (amber, amethyst carnival, amber dark, amethyst, amberina, aqua, bluebell, burnt persimmon, blue & white slag, clear, cobalt, Crown Tuscan, custard, Elizabeth's lime ice, emerald green, forest green, heatherbloom, Henry's blue, ivory, gold, jade, lemon custard, lavender marble slag, lemon opal, milk blue, milk white, opalescent, pink, peach blow, persimmon, ruby, Rose Marie, sapphire, Snow White, teal, tomato, topaz, vaseline).

Known items: **Clear**

Bowl, open

    Flat

        6" d. $15.00

        7" d. 25.00

    Footed, 9" d. 45.00

Butter dish with domed lid and star in base. 55.00

Cake stand on high standard, 9-1/2" d. 85.00

Celery vase with star in base. 40.00

Cheese dish with cover 175.00

Compote with cover

        High standard 95.00

        Low standard 65.00

Creamer

        Applied handle, 4-3/4" h. 55.00

        Pressed handle 25.00

Dish, covered, open, flat .45.00

Goblet 25.00

Lamp, all glass, footed with finger grip and patented *"August 29, 1876"* 135.00

Pickle dish, oval 15.00

Pitcher, water, applied handle, 1/2-gal. 150.00

Plate

    Bread with *"Sheaf of Wheat"* center. 35.00

Dewdrop with Star creamer.

Dewdrop with Star covered sugar.

Known items:	Clear
Table	
4-1/2" d..........................	10.00
5" d...............................	10.00
5-1/4"d............................	10.00
5-1/2" d...........................	10.00
6" d...............................	15.00
6-1/4"d............................	15.00
6-1/2" d...........................	15.00
7" d..............................	15.00
7-1/4"d............................	15.00
7-1/2" d...........................	15.00
7-3/4" d...........................	15.00
8-1/4"d............................	20.00
9" d...............................	20.00
Salt, master, open, footed, 3-1/8" d.	15.00

Known items:	Clear
Sauce dish, round	
Flat	
4" d...............................	5.00
4-1/2" d...........................	5.00
Footed	
4" d...............................	5.00
4-1/2" d...........................	5.00
Spoon holder................................	25.00
Sugar bowl with cover........................	45.00

DEWEY

OMN: Flower Flange.

Non-flint. Indiana Tumbler & Goblet Co., Dunkirk, IN, c. 1898.

Original color production: Amber, blue (scarce), chocolate, clear, emerald green, Nile green, opaque white (difficult to find), vaseline, yellow (dull). Not all items were produced in all colors. Christened *"Dewey"* by the Indiana Tumbler & Goblet Company to honor Admiral Dewey's Spanish-American War triumphs.

Reproductions and Look-a-Likes: Covered butter dish (amber, clear, olive green, milk white, purple carnival, purple slag). Often encountered with the "I.G." insignia of the Imperial Glass Corporation.

Dewey butter dish, sugar bowl.

Dewey covered sugar bowl.

Dewey spoon holder.

Known items:	Amber	Chocolate	Clear	Emerald Green	Vaseline
Bowl, master berry, open, footed, 8" d.......	$85.00	$325.00	$65.00	$90.00	$110.00
Butter dish with cover					
Quarter pound, 4" d.	65.00	200.00	55.00	95.00	125.00
Table size, 5" d.	125.00	725.00	75.00	150.00	135.00
Creamer					
Individual with cover, 4" h.	45.00	110.00	35.00	65.00	75.00
Table size, 5" h.	65.00	525.00	55.00	85.00	110.00
Cruet with original stopper	185.00	2250.00	125.00	225.00	235.00
Mug with handle	55.00	250.00	45.00	75.00	110.00
Parfait	65.00	275.00	55.00	85.00	100.00
Pitcher, water, 1/2-gal.	125.00	—	110.00	175.00	185.00
Plate, round, footed, 7-1/2" d..............	65.00	—	55.00	85.00	95.00
Saltshaker	55.00	650.00	50.00	75.00	95.00
Sauce dish, round, flat....................	10.00	95.00	8.00	20.00	20.00
Spoon holder, 5" h.......................	55.00	325.00	45.00	65.00	75.00
Sugar bowl with cover					
2-1/4" h............................	65.00	135.00	40.00	85.00	95.00
2-1/2" h............................	65.00	200.00	40.00	85.00	95.00
4" d................................	95.00	625.00	85.00	110.00	135.00
Tray, serpentine-shaped					
Large	65.00	850.00	55.00	85.00	95.00
Small.............................	45.00	—	35.00	55.00	75.00
Tumbler, water, flat	65.00	1,250.00	55.00	85.00	95.00

DIAGONAL BAND

AKA: Diagonal Block and Fan.

Non-flint. Maker unknown, c. 1875-1885.

Original color production: Amber, apple green, clear.

Reproductions and Look-a-Likes: None known.

Diagonal Band water pitcher.

Known items:	Amber	Apple Green	Clear
Butter dish with cover...........	$65.00	$110.00	$45.00
Cake stand on high standard.....	125.00	175.00	95.00
Celery vase....................	45.00	65.00	35.00
Champagne....................	75.00	100.00	55.00
Compote on high standard			
Covered			
7" d..................	75.00	110.00	65.00
7-1/4" d..............	85.00	125.00	75.00
Open, 7-1/2" d..........	45.00	55.00	35.00
Creamer......................	35.00	45.00	25.00
Goblet.......................	40.00	55.00	35.00
Pickle dish, oval, 6-7/8" l........	15.00	20.00	15.00

Known items:	Amber	Apple Green	Clear
Pitcher			
Milk, 1-qt.	75.00	110.00	65.00
Water, 1/2-gal.	65.00	100.00	55.00
Plate			
Rectangular, bread,			
handled............	45.00	65.00	35.00
Round, 6" d...........	20.00	25.00	15.00
Sauce dish, round			
Flat	5.00	10.00	5.00
Footed	5.00	10.00	5.00
Spoon holder	30.00	40.00	25.00
Sugar bowl with cover...........	40.00	55.00	35.00
Wine	20.00	35.00	15.00

DIAMOND AND SUNBURST

OMN: Bryce No. 77. **AKA:** Diamond Sunburst, Plain Sunburst.

Non-flint. Bryce Brothers, Pittsburgh, PA, c. 1882. Designed by John Bryce and patented December 22, 1974 under patent No. 7,948.

Original color production: Clear.

Reproductions and Look-a-Likes: None known.

Diamond and Sunburst goblet.

Known items:	Clear
Butter dish with cover	$45.00
Butter pat	10.00
Cake stand on high standard	95.00
Celery vase	35.00
Champagne	55.00
Compote with cover, 8-1/4" d.	
High standard	85.00
Low standard	55.00
Creamer, 6-1/2" h.	30.00
Cup plate	15.00
Decanter with original stopper	65.00

Known items:	Clear
Eggcup, single, open, pedestaled	25.00
Goblet	30.00
Pickle dish	15.00
Pitcher, water, 1/2-gal.	75.00
Relish dish	15.00
Salt, master, open, footed	25.00
Sauce dish, round, flat	5.00
Spoon holder	25.00
Sugar bowl with cover	35.00
Syrup pitcher	95.00
Tumbler with star-base	25.00
Wine	15.00

DIAMOND CUT WITH LEAF

OMN: AKA: Fine Cut with Leaf.

Non-flint. Windsor Glass Company, Pittsburgh, PA, c. 1887.

Original color production: Amber, blue, canary yellow, clear.

Reproductions and Look-a-Likes: Goblet and wine (clear). Maker unknown.

Diamond Cut with Leaf salt.

Known items:	Amber	Blue	Canary Yellow	Clear
Bowl, open, round, flat, master berry, 8-1/2" d.	$55.00	$75.00	$75.00	$50.00
Butter dish with cover	75.00	95.00	110.00	55.00
Cake stand on high standard	125.00	150.00	150.00	110.00
Compote with cover on high standard	150.00	175.00	185.00	135.00
Creamer	45.00	65.00	65.00	35.00
Eggcup	35.00	45.00	55.00	25.00
Goblet	45.00	55.00	65.00	35.00
Mug with applied handle	110.00	150.00	150.00	85.00
Pickle tray, oval	20.00	25.00	25.00	15.00
Pitcher				
Milk, 1-qt.	95.00	125.00	125.00	85.00

Diamond Cut with Leaf spooner.

Known items:	Amber	Blue	Canary Yellow	Clear
Water, 1/2-gal.	110.00	150.00	150.00	110.00
Platter, bread.	30.00	35.00	35.00	25.00
Saltshaker	85.00	95.00	95.00	55.00
Sauce dish, round, 4-1/4" d.				
Flat.	8.00	8.00	10.00	5.00
Footed.	10.00	10.00	15.00	8.00
Spoon holder	40.00	45.00	50.00	35.00
Sugar bowl with cover	55.00	65.00	75.00	45.00
Tumbler, water, flat	45.00	55.00	65.00	35.00
Wine.	25.00	30.00	35.00	20.00

DIAMOND POINT

OMN: Sharp Diamond. **AKA:** Diamond Point with Ribs, Pineapple, Sawtooth, Stepped Diamond Point.

Flint, non-flint. The Boston & Sandwich Glass Co., Sandwich, MA. New England Glass Co., East Cambridge, MA, c. 1860s. Produced by other glass houses throughout the 1800s.

Original color production: Clear. Amethyst, blue, canary yellow, green opal, colored opaque, opaque white, clambroth, translucent jade green or any other color would be very rare.

Reproductions and Look-a-Likes: Ashtray; footed bonbon; bottles: 22-oz. bitters, bottle, 22-oz. cologne with original stopper; 7-oz. toilet; bowl, open, oval, flat: 10-1/2" l. (celery), 11" l. (celery), with crimped rim, 12" l.; bowl, open, oval, footed, 11" l.; bowl, open, round, flat (finger), 5-1/4" d. (fruit), 6" d. (cereal), 6" d. (preserve), 6-1/2" d. (rose), 8" d. (pickle), 4-part with handle, 8-1/2" d. (sweetmeat), handled, 10" d., 10-1/2" d. (salad), 11-1/2" d., belled, 11-1/2" d., shallow, 11-1/2" d., shallow and cupped 11-1/2" d., 12-1/2" with rolled edge, 12-1/2" d. with flared rim, 12-1/2" d. with rolled edge and crimp, 12" d. with flanged rolled edge, 12" d.; boxes: covered, round 3" d., 4-1/2" d. with foot, square: 4" d.; 10-1/2" d. cake stand on low foot; 13-1/2" h. candelabrum; candlesticks: 4" h., 5" h. with

2-lights, 8" h.; candy dish with covered and foot; 4-1/2" h. claret with square stem; coasters: 3" d. ribbed, plain; cocktails: 4-oz. oyster, 3-1/2-oz. with square stem; compotes: open, oval, footed with patterned stem, handled, 9" l.; round and footed with patterned stem, 4-1/2" d.; 5-1/2" d. round and footed with handle, 6" d. open round with foot and twist stem, 6-1/2" d. open round with foot and belled bowl, 7-1/2" d. open round with foot; open round with foot, 8" d.; 9-1/2" d. open round with foot; creamers: footed with pressed handle, 16-oz. with applied handle, individual; cup and saucer set; decanters with original stoppers: 11-oz., 40-oz.; 10-oz. goblet with square stem; ice bucket; 4-1/2" d. footed ivy ball; marmalade or honey with cover; open divided mayonnaise; 14-oz. mug with applied handle; 2-1/2-oz. mustard with cover; 6" l. handled pickle; pitchers with applied handles, 50-oz., 66-oz., 80-oz. (ball-shaped), 86-oz.; plates, 6" d. (bread and butter), 8-1/2" d. (salad), 10-1/2" d. (dinner) plate-finger-bowl liner, 11-1/2" d. with tab handles; relishes: handled, 2-part 6" l., 2-part 8" l., 2-part 12" l., handled, 3-part, 8" l., 3-part, 11" l., 12" l.; salt dips: oval with handle, round individual, round short; saltshaker; handled sauce boat; sherbets with square stems: 4-1/2" h., 6-1/2" h., sugars: flat, footed, individual; toothpick holder; small tray; tumblers: flat, 2-oz. (whiskey), 5-oz., 7-oz. (old-fashioned), 10-oz. (table); tumblers, footed on square stem: 1-oz., (cordial), 3-oz. (juice), 5-oz., 10-oz. (water), 12-oz. barrel-shaped; 12-oz. (iced tea), 14-oz. barrel-shaped; vases: 5" h., 6" h. footed; 6" h. with crimped rim, 6-1/2" h. squat, 7" h. footed, 10" h. footed; 3-oz. wine on square base.

Known items: **Flint**

Ale glass with knob stem, 6-1/4" h. **$185.00**

Bottle, castor

    Mustard. **85.00**

    Oil with original stopper **135.00**

    Shaker **75.00**

Bowl, flat

    Covered

        5" d.. . . . . **125.00**

        7" d.. . . . . **175.00**

        8" d.. . . . . **200.00**

Diamond Point covered sugar.

Known items: **Flint**

    Open

        5" d. **45.00**

        6" d. **55.00**

        7" d. **65.00**

        8" d. **75.00**

Butter dish with cover **150.00**

Cake stand on high standard

        9" d.. . . . .**450.00**

        10" d.. . . . .**550.00**

        11" d.. . . . .**650.00**

        12" d.. . . . .**850.00**

        14" d.. . . . . **1,250.00**

Candlesticks, 6-1/2" h. pair **650.00**

Carafe with tumbler **750.00**

Celery vase with smooth rim **135.00**

Champagne with knob stem and clear base **95.00**

Claret (jelly glass) **275.00**

Compote

    Covered

        High standard with saucer bowl

            6-1/4" d.. . . . .**200.00**

            7-1/4" d.. . . . .**225.00**

            8-1/4" d.. . . . .**275.00**

Diamond Point pomade jar.

Known items:	Flint
Low standard with saucer bowl	
6-1/4" d.	175.00
7-1/4" d.	200.00
8-1/4" d.	225.00
Open	
High standard	
Deep bowl	
6" d.	55.00
7" d.	65.00
8" d.	75.00
9" d.	95.00
10" d.	110.00
10-1/2" d.	135.00
Saucer-shaped bowl	
6" d.	45.00
7" d.	65.00
8" d.	75.00
Low standard, deep bowl	
6" d.	45.00
7" d.	55.00
7-1/2" d.	65.00
8" d.	75.00
9" d.	85.00
10" d.	110.00

Known items:	Flint
Cordial with knob stem and plain base	150.00
Creamer with applied handle, footed	175.00
Cruet with original stopper	225.00
Decanter	
Bar lip	
1-pt.	110.00
1-qt.	125.00
Patterned stopper	
1-pt.	175.00
1-qt.	200.00
Dish, open, oval, flat	
7" l.	40.00
8" l.	45.00
9" l.	50.00
10" l.	55.00
Eggcup, single, pedestaled	45.00
Goblet with knob stem	
Large (gentleman's)	55.00
Small (lady's)	85.00
Honey dish, round, flat with 10-point star base, 3-1/2" d.	10.00
Lamp, oil, tall	325.00
Mug with applied handle	275.00
Pitcher with applied handle, flat	
Milk	
1/2-pt.	350.00
1-pt.	375.00
1-qt.	400.00
3-pts.	425.00
Water, 1/2-gal.	550.00
Plate, round	
3" d.	35.00
5-1/2" d. with star center	25.00
6" d.	30.00
7" d.	35.00
8" d.	45.00
Pomade jar with cover	425.00
Salt dip	
Open	35.00
Master with cover	250.00
Sauce dish, round, flat with smooth rim, 4-1/4" d.	10.00
Spill holder	55.00
Spoon holder	55.00

Known items:	Flint
Sugar bowl with cover	
Flat, octagonal base	125.00
Footed	110.00
Syrup pitcher	375.00

Known items:	Flint
Tumbler	
Water	55.00
Whiskey, 3-1/4" h.	95.00
Wine with knob stem and plain base	55.00

DIAMOND QUILTED

AKA: Quilted Diamond.

Non-flint. Maker unknown, c. 1880.

Original color production: Amethyst, amber, blue, clear, vaseline.

Reproductions and Look-a-Likes: 8-oz. goblet, milk pitcher, 22-oz. wine (amber, amethyst, blue, clear, green, ruby, vaseline). L.G. Wright Glass Company, New Martinsville, WV. Unmarked.

Diamond Quilted celery vase.

Known items:	Amethyst	Amber	Blue	Clear	Vaseline
Bowl, open, flat					
Oval	$35.00	$15.00	$30.00	$10.00	$45.00
Round					
6" d.	35.00	15.00	25.00	10.00	40.00
7" d.	40.00	15.00	30.00	10.00	45.00
Butter dish with cover	110.00	35.00	100.00	30.00	135.00
Celery vase	85.00	20.00	75.00	20.00	100.00
Champagne, 5-1/2" h.	45.00	20.00	45.00	15.00	65.00
Compote with cover, round					
High standard, 8" d.	175.00	55.00	200.00	55.00	325.00
Low standard	125.00	45.00	150.00	45.00	275.00
Creamer with applied handle	65.00	25.00	75.00	20.00	95.00
Goblet					
Regular stem	45.00	15.00	55.00	15.00	65.00
Short stem	40.00	15.00	50.00	15.00	55.00
Mug	45.00	20.00	40.00	15.00	55.00
Pitcher, water, 1/2-gal.	110.00	35.00	125.00	30.00	225.00
Relish	25.00	15.00	25.00	10.00	35.00
Salt, open, rectangular, flat					
Individual	15.00	8.00	15.00	5.00	20.00
Master	25.00	10.00	25.00	10.00	35.00

Known items:	Amethyst	Amber	Blue	Clear	Vaseline
Sauce dish, round					
Flat with design in base..............	12.50	5.00	10.00	5.00	20.00
Footed	15.00	5.00	12.50	5.00	25.00
Spoon holder, footed....................	40.00	20.00	45.00	20.00	65.00
Sugar bowl with cover	65.00	35.00	55.00	30.00	85.00
Tray, water					
Clover-leaf shape....................	75.00	45.00	65.00	40.00	95.00
Round	55.00	35.00	55.00	30.00	75.00
Tumbler, water, flat	40.00	15.00	35.00	20.00	45.00
Wine.................................	30.00	10.00	30.00	10.00	35.00

DIAMOND THUMBPRINT

AKA: Diamond and Concave.

Flint. Attributed by pioneer research to both the Boston & Sandwich Glass Co., Sandwich, MA. and the Union Glass Co., Somerville, OH, c. 1850s.

Original color production: Clear, amber, amethyst, canary yellow, clambroth, light green, milk white, opaque white, sapphire blue or any other color would be considered rare.

Reproductions and Look-a-Likes: 12" h. covered apothecary; 12" h. basket with applied handle; 5" h. bell; 7-oz. bitters bottle; open bowls: 10" d. belled bowl on low foot, 10" d. shallow open bowl on low foot; flat covered butter dish; flat round, 12" d. cake plate; 6" h. candlestick; 10" h. footed celery vase; open compotes: 6" d. on high standard with ruffled rim, 7" d. on low standard with flared rim; 1-1/2-oz. cordial; 12-oz. footed creamer with pressed handle; 10-oz. goblet; flat footed honey dish; mug with applied handle; 14" d. plate; 7-1/4" l. relish dish; salt shaker; round flat sauce dish; 6-oz. footed sherbet; 6" h. spoon holder; covered sugar bowls: 8" h. patterned base, 8" h. with non-patterned base; tumblers: 9-oz. tumbler (old-fashioned), 5-oz. tumbler (juice); 11" h. swung vase; 6-oz. wine (amber, amethyst, blue, clear, ruby, vaseline). Each permanently marked with "*S.M.*," the insignia of the Sandwich Museum, Sandwich, MA.

Notes: Issued by many factories, the stems of footed items are either bulbous or low-footed while bases may be further ornamented with either concentric circles, plain or elaborate diamond thumbprints. While cruder items are pontil marked, more graceful items are of a later date. Produced from a good quality brilliant flint, handles are of the applied variety and exhibit beautiful crimping.

Diamond Thumbprint celery.

Known items:	Clear
Ale glass with knob stem, 6-1/4" h. (ER)	$2,250.00
Bottle, bitters with applied lip and original pewter stopper	850.00

Diamond Thumbprint compote.

Diamond Thumbprint decanter.

Known items:	Clear
Bowl, round, flat, open, scalloped rim	
5" d.	55.00
6" d.	65.00
7" d.	65.00
8" d.	95.00
Butter dish with cover.	325.00
Cake stand on high standard (R)	
9" d.	650.00
10" d.	850.00
11" d.	1,250.00
12" d.	1,500.00
Celery vase, pedestaled	275.00
Champagne with knob stem	850.00
Claret or jelly glass (R)	1,500.00
Compote, open with scalloped rim (plain or patterned foot)	
High standard	
5" d.	110.00
6" d.	65.00
7" d.	75.00
8" d.	95.00
9" d.	150.00
10" d.	200.00
11-1/2" d. (S)	350.00
Low standard	
5" d.	75.00
6" d.	55.00
7" d.	75.00
8" d.	85.00

Known items:	Clear
9" d.	110.00
10" d.	125.00
Creamer with applied handle	
Bulbous	600.00
Regular with scalloped foot	225.00
Cruet, footed with original stopper (VR)	650.00
Decanter	
Applied bar lip	
1/2-pt.	850.00
1-pt.	175.00
1-qt.	225.00
Original stopper	
1-pt.	325.00
1-qt.	450.00
Dish, open, oval, flat	
7" l.	45.00
8" l.	50.00
9" l.	65.00
10" l.	85.00
Goblet with knob stem (R).	950.00
Honey dish, round, 3-1/2" d., plain or 10-point star center	25.00
Lamp, whale oil, double font (ER)	5,500.00

Known items: **Clear**

Pitcher with applied handle	
Milk, 1-qt.	1,500.00
Water, 1/2-gal.	1,250.00
Sauce dish, round, flat.	15.00
Spoon holder, 6-1/4" h., footed	95.00
Sugar bowl with cover	175.00
Tumbler	
Bar	135.00
Water, flat	150.00
Whiskey	
Applied handle	850.00
No handle	225.00
Wine (R)	550.00

DOLPHIN

AKA: Dolphin Stem.

Non-flint. Hobbs, Brockunier & Company, Wheeling, WV, c. 1880.

Original color production: Clear, clear with frosting.

Reproductions and Look-a-Likes: None known.

Dolphin covered compote.

Dolphin spoon holder.

Known items:	Clear	Clear w/Frosting:
Bowl, covered, oval		
7" l.	$550.00	$850.00
8" l.	650.00	1,000.00
Butter dish with cover	300.00	525.00
Celery vase.	135.00	225.00
Compote with cover on high standard		
7" d.	375.00	650.00
8" d.	425.00	750.00
9" d.	475.00	850.00
Creamer	135.00	200.00
Epergne on high standard with blown tulip vases	1,250.00	2,250.00
Pickle jar with cover	650.00	1,250.00
Pitcher, water, 1/2-gal.	1,250.00	2,250.00
Salt, master.	150.00	225.00
Spoon holder	125.00	175.00
Sugar bowl with cover	300.00	475.00

DOUBLE DAISY

OMN: Chrysanthemum No.408 **AKA:** Rosette Band.

Non-flint. Riverside Glass Works, Wellsburg, WV, c. 1893.

Original color production: Clear, clear with ruby stain.

Notes: Finials are in the form of stylized daisies. Handles are of the applied variety.

Double Daisy four-piece table set.

Known items:	Clear	Clear w/Ruby
Bowl		
Covered, 8-1/4" d.		
with slotted lid	$110.00	$175.00
Open		
7" d.	40.00	55.00
8" d.	50.00	75.00
Butter dish with cover	75.00	135.00
Cake stand on high standard	85.00	375.00
Compote on high standard		
Covered		
5" d.	75.00	150.00
6" d.	85.00	200.00
7" d.	95.00	225.00
8" d.		
Plain lid	110.00	275.00
Slotted lid (R)	150.00	450.00
Open, ruffled rim		
4-1/2" d.	35.00	55.00
5" d.	55.00	85.00
6" d.	65.00	95.00
7" d.	75.00	110.00
Celery vase	55.00	150.00
Cracker jar with cover	150.00	425.00
Creamer, tankard with applied		
handle, 5-1/2" h.	55.00	95.00
Goblet	40.00	85.00
Pitcher, water with applied handle .	95.00	150.00
Salt		
Master, open on 4 stump		
legs (R)	35.00	110.00
Shaker	35.00	65.00
Sauce dish, square, on 4 stump legs	15.00	35.00
Spoon holder	40.00	75.00
Sugar bowl with cover	65.00	110.00
Syrup pitcher	135.00	325.00
Tumbler, water, flat	25.00	50.00
Wine	30.00	55.00

DRAPERY

OMN: Doyle No.30-Lace.

Non-flint. Doyle & Co., Pittsburgh, PA, c. 1870. The United States Glass Co., Pittsburgh, PA, after 1891. Often attributed to the Boston & Sandwich Glass Co., Sandwich, MA, based on shards found at the factory site. Designed by Thomas Bakewell Atterbury and patented under design patent No. 3,854 February 22, 1870.

Original color production: Clear.

Notes: Items employing finely stippled backgrounds incorporate applied handles; those with coarsely stippled backgrounds pressed handles. Finials are in the shape of pseudo pine cones.

Drapery creamer.

Known items:	Clear
Butter dish with cover	$65.00
Compote with cover on high standard, 7-1/4" d.	85.00
Creamer, 5-3/4" h.	
Applied handle	55.00
Pressed handle	35.00
Dish, oval, flat	30.00
Eggcup, open, footed	25.00
Goblet	35.00
Pitcher, water, with applied handle, 1/2-gal.	225.00
Plate, round, 6" d.	35.00
Sauce dish, round, flat, 4" d.	8.00
Spoon holder	35.00
Sugar bowl with cover	55.00
Tumbler, water, flat	45.00

EGG IN SAND

AKA: Bean, Stippled Oval.

Non-flint. Maker unknown, c. 1880s.

Original color production: Clear. Amber, blue or any other color would be rare.

Reproductions and Look-a-Likes: None known.

Egg in Sand water pitcher.

Known items:	Clear
Butter dish with cover	$55.00
Cake stand on high standard	125.00
Compote with cover on high standard (Jelly)	85.00
Creamer	35.00
Dish, flat with *"swan"* center	45.00
Goblet	35.00
Marmalade jar with cover	95.00
Pitcher	
Milk, 1-qt.	55.00
Water, 1/2-gal.	65.00

Known items:	Clear
Platter, rectangular, deep	55.00
Relish tray	25.00
Saltshaker	55.00
Sauce dish, round, flat	8.00
Spoon holder	30.00
Sugar bowl with cover	55.00
Tray	
Bread, octagonal	45.00
Water, round	65.00
Tumbler, water, flat	40.00
Wine	35.00

EGYPTIAN

AKA: Parthenon.

Non-flint. Adams & Co., Pittsburgh, PA, c. 1880.

Original color production: Clear.

Reproductions and Look-a-Likes: 13-1/4", 8-1/4" *"Salt Lake Temple"* bread platter (clear). Embossed *(C) 1983 LDS* signifying "Latter Day Saints."

Known items:	Clear
Bowl, round, flat	
Covered	
8" d.	$225.00
Open	
8" d.	85.00
8-1/2" d.	110.00
Butter dish with cover	275.00
Butter mold, *"pyramid shape"*	550.00
Celery vase	150.00
Compote	
Covered	
High standard, *"sphinx base"*	
7" d.	325.00
8" d.	375.00

Egyptian celery vase.

Egyptian spoon holder.

Known items:	Clear
Low standard	
7" d.	250.00
8" d.	275.00
Open on high standard, 5" d.	110.00
Creamer, 6" h.	55.00
Goblet	
Plain.	75.00
"Ruins of Parthenon"	125.00
Honey dish, round, flat, 3-1/2" d.	20.00
Pickle dish, oblong.	25.00
Pitcher, water, 1/2-gal.	375.00
Plate	
Closed handles	
6" d.	45.00
8" d.	55.00
10" d.	75.00
Pyramid handles, 12" d. (R)	325.00
Platter, 8-1/2" x 13"	
"Cleopatra" center	65.00
"Salt Lake Temple" center	750.00
Relish tray	25.00
Sauce dish	
Flat	
4" d.	15.00
4-1/2" d.	20.00
Footed	
4" d.	20.00
4-1/2" d.	25.00
Spoon holder	45.00
Sugar bowl with cover	225.00

ELLROSE

OMN. AKA: Amberette, Daisy and Button-Paneled-Single Scallop, Daisy and Button-Single Panel, Paneled Daisy, and Paneled Daisy and Button.

Non-flint. George Duncan & Sons, Pittsburgh, PA. Introduced in March 1885. United States Glass Co., Pittsburgh, PA, c. 1892.

Original color production: Clear, clear with amber stain. Clear with ruby stain and the solid colors of canary and blue would be considered scarce.

Reproductions and Look-a-Likes: 6-3/4" h. goblet, 8-1/2" d. round covered bowl, 8-1/2" oval open bowl (clear). Goblet marked "VPNT" within a large "S" signifying the logo Vincent Price National Treasures produced in partnership with Sears, Roebuck & Company. Bowls permanently marked with the Fenton logo.

Known items:	Clear w/Amber
Bowl	
Round	
Covered, collared foot	
7" d.	$225.00
8" d.	250.00
Open	
Collared foot	
7" d.	110.00
8" d.	125.00

Ellrose bread plate.

Ellrose covered butter dish.

Ellrose covered sugar bowl.

Known items:	Clear w/Amber
Flat	
Flared rim	
8" d..	100.00
9" d..	110.00
Scalloped rim	
Deep bowl	
8" d.	110.00
9" d.	125.00
Shallow bowl	
8" d.	100.00
9" d.	125.00
Oval, open, flat	
5" l.	55.00
7" l.	85.00
8" l.	95.00
12" l.	150.00
Square, open	
Flared scalloped rim	
5"	45.00
6"	65.00
7"	85.00
8"	95.00
9"	135.00
Butter dish with cover	
Flat smooth rim	175.00
Scalloped rim	225.00
Butter pat, square (R)	65.00
Cake stand, high standard, 10"	450.00

Known items:	Clear w/Amber
Celery	
Tray	65.00
Vase	95.00
Creamer with applied handle	85.00
Cruet with original stopper	325.00
Goblet	175.00
Gas shade, 9" d.	135.00
Olive dish, 6"	55.00
Pickle dish	65.00
Pitcher with applied handle	
Milk, 3-pts.	375.00
Water, 1/2-gal.	425.00
Plate	
Bread, 11" l.	135.00
Dinner, 7"	65.00

Ellrose creamer.

Empress covered butter dish.

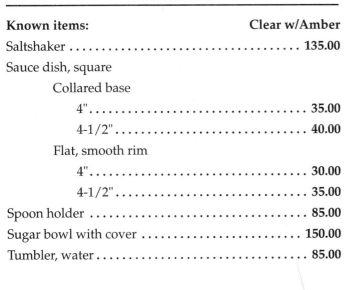

Known items:	Clear w/Amber
Saltshaker	135.00
Sauce dish, square	
Collared base	
4"	35.00
4-1/2"	40.00
Flat, smooth rim	
4"	30.00
4-1/2"	35.00
Spoon holder	85.00
Sugar bowl with cover	150.00
Tumbler, water	85.00

EMPRESS

OMN: Riverside No. 492. **AKA:** Double Arch. Non-flint. Riverside Glass Works, Wellsburgh, WV, c. 1898.

Original color production: Clear, emerald green (plain, gilded). Amethyst or any other color would be considered rare.

Reproductions and Look-a-Likes: None known.

Empress spoon holder, sugar bowl, and creamer.

Known items:	Clear	Emerald Green
Bowl		
Open		
Plain rim		
8-1/2" d., master berry	$75.00	$125.00
7" d.	55.00	85.00
Scalloped rim		
7" d.	75.00	125.00
Butter dish with cover	85.00	125.00
Cake stand	200.00	325.00
Celery vase	200.00	325.00
Compote, on high standard		
Covered		
5" d.	200.00	300.00
6" d.	250.00	375.00
7" d.	275.00	425.00
Open		
4-1/2" d. (jelly)	75.00	135.00
5" d.	150.00	250.00
6" d.	175.00	275.00
7" d.	200.00	300.00
8" d.	225.00	325.00
Cup, custard or punch	75.00	135.00
Creamer		
Breakfast	75.00	125.00
Table size, 5-1/4" h.	50.00	85.00
Cruet with original stopper	135.00	250.00

Known items:	Clear	Emerald Green
Lamp, oil		
Finger (2 sizes)	110.00	225.00
Stand (3 sizes)	135.00	250.00
Mustard, covered	175.00	275.00
Pickle dish	30.00	45.00
Pitcher, water with applied handle,		
1/2-gal.	175.00	275.00
Plate, small	35.00	55.00
Salt		
Individual	75.00	135.00
Master	110.00	175.00

Known items:	Clear	Emerald Green
Shaker	50.00	85.00
Sauce dish, round, 4-1/2" d	20.00	35.00
Spoon holder	40.00	65.00
Sugar bowl with cover		
Breakfast	85.00	135.00
Table	65.00	110.00
Sugar shaker	55.00	125.00
Syrup pitcher	225.00	425.00
Toothpick holder	110.00	225.00
Tray, cruet or spoon	45.00	75.00
Tumbler, water, flat	30.00	50.00

ESTHER (Riverside)

OMN: Esther Ware. **AKA:** Tooth and Claw. Non-flint. Riverside Glass Works, Wellsburgh, WV, c. 1896.

Original color production: Clear, emerald green (plain, gilded), clear with ruby stain, clear with enameled flowers (often souvenired). **???SHOULD AMBER BE MENTIONED HERE???**

Reproductions and Look-a-Likes: None known.

Esther covered butter dish.

Esther bulbous water pitcher.

Esther Amber Stained Goblet

Esther rare four-bottle castor set in original holder.

Esther ruby stained wine.

Known items:	Clear	Clear w/Amber	Clear w/Ruby	Green
Bowl, open, footed with scalloped rim				
7" d.	$75.00	$135.00	$135.00	$110.00
8" d. master berry	55.00	110.00	110.00	85.00
Butter dish, with cover, 7-3/4" d.	85.00	175.00	175.00	135.00
Cake stand on high standard, 10-1/2" d.	125.00	275.00	250.00	175.00
Castor set 4-bottles				
Flat stand	550.00	1,250.00	1,000.00	850.00
Revolving stand	750.00	1,500.00	1,250.00	1,000.00
Celery				
Tray	75.00	135.00	150.00	100.00
Vase	175.00	325.00	300.00	250.00
Cheese dish with cover	175.00	350.00	325.00	275.00
Compote on high standard				
Covered				
5" d.	85.00	175.00	175.00	135.00
6" d.	100.00	200.00	200.00	150.00
7" d.	135.00	275.00	300.00	200.00
Open with scalloped rim				
4-1/2" d. (Jelly)	55.00	110.00	110.00	85.00
5" d.	55.00	110.00	110.00	85.00
6" d.	75.00	135.00	135.00	110.00
7" d. fluted style	135.00	250.00	275.00	200.00
7" d. regular style	110.00	200.00	200.00	175.00
Cracker jar with cover	175.00	325.00	300.00	250.00
Creamer				
Breakfast	75.00	135.00	125.00	110.00
Table size	55.00	110.00	110.00	85.00

Known items:	Clear	Clear w/Amber	Clear w/Ruby	Green
Cruet with original stopper				
Large	175.00	350.00	325.00	250.00
Small	135.00	275.00	275.00	200.00
Goblet, 6" h.	125.00	175.00	175.00	150.00
Mustard with cover	75.00	150.00	175.00	110.00
Pickle dish	45.00	85.00	85.00	65.00
Pitcher, water, bulbous with applied handle	150.00	325.00	350.00	275.00
Plate, round				
5-1/2" d.	35.00	65.00	65.00	50.00
8" d.	95.00	175.00	175.00	125.00
10" d.	110.00	225.00	200.00	150.00
Relish tray				
Large	65.00	135.00	135.00	110.00
Small	55.00	110.00	100.00	85.00
Rose bowl	75.00	175.00	150.00	110.00
Salt				
Individual	55.00	110.00	125.00	85.00
Shaker	50.00	95.00	95.00	55.00
Sauce dish, round, cupped, 4" d.	20.00	45.00	40.00	35.00
Spoon holder	50.00	95.00	95.00	75.00
Sugar bowl with cover				
Breakfast	85.00	175.00	165.00	135.00
Table	75.00	135.00	135.00	110.00
Syrup pitcher (R)	550.00	1,250.00	1,500.00	750.00
Toothpick holder	110.00	225.00	225.00	175.00
Tray, cruet	55.00	110.00	125.00	85.00
Tumbler, water, flat	35.00	65.00	65.00	50.00
Vase	75.00	135.00	150.00	110.00
Wine	55.00	100.00	110.00	85.00

EUGENIE

Flint. McKee Brothers, Pittsburgh, PA, c. 1859.

Original color production: Clear.

Reproductions and Look-a-Likes: None known.

Known items:	Clear
Bottle, castor	
Mustard	$85.00
Oil with original stopper	125.00
Shaker	75.00

Known items:	Clear
Bowl with cover	
7" d.	175.00
9" d.	200.00
Celery vase	225.00
Champagne	175.00

Eugenie low-footed covered bowls.

Eugenie rare covered sugar bowl.

Eugenie wine.

Eugenie celery vase.

Known items: **Clear**

Decanter

    Bar lip

        1-pt. 150.00

        1-qt. 175.00

Eggcup, single, open, pedestaled 65.00

Goblet 85.00

Lamp, whale oil, all glass. .275.00

Sugar bowl with cover and *"dolphin"* finial (VR) 550.00

Tumbler, water, footed, 4-3/4" h. 65.00

Wine 55.00

EUREKA (McKee)

OMN:

Flint. McKee & Brothers, Pittsburgh, PA, c. 1866.

Original color production: Clear.

Reproductions and Look-a-Likes: None known.

Known items: **Clear**

Bowl

    Round with cover, 6" d. $75.00

    Open, oval

        6" l. 25.00

        7" l. 30.00

        8" l. 35.00

        9" l. 45.00

Known items: **Clear**

Compote with cover

    High standard

        7" d. 225.00

        8" d. 275.00

    Low standard

        7" d. 175.00

        8" d. 200.00

Creamer. 250.00

Eureka goblet.

Known items: **Clear**

Butter dish with cover 95.00

Champagne 110.00

Compote

   Covered

      High standard

         6" d 125.00

         7" d 150.00

         8" d 175.00

      Low standard

         6" d 100.00

         7" d 125.00

         8" d 150.00

   Open

      High standard

         6" d 45.00

         7" d 55.00

         8" d 65.00

      Low standard

         6" d 35.00

         7" d 45.00

         8" d 55.00

Creamer, footed with applied handle, 6" h 45.00

Eggcup, single, open, footed 25.00

Goblet 35.00

Pitcher, water with applied handle, 1/2-gal 250.00

Salt, master, open, footed 45.00

Sauce dish, round, flat, 4" d 5.00

Spoon holder 35.00

Known items: **Clear**

Sugar bowl with cover 65.00

Tumbler, water, footed 35.00

Wine 20.00

EUREKA (National)

OMN:

Non-flint. National Glass Co. at McKee Brothers, Jeannette, PA, c. 1901-1904.

Original color production: Clear, clear with ruby stain.

Reproductions and Look-a-Likes: None known.

Eureka (National) creamer.

Known items:	**Clear**	**Clear w/Ruby**
Bottle, cologne with original faceted stopper	$45.00	$225.00
Bowl, round, open, flat		
Straight-sided with scalloped rim, 8" d.	45.00	95.00
Triangular with scalloped rim	30.00	65.00
Butter dish, flat with cover	65.00	175.00
Cake stand on high standard, 10" d.	125.00	650.00
Celery vase	35.00	110.00
Compote on high standard, open		
Belled bowl, 9" d.	35.00	75.00
Round bowl, 4-1/2" d. (Jelly)	20.00	45.00

Known items:	Clear	Clear w/Ruby
Shallow bowl, 10" d.	40.00	85.00
Square bowl, 4-1/2"	25.00	55.00
Creamer	35.00	95.00
Cruet, 8-oz. with original faceted stopper	55.00	275.00
Pickle dish, oblong, handled	15.00	45.00
Pitcher, water	75.00	325.00
Relish dish, oblong with scalloped rim	20.00	45.00
Rose bowl, 5" d.	5.00	75.00
Salt		
Individual, round	10.00	35.00
Master (R)	55.00	125.00
Shaker		
Bulbous	25.00	65.00
Tall	30.00	75.00
Sauce dish, flat		
Round		
4" d.	5.00	20.00
4-1/2" d.	5.00	20.00
Square		
4" d.	8.00	25.00
4-1/2" d.	8.00	25.00
Spoon holder	35.00	75.00
Sugar bowl with cover	45.00	135.00
Syrup pitcher	95.00	425.00
Toothpick holder, 2-1/2" h.	25.00	55.00
Tumbler, water, flat	30.00	75.00
Vase, 9" h.	25.00	55.00

EXCELSIOR

OMN: AKA: Barrel Excelsior, Flare Top Excelsior, Giant Excelsior.

Flint. McKee Brothers, Pittsburgh, PA, c. 1859-1860. Ihmsen & Co., Pittsburgh, PA, c. 1851. Attributed to the Boston & Sandwich Glass Co., Sandwich, MA, based on shards found at the site of the factory.

Original color production: Clear.

Reproductions and Look-a-Likes: Champagne, goblet (Azure blue, clear, cobalt, pink, ruby). Dalzell-Viking Glass Company, New Martinsville, WV. Unmarked.

Excelsior true open footed bowl.

Excelsior bitters bottle and ale glass.

Known items:	Clear
Ale glass	$135.00
Bottle	
Bar	75.00
Bitters	175.00
Medicine	85.00
Water with tumbler (**Carafe**)	650.00
Bowl, round, flat	
Covered	150.00
Open, 10" d.	75.00

Excelsior carafe.

Excelsior rare water pitcher.

Known items:	Clear
Butter dish with cover	175.00
Candlesticks	
8-1/4" h., each	275.00
9-1/2" h., each	325.00
Celery vase, knob stem	95.00
Champagne	85.00
Claret (jelly glass)	275.00
Compote	
Covered on low standard	175.00
Open on standard with scalloped rim	
7-1/2" d.	85.00
10-1/2" d. (VR)	650.00
Creamer	
Table size, 6-1/2" h.	225.00
Made from a tumbler	350.00
Decanter	
Bar lip	
1-pt.	110.00
1-qt.	135.00
With original stopper	
1-pt.	250.00
1-qt.	275.00
Dish, open, oval, flat	45.00
Eggcup	
Double, open	125.00

Known items:	Clear
Single	
Covered	325.00
Open, knob stem	30.00
Goblet (2 styles)	65.00
Lamp, whale oil	
Hand	150.00
High standard	275.00
Peg font with Maltese cross on candlestick	
base (VR)	575.00
Mug with applied handle	225.00
Pickle jar with cover	325.00
Pitcher	
Milk	
1-pt.	950.00
1-qt.	1,250.00
Water, 1/2-gal.	1,000.00
Salt, master, open, footed	35.00
Spill holder	75.00
Spoon holder	65.00
Sugar bowl with cover and double-knob finial	175.00
Syrup pitcher with applied handle	350.00

Known items:	Clear
Tumbler	
Flat	
1/3-qt.	95.00
1/2-pt., ship's	135.00

Excelsior tumbler.

Eyewinker cake stand.

Known items:	Clear
Footed	
1/3-gill	65.00
1/3-pt.	75.00
1/3-qt.	85.00
Water	85.00
Whiskey	95.00
Wine	45.00

EYEWINKER

AKA: Cannon Ball, Crystal Ball, Winking Eye.

Non-flint. Attributed to the Dalzell, Gilmore & Leighton Glass Co., Findlay, OH, c. 1889.

Original color production: Clear.

Reproductions and Look-a-Likes: ash trays: 4-1/2, 7"; bowls: open footed: 5" with four-toes, 10" open; covered butter dish; compotes: covered: 4", 5" with low foot, 6", 7-1/2"; compotes: open 5", 6" on high foot; covered honey dish; covered marmalade jar; creamer; fairly lamp; goblet; milk pitcher; pickle tray; salt dip; salt and pepper; 4" sauce dish; sherbet; sugar bowl with cover; toothpick holder; tumbler; vases: 6" h., vase 8" h., water pitcher, wine (clear, colors). L.G. Wright Glass Company, New Martinsville, WV, unmarked.

Known items:	Clear
Banana dish	
Flat with upturned sides, 7-1/4"	$110.00
High standard with up turned sides	
5"	125.00
7"	135.00
8-1/2"	150.00
9"	175.00
10"	225.00
10" (made from cake stand)	450.00
Bowl, flat	
Covered, 9" d.	275.00
Open, round or square	
5" d.	45.00
6" d.	65.00
7" d.	85.00
8" d.	125.00
9" d.	150.00
10-1/2" d.	175.00
Butter dish, covered	150.00
Cake stand, high standard	
8" d.	95.00
9-1/2" d.	150.00
10" d.	275.00
Celery vase	175.00
Compote, high standard	
Covered, round bowl	
4" d.	100.00
5" d.	150.00

Eyewinker covered compote.

Eyewinker goblet.

Known items:	Clear
6" d.	200.00
7" d.	275.00
8" d.	375.00
9" d.	550.00
Open, square bowl with scalloped rim	
4" d.	65.00
5" d.	75.00
6" d.	110.00
7" d.	125.00
8" d.	150.00
9" d.	225.00
10-1/2" d.	375.00
Creamer, 5-1/2" h.	125.00
Cruet with original stopper	275.00
Fruit or orange bowl on high standard, conical shape, open	
9-1/4" d.	350.00
10" d.	425.00
Goblet	135.00
Honey dish, flat, 3-1/2" square	25.00
Lamp, kerosene with patterned font	
Finger, footed	325.00

Known items:	Clear
High standard	
7-1/2" h.	275.00
8-1/2" h.	350.00
9-1/2" h.	425.00
10-1/2" h.	550.00
Marmalade jar with cover	450.00
Pitcher	
Milk, 1-qt.	350.00
Water, 1/2-gal.	450.00
Plate, square with upturned rim	
5"	45.00
7"	65.00
8-1/2"	85.00
9"	95.00
10"	135.00
Saltshaker	150.00
Sauce dish, flat	
Round (2 sizes)	35.00
Square (2 sizes)	45.00
Spoon holder	110.00
Sugar bowl, covered	175.00
Syrup pitcher	325.00
Tumbler, water, flat	95.00

FAN WITH DIAMOND

OMN: McKee No. 3-Shell.

Non-flint. McKee & Brothers, Pittsburgh, PA, c. 1880.

Original color production: Clear.

Reproductions and Look-a-Likes: None known.

Fan with Diamond creamer.

Known items:	Clear
Butter dish with cover	
4-1/8" d.	$35.00
6-1/8" d.	55.00
Compote with cover	
High standard	85.00
Low standard	65.00

Known items:	Clear
Cordial	65.00
Creamer	
Applied handle, 5-1/2" h.	75.00
Pressed handle	35.00
Dish, oval, open, flat, 9" x 5-1/2"	30.00
Eggcup, open, pedestaled	35.00
Goblet	35.00
Pitcher, water, bulbous with applied handle, 1/2-gal.	275.00
Sauce dish, round, flat, 4" d.	5.00
Spoon holder, pedestaled	30.00
Sugar bowl with cover	55.00
Syrup with applied handle	175.00
Wine	30.00

FEATHER

OMN: Cambridge Glass No. 669, McKee's Doric. **AKA:** Cambridge Feather, Feather and Quill, Fine Cut and Feather, Indiana Feather, Indiana Swirl, Prince's Feather, Swirl, Swirl(s) and Feather(s).

Non-flint. Beatty-Brady Glass Co., Dunkirk, IN, c. 1903. Cambridge Glass Co., Cambridge, OH, c. 1902-1903. McKee Glass Co., Jeannette, PA, c. 1896-1901.

Original color production: Clear, clear with amber stain, emerald green, chocolate (water pitcher only). Originally rendered with notable variations and differences in quality.

Reproductions and Look-a-Likes: Goblet (amber, blue, clear).

Known items:	Clear	Green	Amber Stain
Banana dish			
Flat	$125.00	$550.00	—
Footed	450.00	—	—

Feather cake stand.

Feather covered butter dish.

Feather covered compote.

Known items:	Clear	Green	Amber Stain
Bowl, open, flat			
Round			
Scalloped rim, 8" d....	55.00	—	—
Smooth rim			
6" d.	30.00	85.00	95.00
7" d.	40.00	110.00	135.00
Square with scalloped rim,			
8"	225.00	—	—
Butter dish with cover			
Patterned lid rim	55.00	—	—
Plain lid rim	65.00	225.00	350.00
Cake stand on high standard			
8" d.	75.00	225.00	450.00
8-1/2" d.	85.00	235.00	450.00

Known items:	Clear	Green	Amber Stain
9-1/2" d.	110.00	275.00	475.00
10" d.	125.00	325.00	550.00
11" d. (R)	175.00	550.00	850.00
Compote			
Covered			
High standard			
6" d.	125.00	550.00	950.00
7-3/8" d.	175.00	650.00	1,000.00
8-3/8" d.	225.00	1,000.00	1,500.00
Low standard with deep bowl			
6" d.	135.00	550.00	950.00
7" d.	150.00	600.00	1,000.00
8" d.	225.00	1,000.00	1,500.00
8-1/2" d.	275.00	1,500.00	2,500.00
Open,			
Deep bowl, jelly,			
4-1/4" d.	20.00	110.00	135.00
Shallow bowl			
7" d.	85.00	225.00	—
8" d.	95.00	275.00	—
9" d.	110.00	325.00	—
10" d.	150.00	—	—
12" d. (R)	350.00	—	—
Cordial	150.00	325.00	650.00
Creamer 4-5/8" h. (2 styles)	35.00	110.00	225.00
Cruet with original faceted stopper	75.00	350.00	550.00

Feather covered sugar bowl.

Feather open compote on high standard.

Feather dinner plate.

Known items:	Clear	Green	Amber Stain
Dish, open, oval, flat			
7" d.	30.00	95.00	175.00
8-1/2" l.	35.00	110.00	225.00
9-1/4" l. (vegetable)	40.00	125.00	250.00
Goblet	65.00	325.00	250.00
Honey dish, round, flat with smooth rim, 3-1/2" d.	15.00	35.00	65.00
Marmalade jar with cover (R)	750.00	1,500.00	2,000.00

Known items:	Clear	Green	Amber Stain
Pitcher (2 styles)			
Milk, 1-qt	75.00	375.00	475.00
Water, 1/2-gal	65.00	225.00	350.00
Plate			
Cheese plate, round, flat with grooved base for blown lid (R)			
7-3/4" d.	125.00	—	—
8-1/2" d.	150.00	—	—
9-1/4" d.	175.00	—	—
Dinner, 10" d. with scalloped rim	75.00	175.00	225.00
Relish tray, flat	15.00	65.00	85.00
Saltshaker			
Tall	110.00	225.00	375.00
Squat	85.00	150.00	550.00
Sauce dish			
Flat			
Round			
Plain rim			
4" d.	8.00	45.00	75.00
4-1/2" d.	8.00	50.00	85.00
Scalloped rim			
4" d.	12.50	55.00	100.00
4-1/2" d.	15.00	65.00	110.00
Square with scalloped rim			
4" d.	45.00	—	—
4-1/2" d.	55.00	—	—

Known items:	Clear	Green	Amber Stain
Footed, round, smooth rim			
4" d......... 20.00		65.00	95.00
4-1/2" d..... 22.50		75.00	110.00
Spoon holder			
Scalloped rim....... 35.00		110.00	225.00
Smooth rim........ 25.00		—	—
Sugar bowl with cover			
(2 styles) 65.00		150.00	275.00
Syrup pitcher 250.00		650.00	1,500.00
Toothpick holder 150.00		375.00	950.00
Tumbler, water, flat 65.00		125.00	325.00
Wine			
With cut feather design...........15.00		—	—
With scalloped feather design 35.00		150.00	350.00

Feather Duster tumbler.

FEATHER DUSTER

OMN: U.S. Glass No. 15043. **AKA:** Huckle, Rosette Medallion.

Non-flint. The United States Glass Co., Pittsburgh, PA, c. Mid-1895.

Original color production: Clear, emerald green.

Reproductions and Look-a-Likes: None known.

Feather Duster covered butter.

Known items:	Clear	Emerald Green
Bowl, round, flat		
Covered		
5" d.................$35.00		$55.00
6" d.................40.00		60.00

Known items:	Clear	Emerald Green
7" d. 45.00		65.00
8" d. 55.00		75.00
Open		
5" d. 15.00		35.00
6" d. 20.00		40.00
7" d. 25.00		45.00
8" d. 35.00		55.00
Butter dish flat with cover		
Flanged rim 45.00		65.00
Plain rim................ 35.00		55.00
Cake stand on high standard		
8" d.................... 55.00		75.00
9" d.................... 65.00		85.00
10" d................... 85.00		110.00
11" d................... 110.00		125.00
Celery vase 25.00		65.00
Compote, round		
Covered		
High standard		
5" d.............. 45.00		75.00
6" d.............. 55.00		85.00
7" d.............. 65.00		95.00
8" d.............. 85.00		110.00

Known items:	Clear	Emerald Green
Low standard		
5" d.	35.00	55.00
6" d.	45.00	65.00
7" d.	55.00	75.00
8" d.	75.00	85.00
Open		
High standard		
Deep bowl		
5" d.	25.00	45.00
6" d.	30.00	50.00
7" d.	35.00	55.00
8" d.	40.00	65.00
Saucer bowl		
7" d.	25.00	45.00
8" d.	30.00	50.00
9" d.	35.00	55.00
10" d.	45.00	65.00
Low standard, deep bowl		
5" d.	25.00	45.00
6" d.	30.00	50.00
7" d.	35.00	55.00
8" d.	40.00	65.00
Creamer, 5" h.	25.00	45.00
Dish, open, oblong, flat		
7" l.	15.00	25.00
8" l.	20.00	30.00
9" l.	25.00	35.00
Eggcup, single, open	35.00	45.00
Goblet	75.00	125.00
Mug with pressed handle	25.00	45.00
Pickle dish, flat, oblong	15.00	20.00
Pitcher		
Milk, 1-qt.	35.00	55.00
Water, 1/2-gal.	45.00	65.00
Plate		
Rectangular , "McKinley Gold Standard 1896" (R)	325.00	—
Round, 7" d.	25.00	45.00
Platter, bread, rectangular	35.00	55.00
Relish tray	15.00	20.00
Saltshaker	25.00	55.00
Sauce dish, round, flat		
4" d.	5.00	10.00
4-1/2" d.	5.00	10.00
Spoon holder	20.00	45.00

Known items:	Clear	Emerald Green
Sugar bowl with cover	35.00	55.00
Tray, water, round, 11-1/2" d.	45.00	65.00
Tumbler, water, flat	25.00	45.00
Wine	35.00	55.00

FESTOON

Non-flint. Beatty-Brady Glass Co., Donkirk, In. C. 1898.

Original color production: Clear.

Reproductions and Look-a-Likes: None known.

Festoon creamer.

Known items:	Clear
Bowl, open, flat	
Rectangular	
4-1/2" x 7" l.	$45.00
9" l.	55.00
Round	
6" d.	30.00
7" d.	40.00
8" d.	50.00
Butter dish with cover	95.00

Festoon rectangular bowl.

Known items:	Clear
Cake stand on high standard	
9" d.	85.00
10" d.	110.00
Compote, open on high standard	325.00
Creamer, 4-1/2" h.	35.00
Mug	55.00

Known items:	Clear
Pickle	
Castor complete in silver plate frame	150.00
Dish, 9" l.	25.00
Jar, covered	110.00
Pitcher, water, 1/2-gal.	75.00
Plate with plain rim	
7" d.	55.00
8" d.	85.00
9" d.	95.00
Relish tray, 4-1/2" x 7-1/4"	30.00
Sauce dish, round, flat, 4-1/2" d.	10.00
Spoon holder	35.00
Sugar bowl with cover	65.00
Tray, water, round	35.00
Tumbler, water	35.00
Waste bowl	55.00

FINE CUT

OMN: Bryce No. 720. **AKA:** Finecut, Flower in Square.

Non-flint. Bryce Brothers, Pittsburgh, PA, c. 1885. The United States Glass Co., Pittsburgh, PA, c. 1891.

Original color production: Amber, blue, clear, vaseline.

Reproductions and Look-a-Likes: None known.

Fine Cut goblet.

Known items:	Amber	Blue	Clear	Vaseline
Bowl, open, flat, 8-1/4" d.	$35.00	$40.00	$30.00	$45.00
Butter dish with cover	50.00	65.00	45.00	75.00
Cake stand on high standard	95.00	110.00	85.00	125.00
Celery				
Tray	30.00	35.00	25.00	35.00
Vase in silver plated holder	55.00	65.00	45.00	85.00
Compote with cover on				
high standard	95.00	110.00	85.00	135.00

Known items:	Amber	Blue	Clear	Vaseline
Creamer	35.00	40.00	30.00	40.00
Dish, open, oblong, deep (vegetable)	15.00	20.00	15.00	25.00
Finger or waste bowl	20.00	30.00	20.00	35.00
Goblet	30.00	45.00	25.00	45.00
Pitcher, water, 1/2-gal.	95.00	125.00	75.00	125.00
Plate, round				
6" d.	8.00	10.00	5.00	10.00
7" d.	10.00	15.00	10.00	15.00
10" d.	15.00	20.00	15.00	25.00
Relish tray	15.00	20.00	15.00	25.00
Sauce dish, round, flat	5.00	8.00	5.00	10.00
Spoon holder	30.00	35.00	25.00	40.00
Sugar bowl with cover	40.00	45.00	40.00	55.00
Tray, water, round	45.00	55.00	45.00	65.00
Tumbler, water, flat	20.00	30.00	20.00	35.00
Wine	15.00	20.00	15.00	25.00

FINECUT AND BLOCK

Fine Cut and Block covered sugar.

OMN: King's No. 25.

Non-flint. King, Son & Co., Pittsburgh, PA, c. 1890. Traditionally attributed to the Portland Glass Co., Portland, ME, and the Model Flint Glass Co., Findlay, OH.

Original color production: Clear, clear with amber, blue and pink stained blocks; solid colors of amber, blue, canary yellow.

Reproductions and Look-a-Likes: Basket with applied handle; footed bonbon dish; open round footed candle bowl; covered footed candy box; open round compote on high standard with ruffled rim; open round compote on short bulbous standard; footed creamer with pressed handle; open dish with flared rim (nut); goblet; ring holder; tall footed salt shaker; 4" open sugar bowl with scalloped rim and bell-shaped foot; 4-1/2" h. flat bulbous vase with ruffled rim; 7" h. flat swung vase; footed ruffled rim vase; footed bud vase (amethyst, opaque blue, Colonial amber, Colonial blue, Colonial green, carnival, cameo opalescent, custard, clear, dark carnival, dusty rose, Federal blue, heritage green, forget-me-not blue, sea mist green, milk white, orange, periwinkle blue, country peach, ruby, candleglow yellow). Fenton Art Glass Company, Williamstown, WV. Mark: Paper label or embossed either "OV" or with the Fenton logo.

Known items:	Clear	Solid Colors	Amber Blocks	Blue Blocks	Pink Blocks
Bowl, open, flat, round					
Handled					
6" d.	$15.00	$25.00	$35.00	$30.00	$35.00
7" d.	20.00	30.00	40.00	35.00	35.00
8" d.	25.00	35.00	45.00	40.00	40.00
9" d.	30.00	40.00	50.00	45.00	45.00
10" d.	40.00	50.00	65.00	55.00	55.00
Handleless					
6" d.	15.00	25.00	45.00	35.00	35.00
7" d.	20.00	30.00	50.00	40.00	40.00
8" d.	25.00	35.00	65.00	45.00	55.00
Butter dish with cover					
Flat	55.00	—	—	—	—
Footed	75.00	150.00	175.00	150.00	175.00
Cake stand on high standard with galleried rim					
8" d.	65.00	110.00	275.00	—	—
9" d.	75.00	125.00	300.00	—	—
10" d.	85.00	135.00	325.00	—	—
11" d.	110.00	150.00	—	—	—
12" d.	135.00	175.00	—	—	—
Celery tray with turned sides	30.00	85.00	110.00	95.00	100.00
Champagne					
Round bowl	45.00	85.00	150.00	110.00	125.00
Saucer-shaped bowl	35.00	75.00	125.00	95.00	110.00
Claret, round bowl	40.00	85.00	135.00	100.00	125.00
Cologne bottle with original matching stopper					
Bulbous base with long slender neck	25.00	—	—	—	—
Tall, hexagonal shape					
2-oz.	25.00	—	—	—	—
4-oz.	30.00	—	—	—	—
6-oz.	35.00	—	—	—	—
8-oz.	40.00	—	—	—	—
10-oz.	45.00	—	—	—	—
Compote					
High standard					
Covered 8-1/2" d.	95.00	150.00	275.00	225.00	250.00
Open					
4-1/2" d. (jelly)	35.00	75.00	110.00	85.00	95.00
8-1/2" d.	45.00	65.00	85.00	75.00	75.00
Low standard					
Covered	75.00	125.00	225.00	175.00	200.00
Open, 8-1/2" d.	35.00	45.00	55.00	50.00	50.00

Known items:	Clear	Solid Colors	Amber Blocks	Blue Blocks	Pink Blocks
Cordial	65.00	125.00	225.00	175.00	175.00
Creamer	35.00	55.00	85.00	65.00	75.00
Cup, custard	15.00	25.00	45.00	35.00	40.00
Eggcup, single, open	30.00	55.00	65.00	65.00	65.00
Finger or waste bowl, round					
with scalloped rim	25.00	45.00	65.00	50.00	55.00
Goblet					
Large (Gentleman's)	45.00	85.00	110.00	95.00	100.00
Small (Lady's)	40.00	75.00	95.00	85.00	85.00
Jewel or cracker tray	55.00	110.00	135.00	110.00	125.00
Lamp, oil					
Finger	75.00	125.00	225.00	—	—
High standard					
7-1/2" d.	110.00	135.00	275.00	—	—
8-1/2" d.	125.00	150.00	300.00	—	—
9-1/2" d.	150.00	175.00	325.00	—	—
Mug	35.00	65.00	85.00	75.00	75.00
Orange bowl, flat, deep with large point and scallop rim					
8" d.	85.00	175.00	275.00	225.00	250.00
10" d.	125.00	225.00	325.00	250.00	275.00
Pickle jar with cover	95.00	175.00	250.00	200.00	225.00
Pitcher					
Milk, 3-pts.	65.00	110.00	175.00	150.00	150.00
Water, 1/2-gal.	85.00	135.00	225.00	175.00	200.00
Plate, round with scalloped rim					
5-3/4" d.	10.00	20.00	30.00	—	—
6" d.	15.00	25.00	35.00	—	—
7" d.	20.00	30.00	40.00	—	—
Relish tray, rectangular	15.00	35.00	55.00	45.00	50.00
Salt					
Dip, flat with scalloped rim					
Individual	10.00	20.00	30.00	25.00	25.00
Master	30.00	45.00	85.00	75.00	75.00
Shaker, tall	35.00	55.00	75.00	65.00	75.00
Sauce dish, round					
Flat, handled					
4" d.	10.00	10.00	15.00	10.00	10.00
5" d.	10.00	15.00	20.00	15.00	15.00
Footed					
4" d.	5.00	10.00	15.00	10.00	10.00
5" d.	10.00	15.00	20.00	15.00	15.00

Known items:	Clear	Solid Colors	Amber Blocks	Blue Blocks	Pink Blocks
Soap dish, rectangular with bracket for hanging	95.00	—	—	—	—
Soap slab, flat, rectangular	45.00	—	—	—	—
Spice barrel with cover, "Conestoga Wagon" shaped	325.00	550.00	850.00	—	—
Spoon holder	30.00	55.00	75.00	65.00	65.00
Sugar bowl with cover	55.00	110.00	150.00	135.00	135.00
Tray					
Ice cream	75.00	175.00	225.00	200.00	—
Orange bowl underplate	85.00	200.00	250.00	225.00	—
Water	75.00	150.00	200.00	175.00	—
Tumbler, water, flat	35.00	65.00	75.00	55.00	65.00
Wine	30.00	55.00	65.00	65.00	65.00

FINE CUT AND PANEL

Fine Cut and Panel goblet.

OMN: No. 260-Russian. **AKA:** Button and Oval Medallion, Nailhead and Panel.

Non-flint. Bryce Brothers, Pittsburgh, PA, Richards & Hartley Glass Co., Pittsburgh, PA, c. 1889. The United States Glass Co., Pittsburgh, PA, at Factory "B" after 1891.

Original color production: Amber, blue, clear, vaseline.

Reproductions and Look-a-Likes: None known.

Known items:	Amber	Blue	Clear	Vaseline
Bowl, open, round, flat				
Master berry, 7" d.	$40.00	$45.00	$35.00	$55.00
Waste	30.00	35.00	25.00	45.00
Butter dish with cover	50.00	65.00	45.00	75.00
Cake stand on high standard, 10" d.	110.00	135.00	95.00	150.00
Compote on high standard				
Covered	85.00	110.00	75.00	150.00
Open	40.00	45.00	35.00	50.00
Creamer	30.00	35.00	25.00	45.00

Known items:	Amber	Blue	Clear	Vaseline
Cup 15.00		20.00	15.00	20.00
Dish, open, oblong, deep				
7" l. 20.00		25.00	20.00	30.00
8" l. 25.00		30.00	25.00	35.00
9" l. 30.00		35.00	30.00	40.00
Goblet 25.00		35.00	25.00	40.00
Pickle dish, flat. 15.00		20.00	15.00	20.00
Pitcher				
Milk, 1-qt. 55.00		75.00	45.00	85.00
Water, 1/2-gal. 65.00		85.00	55.00	95.00
Plate, dinner, round				
6-1/4" d. 15.00		20.00	15.00	20.00
7-1/4" d. 20.00		25.00	20.00	25.00
Relish tray. 15.00		20.00	15.00	20.00
Sauce dish, square, footed 5.00		10.00	5.00	10.00
Spoon holder 20.00		25.00	20.00	30.00
Sugar bowl with cover 35.00		40.00	35.00	45.00
Tray				
Bread 30.00		30.00	25.00	35.00
Water, round 55.00		65.00	55.00	65.00
Tumbler, water, flat 20.00		25.00	20.00	30.00
Wine. 20.00		25.00	15.00	25.00

FINE RIB

OMN: Reeded. AKA: Fine Rib to Top.

Flint, non-flint. New England Glass Co., East Cambridge, MA, c. 1860s. McKee & Brothers Glass Co., Pittsburgh, PA, c. 1868-1869. Later reissued in non-flint.

Original color production: Clear. Opaque white, translucent white, translucent blue or any other color would be considered rare. Items. Non-flint colored items are of later manufacture.

Reproductions and Look-a-Likes: None known.

Fine Rib wine.

Known items:	Clear
Ale glass $325.00	
Bottle	
Bitters 110.00	
Water with matching tumbler 750.00	

Known items:	Clear
Bowl, flat	
Covered	
5-1/2" d. 150.00	
6" d. 225.00	
7" d. 275.00	

Fine rib true open compote.

Known items: **Clear**

Open
- 5" d. 45.00
- 5-1/2" d. 45.00
- 6" d. 55.00
- 7" d. 65.00
- 8" d. 95.00

Butter dish with cover. 225.00

Castor
- Bottles
  - Mustard 55.00
  - Oil with original stopper. 85.00
  - Shaker 45.00
- Stands (see Bellflower)

Celery vase 150.00

Champagne, 5-1/4" h. 175.00

Compote, round
- Covered
  - High standard
    - Deep bowl
      - 6" d. 375.00
      - 7" d. 450.00
    - Saucer-shaped bowl
      - 6" d. 325.00
      - 7" d. 375.00

Known items: **Clear**

- Low standard
  - Deep bowl
    - 6" d. 275.00
    - 7" d. 350.00
  - Saucer-shaped bowl
    - 6" d. 250.00
    - 7" d. 300.00
- Open
  - High standard
    - Deep bowl
      - 6" d. 65.00
      - 7" d. 75.00
      - 8" d. 95.00
      - 9" d. 110.00
      - 10" d. 175.00
    - Saucer-shaped bowl
      - 6" d. 55.00
      - 7" d. 65.00
      - 8" d. 85.00
  - Low standard
    - Deep bowl
      - 6" d. 45.00
      - 7" d. 55.00
      - 8" d. 75.00
      - 9" d. 95.00
      - 10" d. 125.00
    - Saucer-shaped bowl
      - 6" d. 45.00
      - 7" d. 55.00
      - 8" d. 75.00

Creamer with applied handle. 125.00

Cup, custard, footed. 135.00

Decanter
- With bar lip
  - 1-pt. 95.00
  - 1-qt. 125.00
- With original stopper
  - 1-pt. 375.00
  - 1-qt. 450.00

Eggcup, open, pedestaled 30.00

Goblet
- Plain band around bowl top. 85.00
- Ribbed to bowl top. 95.00

Honey dish, round, flat, 3-1/2" d. 10.00

Known items: **Clear**

Jelly glass (claret), 5" h. 225.00

Lamp, whale oil

    Finger with applied handle (2 styles). 85.00

    High standard

        All glass. 225.00

        Brass stem and marble base 150.00

Pitcher

    Milk, bulbous

        1-pt. 650.00

        1-qt.. . . . . 750.00

    Water with applied handle 1,000.00

Plate, round

    6" d. 85.00

    7" d. 95.00

Salt

    Dip, individual, open 25.00

    Master

        Covered, footed 375.00

        Open, oval, flat 65.00

Sauce dish, round, flat, 4" d.. . . . . 10.00

Spoon holder, pedestaled 65.00

Sugar bowl with cover 175.00

Tumbler

    Bar, 1/2-pt. 65.00

    Gill 85.00

    Taper, 2-Pint 110.00

    Whiskey

        1-1/2" h. applied handle. 150.00

        2-3/4" h. applied handle. 275.00

        3" h.. . . . . 110.00

Wine. 45.00

FISHSCALE

OMN: Coral.

Non-flint. Bryce Brothers, Pittsburgh, PA, c. 1888.
The United States Glass Co., Pittsburgh, PA,
c. 1891-1898.

Original color production: Clear.

Reproductions and Look-a-Likes: None known.

Fishscale dinner plate.

Known items: **Clear**

Ashtray, *"Daisy and Button Slipper"* attached to a Fishscale
    rectangular tray $225.00

Bowl, flat

    Covered, round

        6" d. 55.00

        7" d. 65.00

        8" d. 75.00

        9-1/2" d. 95.00

    Open, round with saucer bowl

        6" d. 20.00

        7" d. 25.00

        8" d. 30.00

        10" d. 45.00

Butter dish with cover 55.00

Cake stand on high standard

    9" d.. . . . . .55.00

    10" d.. . . . . .65.00

    10-1/2" d.. . . . . .75.00

    11" d.. . . . . .95.00

Celery vase, pedestaled 35.00

Compote on high standard

    Covered

        4-1/2" d. (Jelly). .45.00

        6" d. 75.00

        7" d. 85.00

        8" d. 100.00

        9" d. 125.00

        10" d. 150.00

Fishscale sugar bowl, creamer, spoon holder, butter dish.

Fishscale water set.

Fishscale true open compote on high standard.

Known items:	Clear
Open, saucer bowl	
4-1/2" d. (Jelly)	15.00
6" d.	25.00
7" d.	30.00
8" d.	35.00
9" d.	40.00
10" d.	50.00
Creamer	35.00
Goblet	35.00
Lamp, finger, flat with applied finger grip	125.00
Mug, 3-7/8" h.	75.00
Pickle scoop with taper at one end	15.00
Pitcher	
Milk, 1-qt.	45.00
Water, 1/2-gal.	65.00
Plate, square	
7"	25.00
8"	30.00
9"	35.00
10"	45.00

Known items:	Clear
Relish dish, pointed at one end	15.00
Saltshaker (R)	85.00
Sauce dish, 4"	
Flat	5.00
Footed	8.00
Spoon holder	30.00
Sugar bowl with cover	55.00
Syrup pitcher	275.00
Tray	
Condiment, rectangular	65.00
Water, round	45.00
Tumbler, water, flat, 1/2-pt. (R)	125.00
Waste	35.00

FLAMINGO HABITAT

Non-flint. Hobbs, Brockunier.& Co. c. 1880.

Original color production: Clear with acid-etched design.

Reproductions and Look-a-Likes: None known.

Known items:	Clear w/Etching
Bowl, oval, flat	
Covered	
8" l.	$175.00
9" l.	200.00
10" l.	275.00

Flamingo Habitat close up.

Flamingo Habitat covered cheese.

Known items:	Clear w/Etching
Open	
8" l.	85.00
9" l.	95.00
10" l.	110.00
Butter dish with cover.	150.00
Celery vase, pedestaled	125.00
Champagne, 5-1/2" h.	85.00
Cheese dish with blown domed lid	225.00
Claret, 4-1/2" h.	55.00
Compote on high standard	
Covered	
5" d. (Jelly)	110.00
6" d.	85.00
7" d.	100.00
8" d.	150.00
9" d.	225.00
Open	
5" d. (Jelly)	35.00
6" d.	40.00
7" d.	50.00
8" d.	65.00
9" d.	75.00
Cordial, 3-1/4" h.	95.00
Creamer.	75.00
Eggcup.	55.00
Goblet	45.00
Sauce dish, round	
Flat	12.50
Footed	15.00

Known items:	Clear w/Etching
Spoon holder	65.00
Sugar bowl with cover	100.00
Tumbler, water, flat	55.00
Wine, 4" h.	45.00

FLEUR-DE-LIS AND DRAPE

OMN: U.S. Glass No. 15009. **AKA:** Fleur-de-lis and Tassel.

Original color production: Clear, emerald green, milk white.

Reproductions and Look-a-Likes: Wine (amethyst, blue, candy swirl, chocolate, clear, delphinium, firefly, impatient, katydid, orange, opalescent orange, white, willow blue). Crystal Art Glass, Cambridge, OH. Boyd's Crystal Art Glass, Cambridge, OH. Sometimes embossed with a "D" within a heart (signifying Crystal), sometimes embossed with a "B" within a diamond (signifying Boyd's).

Known items:	Clear	Emerald Green
Bottle, water	$65.00	$135.00
Bowl, open, flat		
Berry		
6" d.	15.00	20.00
8" d.	30.00	35.00

Fleur-de-lis and Drape low-footed covered sugar bowl.

Fleur-de-lis and Drape spoon holder, sugar bowl, creamer.

Known items:	Clear	Emerald Green
Finger or waste	25.00	30.00
Butter dish with cover		
Flat	45.00	65.00
Footed with flanged rim	55.00	75.00
Cake stand on high standard		
9" d.	85.00	125.00
10" d.	110.00	135.00
Celery		
Tray, oval	25.00	35.00
Vase	45.00	55.00
Claret	45.00	65.00
Compote		
Covered		
High standard		
5" d.	45.00	55.00
6" d.	55.00	65.00
7" d.	65.00	75.00
8" d.	85.00	95.00
Low standard		
5" d.	40.00	50.00
6" d.	50.00	65.00
8" d.	75.00	95.00

Known items:	Clear	Emerald Green
Open		
High standard		
5" d.	20.00	35.00
6" d.	25.00	40.00
7" d.	30.00	45.00
8" d.	35.00	50.00
Low standard		
5" d.	20.00	35.00
6" d.	25.00	40.00
7" d.	30.00	55.00
8" d.	35.00	50.00
Creamer, 5-3/8" h.	30.00	50.00
Cruet with original stopper	65.00	110.00
Custard cup	15.00	20.00
Dish, open, oblong, flat, 8" l.	15.00	20.00
Goblet	35.00	65.00
Honey dish		
Covered with ribbed lid	225.00	425.00
Round, 3-1/2" d.		
Flat	5.00	15.00
Footed	5.00	15.00
Lamp, oil, tall	135.00	175.00
Mustard with cover	35.00	50.00
Pickle dish, boat shaped	15.00	20.00
Pitcher		
Milk, 1-qt.	45.00	65.00
Water, 1/2-gal.	55.00	85.00
Plate, round		
6" d.	15.00	25.00
7" d.	20.00	30.00
8" d.	25.00	35.00
9" d.	30.00	40.00
10" d.	35.00	45.00

Fleur-de-lis and Drape covered bowl.

Florida seven-piece water set.

Relish tray, oval	15.00	30.00
Saltshaker	30.00	55.00
Sauce dish, round		
Flat		
4" d.................	5.00	5.00
4-1/2" d.............	5.00	5.00
Footed		
4" d.................	5.00	5.00
4-1/2" d.............	5.00	5.00
Saucer (underplate to custard cup) ..	20.00	25.00
Spoon holder	30.00	40.00
Sugar bowl with cover	45.00	55.00
Sugar shaker....................	65.00	85.00
Syrup pitcher	125.00	175.00
Tray, water, round, 11-1/2" d.	55.00	65.00
Tumbler, water, flat	25.00	35.00
Wine..........................	25.00	35.00

FLORIDA

Florida covered butter dish.

OMN: United States Glass No. 15,056-Florida.
AKA: Emerald Green Herringbone (emerald green only), Paneled Herringbone (clear only), Prism and Herringbone.

Non-flint. The United States Glass Co., Pittsburgh, PA, at Factory "B," c. 1898.

Original color production: Clear, emerald green.

Reproductions and Look-a-Likes: 5-3/4" h. goblet, large square plate (amber, amethyst, blue, clear, emerald green, ruby). Unmarked.

Known items:	Clear	Emerald Green
Bowl, round, flat		
Covered	$35.00	$45.00
Open		
7-3/4 " d.............	15.00	20.00
9" d.	20.00	25.00
Butter dish with cover	35.00	40.00
Cake stand on high standard	95.00	175.00
Celery vase.....................	45.00	75.00
Compote on high standard, 6-1/2"		
Covered	35.00	55.00
Open...................	15.00	30.00
Cordial	45.00	100.00
Creamer	25.00	30.00

Florida bowl, open compote, and square relish.

Florida open jelly compote.

Known items:	Clear	Emerald Green
Cruet with original stopper	65.00	325.00
Goblet	35.00	75.00
Mustard pot with cover and attached underplate	35.00	65.00
Pickle dish, oval	15.00	20.00
Pitcher, water, 1/2-gal.	35.00	35.00
Plate, square		
7-1/4"	35.00	45.00
9-1/4"	25.00	35.00
Relish tray		
Oval	15.00	20.00
Square, plate with upturned sides		
6"	15.00	25.00
8-1/2"	20.00	35.00
Saltshaker (R)	65.00	95.00

Known items:	Clear	Emerald Green
Sauce dish, round, square top		
Handled	5.00	5.00
Handleless	5.00	5.00
Spoon holder	25.00	30.00
Sugar bowl with cover	30.00	40.00
Syrup pitcher	95.00	375.00
Tumbler, water, flat	15.00	15.00
Wine	20.00	65.00

FLOWER BAND

AKA: Bird Finial, Frosted Flower Band.

Non-flint. Maker unknown, c. 1870s.

Original color production: Clear, clear with a frosted band. Identified as *"Fruit Band"* when the flowers in the pattern have been substituted with fruit. **Note:** Finials are in the shape of finely sculpted frosted "love birds." All clear pieces are 25% less.

Reproductions and Look-a-Likes: Ashtray, open, round flat 9" d. bowl, candle holder, open compote on high standard, footed creamer with pressed handle, 9-1/2-oz. goblet, footed saltshaker, sherbet, open footed sugar bowl. (Colonial amber, colonial blue, colonial pink, clear, forget-me-not blue, country peach.) Fenton Art Glass Company, Williamstown, WV. Either unmarked or permanently embossed with the Fenton log.

Known items:	Clear w/Frosting
Butter dish with cover	$275.00
Celery vase with double handles	150.00

Flower Band butter dish.

Flower Band covered compote.

Flower Band celery.

Flower Band covered sugar.

Known items:	Clear w/Frosting
Compote with cover	
Collared base	
Oval	325.00
Round	400.00
High standard, round, 8" d.	425.00

Known items:	Clear w/Frosting
Creamer, 6" h.	125.00
Goblet	150.00
Pitcher	
Milk, 1-qt.	325.00
Water, 1/2-gal.	300.00

Known items: Clear w/Frosting

Sauce dish, round

     Flat 25.00

     Footed 45.00

Spoon holder, double-handled 125.00

Sugar bowl with cover 225.00

Flower Band creamer.

Flower Band goblet.

FLUTE

OMN. AKA: Beaded Flute, Bessimer Flute and New England Flute.

Flint, non-flint. Bakewell, Pears & Co., Pittsburgh, PA, c. 1868. McKee & Brothers, Pittsburgh, PA, c. 1859-1864.

Original color production: Clear. Miscellaneous items in amethyst, clear with amber stain (plain, engraved), cobalt blue, deep green or any other color would be considered scarce. Originally distinguished by the number of flutes appearing on an item: six flute, eight-flute, ten-flute, etc.

Reproductions and Look-a-Likes: None known.

Flute seven-piece water set.

Known items: Clear

Ale glass $55.00

Bottle, bitters 75.00

Butter dish with cover 65.00

Candlestick, 4" h. 85.00

Champagne, 5-1/2" h. 45.00

Claret (Jelly glass) 95.00

Compote, open on low standard

     8-1/2" d. 55.00

     9-1/2" d. 65.00

Creamer 45.00

Decanter with bar lip, 1-qt. 100.00

Eggcup, open, footed

     Double 45.00

     Single 25.00

Goblet 35.00

Flute decanter and tumblers.

Flute pint decanter.

Known items:	Clear
Honey dish, round, flat	5.00
Lamp, oil	225.00
Mug with applied handle, 3-1/8" h	65.00
Pitcher, water with applied handle	
Milk, 1-qt	125.00
Water 2-gal	150.00
Sauce dish, round, flat	5.00
Spoon holder	30.00
Sugar bowl with cover	55.00
Syrup pitcher with applied handle	200.00

Known items:	Clear
Water, 4-1/4" h	35.00
Whiskey with applied handle, 3-1/8" h	65.00
Wine	20.00

FLYING STORK

Non-flint. Fort Pitt Glass Works, Pittsburgh, PA, c. 1879.

Original color production: Clear.

Reproductions and Look-a-Likes: None known.

Known items:	Clear
Tumbler	
Bowl, low foot, shallow	
6" d	$55.00
7" d	65.00
8" d	85.00
Butter dish with cover	135.00
Celery vase	95.00
Compote with cover on high standard	225.00
Creamer	65.00
Goblet	110.00
Marmalade jar with cover	150.00
Pitcher, water, 1/2-gal	275.00

Flying Stork covered sugar.

Flying Stork creamer, butter dish, sugar bowl, and spoon holder.

Flying Stork goblet.

Frosted Circle covered butter.

Known items:	Clear
Sauce dish, round, footed	15.00
Spoon holder	55.00
Sugar bowl with cover	110.00

FROSTED CIRCLE

OMN: U.S. Glass No. 15,007-Horn of Plenty. **AKA:** Clear Circle (without frosting).

Non-flint. Bryce Brothers, Pittsburgh, PA, c. 1876. The United States Glass Company, Pittsburgh, PA, after 1891.

Original color production: Clear, clear with frosted circles. Clear with ruby stain or any other color would be considered rare and demand premium prices.

Reproductions and Look-a-Likes: Goblet (Clear). Unmarked.

Known items:	Clear	Clear w/Frosting
Bowl, flat		
Covered		
5" d.	$45.00	$65.00
6" d.	55.00	75.00
7" d.	65.00	85.00
8" d.	75.00	95.00
9" d.	85.00	110.00
Open		
5" d.	10.00	25.00
6" d.	15.00	30.00
7" d.	20.00	35.00
8" d.	35.00	55.00
9" d.	45.00	75.00
Butter dish with cover	65.00	110.00
Cake stand on high standard		
8" d.	75.00	125.00
9" d.	95.00	135.00

Frosted Circle covered sugar.

Frosted Circle cruet with original stopper.

Known items:	Clear	Clear w/Frosting
9-1/2" d.	110.00	150.00
10" d.	125.00	175.00
Celery vase	45.00	65.00
Champagne	75.00	125.00
Compote on high standard		
Covered		
5" d.	65.00	85.00
6" d.	75.00	95.00
7" d.	85.00	110.00
8" d.	110.00	135.00
Open		
5" d.	30.00	50.00
6" d.	35.00	55.00
7" d.	45.00	65.00
8" d.	55.00	85.00
Creamer, footed with pressed handle	35.00	55.00
Cruet with original patterned stopper	65.00	135.00
Cup, custard	25.00	45.00
Goblet	40.00	85.00
Pickle		
Dish, oblong	15.00	30.00
Jar with cover	95.00	175.00
Pitcher, water	85.00	150.00
Plate, round with smooth rim, 7" d.	25.00	45.00
Saltshaker, fall	30.00	50.00

Known items:	Clear	Clear w/Frosting
Sauce, flat	10.00	20.00
Saucer (underplate for custard cup)	20.00	35.00
Spoon holder, footed	30.00	55.00
Sugar bowl with cover	45.00	95.00
Sugar shaker	110.00	175.00
Syrup pitcher with pressed handle	150.00	275.00
Tumbler, water, flat	35.00	65.00
Wine	55.00	75.00

FRANCESWARE HOBNAIL

Non-flint. Hobbs, Brockunier & Co., Wheeling, WV, c. 1880.

Original color production: *Francesware Hobnail* clear & frosted with amber stain. Other colors not priced.

Reproductions and Look-a-Likes: None known.

Known items:	Clear/Frosted w/Amber
Bottle	
Bitters	$175.00
Water	275.00

Francesware Hobnail creamer, toothpick, and finger bowl.

Francesware Hobnail spoon holder and covered butter.

Known items:	Clear/Frosted w/Amber
Bowl, open	
Oval	
7" l.	65.00
8" l.	75.00
9" l.	85.00
Round	
Flat	
8" d.	85.00
10" d.	100.00
Footed on shell feet	
8" d.	325.00
Square	
8"	85.00
9"	95.00
Butter with cover	
Flanged	425.00
Table	110.00
Celery vase	85.00
Creamer, table.	65.00
Cruet with original stopper	500.00
Decanter with original stopper	450.00
Finger or waste bowl.	55.00
Pickle jar and cover	375.00
Pitcher (6 sizes square mouth)	
No. 0 (Miniature)	325.00
No. 1 (Hotel creamer)	225.00
No. 2 (Small milk)	200.00
No. 3 (Large milk)	175.00
No. 4 (Lemonade)	225.00
No. 5 (Water)	275.00

Known items:	Clear/Frosted w/Amber
Saltshaker	175.00
Sauce	
Round, 4-1/2" d.	35.00
Square, 4-1/2"	30.00
Spoon holder	55.00
Sugar bowl with cover	85.00
Syrup.	550.00
Toothpick or child's tumbler	110.00
Tray, water	150.00
Tumbler, water.	65.00

FROSTED CHICKEN

OMN: No. 76 Ware **AKA:** Chick, Chicken.

Non-flint. Riverside Glass Works, Wellsburg, WV, c. Late 1880.

Original color production: Clear (plain, engraved). **Note:** Finials are in the shape of finely sculpted frosted "chicks."

Reproductions and Look-a-Likes: None known.

Known items:	Clear
Bowl, oval, flat	
7" l.	$85.00
8" l.	95.00
9" l.	110.00
Butter dish with cover	225.00
Celery vase, double-handled.	75.00

Frosted Chicken covered compote.

Frosted Chicken covered sugar.

Known items:	Clear
Compote with cover	
High standard	
6" d.	250.00
7" d.	275.00
8" d.	325.00
Low standard	
6" d.	225.00
7" d.	250.00
8" d.	275.00

Frosted Chicken goblet, marmalade, and creamer group.

Known items:	Clear
Creamer	65.00
Eggcup	95.00
Goblet	225.00
Horseradish or mustard, covered with notched lid.	375.00
Marmalade jar with cover	
Flat (VR)	475.00
Footed (R)	350.00
Pitcher	
Milk	225.00
Water	450.00
Salt	
Dip, flat	35.00
Master	
Flat	85.00
Footed	65.00
Shaker with double handles	85.00
Sauce dish, round, footed with double handles	25.00
Spoon holder with double handles	55.00
Sugar bowl with cover	200.00

FROSTED EAGLE

AKA: Frosted Hawk, Old Abe.

Non-flint. Attributed by early researchers to the Crystal Glass Co., Bridgeport, OH, c. 1883.

Original color production: Clear with acid finish (plain, engraved). **Note:** Finials are in the shape of finely sculpted "frosted eagles."

Reproductions and Look-a-Likes: None known.

Frosted Eagle sugar bowl and butter.

Frosted Leaf champagne.

Known items:	Clear w/Frosting
Bowl with cover on collared base, 6" d.	$200.00
Butter dish with cover, 8" d.	
Handled with double-rings	225.00
Handleless	150.00
Celery vase	85.00
Compote with cover on high standard.	250.00
Creamer with pressed handle, 6" h.	75.00
Jam jar with cover	750.00
Pitcher, water, 1/2-gal.	275.00
Salt	
Dip	45.00
Master	125.00
Shaker	55.00
Spoon holder with double handles	65.00
Sugar bowl with cover and double handles	175.00

FROSTED LEAF

Flint. Attributed by early researchers to both the Portland Glass Co., Portland, ME, c. 1873-1874 and the Boston & Sandwich Glass Co., Sandwich, MA, c. 1860.

Original color production: Clear with machine frosted leaves. Amethyst or any other color would be considered very rare.

Reproductions: 4-oz. wine (clear & frosted). Permanently embossed with the "S.I." monogram of the Smithsonian Institution.

Frosted Leaf master salt.

Known items:	Clear w/Frosting
Butter dish with cover	$325.00
Celery vase	275.00
Champagne	375.00
Compote with cover on high standard	450.00
Creamer	550.00

Known items: **Clear w/Frosting**

Decanter,

    1-pt. with cut shoulders and

        matching stopper 475.00

    1-qt. with matching stopper............. 525.00

Eggcup, open, single......................... 125.00

Goblet

    Gentleman's (large)..................... 275.00

    Lady's (small)......................... 225.00

Lamp, oil, brass stem with milk white base 350.00

Pitcher, water with applied handle, 2-gal. (ER) ...3,500.00

Salt, master, footed 95.00

Sauce dish, flat, 4" d........................ 25.00

Spoon holder 175.00

Sugar bowl with cover 275.00

Tumbler

    Flat 225.00

    Footed............................... 150.00

Wine...................................... 175.00

Frosted Ribbon four-piece table set.

FROSTED RIBBON

OMN: Duncan's No. 150. **AKA:** Ribbon.

Non-flint. George Duncan & Sons, Pittsburgh, PA, c. 1878-1886. The United States Glass Co., Pittsburgh, PA, after 1891.

Original color production: Clear, clear & frosted (plain, engraved). Items manufactured by George Duncan & Sons may be identified by the thumbprints on the knob of stemmed items. All clear items are 30-50% less than clear with frosted items.

Reproductions and Look-a-Likes: None.

Known items: **Clear w/Frosting**

Bottle, bitters................................ $75.00

Butter dish with cover, 6" d..................... 65.00

Celery vase, pedestaled 45.00

Champagne................................. 85.00

Claret..................................... 75.00

Compote

    Covered

        High standard

            6" d............................. 55.00

            7" d............................. 65.00

Frosted Ribbon decanter.

Known items: **Clear w/Frosting**

        8" d..............................75.00

        9" d..............................110.00

        10" d.............................125.00

    Low standard with deep bowl

        6" d..............................45.00

        7" d..............................55.00

        8" d..............................65.00

        9" d..............................95.00

        10" d.............................110.00

Open

    High standard

        Deep bowl

            5" d. 20.00

            6" d. 25.00

            7" d. 30.00

            8" d. 35.00

            9" d. 45.00

            10" d. 55.00

Frosted Ribbon etched goblet.

Frosted Ribbon water pitcher.

Known items: **Clear w/Frosting**

Saucer-shaped bowl

 5" d.......................... 20.00

 6" d.......................... 25.00

 7" d.......................... 30.00

 8" d.......................... 35.00

 9" d.......................... 45.00

 10" d.......................... 55.00

Low standard

 5" d.......................... 15.00

 6" d.......................... 20.00

 7" d.......................... 25.00

 8" d.......................... 30.00

 9" d.......................... 35.00

 10" d.......................... 40.00

Cordial.......................... 95.00

Creamer.......................... 45.00

Cup, custard.......................... 20.00

Decanter, 1-qt. with original faceted stopper 110.00

Dish, open, octagonal, flat

 7" l. 15.00

 8" l. 20.00

 9" l. 25.00

Eggcup, open, footed 25.00

Goblet 35.00

Pickle jar, covered 135.00

Pitcher

 Milk, 1-qt.......................... 95.00

 Water, 1/2- (gal.) 85.00

Known items: **Clear w/Frosting**

Salt

 Master, open, footed with scalloped rim.....35.00

 Shaker..................................30.00

Sauce dish, round

 Flat

  Flared, scalloped

   4" d...............................10.00

   4-1/2" d...........................12.50

  Straight-sided, scalloped rim, 4" d.......10.00

  Footed with scalloped rim

   4" d. 10.00

   4-1/2" d. 15.00

Sherry 45.00

Spoon holder 40.00

Sugar bowl with cover 55.00

Tumbler, water, flat............................30.00

Wine 45.00

FROSTED STORK

AKA: Flamingo, Frosted Crane.

Non-flint. Crystal Glass Co., Bridgeport, OH, c. 1880s.

Original color production: Clear, clear with frosting. **Note:** Finials are in the shape of finely sculpted "storks."

Reproductions and Look-a-Likes: 11-3/4" l. bread plate; 5-1/4" h. spoon holder (clear, clear with frosting). A.A. Importing Company, Inc., St. Louis, MI. Unmarked., (clear, clear with frosting, vaseline). Goblet (amber, blue, clear) Summit Art Glass Company, Akron, OH. Also, L.G. Wright Glass Company, New Martinsville, WV. Wright goblets are unmarked; Summit goblets are permanently impressed with a "V" within a circle.

Frosted Stork goblet.

Known items:	Clear	Clear w/Frosting
Bowl, open, flat		
Oval, flat	$65.00	$85.00
Round		
Berry		
8" d.	55.00	95.00
9" d.	75.00	110.00
Finger or waste	55.00	75.00
Butter dish with cover	175.00	275.00
Creamer	65.00	95.00
Goblet	125.00	150.00
Marmalade jar with cover	135.00	175.00
Pitcher, water, 1/2-gal.	300.00	350.00
Plate, round, handled, 9" d.	50.00	65.00
Platter, oval, 8" x 11-1/2"		
With *"One-O-One"* border	75.00	125.00
With scenic border	65.00	100.00
Relish tray	45.00	55.00
Sauce dish, round, flat	20.00	25.00

Known items:	Clear	Clear w/Frosting
Spoon holder	65.00	85.00
Sugar bowl with cover	150.00	175.00
Water tray, round	125.00	175.00

FUCHSIA

AKA: Clear Fuchsia.

Non-flint. Maker unknown, c. 1875-1885.

Original color production: Clear.

Reproductions and Look-a-Likes: None known.

Fuchsia spoon holder.

Known items:	Clear
Bowl, open, oval, flat	
7" l.	$30.00
8" l.	35.00
9" l.	45.00
Butter dish with cover	110.00
Celery vase (R)	225.00
Creamer, 5-1/2" h.	85.00
Goblet	55.00
Pickle tray	15.00
Pitcher, water, 1/2-gal.	325.00
Sauce dish, round, flat, 4" d.	10.00
Spoon holder	45.00
Sugar bowl with cover	95.00
Tumbler, footed	85.00

GALLOWAY

OMN: U.S. Glass No. 15,086-Mirror. Jefferson's No. 15,601. **AKA:** Mirror Plate, U.S. Mirror, Virginia, Woodrow.

Non-flint. The United States Glass Co., Pittsburgh, PA, c. 1904. Jefferson Glass Co., Toronto, Canada between 1900 and 1925.

Original color production: Clear, clear with a rose blush (plain, gilded). Clear with ruby stain or any other color would be considered rare. Issued in three conspicuous forms: (a) a "table set" distinguished by straight sides, (b) a "hotel set" distinguished by its distinct squat shapes, and (c) an individual or "berry set" distinguished by its distinct shape and size.

Reproductions and Look-a-Likes: 2-1/2" h. toothpick holder, 6-qt. punch bowl, punch cups, 20" punch bowl underplate (clear, amber, amethyst, blue, green, orange). Trans-World Trading Company, Robinson, IL, Mosser Glass, Inc., Cambridge, OH, United States Glass Company, Tiffin, OH, unmarked.

Galloway castor insert.

Galloway butter tub.

Known items:	Clear	Clear w/Rose stain
Basket with applied handle	$225.00	$550.00
Bottle, water	85.00	275.00
Bowl, flat		
Open		
Belled bowl		
5-1/2" d	25.00	45.00
6-1/2" d	30.00	50.00
7-1/2" d	35.00	55.00
8-1/2" d	40.00	65.00
10" d	65.00	85.00
Rectangular		
6"	25.00	45.00
9"	35.00	55.00
Round		
5-1/2" d	25.00	45.00
6-1/2" d	30.00	50.00
7-1/2" d	35.00	55.00
8-1/2" d	40.00	65.00
9-1/2" d	45.00	65.00
11" d	65.00	85.00
Waste	55.00	110.00

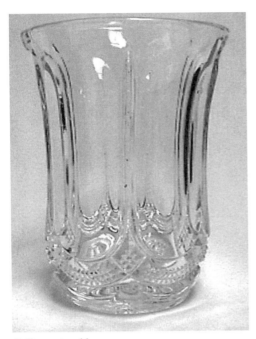

Galloway tumbler.

Known items:	Clear	Clear w/Rose stain
Butter dish with cover		
Hotel size	95.00	225.00
Quarter pound	65.00	150.00
Table size	75.00	175.00
Butter Tub	75.00	
Cake stand on high standard		
8-1/2" d.	125.00	375.00
9" d.	135.00	400.00
10" d.	150.00	425.00
Celery vase	65.00	95.00
Compote, open on high standard, deep bowl		
5-1/2" d.	35.00	65.00
6-1/2" d.	40.00	75.00
7-1/2" d.	45.00	85.00
8" d.	65.00	95.00
8-1/2" d.	75.00	100.00
9" d.	85.00	125.00
10" d.	110.00	175.00
Cracker jar with original lid		
Britannia lid (R)	325.00	650.00
Patterned lid. (R)	450.00	1,250.00
Creamer		
Hotel size	85.00	150.00
Individual size	25.00	55.00
Table size, tankard shape, 4-1/2" h.	35.00	85.00

Known items:	Clear	Clear w/Rose stain
Cruet with original stopper, 5-oz.	65.00	150.00
Cup, custard	15.00	35.00
Dish, open, flat		
Oblong		
8" l	30.00	55.00
9" l	35.00	60.00
10" l	40.00	65.00
11" l	55.00	75.00
Oval		
Crimped rim		
6-1/2" l	25.00	55.00
8-1/2" l	30.00	65.00
Ledged rim, 5-1/4"	25.00	55.00
Plain rim		
5-1/4"	20.00	45.00
8-1/2"	30.00	50.00
9-1/2"	35.00	55.00
10"	45.00	65.00
Goblet		
Flared bowl	125.00	250.00
Straight-sided bowl	110.00	225.00
Jelly, flat, handled, 5"	25.00	40.00
Lemonade, tall with handle	45.00	85.00
Mug with handle	35.00	65.00
Olive dish, round		
Handled, 5-1/4"	25.00	45.00
Handleless, 5-1/4"	20.00	40.00
Tri-cornered, 5-3/4"	30.00	50.00
Pickle		
Castor, complete in silver plate holder	175.00	375.00
Dish, 8-1/2" l	15.00	45.00
Jar, silverplate lid	85.00	150.00
Pitcher		
Ice jug with applied handle, 2-quarts	225.00	375.00
Milk, 1-quart	75.00	175.00
Tankard		
Large	135.00	275.00
Medium	110.00	250.00
Small	85.00	225.00

Galloway four-piece table set.

Known items:	Clear	Clear w/Rose stain
Plate, round		
4" d.	55.00	85.00
5" d.	65.00	95.00
6" d.	75.00	110.00
8" d.	95.00	125.00
Punch bowl with foot, 15" d.	325.00	750.00
Punch bowl underplate	175.00	375.00
Relish tray	15.00	35.00
Rose bowl	75.00	125.00
Salt		
Dip		
Individual, oblong	25.00	45.00
Master, flat		
Oblong	55.00	95.00
Round	95.00	225.00
Shaker		
Squat, bulbous base	35.00	95.00
Tall, bulbous	25.00	65.00
Sauce dish, round, flat		
Flared, belled bowl		
4" d.	10.00	20.00
4-1/2" d.	10.00	20.00
Straight-sided bowl		
4" d.	10.00	20.00
4-1/2" d.	10.00	20.00
Sherbet, footed, 3-1/4" h.	25.00	55.00
Spoon holder		
Hotel size	85.00	150.00
Table size	35.00	85.00

Known items:	Clear	Clear w/Rose stain
Sugar bowl with cover		
Hotel size, 7-1/4" h.	95.00	175.00
Individual, open, oval, flat	25.00	55.00
Table size, 7-1/4" h.	65.00	125.00
Sugar shaker	95.00	225.00
Syrup pitcher		
7-oz.	95.00	250.00
10-oz.	110.00	275.00
Toothpick holder	20.00	65.00
Tray, water		
8-1/2" d.	135.00	375.00
10" d.	150.00	425.00
Tumbler with pressed or ground base, water, table size, 4" h.	30.00	65.00
Vase		
Bulbous base with tapered center with flared rim, 8" h.	45.00	85.00
Cylindrical shaped with pulled rim, 11" h.	55.00	125.00
Straight sided, swung		
5-1/2" h.	55.00	—
18" h.	125.00	—
Wine	20.00	55.00

GARDEN OF EDEN

AKA: Fish, Lotus, Lotus and Serpent, Lotus with Serpent, Turtle.

Non-flint. Maker unknown. c. late 1870s, early 1880s.

Original color production: Clear.

Reproductions and Look-a-Likes: None known.

Garden of Eden water pitcher.

Garden of Eden goblet.

Known items:	Clear
Butter dish with cover	
Plain stem	$75.00
Serpent stem	125.00
Cake stand on high standard	135.00
Compote, open on high standard with shallow bowl	
6-1/2" d.	45.00
7-3/4" d.	65.00
8-1/2" d.	75.00
9-1/2" d.	95.00
Creamer	
Individual, 3-1/2" h.	25.00
Table size, 5" h.	55.00
Eggcup, open, single	45.00

Known items:	Clear
Goblet	
Plain stem	85.00
Serpent stem	375.00
Honey dish, round, flat	10.00
Mug	45.00
Pickle dish, oval	25.00
Pitcher, water, 1/2-gallon	125.00
Plate	
Oval, bread, handled with *"Give Us This Day Our Daily Bread"* center	45.00
Round, handled, 6" d.	25.00
Relish dish, oval, flat	
Handled	15.00
Handleless	20.00
Sauce dish, round	
Flat	5.00
Footed	8.00
Spoon holder	40.00
Sugar bowl with cover	85.00

GARFIELD DRAPE

> **AKA:** Canadian Drape.
>
> Non-flint. Attributed by early researchers to Adams & Co., Pittsburgh, PA.
>
> **Original color production:** Clear.
>
> **Reproductions and Look-a-Likes:** None known.

Garfield Drape flared celery vase.

Known items:	Clear
Bowl, open, flat	$30.00
Butter dish with cover	125.00
Cake stand on high standard, 9-1/2" d.	200.00
Celery vase, 8-1/2" h.	
Flared	110.00
Straight-sided	85.00
Compote	
Covered	
High standard, 8" d.	225.00
Low standard, 6" d.	150.00
Open on high standard, 8-1/2" d.	75.00
Creamer, 5-1/2" h.	
Applied handle	95.00
Pressed handle	45.00

Known items:	Clear
Goblet	
Large (Gentleman's)	85.00
Small (Lady's) (R)	150.00
Honey dish, round, flat	15.00
Lamp, oil on high standard	275.00
Pickle dish, oval	20.00
Pitcher, bulbous with applied handle	
Milk, 1-quart	150.00
Water, 1/2-gallon	225.00
Plate, bread, 11" d.	
"Memorial portrait of Garfield"	45.00
"We Mourn Our Nation's Loss" center	65.00
"Star" center	45.00
Relish tray, oval	20.00
Sauce dish, round, 3-1/2" d.	
Flat	10.00
Footed	15.00
Spoon holder	40.00
Sugar bowl with cover	95.00
Tumbler, water	
Flat	85.00
Footed	65.00

GEORGIA

> **OMN:** U.S. Glass No. 15076-Georgia.
> **AKA:** Peacock Eye, Peacock Feather(s).
>
> Non-flint. Richards & Hartley Glass Co., Pittsburgh, PA. The United States Glass Co., at Factory "E," c. 1902.
>
> **Original color production:** Clear. Blue or any other color would be considered rare.
>
> **Reproductions and Look-a-Likes:** None known.

Known items:	Clear
Bowl, open, round, flat	
5" d.	$15.00
6" d.	20.00
7" d.	35.00
8" d.	45.00

Georgia covered butter dish.

Georgia deep open bowl.

Known items:	Clear
Butter dish with cover	
Quarter pound	55.00
Table size	65.00
Cake stand on high standard	
8-1/2" d.	55.00
9" d.	65.00
10" d.	75.00
11" d.	125.00
Celery, boat shaped	25.00
Compote on high standard	
Covered	
5" d.	55.00
6" d.	65.00
7" d.	75.00
8" d.	110.00
Open	
Deep bowl	
5" d.	20.00
6" d.	25.00
7" d.	30.00
8" d.	40.00
Shallow bowl, saucer-shaped	
8" d.	35.00
9" d.	45.00
10" d.	5.00
Creamer	
Individual, 2" h. (R)	95.00
Table, 4-1/4" h.	45.00
Cruet, 8-1/4" h. with original stopper	65.00

Known items:	Clear
Decanter, 14-oz. with original stopper	85.00
Lamp, oil	
Chamber on short foot, 7" h.	150.00
Flat with ring handle, 5-3/4" h.	85.00
High standard	
7-1/2" h.	125.00
8-1/2" h.	150.00
9-1/2" h.	225.00
Mug	35.00
Pickle dish, oblong with pointed ends	15.00
Pitcher, water, 1/2-gallon	85.00
Plate, 5-1/4" d.	35.00
Preserve dish, 8" l. with pointed ends	20.00
Relish tray	15.00
Saltshaker	35.00
Sauce dish, round, flat	
4" d.	10.00
4-1/2" d.	10.00
Spoon holder	45.00
Stand, condiment, salt and pepper	30.00
Sugar bowl with cover	65.00
Sweetmeat, deep bowl on low standard	
Covered	75.00
Open	30.00
Syrup pitcher	110.00
Tumbler, water, flat	40.00

Georgia water pitcher.

Giant Bull's Eye goblet.

GIANT BULL'S EYE

OMN: Bellaire No. 151, U.S. Glass No. 157.
AKA: Bull's Eye and Spearhead, Bull's Eye Variation, Concave Circle, Excelsior.

Non-flint. Bellaire Goblet Co., Bellaire, OH, c. 1889. Model Flint Glass Co., c. 1891. The United States Glass Co., Pittsburgh, PA, after 1891.

Original color production: Clear.

Reproductions and Look-a-Likes: None known.

Known items:	Clear
Bottle	
Brandy with original patterned stopper	
12-oz.	$35.00
16-oz.	45.00
22-oz.	55.00
Perfume with original patterned stopper	30.00
Bowl, open, flat, 8" d.	35.00
Butter dish with cover	55.00
Cake stand on high standard	125.00
Cheese dish with cover	175.00

Known items:	Clear
Compote on high standard	
Covered	95.00
Open	
Flared rim	45.00
Scalloped rim	55.00
Condiment set (cruet, salt/pepper shakers, mustard)	175.00
Creamer	35.00
Cruet with original patterned stopper	65.00
Decanter with original patterned stopper	
Claret	75.00
Wine	65.00
Goblet	40.00
Mustard, metal screw lid	35.00
Lamp, night with tall domed shade, "*Remington*"	375.00
Pitcher with pressed handle	
Claret, 7" h.	75.00
Water, 1/2-gal.	85.00
Relish tray	15.00
Sauce dish, round, flat, 4" d.	5.00
Saltshaker	30.00
Spoon holder	30.00
Sugar bowl with cover	55.00

Known items:	Clear
Syrup pitcher	
Large	110.00
Small	95.00
Tray, round	
Water	50.00
Wine	40.00
Tumbler, water, flat	35.00
Vase	
7" h.	25.00
8" h.	30.00
9" h.	35.00
Wine	20.00

GIBSON GIRL

OMN: Medallion.

Non-flint. McKee-Jeannette Glass Company, c. 1904.

Original color production: Clear, clear with frosted medallions. Rare examples are known in clear with gilded medallions.

Reproductions and Look-a-Likes: None known.

Gibson Girl spoon holder, butter dish, sugar bowl, and creamer.

Gibson Girl rare gilded spoon holder.

Gibson Girl seven-piece berry set with bowl depicting Gibson Girl motif.

Gibson Girl seven-piece water set.

Known items:	Clear	Clear w/Frosting
Bowl, master berry, round, flat	$150.00	$250.00
Butter dish with cover	325.00	450.00
Creamer	110.00	175.00

Known items:	Clear	Clear w/Frosting
Pitcher, water	650.00	1,000.00
Relish tray, oval	150.00	225.00
Saltshaker	175.00	225.00

Gibson Girl close-up.

Gibson Girl tumbler.

Gibson Girl oval relish.

Gibson Girl water pitcher.

Known items:	Clear	Clear w/Frosting
Sauce dish, round, flat. 35.00		50.00
Spoon holder 100.00		175.00

Known items:	Clear	Clear w/Frosting
Sugar bowl with cover 250.00		350.00
Tumbler, water. 100.00		135.00

GONTERMAN

OMN: Duncan No. 95.

Non-flint. George Duncan's Sons, Pittsburgh, PA, c. 1887-1890.

Original color production: Amber stain with frosting.

Reproductions and Look-a-Likes: None known.

Gonterman sugar bowl, creamer, and footed butter dish.

Gonterman rare goblet.

Gonterman spoon holder.

Known items:	Amber w/Frosting
Bowl, open	
Flat	
7" d.	$175.00
8" d.	225.00
Footed	
7" d.	200.00
8" d.	225.00
Butter dish with cover	325.00
Cake stand on high standard, 10" d.	650.00
Celery vase, pedestaled	175.00
Compote, round on high standard	
Covered	
5" d.	350.00
7" d.	450.00
8" d.	650.00
Open	
5" d.	150.00
7" d.	200.00
8" d.	250.00
Creamer	175.00

Known items:	Amber w/Frosting
Goblet (R)	1,000.00
Pickle jar	
In silver-plated caster frame	950.00
With original glass lid	675.00
Pitcher	
Milk, 1-qt.	650.00
Water, 1/2-gal.	850.00
Saltshaker	325.00

Gonterman water pitcher.

Good Luck close up.

Known items:	Amber w/Frosting
Sauce dish, round	
Flat	
3-1/2" d.	45.00
4" d.	50.00
4-1/2" d.	55.00
Footed	
4" d.	50.00
4-1/2" d.	55.00
Spoon holder	150.00
Sugar bowl with cover	275.00

GOOD LUCK

AKA: Horseshoe, Prayer Mat, Prayer Rug.

Non-flint. Adams & Co., Pittsburgh, PA, c. 1881, the pattern was designed by Mr. Samuel G. Vogeley.

Original color production: Clear. Amber or any other color would be considered very rare.

Reproductions and Look-a-Likes: Small oval bread platter with single horseshoe handle (clear). Unmarked.

Known items:	Clear
Bowl, oval, flat	
Open	
8" l.	$35.00
9-1/4" l.	40.00
10-1/4" l.	45.00
Covered	
7" l.	175.00
8" l.	200.00
9" l.	225.00
Butter dish with cover	125.00
Cake stand on high standard	
8" d.	275.00
9" d.	150.00
10" d.	175.00
Celery vase	
Knob stem	110.00
Plain stem	75.00
Cheese dish with cover and *"woman churning"* center in base.	325.00
Compote	
Covered	
High standard	
7-1/2" d.	225.00
8" d.	250.00
Low standard	
7-1/2" d.	150.00
8" d.	200.00

Good Luck double-handled bread plate.

Good Luck waste bowl.

Known items:	Clear
Open on high standard, 11" d.	275.00
Creamer	
Hotel, flat (VR)	275.00
Table size, footed	35.00
Finger or waste bowl, round	125.00
Goblet	
Knob stem	75.00
Plain stem	45.00
Marmalade jar with cover	325.00
Pickle dish	25.00
Pitcher	
Milk, 1-qt.	150.00
Water, 1/2-gal.	125.00
Plate	
7" d.	65.00
7-1/4" d.	75.00
8-1/4" d.	85.00
10-1/4" d.	110.00
Relish	
Tray 7" l.	20.00
Wheelbarrow-shaped with attached pewter wheel, 8" l.	150.00
Salt	
Individual, horseshoe-shaped	25.00
Master	
Horseshoe-shaped	35.00
Round with design from base to rim (R)	150.00
Wheelbarrow-shaped with attached pewter wheel	125.00

Known items:	Clear
Sauce dish, round	
Flat	
3-3/4" d.	8.00
4" d.	8.00
4-1/4" d.	8.00
Footed	
3-3/4" d.	8.00
4" d.	10.00
4-1/4" d.	10.00
Spoon holder	35.00
Sugar bowl with cover	125.00
Tray	
Bread, single horseshoe handles, 10" x 14"	35.00
Water, double horseshoe handles	175.00
Wine (R)	275.00

GOOSEBERRY

Non-flint. Manufacturer unknown.

Original color production: Clear, milk white.

Reproductions and Look-a-Likes: Goblet (clear) mug with pressed handle (milk white), wine (clear). Unmarked.

Gooseberry milk white creamer.

GOTHIC

AKA: Cathedral.

Flint. Maker unknown. Attributed by early researchers to the Union Glass Co., Somerville, MA, c. 1860s.

Original color production: Clear.

Reproductions and Look-a-Likes: None known.

Gothic celery vase.

Known items:	Clear	Milk White
Bowl, open, flat, master berry	$45.00	$65.00
Butter dish with cover............	75.00	95.00
Cake stand on high standard.....	175.00	—
Compote with cover on high standard		
6" d.	95.00	110.00
7" d.	125.00	150.00
8" d.	150.00	175.00
Creamer, 5" h...................	45.00	55.00
Goblet	55.00	65.00
Lemonade glass with applied		
handle	85.00	—
Mug with pressed handle........	45.00	55.00
Pitcher, water with applied handle,		
1/2-gal.	375.00	550.00
Sauce dish, round, flat...........	10.00	15.00
Spoon holder	35.00	45.00
Sugar bowl with cover	65.00	75.00
Syrup pitcher	225.00	325.00
Tumbler, water, flat	55.00	65.00

Known items:	Clear
Bowl, open, flat with scalloped rim	
7" d.	$95.00
8" d.	110.00
Butter dish with cover	175.00
Castor bottle	
Mustard	45.00
Oil with original stopper..................	65.00
Shaker.................................	55.00
Celery vase....................................	350.00
Champagne	325.00

Known items:	Clear
Compote	
Covered	
High standard	
7" d. 275.00	
8" d. 325.00	
Low standard, 8" d. 225.00	
Open	
High standard, 8" d. 135.00	
Low standard	
7" d. 75.00	
8" d. 85.00	
Creamer. 225.00	
Eggcup, single, open 35.00	
Goblet	
Plain base 65.00	
Rayed base 75.00	
Lamp, oil, brass stem and marble base (R) 750.00	
Pickle dish, oval, 7" l. 35.00	
Plate (R). 150.00	
Salt, aster, open, footed 85.00	
Sauce dish, round, flat, 4" d. 15.00	
Spoon holder, pedestaled 65.00	
Sugar bowl with cover 175.00	
Tumbler, water, flat 150.00	
Wine. 110.00	

Gothic celery vase.

GOTHIC (McKEE)

OMN. AKA: Spearpoint Band.

Non-flint. McKee-Jeannette Glass Company, Jeannette, PA, c. 1904.

Original color production: Clear, clear with ruby stain.

Reproductions and Look-a-Likes: None known.

Known items:	Clear	Clear w/Ruby
Bowl		
Berry, open with scalloped rim. \$45.00		\$125.00
Fruit, open, flat 45.00		110.00

Known items:	Clear	Clear w/Ruby
Vegetable, oblong, flat with scalloped rim..... 25.00		45.00
Butter dish with cover and pyramid-shaped finial.. 45.00		110.00
Celery vase. 35.00		85.00
Compote, open on high standard with scalloped rim (Jelly).20.00		55.00
Creamer, 4-1/4" h. 30.00		55.00
Eggcup, single, open, footed 25.00		55.00
Pitcher, water, 1/2-gallon 75.00		150.00
Relish tray 15.00		35.00
Saltshaker, tall 25.00		65.00
Sauce dish, round, flat 5.00		25.00
Spoon holder with scalloped rim .. 30.00		65.00
Sugar bowl with cover 35.00		75.00
Toothpick holder. 20.00		85.00
Tumbler, water, flat. 20.00		55.00
Wine 15.00		45.00

GRAND

OMN: New Grand. **AKA:** Diamond Medallion, Fine Cut and Diamond, Fine Cut Medallion.

Non-flint. Bryce, Higbee & Co., Pittsburgh, PA, c. 1885.

Original color production: Clear. Clear with ruby stain or any other color would be considered rare.

Reproductions and Look-a-Likes: None known.

Grand water set.

Grand covered butter dish.

Grand covered compote.

Known items:	Clear
Bowl	
Covered, 6" d.	
Flat	$45.00
Low footed	65.00
Open, low footed	
6" d.	25.00
7" d.	30.00
Butter dish with cover, 6-1/4" d.	
Flat	45.00
Footed	55.00
Cake stand on high standard	
8" d.	55.00
8-1/2" d.	65.00
10" d.	85.00

Known items:	Clear
Celery vase	35.00
Compote	
Covered	
High standard	
5-1/2" d.	75.00
6" d.	65.00
7" d.	75.00
7-1/2" d.	85.00
8" d.	100.00
Low standard	
6" d.	55.00
7" d.	65.00
8" d.	85.00
Open	
High standard	
6" d.	25.00
7" d.	30.00
8" d.	35.00
9" d.	45.00
Low standard	
6" d.	20.00
7" d.	25.00
8" d.	35.00
Cordial, 2" h.	95.00

Grand covered sugar bowl.

Grand goblet.

Known items: **Clear**

Creamer, 5" h.		30.00
Decanter with original stopper		150.00
Dish, oval, open, flat		
	7" l.	20.00
	8" l.	25.00
	9" l.	30.00
Goblet		
	Plain stem	25.00
	Ring stem	30.00
Mug		45.00

Known items: **Clear**

Pitcher, water with applied handle, 1/2-gal.		65.00
Plate with scalloped rim		
	10" d.	25.00
	11" d.	30.00
Relish dish, oval, 7-1/2" l.		15.00
Saltshaker		35.00
Sauce dish, round, 4" d.		
	Flat with plain rim	5.00
	Footed with scalloped rim	5.00
Sherbet		20.00
Spoon holder		25.00
Sugar bowl		
	Plain rim	40.00
	Scalloped rim	45.00
Syrup pitcher		175.00
Tray, water, round		55.00
Waste bowl with collared base		35.00
Wine		30.00

GRAPE AND FESTOON

OMN: Doyle No. 25, Wreath.

Non-flint. The Boston & Sandwich Glass Co., Sandwich, MA, c. 1880s. Doyle & Co., Pittsburgh, PA. The United States Glass Company, Pittsburgh, PA, c. 1891.

Original color production: Clear. Produced in four noticeable variations: with (a) clear leaf, (b) stippled grape, (c) stippled leaf and (d) veined leaf.

Reproductions and Look-a-Likes: None known.

Grape and Festoon creamer.

Known items:	Clear
Bowl, open, flat, 6" d.	$25.00
Butter dish with cover	65.00
Celery vase	55.00
Compote with cover	
High standard, 8" d.	150.00
Low standard	65.00
Creamer applied handle	45.00
Presser Handle	35.00
Eggcup, single, open (2 styles)	30.00
Goblet	35.00
Lamp, oil, 7-1/2" h.	125.00
Pickle tray, oval	15.00
Pitcher with applied handle	
Milk, 1-qt.	200.00
Water, 1/2-gal.	175.00
Plate, 6" d.	35.00
Relish tray, oval	15.00
Salt, master, open, footed	35.00
Sauce dish, round, flat, 4" d.	5.00
Spoon holder	35.00
Sugar bowl with cover	75.00
Wine	55.00

Grape Band goblet.

Known items:	Non-flint
Creamer with applied handle	65.00
Eggcup, single, open, footed	30.00
Goblet	35.00
Pickle dish, scoop-shaped	15.00
Pitcher, water, 1/2-gal.	195.00
Plate, round, 6" d.	30.00
Salt, master, open, footed	35.00
Spoon holder	35.00
Sugar bowl with cover	65.00
Tumbler, water, flat	35.00
Wine	35.00

GRAPE BAND

AKA: Ashburton with Grape Band, Early Grape Band, Vine.

Flint, non-flint. Bryce, Walker & Co., Pittsburgh, PA, c. 1869. Designed by John Bryce and patented under patent No.3,716, October 19, 1869 for Bryce, Walker & Company. Add 25-50% more for flint items.

Original color production: Clear.

Known Reproductions and Look-a-Likes: None known.

Known items:	Non-flint
Butter dish with cover	$85.00
Compote	
Covered	
High standard	125.00
Low standard	95.00
Open on high standard	45.00

GRASSHOPPER

AKA: Locust, Long Spear.

Non-flint. Riverside Glass Works, Wellsburg, WV, c. 1883.

Original color production: Clear. Amber, blue, vaseline or any other color would be considered rare. Issued either plain or footed, the design is found in three conspicuous forms: (a) with insect, (b) without insect, and (c) with long spear.

Reproductions and Look-a-Likes: 8-oz. goblet (clear). L.G. Wright Glass company, New Martinsville, WV. Unmarked.

Grasshopper covered sugar bowl.

Grasshopper creamer.

Known items:	Clear
Bowl,	
Covered, low	$135.00
Open, footed	
Deep	85.00
Shallow with flared rim	75.00
Butter dish with cover	225.00
Celery vase	
With insect	225.00
Without insect	55.00
Compote with cover on high standard	
7" d.	225.00
8-1/2" d.	275.00
Creamer, 5-1/2" h.	
With insect	135.00
Without insect	35.00
Goblet (repro. by Wright not made originally)	20.00
Marmalade jar with cover	
With insect	175.00
Without insect	95.00

Known items:	Clear
Pickle dish	25.00
Pitcher, water, 1/2-gal.	275.00
Plate, round, footed	
8-1/2" d.	45.00
9" d.	55.00
10-1/2" d.	65.00
Salt	
Master	75.00
Shaker (R)	85.00
Sauce dish, round	
Flat	15.00
Footed	20.00
Spoon holder	
With insect	125.00
Without insect	45.00
Sugar bowl with cover	
With insect	175.00
Without insect	65.00

HAIRPIN

AKA: Early Loop, Hairpin Plain, Hairpin with Rayed Base, Sandwich Loop.

Flint. The Boston & Sandwich Glass Company, Sandwich, MA, c. 1850.

Original color production: Clear, milk white.

Reproductions and Look-a-Likes: None known.

Hairpin castor.

Hairpin covered compote.

Known items:	Clear	Milk White
Butter dish with cover	$150.00	$375.00
Castor bottle		
Mustard	75.00	—
Oil with original stopper	110.00	—
Shaker	65.00	—
Celery vase	75.00	275.00

Known items:	Clear	Milk White
Champagne	125.00	350.00
Compote on high standard		
Covered		
Large	225.00	650.00
Small (Jelly)	135.00	450.00
Open	55.00	375.00
Creamer	110.00	275.00
Eggcup, single, open, footed	35.00	95.00
Goblet		
Plain base	55.00	125.00
Rayed base	65.00	150.00
Mug, whiskey with handle, 3-1/4" h.	125.00	575.00
Salt, master, with cover	175.00	675.00
Sauce dish, round, flat	10.00	25.00
Spoon holder	45.00	125.00
Sugar bowl with cover	125.00	325.00
Tumbler		
Water	65.00	150.00
Whiskey	55.00	125.00
Wine	35.00	110.00

HALEY'S COMET

OMN: Etruria.

Non-flint. Model Flint Glass Company, Findlay, OH, c. 1891.

Original color production: Clear (plain, engraved). Clear with ruby stain or any other color would be considered rare.

Reproductions and Look-a-Likes: None known.

Haley's Comet goblet.

Known items:	Clear
Bowl	
Covered with 3-legs, 4" d.	$55.00
Open, flat	
7" d.	30.00
8" d.	35.00
Butter dish with cover	95.00
Cake stand on high standard	135.00
Celery vase	45.00

Known items:	Clear
Compote on high standard	
Covered	
6" d.	55.00
7" d.	65.00
8" d.	75.00
Open	
6" d.	30.00
7" d.	35.00
8" d.	40.00
Creamer	35.00
Cruet with original stopper	65.00
Cup, punch	15.00
Dish, candy	20.00
Goblet	
Gentleman's	45.00
Lady's cupped bowl	95.00
Pitcher	
Milk, 1-qt	65.00
Water, 1/2-gal.	85.00
Saltshaker	35.00
Sauce dish, round, 4" d.	10.00
Spoon holder	30.00
Sugar bowl with cover	75.00
Tray, water, round, 8" d.	55.00
Tumbler, water, flat	30.00
Wine	20.00

HAMILTON

OMN: Cape Cod's No. 64. **AKA:** Cape Cod.

Flint. Cape Cod Glass Co., Sandwich, MA, c. 1860s.

Original color production: Clear. Deep blue or any other color would be considered rare. Unlike *Hamilton with Leaf*, which contains a vine of frosted leaves, the vine in *Hamilton* has been replaced by a motif of crosshatching.

Reproductions and Look-a-Likes: None known.

Hamilton tumbler.

Hamilton water pitcher.

Known items: **Clear**

Butter dish with cover.........................$150.00

Castor bottle

    Mustard................................. 65.00

    Oil with original stopper 75.00

    Shaker 55.00

Champagne, 4-1/4" h......................... 225.00

Compote

    Covered on low standard, 6" d........... 175.00

    Open

        High standard

           7" d............................. 125.00

           8" d............................. 135.00

Creamer

    Applied handle 225.00

    Pressed handle......................... 65.00

Decanter with original patterned stopper 675.00

Eggcup, single, open, footed, 3-1/2" h. 35.00

Goblet, 6" h. 45.00

Hat, made from a tumbler (ER) 2,500.00

Mug, whiskey, flat with applied handle, 3" h....... 350.00

Pitcher, water with applied handle, 1/2-gal.......1,800.00

Salt, master, open, footed with smooth rim......... 45.00

Sauce dish, round, flat

    Plain rim

        4" d................................. 10.00

        4-7/8" d............................. 10.00

Known items: **Clear**

    Scalloped rim

        4" d. 10.00

        5" d. 12.50

Spoon holder

    Plain rim..............................55.00

    Scalloped rim 45.00

Sugar bowl with cover.........................150.00

Syrup pitcher with applied handle 950.00

Tumbler, flat

    Water, 3-1/2" h........................85.00

    Whiskey, 3" h. 125.00

Wine, 3-1/4" h..................................110.00

HAMILTON WITH LEAF

AKA: Hamilton with Frosted Leaf.

Flint. Cape Cod Glass Company, Sandwich, MA, c. 1860s.

Original color production: Clear, clear with frosting. Unlike *Hamilton* which contains a band of crosshatching, the band in *Hamilton* has been replaced by a molded vine of leaves.

Reproductions and Look-a-Likes: None known.

Hamilton with Leaf tumbler.

Hamilton with Leaf spoon holder.

Known items:	Clear	Clear w/Frosting
Butter dish with cover.........	$150.00	$225.00
Champagne....................	275.00	375.00
Compote		
Covered on high standard .	175.00	275.00
Open		
High standard........	135.00	225.00
Low standard	75.00	95.00
Creamer		
Applied handle	225.00	250.00
Pressed handle...........	85.00	110.00
Eggcup, single, open.............	45.00	75.00
Goblet	85.00	125.00

Known items:	Clear	Clear w/Frosting
Honey dish, round, flat	15.00	15.00
Lamp, oil, stand................	225.00	275.00
Salt, master, open, footed.........	55.00	65.00
Sauce dish, round, flat, 4" d.	10.00	15.00
Spoon holder	95.00	125.00
Sugar bowl with cover	175.00	225.00
Tumbler, flat		
Water	135.00	150.00
Whiskey with applied		
handle	150.00	225.00
Wine	95.00	125.00

HANOVER

OMN: AKA: Block with Stars, Blockhouse, Hanover Star.

Non-flint. Richards & Hartley Glass Co., Tarentum, PA, c. 1888. The United States Glass Company, Pittsburgh, PA. after 1891.

Original color production: Amber, blue, clear, vaseline.

Reproductions and Look-a-Likes: None known.

Hanover hard-to-find etched covered sugar bowl.

Hanover true open compotes and covered butter dish.

Known items:	Amber	Blue	Clear	Vaseline
Bowl, open, round, flat				
7" d...............................$25.00	$30.00	$20.00	$30.00
8" d...............................30.00	35.00	25.00	35.00
10" d...............................35.00	40.00	30.00	40.00
Butter dish with cover.........................50.00	55.00	45.00	65.00
Cake stand on high standard, 10" d..............95.00	110.00	85.00	125.00
Celery vase 35.00	45.00	30.00	50.00
Cheese dish with cover, 10" d..................100.00	125.00	95.00	135.00
Compote				
Covered				
High standard				
7" d............................85.00	125.00	75.00	135.00
8" d............................95.00	135.00	85.00	150.00
Low standard				
7" d............................65.00	85.00	55.00	95.00
8" d............................75.00	95.00	65.00	110.00
Creamer with pressed handle 35.00	45.00	30.00	45.00
Cruet with original stopper 65.00	85.00	55.00	85.00
Goblet 35.00	45.00	30.00	50.00
Mug with pressed handle				
Large 35.00	45.00	30.00	45.00
Small.......................................30.00	40.00	25.00	40.00
Pitcher with pressed handle				
Milk, 1-qt. 65.00	85.00	55.00	85.00
Water, 1/2-gal. 75.00	95.00	65.00	100.00
Plate, round				
4" d.......................................15.00	20.00	15.00	20.00
6" d.......................................20.00	25.00	20.00	25.00
10" d......................................30.00	35.00	30.00	35.00
Platter 35.00	40.00	35.00	40.00
Sauce dish, round, footed......................5.00	8.00	5.00	10.00
Spoon holder 30.00	35.00	25.00	35.00

Known items:	Amber	Blue	Clear	Vaseline
Sugar bowl with cover	40.00	50.00	35.00	55.00
Tumbler, water, flat	30.00	35.00	25.00	40.00
Wine...	20.00	25.00	20.00	25.00

Hanover high-standard cake stand.

Hartley etched plate.

HARTLEY

OMN: U.S. Glass No. 900. AKA: Daisy and Button with Oval Panels, Paneled Diamond Cut and Fan.

Non-flint. Richards & Hartley Glass Co., Tarentum, PAS, c. 1887. The United States Glass Company, Pittsburgh, PA, c. 1891.

Original color production: Amber, blue, canary, clear (plain, engraved).

Reproductions and Look-a-Likes: None known.

Hartley etched covered sugar.

Known items:	Amber	Blue	Canary	Clear
Bowl, open, round				
Flat				
6" d.............................	$20.00	$25.00	$30.00	$15.00
7" d.............................	25.00	30.00	35.00	20.00
8" d.............................	30.00	35.00	40.00	25.00
9" d.............................	40.00	45.00	50.00	35.00

Hartley etched plate.

Hartley etched true open compote.

Known items:	Amber	Blue	Canary	Clear
Footed, 7" d.	30.00	35.00	35.00	25.00
Bread plate, tri-lobed	20.00	25.00	30.00	20.00
Butter dish with cover	45.00	65.00	75.00	45.00
Cake stand on high standard, 10" d.	85.00	110.00	125.00	75.00
Celery vase	35.00	45.00	45.00	30.00
Compote				
Covered				
High standard				
7" d.	75.00	110.00	110.00	65.00
8" d.	85.00	125.00	135.00	75.00
Low standard, 7-1/4" d.	65.00	75.00	75.00	55.00
Open on high standard				
7" d.	35.00	45.00	45.00	35.00
8" d.	40.00	50.00	50.00	40.00
Creamer	30.00	40.00	45.00	30.00
Dish, center piece	25.00	35.00	35.00	25.00
Goblet	35.00	45.00	45.00	30.00
Pitcher with pressed handle				
Milk, 1-qt.	85.00	110.00	110.00	85.00
Water, 1/2-gal.	95.00	125.00	125.00	95.00

Hartley etched sugar bowl, spoon holder, butter dish, and creamer.

Known items:	Amber	Blue	Canary	Clear
Plate, dinner	25.00	30.00	35.00	25.00
Relish tray	15.00	20.00	20.00	15.00
Sauce dish, round, flat, 4" d.	5.00	8.00	10.00	5.00
Spoon holder	30.00	35.00	35.00	25.00
Sugar bowl with cover	40.00	55.00	55.00	35.00
Tumbler	30.00	35.00	35.00	25.00
Wine	20.00	25.00	30.00	20.00

HARVARD YARD

OMN: AKA: Tarentum's Harvard.

Non-flint. Tarentum Glass Company, Tarentum, PA, c. 1896.

Original color production: Clear (plain, gilded). Emerald green, pink, clear with ruby stain, or any other color would be considered scarce.

Reproductions and Look-a-Likes: None known.

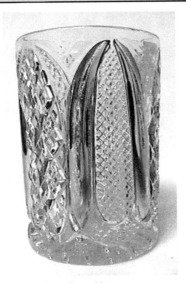

Harvard Yard tumbler.

Known items:	Clear:
Bowl, round (various sizes)	$25.00
Butter dish with cover	45.00
Cake stand on high standard	75.00
Condiment set, complete	95.00
Cordial	25.00

Known items:	Clear
Creamer	25.00
Decanter, wine with original stopper	55.00
Eggcup, open, single, footed	25.00
Goblet	35.00
Jug	75.00
Pitcher, water, 1/2-gal.	85.00
Plate, round, 10" d.	15.00
Salt	
Dip, individual, 1-1/4" d.	5.00
Shaker	25.00
Sauce dish, round, flat	5.00
Spoon holder	25.00
Sugar bowl with cover	35.00
Toothpick holder	20.00
Tray, oval, flat	35.00
Tumbler, water, flat	25.00
Wine	15.00

HEART WITH THUMBPRINT

OMN: Tarentum's Hartford. **AKA:** Bull's Eye in Heart, Columbia, Columbian, Heart and Thumbprint.

Non-flint. Tarentum Glass Company, Tarentum, PA, c. 1898.

Original color production: Clear, clear with ruby stain, emerald green (plain, gilded). Nile green, cobalt blue, custard, or any other color was experimental and is considered rare.

Reproductions and Look-a-Likes: None known.

Heart with Thumbprint oil lamp.

Heart with Thumbprint cordial, wine, and water tumbler.

Known items:	Clear	Clear w/Ruby	Emerald Green
Banana boat, flat with upturned sides			
Large, 11-1/4" l ...$200.00		$550.00	—
Small 10" l. 150.00		450.00	—
Bottle			
Barber 125.00		—	—
Cologne......... 150.00		—	—
Bowl, open, flat with scalloped rim			
Round			
6" d. 35.00		175.00	150.00
9" d. 45.00		225.00	200.00
Square			
7" 55.00		175.00	150.00
9-1/2" 65.00		225.00	175.00
10" 95.00		450.00	225.00
Butter dish with cover and flanged base, 8" d. 225.00		550.00	400.00
Cake stand on high standard, 9" d................... 650.00		1,500.00	—
Carafe 325.00		550.00	—
Card tray, flat with upturned sides.......... 25.00		65.00	55.00
Celery vase 95.00		275.00	
Compote, open on high standard with scalloped rim			
7-1/2" d. 375.00		1,000.00	—
8-1/2" d. 450.00		1,250.00	1,500.00

Known items:	Clear	Clear w/Ruby	Emerald Green
Cordial, 3" h. 175.00		650.00	550.00
Creamer			
Individual 20.00		45.00	40.00
Table size 135.00		275.00	225.00
Cruet with original faceted stopper................150.00		—	—
Finger bowl 85.00		—	—
Goblet 95.00		550.00	375.00
Hair receiver with metal cover.................125.00		225.00	175.00
Ice bucket 110.00		—	—
Lamp, oil			
Finger			
Flat.........125.00		—	225.00
Footed.......150.00		—	275.00
Stand			
7-1/2" h. 225.00		—	350.00
8-1/2" h. 275.00		—	450.00
9-1/2" h. 325.00		—	550.00
Mustard pot with original silver plate cover..............95.00		—	125.00
Pitcher, water, bulbous with applied handle (R) 2,800.00		—	—
Plate, round			
6" d................25.00		55.00	45.00
10" d..............55.00		110.00	95.00
12" d..............95.00		—	—

Heart with Thumbprint finger bowl.

Heart with Thumbprint punch cup and individual creamer.

Heart with Thumbprint goblet.

Heart with Thumbprint rose bowl.

Known items:	Clear	Clear w/Ruby	Emerald Green
Powder jar w/original silver-plate cover	95.00	—	—
Punch cup	35.00	55.00	45.00
Rose bowl			
Large	95.00	175.00	—
Small	75.00	150.00	—
Sauce dish, round with ruffled rim (several sizes)	20.00	45.00	40.00
Spoon holder	95.00	225.00	175.00
Sugar bowl			
Individual, true open with double-handles	25.00	45.00	35.00

Known items:	Clear	Clear w/Ruby	Emerald Green
Table size with cover	175.00	325.00	275.00
Syrup pitcher			
Large	200.00	—	—
Small	175.00	—	—
Tray, condiment, 8-1/4" l.	55.00	85.00	65.00
Tumbler, water, flat	75.00	125.00	100.00
Vase			
6" h.	35.00	150.00	95.00
10" h.	65.00	175.00	150.00
Wine	65.00	450.00	225.00

Heart with Thumbprint syrup.

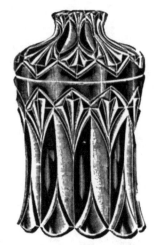

Heavy Gothic covered pickle jar.

HEAVY GOTHIC

OMN: U. S. Glass No. 15,014. **AKA:** Whitton.

Non-flint. Columbia Glass Company, Findlay, OH, c. 1890. The United States Glass Company, Pittsburgh, PA, c. 1891.

Original color production: Clear, clear with ruby stain. Green or any other color would be considered rare.

Reproductions and Look-a-Likes: 6-1/4" h. goblet (amber, blue, clear). Permanently embossed with a capital script "R" surrounded by "(C) RED—CLIFF C USA." designating the Red-Cliff Distributing Company, Chicago, IL.

Known items:	Clear	Clear w/Ruby
Bowl, flat		
Covered, round		
5" d.	$45.00	$75.00
6" d.	55.00	85.00
7" d.	65.00	95.00
8" d.	75.00	110.00

Known items:	Clear	Clear w/Ruby
Open		
Belled bowl		
5-1/2" d.	15.00	35.00
6-1/2" d.	20.00	40.00
7-1/2" d.	25.00	45.00
9" d.	30.00	50.00
Flared bowl		
5-1/2" d.	15.00	35.00
6-1/2" d.	20.00	40.00
7-1/2" d.	25.00	45.00
8-1/2" d.	30.00	50.00
10" d.	45.00	65.00
Butter dish with cover and flanged base.	45.00	150.00
Cake stand on high standard		
9" d.	85.00	225.00
10" d.	110.00	250.00
Celery vase.	35.00	125.00
Claret.	55.00	95.00
Compote on high standard		
Covered		
5" d.	55.00	95.00
6" d.	65.00	110.00
7" d.	75.00	125.00
8" d.	85.00	150.00

241

Thumbprint. Rare flint true open compote.

Bellflower. "Single vine" decanter with matching patterned stopper.

Bird and Strawberry. Spoon holder, clear with enamel decoration.

Broken Column. Very rare clear with ruby stain covered cracker jar.

242

Bullet Emblem. *Exceptionally rare covered sugar bowl retaining its original red, white, and blue decoration.*

Bullet Emblem. *Exceptionally rare covered butter dish retaining its original red, white, and blue decoration.*

Cabbage Leaf. *Clear and frosted celery vase.*

Color Setting. *An interesting assembly of early American pattern glass consisting of an amber Rose in Snow water pitcher, rare blue Rosette spoon holder, emerald green California wine and clear with ruby stain and etching King's Crown master berry bowl.*

Delaware. *Cranberry with gilding seven-piece water set, consisting of the tankard pitcher and six matching tumblers.*

Deer and Dog. *Rare covered oval bowl, enhanced with fine plate-etching.*

Frosted Dog. *Low-footed etched covered butter dish with frosted finial.*

Frosted Chicken. *Rare clear with frosting covered marmalade.*

Frosted Eagle. *Covered sugar bowl and butter dish with matching etching.*

Heart and Thumbprint.
Green stand lamp.

Horn of Plenty. *Matching pair of flint celery vases.*

Jumbo. *Round butter dish.*

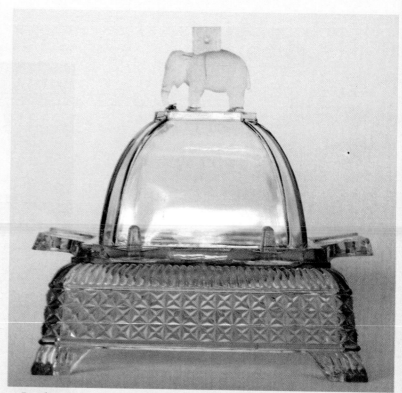

Jumbo. *Scarce square-shaped covered butter dish with frosted elephant finial.*

King's Crown. *Rare clear with ruby stain four-bottle castor in original holder.*

King's Crown. *Rare clear with ruby stain square covered honey dish.*

Klondike. *Cruet set consisting of the cruet, salt- and pepper shaker, and toothpick holder on under tray.*

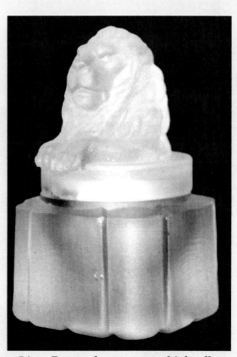

Lion. *Extremely rare covered inkwell.*

Lion. *High-standard compote with the unusual addition of "Garden Harvest" etching.*

Lion. *Very rare oil lamp with clear lion heads.*

Log Cabin. *Rare blue covered Lutted's cough box counter display.*

Log Cabin. *Sugar, spooner, and creamer in clear glass.*

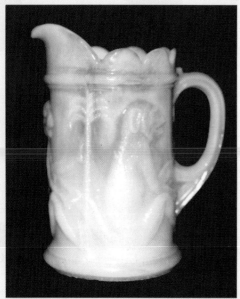

Monkey. *Rare opalescent table creamer.*

Monkey. *Exceptionally rare clear with enamel decoration covered sugar bowl.*

Mario. *Scarce clear with amber stain barber bottle.*

Plume. *Clear with ruby stain covered butter dish.*

Princess Feather. *Rare opal-colored covered sugar bowl.*

Rose Sprig. *Hard-to-find blue high-standard covered compote.*

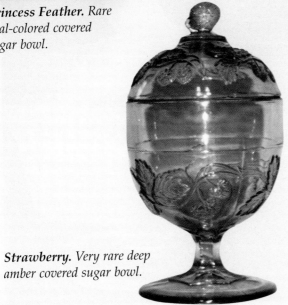

Strawberry. *Very rare deep amber covered sugar bowl.*

Shell and Jewel. *Seven-piece green water set in deep emerald green.*

Three Face. Goblet enhanced with etching.

Thumbprint. Rare flint water pitcher with applied handle.

U.S. Coin. Rare covered butter dish with frosted coins.

Viking. Scarce large apothecary jar with original stopper.

Westward Ho. Low-standard oval covered compote.

Heavy Gothic syrup.

Heavy Gothic true open compote.

Known items:	Clear	Clear w/Ruby
Open		
Belled bowl		
5-1/2" d.	15.00	35.00
6-1/2" d.	20.00	40.00
7-1/2" d.	35.00	55.00
8-1/2" d.	45.00	65.00
9" d.	55.00	75.00
Flared bowl		
5-1/2" d.	15.00	35.00
6-1/2" d.	20.00	45.00
7-1/2" d.	35.00	55.00
8-1/2" d.	45.00	65.00
Creamer	30.00	50.00
Dish, open, oblong, flat		
7" l.	15.00	35.00
8" l.	20.00	40.00
9" l.	25.00	45.00
Goblet, 6-1/4" h.	30.00	85.00
Honey dish with cover and low foot on underplate		
With notch in lid		
4" d.	75.00	150.00
5" d.	85.00	175.00
Without notch in lid		
4" d.	55.00	110.00
5" d.	65.00	135.00
Lamp, oil, stand	110.00	—
Pickle jar with cover	95.00	175.00

Known items:	Clear	Clear w/Ruby
Pitcher, water, 1/2-gal.	85.00	275.00
Saltshaker, tall	25.00	55.00
Sauce dish		
Flat with scalloped rim		
Belled bowl		
4" d.	5.00	15.00
4-1/2" d.	5.00	20.00
5" d.	5.00	20.00
Scalloped bowl		
4" d.	5.00	15.00
4-1/2" d.	5.00	20.00
5" d.	5.00	20.00
Footed		
4" d.	5.00	15.00
4-1/2" d.	8.00	20.00
5" d.	10.00	20.00
Spoon holder	30.00	65.00
Sugar bowl with cover		
Breakfast size (known as the "berry")	25.00	50.00
Table size	40.00	85.00
Sugar shaker	65.00	225.00
Syrup pitcher	95.00	275.00
Tumbler, water, flat	25.00	55.00
Wine	15.00	35.00

HENRIETTA

> **OMN:** Columbia Glass No. 14. **AKA:** Big Block, Diamond Block, Hexagon Block.
>
> Non-flint. Columbia Glass Company, Findlay, OH, c. 1889. The United States Glass Co., Pittsburgh, PA. at Factory "J," c. 1891-1892.
>
> **Original color production:** Clear (plain, engraved). Clear with ruby stain, emerald green or any other color would be considered rare.
>
> **Reproductions and Look-a-Likes:** None known.

Henrietta cracker jar.

Known items:	Clear
Bowl, open	
Rectangular, 8" l.	$25.00
Round, deep	
7" d.	20.00
8" d.	25.00
9" d.	35.00
Butter dish with cover.	50.00
Cake stand on high standard, 10" d.	85.00
Castor set, 2-bottles in silver plate holder	75.00

Known items:	Clear
Celery	
Tray, 8" l.	20.00
Vase.	35.00
Compote, open on high standard with scalloped bowl	45.00
Cracker jar with cover	95.00
Creamer	
Individual	15.00
Table size	35.00
Cruet with original stopper.	55.00
Cup, custard, footed and handled	15.00
Dish, open	
Bone, crescent shape	25.00
Bonbon.	15.00
Oblong, shallow	
7".	15.00
8".	18.00
Olive, shallow	15.00
Jar, with cover, marked "Confection"	75.00
Lamp, oil	95.00
Mustard jar with original nickel plate top	35.00
Pickle jar with cover	85.00
Pitcher, water with applied handle	
Bulbous, 1/2-gal.	85.00
Tankard	100.00
Plate, bread, oval.	25.00
Rose bowl.	30.00
Salt	
Dip	
Individual	5.00
Shaker	
Hotel size	45.00
Table size.	25.00
Sauce dish, round, flat, 4-1/2" d.	5.00
Saucer	15.00

Henrietta four-piece table set.

Known items:	Clear
Shade, electric	45.00
Spoon holder	30.00
Sugar bowl with cover	40.00
Sugar shaker	75.00
Syrup pitcher	95.00
Tumbler, water, 2-pt.	25.00
Vase	
5" h.	25.00
7" h.	30.00
9" h.	35.00

HEXAGON BLOCK

OMN: Hobbs' No. 335. **AKA:** Henrietta.

Non-flint. Hobbs, Brockunier & Company, Wheeling, WV, c. 1889. The United States Glass Company, Pittsburgh, PA, after 1891.

Original color production: Clear, clear with amber stain, clear with ruby stain (plain, engraved). A majority of the items encountered have scalloped, circular feet.

Reproductions and Look-a-Likes: None known.

Hexagon Block cracker jar.

Hexagon Block footed celery vase.

Known items:	Clear	Clear w/Ruby	Clear w/Amber
Bowl, open, round, flat			
Berry			
Deep bowl with point and scallop rim			
7" d.	$20.00	$35.00	$35.00
8" d.	25.00	45.00	45.00
9" d.	30.00	65.00	75.00
Shallow bowl			
7" d.	20.00	35.00	35.00
8" d.	25.00	45.00	45.00
9" d.	30.00	65.00	75.00
Butter dish with cover and flanged base	45.00	150.00	175.00
Celery vase	35.00	85.00	95.00
Compote			
Covered on high standard with smooth rim			
Deep bowl with smooth rim			
7" d.	65.00	135.00	135.00
8" d.	75.00	150.00	150.00
Saucer-shaped bowl with scalloped rim			
8" d.	55.00	125.00	125.00
9" d.	65.00	135.00	150.00
Open with high standard and point and scallop rim			
Deep bowl			
7" d.	35.00	45.00	45.00
8" d.	40.00	55.00	55.00
Saucer-shaped bowl			
8" d.	35.00	45.00	45.00
9" d.	40.00	55.00	65.00

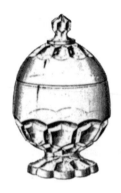

Hexagon Block sugar bowl, spoon holder, butter dish, and creamer.

Known items:	Clear	Clear w/Ruby	Clear w/Amber
Cracker jar with original lid	275.00	450.00	475.00
Creamer with applied handle	35.00	55.00	65.00
Cup, custard, footed with applied handle	25.00	35.00	40.00
Finger bowl, round with point and scallop rim	20.00	40.00	45.00
Goblet	30.00	65.00	65.00
Pickle jar with cover	65.00	150.00	175.00
Pitcher, footed with applied handle			
Milk, 1-qt.	85.00	150.00	150.00
Water			
Bulbous, 2-gal.	75.00	175.00	175.00
Tankard, 3-pts.	65.00	150.00	150.00
Saltshaker	30.00	55.00	55.00

Known items:	Clear	Clear w/Ruby	Clear w/Amber
Sauce dish, round, flat with point and scallop rim			
4" d.	5.00	15.00	20.00
4-1/2" d.	5.00	15.00	20.00
Spoon holder	30.00	50.00	55.00
	40.00	85.00	95.00
Sugar bowl with cover	30.00	50.00	55.00
Syrup pitcher	85.00	275.00	275.00
Tumbler, water, flat	25.00	45.00	45.00

Hexagon Block syrup.

HIDALGO

OMN: Adams' No. 5. **AKA:** Frosted Waffle, Waffle-Red Top.

Non-flint. Adams & Company, Pittsburgh, PA, c. 1880. The United States Glass Company, Pittsburgh, PA, c. 1891.

Original color production: Clear with ground panels (plain, engraved). Clear with amber stain, clear with ruby stain, or any other color would be considered rare. Add 50% more for colored stain items.

Reproductions and Look-a-Likes: None known.

Known items:	Clear w/Frosted Panels
Bowl, open, square, berry, master, 10"	$35.00
Butter dish with cover	45.00
Celery vase	35.00

Hidalgo water set.

Known items:	Clear w/Frosted Panels
Compote	
Covered	
High standard	
6" d.	75.00
7-1/2" d.	85.00
Low standard	
6" d.	55.00
7-1/2" d.	65.00
Open	
High standard	
6" d.	25.00
7-1/2" d.	35.00
10" d.	55.00
11" d.	65.00
Creamer	35.00
Cruet with original stopper	85.00
Cup and saucer set	65.00
Finger or waste bowl	25.00
Goblet	20.00
Pickle dish, boat shaped	15.00
Pitcher	
Milk, 1-qt.	55.00
Water with applied rope handle, 1/2-gal.	65.00
Plate, bread with cupped edge, 10" sq.	30.00
Salt	
Master, square	35.00
Shaker	30.00
Sauce dish, flat, square with tab handle	5.00
Spoon holder	25.00
Sugar bowl with cover	35.00

Known items:	Clear w/Frosted Panels
Sugar shaker	55.00
Syrup pitcher	85.00
Tray, water	55.00
Tumbler, water, flat	20.00

HOBBS' BLOCK

OMN: Hobbs No. 330. **AKA:** Divided Squares.

Non-flint. Hobbs, Brockunier & Company, Wheeling, WV, c. 1888. The United States Glass Company, Pittsburgh, PA, c. 1891.

Original color production: Clear, clear with amber stain, clear with acid finish, clear with acid finish, and amber stain. Issued in two conspicuous forms: (a) plain design and (b) starred design.

Reproductions and Look-a-Likes: Handled basket; bowls: (open, round, flat) 9" d. bowl, 10" d. with cupped bowl, 10-1/2" d. with flared rim, 11" d. round bowl with flared rim, 9" sq. flat open bowl, butter set; footed cake plate; canasta set; candle holders: handled, square, flared; celery vase; footed candy box; 4-5/8" h. open compote on high standard; condiment set; console sets: 3-piece, square, flared, cupped; creamer; cruet; desserts: square, flared, cupped; bonbon dish; jam and jelly set; handled jugs: 70-oz., 6" h., 6-1/2" h.; mayonnaise set; mustard and spoon; relish dish; saltshaker; spoon holder; sugar bowl; 10-1/2" l. pickle tray; sandwich tray; tumblers: 9-oz., 10-oz., 12-oz.; 3-piece vanity set; vases: 6" h., 6-1/2" h., 8-1/2" h., 9" h. (amber, clear, goldenrod, green pastel, Jamestown blue, lilac, light green, milk white, peach crest, rose pastel, silver Jamestown, turquoise). Fenton Art Glass Company, Williamstown, WV. Permanently unmarked.

Known items:	Clear	Clear w/Amber	Frosted w/Amber
Bottle, water	$45.00	$75.00	$125.00
Bowl, open, oval, flat with scalloped rim			
7" l.	25.00	35.00	45.00
8" l.	30.00	40.00	50.00

Hobbs' Block goblet.

Known items:	Clear	Clear w/Amber	Frosted w/Amber
9" l.	.35.00	45.00	55.00
10" l.	.40.00	50.00	65.00
Butter dish with cover.	.55.00	85.00	135.00
Celery tray, boat shaped . . .	.35.00	75.00	110.00
Creamer, oval, flat with applied handle.	.35.00	55.00	75.00
Cruet with original stopper	65.00	150.00	275.00
Finger bowl, round with scalloped rim	.35.00	55.00	85.00
Goblet	.55.00	85.00	135.00
Pitcher, water, tankard with applied handle, 1/2-gal.	85.00	175.00	275.00
Saltshaker, tall	.35.00	65.00	95.00
Sauce dish, oval, flat with scalloped rim, 4-1/2" . . .	.5.00	10.00	15.00
Spoon holder	.35.00	45.00	75.00
Sugar bowl with cover . . .	.45.00	65.00	110.00
Syrup pitcher	.95.00	225.00	325.00
Tumbler, water, flat	.25.00	45.00	65.00

HOLLY

Non-flint. Original manufacturer unknown, c. 1860s, early 1870s. Often attributed to the Boston & Sandwich Glass Company, Sandwich, MA, based on the shards found at the factory site.

Original color production: Clear.

Reproductions and Look-a-Likes: None known.

Holly cake stand.

Known items:	Clear
Bowl with cover, round, flat	
7" d.	$225.00
8" d.	275.00
Butter dish with cover, 6-1/4" d.	275.00
Cake stand on high standard	
8-1/2" d.	200.00
9-1/2" d.	225.00
11" d.	275.00
12-1/4" d	450.00
Celery vase.	250.00
Compote with cover	
High standard	
6-1/4" d.	275.00
7" d.	325.00
8-3/4" d.	350.00
9-1/2" d.	650.00

Holly covered compote.

Holly water pitcher.

Known items:	**Clear**
Low standard	
6-1/4" d.............................	250.00
7" d.................................	275.00
8" d.................................	300.00
8-1/4" d.............................	325.00
9-1/2" d.............................	450.00
Creamer, footed with applied handle.............	225.00
Dish, oval, flat	
7" l.................................	65.00
8" l.................................	75.00
9" l.................................	85.00
Eggcup, open, single, footed with smooth rim.....	135.00
Goblet	275.00
Pitcher, water, bulbous with circular foot, 2-gal.....	475.00
Salt, oval, flat 3-1/4" l......................	275.00
Sauce dish, round, flat	
4" d.	35.00
5" d.	45.00
Spoon holder	125.00
Sugar bowl with cover	250.00
Syrup pitcher (R)	325.00
Tumbler, water	
Flat................................	225.00
Footed	200.00
Wine................................	225.00

HONEYCOMB

OMN: Bellaire No. 40. Cape Cod No. 96. Central No. 136. Cincinnati. Cincinnati Honeycomb. Doyle No.500. New York. O'Hara No. 3. Vernon, **AKA:** Honeycomb External, Midget New York, Thousand Faces.

Flint, non-flint. Bakewell, Pears & Company, Pittsburgh, PA, c. 1875. Bellaire Goblet Company, Bellaire, OH, c. 1889-1890. Boston Silver & Glass Company, East Cambridge, MA, c. 1869. Doyle & Company, Pittsburgh, PA, c. 1880s.

Gillinder & Sons, Philadelphia, PA, c. 1865. Grierson & Company, Pittsburgh, PA, c. 1875. J.B. Lyon & Company, Pittsburgh, PA. McKee Brothers (stemmed items only), Pittsburgh, PA, c. 1880. New England Glass Company, East Cambridge, MA. O'Hara Glass Company, Pittsburgh, PA. United States Glass Company, Pittsburgh, PA.

Original color production: Clear (plain, engraved). Amber, apple green, blue, emerald green, opaque white, opaque green, pink, fiery opalescent, or any other color would be considered exceedingly rare in flint. Issued in two conspicuous forms: (a) New York (design on upper portion of item) and (b) Vernon (design completely covers item).

Reproductions and Look-a-Likes: Bowls: 4-1/4" d. round open berry bowl with ruffled rim; 7-1/2" d. round open berry bowl; rectangular butter dish; clarets: knob stem, tall stem; 24-oz. cocktail shaker; 1-oz. footed cordial; creamer with pressed handle; footed cup with pressed handle; cup and saucer set; flat bulbous decanter; finger bowl with underplate; goblets: 11-oz., 13-oz.; ice bucket with metal handle; footed nut cup with flared bowl; water pitchers: 32-oz. water pitcher with ice lip, 54-oz. water pitcher with ice lip, 32-oz., 5" h. flat water pitcher, 48-oz., 9" h. footed water pitcher; plates: 6" d. bread and butter plate; 6" d. (sherbet), 8" d. (luncheon), 8" d. (salad plate), 10" d. (service plate), 11" d. (platter), 11" d. (3-compartment plate), 4" sq. refrigerator dish; footed saltshaker; sherbets: 5-oz. footed, 6-oz. footed; sugar bowls: covered sugar bowl, open sugar bowl with double handles; sugar shaker; toothpick holder; tumblers: 1-oz., 2" h. flat whiskey, 2-1/2" h. whiskey, 5-oz. juice, 7-oz. 4-1/4" h. footed, 7" h. footed, 9-oz., 3-1/4" h. flat whiskey, 9-oz. flat water, 9-oz. footed water, 10-oz. lemonade, 12-oz. iced tea, 2-oz. flat tumbler; wine. Fenton Art Glass Company, Williamstown, WV: (Amber, black, clear, green, moonstone, pink, royal blue, ruby, topaz). Unmarked. Jeannette Glass Company, Jeannette, PA: (carnival, green, pink). Unmarked. Viking Glass Company, New Martinsville, WV: (amber, blue, brown, green, ruby). Unmarked.

Honeycomb assortment of castors.

Known items:

	Flint
Ale	
6" h.	$65.00
7" h.	75.00
8" h. with knob stem	125.00
Bottle	
Barber	95.00
Bitter (New York)	75.00
Castor (New York)	

	Flint
Mustard	45.00
Oil with original stopper	65.00
Shaker	35.00
Catsup (New York)	55.00
Pepper or saloon (New York)	45.00
Water with tumbler (New York)	325.00
Bowl	
Covered	
Collared base	
6" d.	110.00
7" d.	125.00
8" d.	150.00
9" d.	175.00
Flat	
5-1/2" d.	95.00
6" d.	110.00
7" d.	125.00
8" d.	150.00
Open, flat	
Oval, 7-1/4" l., dated *"May 11, 1869"*	125.00
Round	
Collared base	
Deep bowl	
6" d.	35.00
7" d.	45.00

Honeycomb creamer.

Honeycomb oil lamp.

Known items:	Flint
8" d..	55.00
9" d..	75.00
Saucer-shaped bowl	
7" d..	35.00
8" d..	45.00
9" d..	55.00
10" d..	75.00
Flat, deep bowl	
5" d..	35.00
6" d..	45.00
7" d..	55.00
8" d..	75.00
Butter dish with cover..	75.00
Butter pat	25.00
Cake stand on high standard	
8" d.	110.00
9-1/2" d.	175.00
10-1/2" d.	225.00
11-1/4" d.	250.00
Candlestick.	175.00
Celery vase	
Scalloped rim.	45.00
Smooth rim.	45.00

Known items:	Flint
Champagne	55.00
Claret.	65.00
Compote, round	
Covered	
High standard	
Deep bowl	
6" d..	95.00
7" d..	110.00
8" d..	125.00
9" d..	150.00
10" d..	175.00
Saucer-shaped bowl	
6" d..	95.00
7" d..	110.00
8" d..	125.00
Low standard with saucer-shaped bowl	
6" d..	75.00
7" d..	85.00
8" d..	110.00
Open	
High standard	
Deep bowl	
6" d.	35.00
7" d.	40.00

Honeycomb goblet and champagne.

Known items:	Flint
8" d.	50.00
9" d.	65.00
10" d.	85.00
Saucer-shaped bowl	
6" d.	35.00
7" d.	40.00
8" d.	50.00
Low standard	
Deep bowl	
6" d.	35.00
7" d.	40.00
8" d.	45.00
9" d.	55.00
10" d.	65.00
Saucer-shaped bowl	
6" d.	35.00
7" d.	40.00
8" d.	45.00
Cordial	
3" h. (R)	125.00
3-1/2" h.	75.00
Creamer	
Applied handle	85.00
Pressed handle	35.00
Cup, custard, footed with applied handle	85.00
Decanter	
Bar lip	
1-pt.	65.00
1-qt.	95.00
With original honeycomb stopper	
1-pt.	85.00
1-qt.	110.00

Known items:	Flint
Dish, flat	
Oval, open	
7" l.	20.00
8" l.	25.00
9" l.	35.00
10" l.	45.00
Eggcup, single, open, footed	
Flared bowl	20.00
Straight-sided bowl	20.00
Finger bowl, round	65.00
Goblet	30.00
Honey dish, round, flat	
3" d.	10.00
3-1/2" d.	10.00
Lamp	
All glass	225.00
Glass font with marble base	175.00
Mug	
2-pt.	65.00
Beer	55.00
Pony	55.00
Pickle jar with cover	225.00
Pitcher with applied or pressed handle	
Milk, 1-qt.	150.00
Water, bulbous	
Dated on handle "Pat. 1865," 2-gal.	125.00
Plain, undated handle, 2-gal.	175.00
3-pt.	150.00
Pomade jar with cover	135.00
Relish dish	30.00

Honeycomb true open compote.

Known items: Flint

Salt

    Dip

        Individual

            Oblong 10.00

            Round 10.00

        Master with foot

            Covered 135.00

            Open, round, flat 30.00

Sauce dish, round, flat, 4" d. 10.00

Spill holder 45.00

Spoon holder 35.00

Sugar bowl with cover 75.00

Syrup pitcher

    1/2-pt. 250.00

    1-pt. 275.00

    3-pts. 300.00

    1-qt. 325.00

Tumbler

    1/2-pt. 45.00

    1/3-pt. 55.00

Lemonade 65.00

Water

    Flat. 65.00

    Footed 45.00

Whiskey

    Applied handle 125.00

    No handle. 55.00

Known items: Flint

Twine holder 525.00

Wine 20.00

HORN OF PLENTY

OMN: Comet. **AKA:** Peacock Tail.

Flint, non-flint. Bryce, McKee & Company, Pittsburgh, PA, c. 1850s. McKee & Brothers, Pittsburgh, PA, c. 1850-1860.

Original color production: Clear. Amber, amethyst, brilliant blue, canary yellow, clear edge with color, milk white or any other color in flint would be considered rare.

Reproductions and Look-a-Likes: Goblet (clear, colors), hat (clear), 11-1/2" h. lamp (amber, amethyst, blue, green-solid colors or attached to milk white bases) , pitcher, 8-oz. tumbler (amber, clear). Unmarked. **Note:** Goblet produced by the L.G. Wright Glass Company, New Martinsville, WV.

Horn of Plenty celery vase.

Horn of Plenty champagne.

Horn of Plenty creamer.

Known items:	Clear
Bottle	
Medicine with applied lip	
4-1/4" h.	$150.00
6" h.	175.00
7-1/8" h.	225.00
8-3/8" h.	275.00
10-1/4" h.	350.00
Bowl, open, round	
Flat	
7-1/8" d.	110.00
8-1/2" d.	135.00
Footed, 8-1/2" d.	175.00
Butter dish with cover	
With *"acorn"* finial	250.00
With *"Washington Head"* finial (R)	750.00
With conventional finial	225.00
Cake stand on high standard	2,800.00
Celery vase	275.00
Champagne	200.00
Claret or jelly glass, 4-7/8" h. (VR)	1,250.00
Compote	
Round	
Covered on high standard	
With *"acorn"* finial	550.00
With *"Washington Head"* finial (R)	2,750.00
With conventional finial	475.00

Known items:	Clear
Open	
High standard	
6" d.	75.00
7" d.	85.00
8" d.	95.00
9" d.	150.00
10" d.	225.00
12-3/8" d.	650.00
Low standard	
6" d.	45.00
7" d.	55.00
8" d.	65.00
9" d.	85.00
10" d.	135.00
Oval, open on high standard with patterned	
base, 10" l. (VR)	2,500.00
Creamer	
Applied handle	
5-1/2" h.	375.00
6-1/4" h.	325.00
Decanter	
Bar lip	
1-pt., 8-3/8" h.	95.00
1-qt., 10-1/4" h.	110.00

Horn of Plenty decanter.

Horn of Plenty tumbler.

Horn of Plenty covered sugar.

Horn of Plenty high-standard covered compote and flat butter dish.

Known items:	Clear
With original patterned stopper	
1-pint	225.00
1-qt.	275.00
1/2-gal. (VR)	850.00

Known items:	Clear
Dish, flat, oval, open	
7" l.	55.00
8" l.	65.00
8-1/2" l.	75.00
9" l.	85.00

Horn of Plenty true open compote.

Known items:	Clear
10" l.	135.00
11-1/2" l.	225.00
Eggcup, open, pedestaled	
Flared-bowl	45.00
Straight-sided bowl	40.00
Goblet with knob stem	
6" h.	175.00
6-1/4" h.	125.00
Honey casket, rectangular covered dish	
With original under tray	20,000.00
Without under tray	10,000.00
Honey dish, round, 3-1/4" d.	15.00
Lamp	
All glass with hexagonal stem	375.00
Glass font with brass stem and marble base.	200.00
Mug, small with applied handle, 3" h. (R)	850.00
Pitcher with applied handle	
Milk, 1-qt.	1,500.00
Water, 1/2-gal.	950.00
Plate, round with scalloped rim	
6" d.	65.00
6-1/2" d.	75.00
Salt, master, open, oval, flat with scalloped rim	75.00
Sauce dish, round, flat	
4" d.	10.00
5" d.	12.50
Spill holder	55.00
Spoon holder	55.00

Sugar bowl with cover	225.00
Tumbler, flat	
Water, 3-1/4" h.	150.00
Whiskey, 3" h.	175.00
Wine, 4-1/2" h.	225.00

HORSEHEAD MEDALLION+

Non-flint. Maker unknown, c. 1870s.

Original color production: Clear, milk white. Amber, blue or any other color would be considered rare and demand a premium price.

Reproductions and Look-a-Likes: None known.

Horsehead Medallion spoon holder.

Known items:	Clear	Milk White
Butter dish with cover	$250.00	$550.00
Celery vase	125.00	325.00
Compote, covered on high		
standard	550.00	1,250.00
Creamer	150.00	300.00
Eggcup, open	95.00	200.00
Spoon holder	125.00	275.00
Sugar bowl with cover	225.00	425.00

HORSESHOE STEM

Non-flint. O'Hara Glass Company, Pittsburgh, PA, c. 1880. Allegedly designed by Joseph Anderson, superintendent of the O'Hara Glass Company, and patented July 6, 1880.

Original color production: Clear, clear with acid finish (plain, engraved). Add 25-50% for frosted items.

Reproductions and Look-a-Likes: None known.

Horsehoe Stem cake stand.

Known items:	Clear
Butter on standard with cover	$225.00
Cake stand on high standard	
7-1/2" d.	250.00
8-1/2" d.	275.00
9-1/2" d.	325.00
Celery vase	175.00
Compote with cover on low standard	
7-1/2" d.	325.00
8-1/2" d.	375.00
Creamer	125.00
Goblet (plain foot)	150.00
Pitcher	
Milk, 1-qt.	425.00
Water, 1/2-gal.	550.00

Known items:	Clear
Sauce dish, round, footed	25.00
Spoon holder (rayed foot)	125.00
Sugar bowl with cover	175.00

HUBER

OMN: Cape Cod No. 22; Central's No. 139.
AKA: Flaring Huber, Straight Huber.

Flint, non-flint. New England Glass Company, Cambridge, MA, c. 1860. McKee & Brothers, Pittsburgh, PA, c. 1860s.

Bakewell-Pears. Cape Cod Glass Company. George A. Duncan & Sons. J.B. Lyon & Company. King, Son & Company. Richards & Hartley Glass Company. United States Glass Company.

Original color production: Clear (plain, engraved).

Reproductions and Look-a-Likes: None known.

Huber celery vase.

Known items:	Clear
Ale glass	$55.00
Bottle, bitters	85.00

Huber decanter.

Huber covered sugar bowl and celery vase.

Known items:	Clear
Bowl, flat	
Covered, round	
Preserve	
6" d.	75.00
7" d.	80.00
Shallow	
6" d.	65.00
7" d.	75.00
8" d.	85.00
Open	
Oval, smooth rim	
6" l.	20.00
7" l.	25.00
8" l.	30.00
9" l.	35.00
10" l.	45.00
Round	
Medium bowl with smooth rim	
6" d.	20.00
7" d.	25.00
8" d.	30.00
Celery vase	55.00
Champagne	
Hotel (barrel-shaped bowl)	50.00
Table size (straight-sided bowl)	55.00

Known items:	Clear
Compote	
High standard	
Covered	
Medium bowl	
6" d.	110.00
7" d.	125.00
Shallow bowl	
6" d.	95.00
7" d.	110.00
8" d.	135.00
Open	
Deep bowl with scalloped rim	
6" d.	25.00
7" d.	30.00
8" d.	35.00
9" d.	40.00
10" d.	55.00
Medium bowl with smooth rim	
6" d.	25.00
7" d.	30.00
Shallow bowl with smooth rim	
6" d.	25.00
7" d.	30.00
8" d.	45.00

Huber open compote, pitcher, spoon holder, and true open compote.

Known items: **Clear**

Low standard

  Covered with shallow bowl

    6" d. 85.00

    7" d. 95.00

    8" d. 110.00

  Open

    Deep bowl with scallops

      6" d. 20.00

      7" d. 25.00

      8" d. 30.00

      9" d. 35.00

      10" d. 45.00

    Shallow bowl with smooth rim

      6" d. 20.00

      7" d. 25.00

      8" d. 35.00

Creamer with pressed handle 55.00

Custard cup, footed with applied handle 110.00

Decanter, bar

  Bar lip

    1-pt. 55.00

    1-qt. 65.00

  With original patterned stopper

    1-pt. 85.00

    1-qt. 110.00

Eggcup, single, open, footed 15.00

Glass, long slender bowl with short foot (Jelly) 65.00

Known items: **Clear**

Goblet

  Gentleman's (straight-sided bowl, thick stem) 25.00

  Hotel, barrel-shaped bowl 15.00

  Lady's (straight-sided bowl, thin stem) 30.00

Honey dish, round, flat, 3-1/2" d. 5.00

Mug with pressed handle, beer

  1/2-pt. 55.00

  Tall beer 65.00

Huber water pitcher with applied handle.

Known items:	Clear
Pitcher, tall with applied handle	
1-qt.	325.00
3-pts.	275.00
Plate, round with smooth rim	
6" d.	25.00
7" d.	35.00
Salt, master, open with smooth rim	25.00
Sauce dish, round, flat with smooth rim, 4" d.	5.00
Spoon holder	30.00

Known items:	Clear
Sugar bowl with cover	55.00
Tumbler	
Flat	
Water	45.00
Whiskey, 3-1/4" h.	55.00
Footed	35.00
Wine	
Hotel (barrel-shaped bowl)	10.00
Table size (straight-sided bowl)	15.00

HUMMINGBIRD

AKA: Bird and Fern, Fern and Bird, Flying Robin, Hummingbird and Fern, Thunder Bird.

Non-flint. Maker unknown, c. 1880s.

Original color production: Amber, blue, canary yellow, clear.

Reproductions and Look-a-Likes: None known.

Hummingbird covered butter.

Known items:	Amber	Blue	Canary Yellow	Clear
Bowl, waste, 5-1/4" d.	$95.00	—	—	$65.00
Butter dish with cover	95.00	125.00	135.00	75.00
Celery vase	75.00	110.00	110.00	55.00
Compote, open on high standard	85.00	125.00	135.00	65.00
Creamer with pressed handle, 5-1/2" h.	65.00	75.00	75.00	45.00
Goblet	65.00	125.00	135.00	85.00
Pitcher				
Milk, 1-qt.	65.00	95.00	100.00	65.00
Water, 1/2-gal.	110.00	150.00	175.00	110.00
Sauce dish, round				
Flat	10.00	15.00	15.00	10.00
Footed	15.00	20.00	20.00	15.00
Spoon holder	45.00	65.00	65.00	45.00
Sugar bowl with cover	75.00	110.00	125.00	65.00
Tray, water, round	85.00	125.00	125.00	75.00
Tumbler, water, flat	65.00	85.00	85.00	45.00
Wine	—	—	—	65.00

ICICLE

AKA: Single Icicle.

Non-flint. Bakewell, Pears & Company, Pittsburgh, PA, c. 1874. Designed by Washington Beck and patented as patent No. 7,755, September 15, 1874.

Original color production: Clear, milk white. Any other color would be considered very rare.

Reproductions and Look-A-Likes: None known.

Icicle pattern illustration.

Known items:	Clear	Milk White
Butter dish with cover		
Flat with plain rim	$55.00	$110.00
Footed with flanged rim	75.00	150.00
Compote		
Covered on high standard		
6" d.	85.00	175.00
8" d.	110.00	225.00
Open		
High standard		
6" d.	35.00	55.00
8" d.	45.00	65.00
Low standard		
6" d.	35.00	55.00
8" d.	45.00	65.00
Creamer footed with applied handle	85.00	175.00
Dish, open, oval, flat		
7" l.	20.00	35.00
8" l.	25.00	40.00
9" l.	30.00	45.00
Goblet	55.00	110.00
Honey Dish, round, flat, 3-1/2" d. (originally listed as the "individual butter")	10.00	20.00
Lamp, 9" h.	135.00	225.00
Pickle scoop with tapered end	15.00	25.00
Pitcher, water with applied handle, 1/2-gal.	275.00	425.00
Salt, master, open	5.00	8.00
Spoon holder, footed	35.00	65.00
Sugar bowl with cover	75.00	150.00

ILLINOIS

OMN: U.S. Glass No. 15,052. **AKA:** Clarissa, Star of the East.

Non-flint. The United States Glass Company, Pittsburgh, PA, at Factory "G" and Factory "P," c. 1897.

Original color production: Clear. Clear with ruby stain, emerald green, or any other color would be considered scarce. Conspicuously produced in two versions: (a) hotel, (b) table set.

Reproductions and Look-a-Likes: Covered butter dish (amber, blue, clear, pink), 5-1/4" h. celery vase (clear, white opalescent). Unmarked.

Illinois banquet lamp.

Illinois candlestick.

Known items:	Clear
Basket with applied handle	
6-1/2" d.	$95.00
11-1/2" h.	135.00
Bonbon, open on high standard	
5" d.	45.00
8" d.	95.00
Bottle, oil	55.00
Bowl, open, flat	
Round	
5" d.	20.00
8" d.	45.00
Square	
Deep, straight-sided with scalloped rim	
6"	25.00
8"	35.00
9"	45.00
Shallow with flared rim	
5"	20.00
9"	35.00
Finger, round, bulbous with scalloped rim	65.00
Butter dish with cover and high domed lid on flat square base	75.00
Butter pat, individual, square	35.00

Known items:	Clear
Cake stand, square on high standard	
7" (*"bonbon"*)	85.00
11"	175.00
Candlesticks, 9-1/4" h., pair	750.00
Celery	
Tray, rectangular with scalloped rim, 11" l.	30.00
Vase	55.00
Cheese dish with cover	150.00
Compote, square open on high standard	
5"	65.00
9"	135.00
Creamer	
Large (table size)	55.00
Medium	35.00
Small (individual)	35.00
Cruet with original matching stopper	95.00
Dish	
Ice cream, rectangular with scallops, 5" l.	20.00
Olive	15.00
Lamp, oil banquet with matching shade	
High standard with round font	
24"	1,500.00
36"	2,500.00

Illinois spoon holder.

Illinois rare covered straw jar.

Illinois rare milk pitcher.

Illinois breakfast, creamer, spoon holder, and table butter.

Known items:	Clear
Straw jar with blown font insert	950.00
Marmalade or pickle jar with cover	175.00
Olive dish, oblong	15.00
Pickle	
Dish, rectangular, 7-1/4" l.	20.00
Tray, rectangular, 7-1/2" l.	20.00
Pitcher	
Bulbous with applied handle	
1-pt.	95.00
1-1/2-pt.	110.00
1/2-gal.	150.00

Known items:	Clear
With pressed handle, 2-gal.	
Square	175.00
Tankard	
With silver plated rim	110.00
Without silver plated rim	225.00
Plate, 7" d.	
Round	25.00
Square	45.00
Puff box with original cover	85.00
Relish tray, 8-1/2" l.	20.00
Salt, square	
Individual	15.00
Master	35.00
Shaker	
Salt (with neck)	35.00
Tall (without neck)	40.00
Sauce dish, flat, square with scalloped rim	
4"	12.50
4-1/2"	12.50

Known items:	Clear
Spoon holder	
Hotel size	35.00
Table size	45.00
Spoon tray, 8-1/2" l., flat with rounded up sides	30.00
Straw holder with matching cover	450.00
Sugar bowl	
Hotel size, true open	35.00
Individual	25.00
Medium, true open	45.00
Table size with cover	85.00
Sugar shaker	125.00
Syrup pitcher	175.00
Toothpick holder	35.00
Tray, ice cream, rectangular with scalloped rim, 12" l.	55.00
Tumbler, water, flat	35.00
Vase, 6" h.	45.00

INVERTED FERN

Flint. Maker unknown, c. 1860s.

Original color production: Clear.

Reproductions and Look-a-Likes: Goblet (clear, colors). Some are permanently embossed "Made in France."

Inverted fern footed bowl.

Known items:	Clear
Bowl, open, footed with smooth rim	$110.00
Butter dish with cover	225.00

Known items:	Clear
Champagne	225.00
Compote, open on high standard, 8" d.	125.00
Creamer with applied handle	175.00
Eggcup, open, single, footed	
Plain base	35.00
Rayed base	
With coarse ribbing	45.00
With fine ribbing	55.00
Goblet	
Plain base with clear band at top of bowl	55.00
Rayed base	65.00
Honey dish, round, flat, 3-1/2" d.	15.00
Pitcher, water with applied handle, 1/2-gal.	950.00
Plate, round, 6" d.	135.00
Salt, master, open, footed	35.00
Sauce dish, round, flat, 4" d.	10.00
Spoon holder	85.00
Sugar bowl with cover	175.00
Tumbler, water, flat	150.00
Wine	95.00

INVERTED STRAWBERRY

OMN: *Cambridge No. 2870-Strawberry.* **AKA:** Late Strawberry Variant.

Non-flint. Cambridge Glass Company, Cambridge, OH, c. 1912-1918.

Original color production: Clear and emerald green. Items in emerald green and clear with ruby stain are difficult to find and demand a premium price.

Reproductions and Look-a-Likes: Cruet, plate, toothpick holder, tumbler, water pitcher (amethyst, carnival colors, clear, emerald green with gold). Guernsey Glass Company, Cambridge, OH. Unmarked.

Known items:	Clear
Basket with applied handle	$125.00
Bowl, round, flat, master berry, 9-1/4" d.	
Deep	110.00
Shallow	75.00

Inverted Strawberry bowl.

Butter dish with cover	135.00
Celery tray, handled	55.00
Compote, open on a high standard, 5" d	65.00
Creamer	65.00
Cruet with original stopper	25.00
Cup, punch	35.00
Goblet	125.00
Hat (made from tumbler)	135.00
Mug	65.00
Pitcher, water, 1/2-gal.	225.00
Plate, 10" d.	85.00
Relish tray, 7" l.	35.00
Rose bowl	75.00
Salt dip, individual	35.00
Sauce dish, round, flat, 4" d.	25.00
Spoon holder, double handled	75.00
Sugar bowl with cover	95.00
Toothpick holder	45.00
Tumbler, water	55.00

IVY IN SNOW

OMN: Forest. **AKA:** Forest Ware, Ivy in Snow-Red Leaves.

Non-flint. Co-Operative Flint Glass Co., Beaver Falls, PA, c. 1898.

Original color production: Clear, clear with ruby stain. Clear with amber stain, milk white, sapphire blue, or any other color would be considered rare.

Reproductions and Look-a-Likes: Round flat covered bowls: 6" d., 7" d., 8" d.; oval flat open bowls: 7" l., 8" l., 9" l.; round flat open bowl: 4" d., 6" d., 7" d., 8" d.; 5-3/4" d. flat covered butter dish; candlesticks: 4-1/2" h., 7" h.; 8" h. pedestaled celery vase; 3-oz. claret; 6" h. open compote on high standard; 4" h. creamer; cup and saucer set; 4" h. handled custard cup; 8-oz. goblet; 8" l. oval pickle dish; 5-1/2" h. milk pitcher; 36-oz. water pitcher; round plates: 7" d., 10" d.; round flat sauce dish; 5" d. saucer; 5" d. footed sherbet; 6" h. covered sugar bowl; 8-1/4" l. oval tray; tumblers: 3-1/2" h. (water); 4" h. (water), 6" h. (iced tea); vases: 6" h. crimped rim, 6" h. pinched rim, 6" h. swung rim, 8" h. cupped rim, 8" h. pinched rim, 8" h. flared rim; 5-1/2-oz. wine. Clear, milk white. Kemple Glass Works, East Palestine, OH/Kenova, WV. Often embossed with the letter "K" designating Kemple. Phoenix Glass Company, Monaca, PA.

Known items:	Clear	Clear w/Ruby
Bowl, flat		
Covered	$55.00	$175.00
Open		
7" d.	25.00	65.00
8" d.	35.00	85.00
Butter dish with cover	55.00	150.00
Cake stand on high standard, 8" sq.	125.00	375.00
Celery vase	45.00	125.00
Champagne	55.00	135.00
Compote on high standard		
Covered		
6" d.	65.00	175.00
8" d.	75.00	200.00
Open (Jelly)	25.00	75.00

Ivy in Snow covered compote.

Ivy in Snow water pitcher.

Ivy in Snow creamer.

Known items:	Clear	Clear w/Ruby
Creamer		
Squat (table size)	30.00	95.00
Table size, tankard	35.00	110.00
Cup and saucer set	55.00	125.00
Finger bowl	25.00	55.00
Goblet	35.00	225.00
Marmalade jar with cover	95.00	325.00

Known items:	Clear	Clear w/Ruby
Mug	30.00	85.00
Pitcher, flat		
Milk, 1-qt	65.00	375.00
Water, 1/2-gal.	85.00	425.00
Plate		
Cake		
Round	30.00	85.00
Square	45.00	95.00
Dinner		
6" d.	25.00	65.00
7" d.	30.00	75.00
10" d.	40.00	95.00
Relish tray	20.00	45.00
Sauce dish, round, flat, 4" d.	5.00	25.00
Spoon holder	30.00	85.00
Sugar bowl with cover	55.00	150.00
Syrup pitcher	135.00	550.00
Tumbler, water, flat	30.00	75.00
Wine, 4" h.	20.00	85.00

JACOB'S LADDER

OMN: Imperial; U.S. Glass No. 4,778. **AKA:** Maltese.

Non-flint. Bryce, McKee & Company, Pittsburgh, PA. The United States Glass Company, Pittsburgh, PA, c. 1891. Designed by John Bryce and patented under patent No. 9,335, June 13, 1876.

Original color production: Clear. Amber, blue, canary yellow, muddy green, pink or any other color is considered rare.

Reproductions and Look-a-Likes: None known.

Jacob's Ladder goblet and wine.

Known items:	Clear
9-3/4" l.	25.00
10-3/4" l.	.35.00
Round, 9" d.	65.00
Butter dish with cover, 6-1/2" d.	150.00
Cake stand on high standard	
8" d.	75.00
9" d.	85.00
11" d.	110.00
12" d.	150.00
Celery vase	45.00
Compote	
Covered, round with *"Maltese Cross"* finial	
High standard	
6-1/2" d.	135.00
7-1/2" d.	150.00
8-1/2" d.	200.00
9-1/2" d.	250.00
Open	
Round on high standard with scalloped rim	
7" d.	35.00
7-1/2" d.	40.00
8" d.	50.00
8-1/2" d.	55.00

Jacob's Ladder goblet.

Known items:	Clear
Bottle	
Cologne with *"Maltese Cross"* finial	$175.00
Castor	
Mustard	.55.00
Oil with original stopper.	.85.00
Shaker	.45.00
Bowl, flat, open	
Oval	
7-3/4" l.	.15.00
8-3/4" l.	.20.00

Jacob's Ladder four-piece table set and applied handle mug.

Known items:	Clear
9" d.	65.00
9-1/2" d.	75.00
10" d.	85.00
10-1/2" d.	125.00
12" d.	225.00
Oblong with *"Dolphin"* stem (R)	1,250.00
Creamer, 6-1/4" h.	35.00
Cruet with *"Maltese Cross"* finial	175.00
Goblet with knob stem	95.00
Honey dish, round, flat, 3-1/2" d.	10.00
Marmalade jar with cover	325.00
Mug, large with applied handle	375.00
Pickle tray, double-handled	20.00
Pitcher, water, bulbous with applied handle, 1/2-gal.	375.00
Plate, round, 6" d.	30.00
Salt, master, open	25.00
Sauce dish, round	
Flat	
4" d.	5.00
4-1/2" d.	8.00
5" d.	10.00

Known items:	Clear
Footed	
4" d.	8.00
4-1/2" d.	10.00
5" d.	12.50
Spoon holder, 6" h.	35.00
Sugar bowl with cover with *"Maltese Cross"* finial	175.00
Syrup pitcher	
Conventional lid	225.00
Knight's-head finial on lid	275.00

Known items:	Clear
Tumbler, bar, flat, 1/2-pt.	150.00
Wine	35.00

JAPANESE

OMN: AKA: Bird in Ring, Butterfly and Fan, Grace, Japanese Fan.

Non-flint. George Duncan & Sons, Pittsburgh, PA, c. 1880.

Original color production: Clear

Reproductions and Look-a-Likes: None known.

Japanese creamer.

Known items: **Clear**

Bowl, open, round, flat $85.00

Butter dish with cover

      Flat with flanged rim 150.00

      Footed on low standard 225.00

Celery vase 175.00

Compote on high standard with cover

      7" d. 275.00

      8" d. 325.00

Creamer, footed with bamboo handles 55.00

Goblet 225.00

Marmalade or pickle jar with cover 175.00

Pitcher, water, 1/2-gal. (R) 750.00

Sauce dish, round, 4" d.

      Flat. 25.00

      Footed 35.00

Spoon holder 55.00

Sugar bowl with cover 150.00

JASPER

AKA: Belt Buckle, Late Buckle.

Non-flint. Bryce Brothers, Pittsburgh, PA, c. 1880. The United States Glass Co., Pittsburgh, PA, at Factory "B" after 1891.

Original color production: Clear. Blue or any other color would be considered very rare.

Reproductions and Look-a-Likes: Cake stand, 9" d.

Jasper wine.

Known items: **Clear**

Bowl, open, flat

    Oval with deep scalloped bowl

        7" l. $15.00

        8" l. 20.00

        9" l. 25.00

        10" l. 35.00

    Round

        5" d. 15.00

        6" d. 20.00

        7" d. 25.00

        8" d. 30.00

        9" d. 35.00

        10" d. 55.00

Butter dish with cover 65.00

Cake stand on high standard

    8" d. 45.00

    9" d. 65.00

    11" d. 75.00

    12" d. 95.00

Cologne bottle, bulbous, footed with original

    stopper 65.00

Compote on high standard

    Covered

        6" d. (Originally listed as the *"Sweetmeat"*) .55.00

        7" d. 65.00

        8" d. 75.00

        9" d. 95.00

    Open with scalloped rim

        7" d. 25.00

        8" d. 30.00

        10" d. 35.00

        12" d. 55.00

Creamer, 6" h. 35.00

Cruet with applied handle (made from a cologne

    bottle) (R) 175.00

Goblet 35.00

Pickle dish with handle 15.00

Pitcher

    3-pts. 175.00

    1/2-gal. 225.00

Salt, master, open, footed with scalloped rim. 25.00

Sauce dish, round

    Flat

        4" d. 5.00

        4-1/2" d. 5.00

Known items:	Clear
Footed	
4" d.	5.00
4-1/2" d.	5.00

Known items:	Clear
Spoon holder	25.00
Sugar bowl with cover	55.00
Wine	20.00

JERSEY SWIRL

OMN: Windsor Swirl. **AKA:** Swirl, Swirl and Diamonds, Windsor.

Non-flint. The Windsor Glass Company, Pittsburgh, PA, c. 1887.

Original color production: Amber, blue, canary yellow, clear.

Reproductions and Look-a-Likes: Fan-shaped ashtray; 4" d. low-footed covered bowl, 6-1/2" d. open compote on high standard; 11-oz. goblet; plates: 5" d., 10" d.; individual footed salt dip; master salt; 5" d. round, footed sauce dish; 32-oz. wine. (Amber, amethyst, amberina, blue, blue opalescent, clear, canary yellow, green, green satin, ruby, vaseline opalescent). L.G. Wright Glass Company, New Martinsville, WV. Unmarked.

Jersey Swirl goblet.

Know items:	Amber	Blue	Canary	Clear
Bowl, open, round, flat, 9-1/4" d.	$40.00	$55.00	$65.00	$35.00
Butter dish with cover	50.00	75.00	85.00	45.00
Cake stand on high standard, 9" d.	95.00	125.00	135.00	85.00
Compote on high standard, 8" d.				
Covered	150.00	175.00	200.00	150.00
Open with scalloped rim.	95.00	110.00	135.00	95.00
Creamer	35.00	45.00	50.00	30.00
Cruet with original stopper	65.00	85.00	100.00	65.00
Cup	15.00	20.00	25.00	15.00
Goblet				
Gentleman's (buttermilk)	45.00	65.00	75.00	45.00
Lady's	35.00	55.00	65.00	35.00
Marmalade jar with cover covered	125.00	150.00	150.00	110.00
Pitcher, water, 1/2-gal.	95.00	125.00	150.00	85.00
Plate, round				
6" d.	15.00	20.00	20.00	15.00
8" d.	20.00	25.00	25.00	20.00

Know items:	Amber	Blue	Canary	Clear
10" d.	25.00	30.00	30.00	25.00
12" d.	30.00	35.00	35.00	30.00
Salt				
Individual	10.00	15.00	15.00	10.00
Master, open	25.00	35.00	35.00	25.00
Sauce dish, round with collared base, 4-1/2" d.	5.00	10.00	10.00	5.00
Spoon holder	30.00	35.00	40.00	25.00
Sugar bowl with cover covered	40.00	50.00	55.00	35.00
Syrup pitcher	135.00	175.00	225.00	125.00
Tumbler, water, flat	25.00	35.00	35.00	25.00
Wine	20.00	25.00	25.00	15.00

JEWELED MOON AND STARS

OMN: Imperial. **AKA:** Late Moon and Star, Moon and Star Variant, Moon and Star Variation, Moon and Star with Waffle Stem.

Non-flint. Co-Operative Flint Glass Company, Beaver Falls, PA, c. 1896.

Original color production: Clear, clear with acid finish, clear with blue and yellow stain (with either clear or satin moons).

Reproductions and Look-a-Likes: Banana bowl; 12" w. high-standard banana stand; open bowls: low footed open bowl, 8" d. flat bowl, 11" d. flat cupped bowl; flat cake plate; footed cake plate; 11-1/4" d. cake stand; candle holder; celery vase; open compotes on high standards: 8" d. with cupped bowl, 10-1/2" d. with deep bowl; goblet; wine.

Kemple Glass Works, East Palestine, OH (clear, caramel lustre, emerald green, milk white, pearl lustre). Usually embossed with the letter "K" to signify Kemple. Phoenix Glass Company, Monaca, PA. Permanently unmarked.

Jeweled Moon and Stars true open compote.

Known items:	Clear	Clear/ Frosting	Clear/ Color Stain
Bottle, water, 5-pt.	$65.00	$85.00	$125.00
Bowl			
Covered, round, flat			
6" d.	65.00	85.00	125.00
7" d.	75.00	95.00	150.00

Known items:	Clear	Clear/ Frosting	Clear/ Color Stain
Open, flat			
Flared rim			
6" d.	30.00	40.00	50.00
7" d.	35.00	45.00	55.00
Straight-sided bowl			
6" d.	30.00	40.00	50.00
7" d.	35.00	45.00	55.00
8" d.	45.00	55.00	65.00
Bread plate, 6" d.	30.00	35.00	75.00
Butter dish with cover	55.00	75.00	150.00
Cake stand on high standard			
9" d.	110.00	135.00	225.00
10" d.	125.00	150.00	275.00
Celery			
Tray	30.00	40.00	55.00
Vase	45.00	55.00	75.00

Jeweled Moon and Stars tumbler.

Known items:	Clear	Clear/Frosting	Clear/Color Stain
Compote on high standard			
Covered			
6" d. 95.00		125.00	150.00
7" d. 110.00		150.00	175.00
8" d. 135.00		175.00	200.00
Open with scalloped rim			
6" d. 45.00		55.00	75.00
7" d. 55.00		65.00	85.00
Creamer.............. 40.00		45.00	65.00
Cruet with original			
stopper, 6-oz. 75.00		100.00	150.00
Eggcup, single, open ... 35.00		40.00	55.00
Goblet 75.00		95.00	135.00
Pitcher, water, bulbous with applied			
handle, 1/2-gal...... 125.00		150.00	200.00
Plate, round, 6" d. 25.00		30.00	45.00
Relish dish, oval....... 20.00		25.00	40.00
Sauce dish, round, flat.. 8.00		10.00	20.00
Saltshaker, bulbous 35.00		40.00	65.00
Spoon holder 35.00		40.00	55.00
Sugar bowl with cover . 55.00		75.00	95.00
Syrup pitcher with			
glass lip............ 135.00		175.00	225.00
Tray, water, round 65.00		75.00	85.00
Tumbler, water, flat 45.00		55.00	65.00
Wine................ 55.00		65.00	100.00

JUMBO

Non-flint. Type-1: Brilliant Glass Works, Brilliant, OH, c. 1881, Central Glass Co., Wheeling, WV, c. 1885. Type-2: Canton Glass Company, Canton, OH, c. 1883.

Original color production: Clear with acid finished finial. Amber, blue or any other color would be considered very rare. Designed by David Baker and patented September 23, 1884. Items produced at Brilliant & Central can be distinguished by their *"Barnum Head"* handles.

Reproductions and Look-a-Likes: None known.

Jumbo covered compote. (Type-1)

Type-1: With Barnum Head handles.

Known items:	Clear w/Frosting
Butter dish, covered with *"Barnum Head"* handles ...	$650.00
Compote with cover on high standard	
7" d..................................	850.00
8" d..................................	1,100.00
9" d..................................	1,700.00

Jumbo round butter dish. (Type-1)

Jumbo covered sugar (Canton). (Type-2)

Jumbo spoon holder. (Type-2)

Jumbo creamer and covered sugar. (Type 1)

Known items:	Clear w/Frosting

Creamer with *"Barnum Head"* motif at base of
handle 175.00

Pitcher, water, 1/2-gal. with *"Barnum Head"*
motif at base of handle 2,500.00

Sauce dish, round, footed 75.00

Spoon holder with *"Barnum Head"* motif at base of
handles 175.00

Sugar bowl with cover 550.00

Type-2: With circus wagon wheels & cross hatching.

Butter dish, covered with ribbed handles $1,100.00

Celery vase

    With ribbing 550.00

    Without ribbing 350.00

Known items:	Clear w/Frosting

Cheese dish with cover, oblong, 4-toed with
attached bail handle

    With removable ice drainer 1,500.00

    Without ice drainer 850.00

Creamer

    With ribbing 400.00

    Without ribbing 300.00

Pitcher, water, 1/2-gal. 2,500.00

Spoon holder

    With ribbing 400.00

    Without ribbing 250.00

Spoon rack (R)

    No patent date 750.00

    With embossed patent date "PAT SEPT 23 1884"
    on base 1,000.00

Sugar, cover with ribbing 900.00

KANSAS

OMN: U.S. Glass No. 15,072-Kansas. Kokomo No. 8. **AKA:** Jewel and Dewdrop, Jewel with Dewdrop, Jewel with Dewdrops.

Non-flint. The United States Glass Company, Pittsburgh, PA, c. 1901. Kokomo Glass Manufacturing Company, Kokomo, IN, c. 1903. Federal Glass Company, Columbus, OH, c. 1914.

Original color production: Clear (plain, gilded, less often blushed with pink stain).

Reproductions and Look-a-Likes: Small mug, D.C. Jenkins Glass Company, Kokomo, IN. Unmarked.

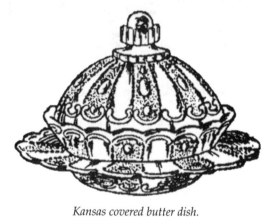

Kansas covered butter dish.

Known items:	Clear
Banana stand, flat with turned-up sides	$110.00
Bowl, round, flat, deep with scalloped rim	
Covered	
6" d.	85.00
7" d.	95.00
8" d.	125.00
Open	
6" d.	30.00
7" d.	40.00
8" d.	45.00

Known items:	Clear
Butter dish with cover	
Flanged with attached under plate	
Notched lid	175.00
Plain lid	125.00
Round, flat without underplate	150.00
Cake stand	
High standard	
8" d.	85.00
9" d.	110.00
10" d.	135.00
Low standard	
8" d.	65.00
9" d.	85.00
10" d.	95.00
Celery vase (R)	125.00
Champagne (VR)	650.00
Compote	
Covered on high standard	
Beading on pedestal base	
6" d.	95.00
7" d.	125.00
8" d.	175.00
Without beading on pedestal	
5" d.	
Notched lid	125.00
Plain lid	85.00
6" d.	
Notched lid	150.00
Plain lid	95.00
Open	
High standard	
Beading on pedestal base	
6" d.	45.00
7" d.	55.00
8" d.	65.00
Without beading on pedestal, 5" d.	55.00

Kansas covered compote on high standard.

Known items:	Clear
Low standard	
Deep scalloped bowl	
6" d.	55.00
7" d.	75.00
8" d.	95.00
Saucer-shaped scalloped bowl	
7-1/2" d.	45.00
8-1/2" d.	55.00
9-1/2" d.	75.00
Creamer with pressed handle	85.00
Cup with handle	30.00
Dish, oval, preserve, 8-1/2" l.	35.00
Goblet	125.00
Mug	
Large	65.00
Small	25.00
Pickle dish, oblong.	25.00
Pitcher with pressed handle	
Milk, 1-qt.	225.00
Water, 1/2-gal.	75.00
Plate, oval	
Bread, oval with *"Give Us This Day Our Daily Bread"* center	75.00
Cake.	95.00
Preserve dish, oval, 8" l.	35.00
Relish tray, oval, 8-1/2" l.	25.00
Saltshaker	55.00

Sauce dish, round, flat with scallops, 4" d.	15.00
Spoon holder	85.00
Sugar bowl with cover	125.00
Syrup pitcher	325.00
Toothpick holder	85.00
Tumbler, flat	
Water	95.00
Whiskey	75.00
Wine	95.00

KENTUCKY

OMN: U.S. Glass No. 15,051-Kentucky.

Non-flint. The United States Glass Company, Pittsburgh, PA, c. 1897.

Original color production: Clear, emerald green. Clear with amber stain, clear with ruby stain, cobalt blue, or any other color is considered rare.

Reproductions and Look-a-Likes: None known.

Known items:	Clear
Bowl, open, round, flat	
7" d.	$20.00
8" d.	35.00
Butter dish with cover	85.00
Cake stand on high standard	
9-1/2" d.	85.00
10-1/2" d.	110.00
Celery	
Tray	
Large	30.00
Small	20.00
Vase.	45.00
Compote on high standard	
Covered	
5" d.	55.00
6" d.	65.00
7" d.	75.00
8" d.	110.00
Open	
5" d.	20.00
6" d.	25.00

Kentucky flat sauce, footed sauce, and handled flat nappy.

Known items:	Clear
7" d.	30.00
8" d.	35.00
Creamer	45.00
Cruet with original stopper	65.00
Cup, custard	10.00
Dish	
Oblong	
7" l.	15.00
8" l.	20.00
9" l.	25.00
10" l.	35.00
Square, open, flat, 5"	15.00
Goblet	95.00
Olive dish, handled	20.00
Pitcher, water, 1/2-gal.	110.00
Plate, square	
7"	35.00
9"	30.00
10"	45.00
Saltshaker	35.00
Sauce dish, square	
Flat	
4"	5.00
4-1/2"	5.00
Footed	
4"	8.00
4-1/2"	8.00
Spoon holder	45.00
Sugar bowl with cover	65.00
Syrup pitcher	110.00
Toothpick holder	35.00
Tumbler, water, flat	40.00
Wine	35.00

KING'S 500

OMN: AKA: Bone Stem, King's Comet (lamps), Parrot, Swirl and Thumbprint.

Non-flint. King Glass Company, Pittsburgh, PA, c. 1891. Designed by William C. King and patented under patent No. 120,505 February 3, 1891. The United States Glass Company, Pittsburgh, PA, at Factory "K," c. 1891-1898.

Original color production: Clear (plain, engraved, less often acid finished, gilded). Clear with ruby stain, green, or any other color would be considered rare.

Reproductions and Look-a-Likes: None known.

King's 500 jug.

King's 500 cologne bottles with original stoppers.

Known items:	Clear	Cobalt Blue
Bowl, open, round, flat		
5" d.	$10.00	$30.00
7" d.	15.00	35.00
8" d.	20.00	40.00
9" d.	35.00	55.00
Butter dish with cover	65.00	225.00
Cake stand, on high standard	95.00	425.00
Castor set complete in silver plate holder		
2 Bottles	65.00	175.00
3 Bottles	95.00	225.00
5 Bottles	125.00	275.00
Celery vase	35.00	125.00
Cologne bottle with original pressed faceted stopper		
1-oz.	35.00	75.00
2-oz.	40.00	85.00
4-oz.	45.00	95.00
6-oz.	55.00	110.00
8-oz.	65.00	125.00
Compote on high standard		
Covered		
Deep bowl		
8" d.	85.00	275.00
9" d.	110.00	325.00

Known items:	Clear	Cobalt Blue
Open		
Deep bowl with smooth rim		
8" d.	35.00	75.00
9" d.	45.00	95.00
Saucer-shaped bowl with smooth rim		
9" d.	30.00	75.00
10" d.	40.00	85.00
Cracker jar with original patterned cover (R)	135.00	525.00
Creamer, bulbous with applied handle		
Individual, flat	20.00	40.00
Table size with low circular foot	35.00	85.00
Cruet with original swirled stopper		
4-oz.	55.00	325.00
8-oz.	65.00	375.00
Cup, custard	15.00	55.00
Dish		
Round with applied finger grip ("Olive dish")	15.00	35.00
Square, flat		
Covered		
7"	75.00	225.00
8"	85.00	250.00
Open		
7"	20.00	65.00
8"	25.00	75.00
Goblet (design appears only on stem)	55.00	225.00
Finger bowl, circular foot with smooth rim	25.00	65.00
Lamp		
Oil		
Hand	85.00	—
Stand		
7-1/4" h.	85.00	—
8-1/4" h.	100.00	—
9-1/4" h.	110.00	—
Pitcher with applied handle		
Bulbous		
3-pts.	65.00	325.00
2-gal.	75.00	350.00
Jug (straight sided)		
3-pts.	55.00	300.00
2-gal.	65.00	325.00

Known items:	Clear	Cobalt Blue
Relish tray	20.00	45.00
Rose bowl	25.00	75.00
Saltshaker (VR)		
Bulbous, squat	35.00	125.00
Tall, straight-sided	40.00	135.00
Sauce dish, round, flat, 4" d.	5.00	25.00
Saucer, 4-1/2" d.	20.00	35.00
Spoon holder	30.00	85.00
Sugar bowl with cover		
Individual	20.00	45.00
Table size	45.00	125.00
Tray, water, round with tab		
handles	55.00	175.00
Syrup pitcher	110.00	375.00
Tumbler, water, flat	25.00	75.00
Whiskey jug, 8-1/2" h. With		
original lock top (VR)	225.00	—
Wine (design appears		
only on stem)	35.00	95.00

KING'S CROWN

OMN: XLCR., Excelsior. **AKA:** Blue Thumbprint, Ruby Thumbprint, Ruby Thumbprint-Clear.

Non-flint. Adams & Company, Pittsburgh, PA, c. 1880. The United States Glass Company, Pittsburgh, PA, at Factory "A," c. 1891.

Original color production: Clear, clear with ruby stain. Clear stained with amethyst, gold, green, yellow (plain, engraved, souvenired).

Reproductions and Look-a-Likes: 5-1/4" sq. ashtray; 9" d. open flat berry bowl; 4-1/4" d. open flat finger bowl; 11-1/2" d. open low-footed bowl with crimped rim; 12-1/2" d. open low-footed bowl; 10-1/4" d. open knob-stem footed fruit bowl; low-standard cake stands: 12" d., 12-1/2" d. without rim; 5-1/2" h. 2-light candle holder; candle sticks: 3-3/4" h., 4" h.; 8-1/2" h.; 6" d. round covered flat candy box; 4-1/2" h. claret; cocktails: 4" h., 4-1/4" h.; high-standard covered compotes: 5" d., 6" d., 8" d.; high-standard open compotes: 5" d., 7" d., 9-3/4" d. with smooth rim, 10-1/4" d.; 2-oz. cordial; bulbous creamer with pressed handle; 3-1/2" h. cup; cup and saucer set; goblets: 5-1/2" h., 5-3/4" h., 9-oz.; juice glasses: 4-oz. with straight bowl, 42-oz.; 24" d. lazy Susan; mayonnaise sets: 3-piece, 4-piece; 4" d. nappy; 24" d. party server; 7-1/2" h. water pitcher; round plates: 5" d. (dinner), 7-3/8" d., 8-1/4" d. (salad), 8-1/2" d., 10" d. plate, 10-1/4" d., 13-1/2" d., 14" d. plate; 10-1/2" d. platter; 13-1/4" d. relish dish; salad sets: 3-piece, 4-piece; 4" d. round flat sauce dish; 6" d. round saucer; punch bowl sets: 10-qt. with round rim, 12-qt. with flared rim; 14" d. round flat 5-part relish; sherbets: 3-1/4" h., 3-1/2" h.; 8-piece snack set; open sugar bowls: double-handled circular footed open sugar bowl, 3" h.; 52-oz. footed sundae; tidbit trays: 2-tier, 3-tier; tumblers: 5-1/2" h. (iced tea), 11-oz. bulbous (iced tea with low circular foot), 12-oz. bulbous (iced tea with knob stem); wines: 3-1/2" h., 4-1/2" h., 4-3/4" h. (Clear, clear with cranberry stain, clear with blue stain, clear with gold, clear with platinum, clear with ruby stain, golden amber, olive green). Imperial Glass Corporation, Bellaire, OH, Indiana Glass Company, Dunkirk, IN, D.C. Jenkins Glass Company, Kokomo, IN, Lancaster Colony Corporation, Lancaster, OH, United States Glass Company, Tiffin, OH. Only permanently marked items are those embossed with the "USG" insignia of the United States Glass Company.

Known items:	Clear	Clear w/Ruby
Banana dish on high standard with folded sides (made from a cake stand) 10" l.	$225.00	$1200.00
Bowl		
Covered with collared base		
5" d.	55.00	175.00
6" d.	65.00	200.00
7" d.	85.00	225.00
8" d.	95.00	275.00
9" d.	110.00	325.00
Open		
Collared base		
Flared bowl		
6" d.	25.00	45.00
7" d.	30.00	55.00
8" d.	35.00	75.00
9-1/2" d.	45.00	110.00

King's Crown covered bowl.

King's Crown mustard.

Known items:	Clear	Clear w/Ruby
Plain rim, round		
5" d.	20.00	40.00
6" d.	25.00	45.00
7" d.	30.00	50.00
8" d.	35.00	75.00
9" d.	55.00	110.00
Flat		
Belled round bowl		
5" d.	20.00	35.00
6" d.	25.00	40.00
7" d.	30.00	45.00
8" d.	35.00	65.00
9" d.	55.00	100.00
Boat-shaped bowl		
8" l.	75.00	175.00
8-1/2" l.	95.00	225.00
10-1/2" l.	125.00	275.00
Flared round bowl		
6-3/4" d.	30.00	55.00
8-1/2" d.	45.00	95.00
Straight-sided bowl		
5" d.	20.00	40.00
6" d.	25.00	45.00
7" d.	30.00	50.00
8-1/2" d.	40.00	65.00
9-1/2" d.	55.00	85.00

Known items:	Clear	Clear w/Ruby
Butter dish with cover	125.00	225.00
Cake stand on high standard		
9" d.	125.00	450.00
10" d.	150.00	550.00
Castor set, 4 bottles with original stoppers in original frame (R)	300.00	850.00
Celery vase	45.00	110.00
Champagne	25.00	65.00
Cheese plate, 7" d.	25.00	55.00
Claret	30.00	75.00
Compote, round		
Covered on high standard		
5" d.	40.00	500.00
6" d.	55.00	600.00
7" d.	65.00	725.00
8" d.	95.00	800.00
9" d.	125.00	900.00
Open		
Belled bowl		
5" d.	25.00	45.00
6" d.	30.00	55.00
7" d.	35.00	65.00
8" d.	45.00	85.00
9" d.	65.00	110.00
10" d.	85.00	275.00

King's Crown water pitcher.

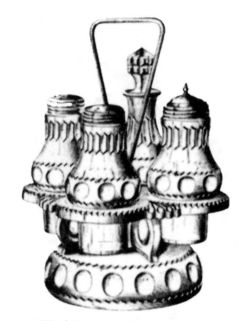

King's Crown four-bottle castor set.

Known items:	Clear	Clear w/Ruby
Flared bowl		
5-1/2" d. 25.00		45.00
6-1/2" d. 30.00		55.00
7-1/2" d. 35.00		65.00
8-1/4" d. 40.00		85.00
9" d. 50.00		95.00
9-1/2" d. 65.00		125.00
10" d. 95.00		275.00
11-1/2" d. 125.00		325.00
Creamer with applied handle		
Individual		
Squat, 3" h. 15.00		35.00
Tankard, 3-1/4" h. 25.00		45.00
Table size, bulbous 45.00		125.00
Custard cup 20.00		45.00
Dish		
Desert, 8" sq. 55.00		325.00
Olive, round with handle. . . 65.00		350.00
Goblet 15.00		55.00
Honey dish, covered with tab		
handles (R) 225.00		1,800.00
Lamp, oil		
Finger 95.00		—

Known items:	Clear	Clear w/Ruby
High standard, all glass, patterned font		
7-1/2" 150.00		—
8-1/2" 175.00		—
9-1/2" 225.00		—
Vase (Parlor) lamp (ER) . . 2,500.00		—
Marmalade jar with cover, 5" h. . . . 175.00		1,250.00
Mustard jar with cover and original		
notched lid, 4" h. 110.00		325.00
Orange or punch bowl, open, footed		
with serrated rim, 12" d. 650.00		1,800.00
Pickle		
Castor, complete in silver		
plated frame 225.00		1,100.00
Jar with cover 200.00		1,200.00
Pitcher with applied handle		
Bulbous		
Milk, 1-qt., 6-1/2" h. . . . 55.00		250.00
Water, 1/2-gal., 8" h. . . . 95.00		375.00
Tankard		
Milk		
7" h. 45.00		135.00
8-3/8" h. 65.00		225.00
Water, 11-1/4" h. 95.00		275.00

King's Crown engraved four-piece table set.

King's Crown footed punch bowl.

King's Crown master berry bowl.

Known items:	Clear	Clear w/Ruby
Preserve dish, oval		
6" l.	15.00	55.00
10" l.	25.00	175.00
Salt		
Individual		
Rectangular	22.50	70.00
Square	40.00	110.00
Master		
Rectangular	75.00	225.00
Square	150.00	325.00
Shaker	25.00	95.00
Sauce dish, flat		
Boat shaped		
4" l.	18.00	65.00
5-1/4" l.	20.00	75.00

Known items:	Clear	Clear w/Ruby
Round		
Belled		
4" d.	5.00	25.00
4-1/2" d.	5.00	30.00
Flared, 5" d.	5.00	35.00
Straight sided		
4" d.	5.00	25.00
4-1/2" d.	5.00	30.00
Saucer	20.00	35.00
Spoon holder, 4-1/4" h.	25.00	65.00
Sugar bowl		
Individual, open	25.00	55.00
Table size with cover	55.00	225.00
Toothpick holder	25.00	35.00
Tumbler, water, flat	30.00	65.00
Wine, 4-3/8" h.	10.00	35.00

KLONDIKE

OMN: Dalzell No. 75 & No. 75D-Amberette.

AKA: English Hobnail Cross, Frosted Amberette, Klondyke.

Non-flint. Dalzell, Gilmore & Leighton Glass Company, Findlay, OH, c. 1898.

Original color production: Clear, clear with acid finish, clear with acid finish and amber stain.

Reproductions and Look-a-Likes: Covered sugar bowl (amber, clear). Unmarked.

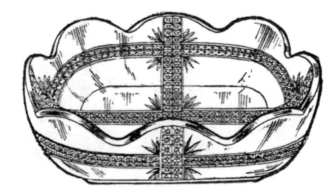

Klondike oblong, flat berry bowl.

Klondike saltshaker.

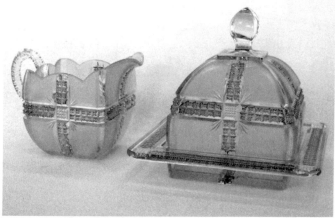

Klondike creamer and butter dish.

Known items:	Clear	Clear w/Amber	Clear /Frosted w/Amber
Bowl, open, flat			
Rectangular			
11"..........	$50.00	$95.00	$225.00
Square			
7"...........	35.00	65.00	150.00
8"...........	40.00	75.00	175.00
9"...........	45.00	85.00	225.00
Butter dish with cover......	95.00	175.00	350.00
Cake stand on high standard,			
8" sq.	125.00	225.00	750.00
Celery			
Tray, oblong	45.00	95.00	175.00
Vase	65.00	110.00	200.00

Known items:	Clear	Clear w/Amber	Clear /Frosted w/Amber
Champagne (R)...........	275.00	375.00	950.00
Creamer	35.00	75.00	225.00
Cruet with original stopper.	150.00	225.00	650.00
Cup, custard..............	20.00	55.00	110.00
Dish, oval, flat, shallow	35.00	95.00	150.00
Goblet	85.00	250.00	650.00
Pitcher, water, 1/2-gal.			
Round, tankard with applied handle ...	175.00	325.00	575.00
Square...........	200.00	350.00	625.00
Relish tray, boat shaped, 9" l..	35.00	95.00	150.00
Saltshaker			
Squat.............	45.00	75.00	275.00
Tall	55.00	85.00	250.00

Klondike spoon holder, butter dish, and creamer.

Klondike spoon holder and sugar bowl.

Known items:	Clear	Clear w/Amber	Clear /Frosted w/Amber
Sauce dish, square, flat	25.00	55.00	135.00
Spoon holder	45.00	85.00	225.00
Sugar bowl with cover	65.00	110.00	275.00
Syrup pitcher	150.00	350.00	1,500.00
Toothpick holder	95.00	200.00	400.00
Tray, flat, 5-1/2" sq.	40.00	85.00	200.00
Tumbler, water, flat	35.00	75.00	150.00
Vase, trumpet shaped			
7" h.	35.00	85.00	175.00
8" h.	40.00	95.00	200.00
9" h.	45.00	110.00	225.00
10" h.	50.00	135.00	250.00
Wine (R)	135.00	225.00	550.00

KOKOMO

OMN: Richards & Hartley No. 190. **AKA:** Bar & Diamond, Jenkins No. 623, R&H Swirl Band.

Non-flint. Richards & Hartley Glass Co., Tarentum, PA, c. 1885. The United States Glass Company, Pittsburgh, PA, c. 1891. Kokomo Glass Co., Kokomo, IN, c. 1901.

Original color production: Clear, clear with ruby stain (plain, engraved).

Reproductions and Look-a-Likes: None known.

Known items:	Clear	Clear w/Ruby
Bowl, open, round		
Flat		
6" d.	$20.00	$45.00
7" d.	25.00	—
8" d.	30.00	—
Footed, 8-1/2" d.	30.00	65.00
Butter dish with cover		
Flat	45.00	125.00
Footed	55.00	—
Cake stand on high standard	85.00	375.00
Celery vase	35.00	75.00
Compote		
Covered on high standard		
5" d.	55.00	125.00
6" d.	65.00	150.00

Kokomo seven-piece wine set on original under tray.

Known items:	Clear	Clear w/Ruby
7" d.	75.00	175.00
8" d.	95.00	225.00
Open		
High standard		
5" d.	25.00	75.00
6" d.	30.00	85.00
7" d.	35.00	95.00
8" d.	45.00	110.00
Low standard		
5" d.	20.00	—
6" d.	25.00	—
7" d.	30.00	—
7-1/2" d.	35.00	—
8" d.	40.00	—
Condiment set (cruet, salt & pepper shakers, under tray)	150.00	550.00
Creamer with applied handle	35.00	75.00
Cruet with original stopper	55.00	325.00
Decanter with original stopper, 9-3/4" h.	45.00	150.00

Known items:	Clear	Clear w/Ruby
Dish, open, oblong		
7" l.	15.00	—
8" l.	20.00	—
9" l.	25.00	—
10" l.	35.00	—
Finger bowl	25.00	—
Goblet	30.00	85.00
Lamp, oil, handled on low foot	95.00	275.00
Pickle dish, oval	15.00	35.00
Pitcher		
Bulbous		
Milk, 1-qt.	65.00	175.00
Water, 1/2-gal.	75.00	200.00
Tankard		
Milk		
2-pt.	45.00	150.00
1-qt.	55.00	175.00
Water, 1/2-gal.	85.00	225.00
Saltshaker	25.00	55.00
Sauce dish		
Flat		
4" d.	5.00	15.00
5" d.	5.00	20.00
Footed		
4" d.	5.00	15.00
5" d.	5.00	20.00
Spoon holder	30.00	65.00
Sugar bowl with cover	45.00	95.00
Syrup pitcher with pressed handle	95.00	325.00
Tray		
Bread, oblong	30.00	85.00
Water, round	35.00	110.00
Tumbler, water, flat	25.00	55.00
Wine	15.00	45.00

LEAF AND DART

OMN: Pride. **AKA:** Double Leaf and Dart.

Non-flint. Richards & Hartley Flint Glass Company, Pittsburgh, PA, c. 1875. The United States Glass Company, Pittsburgh, PA, c. 1891.

Original color production: Clear.

Reproductions and Look-a-Likes: None known.

Leaf and Dart master salt.

Leaf and Dart goblet.

Known items:	Clear
Bowl, open, footed, 8-1/2" d.	$45.00
Butter dish with cover and flanged base, 7" d.	85.00
Celery vase	65.00
Compote	
Covered	
Low standard	85.00
High standard	110.00

Known items:	Clear
Creamer, pedestaled with an applied handle, 6" h.	45.00
Eggcup, single, open	30.00
Goblet	35.00
Honey dish, round, flat	10.00
Lamp, finger, flat	150.00
Pitcher, bulbous with applied handle	
Milk, 1-qt.	225.00
Water, 1/2-gal.	175.00
Relish tray	15.00
Salt, master	
Covered	135.00
Uncovered	35.00
Sauce dish, round, flat, 4" d.	5.00
Spoon holder	30.00
Sugar bowl with cover	65.00
Syrup pitcher with applied handle	250.00
Tumbler, water, footed	35.00
Wine	20.00

LEAF AND FLOWER

OMN: Hobbs' No. 339.

Non-flint. Hobbs, Brockunier & Company, Wheeling, WV, c. 1890. The United States Glass Company, Pittsburgh, PA, c. 1891.

Original color production: Clear, clear with amber stain (plain, acid finished). Clear with ruby stain would be considered very rare.

Reproductions and Look-a-Likes: None known.

Leaf and Flower rare cruet set.

Leaf and Flower seven-piece berry set.

Leaf and Flower breadbasket.

Known items:	Clear w/Amber	Clear/ Frosted w/Amber
Bowl, open, round, flat		
Deep bowl		
5" d.	$25.00	$35.00
7" d.	35.00	55.00
8" d.	45.00	65.00
Shallow saucer-shaped bowl		
7" d.	35.00	55.00
8" d.	45.00	65.00
9" d.	65.00	85.00
Butter dish with cover on flanged base	75.00	135.00

Known items:	Clear w/Amber	Clear/ Frosted w/Amber
Celery		
Basket, flat with rope handle	95.00	150.00
Vase	55.00	110.00
Creamer on low circular foot with applied handle	55.00	95.00
Cruet set, oil bottle, shakers, mustard on leaf shaped tray	250.00	375.00
Finger bowl with scalloped rim	55.00	75.00
Pitcher, water, tankard with low circular foot and applied handle	125.00	225.00
Saltshaker	45.00	75.00
Sauce dish, round, flat, 4" d.	15.00	30.00
Spoon holder, squat	45.00	75.00
Sugar bowl with cover	65.00	110.00
Syrup pitcher	175.00	325.00
Tumbler, water, flat	45.00	65.00

LEAF AND STAR

OMN: New Martinsville No. 711. **AKA:** Tobin.

Non-flint. New Martinsville Glass Manufacturing Company, New Martinsville, WV, c. 1909.

Original color production: Clear (plain, gilded). Clear with ruby stain, iridescent carnival orange, or any other color would be considered rare,

Reproductions and Look-a-Likes: None known.

Leaf and Star covered sugar.

Leaf and Star creamer.

Known items:	Clear
Banana dish on low standard, 8-1/2"	$35.00
Bowl, open, round, footed	
Berry, deep	
Flared bowl, 7" d.	25.00
Scalloped bowl, 8" d.	30.00
Fruit with crimped rim, 10" d.	35.00
Nut	
4" d., with cupped rim	10.00
4-1/2" d.	
Crimped rim	10.00
Flared rim	10.00
Butter dish with cover and flanged base	45.00
Celery	
Tray	20.00
Vase	35.00
Compote, open on high standard (Jelly)	15.00
Creamer, 4-1/2" h.	30.00
Cruet with original faceted stopper, 5-oz.	45.00
Custard cup	10.00
Dish	
Flat	
Bonbon with turned-up sides, 5"	15.00
Ice cream, 6" d.	15.00
Footed, candy with folded sides, 6-1/2" . .	15.00
Dresser jar with original metal lid.	35.00
Goblet	25.00
Hair receiver with original metal lid	35.00
Humidor with original metal lid, 5" h.	75.00
Pitcher, water, 1/2-gal.	
With ice lip	65.00
Without ice lip	50.00

Known items:	Clear
Plate, round	
6" d.	15.00
8" d.	20.00
Relish tray	15.00
Saltshaker.	30.00
Sauce dish, round	
Fat with crimped rim	
4" d.	5.00
4-1/2" d.	5.00
Footed with flared rim	
4" d.	8.00
4-1/2" d.	8.00
Spoon holder	25.00
Sugar bowl with cover	35.00
Toothpick holder.	20.00
Tumbler, water, flat.	20.00
Vase, tulip, 8-1/4" h.	25.00
Wine	15.00

LIBERTY BELL

OMN: AKA: Gillinder's Centennial.

Non-flint: Adams & Co., Pittsburgh, PA, c. 1875. Designed by James C. Gill and patented under patent No. 8,663, September 28, 1875. Manufactured at the Gillinder factory erected at the Philadelphia Exhibition of 1876 and sold as souvenirs, such items as the mugs with snake handles and the "Liberty Bell-shaped" saltshakers are not a part of the original line.

Original color production: Clear. Milk white or any other color would be considered very rare. Designed by James C. Gill and patented under patent No. 8,663, September 28, 1875. Manufactured at the Gillinder factory erected at the Philadelphia Exhibition of 1876 and sold as souvenirs; such items as the mugs with snake handles and the "Liberty Bell-shaped" saltshakers are not a part of the original line.

Reproductions and Look-a-Likes: 7-oz. goblet, 10-oz. goblet, signer's platter (inscribed *"Two Hundred Years Ago 1776-1976 Declaration of Independence"*), freedom platter (inscribed *"Give Us This Day Our Daily Bread"*), and the John Hancock platter (inscribed *"Two Hundred Years Ago 1776-1976 Declaration of Independence"* with Hancock's signature). (Clear). Each permanently embossed "A.H.R.C. Grand Rapids, MI" signifying the American Historical Replica Company, Grand Rapids, MI.

Liberty Bell spoon holder.

Known items:	Clear
Bowl, master berry, open on low foot, 8" d.	$55.00
Butter dish with cover.	135.00
Celery tray, 11-1/4" l. (S)	110.00
Compote, open, round on low collared base	
6" d.	45.00
6-1/4" d.	55.00
Creamer, table size	
Applied clear handle	125.00
Applied reeded handle	150.00

Known items:	Clear
Goblet	25.00
Miniatures	
Butter dish with cover	300.00
Creamer with pressed handle	125.00
Mug with pressed handle, 2" h.	
Inscribed "1776-1876" between two Liberty Bells	225.00
Inscribed "Wheeler & Hayes" (VR)	550.00
Spoon holder (R)	450.00
Sugar bowl with cover	175.00
Mug with snake handle, footed (Gillinder)	550.00
Pickle dish, flat	25.00
Pitcher, water with applied reeded handle, 1/2-gal.	1,250.00
Plate, round, handled	
6" d. (dated)	85.00
8" d.	95.00
10" d.	110.00
Platter	
"100 Years Ago, John Hancock" with twig handles, 13-3/8" l.	55.00
"Signer's Border," 13" l.	85.00
"Thirteen States," 13" l.	75.00
Relish tray, oval	30.00
Salt	
Dip, individual, oval, flat, 2-1/4" l.	35.00
Shaker (Gillinder)	150.00
Sauce dish, round, 4-1/2" d.	
Flat (S)	55.00
Footed	10.00
Spoon holder, 6-1/4" h.	55.00
Sugar bowl with cover	125.00

LILY OF THE VALLEY

OMN: Mayflower. **AKA:** Lily of the Valley on Legs.

Non-flint. Richards & Hartley Flint Glass Company, Tarentum, PA, c. 1870s.

Original color production: Clear. Issued in two conspicuous forms: (a) items having hexagonal stems and applied handles and (b) items having 3 legs and pressed handles.

Lily of the Valley three-legged spooner.

Lily of the Valley rare champagne.

Known items:	Clear
Bowl, open, flat, master berry	$85.00
Butter dish with cover	
Flat	125.00
3-legged	225.00
Cake stand on high standard	350.00
Celery vase, 8" h.	175.00
Champagne, 5" h. (VR)	400.00
Compote with cover on high standard	
7-1/2" d.	175.00
8-1/2" d.	225.00
Creamer	
Pedestaled with applied handle	95.00
3-legged with pressed handle	125.00
Cruet with applied handle	550.00
Dish, oval, flat (3 sizes)	45.00
Eggcup, open, single, footed	75.00
Goblet	150.00
Honey dish, round, flat, 3-1/2" d.	20.00
Pickle scoop, tapered 8" l.	35.00
Pitcher, bulbous with applied handle	
Milk, 1-qt.	275.00
Water, 1/2-gal.	350.00
Salt, master with cover	
Pedestaled	225.00
3-legged	325.00

Known items:	Clear
Sauce dish, round, flat, 4" d.	15.00
Spoon holder	
Pedestaled	65.00
3-legged	110.00
Sugar bowl with cover	
Pedestaled	150.00
3-legged	175.00
Tumbler, water (R)	
Flat	225.00
Footed	150.00
Wine (R)	225.00

LINCOLN DRAPE

AKA: Oval and Lincoln Drape.

Flint, non-flint. The Boston & Sandwich Glass Company, Sandwich, MA, c. 1865-1880.

Original color production: Clear. Cobalt blue, opaque white, green, or any other color would be considered very rare. Issued both with and without the ornamental "tassel" motif.

Reproductions and Look-a-Likes: Miniature oil lamp (clear). Unmarked.

Lincoln Drape eggcup.

Known items:	Clear
Butter dish, covered............................	$225.00
Compote	
Covered on high standard	
6-1/2" d..............................	375.00
7-1/2" d..............................	450.00
Open on low standard	
6" d...................................	125.00
7-1/2" d..............................	175.00
8-1/2" d..............................	225.00

Known items:	Clear
Creamer with applied handle	250.00
Decanter, bar lip..............................	375.00
Eggcup, single, open, footed	75.00
Goblet	
Gentleman's (large), 6" h.	
Plain no tassel	150.00
With tassel	350.00
Lady's (small)........................	275.00
Honey dish, round, flat........................	20.00
Lamp, oil	
All glass	650.00
Marble base with brass stem	325.00
Pitcher, water with applied handle (R)...........	5,500.00
Plate, round, 6" d.	125.00
Salt, master, open, footed	65.00

Spoon holder	.75.00
Sugar bowl with cover	.175.00
Syrup pitcher with applied handle	.325.00
Tumbler, flat.................................	.375.00

LION

AKA: Frosted Lion.

Non-flint. Gillinder & Sons, Philadelphia, PA, c. 1877.

Original color production: Clear with frosting (plain, engraved). Notable characteristics: collared bases, *Lion Head and Tree Trunk* or *Rampant Lion* finials. Clear items without frosting are less common.

Reproductions and Look-a-Likes: Bread plate; covered butter dish; celery vase; covered oval compote; eggcup; goblet; reclining paper weight; round low footed 2-7/8" d. master salt; water pitcher with applied handle; round footed sauce dish; spoon holder; covered sugar bowl (clear, clear with frosting). L.G. Wright Glass Company, New Martinsville, WV, Summit Art Glass Company, Akron, OH, unmarked.

Known items:	Clear/w Frosting
Butter dish with cover	$175.00
Celery vase...................................	.95.00
Cheese dish with cover	.850.00
Cologne bottle with original stopper (VR)	7,500.00
Compote with cover	
Oval on collared base	
6-7/8" l.	.150.00
7-1/4" l.	.175.00
8-1/4" l.	.200.00
Round on collared base	
7" d.	.275.00
8" d.	.325.00
Three-lion face stem	
6" d. (S)	.325.00
7" d.	.225.00
8" d.	.275.00
9" d.	.450.00
Creamer	.85.00
Eggcup, open, single	.125.00

Lion close-up.

Lion close-up of pattern.

Lion covered compote.

Lion covered compote on collared base.

Lion covered marmalade.

Lion covered oval compote.

Lion rare etched wine.

Lion rare covered cheese dish.

Lion syrup.

Known items:	Clear w/Frosting
Goblet	125.00
Marmalade jar with cover	125.00
Pitcher bulbous with applied handle	
Milk, 1-qt.	2,500.00
Water, 1/2-gal.	750.00
Platter, 13" l.	110.00
Pomade jar with cover (ER)	5,500.00
Salt, master, open, rectangular on collared base	575.00
Sauce dish, round on collared base	
4" d.	25.00
4-1/2" d.	30.00
5" d.	65.00
Spoon holder on collared base	85.00

Known items:	Clear w /Frosting
Sugar bowl, with cover on collared base	150.00

Lion water pitcher.

LION AND BABOON

Non-flint. Maker unknown, c. late 1870s, early 1880s.

Original color production: Clear.

Reproductions and Look-a-Likes: None known.

Lion and Baboon spoon holder.

Known items:	Clear
Butter dish with cover	$425.00
Celery vase	275.00

Known items:	Clear
Creamer	225.00
Pitcher with pressed handle	
Milk, 1-qt.	1,250.00
Water, 1/2-gal.	1,000.00
Spoon holder	200.00
Sugar bowl with cover	350.00

LION AND CABLE

Lion and Cable marmalade.

OMN: Richards & Hartley No. 525-Proud Lion. **AKA:** Tiny Lion.

Non-flint. Richards & Hartley Glass Company, Tarentum, PA, c. 1880s.

Original color production: Clear, clear with acid finish (plain, engraved).

Reproductions and Look-a-Likes: 10-1/2" d. round tab-handled bread plate (amber, blue, clear, clear with frosted center). L.G. Wright Glass Company, New Martinsville, WV. Unmarked.

Known items:	Clear
Syrup pitcher, applied handle, original lid	
6-1/2" h. Lid dated *"July 16,'72 - C&W"*	850.00
7-3/8" h. Lid dated *"July 16, '72"*	925.00
9" h., undated lid	1,000.00
Wine (R)	1,250.00

Lion and Cable double-handled plate.

Lion Head covered butter dish.

Known items:	Clear
Butter dish with cover	$135.00
Celery vase, double handled	85.00
Compote, covered	
High standard	
7" d.	125.00
8" d.	150.00
9" d.	175.00
Low standard	
7" d.	85.00
8" d.	100.00
9" d.	125.00
Creamer with pressed handle	55.00
Goblet (R)	175.00
Marmalade jar with cover	135.00
Pitcher, with tiny lion on handle	
Milk, 1-qt.	135.00
Water, 1/2-gal.	150.00
Plate, bread with *"Proud Lion"* center	55.00
Saltshaker, double handled	75.00
Sauce dish, round	15.00
Spoon holder double handled	75.00
Sugar bowl, with cover	125.00

LION HEAD

Non-flint. Gillinder & Sons, Philadelphia, PA, c. 1877.

Original color production: Clear and clear with frosting. Two versions of lids were made: with and without Thumbprints.

Reproductions and Look-a-Likes: None known.

Known items:	Clear w/Frosting:
Butter dish with cover	$110.00
Creamer, table size, cable base without lion	45.00
Compote with cover	
High standard, 3-lion face standard	
6" d.	150.00
7" d.	175.00
8" d.	200.00
9" d.	225.00
Low standard, cable base without lion	
7" d.	125.00
8" d.	150.00
Inkwell, lion head lid (S)	750.00
Marmalade jar with cover, lion-head finial	110.00
Miniatures	
Butter dish with cover, lion-head finial	175.00
Creamer	85.00
Cup and saucer set	110.00
Spoon holder	125.00
Sugar bowl with cover	135.00
Paperweight, lion head	150.00
Sauce dish, round, footed with cable base	
4" d.	5.00
4-1/2" d.	5.00
5" d.	8.00
Spoon holder with cable-edged base	30.00
Sugar bowl with cover	65.00

LOCKET ON A CHAIN

OMN: Heisey No. 160. **AKA:** Stippled Beaded Shield.

Non-flint. A.J. Heisey Company, Inc., Newark, OH, c. 1896.

Original color production: Clear. Clear with ruby stain (plain, gilded). Ruby stained items were decorated by the Oriental Glass Company, Pittsburgh, PA.

Reproductions and Look-a-Likes: None known.

Locket on a Chain goblet.

Locket on a Chain creamer.

Known items:	Clear	Clear w/Ruby
Plate, 8" d.	65.00	135.00
Saltshaker	85.00	175.00
Sauce dish, round, flat, 4" d.	25.00	50.00
Spoon holder	95.00	175.00
Sugar bowl with cover	150.00	325.00
Syrup pitcher (R)	450.00	2,250.00
Toothpick holder (VR)	325.00	1,500.00
Tumbler, water, flat	125.00	225.00
Wine	55.00	175.00

Known items:	Clear	Clear w/Ruby
Bowl, open, flat, master berry, 8" d.	$110.00	$325.00
Butter dish with cover	175.00	375.00
Cake stand on high standard	150.00	—
Celery vase	125.00	275.00
Compote on high standard, 8" d.		
Covered	325.00	850.00
Open, beaded rim	135.00	—
Creamer, 1-pt.	125.00	225.00
Cruet with original stopper (VR)	275.00	1,850.00
Goblet	150.00	650.00
Pickle tray	45.00	95.00
Pitcher, water, 1/2-gal.	375.00	950.00

LOG CABIN

OMN: Central No. 748.

Non-flint. Central Glass Company, Wheeling, WV, c. 1875.

Original color production: Amber, blue, canary, clear.

Reproductions and Look-a-Likes: "Lutteds" covered bowl, creamer, spoon holder, covered sugar bowl (clear, chocolate, cobalt blue). Unmarked. Creamer, spoon holder, sugar bowl produced by the Mosser Glass Works, Cambridge, OH, all items unmarked.

Log Cabin covered cough drop box.

Log Cabin sugar, spooner, and creamer.

Known items:	Amber	Blue	Canary	Clear
Bowl				
Door on base with cover	$1,200.00	$1,800.00	$1,500.00	$450.00
Door missing on base	750.00	1,200.00	850.00	275.00
Butter dish with cover	1,750.00	2,200.00	2,000.00	475.00
Compote with cover on high standard				
6" l.	—	—	—	750.00
7" l.	—	—	—	850.00
8" l.	—	—	—	1,000.00
Creamer	450.00	1,000.00	675.00	175.00
Marmalade jar with cover	1,800.00	2,850.00	2,500.00	550.00
Pitcher, water, 1/2-gal.	2,800.00	4,000.00	3,500.00	850.00
Sauce dish, flat, rectangular	175.00	250.00	225.00	95.00
Spoon holder	425.00	950.00	650.00	125.00
Sugar bowl with cover	1,000.00	1,500.00	1,250.00	325.00

LOOP

OMN: Central's No. 145, O'Hara No. 9, Portland Petal. **AKA:** McKee's O'Hara Pattern, Seneca Loop.

Flint, non-flint. Central Glass Company, Wheeling, WV, c. 1870. Challinor, Taylor & Company, Pittsburgh, PA, c. 1875. Doyle & Company, Pittsburgh, PA, c. 1875. James B. Lyon & Company, Pittsburgh, PA, c. 1860s. McKee Brothers, Pittsburgh, PA, c. 1860s. O'Hara Glass Company, Pittsburgh, PA, c. 1860s. Portland Glass Company, Portland, ME. Boston & Sandwich Glass Company, Sandwich, MA. United States Glass Company, Pittsburgh, PA, c. 1891.

Original color production: Clear. Amethyst, amber, blue, green, opalescent, or any other color would be considered rare.

Reproductions and Look-a-Likes: None known.

Known items:	Flint	Non-Flint
Bottle		
Bitters	$95.00	$45.00
Tumble-up with original		
tumbler (VR)	550.00	—
Bowl, with cover, 9" d.	175.00	75.00
Butter dish with cover		
New style with smooth rim	110.00	45.00
Old style with scalloped rim	135.00	—
Cake stand on high standard	275.00	—
Celery vase	65.00	35.00

Loop goblet.

Known items:	Flint	Non-Flint
Champagne	65.00	35.00
Compote		
High standard		
Covered		
7-1/2" d.	150.00	65.00
9-1/2" d.	175.00	75.00
Open		
Deep bowl		
7" d.	65.00	35.00
9" d.	75.00	40.00
10" d.	110.00	50.00
Shallow bowl		
7" d.	45.00	30.00
8-1/2" d.	55.00	35.00
10" d.	85.00	45.00
Low standard		
Covered		
7-1/2" d.	125.00	55.00
9-1/2" d.	150.00	65.00
Open		
Deep bowl		
7"	45.00	30.00
9" d.	55.00	35.00
10" d.	85.00	40.00
Shallow bowl		
7" d.	40.00	25.00
8-1/2" d.	50.00	30.00
10" d.	75.00	35.00

Known items:	Flint	Non-Flint
Cordial	95.00	20.00
Creamer with applied handle	110.00	45.00
Decanter		
New style with long neck and patterned stopper		
1-pt.	135.00	65.00
1-qt.	150.00	75.00
Old style with short neck		
Bar lip, 1-qt.	65.00	—
Patterned stopper		
1-pt.	175.00	—
1-qt.	200.00	—
Eggcup, single, open	30.00	15.00
Goblet		
Gentleman's	25.00	15.00
Lady's	25.00	15.00
Lamp, oil	225.00	100.00
Pitcher with applied handle		
Milk, 3-pts.	275.00	125.00
Water, 1/2-gal.	375.00	135.00
Plate, round	35.00	25.00
Salt, master, open, footed	25.00	15.00
Spoon holder	35.00	15.00
Sugar bowl with cover		
New style with smooth rim	85.00	45.00
Old style with scalloped rim	95.00	—
Syrup pitcher with applied handle	325.00	125.00
Tumbler, water		
Flat	55.00	25.00
Footed	35.00	15.00
Wine	35.00	15.00

LOOP AND DART

Non-flint. Richards & Hartley Glass Company, Tarentum, PA, c. 1888. Portland Glass Company, Portland, ME, c. 1869. Designed and patented by Annie W. Henderson.

Original color production: Clear.

Reproductions and Look-a-Likes: None known.

Loop and Dart goblet.

Loop and Dart spoon holder.

Known items:	Clear
Bowl, oval, open, flat, 9" l.	$30.00
Butter dish with cover	75.00
Cake stand on high standard, 10" d.	225.00
Celery vase	65.00
Champagne	65.00
Compote with cover, 8" d.	
High standard	125.00
Low standard	95.00
Creamer with applied handle, 6-1/4" h.	55.00
Cruet, footed with applied handle and original stopper	175.00
Cup plate	30.00
Eggcup, single, open	35.00
Goblet	40.00
Lamp, oil	175.00
Pickle tray	15.00
Pitcher, water, bulbous with applied handle, 1/2-gal.	275.00
Plate, 6" d. (R)	55.00
Relish tray	15.00
Salt, master with cover	110.00
Sauce dish, round, 4" d.	
Flat	5.00
Footed	8.00
Spoon holder	35.00
Sugar bowl with cover	65.00

Known items:	Clear
Tumbler, water	
Flat	55.00
Footed	35.00
Wine	35.00

LOOP AND DART WITH DIAMOND ORNAMENT

Flint, non-flint. Maker unknown, c. 1870s.

Original color production: Clear.

Reproductions and Look-a-Likes: None known.

Known items:	Clear
Bowl, open, oval, 9" l.	$25.00
Butter dish with cover	85.00
Celery vase	65.00
Compote	
Covered	
High standard	110.00
Low standard	85.00
Open	
High standard	55.00
Low standard	45.00
Creamer with applied handle	55.00

Loop and Dart with Diamond sugar.

Known items:	Clear
Eggcup, single, open	35.00
Goblet	35.00
Pitcher, water, bulbous with applied handle, 1/2-gal.	275.00
Plate, round, 6" d.	55.00
Relish tray, oval	15.00
Salt, master with cover	125.00
Sauce dish, round, flat	5.00
Spoon holder	35.00
Sugar bowl with cover	75.00
Tumbler, water	
Flat	65.00
Footed	35.00
Wine	30.00

Loop and Dart with Diamond tumbler.

LOOP AND DART, ROUND ORNAMENT

AKA: Portland Loop and Jewel

Flint, non-flint. Portland Glass Company, Portland, ME, c. 1869. Add 100% for flint items.

Original color production: Clear. Designed by W. O. Davis and patented May 11, 1869.

Reproductions and Look-a-Likes: None known.

Loop and Dart with Round Ornament celery vase.

Known items:	Clear
Bowl, open, oval, flat, 9" l.	$35.00
Butter dish with cover	85.00
Celery vase	65.00
Champagne	95.00
Compote with cover, 8" d.	
High standard	125.00
Low standard	110.00
Creamer with applied handle	65.00
Cup plate, 3" d.	30.00
Eggcup, single, open, footed	35.00
Honey dish, round, flat	8.00
Goblet	35.00

Known items: **Clear**

Lamp, oil 175.00

Pickle dish, oval 20.00

Pitcher, water, bulbous with applied handle,
  1/2-gal. 275.00

Plate, round, 6" d. 55.00

Relish tray, oval 15.00

Salt, master, open, footed 55.00

Sauce dish, round, flat

      3-1/4" d. with star base 5.00

      4" d. with loop and dart base. 8.00

Spoon holder 30.00

Sugar bowl with cover

      Cover fits inside base 95.00

      Cover sits over base 75.00

Tumbler

      Flat. 65.00

      Footed 40.00

Wine 30.00

LOOP WITH DEWDROP(S)

OMN: U.S. Glass No. 15,028.

Non-flint. The United States Glass Company, Pittsburgh, PA, c. 1892.

Original color production: Clear.

Reproductions and Look-a-Likes: None known.

Loop with Dewdrops covered butter.

Loop with Dewdrops covered sugar.

Known items: **Clear**

Bowl, open, round, deep

      5" d. $10.00

      6" d. 12.50

      7" d. 15.00

      8" d. 25.00

      9" d. 35.00

Butter dish with cover

      Handleless 45.00

      Tab-handled. 55.00

Cake stand on high standard

      9" d. 75.00

      10" d. 85.00

Celery vase. 35.00

Compote on high standard, round

    Covered

      5" d. 45.00

      6" d. 55.00

      7" d. 65.00

      8" d. 75.00

    Open

      4-1/2" d. 15.00

      5" d. 15.00

      6" d. 20.00

      7" d. 25.00

      8" d. 35.00

Condiment set under tray, handled 25.00

Creamer 30.00

Loop with Dewdrops goblet.

Loop with Dewdrops syrup.

Known items:	Clear
Cup	15.00
Cruet with original stopper	65.00
Dish, open, oval, flat	
7" l.	15.00
8" l.	20.00
9" l.	25.00
Goblet	35.00
Pickle dish, oval, handled.	15.00
Pitcher, water, 1/2-gal.	55.00
Plate, bread, handled.	20.00
Saltshaker	25.00
Sauce dish, round, 4" d.	
Flat	5.00
Footed	5.00

Known items:	Clear
Saucer	20.00
Spoon holder	25.00
Sugar bowl with cover	45.00
Syrup pitcher	95.00
Tumbler, water, flat	30.00
Wine	15.00

LOUISIANA

OMN: U.S. Glass No. 15,053-Louisiana. **AKA:** Granby, Sharp Oval and Diamond.

Non-flint. Bryce Brothers, Pittsburgh, PA, c. 1870s. The United States Glass Company, Pittsburgh, PA, at Factory "B," c. 1898.

Original color production: Clear (clear, less often frosted). Frosted items are worth 25-30% more.

Reproductions and Look-a-Likes: None known.

Louisiana goblet.

Known items:	Clear
Bowl, flat	
Covered, round	
6" d.	$45.00
7" d.	65.00
8" d.	75.00

Known items: **Clear**

   Open

      Round

         6" d. 20.00

         7" d. 25.00

         8" d. 45.00

      Square

         6" sq. 25.00

         7" sq. 35.00

         8" sq. 45.00

         9" sq. 95.00

Butter dish with cover and flanged base 95.00

Cake stand on high standard

      7" d. 65.00

      9" d. 85.00

      10" d. 95.00

Celery vase 45.00

Compote on high standard

   Covered

      6" d. 75.00

      7" d. 95.00

      8" d. 110.00

   Open

      Deep bowl

         5-1/2" d. 35.00

         6" d. 35.00

         7" d. 45.00

         8" d. 55.00

Known items: **Clear**

      Flared bowl, 6" d. 35.00

      Saucer-shaped bowl

         8" d. 55.00

         10" d. 75.00

Creamer 35.00

Dish with cover, handled, 6" d. 75.00

Goblet 35.00

Match holder with attached saucer base 35.00

Mug with handle. 40.00

Mustard with cover and underplate 85.00

Pickle dish, boat shaped. 15.00

Pitcher with pressed handle

      Milk, 1-qt. 65.00

      Water, 1/2-gal. 85.00

Relish tray 15.00

Saltshaker. 40.00

Sauce dish, flat

   Round

      4" d. 8.00

      4-1/2" d. 8.00

   Square

      4" 10.00

      4-1/2" 10.00

Spoon holder 45.00

Sugar bowl with cover 55.00

Tumbler, water, flat. 40.00

Wine 35.00

MAGNET AND GRAPE, FROSTED LEAF

Flint, non-flint. The Boston & Sandwich Glass Company, Sandwich, MA. c. 1860.

Original color production: Clear with frosted leaf.

Reproductions and Look-a-Likes: Goblet (clear, non-flint, unmarked). 6-1/2" goblet, 7" h. pedestaled creamer with applied handle, 8-3/4" h. covered sugar bowl (clear and frosted, sapphire blue). Imperial Glass Company, Bellaire, OH, under license with the Metropolitan Museum of Art, New York City, NY. Permanently marked with the museum's AMMA logo. Eggcup, 3-1/2" h. tumbler and 6-1/4" h. ale or open sugar. Also produced by the Imperial Glass Company under license to the Metropolitan Museum of Art and permanently embossed with the museum's logo, 4-oz. wine (clear and frosted). Imperial Glass Company under license to the Smithsonian Institution, Washington, DC, and permanently embossed with the Smithsonian's "SI" logo. Goblet, wine (clear): L.G. Wright Glass Company, New Martinsville, WV. Unmarked.

Magnet and Grape with Frosted Leaf goblet variant.

Known items:	Clear w/Frosted Leaf
Butter dish with cover	$275.00
Celery vase	375.00
Champagne	350.00
Compote, round	
Covered on high standard, 7-1/2" d.	450.00
Open	
High standard, 7-1/2" d.	150.00
Low standard	95.00
Creamer with applied handle	275.00
Decanter with original stopper	
1-pt.	375.00
1-qt.	425.00

Known items:	Clear w/Frosted Leaf
Goblet	
Low stem	110.00
Regular stem	95.00
Mug with applied handle	950.00
Pitcher with applied handle	
Milk, 1-qt.	1,800.00
Water, 1/2-gal.	1,500.00
Relish dish, oval	75.00
Salt, master, open, footed	95.00
Sauce dish, round, flat, 4" d.	25.00
Spoon holder	125.00
Sugar bowl with cover	225.00
Tumbler, flat	
Water	150.00
Whiskey	325.00
Wine	175.00
Wine jug with dated spigot (ER)	
With inscription	4,500.00
Without inscription	4,000.00

MAGNOLIA

Non-flint. Dalzell, Gilmore & Leighton Company, Findlay, OH, c. 1890.

Original color production: Clear, clear with frosting

Reproductions and Look-a-Likes: None known.

Magnolia tankard water pitcher.

Magnolia covered sugar bowl.

Magnolia syrup.

Magnolia cake standtop.

Known items:	Clear	Clear w/Frosting
Bowl, open, round, flat		
6" d.	$35.00	$65.00
7" d.	45.00	75.00
8" d.	55.00	100.00
Butter with cover	150.00	225.00
Cake plate on high foot	175.00	325.00
Celery vase	125.00	150.00
Creamer	65.00	110.00

Known items:	Clear	Clear w/Frosting
Goblet	85.00	150.00
Pitcher, water with applied handle	150.00	225.00
Saltshaker	45.00	85.00
Sauce dish, round, flat, 4" d.	10.00	20.00
Spoon holder	55.00	95.00
Sugar bowl with cover	85.00	175.00
Syrup	200.00	350.00
Tumbler, water	55.00	85.00

MAINE

> **OMN:** U.S. Glass No. 15,066. **AKA:** Paneled Flower, Paneled Stippled Flower, Stippled Paneled Flower, Stippled Primrose.
>
> Non-flint. The United States Glass Company, Pittsburgh, PA. c. 1899.
>
> **Original color production:** Clear (plain, fire enameled flowers in green, pink and white), emerald green.
>
> **Reproductions and Look-a-Likes:** None known.

Maine covered compote on high standard.

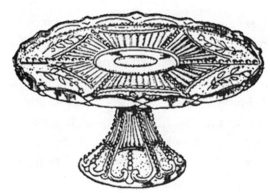

Maine cake stand.

Maine covered sugar bowl.

Known items:	Clear	Emerald Green
Bowl, flat		
Covered, round, 8" d.	$85.00	$135.00
Open		
Flared bowl, 8" d.	35.00	45.00
Oval, 8" l.	35.00	45.00
Round		
6" d.	25.00	30.00
7" d.	30.00	35.00
8" d.	55.00	75.00
Butter dish with cover and		
flanged base	135.00	225.00
Cake stand on high standard		
8" d.	55.00	75.00
9" d.	65.00	85.00
10" d.	75.00	95.00
11" d.	110.00	150.00
Celery vase	65.00	95.00

Known items:	Clear	Emerald Green
Compote		
Covered with high standard,		
5" d. (Jelly)	65.00	85.00
Open		
High standard		
Flared bowl		
8" d.	45.00	55.00
9" d.	55.00	65.00
10" d.	65.00	75.00

Maine water pitcher.

Known items:	Clear	Emerald Green
Round bowl		
5" d.	25.00	35.00
6" d.	35.00	45.00
7" d.	45.00	55.00
8" d.	65.00	85.00
Low standard		
8" d.	45.00	65.00
9" d.	55.00	65.00
Creamer	85.00	125.00
Cruet with original stopper	125.00	325.00
Goblet (VR)	450.00	650.00
Mug with handle	45.00	65.00
Pickle tray, 8" l.	25.00	35.00
Pitcher		
Milk, 1-qt.	85.00	110.00
Water, 1/2-gal.	110.00	150.00
Plate		
Bread, oval, 10" l.	45.00	65.00
Dinner, 10" d.	35.00	55.00
Preserve dish, 8" l.	25.00	35.00
Relish tray	25.00	30.00
Saltshaker	45.00	85.00
Sauce dish, round, flat, 4" d.	15.00	20.00
Spoon holder	75.00	110.00
Sugar bowl with cover	135.00	175.00
Syrup pitcher	125.00	275.00
Toothpick holder	150.00	375.00
Tumbler, water, flat	55.00	75.00
Wine	125.00	175.00

MANHATTAN

OMN: U.S. Glass No. 15,078-New York.

Non-flint. United States Glass Company, Pittsburgh, PA, at Factory "G" and Factory "P," c. 1902.

Original color production: Clear, clear with rose stain. Clear with blue, green, or any other color would be considered scarce. Clear items with color were decorated by the Oriental Glass Company, Pittsburgh, PA.

Reproductions and Look-a-Likes: Flat basket with folded sides and applied handle, 15-piece. Punch set consisting of the 11-oz. one-piece flat punch bowl, 12 punch cups and 23" round underplate with ladle. (Clear. The United States Glass Company, Tiffin, OH). Unmarked. 8-1/2" d. open round flat bowl, creamer, goblet, plates: 6" d., 11" d., round flat 4-1/2" d. sauce dish, footed sherbet, open sugar bowl, iced tea tumbler, wine (amber, clear). Bartlett-Collins Glass Company, Sapulpa, OK. Unmarked.

Manhattan seven-piece water set.

Known items:	Clear	Clear w/ Rose Stain
Basket	$125.00	$375.00
Biscuit jar with cover	150.00	350.00
Bottle, water	75.00	175.00
Bowl, open, round, flat		
Berry		
6" d.	25.00	35.00
7" d.	30.00	45.00

Manhattan creamer, sugar bowl, butter dish, and spoon holder.

Manhattan round plate.

Manhattan true open compote.

Known items:	Clear	Clear w/ Rose Stain
8" d.	35.00	55.00
8-1/2" d.	55.00	65.00
Fruit or vegetable		
9-1/2" d.	40.00	75.00
10" d.	45.00	85.00
11" d.	55.00	95.00
12-1/2" d.	85.00	110.00
Violet	35.00	50.00
Cake stand on high standard		
8" d.	125.00	275.00
9" d.	135.00	300.00
10" d.	150.00	325.00
Celery vase	45.00	95.00
Cheese dish with cover	150.00	325.00
Compote on high standard		
Covered, 9-1/2" d.	225.00	425.00
Open		
Flared rim, 9-1/2" d.	95.00	150.00
Straight-sided bowl	85.00	135.00

Known items:	Clear	Clear w/ Rose Stain
Creamer		
Individual, 2-1/4" h.	20.00	35.00
Table size	45.00	85.00
Cruet with original stopper		
Bulbous	85.00	225.00
Tapered	95.00	250.00
Cup, custard	20.00	45.00
Dish		
Jelly		
Round with handle	15.00	35.00
Triangular with handle	20.00	45.00
Oval with scalloped rim	15.00	45.00
Preserve, 7-1/2" l.	15.00	45.00
Goblet	55.00	150.00
Ice bucket	75.00	125.00
Olive tray	20.00	45.00
Pickle		
Castor in silver plate frame	225.00	375.00

Manhattan tray.

Known items:	Clear	Clear w/ Rose Stain
Dish, flat with pointed ends	25.00	55.00
Jar with original lid	125.00	250.00
Pitcher with applied handle		
Bulbous, water, 1/2-gal.	150.00	275.00
Tankard		
Milk, 1-qt.	125.00	250.00
Water, 1/2-gal.	135.00	275.00
Plate with scalloped rim		
5" d.	10.00	35.00
6" d.	15.00	40.00
8" d.	17.50	45.00
9-1/2" d.	20.00	45.00
10-3/4" d.	25.00	55.00
11" d.	35.00	65.00
12" d.	45.00	95.00
Punch bowl		
Flat	325.00	550.00

Known items:	Clear	Clear w/ Rose Stain
Footed (2-piece)	375.00	650.00
Relish tray, 6" l.	15.00	35.00
Saltshaker		
Café (large bulbous base)	45.00	85.00
Table size (tapered body with slender neck)	55.00	95.00
Shade		
Electric		
Belled-shape	45.00	110.00
Cupped-shape	35.00	95.00
Gas		
Belled-shape	55.00	125.00
Cupped-shape	45.00	110.00
Sauce dish, round		
Flat		
4-1/2" d.	10.00	25.00
5" d.	12.50	25.00
Footed		
4-1/2" d.	15.00	30.00
5" d.	20.00	35.00
Spoon holder	35.00	85.00
Straw jar with cover	550.00	1,250.00
Sugar bowl with cover		
Individual	20.00	40.00
Table size	55.00	100.00
Syrup pitcher	125.00	325.00
Toothpick holder	30.00	150.00
Tray, trinket with folded sides, 5"	25.00	55.00
Tray		
Water	45.00	110.00
Wine	65.00	150.00
Tumbler		
Iced tea	35.00	55.00
Water, flat	30.00	50.00
Vase with twisted stem		
6" h.	20.00	45.00
8" h.	25.00	50.00
Wine	30.00	85.00

MAPLE LEAF

AKA: Leaf, Maple Leaf on Trunk.

Non-flint. Maker unknown. c. 1885.

Original color production: Amber, blue, canary yellow, clear, frosted. Notes: Forms are typically oval in form, feet are log forms and finials are grape and leaf clusters.

Reproductions and Look-a-Likes: Goblet (amber, amethyst, blue, clear, green - plain, frosted). L.G. Wright Glass Company, New Martinsville, WV. Unmarked.

Maple Leaf covered compote.

Known items:	Amber	Blue	Canary Yellow	Clear	Frosted
Bowl, oval open, 4-footed					
5-1/2"	$45.00	$45.00	$45.00	$25.00	$35.00
11"	65.00	75.00	85.00	45.00	55.00
Butter dish, oval, 4-footed	110.00	150.00	175.00	85.00	95.00
Celery vase	100.00	125.00	150.00	75.00	85.00
Compote with cover, footed,					
9" d.	175.00	275.00	325.00	125.00	150.00
Creamer, 4-footed with pressed					
handle	65.00	85.00	95.00	45.00	55.00
Goblet (S).	200.00	250.00	350.00	125.00	175.00
Pitcher, 4-footed					
Milk, 1-qt.	110.00	125.00	175.00	85.00	100.00
Water, 1/2-gal.	125.00	150.00	225.00	100.00	125.00
Plate					
10" d. with maple leaf border and *"diamond"* center	55.00	65.00	75.00	35.00	45.00
10-1/2" d. *"U.S. Grant"* center inscribed *"Let Us Have Peace"* and *"Born April 27 1822. Died July 23 1885"* with maple leaf border	75.00	85.00	95.00	55.00	65.00
Platter, oval with *"diamond"* center. 10-1/2" l.	65.00	75.00	85.00	45.00	55.00
Sauce dish, leaf-shaped with 3 legs					
5"	5.00	10.00	15.00	5.00	5.00
6"	8.00	10.00	15.00	8.00	8.00

Known items:	Amber	Blue	Canary Yellow	Clear	Frosted
Spoon holder, 4-footed 75.00		85.00	95.00	40.00	50.00
Sugar bowl with cover, 4-footed ...85.00		110.00	125.00	65.00	75.00
Tray					
Oblong, 13-1/4" l. 125.00		135.00	175.00	75.00	110.00
Rectangular with leaf rim,					
13-1/4" l. 110.00		125.00	225.00	65.00	100.00
Tumbler, flat 65.00		75.00	95.00	55.00	65.00

MARDI GRAS

OMN: Duncan No. 42, Empire. **AKA:** Paneled English Hobnail with Prisms, Siamese Necklace.

Non-flint. George Duncan's Sons & Company, Washington, PA, c. 1899. Duncan & Miller Glass Company. c. 1898.

Original color production: Clear, clear with ruby stain (plain, gilded). Dark amber, sapphire blue, clear with amber stain, or any other color would be considered rare. Issued in two conspicuous forms: (a) items with a plain rim and (b) items with a ring-and-thumbprint rim).

Reproductions and Look-a-Likes: 2-piece two-gal. punch bowl and 5-oz. punch cups (clear) vases: 8" h. with flared rim, 8" h. with flared rim (milk white). Clear. Duncan & Miller Glass Company. Unmarked. 16-piece punch sets: 13" d., 8-1/2-qt., 2-piece cupped punch bowl with twelve 5-oz. punch cups, underplate and ladle; 14-1/2" d. 8-1/2-qt., 2-piece flared punch bowl with twelve 5-oz. punch cups (clear), The United States Glass Company, Tiffin, OH, unmarked. 15-piece punch set, 8" h. straight-sided bud vase (amber, vaseline). Indiana Glass Company, Dunkirk, IN. Unmarked. Round luncheon plates (amber). Unmarked.

Known items:	Clear	Clear w/Ruby
Banana boat, flat with folded		
sides, 8" l.	$55.00	$275.00
Bon bon dish in silver plate		
holder, 7" l.	40.00	85.00
Bottle		
Bitters, bulbous with		
slender neck, 6-1/4" l....	85.00	225.00
Water, 8-3/4" h.	65.00	135.00

Known items:	Clear	Clear w/Ruby
Bowl, open		
Round		
Flat		
Berry, master 8" d....	45.00	65.00
Deep with scalloped rim		
8-1/2" d..........	25.00	55.00
9" d.............	30.00	75.00
9-1/2" d.........	35.00	85.00
10" d.............	55.00	95.00
Footed		
8" d..............	45.00	85.00
8-1/4" d..........	50.00	95.00
Square, flat with scalloped rim		
6"..................	25.00	65.00
7-3/4"...............	35.00	75.00
Butter dish with cover	125.00	275.00
Butter pat, 3-1/2" d.	15.00	35.00
Cake stand on high standard with turned-down rim		
9-1/2" d................	95.00	275.00
10" d...................	125.00	325.00
11-3/4" d..............	150.00	350.00
Celery tray	35.00	75.00
Champagne		
Cupped bowl...........	45.00	85.00
Saucer-shaped bowl......	35.00	75.00
Claret.......................	55.00	95.00
Cocktail		
Large	25.00	65.00
Small	25.00	65.00
Compote on high standard		
Covered	85.00	225.00
Open		
Deep bowl with scalloped rim		
7-3/4" d.	35.00	75.00
8" d.	40.00	75.00
9-1/4" d.	45.00	85.00
9-3/4" d.	55.00	95.00

Mardi Gras sugar bowl.

Known items:	Clear	Clear w/Ruby Stain
Shallow bowl with scalloped rim, 6" d.....30.00		85.00
Cordial.........................85.00		175.00
Cracker jar with cover...........110.00		250.00
Creamer		
Individual		
Barrel-shaped, 3" h. 20.00		45.00
Oval shape, 2-1/4" h....25.00		65.00
Table size................65.00		125.00
Cruet with original stopper 85.00		275.00
Eggcup, single, open.............25.00		65.00
Epergne in silver plate holder 275.00		—
Finger bowl......................25.00		45.00
Fruit bowl, low footed with shallow scalloped bowl, 10" d. ..65.00		175.00
Goblet 55.00		225.00
Miniatures		
Butter dish with cover, 4-1/4" h. 375.00		650.00
Creamer, 2-7/8" h........125.00		225.00
Honey jug, 2-1/2" h. 85.00		225.00
Rose bowl, 2-1/2" d. 125.00		300.00
Spoon holder, 2-3/4" h.....75.00		150.00
Sugar bowl with cover ...150.00		275.00
Mustard jar with original notched cover, 3-1/4" h. 55.00		95.00
Nappy, flat with handle		
Round		
5" d.................20.00		35.00
6-1/4" d.............25.00		45.00
Triangular		
5" d.................25.00		55.00
6-1/4" d.............30.00		65.00
Olive dish with turned-up sides, 5" l........................15.00		35.00

Known items:	Clear	Clear w/Ruby Stain
Pickle dish, flat		
Round..................20.00		40.00
Square.................20.00		45.00
Pickle jar with cover 110.00		275.00
Pitcher		
Milk, bulbous with applied handle, 1-qt. 150.00		325.00
Water, 1/2-gal.		
Bulbous with applied handle and "Ring and Thumbprint" rim, 8-1/4" h. 175.00		350.00
Straight-sided with applied handle		
Plain rim, 7-3/4" h....150.00		325.00
Silver plate rim, 11" h.............110.00		275.00
Tankard		
"Ring and Thumbprint" rim with pressed handle ..85.00		175.00
Smooth rim with applied handle......110.00		225.00
Plate, round		
5" d.....................20.00		35.00
6" d.....................25.00		40.00
6-1/2" d.................25.00		40.00
7" d.....................30.00		45.00
7-3/4" d.................30.00		45.00
8" d.....................35.00		55.00
Pomade jar with original lid 65.00		125.00
Puff jar, round with cover, 4-3/4" d....................75.00		135.00
Punch bowl, 2-piece, round with scalloped rim		
12-1/4" d 150.00		450.00
14" d..................225.00		550.00
Punch cup, 2" h..................15.00		35.00

Mardi Gras water pitcher with applied handle.

Known items:	Clear	Clear w/Ruby Stain
Relish tray	20.00	40.00
Rose bowl	55.00	95.00
Salt		
Dip		
Individual		
Oval, flat, 2-1/4" l.	5.00	25.00
Round, flat, 1-3/4" d.	5.00	25.00
Shaker		
Bulbous with tall neck	35.00	65.00
Pyramid-shaped	35.00	75.00
Tall with straight sides	45.00	95.00
Sandwich tray in silver plate holder, 11-1/2" d.	110.00	—
Sauce dish		
Round		
Collared base, 5-3/4" d.	10.00	25.00
Flat		
3-3/4" d.	5.00	25.00
4-3/4" d.	8.00	25.00
5-1/2" d.	10.00	25.00
Square, flat, 4"	15.00	30.00
Saucer, round, 5-1/2" d.	25.00	45.00
Shade, gas		
Bullet-shaped, 9" h. with 2-1/4" d. fitter	25.00	175.00

Known items:	Clear	Clear w/Ruby Stain
Straight-sided with flared, scalloped rim. 2-1/4" d. fitter	25.00	175.00
Sherry		
Flared bowl	35.00	75.00
Straight-sided bowl	30.00	65.00
Spoon holder	45.00	95.00
Sugar bowl with cover	75.00	175.00
Syrup pitcher	125.00	375.00
Toothpick holder	35.00	125.00
Tumbler		
Bar	35.00	65.00
Champagne	25.00	55.00
Ice water	40.00	75.00
Water	30.00	65.00
Vase		
Bulbous, 9-3/4" h.	25.00	65.00
Trumpet-shaped		
6-1/2" h.	20.00	75.00
8" h.	25.00	85.00
10" h.	30.00	95.00
Wine	30.00	75.00
Wine or claret jug, bulbous with slender neck, 9-1/4" h.	55.00	110.00

MARIO

OMN: Hobbs Brockunier No. 341 Ware.

Non-flint. Hobbs, Brockunier & Co., Wheeling, WV. c. 1891.

Original color production: Clear, clear with amber or ruby stain. (Plain or etched). Add 35% for etched pieces.

Reproductions and Look-a-Likes: None known.

Known items:	Clear	Clear w/Stain
Bottle, Barber	$50.00	$225.00
Bowl, open, flat		
Crimped rim, 8" d.	45.00	85.00
Plain rim		
7" d.	30.00	55.00
8" d.	40.00	85.00

Mario covered butter dish.

Mario creamer and sugar bowl.

MARYLAND

OMN: U.S. Glass No. 15,049. **AKA:** Inverted Loop(s) and Fan(s), Loop and Diamond, Loop(s) and Fan(s).

Non-flint. Bryce Brothers, Pittsburgh, PA. The United States Glass Company, Pittsburgh, PA. at Factory "B," c. 1897.

Original color production: Clear, clear with ruby stain.

Reproductions and Look-a-Likes: None known.

Maryland seven-piece water set.

Known items:	Clear	Clear w/Stain
Butter dish with cover............55.00		225.00
Celery vase 35.00		110.00
Creamer.........................35.00		110.00
Pitcher, water 110.00		375.00
Saltshaker 25.00		85.00
Sauce, flat		
4-1/2" d. 5.00		25.00
5" d. 8.00		30.00
Spoon holder 30.00		85.00
Sugar bowl with cover 45.00		150.00
Syrup		
2-pt. 95.00		350.00
1-pt. 110.00		375.00
Tumbler, water 25.00		65.00

Known items:	Clear	Clear w/Ruby
Banana dish, flat with		
turned-in sides $55.00		$225.00
Bowl, open, round, flat		
6" d...................15.00		45.00
7" d 20.00		55.00
8" d...................35.00		95.00
Butter dish with cover on flanged		
base.........................65.00		225.00
Cake stand on high standard		
8" d...................45.00		225.00
9" d...................65.00		275.00
10" d...................85.00		325.00
Celery		
Tray...................20.00		55.00
Vase..................45.00		125.00

Maryland goblet.

Known items:	Clear	Clear w/Ruby
Compote on high standard		
Covered		
6" d.	65.00	225.00
7" d.	75.00	275.00
8" d.	110.00	300.00
Open		
Deep bowl		
5" d. (Jelly)	15.00	95.00
6" d.	20.00	110.00
7" d.	25.00	125.00
8" d.	35.00	150.00
Flared bowl (Sweetmeat),		
7" d.	35.00	95.00
Saucer-shaped bowl		
7" d.	25.00	150.00
8" d.	30.00	175.00
10" d.	40.00	200.00
Creamer, 4-1/2" h.	35.00	100.00
Cup, custard	20.00	45.00
Dish, round, preserve, 8" d.	15.00	35.00
Goblet	35.00	225.00
Honey dish, round, flat, 3" d.	8.00	25.00
Jelly dish	15.00	35.00
Olive dish, handled	20.00	45.00
Pickle dish, oval, handled	20.00	45.00

Known items:	Clear	Clear w/Ruby
Pitcher		
Milk, 1-qt.	45.00	225.00
Water, 1/2-gal.	65.00	275.00
Plate		
Bread	35.00	100.00
Dinner, 7" d.	25.00	110.00
Relish tray, oval	20.00	55.00
Saltshaker	45.00	150.00
Sauce dish, round, flat, 4" d.	8.00	25.00
Spoon holder	45.00	110.00
Sugar bowl with cover	55.00	175.00
Toothpick holder (R)	175.00	450.00
Tumbler, water, flat	35.00	75.00
Wine	45.00	125.00

MASCOTTE

OMN: AKA: Dominion, Etched Fern and Waffle, Minor Block.

Non-flint. Ripley & Company, Pittsburgh, PA, c. 1874. The United States Glass Company, Pittsburgh, PA, at Factory "F," c. 1891.

Original color production: Clear (plain, engraved). Amber, milk white or any other color would be considered very rare.

Reproductions and Look-a-Likes: Jars: covered straight-sided cylinder jars on low circular feet: 9-3/4" h., 12" h., 18" h., 23-1/2" h.; flat covered bulbous Egyptian jars with high shoulders: 1/2-pt., 2-pt., 5-pts., 8-pts.; bulbous covered globe jars on low feet: 3-pts., 5-pts., 8-pts.; straight-sided flat covered stack jars: 4-piece, 5-piece. (Clear). Tiffin Glass, Tiffin, OH, unmarked.

Known items:	Clear	Clear w/ Etching
Banana stand on high standard	$175.00	$575.00
Bowl, round, flat		
Covered		
5" d.	45.00	75.00
6" d.	55.00	85.00

Mascotte covered cheese dish.

Mascotte rare sets of pyramid jars.

Known items:	Clear	Clear w/ Etching
7" d.	65.00	95.00
8" d.	75.00	110.00
9" d.	125.00	150.00
Open		
Flared bowl		
5" d.	25.00	35.00
6" d.	30.00	40.00
7" d.	35.00	45.00
8" d.	40.00	50.00
9" d.	65.00	95.00
Straight-sided bowl		
5" d.	25.00	35.00
6" d.	30.00	40.00
7" d.	35.00	45.00
8" d.	40.00	50.00
9" d.	65.00	85.00
Butter dish with cover		
"Maud S"	275.00	450.00
Regular	95.00	150.00
Butter pat	25.00	—
Cake basket with metal handle	110.00	150.00
Cake stand on high standard		
8" d.	55.00	85.00
9" d.	75.00	110.00
10" d.	85.00	125.00
12" d.	110.00	150.00

Known items:	Clear	Clear w/ Etching
Celery		
Tray	25.00	35.00
Vase	40.00	65.00
Cheese dish with cover	150.00	225.00
Compote, round		
Covered		
High standard		
5" d.	65.00	85.00
6" d.	75.00	95.00
7" d.	85.00	110.00
8" d.	100.00	125.00
9" d.	150.00	185.00
Open		
High standard		
Flared bowl		
5" d.	25.00	35.00
6" d.	30.00	40.00
7" d.	35.00	45.00
8" d.	40.00	50.00
9" d.	55.00	65.00
10" d.	65.00	75.00
11" d.	85.00	100.00

Known items:	Clear	Clear w/ Etching
Straight-sided bowl		
5" d.	25.00	35.00
6" d.	30.00	40.00
7" d.	35.00	45.00
8" d.	40.00	50.00
9" d.	55.00	75.00
Low standard with straight-sided bowl, 8" d.	40.00	55.00
Creamer, 6-1/2" h.	45.00	65.00
Goblet	35.00	50.00
Finger or waste bowl.	35.00	50.00
Honey dish, round, flat, 3-1/2" d.	5.00	15.00
Jar, storage		
Bulbous, open on foot ("Fish Globe")	275.00	—
Egyptian Jar, straight sides, 2-oz.	135.00	—
Patent Globe jar, bulbous with cover	225.00	—
Pyramid with cover and under plate		
3 jars high	550.00	—
5 jars high	1,250.00	—
8 jars high	2,250.00	—
Sample bottle with cover, 15" h.	450.00	—
Pitcher, water, 1/2-gal.	95.00	175.00
Plate with turned up sides	25.00	35.00
Platter	55.00	65.00
Salt		
Master	45.00	85.00
Shaker	30.00	45.00
Sauce dish, round, 4" d.		
Flat	5.00	12.00
Footed	8.00	15.00
Spoon holder	35.00	50.00
Sugar bowl with cover	65.00	95.00
Tray, water, round	85.00	125.00
Tumbler, water, flat	30.00	45.00
Wine	25.00	40.00

MASSACHUSETTS

OMN: U.S. Glass No. 15,054-Massachusetts. **AKA:** Arched Diamond Points, Cane Variant, Geneva, Star and Diamonds.

Non-flint. The United States Glass Company, Pittsburgh, PA, at Factory "K," c. 1898.

Original color production: Clear. Odd items may be found in emerald green. Cobalt blue, clear with ruby stain or any other color would be considered rare.

Reproductions and Look-a-Likes: 8-3/4" d. covered butter dish (amberina, blue, clear, green, pink, ruby). Unmarked. Offered by the A.A. Importing Company, Inc., St. Louis, MO, and San Francisco, CA.

Massachusetts juice.

Known items:	Clear
Basket, small with applied handle	
4-1/2" l.	$110.00
9" l.	150.00

Massachusetts syrup pitcher.

Massachusetts mug with pressed handle.

Known items:	Clear
Bottle	
Brandy	**75.00**
Cologne with patterned stopper, 7-1/2" h.	**55.00**
Liqueur	
Individual with cut stopper	**75.00**
Bar sized	
With bar lip	**55.00**
With cut stopper	**95.00**
With original metal shot glass for lid	**125.00**
Tabasco sauce	**55.00**
Water	**65.00**
Wine with patterned stopper, handled (R)	**225.00**
Bowl, open, flat	
Round	**20.00**
Square	
With folded sides	
6"	**15.00**
9"	**35.00**
With pointed sides	
6"	**25.00**
7"	**30.00**
8"	**35.00**
Straight-sided	
7"	**25.00**
9"	**45.00**

Known items:	Clear
Butter dish with cover	**65.00**
Candy dish, oblong	
8" l.	**20.00**
9" l.	**20.00**
Celery	
Tray, 11-7/8" l.	**25.00**
Vase	**65.00**
Champagne	
Saucer-shaped bowl (S)	**45.00**
Square-shaped bowl	**75.00**
Claret	**45.00**
Cocktail	**45.00**
Compote, open on low standard with cupped bowl	**55.00**
Cordial	**125.00**
Creamer	
Individual, 3-1/4" h.	**25.00**
Medium	**35.00**
Table size	**55.00**
Cruet with original patterned stopper	
Large	**65.00**
Small	**45.00**
Cup, custard	**15.00**
Decanter with original patterned stopper	
With high shoulders and short neck	**95.00**
With sloped shoulders and long neck	**95.00**

Massachusetts tankard water pitcher.

Known items:	Clear
Dish	
Almond, oblong, 5" l.	12.50
Bonbon, 5"	15.00
Mayonnaise, handled	30.00
Olive, oblong	
6" l.	15.00
8-1/2" l.	20.00
Goblet	
Round bowl	65.00
Square bowl	85.00
Gravy boat, handled	85.00
Lamp, oil with matching globe	
Banquet size	1,750.00
Table size	650.00
Mug with handle	
Large	55.00
Small	35.00
Mustard jar with original cover	85.00
Pitcher, water, square, 1/2-gal.	
Squat	110.00
Tankard	135.00
Plate	
Round, 8-1/4" d.	
Slightly cupped bowl	30.00
Upward-turned sides	30.00
Square, 6"	35.00

Known items:	Clear
Relish tray, rectangular	
4" l.	10.00
4-1/2" l.	12.50
5-1/2" l.	15.00
6" l.	20.00
Rum jug	
Large	110.00
Medium	95.00
Small	75.00
Saltshaker	
Large (square)	55.00
Medium (bulbous)	35.00
Small (round)	40.00
Sauce dish, flat	
Oval with handle	15.00
Square, 4"	
With pointed sides	8.00
With straight sides	8.00
Sherry	45.00
Spoon holder with double handles	55.00
Sugar bowl	
Covered	
Individual	55.00
Table size	65.00
Open with scalloped rim	30.00
Syrup pitcher	150.00
Toothpick holder(R)	150.00
Tray	
Oblong, 9" l.	35.00
Pin, square, 5" x 5"	20.00
Spoon, flat with rolled sides	20.00
Toast	55.00
Tumbler, flared or straight-sided	
Bar	35.00
Juice (aka: champagne)	35.00
Lemonade	45.00
Pony beer or seltzer	30.00
Shot or whiskey	25.00
Water	
Round	35.00
Square	75.00
Vase, trumpet shaped	
6-1/2" h.	25.00

Known items:	Clear
7" h.	30.00
9" h.	35.00
10" h.	40.00

Known items:	Clear
Wine	
Round bowl	25.00
Square bowl	65.00

MEDALLION

AKA: Hearts and Spades, Spades.

Non-flint. Maker unknown. c. 1885-1895.

Original color production: Amber, apple green, blue, canary yellow, clear.

Reproductions and Look-a-Likes: Covered butter dish (amber, clear, green). Imperial Glass Corporation, Bellaire, OH. Permanently embossed with entwined "IG" signifying Imperial.

Medallion goblet.

Known items:	Amber	Apple Green	Blue	Canary Yellow	Clear
Bowl, waste	$30.00	$45.00	$35.00	$45.00	$25.00
Butter with cover	45.00	65.00	55.00	75.00	45.00
Cake stand on high standard, 9-1/4" d.	95.00	175.00	125.00	175.00	85.00
Celery vase	35.00	55.00	45.00	65.00	35.00
Compote on high standard, covered	75.00	150.00	110.00	150.00	65.00
Creamer	30.00	55.00	45.00	55.00	30.00
Goblet	30.00	55.00	45.00	55.00	25.00
Pickle dish	15.00	25.00	25.00	25.00	15.00
Pitcher, water with pressed handle, 1/2-gal.	55.00	125.00	95.00	125.00	45.00
Relish tray	15.00	25.00	25.00	25.00	15.00
Sauce dish, 4" d.					
Flat	5.00	10.00	8.00	10.00	5.00
Footed	8.00	15.00	10.00	15.00	8.00
Spoon holder	30.00	50.00	40.00	50.00	25.00

Known items:	Amber	Apple Green	Blue	Canary Yellow	Clear
Sugar bowl with cover	40.00	65.00	55.00	75.00	35.00
Tray, water, round	45.00	100.00	75.00	110.00	45.00
Tumbler, water	25.00	45.00	35.00	50.00	20.00
Wine........................	20.00	50.00	35.00	55.00	15.00

MELROSE

AKA: Diamond Beaded Band.

Non-flint. Greensburg Glass Company, Greensburg, PA, c. 1889. The Brilliant Glass Works, Brilliant, OH, c. 1887-1888. McKee Brothers, Jeannette, PA, c. 1901 (chocolate items). John B. Higbee Glass Company, Bridgeville, PA, c. 1907. New Martinsville Glass Company, New Martinsville, WV, c. 1916. Dugan Glass Company (Diamond Glassware Company), Indiana, PA, c. 1915.

Original color production: Clear (plain, engraved). Chocolate (only by McKee Brothers, Jeannette, PA). Clear with ruby stain (plain, engraved) or any other color would be considered rare.

Reproductions and Look-a-Likes: None known.

Melrose water tray.

Melrose etched water set.

Known items:	Clear
Bowl, round, flat	
Master berry........................	$35.00
Waste..............................	30.00

Known items:	Clear
Butter dish with cover	45.00
Cake stand on high standard	75.00
Celery vase, 6" h.................................	35.00
Compote, open, round on a high standard	
6" d.....................................	35.00
7" d.....................................	40.00
9" d.....................................	45.00
Creamer, tankard.................................	30.00
Goblet	25.00
Mug..	25.00
Pickle dish	15.00
Pitcher with applied handle	
Bulbous	
Milk, 1-qt.	45.00
Water, 1/2-gal.	55.00
Tankard	
Milk, 1-qt.	45.00
Water, 1/2-gal.	65.00

Melrose etched high-standard cake stands.

Known items:	Clear
Plate	
7" d.	15.00
8" d.	20.00
Salt	
Individual	5.00
Shaker	30.00
Sauce dish, round, flat.	5.00
Spoon holder	30.00
Sugar bowl with cover	35.00
Tray, water, round, 11-1/2" d.	55.00
Tumbler, water, flat	25.00
Wine	15.00

MICHIGAN

OMN: U.S. Glass No. 15,077-Michigan. **AKA:** Loop and Pillar, Loop with Pillar, Paneled Jewel.

Non-flint. The United States Glass Company, Pittsburgh, PA, at Factory "G," c. 1902.

Original color production: Clear, clear with rose, yellow or blue stain (plain, enamel decorated). Decorated items were produced by the Oriental Glass Company, Pittsburgh, PA. Clear with ruby stain or any other color would be considered rare.

Reproductions and Look-a-Likes: Toothpick holder (amber-light, amber-dark, amberina, amethyst-light, amethyst-dark, apple green, aqua, bittersweet, bittersweet slag, bloody Mary, bluebell, Cambridge pink, caramel, carnival cobalt, clear, concord grape, Crown Tuscan, custard, custard slag, emerald green, fawn, fog, forest green, heliotrope, holly green, ivory, lavender blue, maverick, milk blue, milk white, mint green, mulberry, old lavender, opalescent, peach blow, pearl gray, persimmon, pigeon blood, pink, red Rose Marie, royal violet, rubina, ruby, sapphire, smokey heater, taffeta, teal, toffee, tomato, vaseline). Crystal Art Glass Company, Cambridge, OH. Unmarked or permanently embossed with a "D" within a "heart" signifying the Crystal Art Glass Company. Toothpick holder (butterscotch, candy swirl, chasm blue slag, cathedral blue, frosty blue/orange, Mardi Gras, redwood slag, rubina). Boyd's Crystal Art Glass, Inc., Cambridge, OH. Permanently marked with a "B" within a "diamond" signifying Boyd.

Michigan creamer.

Known items:	Clear	Clear w/Rose
Basket, bride's in silver plate		
holder	$85.00	$175.00
Bottle, water	65.00	200.00

Known items:	Clear	Clear w/Rose
Bowl, round, flat		
Deep		
6" d.....................15.00		45.00
7" d................25.00		55.00
8-1/2" d.............35.00		75.00
Shallow		
With flared rim		
5" d. 15.00		25.00
7-1/2" d...........25.00		35.00
8-1/2" d. 45.00		75.00
10" d. 15.00		95.00
With straight sides		
6" d. 15.00		25.00
7" d. 25.00		35.00
Butter dish with cover		
1/4 pound..............55.00		125.00
Table size...............85.00		175.00
Candlestick (R).................225.00		325.00
Celery vase 55.00		110.00
Compote on high standard		
Covered, round		
Deep bowl, 5" d.		
With notched lid 75.00		135.00
With plain lid 55.00		100.00
Shallow bowl, 5" d.		
(Jelly) 65.00		125.00
Open		
Deep straight-sided bowl		
6" d. 35.00		65.00
7" d. 65.00		95.00
8" d. 85.00		150.00
Shallow flared bowl		
7-1/2" d. 35.00		65.00
8-1/2" d. 45.00		75.00
9-1/2" d. 55.00		85.00
Creamer		
Individual, tankard, 6-oz..30.00		45.00
Table size................55.00		85.00
Cruet with original stopper 95.00		350.00
Cup		
Custard, flared bowl with saucer 15.00		35.00
Sherbet 15.00		35.00

Known items:	Clear	Clear w/Rose
Dish, open, flat		
Oval		
7-1/2" l. 20.00		35.00
9-1/2" l. 25.00		45.00
10-1/2" l. 35.00		65.00
12-1/2" l. 45.00		75.00
Round, handled (Jelly).... 35.00		65.00
Finger bowl 35.00		75.00
Goblet 45.00		125.00
Miniatures		
Butter dish with cover, 5-1/4" d...............150.00		350.00
Creamer 45.00		125.00
Nappy handled, 5-1/4" ...35.00		125.00
Spoon holder, 3" h........50.00		275.00
Stein set		
Individual stein, 2" h. ..12.00		—
Main stein 45.00		—
Sugar bowl, covered......85.00		300.00
Tumbler, water, 2-1/8" h.....10.00		25.00
Mug, lemonade 35.00		65.00
Olive dish, double-handled 15.00		35.00
Pickle dish, oval, double-handled 15.00		30.00
Pitcher		
Milk, 1-qt................65.00		100.00
Water		
Helmet shaped, 3-pts... 75.00		175.00
Tankard, 1/2-gal........95.00		275.00
Punch bowl 250.00		750.00
Relish tray 15.00		35.00
Salt shaker		
Small, short with fluted neck 25.00		85.00
Medium with flared base ...30.00		110.00
Large, table size 40.00		135.00
Sauce dish, round		
Flat		
Flared rim		
4" d...............10.00		35.00
4-1/2" d. 10.00		35.00

Known items:	Clear	Clear w/Rose
Straight-sided bowl		
4" d.	10.00	35.00
4-1/2" d.	10.00	35.00
Footed		
4" d.	15.00	45.00
4-1/2" d.	15.00	45.00
Saucer	10.00	25.00
Spoon holder	55.00	95.00
Sugar bowl		
Individual, open (listed in the catalog as the "sweetmeat sugar") 3-1/2" h.	25.00	45.00
Table-sized with cover	75.00	125.00
Syrup pitcher	125.00	450.00
Toothpick holder	45.00	225.00
Tumbler, water, flat	35.00	65.00
Vase, bud		
6" h.	25.00	45.00
8" h.	30.00	50.00
12" h.	35.00	55.00
13" h.	45.00	85.00
15-1/2" h.	50.00	95.00
16" h.	50.00	95.00
17" h.	85.00	150.00
Wine	35.00	85.00

MINERVA

OMN: AKA: Roman Medallion.

Non-flint. The Boston & Sandwich Glass Company, Sandwich, MA, c. 1870s. Table set made in two styles.

Original color production: Clear.

Reproductions and Look-a-Likes: None known.

Known items:	Clear
Bowl, open	
Rectangular, flat	
7" l.	$30.00
8" l.	35.00
9" l.	45.00

Minerva covered butter dish.

Known items:	Clear
Round on low foot, 8" d.	45.00
Butter dish with cover	95.00
Cake stand on high standard	
8" d.	110.00
10" d.	135.00
10-1/2" d.	150.00
11" d.	275.00
Champagne	750.00
Compote, round	
Covered	
High standard	
7" d.	150.00
8" d.	175.00
Low standard	
7" d.	135.00
8" d.	150.00
Open, 10" d	
High standard	350.00
Low standard	225.00
Creamer	35.00
Goblet	150.00
Honey dish, round, flat	10.00
Marmalade jar with cover	275.00
Pickle dish, oval with "Love's Request is Pickles" inscribed in the base.	35.00

Known items: **Clear**

Pitcher

    Milk, 1-qt. **225.00**

    Water, 1/2-gal. **275.00**

Plate

    Bread, with closed handles

        "Give Us This Day Our Daily Bread"

          center **55.00**

        "Mars" center **75.00**

    Dinner, round

        8" d. **35.00**

        9" d. **45.00**

Platter, oval, 13" l. **110.00**

Sauce dish, round

    Flat

        4-1/4" d. **10.00**

        4-1/2" d. **10.00**

    Footed

        4-1/4" d. **12.50**

        4-1/2" d. **15.00**

Spoon holder **35.00**

Sugar bowl with cover **110.00**

MINNESOTA

OMN: U.S. Glass No. 15,055-Minnesota. **AKA:** Muchness.

Non-flint. The United States Glass Company, Pittsburgh, PA, at Factory "F" and Factory "G," c. 1898.

Original color production: Clear (plain, gilded). Clear with ruby stain, emerald green or any other color would be considered rare.

Reproductions: None known.

Known items: **Clear**

Banana dish, flat with turned up edges, 9" l. $35.00

Basket with applied handle (3 sizes). 125.00

Biscuit jar with cover. 95.00

Bottle, water 55.00

Bowl, open

    Oval, flat

        9-1/2" l. 25.00

        10" l. 30.00

Minnesota butter dish.

Known items: **Clear**

    Pointed ends

        5". 15.00

        6". 20.00

        7". 25.00

        8". 35.00

    Round, flat with flared rim

        6" d. 15.00

        7" d. 20.00

        8" d. 25.00

    Square

        6". 15.00

        7". 25.00

        8". 35.00

    Straight-sided

        6". 15.00

        7". 25.00

        8". 35.00

Butter dish with cover 65.00

Celery tray, oblong

    9" l. 20.00

    13" l. 25.00

Compote, open

    High standard

        Round

            Deep

                Flared bowl

                    7-1/2" d. .45.00

                    8-1/2" d. .65.00

                    9-1/2" d. .85.00

                Straight-sided bowl

                    6" d. 45.00

                    7" d. 55.00

                    8" d. 75.00

Minnesota 4 piece table set.

Known items: **Clear**

Shallow bowl (originally cataloged as
the *"sweetmeat"*) 45.00
Square
Deep
6" 45.00
7" 55.00
8" 75.00
Shallow bowl with folded sides (originally
cataloged as the *"fruit bowl"*)
8" 45.00
9" 65.00
10" 95.00
Low standard, square bowl
6" 25.00
7" 35.00
8" 45.00
9" 65.00
10" 75.00
Creamer with applied handle
Individual (originally cataloged as the
"Jersey" creamer) 20.00
Table size 40.00
Cruet with the original patterned stopper 65.00
Crushed fruit jar with cover 225.00
Cup
Custard 15.00
Lemonade with pressed handle 30.00
Dish
Oblong
Almond, deep with pointed ends 15.00
Bonbon, deep with upturned sides, 5" . . . 15.00
Candy with scalloped sides and pointed ends
7" 15.00
9" 20.00

Known items: **Clear**

Confection, 5" 20.00
Olive
5" l., straight-sided 15.00
6" d., with rounded bowl 15.00
Oval with serrated rim
7" l. 20.00
8" l. 25.00
Rectangular
Cracker with slightly folded sides, 8" l. . . . 30.00
Preserve, 9" l. 20.00
Goblet 45.00
Hair receiver 75.00
Humidor with its original silver plated cover 225.00
Match safe 35.00
Mug with pressed handle 35.00
Pitcher, water with applied handle
Bulbous
1/2-gal. 100.00
3/4-gal. 125.00
Tankard, 1/2-gal. 150.00
Plate
Cheese with upturned sides 25.00
Fruit with serrated rim, 8" d. 35.00
Pomade jar with original cover 75.00
Puff box with original cover 75.00
Relish tray 15.00
Rose bowl 45.00
Salt shaker, bulbous 35.00
Sauce dish, flat, 4"
Flared 5.00
Pointed at each end 8.50
Square 10.00
Straight sided 8.00

Known items: Clear

Spoon holder, bulbous	40.00
Sugar bowl, bulbous with cover	65.00
Syrup pitcher with pressed handle	100.00
Toothpick holder, tri-handled	15.00

Tray

Bread with pointed ends, 13" l.	35.00
Condiment	25.00
Jelly with slightly folded sides, 8" l.	15.00
Mint, round, 6" d.	15.00
Spoon with pointed ends and folded sides, 9" l.	25.00
Water	85.00

Tumbler

Juice	30.00
Water	35.00

Wine	40.00

Missouri covered butter dish.

MISSOURI

OMN: U.S. Glass No. 15,058-Missouri. **AKA:** Palm and Scroll, Palm Leaf and Scroll.

Non-flint. The United States Glass Company, Pittsburgh, PA, c. 1898.

Original color production: Clear, emerald green (plain, gilded). Amethyst, blue, canary yellow or any other color would be considered rare.

Reproductions: None known.

Missouri high standard covered compote.

Known items:	Clear	Emerald Green
Bowl, open, round, flat		
Deep		
6" d.	$15.00	$25.00
7" d.	20.00	35.00
8" d.	30.00	45.00
Shallow		
6" d.	15.00	25.00
7" d.	20.00	35.00
8" d.	30.00	45.00
Butter dish, covered	65.00	125.00

Known items:	Clear	Emerald Green
Cake stand		
High standard		
6" d.	55.00	85.00
8" d.	50.00	65.00
9" d.	55.00	75.00
10" d.	65.00	85.00
11" d.	110.00	175.00
Low standard		
8" d.	35.00	45.00
10" d.	45.00	55.00
Celery vase	55.00	85.00

Missouri milk pitcher.

Known items:	Clear	Emerald Green
Compote on high standard		
Covered		
6" d.	55.00	75.00
7" d.	75.00	95.00
8" d.	95.00	135.00
Open		
Deep bowl		
5" d.	15.00	25.00
6" d.	20.00	35.00
7" d.	35.00	45.00
8" d.	45.00	55.00
Saucer-shaped bowl with scalloped rim		
8" d.	45.00	55.00
9" d.	55.00	65.00
10" d.	65.00	85.00
Cordial	55.00	125.00
Creamer, 1-pt.	35.00	55.00
Cruet with original stopper	85.00	275.00
Dish, covered, flat		
6" d.	55.00	65.00
7" d.	65.00	75.00
8" d.	75.00	150.00
Goblet	75.00	150.00
Jelly dish, flat, covered with notched lid, 5" d.	55.00	75.00
Mug, pressed handle	45.00	65.00

Known items:	Clear	Emerald Green
Olive dish, rectangular, flat	15.00	25.00
Pickle dish, rectangular	15.00	25.00
Pitcher, pressed handle		
Milk, 1/4-gal.	55.00	110.00
Water, 1/2-gal.	75.00	125.00
Plate, bread, flat, rectangular	25.00	45.00
Relish dish	15.00	25.00
Saltshaker	45.00	85.00
Sauce dish, round, flat, 4" d.	10.00	15.00
Spoon holder	35.00	55.00
Sugar bowl, covered	55.00	75.00
Syrup pitcher	125.00	350.00
Tumbler, water, flat	35.00	55.00
Wine	45.00	95.00

MONKEY

Non-flint. Traditionally attributed to George Duncan & Sons, Pittsburgh, PA, c. 1880s.

Original color production: Clear, opalescent. Clear with enamel decoration, clear with amber stain or any other color would be considered very rare. Notes: Finials are in the shape of finely sculpted monkeys.

Reproductions and Look-a-Likes: 4-3/4" h. spoon holder (amber, clear, most likely other colors). Unmarked. Distributed by A.A. Importing Company, Inc., St. Louis, MO.

Known items:	Clear	Opalescent
Bowl, open, master berry	$325.00	$550.00
Butter dish with cover	650.00	1,250.00
Celery vase (R)	950.00	1,500.00
Creamer	325.00	450.00
Mug (2 styles)	125.00	225.00
Pickle jar with cover	850.00	1,500.00
Pitcher, water, 1/2-gal. (R)	5,500.00	10,000.00
Sauce dish, round, flat	75.00	125.00
Spoon holder	175.00	275.00
Sugar bowl with cover	575.00	650.00

Monkey very rare opal covered butter.

Monkey very rare opal creamer.

Known items:	Clear	Opalescent
Tumbler, water, flat	275.00	375.00
Waste bowl with scalloped rim . . .	325.00	450.00

MOON AND STAR

OMN: Palace. **AKA:** Bull's Eye and Star, Star and Punty.

Non-flint. Adams & Company, Pittsburgh, PA. c. 1888. Co-Operative Flint Glass Company, Beaver Falls, PA. c. 1896. The United States Glass Company, Pittsburgh, PA. c. 1890-1898.

Original color production: Clear, clear with frosted moons, clear with ruby stain (decorated by the Pioneer Glass Company, Pittsburgh, PA).

Reproductions and Look-a-Likes: Ashtrays: round, flat: 4-1/2" d., 6" d., 8" d.; banana dish with folded sides: 9"l., 12" l. on collared base; baskets: 9" h. on collared base with folded sides and solid handle, double-twig handle on collared base with scalloped rim; 6" h. bell; bowls: covered, round on collared base: 7-1/2" d., 10" d.; bowls: open with flared scalloped rim: 7-1/2" d., 8" d.; 7-1/2" l.; covered oval box; covered butter dish: 8-1/2" l. oval quarter-pound with tab handles, 7" d. round flat bowl with unpatterned base; cake stands: high standard with skirted rim, 11" d. low standard with no rim; covered canisters: 1-lb., 2-lb., 3-1/2-lb., 5-lb.; candlesticks: short: 4-1/2" h., tall: 6" h., 9-1/4" h., footed with plain base; covered candy box; covered candy jar; round flat covered cheese dish: 9-1/2" d. with clear domed lid on patterned base, same on non-patterned base; compotes: covered on high standard: 4-1/2" h., 6-1/2" h., 7" h., 8" h., 10" h., 12" h.; compotes: open on high standard: 6" h. with crimped rim, barrel-shaped bowl, crimped edge bowl, rolled edge bowl; compotes: covered on low standard: 6" h., 7-1/2" h.; compote: 5" h. open on low standard with scalloped rim; 7-3/4" h. covered cracker jar; creamers with pressed handle: 3" h. individual, 6-1/4" h. table size; cruet with pressed handle, 3-oz. eggcup, epergne; goblets: 3-oz., 11-oz.; lamps: candle with matching half-shade, 7-1/2" h. with clear base, saucer-base courting with patterned shade, 16" h. electric with base and matching patterned half-shade; 5-1/2" d. round nappy with pressed handle; pitchers: 40-oz., 6-1/2" h. miniature; round flat plates: 8" d. dinner with smooth rim, 13" d. egg; 8" l. 3-part relish; 4" d. ring holder; salt dip; saltshakers: 5" h. bulbous, 4" h. straight; 4-1/2" d. round sauce dish on collared base; 6-oz. sherbert; 4-piece smoke set; 6" h. spoon holder; sugar bowls: 3" h. open individual with double handles and scalloped rim, 7" h. table size; 5" h. sugar shaker; 5" h. syrup pitcher; flat covered tobacco jar; toothpick holder; tumblers: flat: 11-oz. (water), 9-oz. (old-fashioned), 11-oz. (old-fashioned); footed: 10-oz., 13-oz. (iced tea); urn; vases: 6-1/2" h. bud, 7" h. with fluted rim; 9" h., pyramid-shaped; wines: 3-oz., 6-oz. with barrel-shaped bowl. (amber, amethyst, carnival, amberina, blue, blue opalescent, brown, clear, cranberry rose opalescent, green, mint green opalescent, ruby). Unmarked: L.E. Smith Glass Company, Mount Pleasant, PA.

Miniature footed banana stand with folded sides; miniature footed bowls: cupped rim, flared rim; miniature footed candle holders: cupped nappy, plate; miniature pitcher with pressed handle; miniature footed plate; miniature water tumbler (clear, clear carnival, cobalt, cobalt carnival, pink, pink carnival). Weishar Enterprises, Wheeling, WV, signed.

Ashtrays: 5" d., 8-1/2" d.; open bowls: 6" d. with circular foot and crimped rim, 8" d. footed console; 5-3/4" d. round covered butter dish; 12" d. low standard cake stand; 6" h. candlestick; flared champagne; compotes: covered on high standard: 3-1/2" d., 4-1/2" d. (plain or knob-stemmed), 6" d., 6-3/4" d., 8" d. (flared rim, ruffled rim); compote: open on high standard: 8" d. with flared rim, 8-1/2" d. with ruffled rim, 10" d. with scalloped rim; creamer with pressed handle; bulbous decanter with clear stopper; 9-oz. goblet; lamps: 10" h. footed miniature with matching half-shade, 10" d. table size; nappies: 8" l. triangular with handle, 6" d. with crimped rim; 32-oz. water pitcher with pressed handle; relishes: 8" l. rectangular, oval boat-shaped; rose bowl; round flat salt dip; salt shaker; 4-1/4" h. footed sherbert with flared bowls; flat oval soap dish; spoon holder; covered sugar bowls: table sized, low footed; 4-1/2" h. sugar shaker; flat toothpick holder; footed tumblers: 5-oz. (juice), 7-oz. (water), 11-oz. (iced tea); 2-oz. wine (amber, amethyst, blue, blue satin, clear, green, green satin, milk white, pink, pink satin, ruby, ruby satin, vaseline, vaseline opalescent, vaseline satin). L.G. Wright Glass Company, New Martinsville, WV, unmarked.

Moon and Star celery vase.

Known items:	Clear	Clear/ Frosted	Clear w/Ruby
Bottle, water............	$125.00	$275.00	$375.00
Bowl, round, flat			
Covered			
6" d..........	65.00	95.00	150.00
7" d..........	75.00	110.00	175.00
8" d..........	85.00	125.00	200.00
10" d........	325.00	450.00	650.00
Open			
6-1/8" d......	25.00	55.00	85.00
7-1/4" d......	30.00	60.00	110.00
8" d..........	35.00	75.00	125.00
10" d........	65.00	110.00	150.00
12-1/2" d (salad).....	450.00	575.00	750.00
Butter dish with cover	75.00	110.00	275.00
Cake stand on high standard			
9" d........	110.00	150.00	325.00
10-1/8"d	135.00	175.00	350.00
Celery vase...............	55.00	85.00	125.00
Champagne	95.00	125.00	100.00
Cheese dish plate (shaped like small relish)...........	30.00	35.00	45.00
Claret....................	85.00	110.00	175.00

Moon and Star saltshaker.

Moon and Star low-footed covered bowl.

Moon and Star cake stand.

Moon and Star rare ruby-stained low-footed bowl.

Known items:	Clear	Clear/ Frosted	Clear w/Ruby
Compote			
Covered			
Collared base			
6" d.......	85.00	110.00	150.00
7" d.......	95.00	125.00	175.00
8" d......	110.00	150.00	225.00
10" d.....	350.00	450.00	850.00
High standard			
6" d......	110.00	135.00	225.00
7" d......	135.00	175.00	250.00
8" d......	175.00	250.00	275.00
10-1/4" d..	650.00	950.00	1,250.00

Known items:	Clear	Clear/ Frosted	Clear w/Ruby
Open			
Collared base			
Deep bowl			
6" d.....	35.00	65.00	95.00
7" d.....	40.00	75.00	110.00
8" d.....	45.00	85.00	125.00
10" d.....	75.00	110.00	150.00
Shallow bowl			
6-1/2" d..	35.00	65.00	95.00
7-1/2" d..	45.00	75.00	110.00
8-1/2" d..	55.00	85.00	125.00
10-1/2" d.	85.00	125.00	150.00

Moon and Star saltshaker and footed eggcup.

Moon and Star syrup with solid clear applied handle.

Moon and Star water pitcher.

Known items:	Clear	Clear/ Frosted	Clear w/Ruby
High standard			
5-1/2" d. . .45.00	75.00	110.00	
7-1/2" d. . .55.00	85.00	125.00	
8-1/2" d. . .65.00	95.00	1,505.00	
10-1/2" d.100.00	135.00	225.00	
Creamer with applied			
handle 85.00	125.00	175.00	
Cruet with original stopper .225.00	275.00	425.00	
Dish, preserve, open, oblong .30.00	45.00	65.00	
Eggcup, open, single 65.00	95.00	125.00	
Goblet 85.00	125.00	375.00	
Lamp, oil 275.00	325.00	—	
Pickle tray, oval 25.00	30.00	45.00	
Pitcher, water, bulbous with			
applied handle 325.00	375.00	650.00	

Known items:	Clear	Clear/ Frosted	Clear w/Ruby
Relish tray 20.00	35.00	45.00	
Salt			
Dip, individual 10.00	25.00	45.00	
Shaker. 55.00	85.00	135.00	
Sauce dish, round			
Flat			
4" d. 10.00	15.00	25.00	
4-1/2" d. 10.00	15.00	25.00	
Footed			
4" d. 15.00	20.00	25.00	
4-1/2" d. 15.00	20.00	25.00	
Spoon holder 65.00	95.00	150.00	
Sugar bowl with cover 95.00	125.00	175.00	
Syrup pitcher 225.00	275.00	750.00	
Tray, bread			
Oblong 45.00	75.00	125.00	
Rectangular 45.00	75.00	125.00	
Water 110.00	150.00	350.00	
Tumbler, water, footed 75.00	110.00	65.00	
Waste bowl. 65.00	95.00	65.00	

NAIL

OMN: U.S. Glass No. 15,002. **AKA:** Recessed Pillar-Red Top, Recessed Pillar-Thumbprint Band.

Non-flint. Ripley & Company, Pittsburgh, PA, c. 1892. The United States Glass Company, Pittsburgh, PA, c. 1892.

Original color production: Clear, clear with ruby stain (plain, engraved).

Reproductions and Look-a-Likes: None known.

Nail rare etched and ruby-stained water set.

Nail ruby stained goblet.

Known items:	Clear	Clear w/Ruby
Bottle, water	$65.00	$325.00
Bowl		
Berry, round, master, 8" d.	45.00	110.00
Finger	35.00	85.00
Butter dish with cover on flanged base	75.00	225.00

Known items:	Clear	Clear w/Ruby
Cake stand on high standard, 9-1/2" d.	135.00	375.00
Celery vase	45.00	125.00
Claret	30.00	85.00
Compote, open on high standard, jelly	35.00	75.00
Creamer	35.00	95.00
Cruet with original stopper	75.00	375.00
Goblet	45.00	110.00
Mustard pot with the original lid (R)	55.00	125.00
Pitcher, water, 1/2-gal.	100.00	275.00
Saltshaker	35.00	85.00
Sauce dish, round		
Flat	8.00	25.00
Footed	10.00	30.00
Spoon holder	30.00	75.00
Sugar bowl with cover	45.00	150.00
Sugar shaker	65.00	225.00
Syrup pitcher	110.00	275.00
Tray, water, round	65.00	225.00
Tumbler, water	25.00	75.00
Vase, 7" h.	15.00	—
Wine	35.00	95.00

NEW ENGLAND PINEAPPLE

AKA: Loop and Jewel, Pineapple, Sawtooth.

Flint. Traditionally attributed to the New England Glass Company, Cambridge, MA, c. 1855-1870s.

Original color production: Clear. Any colored item would be considered very rare. Company, Williamstown, WV, unmarked.

New England Pineapple lady's goblet.

Known items:	Flint
Bottle	
Castor	
Mustard	$65.00
Oil with original stopper	110.00
Shaker	75.00
Oil (footed)	175.00
Bowl, open, round, flat, 8" d.	125.00
Butter dish with cover	275.00
Champagne, 5-1/4" h.	275.00
Compote	
Covered on high standard	
5" d.	325.00
6" d. (originally cataloged as the *"sweetmeat"*)	375.00
8" d.	650.00

Known items:	Flint
Open	
High standard with scalloped rim	
7" d.	110.00
8-1/2" d.	135.00
Low standard	
7" d.	75.00
8-1/2" d.	95.00
Creamer, footed with applied handle	
6" h.	275.00
7" h.	325.00
Decanter with long neck	
Bar lip	
1-pt.	225.00
1-qt.	275.00
With original stopper	
Handled	
1-pt.	375.00
1-qt.	425.00
Handleless	
1-pt.	350.00
1-qt.	375.00
Eggcup, open, single, footed	45.00
Goblet	
Lady's (small) 5-1/2" h.	175.00
Gentleman's (large)	95.00
Honey dish, round, flat, 3-1/2" d.	15.00
Mug with applied handle	
Water	325.00
Whiskey	425.00
Pickle dish	35.00
Pitcher	
Milk, 1-qt.	1,250.00
Water with applied handle, 1/2-gal.	1,500.00
Plate, round, 6" d.	110.00
Salt, master, open, footed	55.00
Sauce dish, round, flat	10.00
Spill holder	85.00
Spoon holder, footed	65.00
Sugar bowl with cover	
Low footed with smooth rim	225.00
High footed with scalloped rim	275.00
Tumbler	
Bar	135.00

Known items: **Flint**

Water 150.00
Whiskey 225.00
Wine. 175.00

NEW HAMPSHIRE

OMN: U.S. Glass No. 15,084-New Hampshire.
AKA: Bent Buckle, Maiden's Blush, Modiste, Red Loop and Fine Cut.

Non-flint. The United States Glass Company, Pittsburgh, PA, c. 1903.

Original color production: Clear, clear with rose stain. Clear with ruby stain or any other color would be considered rare.

Reproductions and Look-a-Likes: None known.

New Hampshire covered marmalade jar.

New Hampshire water pitcher.

Known items:	Clear	Clear w/Rose
Basket with applied handle,		
7-1/2"	$150.00	$350.00
Biscuit jar, covered.	95.00	275.00
Bottle, carafe.	65.00	135.00

Known items:	Clear	Clear w/Rose
Bowl, open, flat		
Round		
Flared rim		
5-1/2" d.	15.00	35.00
6-1/2" d.	25.00	45.00
7-1/2" d.	35.00	55.00
8-1/2" d.	55.00	85.00
Straight sided		
6-1/2" d.	15.00	35.00
7-1/2" d.	25.00	45.00
8-1/2" d.	35.00	65.00
9-1/2" d.	55.00	85.00
Square		
6-1/2".	25.00	35.00
7-1/2".	35.00	45.00
9-1/2".	55.00	95.00
Butter dish, covered	85.00	175.00
Cake stand on high standard,		
9" d..	110.00	275.00
Celery vase.	55.00	110.00
Cocktail (flared wine).	25.00	55.00
Compote on high standard		
Covered, deep bowl		
6" d.	75.00	135.00
7" d.	85.00	175.00
8" d.	125.00	250.00

New Hampshire sugar bowl, creamer, spoon holder, and butter dish.

New Hampshire covered high compote.

Known items:	Clear	Clear w/Rose
Open		
Deep bowl with flared rim		
6" d.	35.00	85.00
7" d.	45.00	95.00
8" d.	55.00	110.00
9" d.	75.00	125.00
Saucer-shaped bowl, 7" d.	45.00	95.00
Creamer		
Breakfast or individual	25.00	45.00
Table size	45.00	85.00
Cruet with original patterned stopper	85.00	225.00
Cup		
Custard, straight-sided bowl	15.00	35.00
Lemonade, flared bowl	15.00	35.00
Dish, olive		
Diamond shaped, flat with crimped rim	20.00	35.00
Oblong	20.00	35.00

Known items:	Clear	Clear w/Rose
Goblet	30.00	125.00
Marmalade, covered	65.00	150.00
Mug		
Large	45.00	95.00
Medium	35.00	75.00
Pickle dish, oval, 7-1/2" l.	15.00	35.00
Pitcher		
Bulbous with applied handle, 3/4-gal.	225.00	550.00
Squat with pressed handle, 3-pts.	150.00	275.00
Tankard with applied handle, 1/2-gal.	175.00	350.00
Plate, round with smooth rim, 8" d.	35.00	65.00
Relish tray	15.00	35.00
Saltshaker		
Hotel, large, straight sided with fluted neck	35.00	95.00
Small, tapered with fluted neck	35.00	95.00
Table size with no neck	35.00	95.00
Sauce dish		
Round		
Deep		
4" d.	8.00	15.00
4-1/2" d.	8.00	15.00
Shallow, 4" d.	8.00	15.00
Square		
4"	8.00	15.00
4-1/2"	8.00	15.00
Spoon holder	35.00	65.00
Sugar bowl		
Covered		
Breakfast	25.00	45.00
Table size	55.00	95.00

Known items:	Clear	Clear w/Rose
Open, individual with double handles	20.00	45.00
Syrup	85.00	325.00
Toothpick holder	25.00	75.00
Tumbler, water	30.00	65.00
Vase		
6" h., thick stem	25.00	45.00
8" h., twist stem	35.00	55.00
9" h., narrow stem	45.00	65.00
Wine, straight-sided bowl	25.00	55.00

NEW JERSEY

OMN: U.S. Glass No. 15,070-New Jersey. **AKA:** Loop and Drops, Red Loop and Finecut.

Non-flint. The United States Glass Company, Pittsburgh, PA, at Factory "G," Factory "P," and Factory "D," c. 1900-1908.

Original color production: Clear, clear with ruby stain (plain, gilded). Ruby stained and decorated items were produced by the Oriental Glass Company, Pittsburgh, PA.

Reproductions and Look-a-Likes: None known.

New Jersey seven-piece water set.

New Jersey covered butter dish.

Known items:	Clear	Clear w/Ruby
Bottle, water..................	$55.00	$225.00
Bowl, open, scalloped		
Oval		
Pointed ends		
6" l................	20.00	45.00
8" l................	25.00	65.00
10" l................	35.00	85.00
Round ends		
6"	20.00	45.00
8"	25.00	65.00
9"	35.00	85.00
Round		
Cupped rim (deep)		
6" d...............	25.00	55.00
7" d...............	35.00	75.00
8" d...............	45.00	95.00
Saucer shaped (shallow)		
5" d...............	15.00	30.00
8" d...............	35.00	55.00
9" d...............	45.00	65.00
10" d..............	65.00	95.00
Butter dish with cover on flanged base		
Flat	75.00	225.00
Footed (originally cataloged as the *"sweetmeat"*)	125.00	325.00
Cake stand on high standard, 8" d........................	85.00	325.00
Celery		
Tray....................	25.00	55.00
Vase....................	35.00	85.00

New Jersey sugar bowl, creamer, spoon holder, and covered butter.

Known items:	Clear	Clear w/Ruby
Compote, round		
High standard		
Covered		
5" d. (Jelly)	55.00	95.00
6" d.	65.00	110.00
7" d.	85.00	150.00
8" d.	125.00	225.00
Open		
5" d. (Jelly)	25.00	45.00
6" d.	35.00	55.00
7" d.	45.00	75.00
8" d.	65.00	95.00
Low standard, open		
6" d.	30.00	65.00
7" d.	40.00	75.00
8" d.	50.00	95.00
Creamer	45.00	110.00
Cruet with original stopper	65.00	350.00
Dish, open, flat, scalloped rim		
6"	15.00	35.00
8"	20.00	45.00
10"	35.00	65.00
Fruit bowl (sallow)		
Flat		
9-1/2" d.	15.00	35.00
10-1/2" d.	20.00	45.00
12-1/2" d.	35.00	65.00
Footed		
9-1/2" d.	55.00	95.00
10-1/2" d.	65.00	110.00
12-1/2" d.	85.00	135.00
Goblet	55.00	275.00

Known items:	Clear	Clear w/Ruby
Olive dish with pointed ends	15.00	30.00
Pickle tray, rectangular	15.00	30.00
Pitcher		
Milk, bulbous with applied handle, 1-qt.	110.00	275.00
Water		
Bulbous with applied handle, 1/2-gal.	175.00	375.00
Straight sided with pressed handle	85.00	225.00
Plate		
Flat		
Dinner, 8" d.	25.00	65.00
Fruit		
9-1/2" d.	25.00	65.00
10-1/2" d.	35.00	85.00
12" d.	45.00	150.00
Footed	25.00	45.00
Salt- or pepper shaker		
Bulbous	65.00	125.00
Hotel size	65.00	125.00
Sauce dish, round, flat, 4" d.	15.00	35.00
Shade, gas with 4" fitter opening	65.00	225.00
Spoon holder	35.00	85.00
Sugar bowl with cover	65.00	150.00
Syrup pitcher with glass lip		
Straight sided	95.00	350.00
Tapered	95.00	350.00
Toothpick holder	65.00	275.00
Tumbler, water, flat	35.00	85.00
Wine		
Flared bowl	35.00	85.00
Straight-sided bowl	35.00	85.00

NEW YORK

OMN: U.S. Glass No. 15,061-New York. **AKA:** U.S. Rib.

Non-flint. The United States Glass Company, Pittsburgh, PA, c. 1899. Shapes are square.

Original color production: Clear, emerald green. Clear with ruby stain or any other color would be considered rare.

Reproductions and Look-a-Likes: None known.

New York rare emerald green saltshaker.

New York footed vase.

New York punch cup, individual open sugar, and toothpick holder.

Known items:	Clear	Emerald Green
Bowl, master berry	$30.00	$45.00
Butter dish with cover...........	45.00	75.00
Celery vase	35.00	45.00
Creamer		
Breakfast or individual, shell shaped	25.00	35.00
Table size...............	35.00	45.00
Cruet with original patterned stopper	55.00	110.00
Cup, custard or lemonade	10.00	15.00
Dish, olive with tab handle	15.00	20.00
Goblet	55.00	95.00
Pitcher, water	65.00	110.00
Plate, 7" sq.	25.00	35.00

Known items:	Clear	Emerald Green
Punch bowl on stand	250.00	550.00
Relish tray, rectangular	15.00	25.00
Saltshaker (R).................	125.00	175.00
Sauce dish, square...............	5.00	8.00
Spoon holder	35.00	45.00
Sugar bowl		
Breakfast, open	25.00	35.00
Table size with cover	45.00	65.00
Toothpick holder...............	35.00	65.00
Tumbler, water, flat.............	25.00	35.00
Vase, 9" h.....................	15.00	20.00

O'HARA DIAMOND

OMN: O'Hara's Diamond & U.S. Glass No. 15,001. **AKA:** Ruby Star, Sawtooth and Star.

Non-flint. O'Hara Glass Company, Pittsburgh, PA, c. 1885. The United States Glass Company, Pittsburgh, PA, at Factory "L," c. 1891.

Original color production: Clear, clear with ruby stain.

Reproductions and Look-a-Likes: None known.

O'Hara Diamond syrup.

O'Hara Diamond goblet.

Known items:	Clear	Clear w/Ruby
Bowl, round, flat		
Covered		
5" d.	$35.00	$75.00
6" d.	40.00	85.00
7" d.	45.00	95.00
8" d.	55.00	110.00

Known items:	Clear	Clear w/Ruby
Open with scalloped rim		
5" d.	20.00	45.00
6" d.	25.00	55.00
7" d.	30.00	60.00
8" d.	35.00	75.00
Butter dish with cover	55.00	135.00
Cake stand on high standard		
9" d.	85.00	250.00
10" d.	110.00	325.00
Celery vase	45.00	95.00
Champagne	35.00	85.00
Claret	30.00	75.00
Compote, open on high standard with scalloped rim		
5" d.	45.00	95.00
6" d.	55.00	110.00
7" d.	65.00	125.00
8" d.	85.00	150.00
Condiment under tray	20.00	45.00
Creamer	30.00	65.00
Cruet with original stopper	55.00	225.00
Cup, custard with handle, 2-3/8" h.	15.00	35.00

O'Hara Diamond spoon holder, sugar bowl, butter dish, creamer.

O'Hara Diamond high-standard cake stand.

Known items:	Clear	Clear w/Ruby
Goblet	30.00	85.00
Honey dish, round, flat, 3-1/2" d.	5.00	15.00
Lamp, oil, stand	135.00	—
Pickle dish	15.00	35.00
Pitcher, water, tankard, 1/2-gal.	75.00	225.00
Plate, round		
7" d.	20.00	55.00
8" d.	25.00	65.00
10" d.	35.00	75.00
Salt		
Master, open, flat	25.00	55.00
Shaker	35.00	65.00
Sauce dish, round		
Flat with serrated rim, 4" d.	5.00	25.00
Footed with scalloped rim		
4" d.	5.00	25.00
5" d.	8.00	30.00

Known items:	Clear	Clear w/Ruby
Saucer, 5-1/4" d.	25.00	55.00
Spoon holder	30.00	75.00
Sugar bowl with cover	45.00	110.00
Syrup pitcher	110.00	375.00
Tray, water, round with ruffled rim	55.00	125.00
Tumbler, water, flat	30.00	65.00
Wine	20.00	45.00

ONE-O-ONE

AKA: Beaded 101, One Hundred and One, 1-0-1.

Non-flint. George Duncan and Sons, Pittsburgh, PA, c. 1885.

Original color production: Clear.

Reproductions and Look-a-Likes: Goblet (clear, colors). Unmarked.

Known items:	Clear
Butter dish with cover	$150.00
Cake stand on high standard, 9" d.	175.00
Celery vase, pedestaled, 8-1/8" h.	85.00
Compote with cover	
High standard	
7" d.	125.00
8" d.	150.00
Low standard	
7" d.	95.00
8" d.	125.00

One-O-One goblet.

One-O-One oil lamp.

Known items:	Clear
Creamer	45.00
Goblet	
Double band top	65.00
Single band top	110.00
Lamp, oil	
Hand, flat with handle	85.00
High standard	
7-1/2" h.	135.00
8-1/2" h.	150.00
9-1/2" h.	175.00
Pickle dish, oval	
Collared	25.00
Flat with taper at one end	20.00
Pitcher, water, bulbous with applied handle, 1/2-gal.	375.00
Plate	
Bread, round	
"One-O-One" border and *"Give Us This Day Our Daily Bread"* center	45.00
Scalloped rim	35.00
Dinner, round	
6" d.	25.00
7" d.	35.00
8" d.	45.00
9" d.	65.00

Known items:	Clear
Relish tray, oval	15.00
Sauce dish, round, plain rim, rayed or star base, 4" d.	
Flat	12.50
Footed	15.00
Spoon holder	55.00
Sugar bowl with cover	125.00
Wine	95.00

OPEN ROSE

AKA: Moss Rose.

Non-flint. Maker unknown, c. 1870s.

Original color production: Clear.

Reproductions and Look-a-Likes: Goblet spoon holder (amber, blue, clear, green). Mosser Glass, Inc., Cambridge, OH. Unmarked.

Known items:	Clear
Bowl, open	
Oval, flat, vegetable, 9" l.	25.00
Round, flat	
5" d.	20.00
7" d.	25.00

Open Rose spoon holder.

Known items: **Clear**

Item	Clear
Butter dish with cover	65.00
Cake stand on high standard	175.00
Celery vase	65.00
Compote, round	
Covered on high standard	
6" d.	95.00
7" d.	110.00
8" d.	135.00
9" d.	175.00
Open on low standard	
6" d.	75.00
7" d.	85.00
7-1/2" d.	110.00
8" d.	125.00
9" d.	150.00
Creamer	65.00
Eggcup, single, open	35.00
Goblet	
Lady's (small)	65.00
Gentleman's (large)	45.00
Pitcher, bulbous with applied handle	
Milk, 1-qt.	225.00
Water, 3-pts.	250.00
Relish tray, oval	15.00
Salt, master, open, footed with cable edge	45.00
Sauce dish, round, flat, 4" d.	5.00

Known items: **Clear**

Item	Clear
Spoon holder	35.00
Sugar bowl with cover	65.00
Tumbler, water, flat	75.00

OREGON

> **OMN:** U.S. Glass No. 15,073-Oregon. **AKA:** Beaded Loop(s), Beaded Ovals.
>
> Non-flint. The United States Glass Company, Pittsburgh, PA, c. 1891.
>
> **Original color production:** Clear.
>
> **Reproductions and Look-a-Likes:** Covered butter dish unmarked. Covered sugar bowl (milk white, clear iridescent carnival). Permanently embossed with the Imperial "IG" insignia.

Oregon celery vase.

Known items: **Clear**

Item	Clear
Bottle, water	$65.00
Bowl, round, flat	
Oval, open	
7-1/2" l.	20.00
9-1/2" l.	30.00
11-1/2" l.	45.00
12-1/2" l.	64.00

Oregon goblet.

Known items:	Clear
Round	
Covered	
6" d.	45.00
7" d.	55.00
8" d.	75.00
Open	
6" d.	15.00
7" d.	20.00
8" d.	35.00
Butter dish with cover	
English (low with attached underplate)	95.00
Flanged rim	65.00
Plain rim	45.00
Cake stand on high standard	
6" d.	65.00
7-1/2" d.	45.00
8" d.	55.00
8-1/2" d.	65.00
9" d.	85.00
10" d.	100.00
Celery vase	45.00
Compote, round	
Covered on high standard	
5" d.	55.00
6" d.	65.00
7" d.	75.00
8" d.	95.00
Open	
High standard	
Deep bowl	
5" d.	25.00
6" d.	25.00

Known items:	Clear
8" d.	30.00
9" d.	40.00
Saucer-shaped bowl (originally known as the *"fruit bowl"*)	
7-1/4" d.	35.00
8-1/2" d.	?????
10" d.	55.00
Low standard	
5" d.	20.00
6" d.	25.00
7" d.	30.00
8" d.	35.00
9" d.	40.00
Creamer	
Flat	35.00
Footed	45.00
Cruet with original stopper	65.00
Goblet	45.00
Honey dish, round, flat, 3-1/2" d.	15.00
Horse radish with cover	95.00
Mug with pressed handle	55.00
Olive dish, boat shaped	15.00
Pickle dish, boat shaped	15.00
Pitcher	
1-pt.	45.00
Milk, 1-qt.	55.00
Water, 1/2-gal.	75.00
Plate, bread, oval, 11" l.	35.00
Relish tray	15.00
Salt	
Master, open	45.00
Shaker, bulbous	45.00
Sauce dish, round, 4" d.	
Flat	10.00
Footed	15.00
Spoon holder	
Flat	35.00
Footed	45.00
Sugar bowl with cover	45.00
Syrup pitcher	110.00
Toothpick holder	65.00
Tumbler, water, flat	30.00
Vase	35.00
Wine	75.00

PALM LEAF FAN

Non-flint. Bryce, Higbee Glass Company, Bridge-port, PA, c. 1904.

Original color production: Clear. Occasionally found in carnival colors.

Reproductions and Look-a-Likes: None known.

Palm Leaf Fan true open compote.

Known items:	Clear
Banana bowl	
Flat	$45.00
High standard	75.00
Bowl, open	
Oval, 7-1/2" x 10"	50.00
Round	
6-1/2"	25.00
8"	30.00

Known items:	Clear
Shallow	
6-1/2"	25.00
9-3/4"	35.00
Square	
5"	20.00
6"	25.00
7-1/2"	30.00
9"	35.00
Butter, covered	65.00
Cake Stand	60.00
Celery	
Tray	35.00
Vase	45.00
Compote, open on high standard	
5" jelly	30.00
8"	45.00
Card receiver	
Flat	30.00
Footed (often sold as a child's cake or banana stand)	45.00
Creamer	
Large	45.00
Small	35.00
Cruet with original stopper	65.00
Goblet	45.00
Marmalade Jar	65.00
Mug	35.00
Pickle, oval	30.00
Pitcher	
Milk	65.00
Water	85.00
Plate, round	
5-1/2"	15.00
7-1/2"	20.00
9-1/2"	25.00
10-1/2"	30.00
Square, 7"	30.00

Known items: Clear

Rose bowl

  Flat

    4" 35.00

    6" 40.00

  Footed

    7" h. 40.00

    9" h. 45.00

Salt

  Dip, individual 10.00

  Shaker 30.00

Soup bowl, flat rim soup, 6-1/2" 40.00

Sugar with cover

  Large 40.00

  Small 35.00

Tumbler (two styles) 35.00

Vase, footed

  6" h. 20.00

  9" h. 30.00

  12" h. 40.00

Wine. 65.00

PALMETTE

AKA: Hearts and Spades, Spades.

Non-flint. Attributed to Bryce, Walker & Co., Pittsburgh, PA, c. 1870s.

Original color production: Clear. Milk white or any other color would be considered rare.

Reproductions and Look-a-Likes: None known.

Known items: Clear

Bowl, open

  Oval, flat

    7-7/8" l. $35.00

    8-5/8" l. 45.00

    9-3/8" l. 55.00

  Round, low footed

    6" d. 45.00

    9" d. 65.00

Palmette creamer.

Palmette oil lamp.

Known items: Clear

Butter dish with cover

  With hexagonal knob finial, 6-1/4" d. 85.00

  Without handles, 6-1/4" d. 75.00

  With tab handles. 125.00

Cake plate, flat with tab-handles, 9" d. 35.00

Cake stand on high standard

  9-1/2" d. 325.00

  10-1/2" d. 375.00

Palmette tumbler.

Known items:	Clear
Castor set, 5 bottles complete in silver plate holder	275.00
Celery	
Tray	25.00
Vase	75.00
Champagne, 4-1/4" h. (R)	475.00
Compote, round	
Covered	
High standard	
7" d.	110.00
7-1/4" d.	125.00
8-1/2" d.	150.00
9-3/4" d.	275.00
Open	
High standard, 8" d.	65.00
Low standard	
5-1/2" d.	55.00
7" d.	65.00
Creamer, footed with applied handle, 6" h.	85.00
Cruet, footed with applied handle and original *Maltese Cross* finial (VR)	325.00
Cup plate, 3-3/8" d.	55.00
Eggcup, open, single, 4" h.	45.00
Goblet	55.00
Honey dish, round, flat, 3-1/4" d.	10.00
Lamp, oil	
Composite with marble base, patterned font and No. 2 collar	110.00

Known items:	Clear
All glass	
8-1/2" h. with 6-sided foot and No. 1 collar	150.00
9-1/2" h. with 6-sided foot and No. 1 collar	175.00
10" h.	225.00
Pickle scoop, oval	15.00
Pitcher, bulbous with applied handle	
Milk, 1-qt. (R)	325.00
Water, 1/2-gal., 9" h. (R)	350.00
Salt	
Master, open	
Flat, round (R)	225.00
Footed with smooth rim	35.00
Shaker Bulbous, tall	125.00
Saloon (oversized)	95.00
Sauce dish, round, flat	
4" d.	5.00
4-1/2" d.	5.00
Spoon holder	45.00
Sugar bowl with cover	85.00
Syrup pitcher with applied handle	175.00
Tumbler, water	
Flat, 4" h.	125.00
Footed, 5" h.	65.00
Wine, 4-1/4" h. (R)	135.00

PANELED DAISY

Paneled Daisy high standard cake stand, covered compote, and true open compote.

OMN: Brazil. **AKA:** Daisy and Panel.

Non-flint. Bryce Brothers, Pittsburgh, PA, c. 1888. The United States Glass Company, Pittsburgh, PA, at Factory "B," c. 1891.

Original color production: Clear. Clear with amber or ruby stain or any other color would be considered rare.

Reproductions and Look-a-Likes: High standard covered compote (blue opalescent, blue satin, Burmese, clear, country peach, custard, dusty rose, forget-me-not blue, French opalescent, lime sherbet, orange carnival, periwinkle blue, shell pink, teal marigold); goblet (clear); relish dish (clear); toothpick holder (blue opalescent, cameo opalescent, clear, ebony); tumbler (amber, blue, clear, milk white, pink, ruby). John E. Kemple Glass Works, Kenova, WV, L.G. Wright Glass Company, New Martinsville, WV; Fenton Art Glass Company, Williamstown, WV, unmarked.

Paneled Daisy sugar shaker.

Paneled Daisy flat open bowl.

Known items:	Clear
Bottle, water	$85.00
Bowl, open	
Flared rim	
6" d.	20.00
7" d.	25.00
8" d.	35.00
Shallow	
7" d.	25.00
8" d.	30.00
9" d.	40.00
10" d.	55.00
Waste	40.00

Known items:	Clear
Butter dish with cover	
Flat	55.00
Footed with flanged rim	75.00
Cake stand on high standard	
8" d.	65.00
9" d.	75.00
10" d.	85.00
11" d.	125.00
Celery vase	45.00
Compote, round on high standard	
Covered	
5" d.	65.00
6" d.	75.00
7" d.	85.00
8" d.	110.00
Open with scalloped rim	
7" d.	25.00
8" d.	30.00
9" d.	35.00
10" d.	40.00
11" d.	50.00
Creamer	35.00

Paneled Daisy syrup, carafe, and saltshaker.

Known items:	Clear
Dish, open, oval, flat	
7" l.	20.00
8" l.	25.00
9" l.	30.00
10" l.	35.00
Goblet	35.00
Mug with handle	45.00
Pickle scoop	15.00
Pitcher, water, 1/2-gal.	95.00
Plate	
Round	
7" d.	30.00
9" d.	35.00
Square	
9-1/2"	30.00
10"	35.00
Relish tray	15.00
Saltshaker, tall	45.00
Sauce dish, round with flared rim	
Flat	
4" d.	5.00
4-1/2" d.	8.00
Footed	
4" d.	8.00
4-1/2" d.	10.00
Spoon holder	35.00
Sugar bowl with cover	55.00
Sugar shaker	75.00
Syrup pitcher	175.00
Tray, water, round	45.00
Tumbler, water, flat	35.00

PANELED FORGET-ME-NOT

OMN: Bryce's Regal, U.S. Glass No. 24. **AKA:** No. 29. Non-flint. Bryce Brothers, Pittsburgh, PA, c. 1875. The United States Glass Company, Pittsburgh, PA, at Factory "B," c. 1891.

Original color production: Amber, blue, clear. Amethyst, green, or any other color would be considered very rare.

Reproductions and Look-a-Likes: None known.

Paneled Forget-Me-Not celery vase.

Known items:	Amber	Blue	Clear
Bowl, covered, round	$65.00	$125.00	$55.00
Butter dish, covered	75.00	150.00	65.00
Cake stand on high standard			
8" d.	75.00	125.00	65.00
9" d.	85.00	150.00	75.00
10" d.	95.00	175.00	85.00
11" d.	110.00	200.00	110.00
12" d.	135.00	250.00	125.00
Celery vase	135.00	225.00	95.00
Compote, round on high standard			
Covered			
7-3/8" d.	110.00	225.00	85.00
8" d.	135.00	275.00	100.00
8-1/2" d.	150.00	325.00	125.00

Known items:	Amber	Blue	Clear
Open			
8" d. 55.00		110.00	35.00
9-1/2" d. 65.00		125.00	45.00
10" d. 75.00		150.00	55.00
Creamer.......................55.00		95.00	35.00
Cruet with the original stopper...... —		—	275.00
Goblet 110.00		275.00	45.00
Jam jar with cover 225.00		325.00	135.00
Pickle tray, boat-shaped 25.00		35.00	20.00
Pitcher			
Milk, 1-qt. 125.00		275.00	65.00
Water, 1/2-gal. 175.00		325.00	95.00
Relish tray tapered at one end.....35.00		55.00	25.00
Saltshaker .... —		—	110.00
Sauce dish, round, 4" d.			
Flat...................15.00		20.00	10.00
Footed 15.00		20.00	10.00
Spoon holder 55.00		85.00	35.00
Sugar bow with cover...........85.00		150.00	55.00
Tray, bread, oval................45.00		65.00	35.00
Wine.........................175.00		250.00	125.00

PANELED GRAPE

> **OMN:** Kokomo-Jenkins No. 507. **AKA:** Heavy Paneled Grape, Maple.
>
> Non-flint. The Kokomo Glass Manufacturing Company, Kokomo, IN, c. 1904.
>
> **Original color production:** Clear.
>
> **Reproductions and Look-a-Likes:** Too numerous to mention.

Known items:	Clear
Ale glass with knob stem, 6-1/4" h.	$65.00
Bowl, round with cover, flat, 8" d................	95.00
Butter dish with cover...........................	85.00
Celery vase	75.00
Compote, round	
Covered on high standard	
4" d....................................	85.00
8" d....................................	125.00
Open on low standard, 6-1/2" d.	45.00

Paneled Grape ale glass.

Known items:	Clear
Creamer	
With plain handle........................	65.00
With vine handle	65.00
Cup, sherbet, handled	25.00
Dish, oval, open, flat..........................	45.00
Goblet	45.00
Pitcher	
Milk, 1-qt................................	95.00
Water, 1/2-gal............................	110.00
Relish, oval..................................	25.00
Saltshaker....................................	65.00
Sauce dish	
Flat	15.00
Footed..................................	20.00
Spoon holder	45.00
Sugar bowl with cover	75.00
Syrup pitcher (2 styles)	175.00
Toothpick holder..............................	45.00
Tumbler	
Jelly....................................	40.00
Lemonade	55.00
Water	45.00
Wine	45.00

PANELED STRAWBERRY

OMN: Indiana Glass No. 127. **AKA:** Strawberry with Roman Key Band.

Non-flint. Indiana Glass Co., Dunkirk, IN, c. 1911.

Original color production: Clear and clear with colored stain.

Reproductions and Look-a-Likes: None known.

Paneled Strawberry creamer.

Paneled Strawberry covered sugar.

Paneled Strawberry spoon holder.

Known items:	Clear w/Stain
Bowl, open, round, flat, 8" d.	$65.00
Butter dish with cover	95.00
Creamer	55.00
Goblet	75.00
Pitcher, water, 1/2-gal.	110.00
Sauce, flat	15.00
Spoon holder	55.00
Sugar bowl with cover	85.00
Tumbler	30.00

PANELED THISTLE

OMN: Delta. **AKA:** Canadian Thistle.

Non-flint. J.B. Higbee Glass Company, Bridgeville, PA, c. 1910. The Jefferson Glass Company, Toronto, Ontario, Canada. Signed Higbee pieces bear their trademark of a "bee" with the letters "H.I.G." embossed across its wings. Add 25-50% for marked items.

Original color production: Clear. Clear with ruby stain or any other color would be considered very rare.

Reproductions and Look-a-Likes: Basket with applied handle and flared sides: bowls: covered with double-handle; bowls, open: 7-1/2" d. with deep bowl, 5-1/2" d. with shallow flared bowl, 7" d.; bowl: 5" l. open 4-toed oval; flat covered butter dish with flanged base; 10" d. high-standard cake stand; round handled candle holder; double-handled celery vase; round high-standard compote: covered, 4" d., 6" d.; round 6" d. high-standard open compote with scalloped flared rim; creamer with pressed handle: berry on low circular foot, table-sized on 4-feet; flat bulbous cruet with pressed handle; punch cup; rectangular flat nut dish; 5-3/8" h. goblet; 4-footed covered square honey dish; fairy lamp; round flat handled nappy; water pitcher with pressed handle; plates: round: 7" d. with rolled sides, 7-1/2" d., 10" d.; plates: square 7-1/2"; 8" l. flat oval relish; salt dip: round individual, 3-footed individual; bulbous flat based saltshaker; round flat sauce dishes: handled, non-handled; round footed sherbet; double-handled spoon holder; sugar bowls: covered: berry, table-size with handles, 3-handles; flat bulbous sugar shaker; toothpick holder; water tumbler, wine (amber, amethyst, amberina, blue, clear, clear satin, green, ice pink, rubina, ruby). L.G. Wright Glass Company, New Martinsville, WV. Either unmarked or marked with an irregular elongated "Bee."

Paneled Thistle spoon holder.

Paneled Thistle goblet.

Known items:	Clear
Banana dish	
Flat with folded sides, 10-1/4" l.	$65.00
Footed on stand (made from cake stand)	
6" l.	350.00
9-1/2" l.	275.00
Basket with applied handle	85.00
Bowl, open	
Rectangular, 7" l.	45.00
Round with foot	
6-1/2" d.	15.00
7" d.	20.00
7-1/2" d.	25.00
8" d.	30.00
8-1/2" d.	35.00
9" d.	55.00
Butter dish with cover and double handles, 5-3/4" d.	110.00

Known items:	Clear
Cake stand on high standard	
6" d.	110.00
9" d.	65.00
9-1/2" d.	75.00
10" d.	95.00
Celery	
Tray	35.00
Vase with double handles	65.00
Champagne	35.00
Compote, open, round on high standard with scalloped rim	
5" d. (Jelly)	45.00
7-1/2" d.	55.00
8" d.	65.00
9" d.	75.00
Creamer	55.00
Cruet with original stopper	85.00
Cup, sherbet with handle	25.00
Goblet	
Flared bowl	85.00
Straight-sided bowl	75.00
Honey dish with cover, 5" x 5"	110.00
Mug with handle	45.00
Pitcher	
Milk, 1-qt.	60.00
Water	
3-pts.	125.00
2-gal.	275.00

Paneled Thistle round berry, creamer, and covered honey dish.

Paneled Thistle milk pitcher.

Known items:	Clear
Plate	
Round	
7" d.	45.00
8-1/4" d.	35.00
9-1/4" d.	45.00
10-1/4" d.	65.00
Square, 7-1/4"	55.00
Relish tray, oval	
7-1/2" l.	30.00
8-1/4" l.	35.00
Rose bowl	
5" d.	55.00
6" d.	65.00
Salt	
Dip, individual	25.00
Master, open, footed	35.00
Shaker	65.00

Known items:	Clear
Sauce dish, round	
Flat, 4-1/2" d.	15.00
Footed, 4-1/2" d.	20.00
Spoon holder with double handles	85.00
Sugar bowl with cover and double handles	95.00
Toothpick holder	65.00
Tumbler, water	55.00
Vase	
Footed	
5" h.	25.00
9-1/4" h.	65.00
Swung, various sizes	110.00

PAVONIA

OMN: AKA: Pineapple Stem.

Non-flint. Ripley & Company, Pittsburgh, PA, c. 1885-1886. The United States Glass Company, Pittsburgh, PA, at Factory "F," c. 1891.

Original color production: Clear, clear with ruby stain (plain, engraved). Known engravings including. No. 106-Oak Leaf and Acorn, No. 77-Leaf Band, No. 119-Wading Bird in Marsh, No. 158-Silhouetted Oak Leaf and Acorn, and No. 118-Bird with Oak Leaf and Acorn. Issued in two conspicuous forms: (a) Table (with footed base) and (b) Hotel (unfooted).

Reproductions and Look-a-Likes: None known.

Known items:	Clear	Clear w/Etching	Clear w/Ruby
Bowl, open, flat			
Finger, ruffled blown with matching ruffled under plate	$35.00	$65.00	$150.00
Round with plain rim			
5" d.	15.00	25.00	35.00
6" d.	20.00	30.00	45.00
7" d.	25.00	35.00	55.00
8" d.	35.00	55.00	85.00
Waste	30.00	45.00	65.00

Pavonia etched goblet.

Known items:	Clear	Clear w/Etching	Clear w/Ruby
Butter dish with cover			
Hotel with			
ruffled base ...45.00		65.00	150.00
Table size with			
plain base 50.00		75.00	175.00
Cake plate, 10" d........25.00		30.00	45.00
Cake stand on high standard			
8" d. 95.00		125.00	150.00
9" d...........110.00		150.00	200.00
10" d. 135.00		175.00	225.00
Celery vase 30.00		45.00	85.00
Compote on high standard, round			
Covered			
5" d. (Jelly).35.00		55.00	85.00
6" d. 40.00		65.00	95.00
7" d. 45.00		75.00	110.00
8" d. 55.00		85.00	125.00
9" d. 65.00		110.00	150.00
10" d. 75.00		135.00	200.00
Open			
5" d. (Jelly).15.00		30.00	45.00
6" d. 20.00		30.00	55.00
7" d. 25.00		35.00	65.00
8" d. 30.00		45.00	75.00

Known items:	Clear	Clear w/Etching	Clear w/Ruby
9" d. 40.00		55.00	85.00
10" d. 50.00		75.00	110.00
Creamer			
Hotel.........25.00		40.00	85.00
Table 30.00		45.00	95.00
Cup, custard with			
applied handle 15.00		25.00	35.00
Dish, open, oblong, flat			
7" l. 15.00		25.00	40.00
8" l. 20.00		30.00	45.00
9" l. 25.00		35.00	50.00
Goblet 25.00		40.00	55.00
Mug with handle,			
4-1/4" h............20.00		35.00	50.00
Pickle dish			
Oblong 15.00		25.00	35.00
Square.........15.00		25.00	35.00
Pitcher			
Jug			
Milk, 1-qt..55.00		75.00	135.00
Water,			
1/2-gal...65.00		85.00	150.00
Tankard with			
applied handle			
Lemonade. 55.00		85.00	150.00
Milk, 1-qt..45.00		110.00	175.00
Water, 1/2-gal.,			
12" h.....65.00		125.00	225.00
Plate, 6-1/2" d.........15.00		25.00	35.00
Salt			
Dip, individual,			
round 5.00		—	25.00
Master, round ..20.00		—	65.00
Shaker, tall 25.00		55.00	65.00
Sauce dish, round			
Flat			
3" d........5.00		10.00	15.00
3-1/2" d....5.00		10.00	15.00
4" d........5.00		10.00	20.00
4-1/2" d....5.00		10.00	20.00
Footed			
3" d........5.00		10.00	20.00
3-1/2" d..5.00		10.00	20.00
4" d........5.00		10.00	22.50
4-1/2" d....5.00		10.00	25.00

Pavonia etched creamer, butter dish, sugar bowl, and spoon holder.

Known items:	Clear	Clear w/Etching	Clear w/Ruby
Saucer	15.00	30.00	45.00
Spoon holder			
Hotel	25.00	40.00	75.00
Table	30.00	45.00	85.00
Sugar bowl with cover			
Hotel	35.00	55.00	110.00
Table	45.00	65.00	125.00
Tray			
Bread	25.00	40.00	75.00
Water	55.00	95.00	150.00
Tumbler, water	20.00	35.00	55.00
Wine	15.00	35.00	45.00

PENNSYLVANIA

OMN: U.S. Glass **No. 15,048**
Pennsylvania. **AKA:** Balder, Hand, Kamoni.

Non-flint. United States Glass Company, Pittsburgh, PA, c. 1898.

Original color production: Clear. Clear with ruby stain, emerald green, or any other color would be considered rare.

Reproductions and Look-a-Likes: Spoon holder (Clear). Unmarked.

Known items:	Clear
Biscuit jar with cover	$110.00
Bottle, water	55.00
Bowl, open, flat	
Round	
Pointed-ends bowl	
6" d.	20.00
7" d.	25.00

Pennsylvania covered sugar bowl.

Known items:	Clear
8" d.	30.00
9" d.	55.00
Shallow bowl with scalloped rim	
5" d.	20.00
7" d.	25.00
8" d.	30.00
9" d.	35.00
Straight-sided bowl	
6" d.	20.00
7" d.	25.00
8" d.	40.00
9" d.	55.00
Square	
6"	20.00
7"	25.00
8"	40.00
9"	55.00

Pennsylvania rare flat punch bowl.

Known items:	Clear
Butter dish with cover	
Hotel size, straight-sided base with low domed lid	110.00
Table size, flat flanged base with high domed lid	55.00
Celery	
Tray, oblong	15.00
Vase	65.00
Champagne (VR)	150.00
Cheese dish with cover	95.00
Claret (VR)	125.00
Compote, open, round on high standard with ruffled rim (Jelly)	55.00
Creamer, table size	35.00
Cruet with original patterned stopper	55.00
Cup, custard with applied (originally cataloged as the *"lemonade"*)	15.00
Decanter with the original patterned stopper	
Handled	175.00
Handleless	100.00
Goblet	30.00
Ice tub	45.00
Jelly, round, single-handled	15.00

Known items:	Clear
Miniatures	
Butter dish with cover	150.00
Creamer	55.00
Spoon holder	55.00
Sugar bowl with cover	110.00
Olive dish, round	15.00
Pickle	
Jar with cover	135.00
Tray, oblong	15.00
Pitcher	
Bulbous	
Milk, 1-1/2-pts.	85.00
Water, 1/2-gal.	95.00
Tankard, water, 1/2-gal.	135.00
Plate, round	
7" d., round with scalloped rim (originally cataloged as the *"cheese plate"*)	35.00
8" d.	45.00
Punch bowl, flat	550.00
Salt	
Dip, individual	10.00
Master	45.00
Shaker	
Bulbous	
Large with short neck	40.00
Medium with short neck	35.00
Small with tall neck	30.00
Straight-sided	35.00
Sauce dish, flat, 4"	
Round	
Deep	
Eight-sided	8.00
Straight-sided	8.00
Shallow bowl with scallops	5.00
Spoon holder	45.00

Pennsylvania sugar bowl, creamer, spoon holder, butter dish.

Known items: **Clear**

Sugar bowl

    Table size

        Covered, flat **55.00**

        Open with handles **25.00**

Syrup pitcher

    Bulbous with inside glass lid.............. **85.00**

    Tapered **110.00**

Toothpick holder **55.00**

Tumbler, flat

    Juice (originally cataloged as the
        "champagne") **15.00**

    Water (originally cataloged as the
        "Taper Water") **30.00**

    Whiskey **15.00**

Wine...................................... **15.00**

Picket spoon holder.

PICKET

AKA: London, Picket Fence.

Non-flint. King Glass Company, Pittsburgh, PA, c. 1890s.

Original color production: Clear. Amber, apple green, blue or any other color would be considered rare.

Reproductions and Look-a-Likes: None known.

Known items: **Clear**

Bowl, 4-footed, square

    Berry, 6-1/2" **$35.00**

    Finger or waste **55.00**

Butter dish with cover....................... **175.00**

Cake stand on high standard.................. **275.00**

Celery vase **95.00**

Compote

    Covered

        High standard

            6" sq.......................... **125.00**

            7" sq.......................... **150.00**

            8" sq.......................... **225.00**

Known items: **Clear**

    Low standard

        6"sq.............................. **100.00**

        7"sq.............................. **125.00**

        8"sq.............................. **175.00**

Open

    High standard, scalloped rim

        6"sq.............................. **55.00**

        7"sq.............................. **65.00**

        8"sq.............................. **95.00**

        10"sq............................. **150.00**

    Low standard, scalloped rim

        6"sq.............................. **50.00**

        7"sq.............................. **60.00**

        8"sq.............................. **75.00**

Creamer, 5" h. **85.00**

Goblet **65.00**

Jam or pickle jar with cover................... **125.00**

Match holder **55.00**

Pitcher, water, 4-footed, 2-gal................. **175.00**

Plate, bread, oval, 13" l.

    "Stuart's McCormick Reaper" center **135.00**

    "Stuart's Mulberry" center **135.00**

    Small.................................. **55.00**

Known items: Clear

Salt

    Dip, individual, 4-legged **15.00**

    Master, oblong, flat **55.00**

Sauce dish, square

    Flat, handled **15.00**

    Footed, no handle **20.00**

Spoon holder **75.00**

Sugar bowl with cover **135.00**

Tray, water, rectangular. **150.00**

Wine (VR) **375.00**

PLEAT AND PANEL

OMN: Derby.

Non-flint. Bryce Brothers, Pittsburgh, PA, c. 1882. The United States Glass Company, Pittsburgh, PA, c. after 1891.

Original color production: Clear. Amethyst, amber, blue, green, milk white, or any other color would be considered very rare. Two recognizable goblets produced: (a) one with even vertical bars in the design and (b) one with extended vertical bars in the design.

Reproductions and Look-a-Likes: Goblet, 7" sq. plate (clear), unmarked.

Known items: Clear

Bowl

    Covered, flat

        7" sq. **$85.00**

        8" sq. **110.00**

        9" sq. **135.00**

    Open, flat

        5" sq. **75.00**

        6" sq. **30.00**

        7" sq. **35.00**

        8" sq. **65.00**

        9" sq. **95.00**

    Waste, 4-3/4" sq. (R) **150.00**

Butter dish with cover

    Low footed with tab handles, 6" sq. **250.00**

    Flat without handles, 6" sq. **150.00**

Pleat and Panel goblet.

Pleat and Panel plate.

Known items: Clear

Butter pat, 3-1/2" sq. (R) **150.00**

Cake stand on high standard

    8" sq. **95.00**

    9" sq. **125.00**

    10" sq. **225.00**

Celery vase, 8" h. **35.00**

Compote

    Covered

        High standard

            6" sq. **85.00**

            7" sq. **110.00**

Pleat and Panel covered marmalade.

Pleat and Panel covered butter.

Known items: **Clear**

Footed on low foot

    7" l.....................................125.00

    8" l.....................................150.00

    9" l.....................................185.00

Open, flat

    7" l.....................................35.00

    8" l.....................................40.00

    9" l.....................................45.00

Goblet, 6" h.

    With plain ribs.........................40.00

    With extended ribs 35.00

Lamp, oil, all glass

    Alternating clear and frosted font panels

        7-1/2"h..............................225.00

        8-1/2" h.............................275.00

        9-1/2" h.............................325.00

    Clear font, 9-1/4" h. 150.00

    Faceted font, 8" h......................125.00

Marmalade jar with cover 250.00

Marmalade set, 2 covered jars on underplate..... 1,250.00

Pickle dish, handled, 9-1/2" l....................20.00

Pitcher

    Milk, 1-qt., 7" h.......................150.00

    Water, 1/2-gal.........................110.00

Plate, square

    5".....................................75.00

    6".....................................45.00

    7".....................................25.00

    8".....................................85.00

    10"....................................125.00

Pleat and Panel covered serving dish.

Known items: **Clear**

    8" sq.................................. 150.00

    9" sq.................................. 225.00

Low standard

    6" sq.................................. 95.00

    7" sq.................................. 125.00

    8" sq.................................. 175.00

    9" sq.................................. 250.00

Creamer, 6-1/2" h. 30.00

Dish, serving, oblong

    Covered

    Flat

        7" l.............................. 100.00

        8" l.............................. 135.00

        9" l.............................. 175.00

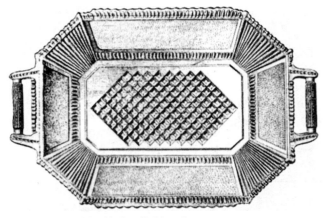

Pleat and Panel double-handled bread tray.

Known items:	Clear
Platter, bread, 13" l.	
Closed handled	35.00
Open handled	55.00
Salt	
Master, oblong with clear panels	45.00
Shaker, 3-1/4" h. (S)	175.00
Sauce dish, square	
Flat with tab handle	
3-1/2" sq.	10.00
4" sq.	12.50
5" sq.	20.00
Footed	
3-1/2" sq.	10.00
4" sq.	15.00
5" sq.	20.00
Spoon holder	30.00
Sugar bowl with cover	150.00
Syrup pitcher with patented lid (VR)	950.00
Tray, water, double handled, 14-1/2" l.	375.00
Wine, 4-1/4" h. (R)	325.00

PLUME

OMN: Adams' No. 3.

Non-flint. Adams & Company, Pittsburgh, PA, c. 1890. The United States Glass Company, Pittsburgh, PA. at Factory "A," c. 1891. Square bowl & sauce made by Indiana Glass Company, Dunkirk, IN, c. 1915.

Original color production: Clear, clear with ruby stain (plain, engraved).

Reproductions: Barrel-shaped goblet (clear, clear with frosting). L.G. Wright Glass Company, New Martinsville, WV, unmarked.

Plume etched covered bowl.

Known items:	Clear	Clear w/Ruby
Bottle, bitters (atypical vertical design)	$95.00	$325.00
Bowl		
Collared base		
Covered, round		
6" d.	110.00	225.00
7" d.	125.00	250.00
8" d.	150.00	275.00
Open		
Round		
Bell bowl with plain rim		
6" d.	25.00	75.00
7" d.	30.00	85.00
8" d.	45.00	95.00
Flared bowl		
With plain rim		
7" d.	30.00	85.00
8" d.	35.00	95.00
9" d.	45.00	100.00

Plume four-piece table set.

Plume ruby-stained creamer.

Plume high-standard cake stand.

Known items:	Clear	Clear w/Ruby
With scalloped rim		
7" d. 35.00		95.00
8" d. 45.00		100.00
9" d. 65.00		125.00
Square, flat, 8". 55.00		—
Butter dish with cover on collared		
base 75.00		225.00
Cake stand on high standard		
9" d. 125.00		325.00
10" d. 150.00		375.00
Castor, pickle in silver plated		
holder 225.00		650.00
Celery vase		
With horizontal plume		
design 65.00		125.00
With vertical plume		
design 55.00		—
Compote, round		
Covered on high standard		
6" d. 125.00		250.00
7" d. 150.00		275.00
8" d. 175.00		325.00

Known items:	Clear	Clear w/Ruby
Open on high standard		
Belled bowl		
Scalloped rim		
7" d. 45.00		95.00
8" d. 55.00		120.00
9" d. 65.00		125.00
Smooth rim		
6" d. 35.00		75.00
7" d. 45.00		95.00
8" d. 55.00		110.00
Straight-sided bowl		
Flared smooth rim		
8" d. 45.00		95.00
9" d. 55.00		110.00
10" d. 75.00		150.00
Scalloped rim		
6" d. 55.00		95.00
7" d. 65.00		110.00
8" d. 85.00		135.00
Creamer with applied handle 55.00		95.00

Known items:	Clear	Clear w/Ruby
Goblet	45.00	110.00
Ice tub	75.00	325.00
Lamp, oil, hand	175.00	—
Pickle dish	20.00	45.00
Pitcher, water		
Bulbous		
Horizontal plumes	125.00	475.00
Vertical plumes and applied handle (originally cataloged as the *"Cider Pitcher"*)	85.00	325.00
Tankard with vertical plumes, 1/2-gal.	110.00	375.00
Sauce dish		
Round, 4"		
Flat	10.00	25.00
Footed	15.00	35.00
Square, 4-3/4"	15.00	—
Spoon holder	35.00	95.00
Sugar bowl with cover	85.00	175.00
Syrup pitcher	125.00	375.00
Tray, water, round	75.00	225.00
Tumbler, water		
Horizontal plumes	30.00	110.00
Vertical plume design (blown rather than pressed)	25.00	55.00
Waste bowl	55.00	125.00

POINTED JEWEL

OMN: U.S. Glass #15006 **AKA:** Long Diamond, Pointed Jewels, Spear Point

Non-flint. Columbia Glass Co., Findlay, OH, c. 1888. The United States Glass Co., Pittsburgh, PA, after c. 1892 at Factory "J" and Factory "N."

Original color production: Clear. Scarce in clear with ruby stain. Add 100% for clear with ruby stained items.

Reproductions and Look-a-Likes: Creamer, tankard.

Pointed Jewel covered square honey dish.

Known items:	Clear
Bottle, cologne with original stopper	$85.00
Bowl, flat	
Covered	
6" d.	65.00
7" d.	85.00
8" d.	95.00
9" d.	150.00
Open, flared	
6" d.	25.00
7" d.	30.00
8" d.	35.00
9" d.	45.00
10-1/2" d.	75.00
Butter dish with cover	
Flanged	75.00
Handled	95.00
Cake stand on high standard, 10" d.	150.00
Celery vase	65.00
Compote on high standard	
Covered	
4-1/2" d.	55.00
6" d.	85.00
7" d.	110.00
8" d.	150.00
9" d.	225.00

Pointed Jewel master berry bowl.

Known items:	Clear
Open	
Flared	
7" d.	55.00
8" d.	65.00
9" d.	85.00
10-1/2" d.	110.00
Straight-sided	
4-1/2" d.	25.00
6" d.	35.00
7" d.	45.00
8" d.	55.00
9" d.	75.00
Creamer	
Table	45.00
Tankard	20.00
Cup, custard or punch	20.00
Dish, open, rectangular	
7"	25.00
8"	30.00
9"	35.00
Goblet	30.00
Honey dish with cover, square (VR)	250.00
Miniatures	
Butter with cover	175.00
Creamer	85.00
Spoon holder	150.00
Sugar bowl with cover	135.00
Mug	35.00
Pitcher	
Milk	150.00
Water, tankard	110.00
Saltshaker	65.00
Sauce	
4" d.	5.00
4-1/2" d.	8.00

Known items:	Clear
Saucer	35.00
Spoon holder	45.00
Sugar bowl with cover	65.00
Tumbler, water	35.00
Wine	25.00

POLAR BEAR

AKA: Alaska, Arctic, Frosted Polar Bear, Ice Berg, North Pole, Polar Bear and Seal.

Non-flint. Traditionally attributed to the Crystal Glass Company, Bridgeport, OH, c. 1883.

Original color production: Clear, clear with frosting.

Reproductions and Look-a-Likes: Goblet (amber, blue, clear). Summit Art Glass Company, Rootstown, OH. When marked, items are impressed with a "V" within a circle designating the Summit Art Glass Company.

Polar Bear goblet.

Known items:	Clear w/Frosting
Goblet	$225.00
Ice bucket	150.00
Pitcher, water	1,250.00
Tray, water	350.00

Polar Bear oval water tray.

Known items:	Clear
Butter dish with cover	$75.00
Cake stand on high standard	
8" d.	85.00
11" d.	150.00
Creamer	35.00
Goblet	
With flat ear of corn	75.00
With raised ear of corn.	35.00
Pitcher, water, bulbous with applied handle,	
1/2-gal.	150.00
Sauce dish, round, flat	5.00
Spoon holder	30.00
Sugar bowl with cover	55.00
Wine	35.00

POPCORN

Non-flint. Traditionally attributed to the Boston & Sandwich Glass Company, Sandwich, MA, c. late 1860s.

Original color production: Clear. Goblet produced in two conspicuous forms: (a) with flat ear of corn and (b) with raised ear of corn.

Reproductions and Look-a-Likes: None known.

Popcorn bulbous water pitcher.

PORTLAND

OMN: U.S. Glass No. 15,121. **AKA:** U.S. Portland.

Non-flint. Portland Glass Company, Portland, ME, c. late 1870s. The United States Glass Company, Pittsburgh, PA, c. 1910.

Original color production: Clear. Clear with ruby stain or any other color would be considered rare.

Reproductions and Look-a-Likes: Creamer nut dish, pickle tray, relish sugar bowl (clear). Wheaton-Craft Giftware, Millville, NJ. Unmarked.

Known items:	Clear
Basket with applied handle.	$95.00
Biscuit jar with cover	110.00
Bottle, water.	55.00
Boudoir set (complete)	225.00
Bowl, round	
Open	
6" d.	20.00
7" d.	25.00
8" d.	30.00
Covered with notch lid, footed.	135.00
Candlestick	
Cupped, 7" h.	110.00
Flared, 7" h.	95.00

Portland sugar bowl, spoon holder, butter dish, and creamer.

Known items:	Clear
Regular	
9" h.	85.00
10-1/2" h.	100.00
With saucer foot.	125.00
Cake stand on high standard, 10-1/2" d.	85.00
Carafe	55.00
Celery	
Tray	15.00
Vase	35.00
Compote, round	
Covered on high standard	
6" d.	85.00
7" d.	95.00
8" d.	110.00
Open	
High standard	
Flared bowl	
7" d.	30.00
8" d.	35.00
9-1/2" d.	45.00
Straight-sided bowl	
6" d.	30.00
7" d.	35.00
8" d.	45.00
Low standard	
6" d.	25.00
7" d.	30.00
8" d.	40.00
Creamer	
Breakfast, oval	20.00
Table	35.00
Tankard, 6-oz.	30.00
Cruet with either faceted or patterned stopper	65.00

Known items:	Clear
Cup, custard with handle	15.00
Decanter, 1-qt. with handle and original stopper	65.00
Dish, open, oval, flat	
6" l.	15.00
7-1/2" l.	20.00
9" l.	25.00
10-1/2" l.	30.00
12-1/2" l	35.00
Finger bowl	25.00
Goblet	35.00
Jam jar with silver plate cover.	95.00
Lamp, oil, all glass, 9" h.	125.00
Olive dish, oval, 5-1/2" l.	20.00
Pickle dish, boat-shaped	15.00
Pin tray	15.00
Pitcher, water, 1/2-gal.	
Bulbous	85.00
Tankard	65.00
Pomade jar with silver plate cover.	25.00
Puff box with silver plate cover	30.00
Punch bowl, footed, 15" d.	175.00
Relish tray with handle	15.00
Ring stand (R)	135.00
Saltshaker	25.00
Sardine box, 4-1/2"	45.00
Sauce dish, flat	
Oval	5.00
Round, 4" d.	
Flared bowl	5.00
Straight-sided bowl	5.00
Square, 4"	5.00
Spoon holder	
Large	35.00
Small	30.00

Known items: — Clear

Sugar bowl
      Breakfast, oval, open..................... 35.00
      Table size with cover..................... 65.00
Sugar shaker................................... 40.00
Syrup pitcher
      6-oz.. 95.00
      16-oz...................................... 110.00
Toothpick holder 20.00
Tray, boudoir, oval, 11" l..................... 25.00
Tumbler, water, flat 25.00
      Vase
        Deep
          6" h.......................... 30.00
          9" h.......................... 30.00
        Regular 30.00
Wine... 20.00

POWER AND SHOT

AKA: Horn of Plenty, Powder Horn and Shot.

Flint, non-flint. Traditionally attributed to the Boston & Sandwich Glass Company, Sandwich, MA, based on shards found at the factory site.

Original color production: Clear.

Reproductions and Look-a-Likes: None known.

Known items: — Clear

Butter dish with cover
      Flat.................................... $125.00
      Footed 150.00
Cake stand on high standard.................... 55.00
Castor bottle................................... 45.00
Celery vase 250.00
Compote with cover
      High standard 175.00
      Low standard........................ 135.00
Creamer with applied handle 95.00
Eggcup, open, single, footed 65.00

Known items: — Clear

Goblet 85.00
Pitcher, water, 1/2-gal. with applied handle....... 325.00

Powder and Shot goblet.

Known items: — Clear

Salt, master, open, footed........................55.00
Sauce dish, round, flat 15.00
Spoon holder 55.00
Sugar bowl with cover 110.00

PRESSED DIAMOND

OMN: Central No. 775. **AKA:** Block and Diamond, Zephyr.

Non-flint. Central Glass Company, Wheeling, WV, c. 1885. The United States Glass Company, Pittsburgh, PA. at Factory "O," c. 1891.

Original color production: Amber, blue, canary, clear.

Reproductions and Look-a-Likes: None known.

Pressed Diamond water pitcher.

Known items:	Amber	Blue	Canary	Clear
Bowl, open, round, flat				
5" d.	$20.00	$25.00	$25.00	$15.00
6" d.	25.00	30.00	30.00	20.00
7" d.	30.00	35.00	35.00	25.00
8" d.	40.00	45.00	45.00	35.00
Butter dish with cover.	55.00	65.00	75.00	45.00
Butter pat	15.00	15.00	20.00	10.00
Cake stand on low foot				
8" d.	65.00	85.00	95.00	55.00
9" d.	75.00	95.00	110.00	65.00
10" d.	85.00	125.00	135.00	75.00
12" d.	100.00	150.00	175.00	95.00
Celery vase	40.00	55.00	65.00	35.00
Compote on high standard				
High standard				
7" d.	75.00	85.00	95.00	65.00
8" d.	95.00	125.00	135.00	85.00
Low standard				
8" d.	35.00	45.00	45.00	35.00
9" d.	45.00	55.00	55.00	45.00
10" d.	55.00	65.00	65.00	55.00
11" d.	65.00	85.00	85.00	65.00
12" d.	75.00	100.00	100.00	75.00
Creamer.	35.00	45.00	45.00	25.00
Cruet with original patterned stopper	125.00	150.00	175.00	65.00
Cup, custard with applied handle.	15.00	20.00	20.00	15.00
Finger bowl.	25.00	30.00	25.00	25.00
Goblet	45.00	95.00	110.00	35.00
Pitcher, water, 1/2-gal.	85.00	150.00	175.00	65.00
Salt				
Dip, individual	10.00	15.00	15.00	5.00
Shaker, tall.	30.00	35.00	35.00	25.00
Sauce dish, round, flat.	5.00	10.00	10.00	5.00
Spoon holder	30.00	40.00	40.00	25.00
Sugar bowl with cover	45.00	65.00	75.00	35.00
Tumbler, water.	25.00	50.00	55.00	20.00
Wine.	20.00	75.00	65.00	20.00

PRESSED LEAF

OMN: N.P.L. **AKA:** New Pressed Leaf.

Flint, non-flint. McKee Brothers, Pittsburgh, PA, c. 1868. Central Glass Company, Wheeling, WV, c. 1881.

Original color production: Clear. Designed by H.S. McKee and patented under U.S. patent No. 2,825 November 5, 1867. Flint items are worth about 50-100% of non-flint prices quoted.

Reproductions and Look-a-Likes: None known.

Pressed Leaf creamer, spoonholder, butterdish.

Pressed Leaf bulbous water pitcher.

Known items:	Clear Non-flint
Butter dish with cover	$95.00
Cake stand	
High standard, 10-1/2" h.	150.00
Low standard, 6-1/2" h.	150.00
Champagne, 5-1/4" h.	125.00
Claret, 4-1/2" h.	45.00
Compote	
Covered	
High standard	
6" d.	75.00
7" d.	95.00
8" d.	110.00

Known items:	Clear Non-flint
Low standard	
6" d.	65.00
7" d.	75.00
8" d.	95.00
Open	
High standard	
6" d.	45.00
7" d.	55.00
8" d.	65.00
Low standard	
6" d.	35.00
7" d.	45.00
8" d.	55.00
Creamer with applied handle	85.00
Dish, open, oval, flat	
5" l.	15.00
6" l.	20.00
7" l.	25.00
8" l.	30.00
9" l.	40.00
Eggcup, open, single, footed	25.00
Goblet	
5-3/4" h.	30.00
6" h.	35.00
Lamp, oil, handled	95.00
Pitcher, water, 1/2-gal.	175.00
Salt, master, open, footed, smooth or fluted rim, 3" h.	30.00
Sauce dish, round, flat	
4" d.	10.00
4-1/2" d.	10.00
Spoon holder	35.00
Sugar bowl with cover	85.00
Wine, 4" h.	35.00

PRIMROSE

OMN: Canton No. 10. **AKA:** Stippled Primrose.

Non-flint. The Canton Glass Company, Canton, OH, c. 1885.

Original color production: Amber, blue, canary yellow, clear, apple green (scarce). Milk white, purple slag, opaque black, or any other color would be considered rare.

Reproductions and Look-a-Likes: None known.

Primrose milk pitcher.

Primrose close up.

Known items:	Amber	Blue	Canary Yellow	Clear	Green
Bowl, open, round, flat, master berry	$40.00	$45.00	$55.00	$35.00	$45.00
Butter dish with cover	65.00	75.00	85.00	55.00	75.00
Cake plate with double handles, 9" d.	45.00	55.00	65.00	35.00	55.00
Cake stand on high standard, 10" d.	150.00	175.00	200.00	125.00	175.00
Compote, covered, round					
High standard					
6" d.	75.00	95.00	110.00	65.00	95.00
7-1/2" d.	85.00	110.00	150.00	75.00	125.00
8" d.	95.00	125.00	175.00	85.00	150.00
9" d.	125.00	175.00	200.00	110.00	175.00
Low standard					
6" d.	65.00	95.00	110.00	55.00	95.00
7-1/2" d.	75.00	110.00	135.00	65.00	125.00
8" d.	85.00	135.00	175.00	75.00	150.00
Cordial	50.00	45.00	65.00	40.00	45.00
Creamer	45.00	65.00	85.00	35.00	75.00
Eggcup, open, single	45.00	65.00	75.00	35.00	85.00

Known items:	Amber	Blue	Canary Yellow	Clear	Green
Goblet					
With knob stem	55.00	75.00	95.00	45.00	85.00
With plain stem	40.00	55.00	75.00	35.00	65.00
Lamp, finger	—	—	—	225.00	—
Pickle dish.	20.00	30.00	35.00	15.00	30.00
Pitcher					
Milk, 1-qt.	55.00	75.00	125.00	45.00	85.00
Water, 1/2-gal.	75.00	95.00	150.00	65.00	110.00
Plate					
4-1/2" d. (Toddy).	10.00	20.00	20.00	10.00	20.00
6" d.	15.00	25.00	30.00	15.00	25.00
7" d.	20.00	35.00	40.00	20.00	35.00
8" d.	30.00	45.00	55.00	25.00	45.00
Platter, oval, 12" l.	40.00	55.00	65.00	35.00	55.00
Relish tray	20.00	25.00	30.00	15.00	25.00
Sauce dish, round					
Flat					
4" d.	8.00	12.50	15.00	5.00	15.00
5-1/2" d.	10.00	15.00	20.00	8.00	20.00
Footed					
4" d.	8.00	15.00	18.00	5.00	18.00
5-1/2" d.	10.00	18.00	20.00	8.00	20.00
Spoon holder	35.00	55.00	75.00	30.00	65.00
Sugar bowl with cover	65.00	95.00	125.00	55.00	110.00
Tray, water.	55.00	85.00	100.00	45.00	95.00
Waste bowl	45.00	65.00	75.00	35.00	75.00
Wine.	30.00	45.00	55.00	20.00	55.00

PRINCESS FEATHER

OMN: Rochelle. **AKA:** Lacy Medallion, Prince's Feather.

Flint, non-flint. Bakewell, Pears & Company, Pittsburgh, PA, c. late 1870s. The United States Glass Company, Pittsburgh, PA, c. after 1891.

Original color production: Clear. Opaque white, opaque blue, or any other color would be considered very rare.

Reproductions and Look-a-Likes: Goblet, spoon holder (clear non-flint). **Note:** Goblet produced by the L.G. Wright Glass Company, New Martinsville, WV, in clear, non-flint, unmarked.

Princess Feather rare opal sugar bowl.

Princess Feather spoon holder.

Known items: **Clear**

Bowl

    Round

        Covered with collared base $125.00

    Open

        Collared base 45.00

        Flat, 6" d. 25.00

        Oval, flat with plain rim

            6" l. 25.00

            7" l. 30.00

            8" l. 35.00

            9" l. 45.00

Butter dish with covered 75.00

Cake plate with closed handles, 9" d. 35.00

Celery vase (S) 110.00

Compote with cover, round

    High standard

        6" d. 150.00

        7" d. 175.00

        8" d. 225.00

    Low collared base

        6" d. 125.00

        7" d. 150.00

        8" d. 175.00

Creamer with applied handle 75.00

Dish, oval, flat, covered 110.00

Known items: **Clear**

Eggcup, single, open, footed 45.00

Goblet 45.00

Honey dish, round, flat, 3" d. 10.00

Pitcher

    Milk, 1-qt. 275.00

    Water, 1/2-gal. 250.00

Plate, round

    6" d. 25.00

    7" d. 30.00

    8" d. 35.00

    9" d. 45.00

Relish tray 20.00

Salt, master, open, footed. 35.00

Sauce dish, round, 4" d.

    Flat 5.00

    Footed. 8.00

Spoon holder 35.00

Sugar bowl with cover 75.00

Wine 45.00

PRISCILLA, DALZELL'S

OMN: Alexis. **AKA:** Late Moon and Star, Stelle, Sun and Star.

Non-flint. Dalzell, Gillmore & Leighton, Findlay, OH, c. late 1880s. National Glass Company, Pittsburgh, PA, c. 1899.

Original color production: Clear. Clear with ruby stain or any other color would be considered very rare.

Reproductions and Look-a-Likes: 12" h. handled basket with flared rim; bowls open round flat: 9" d. with cupped rim, 10-1/2" d. with flared rim; cocktail; creamer with pressed handle; 6" d. handled bonbon dish with ruffled rim; goblet; round flat plates: 11" d. with rolled edge, 6" d. with smooth rim, 8" d. with smooth rim, 12-1/2" d. with smooth rim; 4" h. sherbet; open double-handled sugar bowl; wine (clear, dusty rose, emerald green, light blue, Salem blue). Fenton Art Glass

Company, Williamstown, WV, unmarked or embossed with the familiar Fenton logo.

7" flat ashtray; round low footed bowls: 4" d. with cover; open: 4" d. with scalloped rim; 6-1/2" d. with crimped rim; 8-oz. goblet; 8" d. plate; 4" d. rose bowl; 5", 5-1/2" d. round flat sauce dish; sherbet; toothpick holder; 3-oz. wine (amber, amethyst, clear, clear with ruby stain, green, ruby). L.G. Wright Glass Company, New Martinsville, WV, unmarked.

Priscilla double relish.

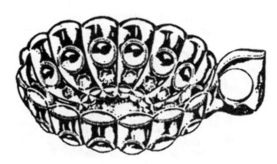

Priscilla handled nappy.

Priscilla covered sugar bowl.

Known items:	Clear
Banana stand on high standard	$175.00
Biscuit jar with cover	225.00
Bowl	
Covered, round, 7" d.	85.00
Open, flat	
Round	
7" d.	25.00
7-1/2" d.	30.00
8" d.	35.00
10-1/4" d.	55.00
Square	
8"	45.00
9-1/4"	55.00
Cake stand on high standard	
6-1/2" d.	75.00
9-1/2" d.	135.00
10" d.	150.00

Known items:	Clear
Celery vase	55.00
Compote on high standard	
Covered	
5" d. (Jelly)	55.00
7" d.	85.00
8" d.	150.00
9" d.	225.00
Open	
With flared rim, 10" sq.	110.00
With scalloped rim	
5" d.	35.00
7" d.	45.00
8" d.	65.00
8-1/2" d.	75.00
10" d.	95.00
With smooth rim, 5" d. (Jelly)	25.00
Condiment tray	35.00
Creamer	
Individual, 3" h.	25.00
Table size	45.00
Cruet with original stopper 1	10.00
Cup	20.00
Goblet	85.00
Mug	35.00

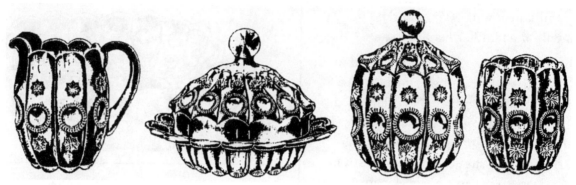

Priscilla four-piece table set.

Priscilla spoon holder.

Priscilla spoon holder.

Known items:	Clear
Pickle dish	15.00
Pitcher, water with applied handle, 1/2-gal.	
Bulbous	175.00
Tankard	225.00
Plate, round	35.00
Relish dish	15.00
Rose bowl	55.00
Sauce dish, flat	
Round	
4" d	15.00
4-1/2" d	55.00
Sugar bowl with cover	17.50
Square	
4"	18.00
4-1/2"	22.50
Saucer	15.00
Spoon holder	40.00
Saltshaker	75.00

Known items:	Clear
Syrup pitcher	135.00
Toothpick holder	45.00
Tumbler, water	50.00
Wine	75.00

PRISCILLA (FOSTORIA)

OMN: Fostoria's No. 676. **AKA:** Acanthus Leaf.

Non-flint. The Fostoria Glass Company, Fostoria, OH, c. 1898.

Original color production: Clear, emerald green (plain, gilded). Minor production in custard and milk white.

Reproductions and Look-a-Likes: None known.

Priscilla (Fostoria) four-piece table set.

Priscilla (Fostoria) celery vase.

Priscilla (Fostoria) master berry.

Known items:	Clear	Emerald Green
Bottle, water	$85.00	$125.00
Bowl, open, flat, round, 8-1/2" d.	55.00	85.00
Butter dish with cover	125.00	225.00
Cake stand on high standard	275.00	650.00
Celery vase	110.00	135.00
Compote, round on high standard		
Covered	150.00	250.00
Open	75.00	95.00
Creamer with applied handle	65.00	85.00
Cruet with original stopper	125.00	275.00
Cup, sherbet	15.00	20.00
Eggcup, single, open	35.00	65.00

Known items:	Clear	Emerald Green
Goblet (S)	65.00	110.00
Lamp, oil	125.00	250.00
Marmalade jar with cover	85.00	175.00
Pickle dish	20.00	30.00
Pitcher, water, tankard with applied handle, 2-gal.	175.00	325.00
Saltshaker		
Large with bulbous neck	35.00	65.00
Small with bulbous base and narrow neck	25.00	45.00
Sauce dish, round, flat, 4-1/2" d.	10.00	15.00
Spoon holder	55.00	75.00
Sugar bowl with cover	85.00	110.00
Syrup pitcher	150.00	425.00
Toothpick holder	65.00	225.00
Tumbler, water	55.00	95.00
Vase	45.00	55.00

QUEEN

OMN: AKA: Daisy and Button with Pointed Panels, Daisy with Depressed Button, Paneled Daisy and Button, Pointed Panel Daisy and Button, Sunk Daisy and Button.

Non-flint. McKee Glass Company, Jeannette, PA, c. 1894.

Original color production: Amber, apple green, blue, canary yellow, clear.

Reproductions and Look-a-Likes: Master berry bowl, high-standard cake stand, spoon holder, water pitcher, tumbler, (cobalt blue, dark amber, vaseline, green), unmarked.

Queen goblet.

Known items:	Amber	Apple Green	Blue	Canary Yellow	Clear
Basket, applied handle $125.00		$175.00	$150.00	$225.00	$95.00
Bowl, open, round, flat,					
master berry, 8-1/2" d. 35.00		55.00	55.00	65.00	30.00
Butter dish					
Domed cover. 50.00		75.00	75.00	85.00	45.00
Tapered cover 65.00		125.00	110.00	135.00	55.00
Cake stand on high standard					
8" d. 55.00		95.00	85.00	100.00	45.00
9" d. 75.00		125.00	110.00	125.00	65.00
10" d. .95.00		135.00	125.00	150.00	85.00
Cheese dish with cover. 65.00		75.00	85.00	95.00	65.00
Claret. 30.00		95.00	85.00	95.00	35.00
Compote with cover on high					
standard 85.00		125.00	110.00	135.00	75.00
Creamer .30.00		50.00	45.00	55.00	30.00

Queen four-piece table set.

Known items:	Amber	Apple Green	Blue	Canary Yellow	Clear
Dish, open, oval					
7" l.	20.00	30.00	30.00	35.00	20.00
9" l.	25.00	35.00	35.00	40.00	25.00
Goblet	35.00	55.00	45.00	50.00	30.00
Pickle tray, oval	15.00	20.00	20.00	20.00	15.00
Pitcher					
Milk, 1-qt.	45.00	65.00	50.00	75.00	45.00
Water, 1/2-gal.	55.00	85.00	65.00	95.00	55.00
Platter, bread	20.00	30.00	30.00	35.00	25.00
Saltshaker	25.00	45.00	35.00	45.00	25.00
Sauce dish, round, 4" d.					
Flat	5.00	10.00	8.00	10.00	5.00
Footed	8.00	15.00	10.00	15.00	8.00
Spoon holder	25.00	35.00	35.00	40.00	25.00
Sugar bowl with cover	35.00	55.00	45.00	55.00	35.00
Tumbler, water, flat	30.00	45.00	40.00	45.00	25.00
Wine	30.00	45.00	35.00	40.00	25.00

QUEEN ANNE

AKA: Bearded Man, Neptune, Old Man, Old Man of the Woods, Santa Claus.

Non-flint. LaBelle Glass Company, Bridgeport, OH, c. 1880. Designed by Andrew H. Boggs and patented under U.S. patent No. 12,006 November 2, 1880.

Original color production: Clear (plain, engraved). Amber or any other color would be considered rare. Add 25% for frosted items.

Reproductions and Look-a-Likes: None known.

Known items:	Clear
Bowl, covered, oval, flat	
8" l.	$95.00
9" l.	115.00
Butter dish with cover	85.00
Casserole, round with cover	
7" d.	135.00
8" d.	175.00
Celery vase	65.00

Queen Anne butter dish, creamer, spoon holder and sugar bowl.

Known items: **Clear**

Compote, round

    Covered

        High standard

            7" d. 150.00

            8" d. 175.00

Low standard, 9" d. 135.00

Creamer.................................... 55.00

Eggcup, open, single 45.00

Pitcher

    Milk, 1-qt. 275.00

    Water, 1/2-gal. 225.00

Plate, bread 65.00

Saltshaker, footed......................... 85.00

Sauce dish, round, footed................... 15.00

Spoon holder 45.00

Sugar bowl with cover 85.00

Syrup pitcher 375.00

QUESTION MARK

OMN: Richards and Hartley No. 55. **AKA:** Oval Loop.

Non-flint. Richard and Hartley Glass Company, Tarentum, PA, c. 1888. The United States Glass Company, Pittsburgh, PA, at Factory "F," c. 1892.

Original color production: Clear. Clear with ruby stain or any other color would be considered rare.

Known items: **Clear**

Bowl

    Collared base, open, round

        7" d................................. $35.00

        8" d................................. 45.00

Question Mark chamber stick.

Known items: **Clear**

    Flat, open, oblong

        5" l. 15.00

        6" l. 20.00

        7" l. 20.00

        8" l. 25.00

        9" l. 30.00

        10" l. 35.00

Butter dish with cover 65.00

Candlestick, chamber with finger grip 110.00

Celery vase...................................35.00

    Compote, round

        Covered, high standard

            7" d.................................75.00

            8" d.................................95.00

        Open

            High standard

                7" d.................................45.00

                8" d.................................55.00

            Low standard

                7" d.................................35.00

                8" d.................................45.00

Question Mark sugar shaker, covered compote, and saltshaker.

Question Mark tumbler, tankard pitcher, goblet, and wine.

Known items:	Clear
Creamer	40.00
Goblet	35.00
Pickle jar with cover	110.00
Pitcher	
Bulbous	
Milk, 1-qt	65.00
Water, 1/2-gal	75.00
Tankard	
Milk, 1-qt	55.00
Water, 1/2-gal	65.00

Known items:	Clear
Saltshaker	30.00
Sauce dish, round, 4" d.	
Collared base	8.00
Footed	10.00
Spoon holder	35.00
Sugar bowl with cover	55.00
Sugar shaker	65.00
Tray, bread	35.00
Tumbler, water, flat	30.00
Wine	20.00

RAINDROP

OMN: Dot.

Non-flint. Doyle & Company, Pittsburgh, PA, c. 1885. The United States Glass Company, Pittsburgh, PA. at Factory "D," c. 1891.

Original color production: Amber, apple green, blue, canary yellow, clear. Odd items found in milk white, opaque blue and opaque white.

Reproductions and Look-a-Likes: None known.

Raindrop master berry bowl in purple marble slag.

Known items:	Amber	Blue	Canary Yellow	Clear
Bowl				
Finger, round with underplate	$35.00	$45.00	$55.00	$25.00
Master berry, 9" d.	25.00	35.00	45.00	20.00
Butter dish with cover	45.00	55.00	65.00	45.00
Cake plate, round	15.00	25.00	30.00	15.00
Compote with cover				
High standard	55.00	65.00	75.00	55.00
Low standard	45.00	55.00	65.00	45.00
Creamer	20.00	35.00	45.00	20.00
Cup and saucer set	45.00	55.00	75.00	35.00
Eggcup, double, open........................	25.00	45.00	85.00	20.00
Pickle dish, oval............................	15.00	20.00	25.00	10.00
Pitcher, water with pressed handle, 1/2-gal.	45.00	55.00	75.00	40.00
Plate				
Alphabet bordered.......................	40.00	65.00	85.00	30.00
Dinner	15.00	25.00	30.00	15.00
Relish tray, oval	10.00	15.00	20.00	10.00
Sauce dish, round				
Flat...................................	5.00	8.00	10.00	5.00
Footed	5.00	10.00	15.00	5.00
Spoon holder	30.00	35.00	45.00	30.00

Known items:	Amber	Blue	Canary Yellow	Clear
Sugar bowl with cover	35.00	45.00	55.00	35.00
Syrup pitcher	85.00	100.00	125.00	65.00
Tray, water, round	30.00	45.00	55.00	30.00
Tumbler, water	20.00	30.00	35.00	15.00
Wine	10.00	25.00	30.00	10.00

RED BLOCK

OMN: Bryce No. 175, Captain Kid-150, Central's No. 881, Central's No. 893, Doyle No. 250, Duncan's No. 328, Eva, Fostoria No. 140, Pioneer's No. 250, Virginia-140. **AKA:** Barreled Block, Clear Block.

Non-flint. Bryce Brothers, Pittsburgh, PA. Central Glass Company, Wheeling, WV. Doyle & Company, Pittsburgh, PA, c. 1885. Fostoria Glass Company, Fostoria, OH, c. 1890. George Duncan & Sons, Pittsburgh, PA. Model Flint Glass Works, Albany, IN. Pioneer Glass Works, Pittsburgh, PA, c. 1890.

Original color production: Clear, clear with amber stain, clear with ruby stain.

Reproductions and Look-a-Likes: Goblet, wine (amber, blue, ruby stain, iridescent amethyst, iridescent blue, orange, carnival colors), unmarked.

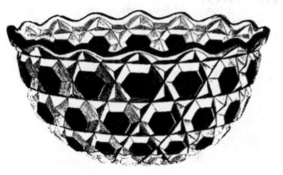

Red Block clear with ruby master berry bowl.

Red Block clear with ruby covered butter dish.

Known items:	Clear	Clear w/Ruby
Banana dish, flat with folded sides	$35.00	$125.00
Bottle, cologne with ruffled rim and original swirl stopper	55.00	110.00

Known items:	Clear	Clear w/Ruby
Bowl, open, flat		
Round		
6" d.	15.00	35.00
8" d.	35.00	55.00
9" d.	45.00	95.00
10" d. (shallow)	55.00	110.00
Square		
5"	25.00	55.00
6"	30.00	65.00
8"	45.00	125.00
Cake stand on high standard	125.00	850.00
Celery		
Tray	25.00	55.00
Vase	35.00	125.00
Cheese dish with cover and underplate	125.00	450.00
Compote, covered on high standard	65.00	275.00
Creamer		
Individual, 3" h.	25.00	35.00
Table size	35.00	85.00
Cream pot with notched cover	125.00	650.00
Cruet with original stopper	45.00	225.00
Cup, custard, handled (known as the "handled ice") (S)	20.00	75.00

Red Block clear with ruby stain water pitcher.

Known items:	Clear	Clear w/Ruby
Dish, open, oblong, flat		
8" l.	25.00	55.00
9" l.	30.00	75.00
10" l.	35.00	95.00
Goblet	20.00	35.00
Lamp, oil		
High standard		
with patterned font		
8" h.	150.00	—
9" h.	175.00	—
Miniature (known as the *"Annie Rooney"*). Red Block base with Artichoke shade	150.00	—
Parlor with matching shade	750.00	6,500.00
Mug with handle	15.00	35.00
Mustard jar with original notched lid.	45.00	110.00
Pickle caster, silverplate frame, lid & tongs	175.00	1,250.00
Pitcher, water		
Bulbous with applied handle	125.00	450.00
Straight-sided with pressed handle	55.00	175.00
Plate, 10" d.	35.00	110.00
Relish tray, 8" l.	20.00	45.00

Known items:	Clear	Clear w/Ruby
Rose bowl		
Large	45.00	125.00
Small	35.00	85.00
Salt		
Dip, individual (R)	15.00	35.00
Master, open, flat (R)	35.00	125.00
Shaker (R)	30.00	175.00
Sauce dish, round, flat		
4-1/2" d.	5.00	25.00
5" d.	8.00	35.00
Spoon holder, handled	25.00	45.00
Sugar bowl, covered and double handles.	35.00	65.00
Syrup pitcher (2 styles)	55.00	325.00
Tray		
Ice cream, rectangular, 8" x 12-1/2"	55.00	350.00
Water, round	45.00	125.00
Tumbler, water, flat	15.00	35.00
Waste or finger bowl.	25.00	65.00
Wine, 4" h.	12.50	25.00

REVERSE 44

OMN: U.S. Glass No. 15,140-Athenia.
AKA: Paneled 44.

Non-flint. The United States Glass Company, Pittsburgh, PA, c. 1912.

Original color production: Clear (plain, gilded, platinum stained & color stains of green, maidens blush & yellow). Blue or any other color would be considered rare. Often the bases of items are embossed with the "U.S.G." insignia of the United States Glass Company. For clear with gold, add 20% to the all clear price; for items with green, yellow and maidens' blush, add 75% to the all clear price.

Reproductions and Look-a-Likes: None known.

Reverse 44 tumbler with platinum stain.

Reverse 44 true open compote with platinum stain.

Known items:	Clear	Clear w/ Platinum
Basket with applied reeded handle		
6" $50.00		$135.00
7" 75.00		175.00
Bonbon dish		
Flat, covered, 5" d........55.00		150.00
Footed, handled, 4" d......35.00		85.00
Bowl, open		
Flat, round		
Flared bowl		
6" d. 35.00		75.00
7" d. 45.00		95.00
8" d. 55.00		110.00
Shallow bowl (salad),		
6" d................35.00		65.00
Straight-sided bowl, deep		
6" d. 35.00		65.00
7" d. 45.00		95.00
8" d. 55.00		110.00
Footed, round		
Flared bowl		
5-1/2" d. 35.00		65.00
8-1/2" d. 45.00		95.00
Straight-sided bowl,		
7" d..................45.00		110.00
Butter dish with cover...........85.00		225.00
Butter pat, 33" d. (VR)...........125.00		325.00

Known items:	Clear	Clear w/ Platinum
Candlestick		
4" h. 65.00		225.00
7" h. 110.00		325.00
Celery		
Tray....................35.00		65.00
Vase...................55.00		125.00
Compote, open, round		
High standard		
4-1/2" d. 45.00		95.00
5-1/2" d. 55.00		125.00
6-1/2" d. with rolled		
edge................65.00		150.00
Low standard		
Handled		
3" d................25.00		45.00
5" d................30.00		55.00
6" d................35.00		75.00
No handle		
4-1/2" d. 25.00		50.00
5-1/2" d. 30.00		65.00
Creamer, footed		
After dinner.............30.00		65.00
Berry...................25.00		55.00
Table size 30.00		75.00
Tankard 35.00		85.00
Cruet with original stopper.......85.00		350.00

Known items:	Clear	Clear w/ Platinum Stain
Cup, custard		
Crimped, ground bottom	25.00	65.00
Ground bottom	20.00	55.00
Dish, open, flat		
Almond	15.00	30.00
Iced olive set	20.00	40.00
Nut, 5" d.	20.00	40.00
Olive, 6" d.	25.00	55.00
Shallow bowl, 8" d.	45.00	110.00
Finger bowl	35.00	75.00
Goblet	35.00	110.00
Pickle dish, 8" l.	20.00	45.00
Pitcher		
Jug with pressed handle, 1/2-gal.	110.00	250.00
Tankard, footed with pressed handle	95.00	175.00
Plate, round, 5-1/2" d.	25.00	55.00
Puff box, covered, footed	65.00	175.00
Rose bowl	45.00	110.00
Salt		
Individual	45.00	125.00
Master, open, footed with double handles	65.00	175.00
Shaker, tall	45.00	85.00
Sauce dish		
Flat		
Flared bowl		
4" d.	10.00	25.00
4-1/2" d.	10.00	25.00
Straight-sided bowl		
4" d.	10.00	25.00
4-1/2" d.	10.00	25.00
Footed		
Flared bowl		
4" d.	15.00	35.00
4-1/2" d.	15.00	35.00
Straight-sided bowl		
4" d.	15.00	35.00
4-1/2" d.	15.00	35.00
Sherbet, footed with handle	35.00	65.00
Spoon holder with double-handles	35.00	65.00

Known items:	Clear	Clear w/ Platinum Stain
Sugar bowl		
After dinner	30.00	55.00
Breakfast	35.00	65.00
Berry, true open	30.00	65.00
Powdered sugar with original cover	55.00	110.00
Table size with cover	45.00	95.00
Sundae		
High footed	20.00	45.00
Low footed	20.00	45.00
Syrup pitcher	225.00	650.00
Toothpick holder, footed with double handles	35.00	55.00
Tumbler		
Iced tea with ground bottom	35.00	65.00
Lemonade, tall with handle	55.00	135.00
Water, flat with ground bottom	25.00	65.00
Vase, 11" h., handled	45.00	95.00

REVERSE TORPEDO

OMN: Dalzell No. 490D. **AKA:** Bull's Eye and Diamond Point, Bull's Eye Band, Bull's Eye with Diamond Point, Diamonds and Bull's Eye Band, Pointed Bull's Eye.

Non-flint. Dalzell, Gilmore & Leighton Glass Company, Findlay, OH, c. 1892.

Original color production: Clear (plain, engraved).

Reproductions and Look-a-Likes: None known.

Known items:	Clear
Banana stand with folded sides on high standard, 9-3/4"	$175.00
Biscuit jar with original cover	325.00
Bowl, open, round, flat	
Fruit, 10-1/2" d.	85.00

Reverse Torpedo spoon holder, covered butter dish, creamer.

Reverse Torpedo covered sugar bowl.

Reverse Torpedo true open jelly compote.

Known items: **Clear**

Piecrust rim, 9" d. **95.00**

Shallow, 8-1/2" d. **65.00**

Smooth rim

    5-1/2" d. **45.00**

    7-1/2" d. **55.00**

Butter dish with cover on flanged rim **110.00**

Cake stand on high standard. **175.00**

Celery vase **65.00**

Compote on high standard, round

    Covered

        4" d. (Jelly) **85.00**

        5" d. **65.00**

        6" d. **75.00**

        7" d. **95.00**

        8" d. **110.00**

        9" d. **125.00**

        9-1/2" d. **150.00**

        10" d. **225.00**

    Open with pie-crust rim

        4" d. (Jelly) **55.00**

        5" d. **35.00**

        6" d. **45.00**

        7" d. **55.00**

        8" d. **65.00**

        9" d. **75.00**

Known items: **Clear**

    9-1/2" d. **85.00**

    10" d. **110.00**

Creamer, tankard with applied handle **65.00**

Dish, open, round, flat with scalloped rim

    11" d. **75.00**

    11-1/2" d. **85.00**

Goblet **110.00**

Honey dish, with cover, square **425.00**

Jam jar with cover. **135.00**

Lamp, oil (several sizes). **150.00**

Pitcher, water, tankard with applied handle

    Milk, 1-qt. **175.00**

    Water, 1/2-gal. **225.00**

Plate. **35.00**

Relish dish **25.00**

Known items:	Clear
Saltshaker	75.00
Sauce dish, flat	
Round	15.00
Square	20.00
Spoon holder	55.00
Sugar bowl with cover	100.00
Syrup pitcher	275.00
Tumbler, water, flat	75.00

Known items:	Clear
Creamer with applied handle	225.00
Goblet	
Straight-sided bowl with 3" marginal band around bowl	75.00
Straight-sided bowl	65.00
Plate, 6" d. with serrated rim and star center	55.00
Sauce dish, round, flat	10.00
Spoon holder	45.00
Sugar bowl with cover	150.00
Wine	65.00

RIBBED GRAPE

AKA: Raisin.

Flint. Traditionally attributed to the Boston & Sandwich Glass Company, Sandwich, MA, c. 1850.

Original color production: Clear. Deep blue peacock green, milk white, opaque, sapphire blue, or any other color would be considered rare.

Reproductions and Look-a-Likes: None known.

Ribbed Grape open compote.

Known items:	Clear
Butter dish with cover	$175.00
Compote, round	
Covered on high standard, 6" d.	325.00
Open on low standard	
7-3/4" d.	75.00
8" d.	85.00

RIBBED IVY

Flint. Traditionally attributed to the Boston & Sandwich Glass Company, Sandwich, MA, c. 1850.

Original color production: Clear. Some pieces can be found with course rib background.

Reproductions and Look-a-Likes: None known.

Ribbed Ivy open footed compote.

Known items:	Clear
Bottle, castor	
Mustard	$55.00
Oil with original stopper	75.00
Shaker	50.00

Known items: **Clear**

Bowl, open, round, flat

    6" d. 45.00

    8-1/2" d. 75.00

Butter dish with cover.......................... 150.00

Celery vase (ER)............................. 1,250.00

Champagne, 5-1/8" h.......................... 225.00

Compote, round

Covered, high standard, sweetmeat, 6" d. 225.00

    Open

        High standard

            Rope edge

                Patterned foot

                    7-1/4" d.................... 135.00

                    7-1/2" d.................... 150.00

                Plain foot

                    7-1/4" d.................... 175.00

                    7-1/2" d.................... 200.00

            Scalloped rim

                Patterned foot

                    7" d....................... 125.00

                    8" d....................... 150.00

                Plain foot

                    7" d....................... 150.00

                    8" d....................... 175.00

        Low standard

            Rope edge

                Patterned foot

                    7-1/4" d.................... 125.00

                    7-1/2" d.................... 135.00

                Plain foot

                    7-1/4" d.................... 150.00

                    7-1/2" d.................... 175.00

            Scalloped rim

                Patterned foot

                    7" d....................... 110.00

                    8" d....................... 125.00

                Plain foot

                    7" d....................... 125.00

                    8" d....................... 150.00

Known items: **Clear**

Creamer, footed with applied crimped handle 225.00

Decanter

    Bar lip

        Cordial decanter, 5-1/8" h.............. 425.00

        Bitters, 7-1/4" h...................... 375.00

        Pt............................... 275.00

        Qt............................... 250.00

    Original Stopper

        Cordial decanter...................... 650.00

        Bitters............................. 575.00

        Pt............................... 450.00

        Qt............................... 675.00

Eggcup, single, open 35.00

Goblet, 6" h.

    Barrel bowl 275.00

    Straight-sided bowl 55.00

Hat made from a tumbler (ER) 3,500.00

Honey dish, round, flat, 3-1/2" d. 15.00

Lamp, oil with *Ribbed Ivy* font

    Brass standard with marble base 175.00

    Milk white standard..................... 225.00

Pitcher, water, 1/2-gal...................... 1,800.00

Salt, master, footed

    Covered 325.00

    Open

        With beaded rim 55.00

        With scalloped rim.................... 175.00

Sauce dish, round, flat, 4" d. 10.00

Spoon holder 45.00

Sugar bowl with cover

    Exterior pattern on lid 325.00

    Interior pattern on lid 150.00

Tumbler

    Water, 3-1/2" h........................ 125.00

    Whiskey, 2-3/4" h.

        With applied handle 375.00

        With no handle....................... 85.00

Wine, 4" h. 95.00

RIBBED PALM

OMN: McKee's Sprig. **AKA:** Oak Leaf.

Flint. McKee Brothers, Pittsburgh, PA, c. 1863.

Original color production: Clear. Patented by Frederick McKee under U.S. Patent No. 1,748 April 21, 1863.

Reproductions and Look-a-Likes: Goblet (clear). L.G. Wright Glass Company, New Martinsville, WV, unmarked.

Ribbed Palm flat covered butter dish.'

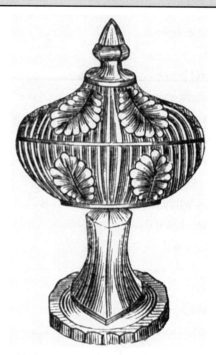

Ribbed Palm covered compote.

Ribbed Palm water pitcher with applied handle.

Known items:	Clear
Butter dish with cover	$175.00
Celery vase	95.00
Champagne	175.00
Compote, round	
High standard	
Covered, 6" d. (originally cataloged as the "Sweetmeat")	275.00
Open	
7" d.	200.00
8" d.	225.00
10" d.	275.00
Low standard, 8-1/8" d.	150.00

Known items:	Clear
Creamer with applied handle	250.00
Dish, open, flat with scalloped rim	
6" d.	55.00
7" d.	65.00
8" d.	75.00
9" d.	85.00
Eggcup, single, open	45.00
Goblet (2 types)	55.00

Known items:	Clear
Lamp, oil	275.00
Pitcher, water with applied handle, 9" h., 1/2-gal.	450.00
Plate, 6" d.	65.00
Master salt, open, footed	45.00
Sauce dish, round, flat, 4" d.	15.00
Spoon holder	55.00
Sugar bowl with cover	150.00
Tumbler, 1/2-pt.	135.00
Wine	75.00

RIBBON (Bakewell)

AKA: Frosted Ribbon, Rebecca at the Well, Simple Frosted Ribbon.

Non-flint. Bakewell, Pears & Company, Pittsburgh, PA, c. 1870.

Original color production: Clear and frosted.

Reproductions and Look-a-Likes: goblet (clear, unmarked). L.G. Wright Glass Company, New Martinsville, WV. 6-1/2" d. low-footed covered compote; 9-3/4" d. Rebecca at the Well open compote; oblong compote with scalloped rim and dolphin stem; candlestick (clear, copper blue, olive green -plain, frosted). Fostoria Glass Company, Fostoria, OH, in association with the Henry Ford Museum, Dearborn, MI. Permanently marked with the museum's "HFM" insignia.

Known items:	Clear
Bottle, cologne with original patterned stopper	$150.00
Bowl, round	
Master berry	65.00
Waste	95.00
Butter dish with cover	85.00
Cake stand on high standard, 8-1/2" d.	325.00
Celery vase	65.00
Champagne	275.00
Cheese dish with cover	325.00
Compote, round	
Covered	
High standard	
6" d.	75.00
7" d.	85.00
8" d.	100.00

Ribbon true open compote with "Dolphin" standard.

Ribbon goblet.

Known items:	Clear
Low standard	
6" d.	65.00
7" d.	75.00
8" d.	85.00
Open	
Scalloped rim	
6-1/2" d.	35.00
7-1/2" d.	45.00
8-1/2" d.	55.00

Ribbon wine.

RIBBON CANDY

OMN: U.S. Glass No. 1,010. **AKA:** Bryce, Double Loop Figure Eight.

Non-flint. Bryce Brothers, Pittsburgh, PA, c. 1885. The United States Glass Company, Pittsburgh, PA, at Factory "B," c. 1891.

Original color production: Clear. Green or any other color would be considered rare.

Reproductions and Look-a-Likes: None known.

Ribbon Candy syrup.

Known items:	Clear
With *"Dolphin"* standard	
Round bowl	
8-1/2" d.	275.00
10-1/2" d.	325.00
Oblong bowl, 8" l.	225.00
With *"Rebecca at the Well"* standard	850.00
Creamer	45.00
Goblet	45.00
Pickle jar with original cover	325.00
Pitcher	
Milk, 1-qt.	110.00
Water, 1/2-gal.	125.00
Plate, round	65.00
Platter, oblong with cut corners, 13" l.	125.00
Sauce dish, round	
Flat with tab-handle	15.00
Footed without handle	20.00
Spoon holder	35.00
Sugar bowl with cover	75.00
Tray, water, 16-1/4" l.	450.00
Wine (R)	225.00

Known items:	Clear
Bowl, open, flat	
Oval, open, 8" l.	$35.00
Round	
6" d.	20.00
8" d.	35.00
Butter dish with cover	
Flat	65.00
Footed	95.00
Cake stand on high standard	
Child's miniature, 6-1/2" d.	65.00
Table size	
8" d.	55.00
9" d.	65.00
10" d.	75.00

Ribbon Candy cruet, sugar, two butters and creamer.

Ribbon Candy footed covered bowl.

Known items:	Clear
Celery vase	55.00
Claret	150.00
Compote, round	
Covered	
High standard	
5" d.	65.00
6" d.	75.00
7" d.	95.00
8" d.	135.00
Low standard	
5" d.	55.00
6" d.	65.00
7" d.	85.00
8" d.	110.00
Open	
High standard	
6" d.	35.00
7" d.	40.00

Known items:	Clear
8" d.	45.00
10" d.	65.00
Low standard	
5" d.	20.00
6" d.	25.00
7" d.	30.00
8" d.	40.00
10" d.	55.00
Cordial	175.00
Creamer	45.00
Cruet with original stopper	125.00
Cup and saucer set	85.00
Goblet	135.00
Honey dish with cover, square (VR)	450.00
Pickle dish, boat-shaped	15.00
Pitcher	
Milk, 1-qt.	55.00
Water, 1/2-gal.	85.00
Plate, round	
6" d.	25.00
7" d.	35.00
8" d.	45.00
9" d.	55.00
10" d.	65.00
11" d.	95.00
Relish dish, oval	15.00
Saltshaker	85.00
Sauce dish, round	
Flat	
3-1/2" d.	8.00
4" d.	10.00
4-1/2" d.	12.50

Known items:	Clear
Footed	
3-1/2" d.	10.00
4" d.	12.50
4-1/2" d.	15.00
Spoon holder	35.00
Sugar bowl with cover	65.00
Syrup pitcher	275.00
Tumbler, water, flat	65.00
Wine	110.00

RICHMOND (Nickel-Plate)

OMN: Nickel-Plate No. 76. **AKA:** Akron Block, Bars and Buttons.

Non-flint. Nickel-Plate Glass Company, Fostoria, OH, c. 1889.

Original color production: Clear. Clear with ruby stain or any other color would be considered rare and demand a premium price.

Reproductions and Look-a-Likes: None known.

Known items:	Clear
Bowl, master berry, round, flat	$55.00
Butter dish with cover	135.00
Cheese dish with cover	175.00
Celery vase	65.00
Creamer	45.00
Cruet with original stopper	55.00
Finger bowl	35.00
Goblet	35.00
Pitcher	
Milk, 2-pints	95.00
Water	
Bulbous with applied handle, 1/2-gal.	110.00
Straight-sided with pressed handle, 3-pts.	95.00
Tankard	85.00
Sauce dish, round, flat	5.00
Saltshaker	30.00
Spoon holder	45.00
Sugar bowl with cover	85.00
Tumbler, water	35.00
Wine	20.00

Richmond (Nickel Plate) covered butter dish.

Richmond (Nickel Plate) creamer..

RICHMOND (Richards & Hartley)

OMN: AKA: Square Tulip with Sawtooth.

Non-flint. Richards & Hartley Glass Company, Tarentum, PA, c. 1888. Reissued by the United States Glass Company, Pittsburgh, PA, c. 1891.

Original color production: Clear.

Reproductions and Look-a-Likes: None known.

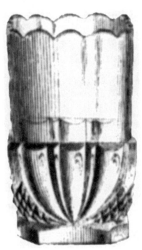

Richmond (Richards and Hartley) creamer.

Richmond (Richards and Hartley) spoon holder.

Known items:	Clear
Butter dish with cover	$65.00
Compotes, covered	
7" d.	75.00
8" d.	95.00

Richmond (Richards and Hartley) wine.

Known items:	Clear
Creamer	35.00
Cruet with the original stopper	55.00
Goblet	65.00
Pitcher with applied handle	
Milk, 1-qt	110.00
Water 1/2-gal.	85.00
Sauce dish	5.00
Spoon holder	35.00
Sugar bowl with cover	55.00
Sugar shaker	95.00
Tumbler, water	45.00
Wine	35.00

RISING SUN

OMN: U.S. Glass No. 125,110-Sunshine. **AKA:** Sunrise.

Non-flint. The United States Glass Company, Pittsburgh, PA, c. 1908.

Original color production: Clear, clear with green or rose stain. Clear with ruby stain or any other color would be considered rare.

Reproductions and Look-a-Likes: None known.

Rising Sun covered butter dish.

Rising Sun double-handled covered sugar bowl.

Rising Sun double-handled spoon holder.

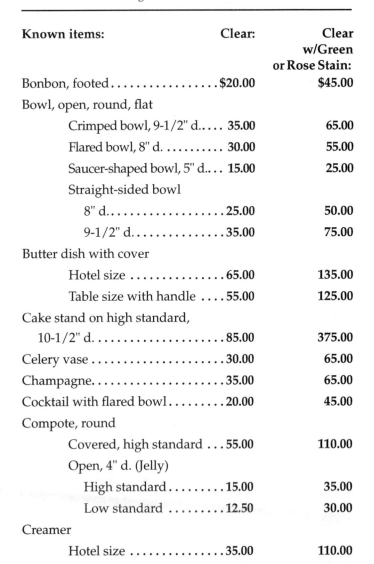

Known items:	Clear:	Clear w/Green or Rose Stain:
Bonbon, footed	$20.00	$45.00
Bowl, open, round, flat		
Crimped bowl, 9-1/2" d.	35.00	65.00
Flared bowl, 8" d.	30.00	55.00
Saucer-shaped bowl, 5" d. . . .	15.00	25.00
Straight-sided bowl		
8" d.	25.00	50.00
9-1/2" d.	35.00	75.00
Butter dish with cover		
Hotel size	65.00	135.00
Table size with handle	55.00	125.00
Cake stand on high standard,		
10-1/2" d.	85.00	375.00
Celery vase	30.00	65.00
Champagne.	35.00	65.00
Cocktail with flared bowl	20.00	45.00
Compote, round		
Covered, high standard . . .	55.00	110.00
Open, 4" d. (Jelly)		
High standard	15.00	35.00
Low standard	12.50	30.00
Creamer		
Hotel size	35.00	110.00
Table size.	30.00	85.00
Cruet with original stopper	55.00	135.00
Cup, custard with handle.	10.00	25.00
Dish, open		
Three-handled, 4-1/2" d.		
(Jelly).	15.00	35.00

Known items:	Clear:	Clear w/Green or Rose Stain:
Handleless with ruffled		
edge	15.00	35.00
Goblet	25.00	55.00
Pickle dish, boat shaped.	15.00	30.00
Pitcher		
Bulbous, water, 2-gal.	65.00	150.00
Tankard		
Milk, 1-qt.	45.00	110.00
Water, 1/2-gal.	55.00	125.00
Relish tray	15.00	30.00
Saltshaker.	30.00	55.00
Sauce dish, round, flat, 4" d.		
Flared	5.00	12.50
Straight-sided	5.00	12.50
Spoon holder		
Hotel size.	35.00	95.00
Table size	30.00	85.00
Sugar bowl with cover		
Hotel size, three-handled . . .	45.00	125.00

Known items:	Clear:	Clear w/Green or Rose Stain:
Table size with double handles	40.00	110.00
Sugar dispenser, commercial	125.00	—
Toothpick holder	20.00	35.00
Tumbler		
Champagne	20.00	35.00
Flared rim	22.50	55.00
Straight-sided	20.00	45.00
Whiskey	15.00	35.00
Vase, 7" h.	15.00	45.00
Wine with straight-sided bowl	15.00	35.00

ROANOKE

OMN: AKA: Late Sawtooth.

Non-flint. Ripley & Company, Pittsburgh, PA, c. 1885. The United States Glass Company, Pittsburgh, PA. at Factory "F" after 1891.

Original color production: Clear, clear with ruby stain. Canary yellow, emerald green or any other color would be considered rare.

Reproductions and Look-a-Likes: None known.

Known items:	Clear	Clear w/Ruby
Bowl, open, round, flat		
Deep		
Round sides	$25.00	$45.00
Straight-sided	30.00	50.00
Shallow		
Pinched sides	25.00	45.00
Round sides	30.00	50.00
Butter dish with cover		
Flat	45.00	65.00
Footed	65.00	85.00
Cake stand on high standard with curled scalloped rim		
6" d.	75.00	125.00
9" d.	85.00	175.00
10" d.	100.00	225.00

Known items:	Clear	Clear w/Ruby
Compote, round		
Covered on high standard		
5" d.	45.00	85.00
6" d.	55.00	75.00
7" d.	65.00	85.00
8" d.	75.00	110.00
Open with scalloped rim		
Deep bowl		
5" d.	15.00	35.00
6" d.	25.00	45.00
7" d.	30.00	50.00
8" d.	35.00	65.00
Saucer-shaped bowl		
6" d.	25.00	45.00
7" d.	30.00	50.00
8" d.	35.00	55.00
9" d.	45.00	75.00
Creamer		
Flat	25.00	45.00
Footed	35.00	75.00
Dish, flat		
Oblong		
7" l.	15.00	35.00
8" l.	20.00	40.00
9" l.	25.00	45.00
Goblet	30.00	65.00
Pitcher, water		
Jug, 1/2-gal.	45.00	110.00
Tankard with applied handle, 1/2-gal.	50.00	125.00
Rose bowl	25.00	—
Salt, round, flat		
Individual	5.00	15.00
Master	25.00	55.00
Sauce dish, round		
Flat	5.00	15.00
Footed	5.00	15.00
Spoon holder		
Flat	20.00	40.00
Footed	25.00	50.00
Sugar bowl with cover		
Flat	35.00	55.00
Footed	45.00	75.00

Roanoke sugar bowl, creamer, footed butter dish, and spoon holder.

Known items:	Clear	Clear w/Ruby
Tumbler, water, flat	20.00	40.00
Wine	15.00	35.00

ROMAN KEY

AKA: Frosted Roman Key, Frosted Roman Key with Ribs, Grecian Border, Greek Key, Plain Roman Key.

Flint. The Union Glass Company, Somerville, MA, c. 1860s.

Original color production: Clear, clear with machine frosting. All clear pieces are considered scarce and are 25% less then clear with frosted.

Reproductions and Look-a-Likes: None known.

Roman Key champagne.

Known items	Clear w/Frosting
Bowl, open, round, flat with cable edge	
8" d.	$65.00
9-1/2" d.	75.00
10" d.	125.00
Butter dish with cover.	225.00
Castor bottle	
Mustard.	75.00
Oil with original stopper	110.00
Shaker	65.00
Celery vase	225.00
Champagne.	125.00

Known items	Clear w/Frosting
Compote, open, round with cable-edge rim	
High standard	
8" d.	95.00
9" d.	110.00
10" d.	125.00
Low standard	
7" d.	55.00
8" d.	75.00
Creamer with applied handle, 6" h.	225.00
Decanter	
Bar lip	
1-pt.	225.00
1-qt.	200.00

Roman Key decanter with stopper.

Known items	Clear w/Frosting
With original stopper	
1-pt.	425.00
1-qt.	375.00
Dish, preserve, round	45.00
Eggcup, single, open	
Handled	275.00
Handleless	55.00
Goblet	65.00
Lamp, oil	325.00
Mustard jar with original cover	150.00
Pickle dish	35.00
Pitcher	
Milk, 1-qt.	1,500.00
Water, 1/2-gal.	1,250.00
Plate, 6" d.	65.00
Relish dish, oval with cable-edge, 9-1/4" l.	45.00
Salt, master, open	55.00
Sauce dish, round, flat, 4" d.	15.00
Spoon holder	65.00
Sugar bowl with cover	
With hexagonal stem	175.00
With octagonal stem	175.00

Known items	Clear w/Frosting
Tumbler, bar	
Flat	150.00
Footed	110.00
Wine	95.00

ROMAN ROSETTE

OMN: U.S. Glass No. 15,030.

Non-flint. Bryce, Walker & Company, Pittsburgh, PA, c. 1875-1885. The United States Glass company, Pittsburgh, PA, at Factory "A," c. 1894. Attributed by early researchers to the Portland Glass company, Portland, ME.

Original color production: Clear, clear with ruby stain. Clear with amber stain or any other color would be considered rare.

Reproductions: Goblet (clear), unmarked.

Roman Rosette bulbous syrup.

Known items:	Clear	Clear w/Ruby
Bowl, open, round, flat with smooth rim		
5" d.	$15.00	—
5-1/2" d.	15.00	—
7" d.	25.00	—
8" d.	35.00	—
8-1/2" d.	40.00	125.00

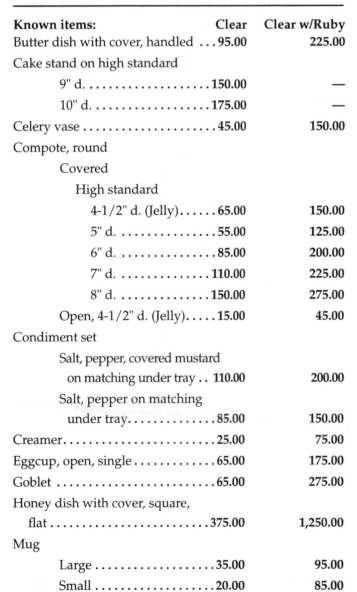

Roman Rosette covered butter.

Roman Rosette three-bottle castor set.

Known items:	Clear	Clear w/Ruby
Butter dish with cover, handled . . .	95.00	225.00
Cake stand on high standard		
9" d.	150.00	—
10" d.	175.00	—
Celery vase	45.00	150.00
Compote, round		
Covered		
High standard		
4-1/2" d. (Jelly)	65.00	150.00
5" d.	55.00	125.00
6" d.	85.00	200.00
7" d.	110.00	225.00
8" d.	150.00	275.00
Open, 4-1/2" d. (Jelly)	15.00	45.00
Condiment set		
Salt, pepper, covered mustard on matching under tray . .	110.00	200.00
Salt, pepper on matching under tray	85.00	150.00
Creamer	25.00	75.00
Eggcup, open, single	65.00	175.00
Goblet	65.00	275.00
Honey dish with cover, square, flat	375.00	1,250.00
Mug		
Large	35.00	95.00
Small	20.00	85.00

Known items:	Clear	Clear w/Ruby
Mustard jar with original notched metal cover	25.00	45.00
Pickle dish, boat-shaped	20.00	55.00
Pitcher		
Milk, 1-qt.	75.00	325.00
Water, 1/2-gal.	95.00	375.00
Plate		
Bread, oval, 10" l.	30.00	95.00
Dinner, round		
7" d.	35.00	85.00
7-1/2" d.	35.00	85.00
Preserve dish, oval, flat		
7" l.	25.00	85.00
8" l.	30.00	95.00
9" l.	35.00	110.00
Saltshaker	25.00	45.00
Sauce dish, round		
Flat		
4" d.	5.00	20.00
4-1/2" d.	5.00	20.00
Footed		
4" d.	8.00	25.00
4-1/2" d.	8.00	25.00
Spoon holder	25.00	75.00
Sugar bowl with cover	55.00	150.00
Syrup pitcher	275.00	550.00
Tray, underplate for salt & pepper . . .	25.00	50.00
Wine, 4" h.	65.00	175.00

ROSE IN SNOW

OMN: Bryce No. 125. **AKA:** Rose.

Non-flint. Produced in two conspicuous forms: (a) Round: Ohio Glass Company, Somerville, OH, (b) Square: Bryce Brothers, Pittsburgh, PA, c. 1880s. The United States Glass Company, Pittsburgh, PA, after 1891.

Original color production: Amber, blue, canary yellow, clear.

Reproductions and Look-a-Likes: 5-1/2" d. bottle (amber, amethyst, blue, green by Clevenger Brothers, Clayton, NJ). Goblet, *"In Fond Remembrance"* mug with pressed handle, pickle dish, 9" d. round plate (amber, blue, canary yellow, clear). Unmarked. Covered sugar bowl (amber, blue, canary yellow, clear, doeskin milk white, sunset ruby). Imperial Glass Corporation, Bellaire, OH. Permanently embossed "IG." Clear and colored covered sugar bowls were also produced by the Imperial Glass Corporation for Vincent Price National Treasures in association with Sears, Roebuck & Company, which were permanently embossed with the "VPNT" monogram within a large "S."

Rose in Snow low standard covered compote.

Rose in Snow creamer.

Known items:	Amber	Blue	Canary Yellow	Clear
Bottle, bitters with the original stopper (3 sizes) .... —	—	—	—	$135.00
Bowl, open				
Oval				
8" d. 175.00	175.00	200.00	200.00	125.00
9" d. 200.00	200.00	225.00	225.00	150.00
10" d. 225.00	225.00	250.00	250.00	175.00
Square				
Flat				
8" . . . . —	—	—	—	45.00
9" . . . . —	—	—	—	55.00
Footed				
8" . . . . —	—	—	—	110.00
9" . . . . —	—	—	—	125.00
Butter dish with cover				
Collared base 110.00	110.00	175.00	200.00	65.00

Rose in Snow mug.

Rose in Snow tumbler.

Known items:	Amber	Blue	Canary Yellow	Clear
Flat				
Round				
Without rim 75.00		125.00	125.00	45.00
With scalloped rim 85.00		150.00	150.00	55.00
Square . . . . —		—	—	45.00
Cake stand on high standard, 9" 150.00		225.00	250.00	110.00
Compote				
Covered				
High standard, 8" d. 150.00		200.00	225.00	100.00
Low standard, 7" d. 135.00		175.00	200.00	95.00
Open, high standard				
6" d. 65.00		95.00	100.00	25.00
7" d. 125.00		150.00	175.00	55.00
8-1/2" d. 150.00		200.00	225.00	75.00
Creamer				
Round 85.00		125.00	135.00	30.00
Square . . . . —		—	—	45.00
Goblet 50.00		75.00	85.00	45.00
Marmalade jar with original cover 225.00		325.00	375.00	150.00
Mug				
Embossed "In Fond Remembrance" with				
pressed handle 45.00		55.00	55.00	35.00
Large with applied handle 95.00		135.00	150.00	65.00
Pickle dish, oval				
Double, 8-1/2" l. 175.00		200.00	225.00	85.00
Single with handle 95.00		110.00	125.00	20.00

Rose in Snow pattern close up.

Rose in Snow rare covered toddy.

Known items:	Amber	Blue	Canary Yellow	Clear
Pitcher, water, bulbous with applied handle,				
1/2-gal. 225.00	325.00	350.00	150.00
Plate, round				
5" d. 85.00	110.00	125.00	45.00
6" d. 45.00	55.00	65.00	25.00
7" d. 65.00	75.00	85.00	35.00
9" d. 75.00	95.00	95.00	45.00
10" d. 40.00	45.00	50.00	35.00
Sauce dish				
Round				
Flat 10.00	15.00	18.00	8.00
Footed. 15.00	18.00	20.00	10.00
Square				
Flat .... —	—	—	10.00
Footed. .... —	—	—	15.00
Spoon holder				
Round 75.00	95.00	110.00	30.00
Square .... —	—	—	35.00
Sugar bowl with cover				
Round 110.00	135.00	150.00	45.00
Square .... —	—	—	45.00
Sweetmeat with cover, 5-3/4" d. 175.00	225.00	250.00	95.00
Toddy jar with matching cover and underplate				
(R) 275.00	375.00	425.00	175.00
Tumbler, water, flat 95.00	125.00	135.00	45.00

ROSE SPRIG

Non-flint. Campbell, Jones and Company, Pittsburgh, PA, c. 1886. Designed by Henry Franz and patented May 25, 1886.

Original color production: Amber, blue, canary yellow, clear.

Reproductions and Look-a-Likes: Goblet, sleigh-shaped salt dip, dated "1888" (amber, blue, canary yellow, clear), unmarked. L.G. Wright Glass Company, New Martinsville, WV.

Rose Sprig footed sauce.

Known items:	Amber	Blue	Canary Yellow	Clear
Biscuit jar with domed lid (VR)	$275.00	$375.00	$425.00	$225.00
Bowl, open, sietz-bath shaped	55.00	65.00	75.00	45.00
Cake stand on high standard, 9" d.	150.00	175.00	175.00	135.00
Celery vase	75.00	95.00	110.00	65.00
Compote, round				
Covered				
High standard				
7" d.	125.00	150.00	175.00	110.00
8" d.	150.00	175.00	200.00	125.00
Low standard	100.00	125.00	135.00	85.00
Open				
High standard				
7" d.	50.00	65.00	75.00	45.00
8" d.	55.00	75.00	85.00	55.00
Low standard				
7" d.	40.00	45.00	50.00	35.00
8" d.	50.00	55.00	55.00	45.00
Creamer with pressed handle	55.00	65.00	65.00	45.00
Dish, open, oblong, 9" l.	35.00	40.00	40.00	30.00
Goblet	55.00	85.00	95.00	45.00
Mug with applied handle	75.00	95.00	110.00	55.00
Nappy, square, handled, 6"	30.00	35.00	35.00	25.00
Pickle dish, oval	30.00	35.00	35.00	25.00
Pitcher with pressed handle				
Milk, 1-qt.	75.00	95.00	100.00	65.00
Water, 1/2-gal.	85.00	110.00	125.00	75.00
Plate, square				
6"	30.00	35.00	35.00	30.00
6-1/2"	35.00	40.00	40.00	35.00

Rose Sprig high standard covered compote.

Known items:	Amber	Blue	Canary Yellow	Clear
8"	40.00	45.00	45.00	40.00
10-1/2"	45.00	50.00	50.00	45.00
Punch bowl on foot with scalloped rim	175.00	250.00	275.00	150.00
Relish tray, boat shaped	30.00	35.00	35.00	25.00
Salt, sleigh shaped dated "1888"	85.00	125.00	135.00	85.00
Sauce dish; Flat, sietz-bath shape	20.00	25.00	30.00	20.00
Footed	15.00	20.00	20.00	15.00
Spoon holder	40.00	55.00	55.00	35.00
Sugar bowl with cover	75.00	95.00	100.00	65.00
Tray, water	55.00	75.00	85.00	55.00
Tumbler, water, flat	40.00	65.00	75.00	35.00
Wine	65.00	95.00	125.00	55.00

ROSETTE

OMN: Magic.

Non-flint. Bryce Brothers, Pittsburgh, PA, c. late 1880s. The United States Glass Company, Pittsburgh, PA, at Factory "B," c. 1891.

Original color production: Clear. Items in amber, blue or canary would be rare.

Reproductions and Look-a-Likes: None known.

Known items:	Clear
Bowl, round	
Covered, flat, 7" d.	$55.00
Open, flat	
Vegetable	25.00
Waste	30.00
Butter dish with cover	55.00
Cake stand on high standard	
7" d.	55.00
9" d.	65.00
10" d.	75.00
11" d.	110.00
Celery vase	35.00

Rosette sugar bowl, creamer, spoon holder, and butter dish.

Rosette saltshaker.

Known items:	Clear
Compote on high standard, round	
Covered	
6" d.	55.00
7" d.	65.00
8" d.	75.00
Open with saucer-shaped bowl	
4-1/2" d. (Jelly)	15.00
6" d.	25.00
7" d.	30.00
8" d.	35.00
9" d.	40.00
10" d.	55.00
11-1/2" d.	65.00
Creamer, 5-1/4" h.	30.00
Goblet	35.00
Mug with pressed handle	20.00
Pickle tray, fish-shaped	15.00
Pitcher	
Milk, 1-qt.	45.00
Water, 1/2-gal.	65.00

Known items:	Clear
Plate	
Bread, oval with tab handles, 9" l.	25.00
Dinner, round, 7" d.	20.00
Saltshaker	45.00
Sauce dish, round, flat, handled, 4" d.	5.00
Spoon holder	30.00
Sugar bowl with cover	45.00
Sugar shaker	65.00
Tray, water, round, 10-1/4" d.	35.00
Tumbler, water, flat	35.00
Wine	45.00

ROYAL CRYSTAL

OMN: Tarentum's Atlanta. **AKA:** Diamond and Teardrop, Shining Diamonds.

Non-flint. The Tarentum Glass Company, Tarentum, PA, c. 1894.

Original color production: Clear, clear with ruby stain.

Reproductions and Look-a-Likes: Cake stand, 7" d.

Royal Crystal bulbous water pitcher with applied handle.

Known items:	Clear	Clear/w Ruby
Bowl, open, flat		
Rectangular		
7" l.	$25.00	$45.00
8-1/4" l.	30.00	50.00

Royal Crystal covered sugar.

Royal Crystal creamer, water pitcher, and syrup.

Royal Crystal round dinner plate.

Known items:	Clear	Clear/w Ruby
Round, open, flat with smooth rim		
Flared bowl		
5" d.	20.00	40.00
6" d.	20.00	40.00
7" d.	25.00	45.00
8" d.	30.00	50.00
Straight-sided bowl		
5" d.	20.00	40.00
6" d.	20.00	40.00
7" d.	25.00	45.00
8" d.	30.00	50.00
Square, 7-1/2"	25.00	65.00
Bottle		
Cologne, 4-oz. with original patterned stopper	45.00	125.00
Water, carafe, 5-pt.	65.00	150.00
Butter dish with cover	55.00	125.00
Cake stand on high standard		
9" d.	65.00	150.00
9-1/4" d.	75.00	175.00
10" d.	95.00	225.00
Celery vase	30.00	50.00
Compote open on high standard		
6" d.	30.00	40.00
7" d.	40.00	50.00
Cracker jar with cover	110.00	135.00
Creamer, 5-1/4" h.	35.00	60.00

Known items:	Clear	Clear/w Ruby
Cruet with original patterned stopper		
5-oz.	45.00	110.00
8-oz.	55.00	125.00
Dish, round, flat, handled		
4" d.	15.00	35.00
4-1/2" d.	20.00	40.00
5" d.	25.00	45.00
Goblet	110.00	150.00
Jar, candy with original cover, 5-1/4" h.	65.00	110.00
Pitcher with applied handle		
Bulbous		
Milk, 1-qt.	75.00	135.00
Water, 1/2-gal.	95.00	175.00
Tankard, water, 1/2-gal., 9-1/2" h.	110.00	200.00
Plate		
Oval, bread	40.00	65.00
Round, 6" d.	15.00	30.00
Saltshaker	35.00	55.00
Sauce dish, round		
Flat		
4" d.	8.00	20.00
4-1/2" d.	10.00	20.00
Footed		
4" d.	10.00	20.00
4-1/2" d.	12.50	20.00
Spoon holder	30.00	55.00

Known items:	Clear	Clear/w Ruby
Sugar bowl		
Individual, open	20.00	45.00
Table size with cover	45.00	95.00
Syrup pitcher	75.00	175.00
Toothpick holder	30.00	75.00
Tumbler, water, flat, 4" h.	25.00	45.00
Wine, 4" h.	35.00	55.00

RUSTIC

OMN: Rustic **AKA:** Drapery Variant, Long Tidy, Short Tidy, Stayman, Tidy.

Flint, non-flint. McKee Bros., Pittsburgh, PA, 1871.

Original color production: Clear.

Reproductions and Look-a-Likes: None known.

Rustic water pitcher.

Known items:	Clear
Butter dish with cover	$75.00
Compote with cover	
High standard	
6" d.	125.00
8" d.	150.00
Low standard, 8" d.	65.00
Creamer	55.00
Dish, oval, flat	
7" l.	25.00
8" l.	30.00
9" l.	35.00
Eggcup	35.00
Goblet	
Long design	45.00
Short design	35.00
Pitcher with applied handle, water, 1/2-gallon	275.00
Relish, scoop	15.00
Salt, master, pedestaled	30.00
Sauce dish, 4" d.	5.00
Spoon holder	35.00
Sugar bowl with cover	65.00

Rustic four-piece table set.

SAINT BERNARD

OMN: Fostoria's No. 450-Czar.

Non-flint. The Fostoria Glass Company, Fostoria, OH, c. 1894.

Original color production: Clear (plain, engraved). **Note:** Finials are finely sculpted frosted dogs in the shape of a Saint Bernard.

Reproductions and Look-a-Likes: None known.

Saint Bernard covered butter dish.

Saint Bernard covered sugar bowl.

Saint Bernard high-standard compote.

Known items:	Clear
Bowl, master berry, open, round, 8" d.	$85.00
Butter dish with cover	225.00
Cake stand on high standard	150.00
Celery vase	65.00
Compote, round	
Covered with dog finial	
High standard	
7" d.	275.00
8" d.	325.00

Known items:	Clear
Low standard	175.00
Open	
6" d.	55.00
7" d.	65.00
8" d.	85.00
Creamer	75.00
Goblet	65.00
Jam jar with original cover with dog finial	175.00
Pickle dish, oval, flat	45.00
Pitcher, water, 1/2-gal.	
Bulbous	175.00
Tankard	150.00
Saltshaker	55.00
Sauce dish, round, flat.	20.00
Spoon holder	45.00
Sugar bowl with original cover with dog finial	150.00
Tumbler, water	45.00

Known items:	Clear
Butter Dish with cover	$550.00
Champagne, 5-3/8" h. (VR)	1,000.00
Compote, open	
"Dolphin" standard (VR)	4,500.00
High Standard with scalloped bowl	
8" d.	450.00
9" d.	550.00
Creamer with applied handle	475.00
Decanter with original patterned stopper	
1-pt.	275.00
1-qt.	325.00
Goblet (VR)	450.00
Lamp, whale oil.	225.00
Pitcher, water with applied handle (VR)	8,500.00
Relish dish, oblong	85.00
Sugar bowl, covered (R).	425.00
Spoon holder	85.00
Wine, 4-5/8" h. (R)	350.00

SANDWICH STAR

Flint. Traditionally attributed to the Boston & Sandwich Glass Company, Sandwich, MA, c. 1850.

Original color production: Clear. Amethyst, jade green, opaque blue, opaque lavender, electric blue, clambroth or any other color would be considered very rare.

Reproductions and Look-a-Likes: None known.

Sandwich Star spill.

SAWTOOTH

OMN: Bryce's Diamond Point, Gillinder's Diamond, McKee's Diamond, Gillinder No. 56, Cambridge Sawtooth. **AKA:** Crossett Sawtooth, Lumberton Sawtooth, Mitre Diamond, Pineapple, Mitre.

Flint, non-flint. New England Glass Company, East Cambridge, MA, c. 1865-1885. The Bryce Group (Bryce, Richards; Bryce, Walker; Bryce Brothers), Pittsburgh, PA, c. 1854-1890s. James B. Lyon & Company, Pittsburgh, PA, c. early 1860s; McKee & Brothers, Pittsburgh, PA, c. 1859-1865; Gillinder & Sons, Philadelphia, PA; Union Glass Company, Somerville, MA; The United States Glass Company, Pittsburgh, PA, c. 1891.

Original color production: Clear, milk white. Deep sapphire blue, amethyst, amber, fiery opalescent, medium blue, opaque blue, canary yellow, translucent white, translucent blue, translucent jade green or any other color in flint would be considered very rare.

Reproductions: 5-1/2" d. ashtray, open bowls on circular foot: 9-3/4" d. with straight-sided bowl; 11-1/2" d. with scalloped rim, 13-1/4" d. with flared rim; 10" d. high-standard cake stand; 6" d. covered chalice; high-standard covered compotes: covered, open: with plain rim, with scalloped rim; goblet, 14" d. plate; flat sauce dishes: with plain rim, with scalloped rim; iced tea tumbler (blue satin, clear, clear with ruby stain. Indiana Glass Company, Dunkirk, IN, unmarked.

High-standard banana stand, 6-1/2" d. covered butter dish; low-standard cake stand; high-standard compotes: covered: 9-1/2" h., 10" h., 13" h., 14" h., 15" h. open, 9" h. with flared bowl (amber, antique green, Bermuda blue, Brandywine blue, clear, deep rich ruby, green marble, golden sunset, laurel green, milk white, olive green, purple marble, ruby). Westmoreland Glass Company, Grapeville, PA. Unmarked or embossed with the Westmoreland "WG" insignia.

Sawtooth covered salt.

Known items:	Flint	Non-flint
Bottle, water with matching		
tumbler	$225.00	—
Bowl, round		
Covered		
6" d.	95.00	65.00
7" d.	125.00	75.00

Sawtooth milk pitcher.

Known items:	Flint	Non-flint
Open, flat		
6" d.	35.00	20.00
7" d.	40.00	25.00
8" d.	50.00	30.00
9" d.	55.00	35.00
10" d.	75.00	40.00
11" d.	85.00	—
12" d.	135.00	—
Butter dish with cover	135.00	45.00
Cake stand on high standard		
9" d.	225.00	75.00
10" d.	250.00	85.00
11" d.	300.00	125.00
12" d.	375.00	—
14" d.	450.00	—
Celery vase, 10" h.	65.00	30.00
Champagne with knob stem	65.00	35.00
Compote, round		
Covered		
High standard		
Deep bowl		
6" d.	125.00	45.00
7" d.	135.00	50.00
8" d.	150.00	55.00
9" d.	175.00	65.00

Sawtooth four-piece table set and tumbler.

Known items:	Flint	Non-flint
9-1/2" d.	175.00	75.00
10" d.	375.00	—
Shallow bowl		
6" d.	85.00	40.00
7" d.	100.00	45.00
Low standard		
Deep bowl		
7" d.	95.00	40.00
8" d.	110.00	45.00
9" d.	125.00	55.00
10" d.	225.00	—
Shallow bowl		
6" d.	65.00	35.00
7" d.	75.00	40.00
Open		
High standard with flared bowl and sawtooth rim		
Deep bowl		
6" d.	35.00	15.00
7" d.	45.00	25.00
8" d.	50.00	30.00
9" d.	55.00	35.00
10" d.	65.00	45.00
Shallow bowl		
6" d.	35.00	55.00
7" d.	45.00	65.00
Low standard with deep bowl		
6" d.	35.00	20.00
7" d.	45.00	25.00
8" d.	55.00	30.00
9" d.	65.00	35.00
10" d.	80.00	45.00
Creamer, table size		
With applied handle	110.00	65.00
With pressed handle	—	35.00

Known items:	Flint	Non-flint
Cruet with original stopper	110.00	45.00
Decanter with original shopper, 1-qt.	85.00	45.00
Dish, open, flat		
Oval		
5" l.	30.00	15.00
6" l.	35.00	25.00
7" l.	40.00	30.00
Eggcup, single		
Covered	225.00	135.00
Open	35.00	20.00
Gas shade	—	35.00
Goblet		
Knob stem	55.00	20.00
Plain stem	45.00	15.00
Honey dish, round, flat	10.00	5.00
Lamp, oil (several sizes)	275.00	—
Miniatures:		
Butter dish with cover	—	75.00
Creamer	—	55.00
Spoon holder	—	50.00
Sugar bowl with cover	—	65.00
Pitcher		
Milk, 1-qt.		
With applied handle	150.00	85.00
With pressed handle	—	35.00
Water, 1/2-gal.		
With applied handle	175.00	—
With pressed handle	—	45.00
Plate, round, 6-1/2" d.	55.00	25.00
Pomade jar with original cover	95.00	45.00
Salt		
Master, footed		
Covered	150.00	65.00
Open with sawtooth rim	35.00	15.00

Known items:	Flint	Non-flint
Sauce dish, round, flat		
4" d.	5.00	5.00
4-1/2" d.	8.00	5.00
5" d.	10.00	5.00
Spill holder	65.00	—
Spoon holder		
With plain base	45.00	25.00
With rayed base	55.00	25.00
Sugar bowl with cover	95.00	35.00
Tray, water, round		
10" d.	—	65.00
11" d.	—	75.00
12" d.	—	85.00
14" d.	—	95.00
Tumbler, water		
Flat	85.00	35.00
Footed	55.00	25.00
Wine		
With knob stem	45.00	15.00
With plain stem	35.00	10.00

SAWTOOTHED HONEYCOMB

OMN: Steimer's Diamond, Union's Radiant.
AKA: Chickenwire, Sawtooth Honeycomb, Serrated Block and Loop.

Non-flint. The Steimer Glass Company, Buckhannon, WV, c. 1906. The Union Stopper Company, Morgantown, WV, c. 1906.

Original color production: Clear, clear with ruby stain (plain, gilded).

Reproductions and Look-a-Likes: None known.

Known items:	Clear	Clear w/Ruby
Bowl, flat, open		
Round, master berry	$45.00	$175.00
Oval		
8-7/8" l.	35.00	95.00
9-5/8" l.	45.00	110.00
10-3/8" l.	55.00	125.00

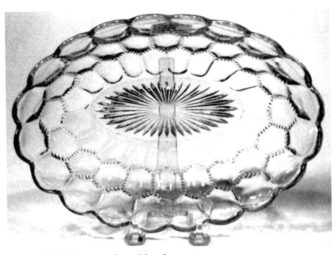

Sawtoothed Honeycomb oval bowl.

Known items:	Clear	Clear w/Ruby
Butter dish with cover	65.00	225.00
Celery vase	40.00	110.00
Compote, open on high standard	35.00	85.00
Creamer with pressed handle	45.00	95.00
Cruet with original stopper	65.00	275.00
Dish, bonbon, triangular shaped		
with handle	20.00	45.00
Goblet	45.00	135.00
Orange bowl, 14-1/2" d.		
Flat	125.00	475.00
Footed	150.00	650.00
Pitcher with pressed handle		
Milk, 2-pts.	65.00	175.00
Water, 1/2-gal.	75.00	200.00
Saltshaker	35.00	95.00
Sauce dish, round		
Flat		
4" d.	8.00	20.00
4-1/2" d.	8.00	20.00
Footed		
4" d.	10.00	25.00
4-1/2" d.	10.00	25.00
Spoon holder	40.00	85.00
Sugar bowl		
Covered	55.00	175.00
Open with double		
handles	30.00	65.00
Syrup pitcher	96.00	275.00
Toothpick holder	30.00	175.00
Tumbler, water, flat	20.00	65.00

SAXON

OMN: AKA: Saxon-Engraved.

Non-flint. Adams & Company, Pittsburgh, PA, c. 1888. The United States Glass Company, Pittsburgh, PA, c. 1892.

Original color production: Clear, clear with ruby stain (plain, engraved). Add 100% for ruby stained items.

Reproductions and Look-a-Likes: None known.

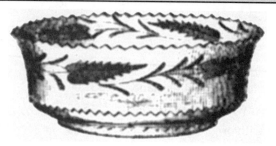

Saxon etched master berry bowl.

Known items:	Clear
Bowl, round	
Flat	
Covered	
5" d.	$35.00
6" d.	40.00
7" d.	45.00
8" d.	50.00
9" d.	65.00
Open	
Belled bowl with scalloped rim	
5" d.	15.00
6" d.	20.00
7" d.	20.00
8" d.	25.00
9" d.	30.00
Flared bowl	
7-1/2" d.	20.00
9" d.	20.00
10" d.	25.00
11-1/2" d.	35.00

Known items:	Clear
Low standard	
Covered	
5" d.	45.00
6" d.	50.00
7" d.	55.00
8" d.	65.00
9" d.	75.00
Open	
Belled bowl	
5" d.	15.00
6" d.	20.00
7" d.	20.00
8" d.	25.00
9" d.	30.00
Shallow bowl with scalloped rim	
6-1/2" d.	20.00
7-1/2" d.	25.00
9" d.	25.00
10" d.	30.00
11-1/2" d.	35.00
Bread platter, oval, handled, 12" l.	30.00
Butter dish with cover	45.00
Cake stand on high standard	
9" d.	65.00
10" d.	75.00
Celery vase	25.00
Claret	25.00
Compote	
Covered on high standard	
5" d.	55.00
6" d.	65.00
7" d.	75.00
8" d.	85.00
Open	
On high standard	
Belled bowl	
5" d.	20.00
6" d.	20.00
7" d.	25.00
8" d.	30.00
9" d.	40.00
Shallow bowl with scalloped rim	
6-1/2" d.	20.00
7-1/2" d.	25.00

Saxon etched cruet, goblet, water pitcher, and covered cracker.

Known items:	Clear
9" d.	30.00
10" d.	35.00
11-1/2" d.	40.00
On low standard, 8" d.	30.00
Creamer	30.00
Cruet with applied handle and original stopper	45.00
Dish, open, oval, flat	
7" l.	15.00
8" l.	15.00
9" l.	30.00
Eggcup, open, single	15.00
Finger bowl	15.00
Goblet	25.00
Mug with handle	20.00
Pickle tray, rectangular	10.00
Pitcher	
Milk, 1-qt.	35.00
Water, 1/2-gal.	45.00
Plate, round, 6" d.	15.00
Salt	
Individual	5.00
Master	15.00
Shaker	25.00
Sauce dish, round	
Flat	
3" d.	5.00
4" d.	5.00
4-1/2" d.	5.00

Known items:	Clear
Footed	
3" d.	8.00
4" d.	8.00
4-1/2" d.	8.00
Spoon holder	20.00
Sugar bowl with cover	35.00
Syrup pitcher	65.00
Toothpick holder	25.00
Tray, water, round	40.00
Tumbler, water, flat	20.00
Wine	15.00

SCALLOPED SIX POINT(S)

OMN: Duncan's No. 30. **AKA:** Divided Medallion with Diamond Cut.

Non-flint. George Duncan's Sons & Company, Washington, PA. Production continued by the Duncan & Miller Glass Company, c. 1897.

Original color production: Clear. Clear with ruby stain or any other color would be considered rare.

Reproductions and Look-a-Likes: None known.

Known items:	Clear
Bowl, open, flat, 9" d.	
Round	$35.00
Square	45.00

Scalloped Six Points covered cracker.

Scalloped Six Points toothpicks.

Known items:	Clear
Butter dish with cover	65.00
Butter pat	15.00
Cake stand on high standard	
Round	95.00
Square	125.00
Celery	
Tray	25.00
Vase	35.00
Claret	
Cupped bowl	35.00
Round bowl	30.00
Cocktail	35.00
Compote, open, round	
High standard	45.00
Low standard	35.00
Cordial	65.00
Cracker jar with cover	95.00
Creamer	
Individual	15.00
Table size	45.00
Cruet with original stopper	55.00
Cup	
Custard	15.00
Sherbet	15.00
Eggcup, open, single	30.00
Goblet	
Cupped bowl	45.00
Straight-sided bowl	35.00
Mustard pot with original lid	25.00
Nappy with handle	15.00

Known items:	Clear
Pickle	
Dish	20.00
Jar with original cover	85.00
Pitcher, water with applied handle, 1/2-gal.	
Bulbous	110.00
Tankard	95.00
Plate, ice cream	20.00
Rose bowl	45.00
Salt	
Dip, individual	8.00
Shaker	30.00
Sherry	
Flared bowl	30.00
Straight-sided bowl	25.00
Spoon holder	35.00
Sugar bowl with cover	
Individual	15.00
Table size	45.00
Syrup pitcher	95.00
Toothpick holder	
Conventional	40.00
Cuspidor	55.00
Tumbler, flat	
Bar	25.00
Champagne	20.00
Water	30.00
Vase, bouquet	
6" h.	15.00
8" h.	25.00

Scalloped Six Points syrup.

Scalloped Tape goblet.

Known items:	Clear
Wine	
Cupped bowl	25.00
Straight-sided bowl	15.00

SCALLOPED TAPE

AKA: Jewel Band, Jeweled Band.

Non-flint. Maker unknown, c. 1880s.

Original color production: Clear. Amber, blue, canary yellow, light green, or any other color would be considered scarce.

Reproductions and Look-a-Likes: None known.

Known items:	Clear
Butter dish with cover	$35.00
Cake stand on high standard	75.00
Celery vase	30.00

Known items:	Clear
Compote, round on high standard, 8" d.	
Covered	45.00
Open	25.00
Creamer with pressed handle	25.00
Dish with cover, rectangular, 8"	75.00
Eggcup, open, single	15.00
Goblet	25.00
Pitcher with pressed handle	
Milk, 1-qt.	35.00
Water, 1/2-gal.	45.00
Plate	
Bread, oval with *"Bread is the Staff of Life"* center	35.00
Dinner, 6" d.	15.00
Relish tray	10.00
Sauce dish, round, 4" d.	
Flat	5.00
Footed	5.00
Spoon holder	25.00
Sugar bowl with cover	35.00
Tray, 6" x 7"	35.00
Wine	15.00

SCROLL

OMN: Lily. AKA: Stippled Scroll.

Non-flint. George Duncan & Sons, Pittsburgh, PA, c. 1870s.

Original color production: Clear.

Reproductions and Look-a-Likes: None known.

Scroll eggcup.

Known items:	Clear
Butter dish with cover	$45.00
Celery vase	35.00
Compote, round, 7" d.	
Covered	
On high standard	85.00
On low standard	65.00
Open on high standard	35.00
Creamer with applied handle	45.00
Eggcup, single, open	25.00
Goblet	35.00
Pitcher, water	135.00
Salt, master, open footed	25.00
Spoon holder	30.00
Sugar bowl with cover	45.00
Tumbler, water, footed	20.00
Wine	15.00

SEASHELL

AKA: Boswell.

Non-flint. Original maker unknown, c. 1870s.

Original color production: Clear. (Plain, frosted, engraved.)

Reproductions and Look-a-Likes: None known.

Seashell creamer.

Known items:	Clear
Butter dish with cover	$125.00
Cake stand on high standard	225.00
Celery vase	75.00
Champagne	125.00
Compote, covered, high standard	225.00
Creamer with pressed handle	55.00
Goblet	85.00
Pitcher with pressed handle	
Milk, 1-qt.	95.00
Water, 1/2-gal.	150.00
Saltshaker	45.00
Sauce dish, round, footed	15.00
Spoon holder	45.00
Sugar bowl with cover	110.00
Wine	55.00

Seashell spoon holder.

SEDAN

AKA: Paneled Star and Button

Non-flint. Original maker unknown, c. 1870s.

Original color production: Clear.

Reproductions and Look-a-Likes: None known.

Known items:	Clear
Bowl, master berry, open, round, flat	$25.00
Butter dish with cover	35.00
Celery	
Tray	15.00
Vase	30.00
Compote, round	
Covered on high standard, 8-1/2" d.	45.00
Open on low standard with scalloped rim	25.00
Creamer	25.00
Goblet	25.00
Mug	20.00
Pickle tray with double handles	15.00
Pitcher, water, 1/2-gal.	45.00
Relish tray	10.00
Saltshaker	25.00

Known items:	Clear
Sauce dish, round, flat	5.00
Spoon holder	20.00
Sugar bowl with cover	35.00
Tumbler, water, flat	20.00
Wine	15.00

SHELL AND JEWEL

OMN: Westmoreland's Victor; Fostoria's No. 618. **AKA:** Jewel and Shell, Late Nugget, Nugget.

Non-flint. The Westmoreland Specialty Glass Company, Grapeville, PA, c. 1893. The Fostoria Glass Company, Fostoria, OH, c. 1898. **Note:** Fostoria only made the water pitcher with a stippled foot.

Original color production: Clear. Odd items have been noted in amber, cobalt blue, green, blue opaque, milk white and carnival irridized orange and green.

Reproductions and Look-a-Likes: There is another pattern similar to this called Nugget that has a plain rim and is of a lesser quality glass.

Shell and Jewel creamer and spoon holder.

Known items:	Clear
Banana dish on high standard, 10" l. (S)	$450.00
Bowl, open, round, flat	
6" d.	35.00
8" d.	85.00

Shell and Jewel clear water pitcher.

Known items:	Clear
Butter dish with cover	135.00
Cake stand on high standard, 10" d	275.00
Creamer with pressed handle	45.00
Dish, open, oval, flat	
7" l	45.00
8" l	75.00
Hat made from a tumbler (R)	550.00
Honey dish with cover, round	65.00
Orange bowl on high standard	375.00
Pitcher	
Plain foot	35.00
Stippled foot (R)	275.00
Sauce dish, round, flat, 4-1/2" d	25.00

Known items:	Clear
Spoon holder	45.00
Sugar bowl with cover	95.00
Tray, water, round	350.00
Tumbler, water, flat	20.00

SHELL AND TASSEL

OMN: Duncan No. 555. **AKA:** Hedlin Shell, Shell and Spike, Shell and Tassel-Square.

Non-flint. George A. Duncan & Sons, Pittsburgh, PA, c. 1881. Designed by Augustus H. Heisey and patented July 26, 1881 in two versions: items with frosted corner shells (U.S. patent No. 12,371) and items with clear corner shells (U.S. patent No. 12,372).

Original color production: Clear (plain, engraved). Amber, blue, canary yellow, or any other color would be considered rare. Manufactured in two conspicuous forms: (a) square with shell finial and scalloped rims often signed "Duncan & Sons" entwined on the bases of cake stands and compotes, and (b) round with frosted dog finials and smooth rims.

Reproductions and Look-a-Likes: Butter with cover, footed, goblet (amber, blue & clear). L.G. Wright Glass Company, New Martinsville, WV, unmarked.

Shell and Tassel round water pitcher.

Shell and Tassel round four-piece table set.

Shell and Tassel goblet.

Shell and Tassel square creamer.

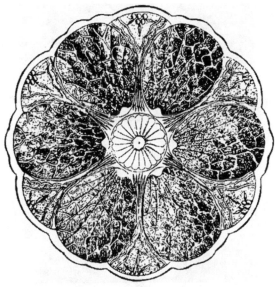

Shell and Tassel rare torte plate.

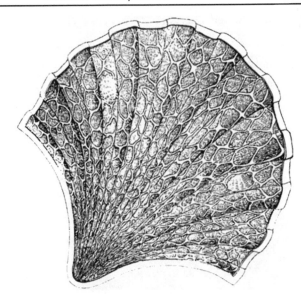

Shell and Tassel rare shell-shaped plate.

Known items:	Clear
ROUND: with collared bases and frosted dog finials. Most items are handled.	
Butter dish with cover.	$225.00
Celery vase	125.00
Creamer.	65.00
Pitcher, water with pressed handle, 1/2-gal.	175.00
Spoon holder	55.00
Sauce dish, 4" d.	15.00
Sugar bowl with cover	175.00

SQUARE: with "shell" finials and scalloped rims.

Bowl
    Covered on collared base

6" d.	$175.00
7" d.	200.00
8" d.	325.00

Known items:	Clear
Open	
Berry	
Oblong on collared base	
Deep, 12" l.	55.00
Shallow with flared bowl, 12" l.	75.00
Shell-shaped on three shell feet,	
7-1/2"	550.00
Butter dish with cover, footed.	150.00
Butter pat, shell-shaped	85.00
Cake stand on high standard	
6" sq.	125.00
7" sq.	85.00
8" sq.	95.00
9" sq.	110.00
10" sq.	150.00

Shell and Tassel high-standard cake stand.

Shell and Tassel bread plate.

Shell and Tassel celery vase.

Known items:	Clear
Celery vase, footed	175.00
Compote, true open on high standard	
5" (Jelly)	95.00
6"	55.00
7"	65.00
8"	85.00
9"	95.00
10"	125.00
Creamer, footed with pressed handle	85.00
Dish, open , rectangular	
7"	45.00
8"	55.00
9"	65.00
10"	85.00
Goblet	
Knob stem	65.00
Plain Stem	150.00
Mug	85.00
Pickle jar with original cover	550.00
Pitcher, water, 1/2-gal.	325.00
Plate, fan-shaped, 12"	
Fruit with clear shell feet	650.00
Tart flat, no feet	475.00
Round (*Oyster*), 9-1/2" d.	550.00
Platter	
Oblong, berry	110.00
Square, bread, with shell handles	85.00

Known items:	Clear
Salt	
Individual, shell shaped	45.00
Shaker (R)	325.00
Sauce dish	
Flat with tab handle	
Shell shaped, 4-1/2"	15.00
Square	
4"	20.00
4-1/2"	25.00
Footed, square	
3"	15.00
4"	20.00
5"	25.00

Known items: | | | **Clear**
Spoon holder, footed 85.00
Sugar bowl with cover 175.00
Tray, ice cream, rectangular with tab handles 125.00
Tumbler
    Soda
        10-oz. 110.00
        13-oz. 125.00
        18-oz. 150.00
    Water, 9-oz. 100.00
Vase, footed with scalloped rim, 7-1/2" h. (R) 175.00

Sheraton water pitcher.

SHERATON

OMN: Ida.

Non-flint. Bryce, Higbee & Company, Pittsburgh, PA, c. 1885.

Original color production: Amber, blue, clear.

Reproductions and Look-a-Likes: None known.

Known items:	Amber	Blue	Clear
Bowl, open, round, flat, 8" d.	$30.00	$35.00	$25.00
Butter dish with cover.	75.00	85.00	65.00

Known items:	Amber	Blue	Clear
Celery vase	35.00	40.00	35.00
Compote, round			
Covered on high standard			
with shallow bowl, 7" d. . . .	95.00	110.00	85.00
Open, 7" d.			
On high standard. . . .	40.00	45.00	35.00
On low standard	35.00	40.00	30.00

Sheraton goblet.

Known items:	Amber	Blue	Clear
Creamer	40.00	45.00	35.00
Dish, open, flat			
Eight-sided	40.00	40.00	35.00
Round.	30.00	30.00	30.00
Goblet	45.00	50.00	35.00

Sheraton seven-piece water set.

Sheraton wine.

Known items:	Amber	Blue	Clear
Pitcher			
Milk, 1-qt., 7" h.	55.00	65.00	45.00
Water, 1/2-gal., 9" h.	65.00	75.00	55.00
Plate, bread, 9-3/4" l.	35.00	35.00	35.00
Platter, oblong	45.00	50.00	45.00
Relish tray with double handles	15.00	20.00	15.00
Salt dish, round, 3-1/2" d.			
Flat	8.00	10.00	8.00
Footed	10.00	12.50	10.00
Spoon holder	35.00	40.00	30.00
Sugar bowl with cover	50.00	65.00	45.00
Tumbler, water, flat	35.00	45.00	30.00
Wine	30.00	40.00	25.00

SHOSHONE

OMN: U.S. Glass No. 15,046-Victor. **AKA:** Blazing Pinwheels, Floral Diamond.

Non-flint. The United States Glass Company, Pittsburgh, PA, c. 1895-1896.

Original color production: Clear, clear with ruby stain, clear with amber stain, emerald green. Individual pieces may be found in cobalt blue and *"Gainsborough"* olive green.

Reproductions and Look-a-Likes: None known.

Shoshone tab-handled ice bucket.

Known items:	Clear	Clear w/Amber	Clear w/Ruby	Green
Banana stand on high standard with folded sides	$65.00	$150.00	$175.00	$85.00
Bowl				
Round				
Collared base with scalloped rim				
Belled bowl				
7" d.	35.00	85.00	95.00	45.00
8" d.	45.00	95.00	110.00	55.00
Straight-sided bowl				
7" d.	35.00	85.00	95.00	45.00
8" d.	45.00	95.00	110.00	55.00

Shoshone clear with ruby spoon holder.

Shoshone banana stand.

Known items:	Clear	Clear w/Amber	Clear w/Ruby	Green
Flat				
Flared bowl				
5" d.	25.00	75.00	85.00	35.00
6" d.	30.00	85.00	95.00	40.00
7" d.	35.00	95.00	110.00	45.00
8" d.	45.00	100.00	125.00	55.00
Straight-sided bowl				
6" d.	25.00	75.00	85.00	35.00
7" d.	30.00	85.00	95.00	40.00
8" d.	35.00	95.00	110.00	45.00
Square with scalloped rim, 8" d.	55.00	110.00	125.00	65.00
Butter dish with high-domed lid on flanged base	55.00	100.00	110.00	65.00
Cake stand on high standard				
9" d.	55.00	125.00	150.00	75.00
10" d.	65.00	150.00	175.00	85.00
11" d.	85.00	175.00	200.00	110.00
Celery vase	35.00	110.00	125.00	75.00
Compote				
Covered on high standard				
6" d.	85.00	150.00	175.00	110.00
7" d.	95.00	175.00	200.00	125.00
8" d.	110.00	200.00	225.00	150.00
Open, square with scalloped rim, 5-1/4"				
On high standard	20.00	75.00	85.00	30.00
On low standard	15.00	65.00	75.00	25.00

Shoshone low-footed covered bowl.

Shoshone footed punch bowl.

Known items:	Clear	Clear w/Amber	Clear w/Ruby	Green
Creamer, bulbous				
Individual	25.00	65.00	65.00	30.00
Table size	45.00	110.00	125.00	55.00
Dish				
Jelly, flat with double-handles	15.00	45.00	50.00	20.00
Flat with turned up sides, 6"	20.00	55.00	65.00	25.00
Oblong, 7"	15.00	45.00	55.00	20.00
Rectangular, 7" l.	20.00	55.00	65.00	25.00
Goblet	95.00	225.00	250.00	150.00
Horseradish with original cover	45.00	150.00	175.00	75.00
Ice tub, straight-sided with tab handles	40.00	110.00	125.00	85.00
Pickle tray, oblong	20.00	45.00	45.00	25.00
Pitcher, water with applied handle, 1/2-gal.				
Bulbous	95.00	275.00	300.00	150.00
Tankard	65.00	250.00	275.00	125.00
Plate				
7" d.	35.00	135.00	150.00	55.00
7-1/2" d., (originally cataloged as the "*sweetmeat*")	40.00	150.00	175.00	65.00
Salt				
Master, round, flat with scalloped rim (R)	45.00	225.00	275.00	75.00
Shaker, tall	35.00	95.00	95.00	55.00
Sauce dish, round, flat, 4" d.	10.00	35.00	35.00	15.00
Spoon holder	35.00	95.00	125.00	45.00
Sugar bowl with cover				
Medium	45.00	110.00	125.00	55.00
Table size	55.00	135.00	150.00	75.00
Toothpick holder	25.00	225.00	225.00	85.00
Tumbler, water, flat	35.00	75.00	85.00	55.00
Wine	20.00	65.00	75.00	30.00

SHRINE

OMN: Orient. AKA: Jewel with Moon and Star, Jeweled Moon and Star, Little Shrine, Moon and Star with Waffle.

Non-flint. Beatty-Brady Glass Company, Dunkirk, IN, c. 1896. Indiana Glass Company, Dunkirk, IN, c. 1904.

Original color production: clear.

Reproductions and Look-a-Likes: None known.

Shrine 1 gallon water pitcher.

Shrine saltshaker

Shrine sugar bowl, jelly compote, creamer, and spoon holder.

Known items:	Clear
Bowl, open, round, flat	
6-1/2" d.	$30.00
8-1/2" d.	35.00
9-1/2" d.	55.00
Butter dish with cover	95.00
Cake stand on high standard, 8-1/2" d.	135.00
Celery vase	75.00
Compote, open on high standard (Jelly)	20.00
Creamer	45.00
Goblet	85.00
Mug with pressed handle	65.00
Pickle tray	20.00
Pitcher, water	
1/2-gal.	45.00
1 gal. (R)	325.00
Platter	65.00
Relish tray	20.00

Known items:	Clear
Saltshaker	
Squat	55.00
Tall	95.00
Sauce dish, round, flat, 4" d.	12.50
Spoon holder	45.00
Sugar bowl with cover	85.00
Toothpick holder (R)	150.00
Tumbler, flat	
Lemonade (tall)	55.00
Water (short)	45.00

SHUTTLE

OMN: Indiana Tumbler No. 29. AKA: Hearts of Loch Laven, Ribbed Asterisk and Concave.

Non-flint. Indiana Tumbler and Goblet Company, Greentown, IN, c. 1896. Indiana Glass Company, Dunkirk, IN, c. 1898.

Original color production: Clear. Some items may be found in amber, chocolate glass, cobalt blue, and green.

Reproductions and Look-a-Likes: None known.

Shuttle creamer.

Known items:	Clear
Bowl, master berry, open, round, flat, 8-1/4" d.	$125.00
Butter dish with cover	200.00
Cake stand	150.00
Celery vase	110.00
Champagne	55.00
Cordial	45.00
Creamer	
Table size, 5-1/2" h.	85.00
Tankard, 6" h.	35.00
Cup, custard	10.00
Goblet (S)	110.00
Mug	35.00
Pitcher, water, 1/2-gal.	110.00
Saltshaker	125.00
Sauce dish, round, flat	35.00
Spoon holder	75.00
Sugar bowl with cover	110.00
Tumbler, water, flat	95.00
Wine	10.00

SKILTON

AKA: Early Oregon, Richards & Hartley's Oregon.

Non-flint Richards & Hartley Glass Company, Tarentum, PA, c. 1890. The United States Glass Company, Pittsburgh, PA, after 1891.

Original color production: Clear, clear with ruby stain.

Reproductions and Look-a-Likes: None known.

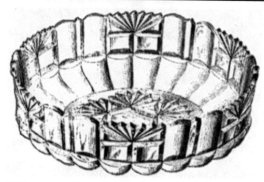

Skilton master berry bowl.

Known items:	Clear	Clear w/Ruby
Bowl, open, flat		
Rectangular		
7" l.	$20.00	$45.00
8" l.	25.00	55.00
9" l.	35.00	75.00
Round		
5" d.	20.00	45.00
6" d.	25.00	55.00
8" d.	45.00	85.00
Butter dish with cover on flanged base	75.00	200.00
Cake stand on high standard	150.00	—
Celery vase	35.00	95.00
Compote, round		
Covered on high standard		
7" d.	85.00	225.00
8" d.	110.00	275.00
Open		
On high standard		
4" d. (Jelly)	15.00	45.00
7" d.	30.00	65.00
8" d.	40.00	75.00
On low standard		
7" d.	25.00	65.00
8" d.	35.00	75.00
Creamer	35.00	75.00
Dish, open, flat		
Oblong		
7" l.		
8" l.	15.00	—
9" l.	15.00	—

Skilton celery vase.

Skilton wine, goblet, water pitcher, and tumbler.

Known items:	Clear	Clear w/Ruby
Olive with handle	20.00	—
Goblet	45.00	110.00
Pickle tray...............	15.00	35.00
Pitcher		
Milk, bulbous, 1-qt........	85.00	225.00
Water, 1/2-gal.		
Bulbous	95.00	235.00
Tankard	110.00	250.00
Saltshaker	35.00	85.00
Sauce dish, round, 4" d.		
Flat.....................	5.00	20.00
Footed	8.00	20.00
Spoon holder	35.00	65.00
Sugar bowl with cover	55.00	125.00
Tray, water, round (S)	85.00	325.00
Tumbler, water, flat	35.00	65.00
Wine...........................	45.00	75.00

SNAIL

OMN: Duncan's No. 360 Ware. **AKA:** Compact, Double Snail, Idaho, Small Comet.

Non-flint. George Duncan & Sons, Pittsburgh, PA, c. 1891. The United States Glass Company, Pittsburgh, PA. at Factory "D," c. 1891. Later produced at Factory "P."

Original color production: Clear, clear with ruby stain (plain, engraved). Deep blue or any other color would be considered rare.

Reproductions and Look-a-Likes: Tankard water pitcher (clear, clear with blush).

Snail syrup.

Known items:	Clear	Clear w/Ruby
Banana stand on high standard		
9" d..................	$250.00	—
10" d..................	275.00	950.00
Basket, cake with pewter handle		
9" d....................	325.00	—
10" d....................	350.00	—
Biscuit jar with cover	425.00	1,500.00

Snail covered butter.

Snail scarce berry set (covered sugar and creamer).

Snail Ruby-stained saltshaker.

Known items:	Clear	Clear w/Ruby
Bowl		
Covered, round on low circular foot		
7" d.	135.00	325.00
8" d.	150.00	375.00
Open		
Round		
Deep		
Flat		
7" d.	30.00	85.00
8" d.	35.00	95.00
9" d.	40.00	110.00
10" d.	65.00	225.00
Footed, 8" d.	40.00	—
Shallow bowl, flat, 10" d.	55.00	200.00
Oval, flat		
7" l.	30.00	85.00
8" l.	35.00	95.00
9" l.	40.00	110.00
Butter dish with cover, 6" d.	125.00	250.00
Cake stand on high standard		
9" d.	135.00	—
10" d.	175.00	—
Celery		
Tray	35.00	55.00
Vase	45.00	110.00

Known items:	Clear	Clear w/Ruby
Cheese dish with matching cover	175.00	375.00
Compote, round on high standard		
Covered		
6" d.	125.00	325.00
7" d.	150.00	350.00
8" d.	225.00	425.00
Open with shallow scalloped bowl		
6" d.	65.00	—
7" d.	75.00	—
8" d.	95.00	—
9" d.	110.00	—
10" d.	150.00	—
Creamer with applied handle		
Individual	55.00	95.00
Table, tankard	75.00	135.00

Snail sugar bowl, butter dish, creamer, spoon holder.

Snail etched goblets, tankard water pitcher, and tumblers.

Known items:	Clear	Clear w/Ruby
Cruet with original patterned stopper	150.00	750.00
Cup, custard with applied handle	35.00	65.00
Finger bowl	75.00	125.00
Goblet	135.00	225.00
Jug in "Double Snail" design		
No. 0	175.00	—
No. 3	200.00	—
No. 4	225.00	—
No. 5	250.00	—
Marmalade with cover	275.00	—
Pitcher with applied handle		
Bulbous, 1-qt.	225.00	375.00
Tankard		
1-pt. (cream)	95.00	200.00
1-1/2-pts. (cream)	135.00	225.00
1/4-gal. (milk)	175.00	275.00
1/2-gal. (water)	225.00	325.00
Plate, round		
5" d.	35.00	—
6" d.	40.00	—
7" d.	65.00	—

Known items:	Clear	Clear w/Ruby
Relish dish, oval, 7" l.	25.00	—
Rose bowl, flat		
3" d.	45.00	110.00
5" d.	55.00	125.00
6" d.	65.00	150.00
7" d.	85.00	175.00
Salt		
Individual	30.00	65.00
Master, round, flat	85.00	175.00
Shaker		
Short, bulbous	65.00	110.00
Tall	75.00	125.00
Sauce dish, round		
Flat		
4" d.	15.00	30.00
4-1/2" d.	15.00	30.00
Footed		
4" d.	20.00	35.00
4-1/2" d.	20.00	35.00
Spoon holder	45.00	95.00
Sugar bowl with cover		
Individual	125.00	—
Table size	95.00	125.00

Known items:	Clear	Clear/w Ruby
Sugar shaker	135.00	375.00
Syrup pitcher with pressed handle	175.00	450.00

Known items:	Clear	Clear/w Ruby
Tumbler, water, flat	45.00	95.00
Vase, swung	250.00	—

SPIREA BAND

OMN: Earl. **AKA:** Nailhead Variant, Spirea, Square and Dot, Squared Dot.

Non-flint. Bryce, Higbee & Company, Pittsburgh, PA, c. 1885.

Original color production: Amber, blue, vaseline, clear.

Reproductions and Look-a-Likes: None known.

Spirea Band footed saltshaker.

Spirea Band wine.

Known items:	Amber	Blue	Clear	Vaseline
Bowl, open, round				
Flat, master berry, open, 8" d.	$25.00	$30.00	$20.00	$35.00
Footed, 8" d.				
Deep bowl	30.00	35.00	25.00	35.00
Shallow bowl	25.00	30.00	20.00	30.00
Butter dish with cover	45.00	55.00	35.00	65.00
Cake stand on high standard				
8" d.	55.00	75.00	45.00	85.00
9" d.	65.00	85.00	55.00	95.00
10" d.	75.00	95.00	65.00	110.00
11" d.	95.00	125.00	85.00	135.00
Celery vase	30.00	35.00	25.00	40.00

Known items:	Amber	Blue	Clear	Vaseline
Compote, round				
Covered				
On high standard				
6" d.........................45.00	55.00	45.00	55.00
7" d.........................55.00	65.00	55.00	65.00
On low standard				
6" d.........................40.00	50.00	40.00	50.00
7" d.........................50.00	65.00	50.00	65.00
Open on high standard, 7" d..............25.00	30.00	25.00	30.00
Creamer with pressed handle 30.00	35.00	30.00	35.00
Goblet 25.00	35.00	20.00	45.00
Honey dish, round, flat......................5.00	8.00	5.00	8.00
Marmalade jar with original cover (R).........125.00	225.00	110.00	250.00
Pickle dish................................10.00	15.00	10.00	20.00
Pitcher, water with pressed handle, 1/2-gal......40.00	65.00	35.00	85.00
Platter, oval				
10-1/2" l. 20.00	25.00	15.00	30.00
11" l. 20.00	25.00	15.00	30.00
Relish tray................................10.00	15.00	10.00	20.00
Salt				
Master 95.00	150.00	55.00	225.00
Shaker 35.00	45.00	25.00	55.00
Sauce dish, round				
Flat 5.00	8.00	5.00	10.00
Footed 5.00	8.00	5.00	12.50
Spoon holder 25.00	35.00	20.00	35.00
Sugar bowl with cover 40.00	45.00	35.00	45.00
Tumbler, water, flat 25.00	35.00	20.00	40.00
Wine......................................30.00	35.00	10.00	35.00

SPRIG

OMN: Bryce's Royal. **AKA:** Indian Tree, Paneled Sprig.

Non-flint. Bryce, Higbee & Company, Pittsburgh, PA, c. 1885.

Original color production: Clear. Deep blue or any other color would be considered very rare.

Reproductions and Look-a-Likes: None known.

Known items:	Clear
Bowl	
Covered, flat, 6" d. $55.00
Open	
6" d. 25.00
10" d., master berry 45.00
Butter dish with cover 75.00
Cake stand on high standard	
8" d...................................75.00
9" d...................................95.00
10" d..................................110.00
Celery vase...................................45.00

Sprig covered low standard coupote.

Known items: **Clear**

Compote
   Covered
      High standard
         6" d. 85.00
         7" d. 110.00
         8" d. 125.00
      Low standard
         6" d. 55.00
         7" d. 75.00
         8" d. 85.00
   Open, ruffled rim on low standard (S)
      7-3/4" d. 85.00
      8-3/4" d. 135.00
Creamer. 35.00
Dish, open, oval, flat
   7" l. 25.00
   8" l. 35.00
   9" l. 45.00
Goblet 45.00
Honey dish, covered, diamond shape with or without
   knife rest
      Flat. 275.00
      Footed 425.00
Mustard, covered, footed 225.00
Pickle
   Dish 15.00
   Jar with original cover 95.00

Known items: **Clear**

Pitcher, water, 1/2-gal. 65.00
Plate, bread, oval. 35.00
Relish tray 15.00
Salt
      Individual 35.00
      Master
         Diamond shape 75.00
         Round, footed. 85.00
Sauce dish, round, 4" d.
      Flat 10.00
      Footed. 15.00
Spoon holder 35.00
Sugar bowl with cover 65.00
Wine 55.00

SQUIRREL

AKA: Squirrel in Bower.

Non-flint. Original maker unknown, c. 1880s.

Original color production: Clear.

Reproductions and Look-a-Likes: None known.

Squirrel covered sugar bowl.

Known items: **Clear**

Bowl, master berry, 8" d. (ER) $550.00
Butter dish with cover 375.00

Known items:	Clear
Creamer	175.00
Goblet (VR)	850.00
Lamp, oil, stand	750.00
Pitcher, water, 1/2-gal.	1,500.00
Sauce dish, round, flat	50.00
Spoon holder	150.00
Sugar bowl with cover	275.00

STAR IN BULL'S EYE

OMN: U.S. Glass No. 15,092.

Non-flint. The United States Glass Company, Pittsburgh, PA, c. 1905.

Original color production: Clear (plain, gilded). Clear with maidens' blush or ruby stain is considered scarce.

Reproductions and Look-a-Likes: None known.

Star in Bull's Eye tumbler.

Known items:	Clear
Bowl, open, flat with flared rim	$35.00
Butter dish with cover	55.00
Cake stand on high standard	85.00
Celery vase	35.00

Star in Bulls Eye toothpick holder.

Known items:	Clear
Compote, round	
Covered on high standard	65.00
Open on low standard with scalloped bowl	30.00
Creamer	35.00
Cruet with original stopper	65.00
Dish, diamond-shaped	15.00
Goblet	30.00
Pitcher, water, 1/2-gal.	65.00
Sauce, cupped	5.00
Spoon holder	30.00
Sugar bowl with cover	45.00
Toothpick holder	
Double	55.00
Single	30.00
Tumbler, water	25.00
Wine	20.00

STATES, THE

OMN: U.S. Glass No. 15,093. **AKA:** Cane and Star Medallion.

Non-flint. The United States Glass Company, Pittsburgh, PA, c. 1905.

Original color production: Clear (plain, gilded, maiden blush stained). Single items may be found in emerald green.

The States sugar bowl, creamer, spoon holder and butter dish.

Known items: **Clear**

Bowl, open, round, flat

No handle, 9-1/4" d. $45.00

Tri-handled, 7" d. 35.00

Butter dish with cover. 85.00

Celery

Tray 25.00

Vase 45.00

Cocktail glass 30.00

Compote, open, round on high standard

7" d. 45.00

9" d. 75.00

Creamer with pressed handle

Individual, oval 15.00

Table size, round 45.00

Cup, punch 10.00

Dish, jelly, flat 15.00

Goblet 45.00

Ice bucket, silverplate rim 65.00

Pickle tray, oblong 15.00

Pitcher, water with pressed handle, 1/2-gal. 85.00

Plate, round, 10" d. 45.00

Punch bowl set, 13" d. 2 part 225.00

Relish tray, diamond-shaped 20.00

Saltshaker 35.00

Sauce dish, flat, tub-shaped, 4" 10.00

Spoon holder 35.00

Sugar bowl

Individual, open 25.00

Table size with cover. 55.00

Syrup pitcher 95.00

Toothpick holder, flat, rectangular 45.00

Tray, 7-1/4" l. 30.00

Tumbler, water, flat 35.00

Wine. 40.00

STEDMAN

Flint, non-flint. McKee Bros., Pittsburgh, PA, 1864.

Original color production: Clear.

Reproductions and Look-a-Likes: None known.

Rare water pitcher with applied handle.

Known items: **Clear**

Bottle, bitters $150.00

Bowl, shell shape (R) 275.00

Butter dish with cover 135.00

Champagne 125.00

Compote

High standard, 8" d. 125.00

Low standard, 8" d. 65.00

Creamer 150.00

Stedman spoon holder, sugar bowl, creamer and butter dish.

Known items:	Clear
Decanter, 1-quart	
Bar lip	125.00
Cut stopper	175.00
Eggcup	55.00
Goblet	75.00
Lamp, oil	
Brass standard and marble base	175.00
Glass patterned standard	250.00
Pitcher with applied handle	
Milk, qt.	950.00
Water, 1/2-gal.	1,000.00
Plate, 6" d.	65.00
Salt, master, oval	45.00
Spoon holder	55.00
Sugar bowl with cover	125.00
Syrup with applied	450.00
Tumbler, water	95.00
Wine	65.00

Stippled Forget-Me-Not wine.

STIPPLED FORGET-ME-NOT

AKA: Dot, Forget-Me-Not in Snow.

Non-flint. Findlay Flint Glass Company, Findlay, OH, c. 1890s.

Original color production: Clear. Amber, blue, milk white, opal, or any other color would be considered scarce.

Reproductions and Look-a-Likes: None known.

Known items:	Clear
Bowl, open, round, flat	
Berry	
7" d.	$45.00
8" d.	65.00
Waste	55.00
Butter dish with cover	125.00
Cake stand	
9" d.	110.00
10" d.	125.00
12" d.	275.00
Celery vase, 8" h.	95.00

Known items:	Clear
Compote, round	
Covered on high standard	
6" d.	110.00
7" d.	125.00
8" d.	150.00
Open on low standard	
6" d.	35.00
7" d.	45.00
8" d.	65.00
Creamer with pressed handle	75.00
Cup with handle	35.00
Dish, oblong	
7" d.	25.00
8" d.	35.00
9" d.	45.00
Goblet	85.00
Lamp, oil, squat with handle	150.00
Miniatures:	
Butter dish with cover	225.00
Creamer	95.00
Spoon holder	125.00
Sugar bowl with cover	150.00
Mug	55.00
Pitcher with pressed handle	
Milk, 1-qt.	135.00
Water, 1/2-gal.	150.00
Plate, round	
6" d.	20.00
7" d.	
With *"Baby Face"* center	75.00
With *"Star"* center	25.00
8" d.	30.00
9" d.	
With *"Kitten"* center	100.00
With *"Star"* center	35.00
Relish dish, oval	25.00
Salt, master, open, oval	65.00
Sauce dish, round	
Flat	8.00
Footed	10.00
Saucer	30.00
Spoon holder	55.00
Sugar bowl with cover	95.00

Known items:	Clear
Syrup pitcher	175.00
Toothpick holder, hat-shaped	150.00
Tray, water with *"wildlife scene"* in center	85.00
Tumbler, water, flat	55.00
Wine	75.00

STIPPLED STAR

OMN: Gillinder's Star.

Non-flint. Gillinder & Sons, Philadelphia, PA, c. 1870. Designed by William F. Gillinder and patented under U.S. Patent No. 3,914 March 22, 1870.

Original color production: Clear. Blue or any other color would be considered rare.

Reproductions and Look-a-Likes: Creamer with pressed handle, 9-oz. goblet, fairy lamp, 3" d. salt dip, covered sugar bowl, round footed toothpick holder, 32-oz. wine (amber, amethyst, amberina, blue, clear, green, ruby). L.G. Wright Glass Company, New Martinsville, WV, unmarked.

Stippled Star spoon holder.

Known items:	Clear
Butter dish with cover	$95.00
Celery vase	55.00

Compote, round on high standard

    Covered, deep bowl

        7" d. 225.00

        8" d. 250.00

    Open, shallow bowl

        7" d. 65.00

        8" d. 75.00

Creamer with applied handle 75.00

Dish, open, oval, flat

    7" l. 25.00

    8" l. 35.00

    9" l. 45.00

Eggcup, open, footed 35.00

Goblet 35.00

Pickle dish. 20.00

Pitcher, water, 1/2-gal. 325.00

Sauce dish, round, 4" d.

    Flat. 8.00

    Footed 10.00

Spoon holder 45.00

Sugar bowl with cover 85.00

Wine. 75.00

Strawberry bulbous water pitcher.

STRAWBERRY

OMN: AKA: Fairfax Strawberry.

Non-flint. Bryce, Walker & Company, Pittsburgh, PA, c. 1870. Designed by John Bryce and patented February 22, 1870.

Original color production: Clear, milk white. Rare in amber.

Reproductions and Look-a-Likes: None known.

Strawberry spoon holder.

Known items:	Clear	Milk White
Bowl, open, flat with smooth rim . .	$45.00	$55.00
Butter dish with cover.	135.00	225.00
Celery vase	225.00	550.00
Compote with cover, round		
High standard		
6-1/4" d.	125.00	175.00
7-1/4" d.	150.00	200.00
8-1/4" d.	175.00	225.00

Known items:	Clear	Milk White
Low standard		
6-1/4" d.	85.00	110.00
7-1/4" d.	100.00	135.00
8-1/4" d.	125.00	150.00
Creamer with applied handle,		
5-3/4" h.	85.00	125.00
Eggcup, single, open	55.00	65.00

Known items:	Clear	Milk White
Goblet 55.00		65.00
Honey dish, round, flat, 3-1/2" d. 15.00		15.00
Pickle tray tapered at one end,		
8-1/2" l......................25.00		30.00
Pitcher, water, bulbous with		
applied handle		
Milk, 1-qt. 425.00		950.00
Water, 1/2-gal. 275.00		750.00
Relish tray, oval 25.00		30.00
Salt, master, open, footed 45.00		55.00
Sauce dish, round, flat............15.00		15.00
Spoon holder 55.00		65.00
Sugar bowl with cover 110.00		150.00
Syrup pitcher with lid...........225.00		450.00
Tumbler, water, flat 135.00		225.00
Wine..........................225.00		325.00

Strawberry and Currant close up.

Strawberry and Currant goblet.

STRAWBERRY AND CURRANT

OMN: Dalzell No. 9D. **AKA:** Currant and Strawberry, Multiple Fruits.

Non-flint. Dalzell, Gillmore & Leighton, Findlay, OH, c. 1890s.

Original color production: Clear.

Reproductions: Creamer, 6-1/2" d. high standard open compote with ruffled rim; 8-oz. goblet; mug; 22-oz. wine (amber, amethyst, blue, blue opalescent, clear, cobalt blue, green, ruby, vaseline, vaseline opalescent). L.G. Wright Glass Company, New Martinsville, WV, unmarked.

Known items:	Clear
Butter dish with cover.........................	$125.00
Celery vase	75.00
Compote, round, covered	
High standard	175.00
Low standard.................................	135.00
Creamer......................................	55.00
Goblet	55.00
Mug with applied handle.....................	65.00
Pitcher	
Milk, 1-qt.	55.00
Water, 1/2-gal.	75.00

Known items:	Clear
Sauce dish, round, footed	10.00
Spoon holder	45.00
Sugar bowl with cover	85.00
Syrup pitcher....................................	225.00
Tumbler, water, flat.............................	55.00

SWAG BLOCK

OMN: Duncan's No. 326 **AKA:** Yoked Spearpoint, Duncan Block.

Non-flint. George Duncan & Sons, Pittsburgh, PA, c. 1888. United States Glass Co., Pittsburgh, PA, at Factory "D" and Factory "P." c. 1891.

Original color production: Clear (plain, engraved). Occasional items may be found in clear with amber or ruby stain (plain or engraved).

Reproductions and Look-a-Likes: None known.

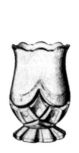

Swag Block spoon holder, sugar bowl, covered butter and creamer.

Swag Block seven-piece water set.

Known items:	Clear
Bowl, open flat	
Oval	
7" l.	$25.00
8" l.	30.00
9" l.	35.00
Round	
6" d.	25.00
7" d.	30.00
8" d.	35.00
9" d.	45.00
Compote on high standard	
Covered	
6" d.	65.00
7" d.	75.00
8" d.	85.00
9" d.	110.00
Open, scalloped rim	
6" d.	30.00
7" d.	40.00
8" d.	45.00
9" d.	55.00

Known items:	Clear
Butter dish with cover, footed	65.00
Cake stand, 10" d.	125.00
Celery vase	55.00
Creamer with applied handle	45.00
Cup, punch	25.00
Egg glass	35.00
Goblet	45.00
Pitcher	
Milk, 1-qt.	75.00
Water, 1/2-gal.	
Bulbous	95.00
Tankard	110.00
Plate, 7" d.	20.00
Sauce, round	
Flat	
4" d.	5.00
4-1/2" d.	8.00
5" d.	10.00
Footed	
4" d.	8.00
4-1/2" d.	10.00
Spoon holder, footed	35.00
Sugar bowl with cover, footed	55.00
Syrup	125.00
Tumbler, water	35.00

SWAN

AKA: Plain Swan, Swan with Mesh.

Non-flint. Traditionally attributed to the Canton Glass Company, Canton, OH, c. 1882.

Original color production: Amber, blue, canary yellow, clear. Designed by David Barker and patented under U.S. Patent No. 12,887 April 18, 1882. Note: Finials are finely sculpted Swans.

Reproductions and Look-a-Likes: None known.

Known items:	Clear
Butter dish with cover	$325.00
Compote, round on high standard	
Covered	450.00
Open	225.00
Creamer, 6" h.	95.00
Dish with cover, oval, flat	575.00
Goblet	350.00
Pickle jar with cover	225.00
Pitcher, water, 1/2-gal.	275.00
Plate, bread, oval with *Bearded Head* handles	125.00
Sauce dish, round, 4" d.	
Flat	20.00
Footed	25.00

Known items:	Clear
Spoon holder with double handles	75.00
Sugar bowl with cover	225.00

Swan goblet.

TACOMA

OMN: Model No. 907. **AKA:** Jeweled Diamond and Fan, Triple X.

Non-flint. Greensburg Glass Company, Greensburg, PA, c. 1894 with production continued by the National Glass Combine at Model Flint Glass Company, Albany, IN, c. 1900.

Original color production: Clear, clear with ruby stain. Odd items may be found in clear with amber stain, and emerald green.

Reproductions and Look-a-Likes: None known.

Tacoma salad bowl.

Tacoma rose bowl.

Known items:	Clear	Clear w/Ruby
Bottle, water	$85.00	$250.00
Bowl, open		
Oval, flat		
7" l.	25.00	85.00
8" l.	30.00	95.00
9" l.	35.00	110.00

Known items:	Clear	Clear w/Ruby
Round		
Berry		
7" d.	35.00	110.00
8" d.	45.00	135.00
Finger or waste with		
smooth rim	25.00	85.00
Punch		
Flat		
12" d.	175.00	—
15" d.	225.00	1,250.00
Pedestaled, plain or		
six-paneled		
12" d.	225.00	—
15" d.	275.00	1,750.00
Square, flat		
7"	35.00	125.00
8"	45.00	150.00
Butter dish with cover, flat, flanged		
base	75.00	175.00
Cake stand on high standard		
9" d.	75.00	275.00
10" d.	95.00	325.00
Celery		
Tray, 11-3/4" l.	30.00	75.00
Vase	55.00	135.00
Compote, open on high standard		
Round		
5" d. (jelly)	20.00	75.00
7" d.	45.00	150.00

Tacoma true open compote on high standard.

Tacoma open compote on high standard.

Known items:	Clear	Clear w/Ruby
8" d.	55.00	175.00
10" d.	75.00	225.00
Square		
7"	55.00	175.00
8"	65.00	200.00
Cracker jar with cover		
5" (AKA tobacco)	135.00	375.00
6"	110.00	350.00
Creamer	40.00	125.00
Cruet with original stopper		
Small	50.00	200.00
Large	55.00	225.00
Cup, punch	15.00	45.00
Decanter, wine with original faceted stopper	125.00	350.00
Dish		
Rectangular		
7" l.	20.00	125.00
8" l.	25.00	135.00
Round, ice cream 5" d.	25.00	65.00
Goblet	35.00	125.00
Pickle jar with cover	125.00	225.00
Pitcher, water, 1/2-gal.		
Bulbous	75.00	250.00
Tankard	85.00	275.00
Plate for finger bowl	20.00	—
Rose bowl		
3-1/2" d.	35.00	85.00
4-1/2" d.	40.00	95.00

Known items:	Clear	Clear w/Ruby
5-1/2" d.	45.00	110.00
6-1/2" d.	55.00	125.00
Salt		
Dip, individual	5.00	35.00
Master	30.00	85.00
Shaker		
Straight sided	35.00	125.00
Tapered	45.00	135.00
Sauce dish, flat		
Round		
4" d.	5.00	20.00
4-1/2" d.	8.00	25.00
Square		
4"	8.00	25.00
4-1/2"	10.00	30.00
Spoon holder	35.00	95.00
Sugar bowl with cover	55.00	175.00
Syrup		
Squat	125.00	325.00
Tall	110.00	275.00
Toothpick holder	25.00	175.00
Tumbler, water, flat	30.00	85.00
Vase		
Swung		
8" h.	35.00	—
11" h.	45.00	—
14" h.	55.00	—
Trumpet shaped		
8" h.	35.00	85.00
10" h.	45.00	110.00
Wine	20.00	55.00

TEARDROP AND TASSEL

AKA: Sampson

Non-flint. Indiana Tumbler & Goblet Co., Greentown, IN, c. 1900.

Original color production: Amber, canary yellow, chocolate, clear, cobalt blue, emerald green, Nile green opaque white. (plain, gilded). All items were not made in all colors.

Reproductions and Look-a-Likes: None known.

Teardrop and Tassel creamer.

Known items:	Amber	Chocolate	Clear	Cobalt Blue	Emerald Green	Nile Green
Bowl, open						
7-1/4" d.	—	—	$50.00	$165.00	—	—
8-1/4" d.	—	700.00	75.00	—	200.00	425.00
Butter dish, covered	275.00	1,250.00	85.00	235.00	250.00	275.00
Compote						
Covered						
4-5/8" d.	—	—	95.00	—	425.00	—
5-1/2" d.	—	—	125.00	—	450.00	—
6-1/2" d.	—	—	160.00	—	475.00	—
7-1/2" d.	—	—	175.00	—	550.00	—
Open, 7-1/2" d.	—	—	40.00	—	375.00	—
Cordial	—	—	275.00	—	475.00	—
Creamer	225.00	375.00	55.00	175.00	175.00	275.00
Goblet	—	—	150.00	—	350.00	—
Pickle dish	125.00	375.00	75.00	150.00	110.00	275.00
Pitcher	325.00	—	95.00	225.00	275.00	1,500.00
Relish dish, oval	165.00	425.00	65.00	235.00	150.00	375.00
Saltshaker	325.00	—	150.00	—	—	425.00
Sauce dish, round, flat						
4" d.	—	225.00	20.00	50.00	—	175.00
4-1/2" d.	—	50.00	20.00	—	85.00	—
Spoon holder	135.00	325.00	65.00	150.00	135.00	225.00
Sugar bowl, covered	250.00	400.00	85.00	175.00	225.00	375.00
Tumbler, water						
Type-1 (Pattern to top)	—	—	65.00	85.00	—	300.00
Type-2	275.00	—	85.00	—	200.00	—
Wine	—	—	225.00	—	300.00	425.00

TENNESSEE

OMN: U.S. Glass No. 15,064-Tennessee.
AKA: Jewel and Crescent, Jeweled Rosette(s), Scrolls with BULL'S EYE.

Non-flint. The United States Glass Company, Pittsburgh, PA, at Factory "K," c.1899.

Original color production: Clear (plain, with colored jewels).

Reproductions and Look-a-Likes: None known.

Tennessee cake stand on high standard.

Tennessee milk pitcher.

Known items:	Clear
Bowl, round, flat	
Covered	
6" d.	$95.00
7" d.	110.00
8" d.	125.00
Open with flared rim	
6" d.	35.00
7" d.	40.00
8" d.	50.00

Known items:	Clear
Butter dish, covered	95.00
Cake stand on high standard	
8-1/2" d.	65.00
9-1/2" d.	85.00
10-1/2" d.	110.00
Celery vase	65.00
Compote, round	
Covered on high standard	
5" d.	75.00
6" d.	95.00
7" d.	110.00
8" d.	125.00
Open	
High standard	
Deep bowl	
5" d.	35.00
6" d.	40.00
7" d.	45.00
8" d.	50.00
Saucer-shaped bowl	
7" d.	45.00
8" d.	55.00
9" d.	65.00
10" d.	85.00
Low standard, 7" d.	45.00
Creamer	55.00
Cruet with applied handle and original stopper	225.00
Goblet (S)	225.00
Mug with handle	45.00
Pickle dish, oblong with double handles	20.00
Pitcher	
Milk, 1-qt.	150.00
Water, 1/2-gal.	225.00

Tennessee sugar bowl, butter dish, spoon holder, and creamer.

Tennessee celery vase, syrup, goblet, and milk pitcher.

Known items:	Clear
Plate, bread, oblong	45.00
Preserve dish, 8" l.	35.00
Relish tray	25.00
Saltshaker	85.00
Sauce dish, round, flat	15.00
Spoon holder	55.00
Sugar bowl, covered	85.00
Syrup pitcher	450.00
Toothpick holder (R)	175.00
Tumbler, water, flat	65.00
Wine	125.00

Tepee true open compote on high standard.

TEPEE

OMN: Duncan No. 128-Arizona. **AKA:** Nemesis, Teepee, Wigwam.

Non-flint. George Duncan's Sons & Company, Washington, PA, c. 1896.

Original color production: Clear. Clear with ruby stain or any other color would be considered rare.

Reproductions and Look-a-Likes: None known.

Known items:	Clear
Bowl, open, round, flat, master berry	$30.00
Butter dish with cover	55.00
Carafe	65.00
Celery vase	35.00
Champagne, saucer bowl	35.00
Cheese dish, covered	85.00
Claret	30.00
Compote, open, round on high standard (Jelly)	20.00
Creamer, 4-1/4" h.	35.00

Tepee goblet.

Known items:	Clear
Cup, custard	10.00
Dish, oval, vegetable	
8-3/4" l.	25.00
9-3/4" l.	35.00
Goblet	35.00
Pitcher, water, 1/2-gal.	75.00
Relish tray	15.00
Sauce dish, round, flat.	5.00
Salt	
Dip, individual	8.00
Shaker	30.00
Spoon holder	30.00
Sugar bowl with cover	45.00
Syrup pitcher	85.00
Toothpick holder	30.00
Tumbler	
Bar	25.00
Juice	15.00
Lemonade	30.00
Water	25.00
Wine	20.00

TEXAS

OMN: U.S. Glass No. 15,067-Texas. **AKA:** Loop with Stippled Panels.

Non-flint. The United States Glass Company, Pittsburgh, PA, at Factory "K", c. 1900.

Original color production: Clear, clear with rose stain (plain, gilded). Clear with ruby stain or any other color would be considered rare.

Reproductions and Look-a-Likes: Individual creamer, individual sugar bowl (amber, amber dark, amethyst, amberina, aqua, blue bell, clear, carnival amethyst, carnival, carnival dark cobalt, cobalt, Cambridge, Crown Tuscan, custard, emerald green, milk blue, milk white, opalescent, peach blow, pine green, red, ruby, sapphire, vaseline, white, willow blue). Crystal Art Glass Company, Cambridge, OH. From 1962 through 1972, each item was identified with a hand-stamped mark. From 1972 through 1978, items were permanently marked with a "D" within a heart signifying the Crystal Art Glass Company. When Bernard Boyd, Cambridge, OH, acquired the Crystal Art Glass Company, the Texas individual creamer and open sugar bowl were issued in delphinium and the mark was changed to an embossed "B" within a diamond signifying Boyd.

Wine (with flared bowl: cobalt blue, willow blue; with straight-sided bowl: clear). Boyd's Crystal Art Glass for the Degenhart Paperweight and Glass Museum. Unmarked.

Known items:	Clear	Clear w/Rose Blush
Bottle, water	$175.00	$350.00
Bowl, round		
Covered on low circular foot		
6" d.	110.00	225.00
7" d.	125.00	250.00
8" d.	175.00	275.00
Open		
Collared base		
6" d.	50.00	95.00
7" d.	60.00	110.00
8" d.	75.00	150.00
Flat, flared rim		
Scalloped		
7-1/2" d.	35.00	85.00
8-1/2" d.	55.00	110.00
9-1/2" d.	75.00	150.00

Texas covered bowl.

Texas covered butter.

Known items:	Clear	Clear w/Rose Blush
Smooth rim		
7-1/2" d. 35.00		85.00
8-1/2" d. 45.00		110.00
9-1/2" d. 85.00		175.00
Bread tray 85.00		175.00
Butter dish with cover. 150.00		325.00
Cake stand on high standard with galleried rim		
9" d. 150.00		325.00
9-1/2" d. 175.00		350.00
10" d. 200.00		375.00
10-1/2" d. 250.00		425.00
11" d. 325.00		550.00
Celery		
Tray, oblong with tab handles, 11-1/2" l. 40.00		85.00
Vase 125.00		275.00
Compote, round on high standard		
Covered		
6" d. 250.00		375.00
7" d. 275.00		400.00
8" d. 325.00		500.00
Open		
With smooth flared rim		
7-1/2" d. 95.00		225.00
8-1/2" d. 110.00		250.00
9-1/2" d. 125.00		325.00
With smooth straight rim		
5" d. 55.00		125.00
6" d. 65.00		150.00

Known items:	Clear	Clear w/Rose Blush
7" d. 85.00		175.00
8" d. 110.00		225.00
Creamer		
Individual 20.00		55.00
Table size with cover and applied handle 125.00		275.00
Cruet with original patterned stopper. 125.00		375.00
Dish, open, round with scalloped rim, 8" d. 65.00		125.00
Goblet 95.00		275.00
Horseradish with original notched cover 150.00		375.00
Olive dish, oblong. 20.00		45.00
Pickle tray, oblong with tab handles, 8-1/2" l. 30.00		85.00
Pitcher, water		
Bulbous with applied handle, 1/2-gal. 375.00		750.00
Straight-sided with inverted design and pressed handle, 3-pts. 225.00		450.00
Plate, round with scalloped rim, 9" d. 110.00		175.00
Relish tray 25.00		55.00
Salt		
Master, open, footed. 125.00		250.00
Shaker		
Hotel (tall). 150.00		325.00
Table (squat) 125.00		200.00

Texas wine.

Texas water pitcher with inverted design.

Known items:	Clear	Clear w/Rose Blush
Sauce dish, round		
Flat		
Round with flared rim, 4-1/2" d.	15.00	35.00
Straight-sided bowl, 4" d.		
Scalloped rim	15.00	45.00
Smooth rim	15.00	30.00
Footed		
Round bowl with smooth rim, 4" d.	20.00	35.00
Straight-sided bowl with flared rim, 5" d.	25.00	55.00

Texas open master berry bowl.

Known items:	Clear	Clear w/Rose Blush
Spoon holder	125.00	275.00
Sugar bowl with cover		
Individual	30.00	65.00
Table size	150.00	275.00
Syrup pitcher	275.00	650.00
Toothpick holder	35.00	150.00
Tumbler, water, flat with inverted design	95.00	175.00
Vase		
6-1/2" h.	25.00	55.00
8" h.	35.00	65.00
9'" h.	45.00	75.00
10" h.	55.00	85.00
Wine	55.00	175.00

TEXAS BULL'S EYE

OMN: Beatty No. 1221 (only tumbler). Bryce's Filley. **AKA:** Bull's Eye Variant, Notched Bull's Eye.

Non-flint. Bryce Brothers, Pittsburgh, PA, c. 1875-1880. A.J. Beatty & Sons, Steubenville, OH, c. 1888. The United States Glass Company, Pittsburgh, PA, after 1891. Also known to have been produced by the Diamond Glass Company, Ltd., Montreal, Quebec, Canada, c. 1902.

Original color production: Clear.

Reproductions and Look-a-Likes: None known.

Texas Bull's Eye creamer.

Texas Bull's Eye spoon holder.

Known items:	Clear
Butter dish with cover.	$65.00
Cake stand on high standard (VR)	175.00
Castor set complete in silver plate holder	225.00
Celery vase	35.00
Champagne, 5" h.	65.00
Creamer.	45.00
Eggcup, open, footed	30.00
Goblet	30.00
Lamp, oil on pedestaled base, 5-1/2" h.	125.00

Known items:	Clear
Pitcher, water, 1/2-gal.	110.00
Sauce dish, round, flat	5.00
Spoon holder	35.00
Sugar bowl with cover	55.00
Tumbler, water	
Flat	35.00
Footed.	20.00
Wine	25.00

THISTLE

AKA: Early Thistle, Scotch Thistle.

Non-flint. Bryce, McKee & Company, Pittsburgh, PA, c. 1872.

Original color production: Clear. Designed by John Bryce and patented April 2, 1872, under U.S. Patent No. 5,742.

Reproductions and Look-a-Likes: Goblet (clear). Maker unknown. Permanently embossed with a clear "R" within a large shield.

Known items:	Clear
Bowl, round with cover, 8" d.	$325.00
Butter dish with cover, 7" d.	225.00
Cake stand on high standard	350.00
Compote	
Covered	
High standard	
6" d.	225.00
7" d.	275.00
8" d.	325.00
Low standard	
6" d.	175.00
7" d.	225.00
8" d.	275.00
Open	
High standard	
6" d.	85.00
7" d.	110.00
8" d.	135.00

Thistle goblet

Known items:	Clear
Low standard	
6" d.	75.00
7" d.	85.00
8" d.	110.00
Creamer with applied handle	150.00
Dish, open, oval, 9" l.	55.00
Eggcup, open, single	85.00
Goblet	125.00
Pickle dish with taper at one end	35.00
Pitcher with applied handle	
Milk, 1-qt.	250.00
Water, 1/2-gal.	325.00
Relish tray, oval	45.00
Salt, master, open, footed	75.00
Sauce dish, round, flat, 4" d.	20.00
Spoon holder	65.00
Sugar bowl with cover	175.00
Syrup pitcher	350.00
Tumbler, water	
Flat	150.00
Footed	85.00
Wine	150.00

THOUSAND EYE

OMN: Richards & Hartley No. 103-Daisy.

Non-flint. Richards & Hartley Glass Company, Tarentum, PA, c.1880. The United States Glass Company, Pittsburgh, PA, at Factory "E," c. 1891.

Original color production: Amber, blue, clear, vaseline, opalescent colors. Produced in two conspicuous forms: (a) stems composed of three knobs (Adams & Company) and (b) plain stems with scalloped feet (Richards & Hartley).

Reproductions and Look-a-Likes: Ball-shaped perfume bottle; 3-1/2" d. ivy bowl; covered puff box; saucer-bowl champagne; cocktail; open compotes: with crimped rim: 5" d., 6" d.; 5-1/2" d. open compote with plain rim; cordial; cruet with applied handle and ball stopper; goblet; hats: 2" h., 4" h.; mug; single knob stem sherbet; toothpick holder; twine holder; tumblers: 2-oz. (whiskey), 5-oz. (juice), 7-oz. (old-fashioned), 10-oz. (water), 12-oz., 14-oz. (iced tea); 3" d. crimped rim vase; wine (amber, amberina, blue, clear, canary yellow, green, ruby). New Martinsville Glass Company and the Viking Glass Company, New Martinsville, WV, unmarked.

Turtle-shaped ashtray; 8" l. flat handled basket; open bowls: 10" d. with double handles, (11" d. (belled), 11" d. (crimped), 11" d. (flared), triangular; turtle-shaped covered cigarette box; candlestick: double, single; 5-oz. claret; 32-oz. cocktail; 5" d. open compote, 1-oz. cordial; creamer; cup and saucer set; 8-oz. goblet; footed mayonnaise; 7-1/2" d. round handled nappy; parfait; pitcher with pressed handle; plates: 6" d., 7" d., 8-1/2" d., 10" d., 14" d.; sectioned relish; footed saltshaker; flat sauce dish; footed sherbet; 3-oz. sherry; open handled sugar bowl; tumblers, flat: 12-oz. (whiskey), 5-oz. (ginger ale), 6-oz. (old-fashioned), 8-oz. (water), 12-oz. (iced tea); tumblers, footed: 5-oz. (ginger ale), 7-oz., 9-oz. (water), 12-oz. (iced tea); 2-oz. wine (clear, clear with ruby stain). Westmoreland Glass Company, Grapeville, PA, unmarked.

Thousand Eye, (Richards & Hartley) pitcher.

Thousand Eye, (Richards & Hartley) twine holder.

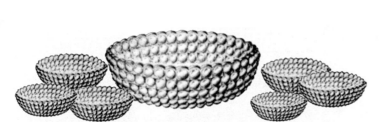

Thousand Eye, (Richards & Hartley) seven-piece berry set.

Thousand Eye, (Richards & Hartley) four-piece table set.

Known items:	Amber	Blue	Clear	Opalescent	Vaseline
Bowl					
Round, open, flat					
5" d.	$10.00	$12.50	$10.00	$20.00	$15.00
6" d.	20.00	25.00	20.00	45.00	35.00
8" d.	30.00	35.00	25.00	85.00	45.00
Butter dish with cover, round, footed					
Dome lid.	75.00	95.00	65.00	275.00	110.00
Flat lid.	95.00	110.00	85.00	325.00	135.00
Celery vase	50.00	65.00	45.00	125.00	85.00
Compote, round, open, low standard, 8" d.	35.00	45.00	35.00	95.00	50.00
Creamer with pressed handle	40.00	45.00	35.00	850.00	50.00
Cruet, with original patterned stopper	135.00	175.00	125.00	350.00	175.00
Pitcher					
Milk, 1-qt.	110.00	135.00	110.00	275.00	150.00
Water, 1/2-gal.	135.00	150.00	135.00	325.00	175.00
Saltshaker, straight-sided	30.00	35.00	30.00	75.00	40.00
Sauce dish, round, footed, 4" d.	8.00	10.00	8.00	20.00	12.50
Spoon holder	35.00	45.00	30.00	85.00	50.00
String holder, 4" h.	185.00	225.00	175.00	650.00	275.00
Sugar bowl with cover	55.00	75.00	55.00	175.00	85.00
Toothpick holder					
Hat shaped.	25.00	35.00	25.00	95.00	40.00
Regular.	20.00	30.00	20.00	75.00	35.00

THOUSAND EYE (Adams)

OMN: Adams' No. 130. **AKA:** Banded Thousand Eye, Three Knob.

Non-flint. Adams & Company, Pittsburgh, PA, c. 1874. The United States Glass Company, Pittsburgh, PA, at Factory "A," c. 1891.

Original color production: Amber, blue, clear, green, vaseline. Produced in two conspicuous forms: (a) stems composed of three knobs (Adams & Company) and (b) plain stems with scalloped feet (Richards & Hartley).

Reproductions and Look-a-Likes: Ball-shaped perfume bottle; 3-1/2" d. ivy bowl; covered puff box; saucer-bowl champagne; cocktail; open compotes: with crimped rim: 5" d., 6" d.; 5-1/2" d. open compote with plain rim; cordial; cruet with applied handle and ball stopper; goblet; hats: 2" h., 4" h.; mug; single knob stem sherbet; toothpick holder; twine holder; tumblers: 2-oz. (whiskey), 5-oz. (juice), 7-oz. (old-fashioned), 10-oz. (water), 12-oz., 14-oz. (iced tea); 3" d. crimped rim vase; wine (amber, amberina, blue, clear, canary yellow, green, ruby). New Martinsville Glass Company and the Viking Glass Company, New Martinsville, WV, unmarked.

Turtle-shaped ashtray; 8" l. flat handled basket; open bowls: 10" d. with double handles, (11" d. (belled), 11" d. (crimped), 11" d. (flared), triangular; turtle-shaped covered cigarette box; candlestick: double, single; 5-oz. claret; 32-oz. cocktail; 5" d. open compote, 1-oz. cordial; creamer; cup and saucer set; 8-oz. goblet; footed mayonnaise; 7-1/2" d. round handled nappy; parfait; pitcher with pressed handle; plates: 6" d., 7" d., 8-1/2" d., 10" d., 14" d.; sectioned relish; footed saltshaker; flat sauce dish; footed sherbet; 3-oz. sherry; open handled sugar bowl; tumblers, flat: 12-oz. (whiskey), 5-oz. (ginger ale), 6-oz. (old-fashioned), 8-oz. (water), 12-oz. (iced tea); tumblers, footed: 5-oz. (ginger ale), 7-oz., 9-oz. (water), 12-oz. (iced tea); 2-oz. wine (clear, clear with ruby stain). Westmoreland Glass Company, Grapeville, PA, unmarked.

Thousand Eye (Adams) compote.

Thousand Eye (Adams) cruet.

Thousand Eye, (Adams) covered honey dish.

Known items:	Amber	Blue	Clear	Green	Vaseline
ABC plate with "clock" center, 6" d.	$75.00	$95.00	$65.00	$125.00	$150.00
Bottle, cologne	100.00	125.00	95.00	150.00	135.00
Bowl					
Carriage-shaped	65.00	150.00	55.00	175.00	225.00
Round, open, flat					
5" d.	10.00	12.50	10.00	20.00	15.00
6" d.	20.00	25.00	20.00	35.00	35.00
8" d.	30.00	35.00	25.00	45.00	45.00
Butter dish with cover, footed	85.00	125.00	65.00	150.00	175.00
Cake stand on high standard					
Closed lattice edge					
10" d.	125.00	150.00	110.00	175.00	175.00
11" d.	135.00	175.00	125.00	185.00	185.00
Open lattice edge					
10" d.	175.00	200.00	175.00	225.00	225.00
11" d.	200.00	225.00	200.00	250.00	250.00
Celery vase	110.00	125.00	95.00	150.00	150.00
Christmas light	45.00	85.00	35.00	95.00	110.00
Compote					
Round					
Covered					
High standard					
6" d.	150.00	175.00	125.00	175.00	175.00
7-1/2" d.	175.00	200.00	150.00	225.00	225.00
8-3/4" d.	275.00	325.00	250.00	350.00	350.00
Low standard					
7-1/2" d.	110.00	135.00	85.00	150.00	175.00
Open					
Round, low standard					
6" d.	25.00	35.00	20.00	35.00	40.00
7" d.	35.00	55.00	25.00	55.00	55.00
8-3/4" d.	55.00	75.00	35.00	75.00	85.00
9-3/4" d.	65.00	85.00	45.00	85.00	95.00
Square, 8"					
High standard	125.00	150.00	95.00	150.00	175.00
Low standard	85.00	95.00	55.00	95.00	110.00
Creamer					
Blown	85.00	125.00	65.00	175.00	175.00
Pressed	35.00	45.00	35.00	55.00	65.00
Cruet with original patterned stopper	85.00	135.00	75.00	175.00	200.00
Cruet stand, holds 2 cruets with center handle	110.00	150.00	100.00	175.00	225.00

Known items:	Amber	Blue	Clear	Green	Vaseline
Eggcup, open, footed	65.00	85.00	55.00	110.00	95.00
Goblet	40.00	55.00	35.00	85.00	65.00
Honey dish with cover, square, 6" x 7-1/4"	135.00	175.00	110.00	225.00	200.00
Inkwell	55.00	85.00	45.00	110.00	125.00
Lamp, kerosene					
High standard					
Matching Thousand Eye patterned font					
12" h.	275.00	450.00	225.00	550.00	550.00
15" h.	325.00	650.00	250.00	750.00	750.00
Non-matching font					
12" h.	150.00	150.00	135.00	175.00	175.00
15" h.	175.00	175.00	150.00	200.00	200.00
On low standard with handle	125.00	135.00	125.00	150.00	175.00
Mug					
2" h.	25.00	35.00	25.00	45.00	45.00
3" h.	35.00	45.00	35.00	55.00	55.00
Pickle dish	20.00	25.00	20.00	25.00	30.00
Pitcher					
Lemonade, blown	175.00	375.00	150.00	450.00	475.00
Milk with cover (sanitary), 7" h. (R)	150.00	250.00	135.00	275.00	250.00
Water					
1/2-gal.	135.00	150.00	125.00	150.00	175.00
1-gal.	175.00	225.00	150.00	225.00	225.00
Plate, square with folded corners					
5"	15.00	25.00	15.00	30.00	35.00
6"	20.00	30.00	20.00	35.00	40.00
7"	25.00	35.00	25.00	40.00	45.00
8"	30.00	45.00	30.00	50.00	55.00
10"	35.00	55.00	35.00	65.00	75.00
Platter					
Oblong, 8" x 11-1/2"	50.00	85.00	40.00	95.00	110.00
Oval, 11" l.	55.00	100.00	45.00	110.00	125.00
Salt					
Master, cart shaped	60.00	95.00	55.00	110.00	125.00
Shaker, banded	35.00	55.00	30.00	75.00	65.00
Sauce dish, round, 4" d.					
Flat	8.00	12.50	5.00	15.00	15.00
Footed	10.00	15.00	8.00	20.00	20.00
Spoon holder	35.00	45.00	35.00	45.00	55.00
Sugar bowl with cover	65.00	85.00	55.00	95.00	100.00
Syrup pitcher	135.00	175.00	125.00	225.00	250.00

Known items:	Amber	Blue	Clear	Green	Vaseline
Toothpick holder, thimble shaped	55.00	85.00	25.00	95.00	110.00
Tray, water					
Oval, 14" l.	95.00	150.00	85.00	175.00	200.00
Round, 12-1/2" d.	100.00	175.00	95.00	200.00	225.00
Tumbler, water, flat	35.00	55.00	30.00	65.00	65.00
Wine	65.00	110.00	55.00	125.00	135.00

THREE FACE

OMN: Duncan No. 400. **AKA:** The Sisters, Three Sisters, Three Graces, Three Fates.

Non-flint. George Duncan & Sons, Pittsburgh, PA, c. 1878.

Original color production: Clear with acid finish. Designed by John Ernest Miller and patented June 18,1878 under U.S. Patent No. 10,727. **Note:** Bases, finials and stems are frosted.

Reproductions and Look-a-Likes: 9" h. candlestick with petal socket; 6" d. high-standard open compote, 9-1/2" h. covered cracker jar; 9-1/2" d. high standard cake stand; saucer-shaped champagne, 3" h. saltshaker (clear and frosted). Imperial Glass Corporation, Bellaire, OH, in accord with the Metropolitan Museum of Glass. Permanently embossed with the "MMA" insignia of the museum.

Covered compote on high standard: 4" d., 6" d.; creamer with head under lip; goblet; oil lamp with plain fond; individual salt dip; saltshaker; round footed sauce dish; sherbet; spoon holder; covered sugar bowl; sugar shaker; toothpick holder; wine (amber satin, blue satin, clear with frosting). L.G. Wright Glass company, New Martinsville, WV, unmarked.

Three Face water pitcher.

Known items:	Clear w/Frosting
Celery vase	
With plain rim (S)	275.00
With fluted rim	200.00
Champagne	
With hollow stem, 4" h.	5,500.00
With solid stem, 5-1/2" h.	450.00
With saucer-bowl and solid stem	2,250.00
Claret, 4-1/2" h.	350.00
Compote, round	
Covered	
High standard	
Beaded rim	
7" d.	1,850.00
8" d.	2,000.00
9" d.	2,500.00
Plain rim	
6" d.	275.00
7" d.	325.00

Known items:	Clear w/Frosting
Biscuit jar with cover	$4,500.00
Butter dish with cover	225.00
Cake stand on high standard	
8" d. (S)	550.00
9" d.	375.00
10" d.	425.00
11" d.	555.00

Three Face rare champagne.

Three Face close up of cake standard.

Three Face etched goblet.

Three Face high-standard cake stand.

Known items:	Clear w/Frosting
8" d.	450.00
9" d.	750.00
Low standard, deep bowl, 6" d.	1,250.00
Open	
High standard	
Beaded rim	
7" d.	1,250.00
8" d.	1,500.00
9" d.	1,750.00
10" d.	3,500.00

Known items:	Clear w/Frosting
Huber paneled bowl, 4-1/2" d. (jelly) (ER)	4,500.00
Plain rim	
6" d.	100.00
7" d.	135.00
8" d.	175.00
9" d.	275.00
10" d.	650.00
Low standard, deep bowl, 6" d.	325.00

Three Face butter dish, creamer, spoon holder, and sugar bowl.

Three Face rare set of etched oil lamps.

Known items:	Clear w/Frosting
Creamer	
With *"face"* under spout	175.00
Without *"face"* under spout	275.00
Goblet	175.00
Lamp, oil, oil, high standard	
Plain font	
7-1/2" h.	325.00
8-1/2" h.	275.00
9-1/2" h.	425.00
Pressed design on font	
7-1/2" h.	1,250.00
8-1/2" h.	1,000.00
9-1/2" h.	1,800.00
Marmalade jar with cover (stag jar with pheasant finial)	375.00
Pitcher	
Milk, 1-qt.	2,250.00
Water, 1/2-gal.	1,250.00
Salt	
Dip, individual	15.00
Shaker	55.00

Known items:	Clear w/Frosting
Sauce dish, round, footed	
4" d.	35.00
4-1/2" d.	35.00
Spoon holder	125.00
Sugar bowl with cover	200.00
Wine, 4" h.	325.00

THREE PANEL

OMN: Richards & Hartley No. 25. **AKA:** Button and Buckle, Paneled Thousand Eye, Thousand Eye Three Panel.

Non-flint. Richards & Harley Glass Company, Tarentum, PA, c. 1880s. The United States Glass Company, Pittsburgh, PA, at Factory "E," c. 1891.

Original color production: Amber, blue, clear, vaseline.

Reproductions and Look-a-Likes: None.

Three Panel covered butter.

Three Panel four-Three panel four-piee table set.

Three Panel spoon holder.

Three Panel low-footed open compotes and ruffled rim celery vase.

Known items:	Amber	Blue	Clear	Vaseline
Bowl, open, round on low foot				
With deep bowl				
8-1/2" d.	$25.00	$35.00	$25.00	$45.00
9-1/2" d.	30.00	40.00	30.00	50.00
10" d.	35.00	50.00	35.00	55.00
With flared rim, 8" d.	30.00	40.00	30.00	50.00
With scalloped rim				
7" d.	25.00	35.00	25.00	45.00
8" d.	30.00	45.00	30.00	55.00
Butter dish with cover				
With flanged cover	95.00	125.00	95.00	125.00
With regular cover	85.00	110.00	85.00	110.00
Celery vase				
With flared rim	35.00	55.00	35.00	65.00
With ruffled rim	45.00	75.00	45.00	85.00
With plain rim	30.00	50.00	30.00	55.00

Known items:	Amber	Blue	Clear	Vaseline
7" d.	25.00	30.00	25.00	35.00
8" d.	30.00	35.00	30.00	40.00
9" d.	35.00	40.00	35.00	45.00
10" d.	40.00	45.00	40.00	55.00
Creamer	35.00	45.00	35.00	50.00
Cruet with applied handle and original stopper (R)	175.00	275.00	150.00	275.00
Goblet	30.00	55.00	25.00	55.00
Mug				
Large	30.00	45.00	25.00	45.00
Small	25.00	40.00	20.00	40.00

Known items:	Amber	Blue	Clear	Vaseline
Pitcher				
Milk, 1-qt.	85.00	125.00	75.00	150.00
Water, 1/2-gal.	75.00	110.00	65.00	125.00
Saltshaker, tall (VR)	65.00	95.00	45.00	100.00
Sauce dish round, footed, 4" d.	5.00	10.00	5.00	15.00
Spoon holder	30.00	45.00	30.00	55.00
Sugar bowl, covered	55.00	85.00	55.00	95.00
Tumbler, water, flat	35.00	65.00	30.00	75.00

THREE STORIES

OMN: Persian. **AKA:** Block and Pleat, Small Block and Prism.

Non-flint. Bryce, Higbee & Company, Homestead, PA, c. 1886.

Original color production: Clear.

Reproductions and Look-a-Likes: None known.

Three Stories goblet.

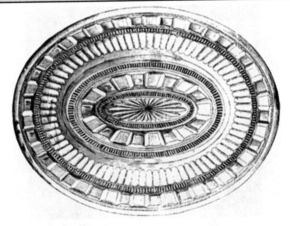

Three Stories platter.

Known items:	Clear
Bowl, open, flat	
Oval	
8" l.	$25.00
9" l.	30.00
10" l.	35.00
Round	
6" d.	20.00
7" d.	30.00
8" d.	40.00
Bread tray, oval	35.00

Known items:	Clear
Butter dish with cover	55.00
Celery vase	45.00
Compote, covered on high standard	
6" d.	55.00
7" d.	65.00
8" d.	85.00
Creamer	35.00
Goblet	35.00
Mug with pressed handle	30.00
Pickle dish, flat with double handles	15.00
Pitcher, water with pressed handle, 2-gal.	85.00
Sauce dish, round	
Flat, 5" d.	5.00
Footed, 4" d.	8.00
Spoon holder	30.00
Sugar bowl with cover	40.00
Tumbler, water, flat	25.00
Wine	15.00

Three Stories celery vase.

THUMBPRINT

AKA: Argus, Argus Thumbprint, Early Thumbprint, Giant Baby Thumbprint, Heavy Argus, Light Argus.

Flint. Bakewell, Pears & Company, Pittsburgh, PA, c. 1850-1860. Various factories including Challinor, King, McKee and Tarentum.

Original color production: Clear. Milk white or any other color would be considered rare.

Reproductions and Look-a-Likes: Flat ashtray: 6-1/2" d., 7" d., oval; baskets: 6-1/2" d. oval, 8" h., handled, 8-1/2" h. with ruffled rim and applied clear handle; bowls, covered: 3-toed oval; bowls, open: flat with scalloped rim, low footed: 8" d. with ruffled rim, 12" d. with ruffled rim; flat covered butter dish: 3-pound oval, round; cake stands: low standard, 13" d. footed with ruffled rim; candle holder: 4" h., 8-1/4" h.; covered candy jar; covered oval 4-toed candy box; 8" h. chalice; chip and dip set; cigarette lighter; compotes: covered on high standard, 7" d. covered on low standard; compotes: open on high standard: with ruffled rim, footed with ruffled rim, footed with plain stem, low footed with ruffled rim; creamer with pressed handle; 8" d.

round flat bonbon dish; 9" h., 3-lily, 4-piece epergne with ruffled rim; 10-oz. goblet; lamp, student with matching shade: 19-1/2" h., 20-1/2" h.; 13-1/2" h. 2-piece lavabo; water pitchers: 2-qt. with ice lip, 34-oz. with plain lip; bulbous 60-oz. with applied handle; hanging planter: 4-1/2" sq., 10"; 8-1/2" d. round plate; 15-piece punch set (2-piece bowl with 12 cups and ladle); 8-1/2" d. 4-part divided relish; saltshakers: bulbous, tall with foot; flat scalloped sauce dish; sherbet; flat covered sugar bowl; tidbit set (2-tier with 9" and 13" plates); tumblers: 6-oz. (flat juice), 12-oz. (water), 13-oz. (footed iced tea); vases: swung footed bud, 8" h. footed with scalloped rim, footed bud with slender neck; 5-oz. wine (Colonial amber, colonial blue, colonial green, colonial pink, clear, cased ruby overlay, ebony, milk white, orange, ruby). Fenton Art Glass Company, Williamstown, WV. When marked, embossed with an "OV" or the Fenton logo.

Thumbprint covered salt.

Known items:	Clear
Ale glass, pony	
Short	$85.00
Tall	400.00
Bottle	
Bitters	95.00
Castor	
Mustard	55.00
Oil with original stopper	95.00
Shaker	65.00

Thumbprint spooner.

Thumbprint open compote.

Known items: **Clear**
Cologne............................ 150.00
Water with tumbler..................... 450.00

Bowl, round
  Covered, flat
    6-1/4" d............................. 125.00
    8" d.................................. 175.00
  Open
    Flat, 8" d. 45.00
    Footed
      5-3/4" d. 45.00
      7-1/4" d. 55.00
      9-1/4" d. 75.00

Butter dish with cover
  Flat.................................. 125.00
  Footed 150.00

Cake stand
  High standard
    8" d................................. 375.00
    9" d................................. 425.00

    10" d................................ 475.00
    11" d................................ 550.00
    12" d................................ 650.00
    13-1/4" d............................ 950.00
    15" d................................1,250.00
  Low standard, 7-3/4" d. 325.00

Celery vase
  With patterned base 325.00
  With plain base 225.00

Thumbprint decanter.

Known items: **Clear**
Champagne 95.00
Claret (jelly glass) 175.00

Compote, round
  Covered
    On high standard
      Dome lid (ball form), double step
      hollow stem
        7" d......................... 4,500.00
        8" d......................... 5,500.00
        10" d........................ 9,500.00

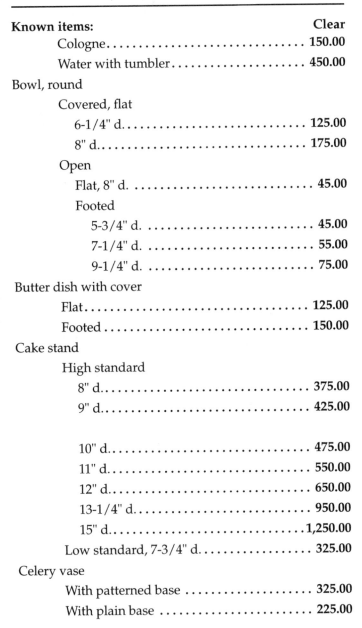

Thumbprint high standard covered compote.

Thumbprint oil lamp on marble base.

Thumbprint tall covered compote.

Known items: **Clear**

Flat lid, double step hollow stem

    6-1/4" d. 550.00

    7-1/4" d. 750.00

    8-1/4" d. 950.00

Flat lid, hexagonal knop stem

    6" d. 125.00

    7" d. 150.00

Known items: **Clear**

    8" d. 225.00

    9" d. 275.00

    On low standard, 7" d. 135.00

    Open, high standard, deep flaring bowls,

      double step hollow stem

      9" d. 450.00

      10-1/2" d. 850.00

      11-1/2" d. 1,250.00

Creamer, 5-3/4" h. 175.00

Decanter

    Bar lip

      Pint. 225.00

      Quart, 10" h. 275.00

    Original stopper

      Pint. 425.00

      Quart 550.00

Eggcup, open, single, pedestaled 65.00

Flip glass, 7" h. 1,200.00

Goblet

    Knob stem 95.00

    Plain stem 135.00

Honey dish, round, flat 15.00

Inkwell with original patterned lid 1,200.00

Mug, whiskey with applied handle

    Flat 150.00

    Footed, 3-1/2" h. 250.00

Paperweight. 650.00

Known items:	Clear
Pitcher, water with applied handle	
Milk, 1-qt.	1,250.00
Water, 1/2-gal.	1,000.00
Plate, round, 8" d.	100.00
Punch bowl on high standard, 14" d., 12" h.	8,500.00
Salt, master, open, footed	45.00
Sauce dish, round, flat.	10.00
Spoon holder	65.00
Sugar bowl with cover	110.00
Syrup pitcher	1,000.00
Tumbler	
Ships, flared rim, heavy base, 4-1/4" h.	275.00
Water	
Flat, 3-1/2" h.	85.00
Footed	
4-1/2" h.	65.00
5" h.	75.00
Whiskey	
Flat	75.00
Footed.	55.00
Wine	
With knob stem	65.00
With plain stem	35.00

Torpedo syrup.

Torpedo saltshaker.

TORPEDO

OMN: Thompson's No. 17. AKA: Fisheye, Pigmy. Non-flint. Thompson Glass Company, Uniontown, PA, c. 1889-1893.

Original color production: Clear, clear with ruby stain (plain, engraved). Black amethyst or any other color would be considered very rare.

Reproductions and Look-a-Likes: None known.

Known items:	Clear	Clear w/Ruby
Banana dish on high standard		
with folded sides, 9-3/4"	$375.00	—
Bowl, round		
Covered, flat		
7" d.	85.00	—
8" d.	110.00	225.00
Open		
Berry, master	45.00	75.00
Finger	55.00	95.00
Vegetable or fruit		
With flared rim		
7" d.	25.00	65.00
8" d.	30.00	85.00
9" d.	40.00	—
9-1/2" d.	45.00	—
With ruffled rim		
5-1/2" d.	35.00	—
10-1/2" d.	65.00	—
Butter dish with cover		
Quarter pound with		
flanged base	110.00	225.00
Table size	75.00	150.00

Torpedo goblet.

Known items:	Clear	Clear w/Ruby
Cake stand on high standard		
9" d.	175.00	—
10" d.	200.00	—
Celery vase	35.00	85.00
Compote, round		
Covered on high standard		
6" d.	85.00	—
7" d.	110.00	—
8" d.	135.00	—
Open on high standard		
4" d. with flared rim		
(Jelly)	55.00	—
7-1/2" d.	35.00	—
8-1/2" d.	45.00	—
9-1/2" d.	55.00	—
Creamer with applied handle		
Hotel size, 5-1/4" h.	95.00	150.00
Table size, 6" h.	65.00	125.00
Cruet with applied handle and		
original patterned stopper	175.00	—
Cup	35.00	55.00
Decanter with original patterned		
stopper, 8" h.	125.00	275.00
Goblet	65.00	95.00
Honey dish, round, flat, 3-1/2" d.	10.00	—
Lamp, oil		
Finger	95.00	—

Known items:	Clear	Clear w/Ruby
Stand on plain base with		
patterned font	125.00	—
Pitcher, tankard with applied handle		
Milk		
7" h. (R)	175.00	275.00
8-1/2" h.	100.00	150.00
Water, 10-1/2" h.,1/2-gal.	125.00	250.00
Rose bowl (S)	85.00	—
Salt		
Individual, round	35.00	55.00
Master, round, flat	75.00	95.00
Shaker		
Squat	65.00	100.00
Tall	75.00	110.00
Sauce dish, round		
Flat		
4-1/2" d.	15.00	25.00
5-1/2" d.	15.00	25.00
Footed		
4-1/2" d.	18.00	—
5-1/2" d.	18.00	—
Spoon holder	45.00	85.00
Sugar bowl with cover	85.00	135.00
Syrup pitcher	125.00	225.00
Tray, water		
Cloverleaf shaped,		
11-3/4"	225.00	—
Round, 10" d.	135.00	—
Tumbler, water, flat	55.00	75.00
Wine	125.00	225.00

TREE OF LIFE

Non-flint. Portland Glass Company, Portland, ME, c. 1870. Hobbs, Brockunier & Company, Wheeling, WV, c. 1879. Sandwich Glass Company, Sandwich, MA, c. 1870s.

Original color production: Clear (plain, engraved). Amber, amethyst, blue (light, dark), canary yellow, cranberry, green, or any other color would be considered rare. Designed by William O. Davis and patented circa 1876. Items may be discovered with the *"Davis"* name interwoven in the pattern of the base or impressed *"P.G.Co."*

Because the design was produced by various glass factories, the pattern can be divided into three categories: (a) **Portland:** The design is separated from the rim by a clear marginal band and covers both stem and base which is conical in shape and only colored items are attributed to Portland manufacture. (b) **Hobbs:** The design covers the entire item without a clear marginal band while bases and stems are unpatterned and items are melon-ribbed with hand stems and ribbed bases. (c) **Sandwich:** While items possess a clear marginal band around the rim like those of Portland manufacture, the design is more strongly defined with well-formed branches and stems which do not extend to either the standard or the base.

Reproductions and Look-a-Likes: 6" d. open bowl with crimped rim; compotes: open with crimped rim, 4" h. covered; 5" d. finger bowl; goblet; 5-1/2" crimped nappy; handled relish tray; 4" d. round sauce dish 3-toes; wine (amber, blue, clear). L.G. Wright Glass Company, New Martinsville, WV, unmarked.

Notes: Wright reproductions are distinguished by the addition of an "eternal flame" finial—an element not found on original pieces.

Tree of Life goblet. (Sandwich)

Tree of Life celery vase. (Portland)

Known items:	Clear
Bowl	
Oval, round, open, flat, master berry	$45.00
Round, open, flat	
Berry, master, 8" d.	55.00
Finger	45.00
Vegetable, 6-1/4" d.	35.00
Butter dish with cover	
Plain	150.00
Set in silver plate holder	175.00
Butter pat, round with scalloped rim	45.00
Celery vase	
Plain	110.00
Set in silver plate holder	135.00
Champagne	150.00
Claret	135.00

Known items:	Clear
Compote, round	
Covered on high standard	225.00
Open, 10" d.	
High standard	175.00
Low standard	125.00
Creamer, 6" h.	
Plain	75.00
Set in silver plate holder	95.00

Known items:	Clear
Dish, open, flat	
Oval	35.00
Rectangular	45.00
Epergne, single lily with under bowl	450.00
Goblet	110.00
Mug	95.00
Pitcher	
Milk, with applied handle, 1-qt.	225.00
Water, 1/2-gal.	
With applied handle	325.00
With pressed handle	85.00

Known items:	Clear
Plate, round, 6" d.	55.00
Salt, master, open, footed	35.00
Sauce dish	
Leaf-shaped	5.00
Round, flat	10.00
Spoon holder	
Plain	55.00
Set in silver plate holder	85.00
Sugar bowl with cover	
Plain	110.00
Set in silver plate holder	150.00
Toothpick holder, footed with scalloped rim	55.00
Tray	
Ice cream, tab-handled	65.00
Water	125.00
Tumbler, footed	65.00
Vase (several sizes)	95.00
Wine	100.00

TREE OF LIFE WITH HAND

OMN: Hobbs' No. 90 & No. 98 **AKA:** Pittsburgh Tree of Life.

Non-flint. Hobbs, Brockunier & Co., Wheeling, WV, c. 1879.

Original color production: Clear.

Reproductions and Look-a-Likes: None known.

Tree of Life with Hand covered compote.

Tree of Life with Hand finger bowl.

Known items:	Clear
Bowl, open, flat	
Oval, 9" l.	$45.00
Round	
Berry, scalloped rim	
6" d.	25.00
8" d.	55.00
10" d.	75.00
Finger or waste	45.00
Butter dish with cover	150.00
Butter pat	35.00
Cake stand (hand base)	325.00
Celery vase	125.00
Compote on high standard	
Covered, 6-1/2" d.	175.00

Tree of Life with Hand creamer.

TRIPLE TRIANGLE

OMN: Doyle No. 76. **AKA:** Triple Triangle-Red Top, Pillar, and Cut Diamond.

Non-flint. Doyle & Company, Pittsburgh, PA, c. 1890. The United States Glass Co., Pittsburgh, PA, at Factory "D" c. 1890-1895.

Original color production: Clear, clear with ruby stain (plain, engraved).

Reproductions and Look-a-Likes: Goblet, wine (clear), unmarked.

Triple Triangle clear with ruby covered butter.

Known items:	Clear
Open on high standard	
Hand base	
4" d.	85.00
6" d.	95.00
8" d.	110.00
10" d.	135.00
Infant Samuel base	275.00
Plain base	
4" d.	30.00
6" d.	35.00
8" d.	45.00
10" d.	65.00
Creamer	85.00
Epergne	
Hand base	
8" d.	425.00
10" d.	475.00
Infant Samuel base	875.00
Plain base	
8" d.	375.00
10" d.	425.00
Gas shade	95.00
Pitcher, water, 1/2-gal.	375.00
Sauce dish	
Flat, 4-1/2" d.	10.00
Footed	25.00
Spoon holder	75.00
Sugar bowl with cover	110.00

Known items:	Clear	Clear w/Ruby
Bowl, open, flat		
Rectangular with scalloped rim		
8" l.	$20.00	$55.00
9" l.	25.00	65.00
10" l.	30.00	95.00
Round		
6" d.	15.00	45.00
7" d.	20.00	55.00
8" d.	25.00	65.00
9" d.	35.00	110.00
Butter dish with cover and double handles	45.00	125.00
Celery vase	30.00	85.00
Creamer with pressed handle	30.00	65.00
Cup, custard with pressed handle	15.00	55.00
Goblet	30.00	65.00
Mug	20.00	45.00
Pickle tray, boat shaped	10.00	45.00

Triple Triangle creamer, butter dish, sugar bowl, and spoon holder.

Triple Triangle clear with ruby covered sugar bowl.

Known items:	Clear	Clear w/Ruby
Pitcher, water with pressed handle, 1/2-gal.	65.00	225.00
Plate, bread, rectangular	35.00	110.00
Sauce dish, round, flat, 5" d.	10.00	30.00
Spoon holder, double handled	25.00	75.00
Sugar bowl with cover	45.00	125.00
Tumbler, water, flat	20.00	55.00
Wine	15.00	45.00

TRUNCATED CUBE

OMN: Thompson No. 77.

Non-flint. Thompson Glass Company, Uniontown, PA, c. 1894.

Original color production: Clear, clear with ruby stain (plain, engraved).

Reproductions and Look-a-Likes: None known.

Truncated Cube creamer.

Known items:	Clear	Clear w/Ruby
Bowl, round, open, flat with folded-scalloped rim, 8" d., master berry	$30.00	$95.00
Butter dish with cover on flanged base	45.00	135.00
Celery vase	30.00	85.00
Cheese dish	55.00	225.00
Creamer with applied handle		
Individual	15.00	35.00
Table size	30.00	85.00
Cruet with pressed handle and original stopper	35.00	125.00
Decanter with original patterned stopper, 12" h.	45.00	225.00
Goblet	25.00	75.00
Pitcher with applied handle		
Milk, 1-qt.	35.00	110.00
Water, 1/2-gal.	40.00	150.00
Saltshaker	20.00	55.00
Sauce dish, round, flat, 4"d.	5.00	20.00
Spoon holder	25.00	65.00
Sugar bowl with cover		
Individual	15.00	35.00
Table size	35.00	110.00
Syrup pitcher with pressed handle		
Squat with design on lower section of body	55.00	150.00

Known items:	Clear	Clear w/Ruby
Tall with design on upper and lower section of body	65.00	175.00
Toothpick holder	20.00	45.00
Tray, water, round	30.00	75.00
Tumbler, water	20.00	45.00
Wine	15.00	35.00

TULIP WITH SAWTOOTH

OMN: Bryce No. 1-Tulip.

Flint, Non-flint. Bryce, Richards & Company, Pittsburgh, PA, c. 1854. United States Glass Company, Pittsburgh, PA, after 1891.

Original color production: Clear. Milk white, opalescent, or any other color would be considered very rare.

Reproductions and Look-a-Likes: Goblet, wine (clear Non-flint), unmarked.

Tulip with Saw Tooth master salt.

Tulip with Saw Tooth covered compote.

Known items:	Flint	Non-Flint
Bottle, cologne with original stopper	$85.00	$45.00
Butter dish with cover	150.00	55.00

Known items:	Flint	Non-Flint
Celery vase	125.00	35.00
Champagne	110.00	35.00
Compote, round		
Covered on high standard		
6" d.	275.00	135.00
7-1/4" d.	325.00	150.00
8-1/2" d.	375.00	175.00
Open on low standard		
6" d. with ruffled rim ...	95.00	45.00
8" d.	55.00	35.00
8-1/2" d.	75.00	—
9" d.	95.00	45.00
Creamer with applied handle	225.00	85.00
Cruet with original stopper and applied handle	225.00	75.00
Decanter		
Bar lip		
1-pt.	110.00	55.00
1-qt.	125.00	65.00
With original stopper		
1-pt.	275.00	—
1-qt.		
With applied handle.	475.00	—
Without handle	225.00	—
Eggcup, pedestaled		
Covered	375.00	

Known items:	Flint	Non-Flint
Open	55.00	25.00
Goblet with knob stem	95.00	35.00
Honey dish, round, flat	10.00	5.00
Mug with applied handle, 3-1/8" h.	325.00	—
Pitcher with applied handle		
Milk	375.00	135.00
Water, water with applied handle	250.00	110.00
Plate, round, 6" d.	65.00	25.00
Pomade jar with original clear stopper	65.00	—
Salt, master, open, footed		
With petaled edge	55.00	15.00
With plain edge	45.00	—
Sauce dish, round, flat	15.00	5.00
Spoon holder	55.00	25.00
Sugar bowl with cover	150.00	45.00
Tumbler		
Water		
Flat	95.00	35.00
Footed	75.00	25.00
Whiskey, 3-1/8" h.	110.00	—
Wine	45.00	25.00

Two Panel covered orange bowl.

TWO PANEL

AKA: Daisy in Panel, Daisy in the Square.

Non-flint. Richards & Hartley Glass Company, Tarentum, PA, c. 1880s. The United States Glass Company, Pittsburgh, PA, at Factory "B," c. 1891.

Original color production: Amber, apple green, blue, clear, vaseline.

Reproductions and Look-a-Likes: Goblet, wine (amber, apple green, blue, clear, vaseline). L.G. Wright Glass Company, New Martinsville, WV, unmarked.

Two Panel covered compote.

Known items:	Amber	Apple Green	Blue	Clear	Vaseline
Bowl, open, oval, flat					
Berry					
5-1/2" l.	$25.00	$35.00	$30.00	$20.00	$35.00
8" l.	30.00	40.00	35.00	25.00	40.00
Cracker	65.00	85.00	75.00	55.00	95.00
Orange, 10" l.					
Covered	175.00	275.00	225.00	150.00	325.00
Open	85.00	125.00	110.00	65.00	150.00
Waste or finger	35.00	45.00	40.00	30.00	55.00
Butter dish with cover	65.00	100.00	95.00	55.00	110.00
Celery Vase	45.00	65.00	55.00	35.00	75.00
Compote, oval on high standard, covered					
6-1/2"	65.00	110.00	95.00	65.00	125.00
8" l.	95.00	135.00	125.00	85.00	150.00
Creamer with pressed handle, 6" h.	30.00	50.00	45.00	20.00	55.00
Goblet	30.00	45.00	45.00	25.00	45.00
Jam jar with cover, oval	75.00	150.00	135.00	65.00	150.00
Lamp, oil					
Finger	95.00	135.00	125.00	65.00	150.00
High Standard					
7-1/2" h.	110.00	135.00	125.00	85.00	150.00
8-1/2" h.	125.00	165.00	150.00	95.00	185.00
9-1/2" h.	150.00	185.00	175.00	110.00	225.00
Mug with pressed handle	30.00	50.00	45.00	20.00	55.00
Pickle dish with handle, 9" l.	25.00	40.00	35.00	20.00	40.00
Pitcher, oval with pressed handle					
Milk, 1-qt.	45.00	110.00	85.00	40.00	125.00
Water, 1/2-gal.	70.00	135.00	110.00	65.00	150.00
Platter					
Bread	25.00	40.00	35.00	20.00	40.00
Ice cream	65.00	100.00	85.00	55.00	110.00
Salt					
Dip, individual, oval	10.00	15.00	15.00	10.00	20.00
Master, oval	25.00	45.00	40.00	20.00	55.00
Shaker (R)	75.00	125.00	95.00	55.00	125.00
Sauce dish, oval					
Flat	5.00	10.00	10.00	5.00	12.50
Footed	8.00	12.50	12.50	8.00	15.00
Spoon holder	30.00	55.00	50.00	25.00	65.00
Sugar bowl with cover	55.00	85.00	75.00	45.00	95.00
Tray, water	100.00	150.00	135.00	75.00	175.00
Tumbler, water, flat	30.00	75.00	55.00	20.00	65.00
Wine	25.00	45.00	35.00	20.00	45.00

U

U.S. COIN

OMN: United States Glass No. 15,005. **AKA:** American Coin, Coin (Dime), Coin (Half Dollar), Frosted Coin, Silver Age, The Silver Age.

Non-flint. The United States Glass Company, Pittsburgh, PA, at Factory "H" and Factory "G." c. 1892.

Original color production: Clear (plain, frosted, or stained with gold or platinum). Clear with amber stain, clear with ruby stain or any other color would be considered very rare.

Reproductions and Look-a-Likes: 6" d. flat covered bowl, 10" l. bread plate; 4" h. candlestick; 6" d. high standard covered compote, 4-1/2" h. creamer; 1-3/4" h. paperweight; 4-3/4" h. footed spoon holder with scalloped rim; 7" h. covered sugar bowl; toothpick holder, tumbler with coin in base (dated 1892), 3-1/2" h. wine.

U.S. Coin water set.

U.S. Coin syrup.

U.S. Coin wine.

Known items:	Clear	Clear w/Frosting
Ale goblet, half dollars, 7" h.....	$425.00	$600.00
Bowl, round, flat		
Covered, plain rim		
6" d.	450.00	650.00
7" d.	375.00	700.00

U.S. Coin rare epergne.

U.S. Coin covered bowl.

Known items:	Clear	Clear w/Frosting
8" d.	500.00	900.00
9" d.	1,800.00	2,500.00
Open, plain rim		
6" d.	350.00	400.00
7" d.	300.00	350.00
8" d.	400.00	450.00
9" d.	1,200.00	1,500.00
Open, scalloped rim		
6" d.	750.00	850.00
7" d.	800.00	900.00
8" d.	950.00	1,200.00
9" d.	1,250.00	1,750.00
Butter dish with cover	450.00	950.00
Cake stand, high standard, 10" d.	400.00	600.00
Celery vase with quarters	275.00	500.00
Champagne, 5-1/2" h. (ex. rare)	2,500.00	3,500.00
Claret, 4-3/4" h.	600.00	900.00
Compote, round		
Covered, straight sided		
High standard		
6" d.	375.00	475.00
7" d.	425.00	600.00
8" d.	600.00	1,200.00
9" d.	2,500.00	4,500.00
Low standard, 6" d.	550.00	750.00
Open		
Flared, high standard		
7" d.	300.00	375.00
8-1/4" d.	350.00	450.00
9-1/2" d.	750.00	950.00
10-1/2" d.	1,000.00	1,500.00

Known items:	Clear	Clear w/Frosting
Plain rim, belled bowl, high standard		
7-1/4" d.	325.00	425.00
8-1/2" d.	375.00	475.00
9-3/4" d.	425.00	575.00
10-1/2" d.	550.00	750.00
Scalloped, high standard, 7" d.	850.00	950.00
Scalloped, low standard		
6" d.	750.00	900.00
7" d.	850.00	1,250.00
Creamer	300.00	550.00
Cruet with original stopper	750.00	1,100.00
Epergne with single lily	1,000.00	1,500.00
Goblet, with dimes, 6-1/2" h.	550.00	600.00
Lamp, oil		
High standard		
Flared or tapered font		
8-1/2" h.	600.00	650.00
9-1/2" h.	600.00	650.00
10" h.	650.00	800.00
Round font, paneled		
8" h.	350.00	400.00
8-1/2" h.	375.00	425.00
9-1/2" h.	425.00	475.00
10" h.	450.00	500.00
11" h.	500.00	550.00
11-1/2" h.	550.00	750.00
Square font (has coins)		
8" h.	400.00	525.00
8-1/2" h.	425.00	550.00

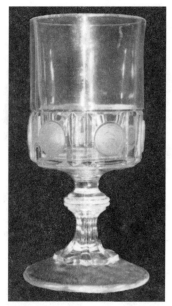

U.S. Coin goblet.

U.S. Coin syrup.

U.S. Coin cruet.

Known items:	Clear	Clear w/Frosting
9-1/2" h.	475.00	600.00
10" h.	500.00	625.00
11" h.	600.00	800.00
11-1/2" h.	750.00	900.00
Footed, plain or round font		
4-7/8" h.	500.00	650.00
5-1/4" h.	525.00	650.00
Mug, beer with pressed handle	450.00	750.00
Pickle dish, oblong.	175.00	225.00
Pitcher with pressed handle		
Milk, 1-qt.	650.00	1,000.00
Water, 1/2-gal.	750.00	1,500.00

Known items:	Clear	Clear w/Frosting
Platter, bread, rectangular (7" x 10")	275.00	450.00
Preserve, 8" x 5"	275.00	325.00
Saltshaker (tall), 3" h.	200.00	300.00
Sauce dish, round		
Plain		
Flat		
3-3/4" d.	125.00	150.00
4-1/4" d.	150.00	175.00
Footed, 3-3/4" d.	150.00	200.00
Scalloped		
Flat		
3-3/4" d.	300.00	400.00
4-1/4" d.	350.00	425.00
Footed, 3-3/4" d.	350.00	450.00
Spoon holder with quarters	200.00	350.00
Sugar bowl with cover	350.00	500.00
Syrup pitcher with original dated pewter lid	850.00	1,250.00
Toothpick holder	125.00	200.00
Tray, water, rectangular, 10" d.	550.00	850.00
Waste bowl	525.00	600.00
Tumbler, water, flat		
Dimes	325.00	375.00
Dollar in base		
1878	125.00	150.00
1879	150.00	175.00
1882	200.00	250.00
Wine	525.00	800.00

UTAH

OMN: U.S. Glass No. 15,080-Utah. AKA: Frost Flower, Frosted Flower, Starlight, Twinkle Star.

Non-flint. The United States Glass Company, Pittsburgh, PA, at Factory "U," c. 1901.

Original color production: Clear (plain, acid finished).

Reproductions and Look-a-Likes: None known.

Utah syrup pitcher.

Utah relish tray.

Known items:	Clear
Bowl	
Oval, flat	
7" l.	$25.00
8" l.	30.00
9" l.	35.00
Round, flat	
Covered	
6" d.	55.00
7" d.	75.00
8" d.	95.00
Open	
6" d.	25.00
7" d.	30.00
8" d.	35.00
Butter dish with cover	
Large	65.00
Small	
With notched lid	85.00
With plain lid	65.00
Cake plate, 9" d.	30.00
Cake stand	
High standard	
7" d.	45.00
9" d.	55.00
10" d.	65.00
Low standard	
9" d.	35.00
10" d.	45.00
11" d.	55.00

Known items:	Clear
Castor under tray (for salt and pepper set)	35.00
Celery vase	45.00
Compote	
Covered on high standard	
Patterned base with plain lid	
6" d.	65.00
7" d.	75.00
8" d.	95.00
Plain base, 5" d.	
Notched lid	85.00
Plain lid	65.00
Open on high standard	
Deep bowl	
Patterned base	
6" d.	30.00
7" d.	35.00
8" d.	40.00
Plain base, 5" d.	25.00
Saucer-shaped bowl with patterned base	
7-1/2" d.	35.00
9" d.	45.00
10" d.	55.00
Creamer	35.00
Cruet with original stopper	65.00
Goblet	35.00
Pickle tray with tab handles	15.00
Pitcher, water	
3-pts.	55.00
1/2-gal.	55.00
Saltshaker, bulbous	30.00
Sauce dish, round, flat, 4" d.	8.00
Spoon holder	35.00
Sugar bowl with cover	45.00
Syrup pitcher	95.00
Tumbler, water, flat	25.00
Wine	25.00

VALENCIA WAFFLE

OMN: Adams No. 85. **AKA:** Block and Star, Hexagonal Block.

Non-flint. Adams & Company, Pittsburgh, PA, c. 1885. The United States Glass Company, Pittsburgh, PA, at Factory "A" after 1891.

Original color production: Amber, apple green, blue, clear, vaseline.

Reproductions and Look-a-Likes: None known.

Valencia Waffle relish, syrup and covered pickle jar.

Known items:	Amber	Apple Green	Blue	Clear	Vaseline
Bowl, master berry, flat, 8" sq.	$35.00	$65.00	$45.00	$25.00	$55.00
Bread plate	30.00	45.00	35.00	25.00	40.00
Butter dish with cover	45.00	85.00	65.00	45.00	75.00
Cake stand on high standard, 10" sq.	110.00	225.00	150.00	85.00	175.00
Castor set in silver plated holder	225.00	325.00	275.00	125.00	375.00
Celery vase	30.00	65.00	45.00	30.00	50.00
Compote					
Covered					
High standard					
6" sq.	75.00	110.00	85.00	65.00	95.00
7" sq.	85.00	125.00	95.00	75.00	110.00
8" sq.	100.00	135.00	110.00	95.00	125.00
Low standard					
6" sq.	60.00	95.00	75.00	55.00	85.00
7" sq.	75.00	110.00	85.00	65.00	95.00
8" sq.	95.00	125.00	100.00	85.00	110.00
Open, scalloped rim, high standard					
5" sq.	30.00	50.00	40.00	30.00	45.00
6" sq.	45.00	65.00	55.00	35.00	65.00
7" sq.	55.00	85.00	65.00	45.00	75.00
8" sq.	65.00	95.00	75.00	55.00	85.00
9" sq.	85.00	125.00	95.00	75.00	110.00
Creamer with applied handle	35.00	55.00	45.00	30.00	55.00

Valencia Waffle goblet.

Valencia Waffle open compote on high standard..

Known items:	Amber	Apple Green	Blue	Clear	Vaseline
Dish, open, oblong, flat					
7" l.	20.00	30.00	25.00	20.00	30.00
8" l.	25.00	35.00	30.00	25.00	35.00
9" l.	30.00	40.00	35.00	30.00	40.00
Goblet	35.00	65.00	45.00	35.00	65.00
Pickle dish, oblong.	20.00	30.00	25.00	15.00	30.00
Pickle jar with cover	125.00	225.00	150.00	110.00	200.00
Pitcher with pressed handle					
Milk, 1-qt.	65.00	175.00	95.00	75.00	150.00
Water, 1/2-gal.	95.00	250.00	125.00	95.00	225.00
Relish dish.	20.00	30.00	25.00	15.00	30.00
Salt					
Master	35.00	75.00	55.00	25.00	85.00
Shaker (tall)	30.00	65.00	45.00	25.00	55.00
Sauce dish, square, 4"					
Flat.	5.00	10.00	8.00	5.00	10.00
Footed	8.00	15.00	10.00	8.00	15.00
Spoon holder	30.00	50.00	35.00	25.00	45.00
Sugar bowl with cover	40.00	75.00	55.00	40.00	65.00
Syrup pitcher	100.00	200.00	135.00	85.00	225.00
Tray, water, 10-1/2" l.	35.00	65.00	55.00	35.00	75.00
Tumbler, water, flat	30.00	50.00	40.00	25.00	45.00

VALENTINE

OMN: Trilby. **AKA:** Vincent Valentine.

Non-flint. The United States Glass Company, Pittsburgh, PA, at Factory "G," c. 1891.

Original color production: Clear.

Reproductions and Look-a-Likes: Match holder, toothpick holder (opalescent and clear colors).

Valentine water pitcher.

Known items:	Clear
Bottle, cologne with original heart-shaped stopper	$225.00
Bowl, open, round, master berry	110.00
Butter dish with cover	225.00
Creamer, 4-1/2" h.	110.00
Goblet	375.00
Pitcher, water with pressed handle, 1/2-gal.	325.00
Sauce dish, round flat, 4-1/2" d.	35.00
Spoon holder	95.00
Sugar bow with cover	175.00
Toothpick holder	125.00
Tumbler, water, flat	110.00
Wall pocket or match safe	65.00

VERMONT

OMN: U.S. Glass No. 15,060-Vermont. **AKA:** Honeycomb with Flower Rim, Inverted Thumbprint with Daisy Band, Vermont Honeycomb.

Non-flint. The United States Glass Company, Pittsburgh, PA, c. 1899-1903.

Original color production: Clear, green (plain, gilded) custard (plain, decorated), chocolate, slag, milk white, blue. Clear with amber stain or any other color would be considered rare.

Reproductions and Look-a-Likes: Toothpick, 2-1/2" h. (Every imaginable color). Boyd's Crystal Art Glass Company, Cambridge, OH. Permanently embossed with a "B" within a diamond.

Vermont covered sugar bowl.

Known items:	Clear	Green
Basket with handle	$45.00	$75.00
Bowl, open, round		
Master berry	55.00	75.00
Finger or waste	45.00	65.00
Butter dish with cover	65.00	125.00
Celery tray	30.00	30.00
Compote, round on high standard		
Covered	95.00	150.00
Open	40.00	65.00

Vermont covered butter dish.

Victoria (Fostoria) syrup.

Known items:	Clear	Green
Creamer with pressed handle	45.00	65.00
Goblet	75.00	135.00
Pickle tray	25.00	30.00
Pitcher, water with pressed handle, 1/2-gal.	85.00	200.00
Saltshaker	45.00	85.00
Sauce dish, round, footed	15.00	20.00
Spoon holder	45.00	75.00
Sugar bowl with cover	65.00	95.00
Toothpick holder	35.00	55.00
Tray, card with handle		
Large	25.00	35.00
Medium	20.00	30.00
Small	15.00	25.00
Tumbler, water, footed	35.00	55.00
Vase	20.00	45.00

Victoria (Fostoria) castor.

VICTORIA (Fostoria)

OMN: Fostoria No. 183.

Non-flint. Fostoria Glass Company, Fostoria, OH, c. 1890.

Original color production: Clear with frosting. Often found with the word "Patent" embossed in the base. All clear 20% less.

Reproductions and Look-a-Likes: None known.

Known items:	Clear w/Frosting
Butter dish with cover	$275.00
Bowl, open, round, flat	
Centerpiece bowl	225.00
Ice cream, shallow	275.00
Master berry, deep	
8" d.	200.00
9" d.	225.00
Candy dip whimsy with handle (ER)	650.00
Celery vase	250.00
Cigar set (cigar holder, cigarette holder, match holder and under tray). Complete (ER)	1,250.00

Victoria Fostoria celery vase.

Known items:	Clear w/Frosting
Creamer with applied handle	135.00
Cruet with applied handle and original faceted stopper	225.00
Custard cup with applied handle	65.00
Fairy lamp (ER)	950.00
Finger bowl with matching underplate	135.00
Ice cream dish, round, flat, very shallow	45.00
Lamp, oil	
Parlor with matching half-shade	3,500.00
Peg	275.00
Mustard with metal top	175.00
Napkin ring (R)	450.00
Nappy, 3-sided with applied handle	125.00
Pickle castor in silver plate frame	225.00
Pickle or banana split dish, canoe-shaped	45.00
Pitcher, bulbous with applied handle	
Milk	650.00
Water	850.00
Relish, leaf shaped	55.00
Rose bowl	
4" d.	95.00
4-1/2" d.	110.00
5" d.	165.00
6" d.	195.00
Saltshaker	135.00
Sauce dish, round, flat	35.00

Known items:	Clear w/Frosting
Saucer or under plate for custard cup	55.00
Spoon holder	110.00
Sugar bowl with cover	225.00
Syrup with applied handle	375.00
Toothpick holder	110.00
Tumbler	
Water	135.00
Whiskey	150.00
Water bottle	375.00

VICTORIA (Pioneer)

OMN: Non-flint. Pioneer Glass Company, Pittsburgh, PA, c. 1892. Designed by Julius Proeger and patented under U.S. Patent No. 21,181, November 24, 1891.

Original color production: Clear, clear with ruby stain. Singular items in chocolate.

Reproductions and Look-a-Likes: None known.

Victoria (Pioneer) decanter.

Known items:	Clear	Clear w/Ruby
Banana dish on high standard	$65.00	$850.00
Bowl, open, flat with smooth rim		
Finger or waste	25.00	55.00

Known items:	Clear	Clear w/Ruby
Master berry, 8" d.	35.00	150.00
Orange with scalloped rim	55.00	225.00
Butter dish with cover, footed with flanged base	55.00	225.00
Cake plate	35.00	135.00
Cake stand on high standard		
9" d.	75.00	325.00
10" d.	110.00	450.00
Celery vase	35.00	150.00
Champagne, 5-1/2" h.	35.00	150.00
Cheese dish with cover and flanged base with high domed lid	75.00	375.00
Cologne bottle, bulbous base with slender neck and original patterned stopper	30.00	125.00
Compote with cover on high standard, 6" d.	65.00	250.00
Cordial	30.00	175.00
Cracker jar with cover	85.00	375.00
Creamer with applied handle, 5" h.	45.00	100.00
Cruet		
Bulbous with long slender spout, pressed handle and original patterned stopper	75.00	325.00
Traditional shape, original patterned stopper	45.00	375.00
Cup, custard	15.00	45.00
Decanter with original patterned stopper	55.00	250.00
Goblet	35.00	125.00
Jam jar attached to under plate, with cover	55.00	175.00
Pickle jar with cover	65.00	275.00
Pitcher		
Bulbous	75.00	325.00
Tankard with applied handle		
Milk, 1-qt.	65.00	225.00
Water, 1/2-gal.	85.00	275.00
Rose bowl, several sizes	25.00	75.00
Saltshaker (fall)	25.00	85.00
Sauce dish, round, flat, 4" d.	8.00	20.00
Saucer, round	15.00	45.00

Known items:	Clear	Clear w/Ruby
Spoon holder	30.00	95.00
Sugar bowl with cover	45.00	150.00
Syrup pitcher	75.00	275.00
Tray, wine, round	25.00	95.00
Tumbler		
Lemonade with applied handle	20.00	65.00
Water, flat	25.00	75.00
Wine	15.00	65.00

VICTORIA (Riverside)

OMN: Riverside No. 431. **AKA:** Draped Top, Draped Rep Top.

Non-flint. Riverside Glass Works, Wellsburg, WV, c. 1895.

Original color production: Clear, clear with ruby stain. Singular items may be found in clear with amber stain.

Reproductions and Look-a-Likes: None known.

Victoria (Riverside) high-standard compote.

Known items:	Clear	Clear w/Ruby
Bowl, open, round, flat, 8" d.	$35.00	$150.00
Butter dish with cover	75.00	275.00
Cake stand on high standard	125.00	650.00

Victoria (Riverside) creamer, butter and sugar bowl.

Known items:	Clear	Clear w/Ruby
Celery vase	35.00	275.00
Compote, round on high standard		
Covered, 6" d.	65.00	350.00
Open, scalloped rim		
4-1/2" d. (jelly)	25.00	175.00
6" d.	50.00	275.00
Condiment under tray	20.00	85.00
Creamer		
Breakfast	25.00	175.00
Individual	20.00	150.00
Table size	35.00	135.00
Cruet with original stopper	65.00	425.00
Goblet	45.00	175.00
Pickle dish	25.00	75.00
Pitcher, water with applied handle,		
1/2-gal., 8" h.	85.00	375.00
Nappy, handled	20.00	55.00
Saltshaker	25.00	110.00
Sauce dish, round, flat, 4-1/2" d.	8.00	45.00
Spoon holder	25.00	125.00
Sugar bowl with cover		
Breakfast	25.00	175.00
Table size	50.00	225.00
Syrup pitcher	85.00	650.00
Toothpick holder	35.00	425.00
Tumbler, water, flat	20.00	85.00

Non-flint. Hobbs, Brockunier & Company, Wheeling, WV, c. 1876. Designed by John H. Hobbs and patented under U.S. Patent No.9,647, November 21, 1876.

Original color production: Clear. Examples in milk white or any other color are rare. **Note:** peculiar to the pattern are the "Viking Heads" that appear on both the feet and the finials of items.

Reproductions and Look-a-Likes: None.

Viking milk white shaving mug.

VIKING

OMN: Hobbs' Centennial. **AKA:** Bearded Head, Bearded Prophet, Old Man of the Mountain(s).

Known items:	Clear
Apothecary jar with cover	$125.00
Bowl, oval with cover	
8" l.	175.00
9" l.	225.00
Butter dish with cover	110.00
Casserole, round with cover	275.00

Viking three-piece table set: butter, creamer, suger bowl.

Viking celery vase.

Viking covered butter dish and sugar bowl.

Known items:	Clear
Celery vase	75.00
Compote, round	
Covered	
On high standard	
7" d.	150.00
8" d.	200.00
9" d.	325.00
On low standard, 9" d.	275.00
Creamer with pressed handle	75.00
Cup, footed with applied handle	85.00
Eggcup, open, single	55.00
Epergne with 4 blown lilies, patent dated (ER)	1,500.00

Known items:	Clear
Marmalade jar with cover	175.00
Mug, shaving (patent dated)	225.00
Pickle dish, oval	45.00
Pitcher, water with pressed handle, 1/2-gal.	225.00
Platter, bread, oval	75.00
Relish tray, oval on foot	30.00
Salt, master, open, footed	55.00
Sauce dish, round, footed	20.00
Spoon holder	55.00
Sugar bowl with cover	95.00
Vase (R)	135.00

VIRGINIA

OMN: U.S. Glass. Glass No. 15,071-Virginia. **AKA:** Banded Portland, Diamond Banded Portland, Maiden's Blush, Portland with Diamond Point.

Non-flint. United States Glass Co., Pittsburgh, PA, at Factory "G," Factory "U," and Factory "E."

Original color production: Clear, clear with rose blush (plain, gilded). Odd items may be found in clear flashed with blue, green, or yellow. Decorated items were produced by the Oriental Glass Co., Pittsburgh, PA.

Reproductions and Look-a-Likes: None known.

Virginia water pitcher.

Virginia syrup.

Known items:	Clear	Clear w/Blush
Bonbon dish, oval, flared rim,		
pointed ends, 5-1/2" l.	$20.00	$30.00
Bowl, flat		
Covered		
6"	45.00	65.00
7"	55.00	75.00
8"	75.00	95.00
Open		
Deep, straight-sided		
with scalloped rim		
6" d.	25.00	45.00
7" d.	35.00	55.00
8" d.	45.00	75.00

Known items:	Clear	Clear w/Blush
Shallow with flared bowl		
7-1/2" d.	30.00	55.00
8-1/2" d.	35.00	65.00
9-1/2" d.	45.00	75.00
10-1/2" d.	65.00	95.00
Butter dish, covered on flanged		
base	65.00	225.00
Cake stand on high standard	95.00	250.00
Candlestick, 9" h.	85.00	175.00
Carafe (also known as the "claret		
jug")	95.00	250.00
Celery		
Tray, oblong with		
scalloped rim		
Pointed ends	25.00	45.00
Straight ends	55.00	95.00
Vase	55.00	95.00
Cologne bottle with original stopper		
Large	85.00	225.00
Small	55.00	150.00
Compote		
High standard		
Covered		
6" d. (Jelly)	55.00	85.00
7" d. (Sweetmeat)	85.00	110.00
8" d.	110.00	150.00
Open		
Flared bowl with		
scalloped rim		
6" d.	25.00	45.00
7" d.	35.00	55.00
8" d.	45.00	75.00
Straight-sided bowl		
6" d.	25.00	45.00
7" d.	35.00	55.00
8" d.	55.00	85.00

Virginia high-standard covered compote.

Known items:	Clear	Clear w/Blush
Low standard, covered, 5-1/4" d.	55.00	85.00
Creamer		
Individual		
Oval	15.00	35.00
Tankard, 6-oz. (also known as the "Jersey Cream")	35.00	75.00
Table size.	45.00	85.00
Cruet with original stopper	65.00	225.00
Cup, custard or lemonade	15.00	35.00
Decanter, handled	85.00	275.00
Dish, open, oval, shallow with scalloped rim		
6"l.	25.00	45.00
7-1/2" l.	30.00	55.00
9"l.	40.00	65.00
10-1/2" l.	50.00	95.00
12-1/2" l.	65.00	125.00
Dresser tray, flat	50.00	150.00
Goblet	45.00	110.00
Jar, dresser, covered	35.00	75.00
Marmalade dish, footed with original notched cover, 4-1/2" d.	65.00	150.00
Nappy, round with handle	20.00	65.00
Olive dish		
Deep, scalloped rim with pointed ends, 5-1/2"	15.00	35.00
Tray, boat shaped	15.00	35.00
Pickle dish, flat, scalloped with pointed ends	15.00	35.00

Known items:	Clear	Clear w/Blush
Pin tray	25.00	45.00
Pitcher, water, tankard, 1/2-gal.	125.00	325.00
Plate, 6" d.	35.00	65.00
Pomade jar with cover	35.00	75.00
Puff box with cover.	35.00	75.00
Punch bowl (R)		
Flat, 13" d.	225.00	550.00
Footed, 15" d.	225.00	650.00
Relish tray		
6-1/2" l.	15.00	25.00
8" l.	20.00	35.00
8-1/4" l.	20.00	30.00
Ring holder with center post (R)	85.00	175.00
Saltshaker		
Café (short)	25.00	65.00
Hotel (tall)	25.00	65.00
Small with long fluted neck	25.00	65.00
Sardine box with original cover (R)	125.00	225.00
Sauce dish, flat		
Oval, 4-1/2" l.	10.00	20.00
Round		
4" d.	10.00	20.00
4-1/2" d.	10.00	20.00
Square, 4"	10.00	20.00
Spoon holder	35.00	85.00
Sugar bowl		
Individual, oval, true open	20.00	35.00
Powdered, covered, flat	45.00	95.00
Table size, covered	55.00	110.00
Sugar shaker	65.00	225.00
Syrup pitcher	85.00	325.00
Toothpick holder	25.00	75.00
Tumbler	35.00	65.00
Vase		
Flared rim, tall foot		
6"h.	20.00	45.00
9"h.	35.00	55.00
Straight rim, short foot, 6" h.	20.00	45.00
Wine	35.00	95.00

WAFFLE

AKA: Paneled Waffle.

Flint. Traditionally attributed to the Boston & Sandwich Glass Company, Sandwich, MA, c. 1850s.

Original color production: Clear. Milk white or any other color would be considered rare.

Reproductions and Look-a-Likes: Goblet (clear).

Waffle goblet.

Known items:	Clear
Bowl, open, oval, flat, 8" l.	$35.00
Butter dish with cover	150.00
Celery vase	110.00
Champagne	275.00
Claret (Jelly glass)	250.00
Compote, round	
Covered	
On high standard	
6" d.	85.00
7" d.	110.00

Known items:	Clear
8" d.	135.00
9" d.	475.00
On low standard	
6" d.	65.00
7" d.	85.00
8" d.	110.00
9" d.	325.00
Open on low standard	
6" d.	45.00
7" d.	55.00
8" d.	65.00
Creamer with applied handle, 6-3/4" h. (S)	325.00
Decanter	
Bar lip	
1-pt.	95.00
1-qt.	100.00
Matching original stopper	
1-pt.	225.00
1-qt.	200.00
Eggcup, open, single, footed	40.00
Goblet with knob stem	175.00
Lamp	
All glass	
Small with applied handle	65.00
Tall without handle	175.00
Glass font with brass stem on marble base	125.00
Mug with applied handle, 3" h.	325.00
Pickle dish, oval with taper at one end	30.00
Pitcher with applied handle	
Milk, 1-qt. (VR)	1,500.00
Water, 1/2-gal. (R)	950.00
Plate, 6" d.	65.00
Relish tray, oblong, 6" l.	35.00
Salt, master, covered, footed	375.00
Sauce dish, round, flat, 4" d.	8.00
Spill holder	55.00
Spoon holder	55.00

Known items:	Clear
Sugar bowl with cover	95.00
Tumbler, flat	
Water	95.00
Whiskey, 3" h.	135.00
Wine	65.00

WAFFLE AND THUMBPRINT

OMN: Palace. **AKA:** Bull's Eye and Waffle, Triple Bulls Eye.

Flint. New England Glass Company, East Cambridge, MA, c. 1868. Curling, Robertson & Company, Pittsburgh, PA, c. 1856. Most likely other glass factories.

Original color production: Clear. Canary yellow, milk white, or any other color would be considered very rare.

Waffle and Thumbprint open compote.

Known items:	Clear
Bowl, open, rectangular, flat, 5" x 7"	$45.00
Butter dish with cover	175.00
Celery vase	175.00
Champagne	275.00
Claret (Jelly glass)	225.00

Waffle and Thumbprint eggcup.

Known items:	Clear
Compote, round	
Covered, 6" d.	
On high standard	275.00
On low standard	200.00
Open, 6" d.	
On high standard	95.00
On low standard	85.00
Creamer with applied handle	225.00
Decanter	
Bar lip	
1-pt.	150.00
1-qt.	135.00
Matching original stopper	
1-pt.	325.00
1-qt.	300.00
Eggcup, open, single, footed	45.00
Goblet	
Bulbous stem	95.00
Heavy stem	110.00
Plain stem	85.00
Lamp	
Hand with applied handle	135.00
Stand	
9-1/2" h.	225.00
11" h.	275.00
Mug, applied handle, 3" h.	425.00

Washington (New England Glass) celery vase.

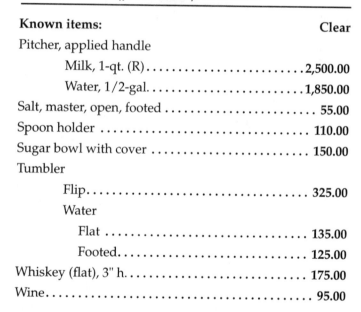

Waffle and Thumbprint decanter.

Known items:	Clear
Pitcher, applied handle	
Milk, 1-qt. (R)	2,500.00
Water, 1/2-gal.	1,850.00
Salt, master, open, footed	55.00
Spoon holder	110.00
Sugar bowl with cover	150.00
Tumbler	
Flip	325.00
Water	
Flat	135.00
Footed	125.00
Whiskey (flat), 3" h.	175.00
Wine	95.00

WASHINGTON (New England Glass)

AKA: Early Washington, Leafy Panel, and Thumbprint.

Flint. New England Glass Company, East Cambridge, MA, c. 1869. Also made in England as some pieces can be found with English registry mark.

Original color production: Clear.

Reproductions and Look-a-Likes: None known.

Known items:	Clear
Ale glass, footed	$450.00
Bottle, bitters	175.00
Bowl, flat	
Round	
Covered	
5" d.	175.00
6" d.	225.00
7" d.	250.00
8" d.	325.00
Open	
5" d.	75.00
6" d.	85.00
7" d.	110.00
8" d.	125.00
Oval	
7" l.	40.00
8" l.	45.00
9" l.	55.00
10" l.	85.00
Butter dish, covered	275.00
Celery vase, low pedestal with smooth rim	225.00
Champagne (ER)	950.00
Claret (jelly glass)	325.00

Known items:	Clear
Compote, round	
Covered	
High standard	
Deep bowl	
6" d.	275.00
7" d.	325.00
8" d.	450.00
Shallow bowl	
6" d.	225.00
7" d.	300.00
8" d.	425.00
Low standard with deep bowl	
6" d.	175.00
7" d.	225.00
8" d.	375.00
Open	
High standard	
Deep bowl	
6" d.	65.00
7" d.	75.00
8" d.	85.00
9" d.	135.00
10" d.	275.00
Shallow bowl	
6" d.	65.00
7" d.	75.00
8" d.	85.00
Low standard	
Deep bowl	
6" d.	45.00
7" d.	55.00
8" d.	65.00
9" d.	125.00
10" d.	200.00
Shallow bowl	
6" d.	65.00
7" d.	75.00
8" d.	85.00
Creamer	325.00
Decanter	
With bar lip	
1-pt.	225.00
1-qt.	250.00

Known items:	Clear
With original stopper	
1-pt.	425.00
1-qt.	475.00
Dish, oval, flat	
Covered, 10" l.	425.00
Open	
Deep	
6" l.	45.00
7" l.	55.00
8" l.	65.00
9" l.	85.00
10" l.	110.00
Shallow	
6" l.	45.00
7" l.	55.00
8" l.	65.00
9" l.	85.00
10" l.	110.00
Eggcup, footed	85.00
Goblet	
Large (Gentleman's)	150.00
Small (Lady's)	135.00
Honey dish, round, flat, 3-1/2" d.	25.00
Lamp with original burner	375.00
Mug	
Beer, pressed handle	175.00
Lemonade, 3-3/4" h., applied handle	325.00
Whiskey, applied handle. 3" h.	425.00
Pitcher	
Milk, 1-qt.	1,500.00
Water	
1/2-gal.	2,800.00
3-pts.	1,500.00
Plate, round, 6" d.	95.00
Salt, master	
Flat, round	85.00
Footed, open	55.00
Sauce dish, round, flat	
4" d.	10.00
5" d.	12.50
Spoon holder	110.50
Sugar bowl, covered	200.00
Syrup pitcher with applied handle	475.00

Known items:	Clear
Tumbler	
Water	
1/3-pt.	110.00
1/2-pt.	125.00
Whiskey, 3-1/8" h.	225.00
Wine	135.00

WASHINGTON (U.S. Glass)

OMN: U.S. Glass No. 15074. **AKA:** Beaded Base, Late Washington.

Non-flint. The United States Glass Company at Factory "K" and Factory "F," Pittsburgh, PA, c. 1901.

Original color production: Clear, clear with ruby stain.

Reproductions and Look-a-Likes: None known.

Washington (U.S. Glass) creamer.

Known items:	Clear	Clear w/Ruby
Bowl, round, flat		
Covered		
5" d.	$45.00	$85.00
6" d.	55.00	95.00
7" d.	65.00	110.00
8" d.	95.00	150.00

Known items:	Clear	Clear w/Ruby
Open		
5" d.	25.00	45.00
6" d.	30.00	50.00
7" d.	35.00	55.00
8" d.	45.00	95.00
Butter dish, covered, footed	125.00	250.00
Cake stand on high standard, 10" d.	95.00	275.00
Celery		
Tray	35.00	75.00
Vase, footed with smooth rim	35.00	110.00
Champagne	75.00	150.00
Claret	55.00	110.00
Compote		
High standard		
Covered, deep flared bowl		
4-1/2" d.	55.00	110.00
5" d.	45.00	85.00
6" d.	55.00	95.00
7" d.	65.00	135.00
8" d.	85.00	225.00
Open		
Low round bowl, smooth rim (known as the *"fruit bowl"*)		
7-1/2" d.	55.00	110.00
8-1/2" d.	65.00	125.00
9-1/2" d.	85.00	150.00
Low standard		
Covered		
5" d.	35.00	55.00
6" d.	45.00	65.00
7" d.	55.00	75.00
8" d.	75.00	110.00
Open		
5" d.	20.00	35.00
6" d.	25.00	40.00
7" d.	30.00	45.00
8" d.	45.00	65.00
Cordial	75.00	150.00
Creamer with applied handle		
Individual	25.00	45.00
Table size	55.00	95.00
Cruet	85.00	275.00

Known items:	Clear	Clear w/Ruby
Cup, custard with applied handle...	15.00	25.00
Dish, rectangular, flat		
6" l.	30.00	45.00
8" l.	35.00	55.00
10" l.	45.00	65.00
Finger or waste bowl, smooth rim, flat	35.00	55.00
Goblet		
Gentleman's (10-oz.)	55.00	95.00
Lady's (8-oz.)	45.00	85.00
Pitcher		
Squat with applied handle		
1/2-pt.	45.00	75.00
1-pt.	55.00	85.00
1-qt.	65.00	110.00
3-pts.	75.00	125.00
Tankard with applied handle		
1/2-pt.	45.00	75.00
1-pt.	55.00	85.00
1-qt.	65.00	110.00
3-pts.	75.00	125.00
Powdered sugar bowl with cover ...	55.00	95.00
Salt		
Individual	15.00	25.00
Master	35.00	65.00
Shaker	45.00	85.00
Sauce dish, round		
Flat		
3" d.	8.00	15.00
3-1/2" d.	8.00	15.00
4" d.	10.00	17.50
4-1/2" d.	12.50	20.00
Footed, 3-1/2" d.	12.50	20.00
Spoon holder, footed	45.00	75.00
Sugar bowl		
Individual, true open, footed	25.00	45.00
Table size with cover	65.00	95.00
Toothpick holder	45.00	95.00
Tumbler, water, flat	35.00	55.00
Wine	35.00	65.00

WASHINGTON CENTENNIAL

AKA: Centennial, Chain with Diamonds, Washington.

Non-flint. Gillinder & Co., Philadelphia, PA, c. 1876.

Original color production: Clear. Opaque, white or any other color would be considered rare. **Note:** Platters can be found both clear and clear with acid-finished centers.

Reproductions and Look-a-Likes: None known.

Washington Centennial celery vase.

Known items:	Clear
Bowl, open, flat	
Oval	
7" l.	$35.00
8" l.	45.00
9" l.	55.00
Round	
7" d.	35.00
8" d.	45.00
9" d.	55.00
Butter dish with cover	
Flat	125.00
Footed	225.00

Washington Centennial spoon holder.

Known items:	Clear
Cake stand on high standard	
8-1/2" d.	65.00
10" d.	95.00
Celery vase, 7-1/2" h.	75.00
Champagne, 5-1/2" h.	225.00
Compote, round on high standard	
Covered	
7" d.	275.00
8" d.	325.00
Open	
7" d.	45.00
8" d.	55.00
9" d.	65.00
10" d.	95.00
Creamer with applied handle	150.00
Dish, pickle, fish shaped	25.00
Eggcup, open, single, footed	45.00
Goblet	95.00
Pitcher with applied handle	
Milk, 1-qt.	225.00
Water, 1/2-gal.	275.00
Plate, 6" d. (R)	125.00
Platter, oval	
With "Carpenter's Hall" center	85.00
With "Independence Hall" center	85.00
With "Washington Head" center	75.00

Known items:	Clear
Relish tray, flat, oval with claw handles marked "Centennial 1776-1876"	45.00
Salt	
Dip, individual, 2" d.	15.00
Master, open, flat, oval	65.00
Shaker	95.00
Sauce dish, round, flat	12.50
Spoon holder	45.00
Sugar bowl, covered	125.00
Syrup pitcher	275.00
Wine	65.00

WEDDING BELLS

OMN: Fostoria No. 789.

Non-flint. Fostoria Glass Company, Moundsville, OH, c. 1900.

Original color production: Clear, clear with rose blush.

Reproductions and Look-a-Likes: Covered sugar bowl (blue-purple).

Wedding Bells toothpick.

Known items:	Clear	Clear w/Blush
Bowl, round		
Finger or waste	$30.00	$95.00
Master berry	35.00	110.00

Known items:	Clear	Clear w/Blush
Butter dish with cover...........	55.00	150.00
Celery vase	30.00	75.00
Compote, round with cover		
On high standard	95.00	275.00
On low standard	65.00	225.00
Creamer with applied handle	45.00	95.00
Cruet with original stopper	55.00	225.00
Cup, sherbet	15.00	35.00
Decanter with original stopper,		
1-qt.........................	75.00	175.00
Pitcher, water with applied handle,		
1/2-gal.		
Bulbous.................	95.00	275.00
Tankard................	75.00	175.00
Punch bowl, flat................	225.00	750.00
Relish tray, rectangular..........	20.00	55.00
Saltshaker	35.00	95.00
Spoon holder	40.00	85.00
Sugar bowl with cover	55.00	125.00
Syrup pitcher	125.00	375.00
Toothpick holder	45.00	110.00
Tumbler, flat		
Water..................	25.00	65.00
Whiskey	20.00	45.00

WEDDING RING

AKA: Double Wedding Ring.

Flint (c. 1860s), Non-flint (c. 1870s). Original maker unknown.

Original color production: Clear.

Reproductions and Look-a-Likes: Goblet, 6" d. plate, footed sherbet, covered sugar bowls, toothpick holders: squat, tall. (blue, clear, pink). Dalzell-Viking Glass Company, New Martinsville, WV, unmarked.

6" d. covered compote; 9-oz. goblet; 4" d. covered jelly; 8" d. round plate; salt dip; round flat sauce dish; sherbet; round flat toothpick; footed tumbler; 5-oz. wine (amber, amethyst, blue, clear, cobalt blue, green, ruby). L.G. Wright Glass Company, New Martinsville, WV, unmarked.

Wedding Ring wine.

Wedding Ring syrup.

Known items:	Clear
Butter with cover	$225.00
Celery vase...................................	275.00
Champagne	225.00
Creamer	
Applied handle.........................	225.00
Pressed handle	75.00
Decanter	
With applied heavy bar lip	175.00
With original stopper....................	325.00

Known items: **Clear**

Goblet

    With faceted knob stem 125.00

    With plain stem 95.00

Lamp, oil, finger, 5" 225.00

Pitcher, water with applied handle, 1/2-gal....... 1,250.00

Relish tray.................................... 50.00

Sauce dish, round, flat........................ 10.00

Spoon holder 95.00

Sugar bowl with cover 150.00

Syrup pitcher with applied handle.............. 325.00

Tumbler, water

    Flat..................................... 110.00

    Footed 75.00

Wine.. 55.00

Westward Ho goblet.

WESTWARD HO

OMN: Pioneer. **AKA:** Tippecanoe.

Non -flint. Gillinder & Sons, Philadelphia, PA, c. 1879.

Original color production: Clear with acid finish.

Reproductions and Look-a-Likes: Footed covered butter, celery vase; compotes: 6" d. covered on high standard; compotes: covered on low standard: 6"l. oval, 4" d. round, 5" d. round; creamer, goblet, footed sherbet, footed covered sugar bowl, tumbler, wine (clear and frosted). L.G. Wright Glass Company, New Martinsville, WV, unmarked.

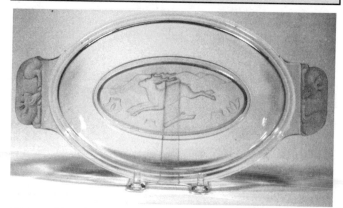

Westward Ho platter.

Known items: **Clear w/Frosting**

Butter dish with cover on high standard $375.00

Celery vase 275.00

Westward Ho covered compote.

Known items: **Clear w/Frosting**

Champagne, 5"h. (VR) 1,200.00

Compote

    Oval, covered, low standard

        6-3/4" l. 250.00

        7-3/4" l. 300.00

        8-3/4" l. 450.00

    Round, covered

    High standard

        6" d. 375.00

        7" d. 400.00

Westward Ho butter dish.

Westward Ho covered marmalade.

Westward Ho close up of finial.

Known items:	Clear w/Frosting
8" d.	550.00
9" d. (R)	1,500.00
Low standard	
6" d.	325.00
7" d.	350.00
8" d.	500.00
9" d. (R)	1,200.00
Creamer with pressed handle	200.00

Known items:	Clear w/Frosting
Goblet	250.00
Lamp, oil from goblet mold (1930s reproduction not made originally)	125.00
Marmalade jar with cover	425.00
Mug with pressed handle	
2" h.	450.00
3-1/2" h.	425.00
Pickle dish, oval	150.00
Pitcher with pressed handle	
Milk, 1-qt.	650.00
Water, 9-1/2" h., 1/2-gal.	450.00
Plate, bread, oval	
Deer handles	375.00
Log Cabin handles	850.00
Sauce dish, round, footed	
3-1/2" d.	35.00
4" d.	30.00
4-1/2" d.	40.00
5" d.	65.00
Spoon holder	175.00
Sugar bowl with cover	300.00
Tumbler (reproduction by L.G. Wright not made originally)	25.00
Wine, 4-1/4" h. (R)	950.00

WHEAT AND BARLEY

OMN: Duquesne. **AKA:** Hops and Barley, Oats and Barley.

Non-flint. Bryce Brothers, Pittsburgh, PA, c. 1880s. The United States Glass Company, Pittsburgh, PA. at Factory "B" after 1891.

Original color production: Amber, blue, clear, canary.

Reproductions and Look-a-Likes: Goblet (clear, colors). L.G. Wright Glass Company, New Martinsville, WV, unmarked.

Wheat and Barley creamer.

Known items:	Amber	Blue	Canary	Clear
Bowl, round, flat				
Covered				
6" d.	$55.00	$65.00	$75.00	$45.00
7" d.	65.00	75.00	85.00	55.00
8" d.	85.00	110.00	125.00	65.00
Open				
6" d.	25.00	30.00	35.00	20.00
7" d.	30.00	35.00	45.00	25.00
8" d.	40.00	55.00	65.00	35.00
Bread plate, handled	30.00	35.00	40.00	25.00
Butter dish with cover	65.00	85.00	90.00	55.00
Cake stand on high standard				
8" d.	65.00	75.00	85.00	55.00
9" d.	75.00	95.00	110.00	65.00
10" d.	110.00	125.00	135.00	95.00
Compote, round				
Covered on high standard				
6" d.				
With handles	95.00	110.00	125.00	85.00
Without handles	65.00	75.00	85.00	55.00
7" d.	75.00	85.00	95.00	65.00
8" d.	110.00	150.00	175.00	95.00
Open on high standard with shallow bowl				
6" d.	30.00	40.00	30.00	30.00
7" d.	35.00	45.00	30.00	35.00
8" d.	40.00	50.00	35.00	45.00
10" d.	45.00	55.00	40.00	65.00
Creamer with pressed handle	35.00	55.00	65.00	35.00
Dish, open, footed, 5" d. (Jelly)	30.00	45.00	55.00	25.00

Wheat and Barley creamer.

Wheat and Barley sugar bowl, creamer, spoon holder, and butter dish.

Wheat and Barley saltshaker.

Wheat and Barley covered sugar.

Known items:	Amber	Blue	Canary	Clear
Goblet	35.00	45.00	50.00	25.00
Mug with pressed handle, large	35.00	50.00	65.00	35.00
Pitcher with pressed handle				
Milk, 1-qt.	55.00	75.00	85.00	45.00
Water, 1/2-gal.	75.00	95.00	110.00	65.00
Plate				
7" d.	20.00	30.00	35.00	15.00
9" d.	25.00	35.00	40.00	20.00
Relish dish	15.00	20.00	25.00	15.00
Saltshaker	45.00	65.00	75.00	35.00
Sauce dish, round, 4" d.				
Flat	10.00	15.00	20.00	5.00
Footed	15.00	25.00	30.00	10.00
Spoon holder	35.00	45.00	55.00	30.00
Sugar bowl with cover	55.00	65.00	75.00	50.00
Syrup pitcher (S)				
1/2-pt.	175.00	225.00	250.00	110.00
1-pt.	200.00	275.00	325.00	125.00
Tumbler, water				
Flat	30.00	40.00	45.00	22.50
Footed	35.00	45.00	55.00	25.00

WILDFLOWER

OMN: Adams No. 140.

Non-flint. Adams & Company, Pittsburgh, PA, c. 1874. The United States Glass Company, Pittsburgh, PA, at Factory "A" c. 1891.

Original color production: Amber, apple green, blue, canary, clear. Table set has 2 different style finials (conventional & tab).

Reproductions and Look-a-Likes: Footed sauce dish with center candleholder; footed covered candy dish (clear, multitude of colors). Crystal Art Glass, Cambridge, OH. Permanently embossed with a "D" within a heart.

Covered candy jar; covered compotes: high standard, low standard; creamer with applied handle; flat oblong master salt; covered sugar bowl (Crown Tuscan, ruby). Mosser Glass, Inc., Cambridge, OH. Permanently embossed with an "M" or an "M" within a circle.

5-1/2" h. creamer with pressed handle; 4" d. low-standard covered compote; 8-oz. goblet; 10-1/2" h. stick candy covered jar; rectangular flat master slat; 9-1/2" square plate; 4" d. round, footed sauce dish; footed covered sugar bowl; 7-1/2" h. footed vase; 22-oz. wine (amber, amethyst, blue, clear, green, ruby, vaseline, vaseline opalescent). L.G. Wright Glass Company, New Martinsville, WV, unmarked.

Wildflower celery vase.

Wildflower seven-piece water set.

Known items:	Amber	Apple Green	Blue	Canary	Clear
Basket, cake, oblong with metal handle on high standard	$125.00	$275.00	$150.00	$175.00	$110.00
Bowl, open, flat					
Round, 6" d.	25.00	35.00	30.00	35.00	25.00
Square, flat					
6"	25.00	35.00	35.00	35.00	25.00
7"	35.00	45.00	45.00	45.00	35.00
8"	45.00	65.00	55.00	55.00	45.00
9"	65.00	85.00	75.00	75.00	65.00
Waste.	55.00	110.00	85.00	95.00	55.00
Butter dish with cover					
With collared base.	65.00	110.00	85.00	95.00	65.00
With flat base.	45.00	75.00	55.00	65.00	45.00

Wildflower cake tray.

Wildflower creamer, butter dish, sugar bowl, and spoon holder.

Known items:	Amber	Apple Green	Blue	Canary	Clear
Cake stand on high standard,					
10-1/2" d. 125.00		225.00	175.00	200.00	135.00
Celery vase 85.00		150.00	125.00	150.00	75.00
Champagne................... 30.00		85.00	45.00	55.00	35.00
Compote					
Covered					
High standard					
6" 65.00		110.00	85.00	95.00	75.00
7" 85.00		150.00	110.00	125.00	85.00
8" 110.00		200.00	150.00	175.00	125.00
Low standard					
6" 65.00		95.00	75.00	85.00	55.00
7" 75.00		125.00	85.00	110.00	65.00
8" 110.00		175.00	125.00	150.00	110.00
Open, square bowl (S)					
High standard					
6" 65.00		110.00	85.00	95.00	55.00
7" 75.00		125.00	95.00	110.00	65.00
8" 110.00		150.00	125.00	135.00	110.00
Creamer with pressed handle ... 30.00		45.00	40.00	45.00	35.00
Dish, open, oblong, flat					
5-3/4" l..................... 15.00		30.00	20.00	25.00	15.00
6-3/4" l..................... 20.00		35.00	25.00	30.00	20.00
7" l........................ 25.00		40.00	30.00	35.00	25.00
7-3/4" l..................... 30.00		50.00	35.00	40.00	30.00
Goblet 35.00		85.00	45.00	65.00	35.00
Pitcher, water with pressed					
handle, 1/2-gal.............. 85.00		175.00	125.00	150.00	75.00
Plate, cake, 10" sq. 25.00		55.00	35.00	45.00	25.00
Plate, oblong, 10" l. 25.00		55.00	40.00	55.00	25.00
Platter with scalloped rim,					
8" x 11"..................... 35.00		75.00	55.00	65.00	35.00
Relish tray, oblong............ 20.00		45.00	35.00	40.00	20.00
Salt					
Master, turtle shaped,					
2-1/8" h................... 85.00		150.00	125.00	150.00	75.00
Shaker...................... 35.00		75.00	45.00	55.00	35.00

Known items:	Amber	Apple Green	Blue	Canary	Clear
Sauce dish					
Round					
Flat					
3-1/2" d. 8.00	15.00	15.00	15.00	5.00
4" d. 8.00	15.00	15.00	15.00	5.00
Footed					
3-1/2" d. 10.00	15.00	15.00	15.00	10.00
4" d. 12.50	20.00	18.00	20.00	12.50
Square, 4-1/2". 15.00	22.50	20.00	22.50	15.00
Spoon holder 30.00	45.00	35.00	45.00	30.00
Sugar bowl with cover 45.00	75.00	50.00	65.00	45.00
Syrup pitcher 150.00	300.00	225.00	275.00	135.00
Tray, water, oval 75.00	225.00	125.00	175.00	85.00
Tumbler, water, flat 30.00	65.00	45.00	55.00	25.00
Wine (S) 75.00	135.00	85.00	125.00	65.00

WILLOW OAK

OMN: Bryce's Wreath. **AKA:** Acorn, Acorn and Oak Leaf, Oak Leaf, Stippled Daisy, Thistle and Sunflower, Willow and Oak.

Non-flint. Bryce Brothers, Pittsburgh, PA, c. 1880. The United States Glass Company, Pittsburgh, PA, at Factory "B," c. 1891.

Original color production: Amber, blue, canary yellow, clear.

Reproductions and Look-a-Likes: None known.

Willow Oak covered compote on high standard.

Known items:	Amber	Blue	Canary Yellow	Clear
Bowl, round, flat				
Covered				
6-1/4" d. $65.00	$95.00	$100.00	$55.00
7-1/4" d. 75.00	110.00	125.00	65.00
8-1/4" d. 95.00	125.00	135.00	85.00
Open				
6-1/4" d. 25.00	35.00	45.00	20.00
7-1/4" d. 30.00	45.00	55.00	25.00
8-1/4" d. 40.00	65.00	75.00	35.00
Butter dish with cover on				
flanged base 55.00	75.00	85.00	50.00
Cake stand on low standard				
8-1/2" d. 75.00	85.00	95.00	55.00
9" d. 95.00	110.00	125.00	65.00

Willow Oak tab-handled plate, celery vase, and handled mug.

Known items:	Amber	Blue	Canary Yellow	Clear
Celery vase	55.00	65.00	75.00	45.00
Compote on high standard				
Covered				
Round				
6-1/4" d.	85.00	95.00	100.00	75.00
7-1/4" d.	95.00	110.00	125.00	85.00
8-1/4" d.	125.00	135.00	150.00	110.00
Square (sweetmeat), 7" sq.	95.00	110.00	125.00	85.00
Open				
7-1/2" d.	30.00	45.00	50.00	25.00
8-1/2" d.	40.00	55.00	65.00	35.00
9-1/2" d.	50.00	65.00	75.00	45.00
10-1/2" d.	65.00	85.00	95.00	55.00
Creamer with pressed handle	45.00	50.00	60.00	35.00
Finger bowl	40.00	65.00	75.00	35.00
Goblet	55.00	75.00	85.00	35.00
Mug, large with pressed handle	45.00	65.00	75.00	30.00
Pitcher with pressed handle				
Milk, 1-qt.	55.00	95.00	110.00	45.00
Water, 1/2-gal.	65.00	110.00	125.00	55.00
Plate, round with tab handles				
7" d.	35.00	45.00	55.00	25.00
9" d.	45.00	55.00	65.00	35.00
10" d., tab handles	55.00	65.00	85.00	45.00
Saltshaker	55.00	75.00	75.00	35.00
Sauce dish, 4"				
Flat, square, handled	15.00	20.00	20.00	10.00
Footed, round	20.00	25.00	25.00	15.00
Spoon holder	35.00	45.00	55.00	30.00
Sugar bowl with cover	65.00	85.00	95.00	45.00
Tray, water, 10-1/2" d.	55.00	65.00	75.00	45.00
Tumbler, water, flat	45.00	65.00	65.00	35.00

WINDFLOWER

Non-flint. Maker unknown, c. late 1870s.

Original color production: Clear.

Reproductions and Look-a-Likes: None known.

Windflower tumbler.

Known items:	Clear
Bowl, open, oval, flat, 8" l., master berry	$35.00
Butter dish with cover	65.00
Celery vase	85.00
Compote, round	
Covered	
On high standard	
7" d.	95.00
8" d.	110.00
On low standard	
7" d.	65.00
8" d.	85.00
Open on low standard	
7" d.	30.00
8" d.	40.00
Creamer with applied handle	55.00
Eggcup, open, single, footed	35.00
Goblet	45.00
Pickle dish, oval, tapered at one end	20.00
Pitcher, water with applied handle, 1/2-gal.	325.00
Salt, master, open, footed	35.00

Known items:	Clear
Sauce dish, round, flat	10.00
Spoon holder	35.00
Sugar bowl with cover	65.00
Tumbler, water, flat	65.00
Wine	45.00

WISCONSIN

OMN: U.S. Glass No. 15,079-Wisconsin.
AKA: Beaded Dewdrop, Prism.

Non-flint. The United States Glass Company, Pittsburgh, PA, at Factory "U."

Original color production: Clear.

Reproductions and Look-a-Likes: Witch's 2-1/4" h. kettle-shaped footed toothpick with side handles (clear, multitude of contemporary colors). Crystal Art Glass Company, Cambridge, OH. Permanently embossed with either a "D" within a heart or a "D" within a diamond. The Guernsey Glass Company, Cambridge, OH, likewise produced similarly shaped toothpick holders that are unmarked.

Low-footed open low standard jelly compotel

Known items:	Clear
Banana stand	$150.00
Bottle, oil with or without handle	225.00
Bowl, flat	
Covered	
Oval, double handled, 6" l.	135.00

Known items:	Clear
Round	
6" d.	85.00
7" d.	110.00
8" d.	135.00
Open	
Oval, double handled	
5-1/2" l.	30.00
6" l.	35.00
Rectangular	
6" l.	35.00
8" l.	45.00
Round, straight sided	
6" d.	35.00
7" d.	45.00
8" d.	65.00
Butter dish, flat, covered	
Double handled	
Notched lid	225.00
Plain lid	150.00
Quarter pound with flanged base (hotel)	
Notched lid	150.00
Plain lid	110.00
Cake stand on high standard	
6-1/2" d.	65.00
8-1/2" d.	75.00
9-1/2" d.	95.00
11-1/2" d.	150.00
Celery	
Tray, rectangular	45.00
Vase	95.00
Compote, round	
Covered on high standard with patterned base	
6" d.	85.00
7" d.	110.00
8" d.	175.00
Open	
High standard with patterned base	
Deep bowl, beaded rim	
6" d.	45.00
7" d.	55.00
8" d.	75.00
Saucer-shaped bowl with beaded rim	
6-1/2" d.	45.00
7-1/2" d.	55.00

Known items:	Clear
8-1/2" d.	65.00
9-1/2" d.	85.00
10-1/2" d.	125.00
Low standard with plain base	
Cone-shaped bowl, 7" d.	55.00
Deep bowl, 5" d.	
Covered	
Notched lid	65.00
Plain lid	55.00
Open with beaded rim	35.00
Condiment under tray	150.00
Creamer with pressed handle	
Individual	45.00
Table size	75.00
Cruet with applied handle and original melon-shaped stopper	225.00
Cup and saucer set	65.00
Cup, custard.	25.00
Goblet	135.00
Jelly dish, round, footed, 5" d.	
Covered	85.00
Open	45.00
Marmalade jar with original patterned cover.	250.00
Mug with pressed handle	75.00
Mustard jar, bulbous with original cover	150.00
Nappy, handled.	35.00
Pickle dish, rectangular	30.00
Pitcher with pressed handle	
Milk, 1-qt.	125.00
Water	
3-pts.	150.00
1/2-gal.	175.00
Plate, square	
5" (confection)	35.00
6-3/4"	40.00
7"	50.00
Saltshaker	
Bulbous	95.00
Tapered.	85.00
Sauce dish, round, flat, 4" d.	20.00
Saucer, round with beaded rim, 5" d.	25.00
Spoon holder	75.00
Sugar bowl	
Hotel, covered, bulbous on low circular foot	95.00

Known items:	Clear
Individual, squat, bulbous with notched lid	150.00
Table size, tall, oval	110.00
Sugar shaker	125.00
Syrup pitcher	275.00

Known items:	Clear
Toothpick holder	45.00
Tumbler, water, flat	75.00
Vase, cylindrical-shape with beaded rim, 6" h.	55.00
Wine	85.00

WOODEN PAIL

AKA: Bucket Set, Oaken Bucket.

Non-flint. Bryce, Higbee & Company, Pittsburgh, PA, c. 1880s. The United States Glass Company, Pittsburgh, PA, c. 1891.

Original color production: Amber, amethyst, blue, canary yellow, clear.

Reproductions and Look-a-Likes: None known.

Wooden Pail water pitcher.

Known items:	Amber	Amethyst	Blue Yellow	Canary	Clear
Butter dish with cover, tab handled	$95.00	$275.00	$150.00	$175.00	$75.00
Creamer, collared base, pressed handle	55.00	150.00	75.00	85.00	45.00
Miniatures:					
Butter dish with cover	—	—	—	—	350.00
Creamer	—	—	—	—	75.00
Spoon holder	—	—	—	—	250.00
Sugar bowl with cover	—	—	—	—	300.00
Pitcher, water with pressed handle, 1/2-gal.	110.00	275.00	175.00	225.00	85.00
Spoon holder	50.00	135.00	65.00	75.00	45.00
Sugar bowl with cover	60.00	200.00	95.00	110.00	55.00
Toothpick or match older (3 sizes)	35.00	85.00	55.00	65.00	30.00
Tumbler	35.00	85.00	45.00	55.00	35.00

Wooden Pail creamer, butter dish, sugar bowl, and spoon holder.

WYOMING

OMN: U.S. Glass No. 15,081-Wyoming.

AKA: Enigma, Bulls Eye.

Non-flint. The United States Glass Company, Pittsburgh, PA. at Factory "U" and Factory "E," c. 1903.

Original color production: Clear.

Reproductions and Look-a-Likes: None known.

Wyoming wine, handled mug, and tumbler.

Known items:	Clear
Saucer-shaped bowl	
7" d.	45.00
8" d.	55.00
9" d.	75.00
10" d.	95.00
Creamer with pressed handle	
Covered, individual tankard	95.00
Open	
Individual tankard	30.00
Table size	85.00
Dish, open, oval, 8" l. (preserve)	35.00
Goblet (R)	450.00
Mug with pressed handle	65.00
Pickle dish, oval, flat with double handles	25.00
Pitcher with pressed handle	
Milk, 1-qt.	125.00
Water, 3-pts.	175.00
Plate, cake	55.00
Saltshaker	
Bulbous	135.00
Straight-sided	125.00
Sauce dish, round, flat, 4" d.	15.00
Spoon holder	110.00
Sugar bowl with cover	175.00
Syrup pitcher	275.00
Tumbler, water, flat	65.00
Wine	125.00

Wyoming covered sugar bowl.

Known items:	Clear
Bowl, open, round	
Flat	
6" d.	$35.00
7" d.	45.00
8" d.	65.00
Footed, deep with ruffled rim.	95.00
Butter dish with cover on flanged base, 9" d.	250.00
Cake stand on high standard	
9" d.	75.00
10" d.	85.00
11" d.	125.00
Compote, round	
Covered, deep bowl	
6" d.	110.00
7" d.	135.00
8" d.	175.00
Open with scalloped rim	
Deep bowl	
6" d.	45.00
7" d.	55.00
8" d.	75.00

Wyoming deep ruffle-rim bowl.

X-RAY

OMN.

Non-flint. Riverside Glass Works, Wellsburg, WV, c. 1896.

Original color production: Clear, emerald green (plain, gilded, enamel decorated). Amethyst, canary yellow, or any other color would be considered rare.

Reproductions and Look-a-Likes: None known.

Known items:	Amethyst	Clear	Emerald Green
Bowl, open, round 8" d. (Master berry)	$75.00	$25.00	$55.00
Butter dish with cover on flanged rim	175.00	45.00	125.00
Celery vase	85.00	25.00	50.00
Compote			
Covered on high standard	225.00	75.00	150.00

Known items:	Amethyst	Clear	Emerald Green
Open on high standard with beaded-scalloped rim, 6" d.	75.00	25.00	55.00
Creamer with applied handle			
Breakfast	55.00	15.00	35.00
Individual	45.00	15.00	30.00
Table size	85.00	35.00	55.00
Cruet with original stopper	275.00	55.00	175.00
Cruet under tray (clover shaped)	110.00	35.00	65.00
Pitcher, water with applied handle, 1/2-gal.	225.00	95.00	150.00
Plate, bread	75.00	30.00	55.00
Saltshaker	85.00	20.00	65.00
Sauce dish, round, flat, 4-1/2" d.	25.00	8.00	20.00
Spoon holder	75.00	30.00	55.00
Sugar bowl			
Individual, open	65.00	15.00	45.00
Table size with cover	110.00	35.00	65.00
Syrup pitcher	425.00	125.00	325.00
Toothpick holder	85.00	20.00	45.00
Tumbler, water, flat	55.00	20.00	35.00

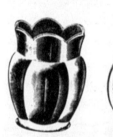

X-Ray spoon holder, sugar bowl, butter dish, and creamer.

ZIPPER

OMN. AKA: Cobb, Late Sawtooth.

Non-flint. Richards & Hartley Glass Co., Tarentum, PA, c. 1888.

Original color production: Clear. Amber, blue, or any other color is rare.

Reproductions and Look-a-Likes: None.

Zipper water pitcher.

Known items:	Clear
Bowl, open, flat, 7" d., round	$15.00
Butter dish with cover	45.00
Celery vase	30.00
Cheese dish, covered	65.00
Compote, covered, 8" d.	
On high standard	65.00
On low standard	55.00
Creamer with pressed handle	
With high foot	45.00
With low foot	30.00
Cruet with original stopper	55.00

Known items:	Clear
Dish, open, oblong, 9-3/8" l.	20.00
Goblet	30.00
Jam jar with cover	55.00
Pitcher with pressed handle	
Milk, 1-qt.	45.00
Water, 1/2-gal.	55.00
Relish tray, 10" l.	15.00
Salt dip, individual	10.00
Sauce dish, round	
Flat	5.00
Footed	5.00
Spoon holder	25.00
Sugar bowl with cover	35.00
Tumbler, water, flat	25.00
Wine (S)	30.00

ZIPPER BLOCK

OMN: Duncan & Sons No. 90. **AKA:** Cryptic, Iowa, Nova Scotia Ribbon and Star.

Non-flint. George Duncan & Sons, Pittsburgh, PA, c. 1887. The United States Glass Company, Pittsburgh, PA. at Factory "D," c. 1891.

Original color production: Clear, clear with ruby stain (plain, engraved). Produced in two conspicuous forms: (a) with and (b) without the stars in the panels.

Reproductions and Look-a-Likes: None known.

Known items:	Clear	Clear w/Ruby
Bowl		
Oblong, open		
With shallow serrated rim		
6" l.	$15.00	$35.00
7" l.	20.00	45.00
8" l.	25.00	55.00

Zipper Block goblet.

Known items:	Clear	Clear w/Ruby
Oval		
With deep serrated bowl		
7" l.	30.00	55.00
8" l.	35.00	65.00
9" l.	40.00	70.00
10" l.	45.00	75.00
With shallow bowl		
5-1/2" l.	10.00	20.00
6-1/2" l.	12.50	25.00
7-1/2" l.	15.00	35.00
8-1/2" l.	20.00	45.00
9-1/2" l.	25.00	50.00
10-1/2" l.	30.00	55.00
11-1/2" l.	45.00	65.00
Round		
Collared base		
Covered		
6" d.	45.00	75.00
7" d.	55.00	85.00
8" d.	65.00	110.00
Open		
6" d.	20.00	35.00
7" d.	25.00	45.00
8" d.	30.00	50.00
Flat with scalloped rim		
5" d. (ice cream)	10.00	25.00
7" d.	5.00	30.00
8" d.	25.00	40.00
9" d.	35.00	45.00

Known items:	Clear	Clear w/Ruby
Butter dish with cover	95.00	225.00
Cake stand on high standard,		
10" d.	125.00	350.00
Celery vase	35.00	125.00
Compote, round on high standard		
Covered		
7" d.	55.00	150.00
8" d.	65.00	175.00
Open with scalloped rim		
7" d.	45.00	125.00
8" d.	50.00	150.00
Creamer with applied handle	40.00	85.00
Goblet	55.00	125.00
Lamp, oil		
No. 90, #1 collar (smallest)		
No. 91, #1 collar	85.00	—
No. 92, #1 or #2 collar	95.00	—
No. 93, #2 collar	135.00	—
No. 94, #3 collar (largest)	175.00	—
Pickle		
Jar with cover	65.00	225.00
Tray, oblong	15.00	30.00
Pitcher with applied handle		
Milk, 1-qt.	125.00	325.00
Water, 1/2-gal.	175.00	425.00
Plate		
Bread, 8"	15.00	65.00
Cheese, 7"	15.00	—
Dinner, 8"	20.00	—
Ice cream, 7"	10.00	45.00
Saltshaker (tall)	65.00	125.00
Sauce dish		
Flat		
4" d.	8.00	25.00
4-1/2" d.	10.00	25.00
Footed		
4" d.	8.00	25.00
4-1/2" d.	10.00	25.00
Spoon holder	30.00	85.00
Sugar bowl with cover		
Hotel size	55.00	110.00
Table size	75.00	150.00
Tumbler, water, flat	30.00	75.00
Waste or finger bowl	15.00	55.00